The Great American Mosaic

The Great American Mosaic

An Exploration of Diversity in Primary Documents

Gary Y. Okihiro, General Editor

Volume 1
African American Experience

Lionel C. Bascom, Volume Editor

 GREENWOOD

AN IMPRINT OF ABC-CLIO, LLC
Santa Barbara, California • Denver, Colorado • Oxford, England

Copyright © 2014 by ABC-CLIO, LLC

Library of Congress Cataloging-in-Publication Data

The great American mosaic: an exploration of diversity in primary documents/Gary Y. Okihiro, general editor.
      volumes cm
Contents: Volume 1. African American Experience/Lionel C. Bascom, volume editor.
ISBN 978-1-61069-612-8 (hardback : acid-free paper)—ISBN
978-1-61069-613-5 (ebook) 1. Cultural pluralism—United States—History—Sources. 2. United States—Race relations—History—Sources. 3. United States—Ethnic relations—History—Sources. 4. Minorities—United States—History—Sources. 5. United States—History—Sources. I. Okihiro, Gary Y., 1945- II. Bascom, Lionel C.
E184.A1G826 2014
305.800973—dc23   2014007428

ISBN: 978-1-61069-612-8
EISBN: 978-1-61069-613-5

18 17 16 15 14   1 2 3 4 5

This book is also available on the World Wide Web as an eBook.
Visit www.abc-clio.com for details.

Greenwood
An Imprint of ABC-CLIO, LLC

ABC-CLIO, LLC
130 Cremona Drive, P.O. Box 1911
Santa Barbara, California 93116-1911

This book is printed on acid-free paper ∞
Manufactured in the United States of America

Contents

Volume 1: African American Experience

Revolutionary War Era and the Early Republic (1760–1830)

Antebellum Slavery (1830–1860)

Civil War and Reconstruction (1861–1877)

Harlem Renaissance through World War II
(1920–1950)

Civil Rights Movement
(1950–1970)

Post–Civil Rights Era and the New Millennium (1970–Present)

General Introduction

Peoples of color—African Americans, Asian and Pacific Islander Americans, Latinas/ Latinos, and Native Americans—were not always included within the American mosaic. In fact, throughout much of the nation's history, peoples of color were not members or citizens of these United States. In 1787, John Jay, a Founding Father and a leading designer of the nation-state, declared in "Concerning the Dangers from Foreign Force and Influence," essays that were part of *The Federalist* papers, that Americans are "one united people—a people descended from the same ancestors, speaking the same language, professing the same religion, attached to the same principles of government, very similar in their manners and customs."

Jay's "one united people" were Europeans, foreigners, who called themselves "persons" and "whites" in the new nation's Constitution, laws, and census. Those not included within that racialized, nationalized category or "the citizen race" in the words of U.S. Supreme Court chief justice Roger Taney in *Dred Scott v. Sandford* (1857), were of "another and different class of persons" and they represented "foreign dangers," threatening disunity and conflict. It is the experiences of those peoples that *The Great American Mosaic: An Exploration of Diversity in Primary Documents* covers in its four volumes. Volume 1 provides a collection of documents exploring the African American experience; Volume 2, the American Indian experience; Volume 3, the Asian American and Pacific Islander experience; and Volume 4, the Latino American experience.

Standard narratives of the nation routinely excluded peoples of color. Only around the mid-20th century did U.S. history textbooks reflect more fully the nation's diversity, highlighting especially the presence of African Americans. Still, the architecture of American history remains white at its core; Native Americans, including American Indians and Pacific Islanders, formed the environment and background for white expansion and settlement, and African and Asian Americans and Latinas/Latinos played minor notes in an anthem devoted to the European nation.

Indeed, the nation, since the English invasion and colonization of America in the 17th century, systematically excluded peoples of color from the privileges and protections accorded Taney's "citizen race." "We, the people" of the U.S. Constitution was never intended to embrace nonwhites; that exclusion is the foundational premise upon which the nation was conceived. Conversely, the inclusion of peoples of color democratized the nation and was truly revolutionary. The American Revolution, by contrast, was not transformative in that the new nation was an extension of the original white settler colonialism that infringed upon these shores.

American Indians

To the invaders, American Indians were impediments to their freedom, especially embodied in the concept of "free" land. Conquest and expulsion were the means of American Indian alienation whereby English foreigners became natives on their sovereign estates, and the land's natives became aliens. The English-drawn border of 1763, despite its porous nature, was indicative of that demarcation, that segregation of "citizens" from "aliens."

The postcolonial nation acknowledged that arrangement in the Treaty of Greenville (1795), which recognized Indian sovereignty in territories not claimed by the United States. In *Worcester v. Georgia* (1832), the U.S. Supreme Court declared the Cherokee nation to be a "foreign state," a condition reaffirmed by Chief Justice Taney in his *Dred Scott* (1857) majority opinion. As Taney wrote, the United States signed treaties with American Indian nations, "under subjection to the white race," and, accordingly, in the United States whites were the "citizen race" and American Indians were "aliens."

That exclusion shifted with the white flood, which by the late 19th century had engulfed the entire continent from sea to shining sea. Following the final bloody wars of conquest waged mainly against Indians of the Great Plains, the U.S. census of 1890 declared in that year, which saw the massacre of Indian men, women, and children at Wounded Knee, that the entire continent had been filled (by whites). President Theodore Roosevelt called those lands, memorably, the "red wastes," and other men called them "virgin land." There were no more frontiers for manly probing and capture.

Conquest achieved, the Dawes Act (1887) sought to dissolve Indian nations and assimilate American Indians as individuals. Soon thereafter, the U.S. Supreme Court affirmed, in *Lone Wolf v. Hitchcock* (1903), the plenary powers of Congress over Indian nations because they constituted "domestic dependent nations." The assimilation continued with U.S. citizenship bestowed in 1924 on those born after that year, and, in 1940, on all American Indians.

Following a brief interlude during the New Deal of the 1930s, the attempt to absorb American Indians politically and culturally continued into the 1950s, when Dillon Myer, as chief of the Bureau of Indian Affairs, pursued the policy called appropriately "termination." Myer had experience with termination, having administered the concentration camps for Japanese Americans as the War Relocation Authority's director during World War II.

American Indians, thus, were at first excluded as "foreign" nations and peoples, and, after conquest, were assimilated and rendered domestic dependencies and dependents.

African Americans

Like American Indians, African Americans were "aliens" excluded from community membership. In 1669, a Virginia colony jury ruled that Anthony Johnson was "a Negroe and by consequence an alien." Race determined citizenship. The postcolonial nation and its founding Constitution (1787) specified that African Americans were not "persons" but "three fifths of all other Persons" and thereby failed to qualify for full representation in the Congress.

In fact, as Chief Justice Taney held in *Dred Scott* (1857): "Negroes of the African race" and their descendants "are not included, and were not intended to be included, under the word 'citizens' in the Constitution, and can therefore claim none of the rights and privileges which that instrument provides for and secures to citizens of the United States." Moreover, Taney pointed out, from the republic's founding, the 1790 Naturalization Act limited citizenship to "free white persons," making clear the distinction between the "citizen race" or whites and "persons of color" or those "not included in the word citizens."

That separation dissolved with the Thirteenth (1865), Fourteenth (1868), and Fifteenth (1870) Amendments to the U.S. Constitution, which, respectively, ended slavery, extended citizenship to all persons born in the United States, and enfranchised men regardless of "race, color, or previous condition of servitude." In 1870, Congress extended to Africans the right of naturalization. African American citizens, although without full equality under Jim Crow, transformed the complexion of the "citizen race" and, thus, the nation. The change was a radical break with the past; it was, in fact, revolutionary.

Still, racial segregation was the primary instrument of the state to secure African American political and economic dependency, and Jim Crow, as was affirmed by *Plessy v. Ferguson* (1896), ruled the land until *Brown v. Board of Education* (1954), which integrated public schools. In *Plessy*, the U.S. Supreme Court ruled that racial segregation in private businesses, conducted under the doctrine of "separate but equal," fulfilled the Fourteenth Amendment's equal protection clause. States routinely denied African American men and, after 1920, women access to the ballot through property and literacy requirements from the end of Reconstruction in the 1870s to the Voting Rights Act of 1965.

Latinas/Latinos

Mexican Americans were a people made through conquest, much like American Indians. In the 1820s and 1830s, Americans, many of them owning slaves, settled in the Mexican province of Texas. These white Protestant settlers, never comfortable in a Catholic republic that sought to end slavery, shook off Mexican control in 1836. In 1845, the United States admitted Texas as a state, an action that helped precipitate the Mexican American War (1846–1848). Driven by Manifest Destiny, an expansionist doctrine that proclaimed the God-given right of the United States to expand across the North American continent, the U.S. government, after defeating Mexico, demanded the cession of almost half of Mexico's territory, land that later formed the entire states of California, Nevada, and Utah, as well as portions of Colorado, Wyoming, Arizona, and New Mexico. The Treaty of Guadalupe Hidalgo (1848), which ended the war, granted U.S. citizenship to Mexican residents of the ceded lands, and Mexicans were thus rendered "white" by treaty. At the same time, many Mexican Americans lost their farms and land, like American Indians, and were widely denied equality in employment, housing, and education on the basis of race, class, and culture.

Judicial decisions commonly cited the contradiction between Mexican whiteness by treaty and Mexicans as a mestizo and "mongrel" race by scientific and common opinion. Further, courts decided, in accordance with the one-drop rule, that is, one drop of nonwhite blood meant a person was considered nonwhite, that children of whites and nonwhites were "colored." This principle was applied in such cases as *In re Camille* (1880), involving a white father and American Indian mother, and *In re Young* (1912), involving a white father and

Japanese mother. Still, as *In re Rodriguez* (1897), the courts were compelled to rule that Mexican Americans were white and thus citizens. At the same time, whiteness in theory disallowed Mexican American claims of racial discrimination in practice, such as the right to a trial of their peers, which, if granted, would end instances of all-Anglo juries ruling on Mexican Americans.

The state segregated Mexican American children in inferior schools on the basis of language and "migrant farming patterns," as was affirmed by a Texas court in *Independent School District v. Salvatierra* (1930). Mexicans emerged from the white race in the 1930 U.S. census and appeared as "Mexicans." The enumeration facilitated the expulsion to Mexico of about half a million Mexican and Mexican Americans from the United States during the Great Depression, when their labor was no longer required. That removal complemented the 1935 Filipino Repatriation Act, which offered Filipino Americans, like Mexican American migrant laborers, free passage to the Philippines.

Asian and Pacific Islander Americans

The 1790 Naturalization Act, which limited U.S. citizenship to "free white persons," excluded Pacific Islanders and Asians, like American Indians and African Americans, from the "citizen race." In the 1850s, California's supreme court chief judge Hugh Murray affirmed the distinction between "a free white citizen of this State" and American Indians, Africans, Pacific Islanders, and Asians, those "not of white blood," in Murray's words. Unlike Native Americans, including American Indians and Pacific Islanders, whose utility to the nation involved mainly their land, Asians were employed, like African and Mexican Americans, as laborers.

As persons "not of white blood," Pacific Islander and Asian men served as slaves and servants to whites; appealed to whites and antislavery societies for manumission; married American Indian, African American, and Mexican women; were counted in the U.S. census as colored and mulatto; fought in African American units in the Civil War; and were buried in colored cemeteries. Like Mexicans, Asians and Pacific Islanders served employers as migrant laborers, mainly in agriculture but also in mines and on railroads; formed unions irrespective of race; and married and produced bicultural children.

Unique among people of color in the United States was the persistent condition of Asians as "aliens ineligible to citizenship" under the 1790 Naturalization Act. Mexicans by treaty and African Americans and American Indians through law acquired U.S. citizenship, albeit absent its full rights and privileges. Unable to naturalize, Asians and Pacific Islanders gained U.S. citizenship by birth under the Fourteenth Amendment. Chinese acquired the right to naturalization in 1943, South Asians and Filipinos in 1946, and Japanese and Koreans not until 1952. Accordingly, the United States denied Asians naturalization rights for more than 160 years, from 1790 to 1952.

Tempering those acts of inclusion were immigration quotas imposed on Asians and Pacific Islanders. Starting in 1929, under the Johnson-Reed Immigrant Act (1924), Congress assigned an annual quota of 100 each to those immigrating from Australia and Melanesia, Bhutan, China, India, Iran, Iraq, Japan, Micronesia, Nepal, New Zealand, Oman, Sāmoa, and Thailand. The law gave to Turkey, straddling Europe and Asia, a quota of 226. Likewise, the law assigned to African nations, from Egypt to South Africa, annual quotas of 100.

European countries, by contrast, which supplied the "citizen race," received quotas of 1,181 (Denmark), 2,377 (Norway), 3,153 (Netherlands), 5,802 (Italy), 17,853 (Irish Free State), 25,957 (Germany), and 65,721 (Great Britain and Northern Ireland). In force until 1965, the Johnson-Reed Act established the nation's first comprehensive, restrictive immigration policy. The act also served to define the nation, its citizens, and its peoples—called a race—by excluding those who were deemed unworthy or even dangerous. In that sense, immigration is a matter of national defense and homeland security.

Imperialism

Conquest did not end with the filling of the continent. The nation, in the late 19th century, extended its imperial reach overseas to the Caribbean and Pacific. Peoples indigenous to and settled upon those territories thereby became Americans, though not fully. After the Spanish-American War of 1898, Puerto Ricans and Filipinos, natives of unincorporated territories, followed divergent paths; Puerto Ricans became U.S. citizens in 1917, and Filipino nationals became Asian aliens in 1934. Contrarily, Hawaiians and Alaska's indigenous peoples, natives of incorporated territories, became U.S. citizens, whereas those in the unincorporated territories of Guam, where "America's day begins," are U.S. citizens while those in American Sāmoa are nationals.

American Mosaic

Founding Father John Jay's "one united people" diversified with the nation's expansion. European immigration during the late 19th century was unlike the usual flow from Great Britain and northern Europe. These new immigrants came from southern and eastern Europe and brought with them different religions, languages, and cultures. Nonetheless, most, through Americanization and assimilation, became members of the white, citizen race.

Peoples of color were not counted among that number at first, and when they became Americans and citizens, they transformed the nation and its peoples from a people descended from the same ancestors to an American mosaic. Racism and segregation, nonetheless, deferred dreams and attenuated the achievement of that revolution. As the documents in these four volumes testify, however, peoples of color are more than minor figures in the nation's narrative; they are central to it, and the documents collected in these volumes shed new light on that history, revealing a more complex, diverse, and troubled American past.

These documents expand upon the standard narratives of nation, which have, for the most part, excluded and marginalized peoples of color. They offer a fuller, more comprehensive understanding of these United States, and are of great consequence for all Americans. They are also important for peoples of color. As Frantz Fanon pointed out in his *The Wretched of the Earth* (1961), colonization denies a people their past, leading to "estrangement" from their history and culture. Freedom requires a recuperation of "the whole body of efforts made by a people in the sphere of thought to describe, justify, and praise the action through which that people has created itself and keeps itself in existence" (p. 233).

We, the people, and descendants of the nation's branching genealogy possess the ability and share the responsibility to shape a more inclusive, equitable, and democratic future.

                                                                        Gary Y. Okihiro

Volume Introduction

African American Experience, volume 1 of *The Great American Mosaic: An Exploration of Diversity in Primary Documents* is an expansive collection of nearly 100 primary sources, documents, speeches, landmark civil rights court rulings, interviews, and articles written by prominent African Americans throughout the history of the United States. The work collected here includes primary memoirs and narratives from the colonial era to the present day.

Significantly, this work contains the important slave narratives collected in the late 1930s and early 1940s by writers of the Work Progress Administration during the New Deal. These documents preserve the voices of countless former slaves in the South, who were maligned after their emancipation as docile participants of bondage, not as survivors of one of the most brutal chapters in human history. The collection also includes the slave narratives of Frederick Douglass, Henry Bibb, and Josiah Henson; excerpts from the *Plessy v. Ferguson* (1896) and *Brown v. Board of Education* (1954) U.S. Supreme Court decisions; selections from Alain Locke's writing on the "New Negro"; excerpts from such landmark civil rights legislation as the Civil Rights Act of 1964 and the Voting Rights Act of 1965; and the speeches of current African American leaders, including Harold Ford Jr., Rev. Al Sharpton, and the first African-American president of the United States, Barack H. Obama.

The collection also includes interviews housed in the Radcliffe College Black Women Oral History Project in the Schlesinger Library. This project has pulled together the speeches of Barack Obama before, during, and after his successful bid to become the first African American president of the United States, as well as the narratives of slaves, orators, civil rights workers, and black pioneers, to tell the stories of African Americans and their journey throughout American history.

Together, these documents follow the public discourse of African American history from slavery through the early years of the second decade of the 21st century. The works span more than 250 years, from Briton Hammon's 1760 narrative of his life to President Obama's remarks on the Trayvon Martin case in the summer of 2013. Each of the documents in this collection is a window on its own time and a record to be read and interpreted by future generations through the window of their own times.

In earlier times, the significance of such a collection would not be missed. Its importance would have been more obvious in 1862, a time before emancipation of black slaves; in 1954, the year segregation was outlawed; and in 1964, when the phrase "civil rights" became the law of the land. This is because the narratives represented in this work were a reflection of daily life in the United States for blacks whose stories were only told in those days by a vibrant black press. In the early years of the 20th century, hundreds of black weeklies, like *The Chicago Defender* and *The Amsterdam News,* and national magazines for blacks, like *Opportunity* and *The Crisis,* were widely published throughout the country. In these publications, blacks were informed daily, weekly, and monthly about their status as second-class citizens.

In 1936, the *Savannah (Ga) Tribune* reported the following story:

> More than two years ago a number of colored citizens of Wilkesboro, North Carolina, were prevented from being registered as voters by the district registrar. The registrar adopted subterfuges to discourage the applicants. In this he failed, because they were determined to become qualified voters. Upon final refusal legal proceedings were resorted to in the federal courts. For this registration refusal, the registrar was found guilty. This was a remarkable case. It is the first time in our knowledge that any one has been convicted for refusing to register colored applicants for voting.

The significance of publications like the *Savannah Tribune* has been diminished by racial progress. Although African American publications continue to be published along with numerous blogs and Web sites on the Internet, African Americans no longer rely on these publications as their main sources of news or history. This is particularly true in academic circles, where black scholars have access to the same libraries and databases as their colleagues.

In 2009, public television anchorwoman Gwen Ifill published *The Breakthrough: Politics and Race in the Age of Obama.* In this book, she noted that there are stark ideological differences between the established civil rights leaders who were prominent in the 1960s and President Obama and black leaders of his generation. In writing about Ifill's book, *The Journal of Blacks in Higher Education* noted that today's black leaders grew up in the midst of civil rights struggles in which they broke barriers and seized power.

Like the readers of this collection, the children of those early civil rights leaders, as Ifill noted, "faced a more tolerant world. They were raised to believe they could do anything. Their schools were integrated and Ivy League colleges came calling for them. They grew up in a world shaped by access instead [of] denial." The black leaders of the current era "have a new outlook where change is possible and race is no longer an important barrier to their success."

Even in these progressive times, it remains abundantly clear that the preservation of primary documents, literature, and historical artifacts like those in *The Great American Mosaic* is vital to the vitality of future scholarship in African American studies, literature, and history. As I was editing this collection, several significant examples of this occurred to me.

Just weeks after the debut of the 1973 blaxploitation film, *The Spook Who Sat by the Door,* by Ivan Dixon and Sam Greenlee, copies of the film disappeared from public view. It was deliberately hidden and nearly forgotten until 2004 when, as Elizabeth Reich noted in the fall 2012 issue of *The African American Review*, "television producer Tim Reid recovered the lone extant negative from the film vault in which Greenlee had hidden it shortly after *Spook's* premiere, sparking renewed interest in the picture." Reid's discovery marked the preservation of a primary film that current and future scholars can add to a growing arsenal of historical markers in African American history, like this volume.

In my 2012 review in *The African American Review* of *Ain't Nothing Like the Real Thing: How the Apollo Theater Shaped American Entertainment,* a Smithsonian Institute book edited by Richard Carlin and Kinshasha H. Conwill, I wrote that the "recent untimely passing of Soul Train godfather and the show's founder Don Cornelius (in February, 2012) offers us another painful reminder that our musical icons are precious and must be preserved for future generations." The Apollo was for many years the flagship of a string of entertainment venues throughout the United States, known as the "Chit'lin Circuit," that were the only places where black entertainers and musicians could appear in most American cities during the years of racial segregation.

Reading *Ain't Nothing Like the Real Thing* helped me relive my high school years growing up in Harlem in the early 1960s, when my brother Chuck used to treat me to a weekly ticket to the Apollo's Wednesday night amateur hour. Every Wednesday night for seven decades, the Apollo helped launch the careers of such notables as Ella Fitzgerald, Sarah Vaughan, Johnny Mathis, and the Jackson Five. This same venue became center stage for comic actors like Lincoln Perry, whose stage name in the 1930s was "Stepin Fetchit," and Eddie Rochester Anderson, who later became known as Rochester and the sidekick to comic Jack Benny. In later years, it was home to comics Jackie "Moms" Mabley and Redd Foxx, who is best known for his later portrayal of the character Fred Sanford in the television series *Sanford and Son.* Just as *Spook* now becomes a historical marker for the Black Power movement of the 1960s and early 1970s, the legacy preserved in *Ain't Nothing Like the Real Thing* notes the struggles and triumphs of African American entertainers and audiences during the many years of segregation.

The documents in *The Great American Mosaic* collection now join this effort as well.

In the fall of 2002, I was visiting my niece Erin, who was an undergraduate at Temple University in Philadelphia. There I met a professor from the Department of African American Studies in the bookstore one afternoon. Erin was a freshman, and we were moving her into one of the new dorms just off Broad Street. She had met this professor during one of the orientations on campus that year and told me that he and I had several things in common. I wasn't sure that was true. I was in my early 50s and an adjunct at a small state college in Connecticut where I taught writing and journalism. He certainly was not an adjunct or a junior member of that department. In those years, this major was no longer the token enterprise it had once been at Temple, at Yale, at Harvard, and at nearby Princeton, where Cornell West had distinguished himself as a leading scholar. No, this Temple brother was clearly a Cornell West type whose hairdo was a cross between the dreadlocks of the 1960s and the muted curly hairstyles worn by some of the young, emerging black academics. His Brooks Brother suits said, "Yes, I am Ivy League," but his hairstyle said, "I'm black and I'm proud," lyrics introduced by singer James Brown from the stage of the Apollo Theater in Harlem back in my time in the 1960s.

As black people, we have always lived with duality, have always been torn between the two poles of safety and emancipation, the pain of being betwixt and between, being the field hand and house servant, the Negro and the New Negro. These choices were dramatized by Booker T. Washington, the famed author of *Up from Slavery,* and W. E. B Du Bois, author of *The Souls of Black Folk* in the 1920s. Martin Luther King emerged as the Great Black Hope of 1963 from the Deep South, and I grew up hearing King's sermons and the self-defense proclamations of Malcolm X at precisely the same time in Harlem.

The brother I met at Temple knew his place, like all of us in the East Coast academia know our places. Although outspoken and vocal, we are still guests of the manor, folks like Nikki Giovanni,

Cornell West, Henry Louis Gates, and I. We also know there is no turning us around because we have all found gathering places on campuses across the country where we can tell accurate versions of our story. This is the significance of a work like this volume. It is history told by participants.

Still, the telling of this history is always going to be a delicate balance between how we see ourselves and how we are seen. That is why our history is forever being rewritten and why *African American Experience* is important in the way it can help pave the way for the new voices that will be writing and rewriting our history in the future. What was the significance of the Emancipation Proclamation? When did the Great Migration of blacks from the South to northern cities begin? What was its significance? I ask these questions wherever I travel, and I am always fascinated by the diversity of the answers I receive.

In the fall of 2002, I was still promoting my book *A Renaissance in Harlem*, when I stopped with Erin to talk about it that afternoon with a colleague at Temple. When I travel or do book signings, I am constantly asked to pinpoint the start of the Harlem Renaissance. It's a difficult question for me to answer. I generally say no one seems to know exactly when it began, although most agree it was probably sometime in the early 1920s. Another question I like to ask is, "When did that trek we call the Great Migration begin?" Millions of southern blacks fled the South in the early years of the 20th century to live in northern cities like Detroit, New York, and Chicago, and it probably began sometime in the early years of the century. When I asked this question that afternoon in the Temple bookstore, my colleague thought about it for a short time, and then said:

> It began one day, somewhere, way down south, when a slave with no last name, let's call him Toby, dropped the reins of the mule he was driving and escaped to the north. That certainly was the beginning of that great migration, maybe the start of the Harlem Renaissance and the beginning of what we now call African-American culture.

I loved the simple chronology. Generally, chronologies are more complicated. In histories, there are no absolutes. At best, the periods approximate periods because there is no definitive way to determine precisely when a period in history began or exactly when it ended.

The documents in *African American Experience* are arranged chronologically into the following seven broad periods:

Revolutionary War Era and the Early Republic (1760–1830)

Antebellum Slavery (1830–1860)

Civil War and Reconstruction (1861–1877)

Jim Crow (1877–1920)

Harlem Renaissance through World War II (1920–1950)

Civil Rights Movement (1950–1970)

Post–Civil Rights Era and the New Millennium (1970–Present)

All documents open with a brief introduction that puts the selection into context for readers, and each document concludes with a source note.

Lionel C. Bascom

Brief Guide to Primary Sources

Primary sources are original, direct, firsthand stories, personal experiences, testimony, and viewpoints that are created during the time period involved. They may include such forms as diaries, journals, letters, personal narratives, government records, graffiti, laws, court cases, plays, novels, poems, architectural plans, maps, memoirs, autobiographies, sound recordings, songs, advertisements, photographs, paintings, prints, speeches, and other material objects. The sources become the raw material that historians, or other scholars, use to create their works in book or article form. Secondary sources are interpretations, which are often made using myriad primary sources.

Primary sources provide readers with a wealth of firsthand information that gets them close to the actual experiences of the historical time period, people, and events. Firsthand material offers a window to a particular time and place, viewpoints, and eyewitness accounts that supplement information and facts typically provided in textbooks and other secondary sources. Primary sources offer readers the raw material of history that has not been analyzed and interpreted.

How to Read and Reflect on Primary Documents

Primary sources in written form, as illustrated by the document selections included in *The Great American Mosaic: An Exploration of Diversity in Primary Documents*, were produced at a particular historical moment and for a particular purpose. These volumes are intended to provide an outlet for the voices of people of color whose experiences and viewpoints are often overlooked or downplayed in the larger American history narrative. Some of these documents were written by an author conscious of a larger audience or with the expectation that they would be published; others were written for personal reasons without the expectation that others would read them. Some documents were intended to persuade, inform, or entertain. Note that documents are based on the particular viewpoints, experiences, and memories of the writer and can reflect selective memories, mistaken information, or deception. The reader is left to evaluate the relevance, reliability, and value of the information and to take into account the analysis and interpretations of secondary sources. The documents in *The Great American Mosaic* provide readers with a variety of firsthand content, ranging from creation myths to legislation to reflections on historical events that provide insights into the experiences of people of color in the United States.

What Questions Should You Ask as You Read?

- Who wrote or produced the document, and what do we know about him or her?
- When and where was the source written or produced, and how does it fit into the timeline of the events and period described?
- Where was the source written or produced? Does that material portray cultural, social, or religious values? What form did it take originally?
- Why was the source material written or produced? What was its creator's intention or purpose? What is the overall tone of the source material?
- Who was the intended audience? How was the document used, and how widely distributed or read was it?
- Overall, how do we evaluate the relevance, reliability, and value of the content? What might the author have left out, intentionally or not?

Revolutionary War Era and the Early Republic

(1760–1830)

A Narrative of the Uncommon Sufferings, and Surprizing Delieverance of Briton Hammon, a Negro Man . . .

(1760)

This insightful narrative about the life and times of a Negro named Briton Hammon was written in the style and form of many European writers of the 18th century. Accounts like Hammon's were rare in 18th-century America and Europe because black slaves, former slaves, and free men of color rarely had the opportunity to get an education. Accounts like this one by Hammon are extremely valuable in modern times because they are first-person accounts of the many hardships suffered by these men and women in a world where being black made them targets of immeasurable cruelties. This account recorded a daily experience that otherwise might be lost in the fog of time and history.

To THE READER,

As my Capacities and Condition of Life are very low, it cannot be expected that I should make those Remarks on the Sufferings I have met with, or the kind Providence of a good GOD for my Preservation, as one in a higher Station; but shall leave that to the Reader as he goes along, and so I shall only relate Matters of Fact as they occur to my Mind—

ON Monday, 25th Day of December, 1747, with the leave of my Master, I went from Marshfield, with an Intention to go a Voyage to Sea, and the next Day, the 26th, got to Plymouth, where I immediately ship'd myself on board of a Sloop, Capt. John Howland, Master, bound to Jamaica and the Bay.—We sailed from Plymouth in a short Time, and after a pleasant Passage of about 30 Days, arrived at Jamaica; we was detain'd at Jamaica only 5 Days, from whence we sailed for the Bay, where we arrived safe in 10 Days. We loaded our Vessel with Logwood, and sailed from the Bay the 25th Day of May following, and the 15th Day of June, we were cast away on Cape-Florida, about 5 Leagues from the Shore; being now destitute of every Help, we knew not what to do or what Course to take in this our sad Condition:—The Captain was advised, intreated, and beg'd on, by every Person on board, to heave over but only 20 Ton of the Wood, and we should get clear, which if he had done, might have sav'd his Vessel and Cargo, and

1

not only so, but his own Life, as well as the Lives of the Mate and Nine Hands, as I shall presently relate.

After being upon this Reef two Days, the Captain order'd the Boat to be hoisted out, and then ask'd who were willing to tarry on board? The whole Crew was for going on Shore at this Time, but as the Boat would not carry 12 Persons at once, and to prevent any Uneasiness, the Captain, a Passenger, and one Hand tarry'd on board, while the Mate, with Seven Hands besides myself, were order'd to go on Shore in the Boat, which as soon as we had reached, one half were to be Landed, and the other four to return to the Sloop, to fetch the Captain and the others on Shore. The Captain order'd us to take with us our Arms, Ammunition, Provisions and Necessaries for Cooking, as also a Sail to make a Tent of, to shelter us from the Weather; after having left the Sloop we stood towards the Shore, and being within Two Leagues of the same, we espy'd a Number of Canoes, which we at first took to be Rocks, but soon found our Mistake, for we perceiv'd they moved towards us; we presently saw an English Colour hoisted in one of the Canoes, at the Sight of which we were not a little rejoiced, but on our advancing yet nearer, we found them, to our very great Surprize, to be Indians of which there were Sixty; being now so near them we could not possibly make our Escape; they soon came up with and boarded us, took away all our Arms, Ammunition, and Provision.

The whole Number of Canoes (being about Twenty,) then made for the Sloop, except Two which they left to guard us, who order'd us to follow on with them; the Eighteen which made for the Sloop, went so much faster than we that they got on board above Three Hours before we came along side, and had kill'd Captain Howland, the Passenger and the other hand; we came to the Larboard side of the Sloop, and they order'd us round to the Starboard, and as we were passing round the Bow, we saw the whole Number of Indians, advancing forward and loading their Guns, upon which the Mate said, "my Lads we are all dead Men," and before we had got round, they discharged their Small Arms upon us, and kill'd Three of our hands, viz. Reuben Young of Cape-Cod, Mate; Joseph Little and Lemuel Doty of Plymouth, upon which I immediately jump'd overboard, chusing rather to be drowned, than to be kill'd by those barbarous and inhuman Savages.

In three or four Minutes after, I heard another Volley which dispatched the other five, viz. John Nowland, and Nathaniel Rich, both belonging to Plymouth, and Elkanah Collymore, and James Webb, Strangers, and Moses Newmock, Molatto. As soon as they had kill'd the whole of the People, one of the Canoes padled after me, and soon came up with me, hawled me into the Canoe, and beat me most terribly with a Cutlass, after that they ty'd me down, then this Canoe stood for the Sloop again and as soon as she came along side, the Indians on board the Sloop betook themselves to their Canoes, then set the Vessel on Fire, making a prodigious shouting and hallowing like so many Devils. As soon as the Vessel was burnt down to the Water's edge, the Indians stood for the Shore, together with our Boat, on board of which they put 5 hands. After we came to the Shore, they led me to their Hutts, where I expected nothing but immediate death, and as they spoke broken English, were often telling me, while coming from the Sloop to the Shore, that they intended to roast me alive. But the Providence of God order'd it otherways, for He appeared for my Help, in this Mount of Difficulty, and they were better to me then my Fears, and soon unbound me, but set a Guard over me every Night. They kept me with them about five Weeks, during which Time they us'd me pretty well, and gave me boil'd Corn, which was what they often eat themselves. The Way I made my Escape from these Villains was this; A Spanish Schooner arriving there from St. Augustine, the Master of which, whose Name was Romond, asked the Indians to let me go on board his Vessel, which they granted. The Way I came to know this Gentleman was, by his being taken last War by an English Privateer, and brought into Jamaica, while I was there knowing me very well, weigh'd Anchor and carry'd me off to the Havanna, and after being there four Days the Indians came after me, and insisted on having me again, as I was their Prisoner;—They made Application to the Governor, and demanded me again from him; in answer to which the Governor told them, that as they had put the whole Crew to Death, they should not have me again, and so paid them Ten Dollars for me, adding, that he would not have them kill any person hereafter, but take as many of them as they could, of those that should be cast away, and bring them to him, for which he would pay them Ten Dollars a-head. At the Havanna I lived with the Governor in the Castle about a Twelve-month, where I was walking thro' the Street, I met with a Press-Gang who immediately prest me, and put me into Goal, and with a Number of others I was confin'd till next Morning, when we were all brought out, and ask'd who would go on board the King's Ships, four of which having been lately built, were bound to Old-Spain, and on my refusing to serve on board, they put me in a close Dungeon, where I was confin'd Four Years and seven months; during which Time I often made application to the Governor, by Persons who came to see the Prisoners, but they never acquainted him with it, nor did he know all this Time what became of me, which was the means of my being confin'd there so long. But kind Providence so order'd it, that after I had been in this Place so long as the Time mention'd above, the Captain of a Merchantman, belonging to Boston, having sprung a Leak was obliged to put into the Havanna to refit, and while he was at Dinner at Mrs. Betty Howard's, she told the Captain of my deplorable Condition, and said she would be glad, if he could by some means or other relieve me; The Captain told Mrs. Howard he would use his best Endeavours for my Relief and Enlargement.

Accordingly, after Dinner, [the Captain] came to the Prison, and ask'd the Keeper if he might see me; upon his Request I was brought out of the Dungeon, and after the Captain had Interrogated me, told me, he would intercede with the Governor for my Relief out of that miserable Place, which he did, and the next Day the Governor sent an Order to release me; I lived with the Governor about a Year after I was delivered from the Dungeon, in which Time I endeavour'd three Times to make my Escape, the last of which proved effectual; the first Time I got on board of Captain Marsh, an English Twenty Gun Ship, with a Number of others, and lay on board conceal'd that Night; and the next Day the Ship being under sail, I thought myself safe, and so made my Appearance upon Deck, but as soon as we were discovered the Captain ordered the Boat out, and sent us all on Shore—I intreated the Captain to let me, in particular, stay on board, begging, and crying to him, to commiserate my unhappy Condition, and added, that I had been confin'd almost five Years in a close Dungeon, but the Captain would not hearken to any Intreaties, for fear of having the Governor's Displeasure, and so was obliged to go on shore, after being on Shore another Twelve month, I endeavour'd to make my Escape the second Time, by trying to get on board of a Sloop bound to Jamaica, and as I was going from the City to the Sloop, was unhappily taken by the Guard, and ordered back to the Castle, and there confined.—However, in a short Time I was set at Liberty, and order'd with a Number of others to carry the Bishop from the Castle, thro' the Country, to confirm the old People, baptize Children, &c. for which he receives large Sums of Money.—I was employ'd in this Service about Seven Months, during which Time I lived very well, and then returned to the Castle again, where I had my Liberty to walk about the City, and do Work for my self;—The Beaver, an English Man of War then lay in the Harbour, and having been informed by some of the Ship's Crew that she was to sail in a few Days, I had nothing now to do, but to seek an Opportunity how I should make my Escape.

Accordingly one Sunday Night the Lieutenant of the Ship with a Number of the Barge Crew were in a Tavern, and Mrs. Howard who had before been a Friend to me, interceded with the Lieutenant to carry me on board: the Lieutenant said he would with all his Heart, and immediately I went on board in the Barge. The next Day the Spaniards came along side the Beaver, and demanded me again, with a Number of others who had made their Escape from them, and got on board the Ship, but just before I did; but the Captain, who was a true Englishman, refus'd them, and said he could not answer it, to deliver up any Englishmen under English Colours.—In a few Days we set Sail for Jamaica, where we arrived safe, after a short and pleasant Passage.

After being at Jamaica a short Time we sail'd for London, as convoy to a Fleet of Merchantmen, who all arrived safe in the Downs, I was turned over to another Ship, the Arcenceil, and there remained about a Month. From this Ship I went on board the Sandwich of 90 Guns; on board the Sandwich, I tarry'd 6 Weeks, and then was order'd on board the Hercules, Capt. John Porter, a 74 Gun Ship, we sail'd on a Cruize, and met with a French 84 Gun Ship, and had a very smart Engagement, A particular Account of this Engagement, has been Publish'd in the Boston News-Papers in which about 70 of our Hands were Kill'd and Wounded, the Captain lost his Leg in the Engagement, and I was Wounded in the Head by a small Shot. We should have taken this Ship, if they had not cut away the most of our Rigging; however, in about three Hours after, a 64 Gun Ship, came up with and took her.—I was discharged from the Hercules the 12th Day of May 1759 (having been on board of that Ship 3 Months) on account of my being disabled in the Arm, and render'd incapable of Service, after being honourably paid the Wages due to me. I was put into the Greenwich Hospital where I stay'd and soon recovered.—I then ship'd myself a Cook on board Captain Martyn, an arm'd Ship in the King's Service. I was on board this Ship almost Two Months, and after being paid my Wages, was discharg'd in the Month of October.—After my discharge from Captain Martyn, I was taken sick in London of a Fever, and was confin'd about 6 Weeks, where I expended all my Money, and left in very poor Circumstances; and unhappy for me I knew nothing of my good Master's being in London at this my very difficult Time.

After I got well of my sickness, I ship'd myself on board of a large Ship bound to Guinea, and being in a publick House one Evening, I overheard a Number of Persons talking about Rigging a Vessel bound to New-England, I ask'd them to what Part of New-England this Vessel was bound? they told me, to Boston; and having ask'd them who was Commander? they told me, Capt. Watt; in a few Minutes after this the Mate of the Ship came in, and I ask'd him if Captain Watt did not want a Cook, who told me he did, and that the Captain would be in, in a few Minutes; and in about half an Hour the Captain came in, and then I ship'd myself at once, after begging off from the Ship bound to Guinea; I work'd on board Captain Watt's Ship almost Three Months, before she sail'd, and one Day being at Work in the Hold, I overheard some Persons on board mention the Name of Winslow, at the Name of which I was very inquisitive, and having ask'd what Winslow they were talking about? They told me it was General Winslow; and that he was one of the Passengers, I ask'd them what General Winslow? For I never knew my good Master, by that Title before; but after enquiring more particularly I found it must be Master, and in a few Days Time the Truth was joyfully verify'd by a happy Sight of his Person, which so overcome me, that I could not speak to him for some Time— My good Master was exceeding glad to see me, telling me that I was like one arose from the Dead, for he thought I had been Dead a great many Years, having heard nothing of me for almost Thirteen Years. I think I have not deviated from Truth, in any particular of this my Narrative, and tho' I have omitted a great many Things, yet what is wrote may suffice to convince the Reader, that I have been most grievously afflicted, and yet thro' the Divine Goodness, as miraculously preserved, and delivered out of many Dangers; of which I desire to retain a grateful Remembrance, as long as I live in the World.

And now, That in the Providence of that GOD, who delivered his Servant David out of the Paw of the Lion and out of the Paw of the Bear, I am freed from a long and dreadful Captivity, among worse Savages than they; And am return'd to my own Native Land, to Shew how Great Things the Lord hoth done for Me; I would call upon all Men, and Say, O Magnifie the Lord with Me, and let us Exalt his Name together!——O that Men would Praise the Lord for His Goodness, and for his Wonderful Works to the Children of Men!

Source: Hammon, Briton. *A Narrative of the Uncommon Sufferings, and Surprizing Delieverance of Briton Hammon, a Negro Man* . . . Boston: Printed and Sold by Green & Russell, in Queen-Street, 1760. Early American Imprints, 1st series, no. 8611.

A Narrative of the Most Remarkable Particulars in the Life of James Albert Ukawsaw Gronniosaw, an African Prince, Written by Himself

(1774)

This narrative was written by a European woman who interviewed Gronniosaw. It is a biography, masked as an autobiography, and it enlightens us about the life of an African prince who was enslaved and lived in Europe and the United States. The curious narrative falls into the category of what is now commonly called "creative nonfiction." Although the text claims that Gronniosaw wrote this account himself, such a claim is often used in the most general sense and rarely takes into account the point of view, impressions, and interpretations of a ghostwriter who may have conducted an interview of the alleged writer and written the account on his behalf.

The authorship of this narrative is authentic in the sense that the true writer admits her role in a preface to the main narrative, although she does so in a contradictory fashion, saying both that she took down what Gronniosaw told her, and that it was penned by the subject himself. This was not uncommon for the period. Nevertheless, these types of accounts are vivid testimonies that in many ways are as accurate as any other form of memoir, meaning they, too, are subject to the editing, interpretation, and perspective of editors, no matter who authored the text. In this account, Gronniosaw's ghostwriter relates a spiritual narrative in memoir form, depicting the European adventures of an African prince.

AN ACCOUNT OF JAMES ALBERT, &C.

I WAS born in the city of *Baurnou*, my mother was the eldest daughter of the reigning King there. I was the youngest of six children, and particularly loved by my mother, and my grand-father almost doted on me. I had, from my infancy, a curious turn of mind; was more grave and reserved, in my disposition, than either of my brothers and sisters, I often teazed them with questions they could not answer; for which reason they disliked me, as they supposed that I was either foolish or insane. 'T was certain that I was, at times, very unhappy in myself: It being strongly impressed on my mind that there was some GREAT MAN of power which resided above the sun, moon and stars, the objects of our worship.—My dear, indulgent mother would bear more with me than any of my friends beside.—I often raised my hand to heaven, and asked her who lived there? Was much dissatisfied when she told me the sun, moon and stars, being persuaded, in my own mind, that there must be some SUPERIOR POWER.—I was frequently lost in wonder at the works of the creation: Was afraid, and uneasy, and restless, but could not tell for what. I wanted to be informed of things that no person could tell me; and was always dissatisfied.—These wonderful impressions began in my childhood, and followed me continually till I left my parents, which affords me matter of admiration and thankfulness. To this moment I grew more and more uneasy every day, insomuch that one Saturday (which is the day on which we kept our sabbath) I laboured under anxieties and fears that cannot be expressed; and, what is more extraordinary, I could not give a reason for it.—I rose, as our custom is, about three o'clock (as we are obliged to be at our place of worship an hour before the sun rise). We say nothing in our worship, but continue on our knees with our hands held up, observing a strict silence till the sun is at a certain height, which I suppose to be about 10 or 11 o'clock in *England*. When, at a certain sign made by the Priest, we get up (our duty being over) and disperse to our different houses.—Our place of meeting is under a large palm tree; we divide ourselves into many congregations; as it is impossible for the same tree to cover the inhabitants of the whole city, though they are extremely large, high and majestic; the beauty and usefulness of them are not to be described; they supply the inhabitants of the country with meat, drink and clothes; the body of the palm tree is very large; at a certain season of the year they tap it, and bring vessels to receive the wine, of which they draw great quantities, the quality of which is very delicious: The leaves of this tree are of a silky nature; they are large and soft; when they are dried and pulled to pieces, it has much the same appearance as the English flax, and the inhabitants of BOURNOU manufacture it for clothing, &c. This tree likewise produces a plant, or substance, which has the appearance of a cabbage, and very like it, in taste almost the same: It grows between the branches. Also the palm tree produces a nut, something like a cocoa, which contains a kernel, in which is a large quantity of milk, very pleasant to the taste: The shell is of a hard substance, and of a very beautiful appearance, and serves for basons, bowls, &c.

I hope this digression will be forgiven.—I was going to observe, that after the duty of our sabbath was over (on the day in which I was more distressed and afflicted than ever) we were all on our way home as usual, when a remarkable black cloud arose and covered the sun; then followed very heavy rain and thunder, more dreadful than ever I had heard: The heavens roared, and the earth trembled at it: I was highly affected and cast down; insomuch that I wept sadly, and could not follow my relations & friends home.—I was obliged to stop, and felt as if my legs were tied, they seemed to shake under me: So I stood still, being in great fear of the MAN of POWER, that I was persuaded, in myself, lived above. One of my young companions (who entertained a particular friendship for me, and I for him) came back to see for me: He asked me why I stood still in such very hard rain? I only said to him that my legs were weak, and I could not come faster: He was much affected to see me cry, and took me by the hand, and said he would lead me home, which he did. My mother was greatly alarmed at my tarrying out in such terrible weather; she asked me many questions, such as what I did so for? And if I was well? My dear mother, says I, pray tell me who is the GREAT MAN of POWER that makes the thunder? She said, there was no power but the sun, moon and stars; that they made all our country.—I then inquired how all our people came? She answered me, from one another; and so carried me to many generations back.—Then says I, who made the *first man*? And who made the first cow, and the first lion, and where does the fly come from, as no one can make him? My mother seemed in great trouble; she was apprehensive that my senses were impaired, or that I was foolish. My father came in, and seeing her in grief asked the cause, but when she related our conversation to him he was exceedingly angry with me, and told me he would punish me severely if ever I was so troublesome again; so that I resolved never to say any thing more to him. But I grew very unhappy in myself; my relations and acquaintance endeavoured, by all the means they could think on, to divert me, by taking me to ride upon goats (which is much the custom of our country) and to shoot with a bow and arrow; but I experienced no satisfaction at all in any of these things; nor could I be easy by any means whatever: My parents were very unhappy to see me so dejected and melancholy.

About this time there came a merchant from the *Gold Coast* (the third city in GUINEA) he traded with the inhabitants of our country in ivory, &c. he took great notice of my unhappy situation, and inquired into the cause; he expressed vast concern for me, and said, if my parents would part with me for a little while, and let him take me home with him, it would be of more service to me than any thing they could do for me.—He told me that if I would go with him I should see houses with wings to them walk upon the water, and should also see the white folks; and that he had many sons of my age, which should be my companions; and he added to all this that he would bring me safe back again soon.—I was highly pleased with the account of this strange place, and was very desirous of going.—I seemed sensible of a secret impulse upon my mind, which I could not resist, that seemed to tell me I must go. When my dear mother saw that I was willing to leave them, she spoke to my father and grandfather and the rest of my relations, who all agreed that I should accompany the merchant to the Gold Coast. I was the more willing as my brothers and sisters despised me, and looked on me with contempt on the account of my unhappy disposition; and even my servants slighted me, and disregarded all I said to them. I had one sister who was always exceeding fond of me, and I loved her entirely; her name was LOGWY, she was quite white, and fair, with fine light hair, though my father and mother were black.—I was truly concerned to leave my beloved sister, and she cry'd most sadly to part with me, wringing her hands, and discovered every sign of grief that can be imagined. Indeed if I could have known when I left my friends and country that I should never return to them again my misery on that occasion would have been inexpressible. All my relations were sorry to part with me; my dear mother came with me upon a camel more than three hundred miles, the first of our journey lay chiefly through woods: At night we secured ourselves from the wild beasts by making fires all around us; we and our camels kept within the circle, or we must have been torn to pieces by the lions, and other wild creatures, that roared terribly as soon as night came on, and continued to do so till morning.—There can be little said in favour of the country through which we passed; only a valley of marble that we came through which is unspeakably beautiful.—On each side of this valley are exceedingly high and almost inaccessible mountains—Some of these pieces of marble are of prodigious length and breadth but of different sizes and colour, and shaped in a variety of forms, in a wonderful manner.—It is most of it veined with gold mixed with striking and beautiful colours; so that when the sun darts upon it, it is as pleasing a sight as can be imagined.—The merchant that brought me from BOURNOU was in partnership with another gentleman who accompanied us; he was very unwilling that he should take me from home, as, he said, he foresaw many difficulties that would attend my going with them.—He endeavoured to prevail on the merchant to throw me into a very deep pit that was in the valley, but he refused to listen to him, and said, he was resolved to take care of me: But the other was greatly dissatisfied; and when we came to a river, which we were obliged to pass through, he purposed throwing me in and drowning me; but the merchant would not consent to it, so that I was preserved.

We travel'd till about four o'clock every day, and then began to make preparations for night, by cutting down large quantities of wood, to make fires to preserve us from the wild beasts.—I had a very unhappy and discontented journey, being in continual fear that the people I was with would murder me. I often reflected with extreme regret on the kind friends I had left, and the idea of my dear mother frequently drew tears from my eyes. I cannot recollect how long we were in going from *Bournou* to the *Gold Coast*; but as there is no shipping nearer to *Bournou* than that city, it was tedious in travelling so far by land, being upwards of a thousand miles.—I was heartily rejoiced when we arrived at the end of our journey: I now vainly imagined that all my troubles and inquietudes would terminate here; but could I have looked into futurity, I should have perceived that I had much more to suffer than I had before experienced, and that they had as yet but barely commenced.

I was now more than a thousand miles from home, without a friend or any means to procure one. Soon after I came to the merchant's house I heard the drums beat remarkably loud, and the trumpets blow—the persons accustom'd to this employ, are oblig'd to go upon a very high structure appointed for that purpose, that the sound might be heard at a great distance: They are higher than the steeples are in *England*. I was mightily pleased with sounds so entirely new to me, and was very inquisitive to know the cause of this rejoicing, and asked many questions concerning it: I was answered that it was meant as a compliment to me, because I was grandson to the King of *Bournou*.

This account gave me a secret pleasure; but I was not suffered long to enjoy this satisfaction, for, in the evening of the same day, two of the merchant's sons (boys about my own age) came running to me, and told me, that the next day I was to die, for the King intended to behead me.—I reply'd, that I was sure it could not be true, for that I came there to play with them, and to see houses walk upon the water, with wings to them, and the white folks; but I was soon informed that their King imagined I was sent by my father as a spy, and would make such discoveries, at my return home, that would enable them to make war with the greater advantage to ourselves; and for these reasons he had resolved I should never return to my native country.—When I heard this, I suffered misery that cannot be described.—I wished, a thousand times, that I had never left my friends and country.—But still the Almighty was pleased to work miracles for me.

The morning I was to die, I was washed and all my gold ornaments made bright and shining, and then carried to the palace, where the King was to behead me himself (as is the custom of the place).—He was seated upon a throne at the top of an exceeding large yard, or court, which you must go through to enter the palace, it is as wide and spacious as a large field in *England*.—I had a lane of

life-guards to go through.—I guessed it to be about three hundred paces. I was conducted by my friend, the merchant, about half way up; then he durst proceed no further: I went up to the King alone—I went with an undaunted courage, and it pleased God to melt the heart of the King, who sat with his scymitar in his hand ready to behead me; yet, being himself so affected, he dropped it out of his hand, and took me upon his knee and wept over me. I put my right hand round his neck, and prest him to my heart.—He set me down and blest me; and added that he would not kill me, and that I should not go home, but be sold for a slave, so then I was conducted back again to the merchant's house.

The next day he took me on board a French brig; the Captain did not chuse to buy me: He said I was too small; so the merchant took me home with him again. The partner, whom I have spoken of as my enemy, was very angry to see me return, and again purposed putting an end to my life; for he represented to the other, that I should bring them into troubles and difficulties, and that I was so little that no person would buy me.

The merchant's resolution began to waver, and I was indeed afraid that I should be put to death: But however he said he would try me once more. A few days after a *Dutch* ship came into the harbour, and they carried me on board, in hopes that the Captain would purchase me.—As they went, I heard them agree, that, if they could not sell me *then*, they would throw me overboard.—I was in extreme agonies when I heard this; and as soon as ever I saw the *Dutch* Captain, I ran to him, and put my arms round him, and said, "Father save me." (for I knew that if he did not buy me, I should be treated very ill, or, possibly murdered) And though he did not understand my language, yet it pleased the Almighty to influence him in my behalf, and he bought me *for two yards of check*, which is of more value *there*, than in *England*. When I left my dear mother I had a large quantity of gold about me, as is the custom of our country, it was made into rings, and they were linked into one another, and formed into a kind of chain, and so put round my neck, and arms and legs, and a large piece hanging at one ear almost in the shape of a pear. I found all this troublesome, and was glad when my new master took it from me.—I was now washed, & clothed in the *Dutch* or *English* manner.—My master grew very fond of me, and I loved him exceedingly. I watched every look, was always ready when he wanted me, and endeavoured to convince him, by every action, that my only pleasure was to serve him well.—I have since thought that he must have been a serious man. His actions corresponded very well with such a character.—He used to read prayers in public to the ship's crew every sabbath day; and when first I saw him read, I was never so surprised in my whole life as when I saw the book talk to my master; for I thought it did, as I observed him to look upon it, and move his lips.—I wished it would do so to me.—As soon as my master had done reading I follow'd him to the place where he put the book, being mightily delighted with it, and when nobody saw me, I open'd it and put my ear down close upon it, in great hope that it would say something to me; but was very sorry and greatly disappointed when I found it would not speak, this thought immediately presented itself to me, that every body and every thing despised me because I was black.

I was exceedingly sea-sick at first; but when I became more accustom'd to the sea, it wore off.— My master's ship was bound for *Barbados*. When we came there, he thought fit to speak of me to several gentlemen of his acquaintance, and one of them exprest a particular desire to see me.—He had a great mind to buy me; but the Captain could not immediately be prevail'd on to part with me; but however, as the gentleman seemed very solicitous, he at length let me go, and I was sold for fifty dollars (*four and six penny pieces in English*.) My new master's name was *Vanborn*, a young gentleman; his home was in *New-England*, in the city of *New-York*; to which place he took me with him. He dress'd me in his livery, & was very good to me. My chief business was to wait at table, and tea, & clean knives, & I had a very easy place; but the servants used to curse & swear surprizingly; which I learnt faster than any thing, 'twas almost the first

English I could speak. If any of them affronted me, I was sure to call upon God to damn them immediately; but I was broke of it all at once, occasioned by the correction of an old black servant that lived in the family.—One day I had just clean'd the knives for dinner, when one of the maids took one to cut bread and butter with; I was very angry with her, and called upon God to damn her; when this old black man told me I must not say so: I ask'd him why? He replied there was a wicked man, call'd the Devil, that liv'd in hell, and would take all that said these words and put them in the fire and burn them.—This terrified me greatly, and I was entirely broke of swearing. Soon after this, as I was placing the china for tea, my mistress came into the room just as the maid had been cleaning it; the girl had unfortunately sprinkled the wainscot with the mop; at which my mistress was angry; the girl very foolishly answered her again, which made her worse, and she called upon God to damn her.— I was vastly concern'd to hear this, as she was a fine young lady, and very good to me, insomuch that I could not help speaking to her: Madam, says I, you must not say so: Why, says she? Because there is a black man, call'd the Devil, that lives in hell, and he will put you in the fire and burn you, and I shall be very sorry for that. Who told you this, replied my lady? Old Ned, says I. Very well was all her answer; but she told my master of it, who ordered that old Ned should be tied up and whipp'd, and was never suffered to come into the kitchen, with the rest of the servants, afterwards.— My mistress was not angry with me, but rather diverted at my simplicity, and, by way of talk, she repeated what I had said to many of her acquaintance that visited her; among the rest, *Freelandhouse*, a very gracious, good minister, heard it, and he took a great deal of notice of me, and desired my master to part with me to him. He would not hear of it at first, but, being greatly persuaded, he let me go; and Mr. *Freelandhouse* gave £50 for me.—He took me home with him, and made me kneel down, and put my two hands together, and prayed for me, and every night and morning he did the same.—I could not make out what it was for, nor the meaning of it, nor what they spoke to when they talked—I thought it comical, but I liked it very well.—After I had been a little while with my new master I grew more familiar, and asked him the meaning of prayer: (I could hardly speak *English* to be understood) he took great pains with me, and made me understand that he pray'd to God, who liv'd in Heaven; that he was my father and *best* friend.—I told him that this must be a mistake; that *my* father lived at *Bournou*, and I wanted very much to see him, and likewise my dear mother, and sister, and I wished he would be so good as to send me home to them; and I added, all I could think of to induce him to convey me back, I appeared in great trouble, and my good master was so much affected that the tears ran down his face.

He told me that God was a great and good Spirit, that [he] created all the world, and every person and thing in it, *Ethiopia*, *Africa* and *America*, and every where. I was delighted when I heard this: There, says I, I always thought so when I lived at home! Now, if I had wings like an eagle, I would fly to tell my dear mother that God is greater than the sun, moon and stars; and that they were made by him.

I was exceedingly pleas'd with this information of my master's, because it corresponded so well with my own opinion; I thought now if I could but get home, I should be wiser than all my country-folks, my grandfather, or father, or mother, or any of them.—But though I was somewhat enlightened, by this information of my master's, yet I had no other knowledge of God than that he was a good Spirit, and created every body, and every thing.—I never was sensible, in myself, nor had any one ever told me, that he would punish the wicked, and love the just. I was only glad that I had been told there was a God, because I had always thought so.

My dear kind master grew very fond of me, as was his lady; she put me to school, but I was uneasy at that, and did not like to go; but my master and mistress requested me to learn in the gentlest terms, and persuaded me to attend my school without any anger at all; that, at last, I came to like it

better, and learnt to read pretty well. My school-master was a good man, his name was *Vanosdore*, and very indulgent to me.—I was in this state when, one Sunday, I heard my master preach from these words out of the *Revelations*, chap. i. v. 7. "*Behold, He cometh in the clouds and every eye shall see him and they that pierc'd Him.*" These words affected me excessively; I was in great agonies because I thought my master directed them to me only; and, I fancied, that he observed me with unusual earnestness—I was farther confirm'd in this belief as I looked round the church, and could see no one person beside myself in such grief and distress as I was; I began to think that my master hated me, and was very desirous to go home, to my own country; for I thought that if God did come (as he said) He would be sure to be most angry with *me*, as I did not know what He was, nor had ever heard of him before.

I went home in great trouble, but said nothing to any body.—I was somewhat afraid of my master; I thought he disliked me.—The next text I heard him preach from was, *Heb.* xii. 14. "*Follow peace with all men, and holiness, without which no man shall see the LORD.*" He preached the law so severely, that it made me tremble.—He said, that GOD would judge the whole world; *Ethiopia*, *Asia*, and *Africa*, and every where.—I was now excessively perplexed, and undetermined what to do; as I had now reason to believe that my situation would be equally bad to go as to stay.—I kept these thoughts to myself, and said nothing to any person whatever.

I should have complained to my good mistress of this great trouble of mind, but she had been a little strange to me for several days before this happened, occasioned by a story told of me by one of the maids. The servants were all jealous, and envied me the regard, and favour shewn me by my master and mistress; and the Devil being always ready, and diligent in wickedness, had influenced this girl to make a lie on me.—This happened about hay harvest, and one day, when I was unloading the waggon to put the hay into the barn, she watched an opportunity, in my absence, to take the fork out of the stick, and hide it: When I came again to my work, and could not find it, I was a good deal vexed, but I concluded it was dropt somewhere among the hay; so I went and bought another with my own money: When the girl saw that I had another, she was so malicious that she told my mistress I was very unfaithful, and not the person she took me for; and that she knew, I had, without my master's permission, ordered many things in his name, that he must pay for; and as a proof of my carelessnes produced the fork she had taken out of the stick, and said, she had found it out of doors—My Lady, not knowing the truth of these things, was a little shy to me, till she mentioned it, and then I soon cleared myself, and convinced her that these accusations were false.

I continued in a most unhappy state for many days. My good mistress insisted on knowing what was the matter. When I made known my situation, she gave me John Bunyan on the holy war, to read; I found his experience similar to my own, which gave me reason to suppose he must be a bad man; as I was convinced of my own corrupt nature, and the misery of my own heart: And as he acknowledged that he was likewise in the same condition, I experienced no relief at all in reading his work, but rather the reverse.—I took the book to my lady, and informed her I did not like it at all, it was concerning a wicked man as bad as myself; and I did not chuse to read it, and I desired her to give me another, wrote by a better man, that was holy, and without sin.—She assured me that John Bunyan was a good man, but she could not convince me; I thought him to be too much like myself to be upright, as his experience seemed to answer with my own.

I am very sensible that nothing but the great power and unspeakable mercies of the Lord could relieve my soul from the heavy burden it laboured under at that time.—A few days after my master gave me Baxter's *Call to the Unconverted*. This was no relief to me neither; on the contrary it occasioned as much distress in me as the other had before done, *as it* invited all to come to *Christ*; and I found myself so wicked and miserable that I

could not come—This consideration threw me into agonies that cannot be described; insomuch that I even attempted to put an end to my life—I took one of the large case-knives, and went into the stable with an intent to destroy myself; and as I endeavoured with all my strength to force the knife into my side, it bent double. I was instantly struck with horror at the thought of my own rashness, and my conscience told me that had I succeeded in this attempt I should probably have gone to hell.

I could find no relief, nor the least shadow of comfort; the extreme distress of my mind so affected my health that I continued very ill for three days, and nights; and would admit of no means to be taken for my recovery, though my lady was very kind, and sent many things to me; but I rejected every means of relief and wished to die—I would not go into my own bed, but lay in the stable upon straw—I felt all the horrors of a troubled conscience, so hard to be born, and saw all the vengeance of God ready to overtake me—I was sensible that there was no way for me to be saved unless I came to *Christ*, and I could not come to Him: I thought that it was impossible He should receive such a sinner as me. The last night that I continued in this place, in the midst of my distress these words were brought home upon my mind, "*Behold the Lamb of God*," I was something comforted at this, and began to grow easier and wished for day that I might find these words in my bible—I rose very early the following morning, and went to my school-master, Mr. Vanosdore, and communicated the situation of my mind to him; he was greatly rejoiced to find me inquiring the way to Zion, and blessed the Lord who had worked so wonderfully for me a poor heathen.—I was more familiar with this good gentleman than with my master, or any other person; and found my self more at liberty to talk to him: He encouraged me greatly, and prayed with me frequently, and I was always benefited by his discourse.

About a quarter of a mile from my master's house stood a large, remarkably fine oak-tree, in the midst of a wood; I often used to be employed there in cutting down trees, (a work I was very fond of) I seldom failed going to this place every day; sometimes twice a day if I could be spared. It was the highest pleasure I ever experienced to sit under this oak; for there I used to pour out all my complaints to the LORD: And when I had any particular grievance I used to go there, and talk to the tree, and tell my sorrows, as if it had been to a friend. Here I often lamented my own wicked heart, and undone state; and found more comfort and consolation than I ever was sensible of before.—Whenever I was treated with ridicule or contempt, I used to come here and find peace. I now began to relish the book my master gave me, Baxter's *Call to the Unconverted*, and took great delight in it. I was always glad to be employed in cutting wood, 'twas a great part of my business, and I followed it with delight, as I was then quite alone and my heart lifted up to GOD, and I was enabled to pray continually; and blessed for ever be his holy name, he faithfully answered my prayers. I can never be thankful enough to Almighty GOD for the many comfortable opportunities I experienced there. . . .

Source: Gronniosaw, James Albert Ukawsaw. *A narrative of the most remarkable particulars in the life of James Albert Ukawsaw Gronniosaw, an African prince, written by himself.* Bath printed: Newport, Rhode-Island, in Queen-Street, 1774. Reprinted and sold by Solomon Southwick [1731–1797]. Early American Imprints, 1st series, no. 13311.

Thomas Jefferson, *Notes on the State of Virginia*
(1782)

Thomas Jefferson has mostly been praised as one of the Founding Fathers of the American Republic. Yet he was also a slave owner who belonged to an elite group of Virginia planters who thought of themselves as liberal slave owners. The following excerpt from Notes on the State of Virginia, *Jefferson's only published work, illustrates a number of contradictions within Jefferson regarding the institution of slavery. For example, Jefferson was behind a vigorous legislative effort to free all slaves born after passage of a law providing for the education or colonization of slaves "in a distant area." This sentiment can be found in several other movements aimed at deporting former slaves to countries and islands outside the United States, including the Caribbean and back to Africa.*

From a slave's point of view, Jefferson was no liberal when it came to slavery. He may have eventually realized it was wrong for a country that upheld freedom as its highest ideal to also condone slavery, but he also opposed assimilating Negroes into the general population. This dilemma does not necessarily constitute the thinking of a liberal. Jefferson supported educating some Negroes, "according to their geniuses," a position which may simply have been motivated by the fact that he, like many planters, had fathered children with his slaves. On the one hand, Jefferson advocated freeing slaves, but on the other, he shared the widely held belief that race mixing was dangerous in a nation built on the backs of slaves. He is known to have supported racist claims that compared blacks to brutish-looking animals and suggested that their dark skin may have been colored by bile.

Nor can Jefferson be considered a liberal by any modern standards held by African Americans. Jefferson is sometimes credited with urging caution and scientific investigation before reaching a final conclusion on racial potentialities. However, the following notes on slavery clearly contradict any of his expressions of sympathy for the "Negro" of his period. To the contrary, inferior characteristics often attributed to blacks throughout the period of slavery and well into the 20th century might easily be attributed to Jefferson himself. These include such clichés as claims that Negroes were shiftless, lazy, and savage, or that they preferred to associate with whites over members of their own race.

By the early 1800s, Virginia leaders looked to the organization of the American Colonization Society as a way of deporting emancipated slaves to offshore colonies that would be supported financially by American funds. This was a position Jefferson supported.

It will probably be asked, why not retain and incorporate the blacks into the state, and thus save the expense of supplying, by importation of white settlers, the vacancies they will leave? Deep rooted prejudices entertained by the whites; ten thousand recollections, by the blacks, of the injuries they have sustained; new provocations; the real distinctions which nature has made; and many other circumstances, will divide us into parties and produce convulsions, which will probably never end but in the extermination of the one or the other race.

To these objections, which are political, may be added others, which are physical and moral. The first difference which strikes us is that of colour. Whether the black of the Negro resides in the reticular membrane between the skin and scarf-skin, or in the scarf-skin itself; whether it proceeds from the colour of the blood, the colour of the bile, or from that of some other secretion, the difference is fixed in nature, and is as real as if its seat and cause were better known to us. And is this difference of no importance? Is it not the foundation of a greater or less share of beauty in the two races?

Are not the fine mixtures of red and white, the expressions of every passion by greater or less suffusions of colour in the one, preferable to that eternal monotony, which reigns in the countenances, that immovable veil of black which covers all the emotions of the other race?

Add to these, flowing hair, a more elegant symmetry of form, their own judgment in favour of the whites, declared by their preference of them, as uniformly as is the preference of the Oranootan for the black women over those of his own species. The circumstance of Superior beauty is thought worthy attention in the propagation of our horses, dogs, and other domestic animals; why not in that of man? Besides those of colour, figure, and hair, there are other physical distinctions proving a difference of race. They have less hair on the face and body. They secrete less by the kidneys, and more by the glands of the skin, which gives them a very strong and disagreeable odour. This greater degree of transpiration renders them more tolerant of heat, and less so of cold than the whites. Perhaps, too, a difference of structure in the pulmonary apparatus, which a late ingenious experimentalist has discovered to be the principal regulator of animal heat, may have disabled them from extricating, in the act of inspiration, so much of that fluid from the outer air, or obliged them in expiration, to part with more of it. They seem to require less sleep. A black after hard labour through the day, will be induced by the slightest amusements to sit up till midnight, or later, though knowing he must be out with the first dawn of the morning. They are at least as brave, and more adventuresome. But this may perhaps proceed from a want of forethought, which prevents their seeing a danger till it be present.

When present, they do not go through it with more coolness or steadiness than the whites. They are more ardent after their female: but love seems with them to be more an eager desire, than a tender delicate mixture of sentiment and sensation. Their griefs are transient. Those numberless afflictions, which render it doubtful whether heaven has given life to us in mercy or in wrath, are less felt, and sooner forgotten with them. In general, their existence appears to participate more of sensation than reflection. To this must be ascribed their disposition to sleep when abstracted from their diversions, and unemployed in labour.

An animal whose body is at rest, and who does not reflect, must be disposed to sleep of course.

Comparing them by their faculties of memory, reason, and imagination, it appears to me that in memory they are equal to the whites; in reason much inferior, as I think one could scarcely be found capable of tracing and comprehending the investigations of Euclid; and that in imagination they are dull, tasteless, and anomalous. It would be unfair to follow them to Africa for this investigation.

We will consider them here, on the same stage with the whites, and where the facts are not apocryphal on which a judgment is to be formed. It will be right to make great allowances for the difference of condition, of education, of conversation, of the sphere in which they move. Many millions of them have been brought to, and born in America. Most of them indeed have been confined to tillage, to their own homes, and their own society: yet many have been so situated, that they might have availed themselves of the conversation of their masters; many have been brought up to the handicraft arts, and from that circumstance have always been associated with the whites. Some have been liberally educated, and all have lived in countries where the arts and sciences are cultivated to a considerable degree, and have had before their eyes samples of the best works from abroad.

The Indians, with no advantages of this kind, will often carve figures on their pipes not destitute of design and merit. They will crayon out an animal, a plant, or a country, so as to prove the existence of a germ in their minds which only wants cultivation. They astonish you with strokes of the most sublime oratory; such as prove their reason and sentiment strong, their imagination glowing and elevated.

But never yet could I find that a black had uttered a thought above the level of plain narration; never saw even an elementary trait of painting or sculpture.

In music they are more generally gifted than the whites with accurate ears for tune and time. . . . Whether they will be equal to the composition of a more extensive run of melody, or of complicated harmony, is yet to be proved. Misery is often the parent of the most affecting touches in poetry. Among the blacks is misery enough, God knows, but no poetry. Love is the peculiar oestrum of the poet. Their love is ardent, but it kindles the senses only, not the imagination. Religion indeed has produced a Phyllis Whately [sic] [Boston poet Phyllis Wheatley] but it could not produce a poet. The compositions published under her name are below the dignity of criticism. The heroes of the Dunciad are to her, as Hercules to the author of that poem.

Ignatius Sancho [ca. 1729–14 December 1780, an Afro-British composer, actor] has approached nearer to merit in composition; yet his letters do more honour to the heart than the head. They breathe the purest effusions of friendship and general philanthropy, and show how great a degree of the latter may be compounded with strong religious zeal. He is often happy in the turn of his compliments, and his style is easy and familiar, except when he affects a Shandean fabrication of words.

But his imagination is wild and extravagant, escapes incessantly from every restraint of reason and taste, and, in the course of its vagaries, leaves a tract of thought as incoherent and eccentric, as is the course of a meteor through the sky. His subjects should often have led him to a process of sober reasoning: yet we find him always substituting sentiment for demonstration. Upon the whole, though we admit him to the first place among those of his own colour who have presented themselves to the public judgment, yet when we compare him with the writers of the race among whom he lived and particularly with the epistolary class, in which he has taken his own stand, we are compelled to enroll him at the bottom of the column.

This criticism supposes the letters published under his name to be genuine, and to have received amendment from no other hand; points which would not be of easy investigation. The improvement of the blacks in body and mind, in the first instance of their mixture with the whites, has been observed by every one, and proves that their inferiority is not the effect merely of their condition of life. We know that among the Romans, about the Augustan age especially, the condition of their slaves was much more deplorable than that of the blacks on the continent of America.

The two sexes were confined in separate apartments, because to raise a child cost the master more than to buy one. Cato, for a very restricted indulgence to his slaves in this particular, took from them a certain price. But in this country the slaves multiply as fast as the free inhabitants. Their situation and manners place the commerce between the two sexes almost without restraint. The same Cato, on a principle of economy, always sold his sick and superannuated slaves. He gives it as a standing precept to a master visiting his farm, to sell his old oxen, old wagons, old tools, old and diseased servants, and every thing else become useless. . . .

The American slaves cannot enumerate this among the injuries and insults they receive.

With the Romans, the regular method of taking the evidence of their slaves was under torture. Here it has been thought better never to resort to their evidence. When a master was murdered, all his slaves, in the same house, or within hearing, were condemned to death. Here punishment falls on the guilty only, and as precise proof is required against him as against a freeman. Yet notwithstanding these and other discouraging circumstances among the Romans, their slaves were often their rarest artists. They excelled too in science, insomuch as to be usually employed as tutors to their masters' children. Epictetus, Terence, and Phaedrus, were slaves. But they were of the race of whites. It is not their condition then, but nature, which has produced the distinction.

The man, in whose favour no laws of property exist, probably feels himself less bound to respect those made in favour of others. When arguing for ourselves, we lay it down as a fundamental, that laws, to be just, must give a reciprocation of right; that, without this, they are mere arbitrary rules of conduct, founded in force, and not in conscience: and it is a problem which I give to the master to solve, whether the religious precepts against the violation of property were not framed for him as well as his slave? And whether the slave may not as justifiably take a little from one, who has taken all from him, as he may slay one who would slay him? That a change in the relations in which a man is placed should change his ideas of moral right or wrong, is neither new, nor peculiar to the colour of the blacks. Homer tells us it was so 2600 years ago.

> Jove fix'd it certain, that whatever day
> Makes man a slave, takes half his worth away.

But the slaves of which Homer speaks were whites. Notwithstanding these considerations which must weaken their respect for the laws of property, we find among them numerous instances of the most rigid integrity, and as many as among their better instructed masters, of benevolence, gratitude and unshaken fidelity. The opinion, that they are inferior in the faculties of reason and imagination, must be hazarded with great diffidence. To justify a general conclusion, requires many observations, even where the subject may be submitted to the anatomical knife, to optical classes, to analysis by fire, or by solvents. How much more then where it is a faculty, not a substance, we are examining; where it eludes the research of all the Senses; where the conditions of its existence are various and variously combined; where the effects of those which are present or absent bid defiance to calculation; let me add too, as a circumstance of great tenderness, where our conclusion would degrade a whole race of men from the rank in the scale of beings which their Creator may perhaps have given them. To our reproach it must be said, that though for a century and a half we have had under our eyes the races of black and of red men, they have never yet been viewed by us as subjects of natural history.

I advance it therefore as a suspicion only, that the blacks, whether originally a distinct race, or made distinct by time and circumstances, are inferior to the whites in the endowments both of body and mind. It is not against experience to suppose, that different Species of the same genus, or varieties of the same species, may possess different qualifications. Will not a lover of natural history then, one who views the gradations in all the races of animals with the eye of philosophy, excuse an effort to keep those in the department of man as distinct as nature has formed them?

This unfortunate difference of colour, and perhaps of faculty, is a powerful obstacle to the emancipation of these people. Many of their advocates, while they wish to vindicate the liberty of human nature are anxious also to preserve its dignity and beauty. Some of these, embarrassed by the question "What further is to be done with them?" join themselves in opposition with those who are actuated by sordid avarice only. Among the Romans emancipation required but one effort. The slave, when made free, might mix with, without staining the blood of his master. But with us a second is necessary, unknown to history. When freed, he is to be removed beyond the reach of mixture.

It is difficult to determine on the standard by which the manners of a nation may be tried, whether [C]atholic, or particular. It is more difficult for a native to bring to that standard the manners of his own nation, familiarized to him by habit. There must doubtless be an unhappy influence on the manners of our people produced by the existence of slavery among us. The whole commerce between master and slave is a perpetual exercise of the most boisterous passions, the most unremitting despotism on the one part, and degrading submissions on the other.

Our children see this, and learn to imitate it; for man is an imitative animal. This quality is the germ of all education in him. From his cradle to his grave he is learning to do what he sees others do. If a parent could find no motive either in his philanthropy or his self love, for restraining the intemperance of passion towards his slave, it should always be a sufficient one that his child is present. But generally it is not sufficient.

The parent storms, the child looks on, catches the lineaments of wrath, puts on the same airs in the circle of smaller slaves, gives a loose to the worst of passions, and thus nursed, educated, and daily exercised in tyranny, cannot but be stamped by it with odious pecularities. The man must be a prodigy who can retain his manners and morals undepraved by such circumstances. And with what execration should the statesman be loaded, who, permitting one half the citizens thus to trample on the rights of the other, transforms those into despots, and these into enemies, destroys the morals of the one part, and the amor patriae of the other. For if a slave can have a country in this world, it must be any other in preference to that in which he is born to live and labour for another; in which he must lock up the faculties of his nature, contribute as far as depends on his individual endeavours to the evanishment of the human race, or entail his own miserable condition on the endless generations proceeding from him. With the morals of the people, their industry also is destroyed. For in a warm climate, no man will labour for himself who can make another labour for him. This is so true, that of the proprietors of slaves a very small proportion indeed are ever seen to labour. And can the liberties of a nation be thought secure when we have removed their only firm basis, a conviction in the minds of the people that these liberties are of the gift of God? That they are not to be violated but with his wrath? Indeed I tremble for my country when I reflect that God is just: that his justice cannot sleep for ever: that considering numbers, nature and natural means only, a revolution of the wheel of fortune, an exchange of situation is among possible events: that it may become probable by supernatural interference! The almighty has no attribute which can take side with us in such a contest.

But it is impossible to be temperate and to pursue this subject through the various considerations of policy, of morals, of history natural and civil. We must be contented to hope they will force their way into every one's mind. I think a change already perceptible, since the origin of the present revolution. The spirit of the master is abating, that of the slave rising from the dust, his condition mollifying, the way I hope preparing, under the auspices of heaven, for a total emancipation, and that this is disposed, in the order of events, to be with the consent of the masters, rather than by their extirpation.

Source: Jefferson, Thomas. *Notes on the State of Virginia,* 1782. The Avalon Project, Yale Law School, New Haven, CT.

Jupiter Hammon, *An Address to the Negroes in the State of New-York* (1787)

Jupiter Hammon is often referred to as "the first black poet in America." Records of his career as a poet are sketchy, and records of his career are obscure. According to various accounts of his life, he was a slave on Long Island, New York, where he lived and worked for the Lloyd family in Lloyd's Neck, not far from Queen's Village, New York. According to the Yale New Haven Teacher's Institute, Hammon was a minister before he became known as a poet. His poetic work first began to appear in print in the 1760s. Reproduced below is Hammon's Address to the Negroes in the State of New-York, *which, while no apology for slavery, offers advice to fellow slaves and reflections upon the nature of relations between blacks and whites.*

AN ADDRESS TO THE NEGROES,

In the State of New York
By Jupiter Hammon,
servant of John Lloyd,: jun, Esq; of the Manor of Queen's Village, Long-Island.

> "Of a truth I perceive that God is no respecter of persons: But in every Nation, he that feareth him and worketh righteousness, is accepted with him."
>
> Acts x. 34, 35.

TO THE MEMBERS OF THE AFRICAN SOCIETY IN THE CITY OF NEW YORK

Gentlemen,

I take the liberty to dedicate an address to my poor brethren to you. If you think it is likely to do good among them, I do not doubt but you will take it under your care. You have discovered so much kindness and good will to those you thought were oppressed, and had no helper, that I am sure you will not despise what I have wrote, if you judge it will be of any service to them. I have nothing to add, but only to wish that "the blessing of many ready to perish, may come upon you."

I am Gentlemen,
Your Servant,
JUPITER HAMMON

. . .

AN ADDRESS TO THE NEGROES IN THE STATE OF NEW YORK

When I am writing to you with a design to say something to you for your good, and with a view to promote your happiness, I can with truth and sincerity join with the apostle Paul, when speaking of his own nation the Jews, and say, "That I have great heaviness and continual sorrow in my heart for my brethren, my kinsmen according to the flesh." Yes my dear brethren, when I think of you, which is very often, and of the poor, despised and miserable state you are in, as to the things of this world, and when I think of your ignorance and stupidity, and the great wickedness of the most of you, I am pained to the heart. It is at times, almost too much for human nature to bear, and I am obliged to turn my thoughts from the subject or endeavour to still my mind, by considering that it is permitted thus to be, by that God who governs all things, who seteth up one and pulleth down another. While I have been thinking on this subject, I have frequently had great struggles in my own mind, and have been at a loss to know what to do. I have wanted exceedingly to say something to you, to call upon you with the tenderness of a father and friend, and to give you the last, and I may say, dying advice, of an old man, who wishes our best good in this world, and in the world to come. But while I have had such desires, a sense of my own ignorance, and unfitness to teach others, has frequently discouraged me from attempting to say any thing to you; yet when I thought of your situation, I could not rest easy.

When I was at Hartford in Connecticut, where I lived during the war, I published several pieces which were well received, not only by those of my own colour, but by a number of the white people, who thought they might do good among their servants. This is one consideration, among others, that emboldens me now to publish what I have written to you. Another is, I think you will be more likely to listen to what is said, when you know it comes from a negro, one your own nation and colour, and therefore can have no interest in deceiving you, or in saying any thing to you, but what he really thinks is your interest and duty to comply with. My age, I think, gives me some right to speak to you, and reason to expect you will hearken to my advice. I am now upwards of seventy years old, and cannot expect, though I am well, and able to do almost any kind of business, to live much longer. I have passed the common bounds set for man, and must soon go the way of all the earth. I have had more experience in the world than the most of you, and I have seen a great deal of the vanity, and wickedness of it. I have great reason to be thankful that my lot has been so much better than most slaves have had. I suppose I have had more advantages and privileges than most of you, who are slaves have ever known, and I believe more than many white people have enjoyed, for which I desire to bless God, and pray that he may bless those who have given them to me. I do not, my dear friends, say these things about myself to make you think that I am wiser or better than others; but that you might hearken, without prejudice, to what I have to say to you on the following particulars.

Ist. Respecting obedience to masters. Now whether it is right, and lawful, in the sight of God, for them to make slaves of us or not, I am certain that while we are slaves, it is our duty to obey our masters, in all their lawful commands, and mind them unless we are bid to do that which we know to be sin, or forbidden in God's word. The apostle Paul says, "Servants be obedient to them that are your masters according to the flesh, with fear and trembling in singleness in your heart as unto Christ: Not with eye service, as men pleasers, but as the servants of Christ doing the will of God from the heart: With good will doing service to the Lord, and not to men: Knowing that whatever thing a man doeth the same shall he receive of the Lord, whether he be bond or free."—Here is a plain command of God for us to obey our masters. It may seem hard for us, if we think our masters wrong in holding us slaves, to obey in all things, but who of us dare dispute with God! He has commanded us to obey, and we ought to do it cheerfully, and freely. This should be done by us, not only because God commands, but because our own peace and comfort depend upon it. As we depend upon our masters, for what we eat and drink and wear, and for all our comfortable things in this world, we cannot be happy, unless we please them. This we cannot do without obeying them freely, without muttering or finding fault. If a servant strives to please his master and studies and takes pains to do it, I believe there are but few masters who would use such a servant cruelly. Good servants frequently make good masters. If your master is really hard, unreasonable and cruel, there is no way so likely for you to convince him of it, as always to obey his commands, and try to serve him, and take care of his interest, and try to promote it all in your power. If you are proud and stubborn and always finding fault, your master will think the fault lies wholly on your side, but if you are humble, and meek, and bear all things patiently, your master may think he is wrong, if he does not, his neighbours will be apt to see it, and will befriend you, and try to alter his conduct. If this does not do, you must cry to him, who has the hearts of all men in his hands, and turneth them as the rivers of waters are turned.

2d: The particular I would mention, is honesty and faithfulness. You must suffer me now to deal plainly with you, my dear brethren, for I do not mean to flatter, or omit speaking the truth, whether it is for you, or against you. How many of you are there who allow yourselves in stealing from your masters. It is very wicked for you not to take care of your masters goods, but how much worse is it to pilfer and steal from them, whenever you think you shall not be found out. This you must know is very wicked and provoking to God. There are none of you so ignorant, but that you must know that this is wrong. Though you may try to excuse yourselves, by saying that your masters are unjust to you, and though you may try to quiet your consciences in this way, yet if you are honest in owning the truth you must think it is as wicked, and on some accounts more wicked to steal from your masters, than from others.

We cannot certainly, have any excuse either for taking any thing that belongs to our masters without their leave, or for being unfaithful in their business. It is our duty to be faithful, not with eye service as men pleasers. We have no right to stay when we are sent on errands, any longer than to do the business we were sent upon. All the time spent idly, is spent wickedly, and is unfaithfulness to our masters. In these things I must say, that I think many of you are guilty. I know that many of you endeavour to excuse yourselves, and say that you have nothing that you can call your own, and that you are under great temptations to be unfaithful and take from your masters. But this will not do, God will certainly punish you for stealing and for being unfaithful. All that we have to mind is our own duty. If God has put us in bad circumstances that is not our fault and he will not punish us for it. If any are wicked in keeping us so, we cannot help it, they must answer to God for it. Nothing will serve as an excuse to us for not doing our duty. The same God will judge both them and us. Pray then my dear friends, fear to offend in this way, but be faithful to God, to your masters, and to your own souls.

The next thing I would mention, and warn you against, is profaneness. This you know is forbidden by God. Christ tells us, "swear not at all," and again it is said "thou shalt not take the name of the Lord thy God in vain, for the Lord will not hold him guiltless, that taketh his name in vain." Now though the great God has forbidden it, yet how dreadfully profane are many, and I don't know but

I may say the most of you? How common is it to hear you take the terrible and awful name of the great God in vain?—To swear by it, and by Jesus Christ, his Son—How common is it to hear you wish damnation to your companions, and to your own souls—and to sport with in the name of Heaven and Hell, as if there were no such places for you to hope for, or to fear. Oh my friends, be warned to forsake this dreadful sin of profaneness. Pray my dear friends, believe and realize, that there is a God—that he is great and terrible beyond what you can think—that he keeps you in life every moment—and that he can send you to that awful Hell, that you laugh at, in an instant, and confine you there for ever, and that he will certainly do it, if you do not repent. You certainly do not believe, that there is a God, or that there is a Heaven or Hell, or you would never trifle with them. It would make you shudder, if you heard others do it, if you believe them as much, as you believe any thing you see with your bodily eyes.

I have heard some learned and good men say, that the heathen, and all that worshiped false Gods, never spoke lightly or irreverently of their Gods, they never took their names in vain, or jested with those things which they held sacred. Now why should the true God, who made all things, be treated worse in this respect, than those false Gods, that were made of wood and stone. I believe it is because Satan tempts men to do it. He tried to make them love their false Gods, and to speak well of them, but he wishes to have men think lightly of the true God, to take his holy name in vain, and to scoff at, and make a jest of all things that are really good. You may think that Satan has not power to do so much, and have so great influence on the minds of men: But the scripture says, "he goeth about like a roaring Lion, seeking whom he may devour—That he is the prince of the power of the air—and that he rules in the hearts of the children of disobedience,—and that wicked men are led captive by him, to do his will." All those of you who are profane, are serving the Devil. You are doing what he tempts and desires you to do. If you could see him with your bodily eyes, would you like to make an agreement with him, to serve him, and do as he bid you. I believe most of you would be shocked at this, but you may be certain that all of you who allow yourselves in this sin, are as really serving him, and to just as good purpose, as if you met him, and promised to dishonor God, and serve him with all your might. Do you believe this? It is true whether you believe it or not. Some of you to excuse yourselves, may plead the example of others, and say that you hear a great many white-people, who know more, than such poor ignorant negroes, as you are, and some who are rich and great gentlemen, swear, and talk profanely; and some of you may say this of your masters, and say no more than is true. But all this is not a sufficient excuse for you. You know that murder is wicked. If you saw your master kill a man, do you suppose this would be any excuse for you, if you should commit the same crime? You must know it would not; nor will your hearing him curse and swear, and take the name of God in vain, or any other man, be he ever so great or rich, excuse you. God is greater than all other beings, and him we are bound to obey. To him we must give an account for every idle word that we speak. He will bring us all, rich and poor, white and black, to his judgment seat. If we are found among those who feared his name, and trembled at his word, we shall be called good and faithful servants. Our slavery will be at an end, and though ever so mean, low, and despised in this world, we shall sit with God in his kingdom as Kings and Priests, and rejoice forever, and ever. Do not then, my dear friends, take God's holy name in vain, or speak profanely in any way. Let not the example of others lead you into the sin, but reverence and fear that great and fearful name, the Lord our God. I might now caution you against other sins to which you are exposed; but as I meant only to mention those you were exposed to, more than others, by your being slaves, I will conclude what I have to say to you, by advising you to become religious, and to make religion the great business of your lives.

Now I acknowledge that liberty is a great thing, and worth seeking for, if we can get it honestly, and by our good conduct, prevail on our masters to set us free: Though for my own part I do not wish to be free, yet I should be glad, if others, especially the young negroes were to be free, for many of us, who are grown up slaves, and have always had masters to take care of us, should hardly know how to take care of ourselves; and it may be more for our own comfort to remain as we are. That liberty is a great thing we may know from our own feelings, and we may likewise judge so from the conduct of the white-people, in the late war. How much money has been spent, and how many lives has been lost, to defend their liberty. I must say that I have hoped that God would open their eyes, when they were so much engaged for liberty, to think of the state of the poor blacks, and to pity us. He has done it in some measure, and has raised us up many friends, for which we have reason to be thankful, and to hope in his mercy. What may be done further, he only knows, for known unto God are all his ways from the beginning. But this my dear brethren is by no means, the greatest thing we have to be concerned about. Getting our liberty in this world, is nothing to our having the liberty of the children of God. Now the Bible tells us that we are all by nature, sinners, that we are slaves to sin and Satan, and that unless we are converted, or born again, we must be miserable forever. Christ says, except a man be born again, he cannot see the kingdom of God, and all that do not see the kingdom of God, must be in the kingdom of darkness. There are but two places where all go after death, white and black, rich and poor; those places are Heaven and Hell. Heaven is a place made for those, who are born again, and who love God, and it is a place where they will be happy for ever. Hell is a place made for those who hate God, and are his enemies, and where they will be miserable to all eternity. Now you may think you are not enemies to God, and do not hate him: But if your heart has not been changed, and you have not become true Christians, you certainly are enemies to God, and have been opposed to him ever since you were born. Many of you, I suppose, never think of this, and are almost as ignorant as the beasts that perish. Those of you who can read I must beg you to read the Bible, and whenever you can get time, study the Bible, and if you can get no other time, spare some of your time from sleep, and learn what the mind and will of God is. But what shall I say to them who cannot read. This lay with great weight on my mind, when I thought of writing to my poor brethren, but I hope that those who can read will take pity on them and read what I have to say to them. In hopes of this I will beg of you to spare no pains in trying to learn to read. If you are once engaged you may learn. Let all the time you can get be spent in trying to learn to read. Get those who can read to learn you, but remember, that what you learn for, is to read the Bible. If there was no Bible, it would be no matter whether you could read or not. Reading other books would do you no good. But the Bible is the word of God, and tells you what you must do to please God; it tells you how you may escape misery, and be happy for ever. If you see most people neglect the Bible, and many that can read never look into it, let it not harden you and make you think lightly of it, and that it is a book of no worth. All those who are really good, love the Bible, and meditate on it day and night. In the Bible God has told us every thing it is necessary we should know, in order to be happy here and hereafter. The Bible is a revelation of the mind and will of God to men. Therein we may learn, what God is. That he made all things by the power of his word; and that he made all things for his own glory, and not for our glory. That he is over all, and above all his creatures, and more above them that we can think or conceive—that they can do nothing without him—that he upholds them all, and will over-rule all things for his own glory. In the Bible likewise we are told what man is. That he was at first made holy, in the image of God, that he fell from that state of holiness, and became an enemy to God, and that since the fall, all the imaginations of the thoughts of his heart, are evil and only evil, and that continually. That the carnal mind is not subject to the law of God, nei-ther indeed can be. And that all mankind, were under the wrath, and curse of God, and must have been for ever miserable, if they had been left to

suffer what their sins deserved. It tells us that God, to save some of mankind, sent his Son into this world to die, in the room and stead of sinners, and that now God can save from eternal misery, all that believe in his Son, and take him for their saviour, and that all are called upon to repent, and believe in Jesus Christ. It tells us that those who do repent, and believe, and are friends to Christ, shall have many trials and sufferings in this world, but that they shall be happy forever, after death, and reign with Christ to all eternity. The Bible tells us that this world is a place of trial, and that there is no other time or place for us to alter, but in this life. If we are Christians when we die, we shall awake to the resurrection of life; if not, we shall awake to the resurrection of damnation. It tells us, we must all live in Heaven or Hell, be happy or miserable, and that without end. The Bible does not tell us of but two places, for all to go to. There is no place for innocent folks, that are not Christians. There is no place for ignorant folks, that did not know how to be Christians. What I mean is, that there is no place besides Heaven and Hell. These two places, will receive all mankind, for Christ says, there are but two sorts, he that is not with me is against me, and he that gathereth not with me, scattereth abroad.— The Bible likewise tells us that this world, and all things in it shall be burnt up—and that "God has appointed a day in which he will judge the world, and that he will bring every secret thing whether it be good or bad into judgment—that which is done in secret shall be declared on the house top." I do not know, nor do I think any can tell, but that the day of judgment may last a thousand years. God could tell the state of all his creatures in a moment, but then every thing that every one has done, through his whole life is to be told, before the whole world of angels, and men. There, Oh how solemn is the thought! You, and I, must stand, and hear every thing we have thought or done, however secret, however wicked and vile, told before all the men and women that ever have been, or ever will be, and before all the angels, good and bad.

Now my dear friends seeing the Bible is the word of God, and every thing in it is true, and it reveals such awful and glorious things, what can be more important than that you should learn to read it; and when you have learned to read, that you should study it day and night. There are some things very encouraging in God's word for such ignorant creatures as we are; for God hath not chosen the rich of this world. Not many rich, not many noble are called, but God hath chosen the weak things of this world, and things which are not, to confound the things that are: And when the great and the rich refused coming to the gospel feast, the servant was told, to go into the highways, and hedges, and compel those poor creatures that he found there to come in. Now my brethren it seems to me, that there are no people that ought to attend to the hope of happiness in another world so much as we do. Most of us are cut off from comfort and happiness here in this world, and can expect nothing from it. Now seeing this is the case, why should we not take care to be happy after death. Why should we spend our whole lives in sinning against God: And be miserable in this world, and in the world to come. If we do thus, we shall certainly be the greatest fools. We shall be slaves here, and slaves forever. We cannot plead so great temptations to neglect religion as others. Riches and honours which drown the greater part of mankind, who have the gospel, in perdition, can be little or no temptations to us.

We live so little time in this world that it is no matter how wretched and miserable we are, if it prepares us for heaven. What is forty, fifty, or sixty years, when compared to eternity. When thousands and millions of years have rolled away, this eternity will be no nigher coming to an end. Oh how glorious is an eternal life of happiness! And how dreadful, an eternity of misery. Those of us who have had religious masters, and have been taught to read the Bible, and have been brought by their example and teaching to a sense of divine things, how happy shall we be to meet them in heaven, where we shall join them in praising God forever. But if any of us have had such masters, and yet have lived and died wicked, how will it add to our misery to think of our folly. If any of us, who have wicked and

profane masters should become religious, how will our estates be changed in another world. Oh my friends, let me entreat of you to think on these things, and to live as if you believed them to be true. If you become Christians you will have reason to bless God forever, that you have been brought into a land where you have heard the gospel, though you have been slaves. If we should ever get to Heaven, we shall find nobody to reproach us for being black, or for being slaves. Let me beg of you my dear African brethren, to think very little of your bondage in this life, for your thinking of it will do you no good. If God designs to set us free, he will do it, in his own time, and way; but think of your bondage to sin and Satan, and do not rest, until you are delivered from it. We cannot be happy if we are ever so free or ever so rich, while we are servants of sin, and slaves to Satan. We must be miserable here, and to all eternity. I will conclude what I have to say with a few words to those negroes who have their liberty. The most of what I have said to those who are slaves may be of use to you, but you have more advantages, on some accounts, if you will improve your freedom, as you may do, than they. You have more time to read God's holy word, and to take care of the salvation of your souls. Let me beg of you to spend your time in this way, or it will be better for you, if you had always been slaves. If you think seriously of the matter, you must conclude, that if you do not use your freedom, to promote the salvation of your souls, it will not be of any lasting good to you. Besides all this, if you are idle, and take to bad courses, you will hurt those of your brethren who are slaves, and do all in your power to prevent their being free. One great reason that is given by some for not freeing us, I understand is, that we should not know how to take care of ourselves, and should take to bad courses. That we should be lazy and idle, and get drunk and steal. Now all those of you, who follow any bad courses, and who do not take care to get an honest living by your labour and industry, are doing more to prevent our being free, than any body else. Let me beg of you then for the sake of your own good and happiness, in time, and for eternity, and for the sake of your poor brethren, who are still in bondage "to lead quiet and peaceable lives in all Godliness and honesty," and may God bless you, and bring you to his kingdom, for Christ's sake, Amen.

Finis

Source: Hammon, Jupiter. *An address to the negroes in the state of New-York*, 1787. New York: Samuel Wood, 1806. American Memory Collection. Library of Congress Rare Book and Special Collections Division.

The Interesting Narrative of the Life of Olaudah Equiano, or Gustavus Vassa, the African
(1789)

Captured in Africa at the age of 11, Olaudah Equiano was sold into slavery but later acquired his freedom. In 1789, he wrote his widely read autobiography, which is excerpted here. The youngest son of a village leader, Equiano was born among the Ibo people in the kingdom of Benin, along the Niger River. His family expected him to follow in his father's footsteps and become a chief, an elder, and a judge. Slavery was an integral part of the Ibo culture, as it was with many other African peoples. Equiano's family owned slaves, but there was also a continual threat of being abducted and becoming someone else's slave. This is what happened one day, while Equiano and his sister were at home alone.

Two men and a woman captured the children. Several days later Equiano and his sister were separated. Equiano continued to travel farther and farther away from home, day after day, month after month, exchanging masters along the way. As it was for all slaves, the Middle Passage (the term often used for the slave routes across the Atlantic Ocean) for Equiano was a long, arduous nightmare. In his autobiography he describes the inconceivable conditions of the slaves' hold: the "shrieks of the women," the "groans of the dying," the floggings, the wish to commit suicide, how those who somehow managed to drown themselves were envied.

The ship finally arrived at Barbados, where buyers purchased most of the slaves. There was no buyer, however, for the young Equiano. Less than two weeks after his arrival, he was shipped off to the English colony of Virginia, where he was purchased and put to work. Less than a month later, he had a new master—Michael Henry Pascal, a lieutenant in the Royal Navy. Under this master, who owned Equiano for the next seven years, Equiano would move to England, educate himself, and travel the world on ships under Pascal's command.

CHAPTER 2

I hope the reader will not think I have trespassed on his patience in introducing myself to him with some account of the manners and customs of my country. They had been implanted in me with great care, and made an impression on my mind, which time could not erase, and which all the adversity and variety of fortune I have since experienced, served only to rivet and record: for, whether the love of one's country be real or imaginary, or a lesson of reason, or an instinct of nature, I still look back with pleasure on the first scenes of my life, though that pleasure has been for the most part mingled with sorrow.

I have already acquainted the reader with the time and place of my birth. My father, besides many slaves, had a numerous family, of which seven lived to grow up, including myself and my sister, who was the only daughter. As I was the youngest of the sons, I became, of course, the greatest favorite with my mother, and was always with her; and she used to take particular pains to form my mind. I was trained up from my earliest years in the art of war: my daily exercise was shooting and throwing javelins, and my mother adorned me with emblems, after the manner of our greatest warriors. In this way I grew up till I had turned the age of eleven, when an end was put to my happiness in the following manner: Generally, when the grown people in the neighborhood were gone far in the fields to labor, the children assembled together in some of the neighboring premises to play; and commonly some of us used to get up a tree to look out for any assailant, or kidnapper, that might come upon us—for they sometimes took those opportunities of our parents' absence, to attack and carry off as many as they could seize. One day as I was watching at the top of a tree in our yard, I saw one of those people come into the yard of our next neighbor but one, to kidnap, there being many stout young people in it. Immediately on this I gave the alarm of the rogue, and he was surrounded by the stoutest of them, who entangled him with cords, so that he could not escape, till some of the grown people came and secured him. But, alas! Ere long it was my fate to be thus attacked, and to be carried off, when none of the grown people were nigh.

One day, when all our people were gone out to their works as usual, and only I and my dear sister were left to mind the house, two men and a woman got over our walls, and in a moment seized us both, and, without giving us time to cry out, or make resistance, they stopped our mouths, and ran off with us into the nearest wood. Here they tied our hands, and continued to carry us as far as they could, till night came on, when we reached a small house, where the robbers halted for refreshment, and spent the night. We were then unbound, but were unable to take any food; and, being quite overpowered by fatigue and grief, our only relief was some sleep, which allayed our misfortune for a short time. The next morning we left the house, and continued traveling all the day. For a long time we had kept the woods, but at last we came into a road which I believed I knew. I had now some hopes of being delivered; for we had advanced but a little way before I discovered some people at a distance, on which I began to cry out for their assistance; but my cries had no other effect than to make them tie me faster and stop my mouth, and then they put me into a large sack. They also stopped my sister's mouth, and tied her hands; and in this manner we proceeded till we were out of sight of these people. When we went to rest the following night, they offered us some victuals, but we refused it; and the only comfort we had was in being in one another's arms all that night, and bathing each other with our tears. But alas! We were soon deprived of even the small comfort of weeping together.

The next day proved a day of greater sorrow than I had yet experienced; for my sister and I were then separated, while we lay clasped in each other's arms. It was in vain that we besought them not to part us; she was torn from me, and immediately carried away, while I was left in a state of distraction not to be described. I cried and grieved continually; and for several days did not eat anything but what they forced into my mouth. At length, after many days' traveling, during which I had often changed masters, I got into the hands of a chieftain, in a very pleasant country. This man had two wives and some children, and they all used me extremely well, and did all they could do to comfort me; particularly the first wife, who was something like my mother. Although I was a great many days' journey from my father's house, yet these people spoke exactly the same language with us. This first master of mine, as I may call him, was a smith, and my principal employment was working his bellows, which were the same kind as I had seen in my vicinity. They were in some respects not unlike the stoves here in gentlemen's kitchens, and were covered over with leather; and in the middle of that leather a stick was fixed, and a person stood up, and worked it in the same manner as is done to pump water out of a cask with a hand pump. I believe it was gold he worked, for it was of a lovely bright yellow color, and was worn by the women on their wrists and ankles.

I was there I suppose about a month, and they at last used to trust me some little distance from the house. This liberty I used in embracing every opportunity to inquire the way to my own home; and I also sometimes, for the same purpose, went with the maidens, in the cool of the evenings, to bring pitchers of water from the springs for the use of the house. I had also remarked where the sun rose in the morning, and set in the evening, as I had travelled along; and I had observed that my father's house was towards the rising of the sun. I therefore determined to seize the first opportunity of making my escape, and to shape my course for that quarter; for I was quite oppressed and weighed down by grief after my mother and friends; and my love of liberty, ever great, was strengthened by the mortifying circumstance of not daring to eat with the free-born children, although I was mostly their companion.

While I was projecting my escape, one day an unlucky event happened, which quite disconcerted my plan, and put an end to my hopes. I used to be sometimes employed in assisting an elderly slave to cook and take care of the poultry; and one morning, while I was feeding some chickens, I happened to toss a small pebble at one of them, which hit it on the middle, and directly killed it. The old slave, having soon after missed the chicken, inquired after it; and on my relating the accident (for I told her the truth, for my mother would never suffer me to tell a lie), she flew into a violent passion, and threatened that I should suffer for it; and, my master being out, she immediately went and told her mistress what I had done. This alarmed me very much, and I expected an instant flogging, which to me was uncommonly dreadful, for I had seldom been beaten at home. I therefore resolved to fly; and accordingly I ran into a thicket that was hard by, and hid myself in the bushes. Soon afterwards my mistress and the slave returned, and, not seeing me, they searched all the house, but not finding me, and I not making answer when they called to me, they thought I had run away, and the whole neighborhood was raised in the pursuit of me.

In that part of the country, as in ours, the houses and villages were skirted with woods, or shrubberies, and the bushes were so thick that a man could readily conceal himself in them, so as to elude the strictest search. The neighbors continued the whole day looking for me, and several times many of them came within a few yards of the place where I lay hid. I expected every moment, when I heard a rustling among the trees, to be found out, and punished by my master; but they never discovered me, though they were often so near that I even heard their conjectures as they were looking about for me; and I now learned from them that any attempts to return home would be hopeless. Most of them supposed I had fled towards home; but the distance was so great, and the way so intricate, that they thought I could never reach it, and that I should be lost in the woods. When I heard this I was seized with a violent panic, and abandoned myself to despair. Night, too, began to approach, and aggravated all my fears. I had before entertained hopes of getting home, and had determined when it should be dark to make the attempt; but I was now convinced it was fruitless, and began to consider that, if possibly I could escape all other animals, I could not those of the human kind; and that, not knowing the way, I must perish in the woods. Thus was I like the hunted deer—Every leaf and every whispering breath, Convey'd a foe, and every foe a death.

I heard frequent rustlings among the leaves, and being pretty sure they were snakes, I expected every instant to be stung by them. This increased my anguish, and the horror of my situation became now quite insupportable. I at length quitted the thicket, very faint and hungry, for I had not eaten or drank anything all the day, and crept to my master's kitchen, from whence I set out at first, which was an open shed, and laid myself down in the ashes with an anxious wish for death, to relieve me from all my pains. I was scarcely awake in the morning, when the old woman slave, who was the first up, came to fight the fire, and saw me in the fireplace. She was very much surprised to see me, and could scarcely believe her own eyes. She now promised to intercede for me, and went for her master, who soon after came, and, having slightly reprimanded me, ordered me to be taken care of, and not ill treated.

Soon after this, my master's only daughter, and child by his first wife, sickened and died, which affected him so much that for sometime he was almost frantic, and really would have killed himself, had he not been watched and prevented. However, in a short time afterwards he recovered, and I was again sold. I was now carried to the left of the sun's rising, through many dreary wastes and dismal woods, amidst the hideous roarings of wild beasts. The people I was sold to used to carry me very often, when I was tired, either on their shoulders or on their backs. I saw many convenient well-built sheds along the road, at proper distances, to accommodate the merchants and travellers, who lay in those buildings along with their wives, who often accompany them; and they always go well armed.

From the time I left my own nation, I always found somebody that understood me till I came to the sea coast. The languages of different nations did not totally differ, nor were they so copious as those of the Europeans, particularly the English. They were therefore easily learned; and, while I was journeying thus through Africa, I acquired two or three different tongues. In this manner I had been traveling for a considerable time, when, one evening, to my great surprise, whom should I see brought to the house where I was but my dear sister! As soon as she saw me, she gave a loud shriek, and ran into my arms—I was quite over-powered; neither of us could speak, but, for a considerable time, clung to each other in mutual embraces, unable to do anything but weep. Our meeting affected all who saw us; and, indeed, I must acknowledge, in honor of those sable destroyers of human rights, that I never met with any ill treatment, or saw any offered to their slaves, except tying them, when necessary, to keep them from running away.

When these people knew we were brother and sister, they indulged us to be together; and the man, to whom I supposed we belonged, lay with us, he in the middle, while she and I held one another by the hands across his breast all night; and thus for a while we forgot our misfortunes, in the joy of being together; but even this small comfort was soon to have an end; for scarcely had the fatal morning appeared when she was again torn from me forever! I was now more miserable, if possible, than before. . . .

Source: The Interesting Narrative of the Life of Olaudah Equiano, or Gustavus Vassa, the African, 1789. The Avalon Project, Yale Law School, New Haven, CT.

Fugitive Slave Act of 1793

Congress enacted the Fugitive Slave Act to ensure the right of slave owners to reclaim their lost human "property." The act created the legal mechanism for masters to recover lost slaves. Signed into law by President George Washington on February 12, 1793, the Fugitive Slave Act opposed every ideal in the U.S. Constitution: free will, the right to happiness, and due process.

Be it enacted That, whenever the Executive authority of any State in the Union, or of either of the Territories Northwest or South of the river Ohio, shall demand any person as a fugitive from justice, of the Executive authority of any such State or Territory to which such person shall have fled, and shall moreover produce the copy of an indictment found, or an affidavit made before a magistrate of any State or Territory as aforesaid, charging the person so demanded with having committed treason, felony, or other crime, certified as authentic by the Governor or Chief Magistrate of the State or Territory from whence the person so charged fled, it shall be the duty of the executive authority of the State or Territory to which such person shall have fled, to cause him or her arrest to be given to the Executive authority making such demand, or to the agent when he shall appear; but, if no such agent shall appear within six months from the time of the arrest, the prisoner may be discharged: and all costs or expenses incurred in the apprehending, securing, and transmitting such fugitive to the State or Territory making such demand, shall be paid by such State or Territory.

SEC. 2. *And be it further enacted*, That any agent appointed as aforesaid, who shall receive the fugitive into his custody, shall be empowered to transport him or her to the State or Territory from which he or she shall have fled. And if any person or persons shall, by force, set at liberty, or rescue the fugitive from such agent while transporting, as aforesaid, the person or persons so offending shall, on conviction, be fined not exceeding five hundred dollars, and be imprisoned not exceeding one year.

SEC. 3. *And be it also enacted*, That when a person held to labor in any of the United States, or in either of the Territories on the Northwest or South of the river Ohio, under the laws thereof, shall escape into any other part of the said States or Territory, the person to whom such labor or service may be due, his agent or attorney, is hereby empowered to seize or arrest such fugitive from labor, and to take him or her before any Judge of the Circuit or District Courts of the United States, residing or being within the State, or before any magistrate of a county, city,

or town corporate, wherein such seizure or arrest shall be made, and upon proof to the satisfaction of such Judge or magistrate, either by oral testimony or affidavit taken before and certified by a magistrate of any such State or Territory, that the person so seized or arrested, doth, under the laws of the State or Territory from which he or she fled, owe service or labor to the person claiming him or her, it shall be the duty of such Judge or magistrate to give a certificate thereof to such claimant, his agent, or attorney, which shall be sufficient warrant for removing the said fugitive from labor to the State or Territory from which he or she fled.

SEC. 4. *And be it further enacted*, That any person who shall knowingly and willingly obstruct or hinder such claimant, his agent, or attorney, in so seizing or arresting such fugitive from labor, or shall rescue such fugitive from such claimant, his agent or attorney, when so arrested pursuant to the authority herein given and declared; or shall harbor or conceal such person after notice that he or she was a fugitive from labor, as aforesaid, shall, for either of the said offences, forfeit and pay the sum of five hundred dollars. Which penalty may be recovered by and for the benefit of such claimant, by action of debt, in any Court proper to try the same, saving moreover to the person claiming such labor or service his right of action for or on account of the said injuries, or either of them.

Source: The Fugitive Slave Act. Annals of Congress, 2nd Cong., 2nd sess., 1413 & 1414, 1793. Law Library of Congress.

A Narrative of the Life and Adventures of Venture: A Native of Africa, but Resident above Sixty Years in the United States of America, Related by Himself (1798)

Kidnapped in Africa at the age of six, Venture Smith was sold to the steward on a slave ship and brought to Connecticut sometime in the early

1730s. At 31 years old, he purchased his freedom with money that he earned "cleaning muskrats and minks, raising potatoes and carrots and fishing."

Later, Smith himself became a slaveholder, owning at least three slaves. When he died at age 77 in 1805, he left a 100-acre farm and three houses in East Haddam, Connecticut. Following is an excerpt from his story, told in his own words.

I was born in Dukandarra, in Guinea, about the year 1729. My father's name was Saungm Furro, Prince of the tribe of Dukandara. My father had three wives. Polygamy was not uncommon in that country, especially among the rich, as every man was allowed to keep as many wives as he could maintain. . . .

The first thing worthy of notice which I remember was, a contention between my father and mother, on account of my father marrying his third wife without the consent of his first and eldest, which was contrary to the custom generally observed among my countrymen. In consequence of this rupture, my mother left her husband and country, and traveled away with her three children to the eastward. I was then five years old. . . .

After five days travel . . . my mother was pleased to stop and seek a refuge for me. She left me at the house of a very rich farmer. I was then, as I should judge, not less than one hundred and forty miles from my native place, separated from all my relations and acquaintance. . . .

My father sent a man and horse after me. After settling with my guardian for keeping me, he took me away and went for home. It was then about one year since my mother brought me here. Nothing remarkable occurred to us on our journey until we arrived safe home.

I found then that the difference between my parents had been made up previous to their sending for me. On my return, I was received both by my father and mother with great joy and affection, and was once more restored to my paternal dwelling in peace and happiness. I was then about six years old.

Not more than six weeks had passed after my return before a message was brought by an inhabitant of the place where I lived the preceding year to my father, that that place had been invaded by a numerous army from a nation not far distant, furnished with musical instrument, and all kinds of arms then in use; that they were instigated by some white nation who equipped and sent them to subdue and possess the country; that his nation had made no preparation for war, having been for a long time in profound peace; that they could not defend themselves against such a formidable train of invaders, and must therefore necessarily evacuate their lands to the fierce enemy, and fly to the protection of some chief; and that if he would permit them they would come under his rule and protection when they had to retreat from their own possessions. He was a kind and merciful prince, and therefore consented to these proposals. . . .

He gave them every privilege and all the protection his government could afford. But they had not been there longer than four days before news came to them that the invaders had laid waste their country, and were coming speedily to destroy them in my father's territories. This affrighted them, and therefore they immediately pushed off to the southward, into the unknown countries there, and were never more heard of.

Two days after their retreat, the report turned out to be but too true. A detachment from the enemy came to my father and informed him, that the whole army was encamped not far out of his dominions, and would invade the territory and deprive his people of their liberties and rights, if he did not comply with the following terms. These were to pay them a large sum of money, three hundred fat cattle, and a great number of goats, sheep, asses, etc.

My father told the messenger he would comply rather than that his subjects should be deprived of their rights and privileges, which he was not then in circumstances to defend from so sudden an invasion. Upon turning out those articles, the enemy pledged their faith and honor that they would not attack him. On these he relied and therefore thought it unnecessary to be on his guard against the enemy. But their pledges of faith and honor proved no better than those of other unprincipled hostile nations; for a few days after a certain relation of the king came and informed him, that the enemy who sent terms of accommodation to him and received tribute to their satisfaction, yet meditated an attack upon his subjects by surprise and that probably they would commence their attack in less than one day, and concluded with advising him, as he was not prepared for war, to order a speedy retreat of his family and subjects. He complied with this advice.

The same night which was fixed upon to retreat, my father and his family set off about the break of day. The king and his two younger wives went in one company, and my mother and her children in another. We left our dwellings in succession, and my father's company went on first. We directed our course for a large shrub plain, some distance off, where we intended to conceal ourselves from the approaching enemy, until we could refresh ourselves a little. But we presently found that our retreat was not secure. For having struck up a little fire for the purpose of cooking victuals, the enemy who happened to be encamped a little distance off, had sent out a scouting party who discovered us by the smoke of the fire, just as we were extinguishing it, and about to eat. As soon as we had finished eating, my father discovered the party, and immediately began to discharge arrows at them. This was what I first saw, and it alarmed both me and the women, who being unable to make any resistance, immediately betook ourselves to the tall thick reeds not far off, and left the old king to fight alone. For some time I beheld him from the reeds defending himself with great courage and firmness, till at last he was obliged to surrender himself into their hands.

They then came to us in the reeds, and the very first salute I had from them was a violent blow on the back part of the head with the fore part of a gun, and at the same time a grasp round the neck. I then had a rope put about my neck, as had all the women in the thicket with me, and were immediately led to my father, who was likewise pinioned and haltered for leading. In this condition we were all led to the camp. The women and myself being pretty submissive, had tolerable treatment from the enemy, while my father was closely interrogated

respecting his money which they knew he must have. But as he gave them no account of it, he was instantly cut and pounded on his body with great inhumanity, that he might be induced by the torture he suffered to make the discovery. All this availed not in the least to make him give up his money, but he despised all the tortures which they inflicted, until the continued exercise and increase of torment, obliged him to sink and expire. He thus died without informing his enemies where his money lay. I saw him while he was thus tortured to death. The shocking scene is to this day fresh in my mind, and I have often been overcome while thinking on it. . . .

The army of the enemy was large, I should suppose consisting of about six thousand men. Their leader was called Baukurre. After destroying the old prince, they decamped and immediately marched toward the sea, lying to the west, taking with them myself and the women prisoners. In the march a scouting party was detached from the main army. To the leader of this party I was made waiter, having to carry his gun, etc. As we were a scouting we came across a herd of fat cattle, consisting of about thirty in number. These we set upon, and immediately wrested from their keepers, and afterwards converted them into food for the army. The enemy had remarkable success in destroying the country wherever they went. For as far as they had penetrated, they laid the habitations waste and captured the people. The distance they had now brought me was about four hundred miles. All the march I had very hard tasks imposed on me, which I must perform on pain of punishment. I was obliged to carry on my head a large flat stone used for grinding our corn, weighing as I should suppose, as much as twenty-five pounds; besides victuals, mat and cooking utensils. Though I was pretty large and stout at my age, yet these burdens were very grievous to me, being only six years and a half old.

We were then come to a place called Malagasco. When we entered the place we could not see the least appearance of either houses or inhabitants, but upon stricter search found, that instead of houses above ground they had dens in the sides of hillocks, contiguous to ponds and streams of water. In these we perceived they had all hid themselves, as I supposed they usually did on such occasions. In order to compel them to surrender, the enemy contrived to smoke them out with faggots. These they put to the entrance of the caves and set them on fire. While they were engaged in this business, to their great surprise some of them were desperately wounded with arrows which fell from above on them. This mystery they soon found out. They perceived that the enemy discharged these arrows through holes on top of the dens, directly into the air. Their weight brought them back, point downwards on their enemies heads, whilst they were smoking the inhabitants out. The points of their arrows were poisoned, but their enemy had an antidote for it, which they instantly applied to the wounded part. The smoke at last obliged the people to give themselves up. They came out of their caves, first putting the palms of their hands together, and immediately after extended their arms, crossed at their wrists, ready to be bound and pinioned. . . .

The invaders then pinioned the prisoners of all ages and sexes indiscriminately, took their flocks and all their effects, and moved on their way towards the sea. On the march the prisoners were treated with clemency, on account of their being submissive and humble. Having come to the next tribe, the enemy laid siege and immediately took men, women, children, flocks, and all their valuable effects. They then went on to the next district which was contiguous to the sea, called in Africa, Anamaboo. The enemies provisions were then almost spent, as well as their strength. The inhabitants knowing what conduct they had pursued, and what were their present intentions, improved the favorable opportunity, attacked them, and took enemy, prisoners, flocks and all their effects. I was then taken a second time. All of us were then put into the castle [a European slave trading post], and kept for market. On a certain time I and other prisoners were put on board a canoe, under our master, and rowed away to a vessel belonging to Rhode Island, commanded by Captain Collingwood, and the mate Thomas Mumford. While we were going to the vessel, our master told us all to appear to the best possible advantage for sale. I was bought on board by one Robert Mumford, steward of said vessel, for four gallons of rum, and a piece of calico, and called Venture, on account of his having purchased me with his own private venture. Thus I came by my name. All the slaves that were bought for that vessel's cargo, were two hundred and sixty.

Source: Smith, Venture. *A Narrative of the Life and Adventures of Venture: A Native of Africa, but Resident above Sixty Years in the United States of America, Related by Himself*. New London: printed by C. Holt, at the BEE-Office, 1798. Reprinted in Middletown, Conn.: J. S. Stewart, printer, 1897.

An Act to Prohibit the Importation of Slaves
(1807)

Article I, Section 9 of the U.S. Constitution protected the transatlantic slave trade for 20 years; no attempt could be made to end the slave trade before January 1, 1808. Accordingly, the U.S. Congress passed this piece of landmark legislation to end the profitable international slave trade on March 2, 1807, and President Thomas Jefferson promptly signed the act, making it law. The act went into effect on January 1, 1808, prohibiting from that time on the importation of African slaves to the United States, although the domestic slave trade continued to thrive until the American Civil War and lax enforcement of the law allowed some slaves to continue to be imported from Africa.

An Act to Prohibit the Importation of Slaves into any Port or Place Within the Jurisdiction of the United States, From and After the First Day of January, in the Year of our Lord One Thousand Eight Hundred and Eight.

Be it enacted by the Senate and House of Representatives of the United States of America in Congress assembled, That from and after the first day of January, one thousand eight hundred and eight, it shall not be lawful to import or bring into the United States or the territories thereof from any foreign kingdom, place, or country, any negro, mulatto, or person of colour, with intent to hold, sell, or dispose of such negro, mulatto, or person of colour, as a slave, or to be held to service or labour.

SECTION 2. And be it further enacted, That no citizen or citizens of the United States, or any other person, shall, from and after the first day of January, in the year of our Lord one thousand eight hundred and eight, for himself, or themselves, or any other person whatsoever, either as master, factor, or owner, build, fit, equip, load or otherwise prepare any ship or vessel, in any port or place within the jurisdiction of the United States, nor shall cause any ship or vessel to sail from any port or place within the same, for the purpose of procuring any negro, mulatto, or person of colour, from any foreign kingdom, place, or country, to be transported to any port or place whatsoever, within the jurisdiction of the United States, to be held, sold, or disposed of as slaves, or to be held to service or labour: and if any ship or vessel shall be so fitted out for the purpose aforesaid, or shall be caused to sail so as aforesaid, every such ship or vessel, her tackle, apparel, and furniture, shall be forfeited to the United States, and shall be liable to be seized, prosecuted, and condemned in any of the circuit courts or district courts, for the district where the said ship or vessel may be found or seized.

SECTION 3. And be it further enacted, That all and every person so building, fitting out, equipping, loading, or otherwise preparing or sending away, any ship or vessel, knowing or intending that the same shall be employed in such trade or business, from and after the first day of January, one

thousand eight hundred and eight, contrary to the true intent and meaning of this act, or any ways aiding or abetting therein, shall severally forfeit and pay twenty thousand dollars, one moiety thereof to the use of the United States, and the other moiety to the use of any person or persons who shall sue for and prosecute the same to effect.

SECTION 4. And be it further enacted, If any citizen or citizens of the United States, or any person resident within the jurisdiction of the same, shall, from and after the first day of January, one thousand eight hundred and eight, take on board, receive or transport from any of the coasts or kingdoms of Africa, or from any other foreign kingdom, place, or country, any negro, mulatto, or person of colour, in any ship or vessel, for the purpose of selling them in any port or place within the jurisdiction of the United States as slaves, or to be held to service or labour, or shall be in any ways aiding or abetting therein, such citizen or citizens, or person, shall severally forfeit and pay five thousand dollars, one moiety thereof to the use of any person or persons who shall sue for and prosecute the same to effect; and every such ship or vessel in which such negro, mulatto, or person of colour, shall have been taken on board, received, or transported as aforesaid, her tackle, apparel, and furniture, and the goods and effects which shall be found on board the same, shall be forfeited to the United States, and shall be liable to be seized, prosecuted, and condemned in any of the circuit courts or district courts in the district where the said ship or vessel may be found or seized. And neither the importer, nor any person or persons claiming from or under him, shall hold any right or title whatsoever to any negro, mulatto, or person of colour, nor to the service or labour thereof, who may be imported or brought within the United States, or territories thereof, in violation of this law, but the same shall remain subject to any regulations not contravening the provisions of this act, which the legislatures of the several states or territories at any time hereafter may make, for disposing of any such negro, mulatto, or person of colour.

SECTION 5. And be it further enacted, That if any citizen or citizens of the United States, or any other person resident within the jurisdiction of the same, shall, from and after the first day of January, one thousand eight hundred and eight, contrary to the true intent and meaning of this act, take on board any ship or vessel from any of the coasts or kingdoms of Africa, or from any other foreign kingdom, place, or country, any negro, mulatto, or person of colour, with intent to sell him, her, or them, for a slave, or slaves, or to be held to service or labour, and shall transport the same to any port or place within the jurisdiction of the United States, and there sell such negro, mulatto, or person of colour, so transported as aforesaid, for a slave, or to be held to service or labour, every such offender shall be deemed guilty of a high misdemeanor, and being thereof convicted before any court having competent jurisdiction, shall suffer imprisonment for not more than ten years nor less than five years, and be fined not exceeding ten thousand dollars, nor less than one thousand dollars.

SECTION 6. And be it further enacted, That if any person or persons whatsoever, shall, from and after the first day of January, one thousand eight hundred and eight, purchase or sell any negro, mulatto, or person of colour, for a slave, or to be held to service or labour, who shall have been imported, or brought from any foreign kingdom, place, or country, or from the dominions of any foreign state, immediately adjoining to the United States, into any port or place within the jurisdiction of the United States, after the last day of December, one thousand eight hundred and seven, knowing at the time of such purchase or sale, such negro, mulatto or person of colour, was so brought within the jurisdiction of the Unified States, as aforesaid, such purchaser and seller shall severally forfeit and pay for every negro, mulatto, or person of colour, so purchased or sold as aforesaid, eight hundred dollars; one moiety thereof to the United States, and the other moiety to the use of any person or persons who shall sue for and prosecute the same to effect: Provided, that the aforesaid forfeiture

shall not extend to the seller or purchaser of any negro, mulatto, or person of colour, who may be sold or disposed of in virtue of any regulation which may hereafter be made by any of the legislatures of the several states in that respect, in pursuance of this act, and the constitution of the United States.

SECTION 7. And be it further enacted, That if any ship or vessel shall be found, from and after the first day of January, one thousand eight hundred and eight, in any river, port, bay, or harbor, or on the high seas, within the jurisdictional limits of the United States, or hovering on the coast thereof, having on board any negro, mulatto, or person of colour, for the purpose of selling them as slaves, or with intent to land the same, in any port or place within the jurisdiction of the United States, contrary to the prohibition of this act, every such ship or vessel, together with her tackle, apparel, and furniture, and the goods or effects which shall be found on board the same, shall be forfeited to the use of the United States, and may be seized, prosecuted, and condemned, in any court of the United States, having jurisdiction thereof. And it shall be lawful for the President of the United States, and he is hereby authorized, should he deem it expedient, to cause any of the armed vessels of the United States to be manned and employed to cruise on any part of the coast of the United States, or territories thereof, where he may judge attempts will be made to violate the provisions of this act, and to instruct and direct the commanders of armed vessels of the United States, to seize, take, and bring into any port of the United States all such ships or vessels, and moreover to seize, take, and bring into any port of the United States all ships or vessels of the United States, wheresoever found on the high seas, contravening the provisions of this act, to be proceeded against according to law, and the captain, master, or commander of every such ship or vessel, so found and seized as aforesaid, shall be deemed guilty of a high misdemeanor, and shall be liable to be prosecuted before any court of the United States, having jurisdiction thereof; and being thereof convicted, shall be fined not exceeding ten thousand dollars, and be imprisoned not less than two years, and not exceeding four years. And the proceeds of all ships and vessels, their tackle, apparel, and furniture, and the goods and effects on board of them, which shall be so seized, prosecuted and condemned, shall be divided equally between the United States and the officers and men who shall make such seizure, take, or bring the same into port for condemnation, whether such seizure be made by an armed vessel of the United States, or revenue cutters "hereof, and the same shall be distributed in like manner, as is provided by law, for the distribution of prizes taken from an enemy: Provided, that the officers and men, to be entitled to one half of the proceeds aforesaid, shall safe keep every negro, mulatto, or person of colour, found on board of any ship or vessel so by them seized, taken, or brought into port for condemnation, and shall deliver every such negro, mulatto, or person of colour, to such person or persons as shall be appointed by the respective states, to receive the same, and if no such person or persons shall be appointed by the respective states, they shall deliver every such negro, mulatto, or person of colour, to the overseers of the poor of the port or place where such ship or vessel may be brought or found, and shall immediately transmit to the governor or chief magistrate of the state, an account of their proceedings, together with the number of such Negroes, mulattoes, or persons of colour, and a descriptive list of the same, that he may give directions respecting such Negroes, mulattoes, or persons of colour.

SECTION 8. And be it further enacted, That no captain, master or commander of any ship or vessel, of less burthen than forty tons, shall, from and after the first day of January, one thousand eight hundred and eight, take on board and transport any negro, mulatto, or person of colour, to any port or place whatsoever, for the purpose of selling or disposing of the same as a slave, or with intent that the same may be sold or disposed of to be held to service or labour, on penalty of forfeiting for every such negro, mulatto, or person of colour, so taken

on board and transported, as aforesaid, the sum of eight hundred dollars; one moiety thereof to the use of the United States, and the other moiety to any person or persons who shall sue for, and prosecute the same to effect: Provided however, That nothing in this section shall extend to prohibit the taking on board or transporting on any river, or inland bay of the sea, within the jurisdiction of the United States, any negro, mulatto, or person of colour, (not imported contrary to the provisions of this act) in any vessel or species of craft whatever.

SECTION 9. And be it further enacted, That the captain, master, or commander of any ship or vessel of the burthen of forty tons or more, from and after the first day of January, one thousand eight hundred and eight, sailing coastwise, from any port in the United States, to any port or place within the jurisdiction of the same, having on board any negro, mulatto, or person of colour, for the purpose of transporting them to be sold or disposed of as slaves, or to be held to service or labour, shall, previous to the departure of such ship or vessel, make out and subscribe duplicate manifests of every such negro, mulatto, or person of colour, on board such ship or vessel, therein specifying the name and sex of each person, their age and stature, as near as may be, and the class to which they respectively belong, whether negro, mulatto, or person of colour, with the name and place of residence of every owner or shipper of the same, and shall deliver such manifests to the collector of the port, if there be one, otherwise to the surveyor, before whom the captain, master, or commander, together with the owner or shipper, shall severally swear or affirm to the best of their knowledge and belief, that the persons therein specified were not imported or brought into the United States, from and after the first day of January, one thousand eight hundred and eight, and that under the laws of the state, they are held to service or labour; whereupon the said collector or surveyor shall certify the same on the said manifests, one of which he shall return to the said captain, master, or commander, with a permit, specifying thereon the number, names, and general description of such persons, and authorizing him to proceed to the port of his destination. And if any ship or vessel, being laden and destined as aforesaid, shall depart from the port where she may then be, without the captain, master, or commander having first made out and subscribed duplicate manifests, of every negro, mulatto, and person of colour, on board such ship or vessel, as aforesaid, and without having previously delivered the same to the said collector or surveyor, and obtained a permit, in manner as herein required, or shall, previous to her arrival at the port of her destination, take on board any negro, mulatto, or person of colour, other than those specified in the manifests, as aforesaid, every such ship or vessel, together with her tackle, apparel and furniture, shall be forfeited to the use of the United States, and may be seized, prosecuted and condemned in any court of the United States having jurisdiction thereof; and the captain, master, or commander of every such ship or vessel, shall moreover forfeit, for every such negro, mulatto, or person of colour, so transported, or taken on board, contrary to the provisions of this act, the sum of one thousand dollars, one moiety thereof to the United States, and the other moiety to the use of any person or persons who shall sue for and prosecute the same to effect.

SECTION 10. And be it further enacted, That the captain, master, or commander of every ship or vessel, of the burthen of forty tons or more, from and after the first day of January, one thousand eight hundred and eight, sailing coastwise, and having on board any negro, mulatto, or person of colour, to sell or dispose of as slaves, or to be held to service or labour, and arriving in any port within the jurisdiction of the United States, from any other port within the same, shall, previous to the unlading or putting on shore any of the persons aforesaid, or suffering them to go on shore, deliver to the collector, if there be one, or if not, to the surveyor residing at the port of her arrival, the manifest certified by the collector or surveyor of the port from whence she sailed, as is herein before directed, to the truth of which, before such officer, he shall swear or affirm, and if the collector or surveyor shall be satisfied therewith, he shall thereupon grant a permit for unlading or suffering such negro, mulatto, or person of colour, to be put on shore, and if the captain, master, or commander of any such ship or vessel being laden as aforesaid, shall neglect or refuse to deliver the manifest at the time and in the manner herein directed, or shall land or put on shore any negro, mulatto, or person of colour, for the purpose aforesaid, before he shall have delivered his manifest as aforesaid, and obtained a permit for that purpose, every such captain, master, or commander, shall forfeit and pay ten thousand dollars, one moiety thereof to the United States, the other moiety to the use of any person or persons who shall sue for and prosecute the same to effect.

Source: An Act to Prohibit the Importation of Slaves. 2 Stat. 426 (1807).

Missouri Compromise
(1820)

Missouri's application for U.S. statehood in 1819 caused considerable controversy because, if it had been admitted as a slave state, Missouri would have tipped the balance in the U.S. Senate toward slave states. Opponents of slavery wanted Missouri to eliminate the institution before being admitted as a state; proponents thought that was a matter for Missouri alone to decide. On March 3, 1820, the

Missouri Compromise, hammered out by U.S. congressman Henry Clay, solved the problem, at least temporarily, by admitting Missouri as a slave state and Maine (formerly part of Massachusetts) as a free state. The law further provided that, Missouri excepted, slavery would be prohibited in the Louisiana Territory north of 36° 30' north latitude and permitted south of that line. Below is an excerpt from the compromise.

Be it enacted by the Senate and House of Representatives of the United States of America, in Congress assembled, That the inhabitants of that portion of the Missouri territory included within the boundaries hereinafter designated, be, and they are hereby, authorized to form for themselves a constitution and state government, and to assume such name as they shall deem proper; and the said state, when formed, shall be admitted into the Union, upon an equal footing with the original states, in all respects whatsoever.

Section 2. And be it further enacted, That the said state shall consist of all the territory included within the following boundaries, to wit: Beginning in the middle of the Mississippi river, on the parallel of thirty-six degrees of north latitude; thence west, along that parallel of latitude, to the St. Francois river; thence up, and following the course of that river, in the middle of the main channel thereof, to the parallel of latitude of thirty-six degrees and thirty minutes; thence west, along the same, to a point where the said parallel is intersected by a meridian line passing through the middle of the mouth of the Kansas river, where the same empties into the Missouri river, thence, from the point aforesaid north, along the said meridian line, to the intersection of the parallel of latitude which passes through the rapids of the river Des Moines, making the said line to correspond with the Indian boundary line; thence east, from the point of intersection last aforesaid, along the said parallel of latitude, to the middle of the channel of the main fork of the said river Des Moines; thence down and along the middle of the main channel of the said river Des Moines, to the mouth of the

same, where it empties into the Mississippi river; thence, due east, to the middle of the main channel of the Mississippi river; thence down, and following the course of the Mississippi river, in the middle of the main channel thereof, to the place of beginning: Provided, The said state shall ratify the boundaries aforesaid; And provided also, That the said state shall have concurrent jurisdiction on the river Mississippi, and every other river bordering on the said state, so far as the said rivers shall form a common boundary to the said state; and any other state or states, now or hereafter to be formed and bounded by the same, such rivers to be common to both; and that the river Mississippi, and the navigable rivers and waters leading into the same, shall be common highways, and for ever free, as well to the inhabitants of the said state as to other citizens of the United States, without any tax, duty, impost, or toll, therefor, imposed by the said state. . . .

Section 4. And be it further enacted, That the members of the convention thus duly elected, shall be, and they are hereby authorized to meet at the seat of government of said territory on the second Monday of the month of June next; and the said convention, when so assembled, shall have power and authority to adjourn to any other place in the said territory, which to them shall seem best for the convenient transaction of their business; and which convention, when so met, shall first determine by a majority of the whole number elected, whether it be, or be not, expedient at that time to form a constitution and state government for the people within the said territory, as included within the boundaries above designated. . . .

Section 5. And be it further enacted, That until the next general census shall be taken, the said state shall be entitled to one representative in the House of Representatives of the United States. . . .

Second. That all salt springs, not exceeding twelve in number, with six sections of land adjoining to each, shall be granted to the said state for the use of said state. . . .

Fifth. That thirty-six sections, or one entire township, which shall be designated by the President of the United States, together with the other lands heretofore reserved for that purpose, shall be reserved for the use of a seminary of learning, and vested in the legislature of said state, to be appropriated solely to the use of such seminary by the said legislature. . . .

Section 8. And be it further enacted, That in all that territory ceded by France to the United States, under the name of Louisiana, which lies north of thirty-six degrees and thirty minutes north latitude, not included within the limits of the state, contemplated by this act, slavery and involuntary servitude, otherwise than in the punishment of crimes, whereof the parties shall have been duly convicted, shall be, and is hereby, forever prohibited: Provided always, That any person escaping into the same, from whom labour or service is lawfully claimed, in any state or territory of the United States, such fugitive may be lawfully reclaimed and conveyed to the person claiming his or her labour or service as aforesaid.

Source: Conference committee report on the Missouri Compromise, March 1, 1820; Joint Committee of Conference on the Missouri Bill, 03/01/1820-03/06/1820; Record Group 128l; Records of Joint Committees of Congress, 1789–1989; National Archives.

John Quincy Adams, Diary Entry on Slavery and the Missouri Compromise (March 3, 1820)

After passage of the Missouri Compromise, President James Monroe assembled his cabinet to ask its members their advice on whether or not he should sign the bills admitting Maine and Missouri to the Union. John Quincy Adams, as secretary of state, was one of those asked to give an opinion regarding the fate of the Missouri Compromise. Although Adams considered slavery a great evil, he recommended that the president sign the bills, believing that, under the Constitution, the federal government had no power to interfere with the institution of slavery. Reproduced here is the March 3, 1820, entry from Adams's diary in which he mentions this meeting, as well as a later discussion with Secretary of War John C. Calhoun of South Carolina, an avid supporter of slavery. In the following excerpt, Adams disagrees with Calhoun on slavery and ultimately decides that "if the Union must be dissolved, slavery is precisely the question upon which it ought to break."

When I came this day to my office, I found there a note requesting me to call at one o'clock at the President's house. It was then one, and I immediately went over. He expected that the two bills—for the admission of Maine, and to enable Missouri to make a constitution—would have been brought to him for his signature, and he had summoned all the members of the administration to ask their opinions, in writing, to be deposited in the Department of State, upon two questions: (1) whether Congress had a constitutional right to prohibit slavery in a territory; and (2) whether the 8th Section of the Missouri bill (which interdicts slavery *forever* in the territory north of thirty-six and a half latitude) was applicable only to the territorial state, or could extend to it after it should become a state. . . .

After this meeting, I walked home with [John C.] Calhoun, who said that . . . in the Southern country . . . domestic labor was confined to the blacks; and such was the prejudice that if he, who was the most popular man in his district, were to keep a white servant in his house, his character and reputation would be irretrievably ruined.

I said that this confounding of the ideas of servitude and labor was one of the bad effects of slavery; but he thought it attended with many excellent consequences. It did not apply to all kinds of labor—not, for example, to farming. He himself had often held the plough; so had his father. Manufacturing and mechanical labor was not degrading. It was only manual labor—the proper work of slaves. No white person could descend to that. And it was the best guarantee to equality among the whites. It produced an unvarying level among them. It not only did not excite but did not even admit of inequalities, by which one white man could domineer over another.

I told Calhoun I could not see things in the same light. It is, in truth, all perverted sentiment—mistaking labor for slavery, and dominion for freedom. The discussion of this Missouri question has betrayed the secret of their souls. In the abstract they admit that slavery is an evil, they disclaim all participation in the introduction of it, and cast it all upon the shoulders of our old Grandam Britain. But when probed to the quick upon it, they show at the bottom of their souls pride and vainglory in their condition of masterdom. They fancy themselves more generous and noblehearted than the plain freemen who labor for subsistence. They look down upon the simplicity of a Yankee's manners, because he has no habits of overbearing like theirs and cannot treat Negroes like dogs.

It is among the evils of slavery that it taints the very sources of moral principle. It establishes false estimates of virtue and vice; for what can be more false and heartless than this doctrine which makes the first and holiest rights of humanity to depend upon the color of the skin? It perverts human reason, and reduces man endowed with logical powers to maintain that slavery is sanctioned by the Christian religion, that slaves are happy and contented in their condition, that between master and slave there are ties of mutual attachment and affection, that the virtues of the master are refined and exalted by the degradation of the slave; while at the same time they vent execrations upon the slave trade, curse Britain for having given them slaves, burn at the stake Negroes convicted of crimes for the terror of the example, and writhe in agonies of fear at the very mention of human rights as applicable to men of color. The impression produced upon my mind by the progress of this discussion is that the bargain between freedom and slavery contained in the Constitution of the United States is morally and politically vicious, inconsistent with the principles upon which alone our Revolution can be justified; cruel and oppressive, by riveting the chains of slavery, by pledging the faith of freedom to maintain and perpetuate the tyranny of the master; and grossly unequal and impolitic, by admitting that slaves are at once enemies to be kept in subjection, property to be secured or restored to their owners, and persons not to be represented themselves, but for whom their masters are privileged with nearly a double share of representation. The consequence has been that this slave representation has governed the Union.

Benjamin portioned above his brethren has ravined as a wolf. In the morning he has devoured the prey, and at night he has divided the spoil. It would be no difficult matter to prove, by reviewing the history of the Union under this Constitution, that almost everything which has contributed to the honor and welfare of the nation has been accomplished in spite of them or forced upon them, and that everything unpropitious and dishonorable, including the blunders and follies of their adversaries, may be traced to them.

I have favored this Missouri Compromise, believing it to be all that could be effected under the present Constitution, and from extreme unwillingness to put the Union at hazard. But perhaps it would have been a wiser as well as a bolder course to have persisted in the restriction upon Missouri, till it should have terminated in a convention of the states to revise and amend the Constitution. This would have produced a new Union of thirteen or fourteen States, unpolluted with slavery, with a great and glorious object to effect; namely, that of rallying to their standard the other states by the universal emancipation of their slaves. If the Union must be dissolved, slavery is precisely the question upon which it ought to break. For the present, however, this contest is laid asleep.

Source: Adams, John Quincy. "Slavery and the Constitution." In *Memoirs of John Quincy Adams, Comprising Portions of his Diary from 1795 to 1848*, Vol. 5, edited by Charles Francis Adams, 4–12. Philadelphia: J. B. Lippincott & Co., 1875.

Thomas Jefferson, Letter to John Holmes
(April 22, 1820)

Concerned about the acrimonious nature of the recent congressional debates regarding the Missouri Compromise, former president Thomas Jefferson wrote this letter to John Holmes, who would soon become a U.S. senator from Maine, on April 22, 1820. The letter is famous because in it Jefferson likened the slavery question to having "the wolf by the ears, and we can neither hold him, nor safely let him go." The former president in this letter correctly predicted that slavery and increased sectionalism would eventually rip the country apart.

I thank you, dear sir, for the copy you have been so kind as to send me of the letter to your constituents on the Missouri question. It is a perfect justification to them. I had for a long time ceased to read newspapers, or pay any attention to public affairs, confident they were in good hands, and content to be a passenger in our bark to the shore from which I am not distant. But this momentous question, like a firebell in the night, awakened and filled me with terror. I considered it at once as the knell of the Union. It is hushed, indeed, for the moment. But this is a reprieve only, not a final sentence. A geographical line, coinciding with a marked principle, moral and political, once conceived and held up to the angry passions of men, will never be obliterated; and every new irritation will mark it deeper and deeper. I can say, with conscious truth, that there is not a man on earth who would sacrifice more than I would to relieve us from this heavy reproach, in any practicable way.

The cession of that kind of property, for so it is misnamed, is a bagatelle which would not cost me a second thought, if, in that way, a general emancipation and expatriation could be effected; and gradually, and with due sacrifices, I think it might be. But as it is, we have the wolf by the ears, and we can neither hold him, nor safely let him go. Justice is in one scale, and self-preservation in the other. Of one thing I am certain, that as the passage of slaves from one state to another would not make a slave of a single human being who would not be so without it, so their diffusion over a greater surface would make them individually happier, and proportionally facilitate the accomplishment of their emancipation, by dividing the burden on a greater number of coadjutors. An abstinence too, from this act of power, would remove the jealousy excited by the undertaking of Congress to regulate the condition of the different descriptions of men composing a state. This certainly is the exclusive right of every state, which nothing in the Constitution has taken from them and given to the general government. Could Congress, for example, say that the non-freemen of Connecticut shall be freemen, or that they shall not emigrate into any other state?

I regret that I am now to die in the belief that the useless sacrifice of themselves by the generation of 1776, to acquire self-government and happiness to their country, is to be thrown away by the unwise and unworthy passions of their sons, and that my only consolation is to be that I live not to weep over it. If they would but dispassionately weigh the blessings they will throw away against an abstract principle more likely to be effected by union than by scission, they would pause before they would perpetrate this act of suicide on themselves, and of treason against the hopes of the world. To yourself, as the faithful advocate of the Union, I tender the offering of my high esteem and respect.

Source: Thomas Jefferson to John Holmes, April 22, 1820. Manuscript letter. Manuscript Division (159). Library of Congress.

The Confessions of Nat Turner, the Leader of the Late Insurrection in Southampton, Virginia

(1832)

In August 1831, a slave named Nat Turner led an ultimately unsuccessful slave insurrection that resulted in the deaths of 55 white people in Southampton County, Virginia. The revolt caused much panic in the South and seriously undermined the southern contention that slaves were contented with their enslavement. A pamphlet titled "The Confessions of Nat Turner, the Leader of the Late Insurrection in Southampton, Virginia, as Fully and Voluntarily Made to Thomas R. Gray," appeared shortly after Turner's trial and execution in November 1831. Dictated by Turner from his jail cell to Southampton attorney Thomas Gray, "The Confession" provides a slave's perspective of the uprising, even though there has been much debate among historians regarding the veracity of Turner's account. The following excerpt is Turner's response when Gray asked him why he led his revolt against slavery.

Sir—You have asked me to give a history of the motives which induced me to undertake the late insurrection, as you call it—To do so I must go back to the days of my infancy. . . . In my childhood a circumstance occurred which made an indelible impression on my mind, and laid the groundwork of that enthusiasm, which has terminated so fatally to many, both white and black, and for which I am about to atone at the gallows. . . . Being at play with other children, when three or four years old, I was telling them something, which my mother overhearing, said it had happened before I was born . . . others being called on were greatly astonished . . . and caused them to say in my hearing, I surely would be a prophet. . . .

For two years [I] prayed continually, whenever my duty would permit—and then again I had [a] . . . revelation, which fully confirmed me in the impression that I was ordained for some great purpose, in the hands of the Almighty. . . .

About this time [around 1825] I had a vision—and I saw white spirits and black spirits engaged in battle, and the sun was darkened—the thunder rolled in the Heavens, and blood flowed in streams. . . .

And on the 12th of May, 1828, I heard a loud noise in the heavens, and the Spirit instantly appeared to me and said the Serpent was loosened, and Christextra had laid down the yoke he had borne for the sins of men, and that I should take it on and fight against the Serpent, for the time was fast approaching when the first should be last and the last should be first.

[Question] Do you not find yourself mistaken now?

[Answer] Was not Christ crucified? And by signs in the heavens that it would be made known to me when I should commence the great work—and until the first sign appeared, I should conceal if from the knowledge of men—And on the appearance of the sign (the eclipse of the sun last February), I should arise and prepare myself, and slay my enemies with their own weapons. And immediately on the sign appearing in the heavens, the seal was removed from my lips, and I communicated the great work laid out before me to do, to four in whom I had the greatest confidence (Henry, Hark, Nelson, and Sam)—It was intended by us to have begun the work of death on the 4th of July last—Many were the plans formed and rejected by us, and it affected my mind to such a degree, that I fell sick, and the time passed without our coming to any determination how to commence—Still forming new schemes and rejecting them, when the sign appeared again, which determined me not to wait longer.

Since the commencement of 1830, I had been living with Mr. Joseph Travis, who was to me a kind master, and placed the greatest confidence in me: in fact, I had no cause to complain of his treatment of me. On Saturday evening, the 20th of August, it was agreed between Henry, Hark, and myself, to prepare a dinner the next day for the men we expected, and then to concert a plan, as we had not yet determined on any. Hark, on the following morning, brought a pig, and Henry brandy, and being joined by Sam, Nelson, Will and Jack, they prepared in the woods a dinner, where, about three o'clock, I joined them . . .

I saluted them on coming up, and asked Will how came he there, he answered, his life was worth no more than others, and his liberty as dear to him. I asked him if he thought to obtain it? He said he would, or lose his life. This was enough to put him in full confidence. Jack, I knew, was only a tool in the hands of Hark, it was quickly agreed we should commence at home (Mr. J. Travis') on that night, and

until we had armed and equipped ourselves, and gathered sufficient force, neither age nor sex was to be spared (which was invariably adhered to). We remained at the feast, until about two hours in the night, when we went to the house and found Austin; they all went to the cider press and drank, except myself. On returning to the house Hark went to the door with an axe, for the purpose of breaking it open, as we knew we were strong enough to murder the family, if they were awakened by the noise; but reflecting that it might create an alarm in the neighborhood, we determined to enter the house secretly, and murder them whilst sleeping. Hark got a ladder and set it against the chimney, on which I ascended, and hoisting a window, entered and came down stairs, unbarred the door, and removed the guns from their places. It was then observed that I must spill the first blood. On which, armed with a hatchet, and accompanied by Will, I entered my master's chamber, it being dark, I could not give a death blow, the hatchet glanced from his head, he sprang from the bed and called his wife, it was his last word, Will laid him dead, with a blow of his axe, and Mrs. Travis shared the same fate, as she lay in bed. The murder of this family, five in number, was the work of a moment, not one of them awoke; there was a little infant sleeping in a cradle, that was forgotten, until we had left the house and gone some distance, when Henry and Will returned and killed it; we got here, four guns that would shoot and several old muskets, with a pound or two of powder. We remained some time at the barn, where we paraded; I formed them in a line as soldiers, and . . . marched them off to Mr. Salthul Francis', about six hundred yards distant.

Sam and Will went to the door and knocked. Mr. Francis asked who was there, Sam replied it was him, and he had a letter for him, on which he got up and came to the door; they immediately seized him, and dragging him out a little from the door, he was dispatched by repeated blows on the head; there was no other white person in the family. We started from there for Mrs. Reese's, maintaining the most perfect silence on our march, where finding the door unlocked, we entered, and murdered Mrs. Reese in her bed, while sleeping; her son awoke, but it was only to sleep the sleep of death, he had only time to say who is that, and he was no more.

From Mrs. Reese's we went to Mrs. Turner's, a mile distant, which we reached about sunrise, on Monday morning. Henry, Austin, and Sam, went to the still, where, finding Mr. Peebles, Austin shot him, and the rest of us went to the house; as we approached, the family discovered us, and shut the door. Vain hope! Will, with one stroke of his axe opened it, and we entered and found Mrs. Turner and Mrs. Newsome in the middle of a room, almost frightened to death. Will immediately killed Mrs. Turner, with one blow of his axe. I took Mrs. Newsome by the hand, and with the sword I had when I was apprehended, I struck her several blows over the head, but not being able to kill her, as the sword was dull. Will turning around and discovering it, dispatched her also. A general destruction of property and search for money and ammunition, always succeeded the murders. By this time my company amounted to fifteen, and nine men mounted, who started for Mrs. Whitehead's. . . . As we approached the house we discovered Mr. Richard Whitehead standing in the cotton patch, near the lane fence; we called him over into the lane, and Will, the executioner, was near at hand, with his fatal axe, to send him to an untimely grave. . . . As I came around to the door I saw Will pulling Mrs. Whitehead out of the house, and at the step he nearly severed her head from her body, with his broad axe. Miss Margaret, when I discovered her, had concealed herself in the corner . . . on my approach she fled, but was soon overtaken, and after repeated blows with a sword, I killed her by a blow on the head, with a fence rail. . . .

'Twas my object to carry terror and devastation wherever we went. . . . I sometimes got in sight in time to see the work of death completed, viewed the mangled bodies as they lay, in silent satisfaction, and immediately started in quest of other victims— Having murdered Mrs. Waller and ten children, we started for Mr. William Williams'—having killed him and two little boys that were there; while engaged in this, Mrs. Williams fled and got some distance from the house, but she was pursued, overtaken, and compelled to get up behind one of the company, who brought her back, and after showing her the mangled body of her lifeless husband, she was told to get down an lay by his side, where she was shot dead. . . .

Our number amounted now to fifty or sixty, all mounted and armed with guns, axes, swords, and clubs. . . . We were met by a party of white men, who had pursued our blood- stained track. . . . The white men, eighteen in number, approached us in about one hundred yards, when one of them fired. . . . I then ordered my men to fire and rush them; the few remaining stood their ground until we approached within fifty yards, when they fired and retreated. . . . As I saw them reloading their guns, and more coming up than I saw at first, and several of my bravest men being wounded, the other became panick struck and squandered over the field; the white men pursued and fired on us several times. . . .

All deserted me but two, (Jacob and Nat,) we concealed ourselves in the woods until near night, when I sent them in search of Henry, Sam, Nelson, and Hark, and directed them to rally all they could, at the place where had had our dinner the Sunday before, where they would find me, and I accordingly returned there as soon as it was dark and remained until Wednesday evening, when discovering white men riding around the place as though they were looking for someone, and none of my men joining me, I concluded Jacob and Nat had been taken, and compelled to betray me. On this I gave up all hope for the present; and on Thursday night after having supplied myself with provisions from Mr. Travis' I scratched a hole under a pile of fence rails in a field, where I concealed myself for six weeks, never leaving my hiding place but for a few minutes in the dead of night to get water which was very near. . . . I know not how long I might have led this life, if accident had not betrayed me, a dog in the neighborhood passing by my hiding place one night while I was out, was attracted by some meat I had in my cave, and crawled in and stole it, and was coming out just as I returned. A few nights after, two Negroes having started to go hunting with the same dog, passed that way, the dog came again to the place, and having just gone out to walk about, discovered me and barked, on which thinking myself discovered, I spoke to them to beg concealment.

On making myself known they fled from me. Knowing when they would betray me, I immediately left my hiding place, and was pursued almost incessantly until I was taken a fortnight afterwards by Mr. Benjamin Phipps, in a little hole I had dug out with my sword, for the purpose of concealment, under the top of a fallen tree.

Source: The Confessions of Nat Turner, the Leader of the Late Insurrection in Southampton, Virginia. Richmond, VA: Thomas R. Gray, 1832. Library of Congress Rare Book and Special Collections Division, African American Odyssey Collection.

Illinois State Legislator Abraham Lincoln Opposes Slavery
(March 3, 1837)

In 1837, at the age of 28, Abraham Lincoln, then an Illinois state legislator, staked out what would become his signature stance on the slavery question. Although he personally despised the institution, he also believed the people of each state should determine whether the institution should exist in their state; Congress ought not to interfere with the state's decision. Thus, when the Illinois legislature passed a resolution condemning slavery and arguing for its abolition by a vote of 77–6, Lincoln, in the following protest of the vote, argued that such an action merely served to whip up fervor in favor of slavery. Leaving the issue alone would allow it to die off in time. The consistency of Lincoln's position on slavery throughout the years is quite remarkable.

Resolutions upon the subject of domestic slavery having passed both branches of the General Assembly at its present session, the undersigned hereby protest against the passage of the same.

They believe that the institution of slavery is founded on both injustice and bad policy; but that the promulgation of abolition doctrines tends rather to increase than to abate its evils.

They believe that the Congress of the United States has the power, under the constitution, to abolish slavery in the District of Columbia; but that that power ought not to be exercised unless at the request of the people of said District.

The difference between these opinions and those contained in the said resolutions, is their reason for entering this protest.

Dan Stone
Abraham Lincoln
March 3, 1837
Representatives from the county of Sangamon

Source: Illinois State Legislator Abraham Lincoln Opposes Slavery, March 3, 1837. TeachingAmericanHistory.org. © 2006 Ashbrook Center for Public Affairs.

Narrative of the Life of Frederick Douglass, An American Slave, Written by Himself
(1845)

From inauspicious beginnings, Frederick Douglass became the most well-known advocate of equal rights in the 19th century. Born into slavery on Maryland's eastern shore in 1818, Douglass was the son of a slave woman and an unknown white man. While working as a ship caulker, he taught himself to read. He escaped slavery, fled to Europe, *and became an abolitionist, orator, and publisher of an influential antislavery newspaper,* The North Star. *The following excerpt is from his memoir, published in 1845.*

A mere look, word, or motion,—a mistake, accident, or want of power,—are all matters for which a slave may be whipped at any time. Does a slave look dissatisfied? It is said, he has the devil in him, and it must be whipped out. Does he speak loudly when spoken to by his master? Then he is getting high-minded, and should be taken down a button-hole lower. Does he forget to pull off his hat at the approach of a white person? Then he is wanting in reverence, and should be whipped for it. Does he ever venture to vindicate his conduct, when censured for it? Then he is guilty of impudence,—one of the greatest crimes of which a slave can be guilty. Does he ever venture to suggest a different mode of doing things from that pointed out by his master? He is indeed presumptuous, and getting above himself. . . .

Source: Narrative of the Life of Frederick Douglass, An American Slave, written by Himself. Boston: Published at the Anti-Slavery Office, 1845. http://www.gutenberg.org/catalog/world/readfile?fk_files=216491.

Frederick Douglass, "Farewell to the British People: An Address Delivered in London, England"

(March 30, 1847)

Former slave Frederick Douglass traveled widely throughout the world in his effort to ensure that slavery would be abolished in the United States. The following excerpt is from a farewell address delivered by Douglass to his British supporters during a valedictory soiree given in his honor at the London Tavern on March 30, 1847. Many distinguished Britons attended the event, and many others, such as novelist Charles Dickens, sent their regrets.

I do not go back to America to sit still, remain quiet, and enjoy ease and comfort. . . . I glory in the conflict, that I may hereafter exult in the victory. I know that victory is certain. I go, turning my back upon the ease, comfort, and respectability which I might maintain even here. . . . Still, I will go back, for the sake of my brethren. I go to suffer with them; to toil with them; to endure insult with them; to undergo outrage with them; to lift up my voice in their behalf; to speak and write in their vindication; and struggle in their ranks for the emancipation which shall yet be achieved.

Source: Foner, Philip S., ed., The Life and Writings of Frederick Douglass. Vol. 1, 102–105. New York: International Publishers, 1950. Permission of International Publishers/New York.

Narrative of the Life and Adventures of Henry Bibb, An American Slave, Written by Himself

(1849)

Henry Walton Bibb was born in Kentucky to a slave mother and a Kentucky state senator, James Bibb. Henry Bibb's master hired young Henry out to several neighboring plantations, where he was often treated inhumanely. As an adult, Bibb was traded frequently, and he lived in at least seven southern states. After trying to escape several times, he finally reached Canada in 1837, only to return shortly thereafter to see his wife. His many later attempts to escape from slavery with his family were unsuccessful, and the family was permanently separated in 1840. Bibb's final experience in slavery was with a humane Cherokee owner in the Indian Territory of Kansas or Oklahoma. On the night of his owner's death, Bibb made a final, successful escape through Missouri and Ohio. He eventually settled in Detroit in 1841 and became an active abolitionist and lecturer. Bibb and his second wife, abolitionist Mary Miles, were married in 1848 and fled to Canada after passage of the Fugitive Slave Act of 1850. Known as one of the most effective antislavery lecturers of his time, Bibb continued to be a leader in the black community in Canada.

Henry W. Bibb's autobiography, Narrative of the Life and Adventures of Henry Bibb, An American Slave *(1849), elaborates on his life story, which he presented during his antislavery lectures. The* Narrative, *which is excerpted here, describes Bibb's childhood as a slave and his many experiences in slavery. The text ends shortly after he secured his freedom.*

CHAPTER 1

Sketch of my Parentage.—Early separation from my Mother.—Hard Fare.—First Experiments at running away.—Earnest longing for Freedom.—Abhorrent nature of Slavery.

I was born May 1815, of a slave mother, in Shelby County, Kentucky, and was claimed as the property of David White Esq. He came into possession of my mother long before I was born. I was brought up in the Counties of Shelby, Henry, Oldham, and Trimble. Or, more correctly speaking, in the above counties, I may safely say, I was flogged up; for where I should have received moral, mental, and religious instruction, I received stripes without number, the object of which was to degrade and keep me in subordination. I can truly say, that I drank deeply of the bitter cup of suffering and woe. I have been dragged down to the lowest depths of human degradation and wretchedness, by Slaveholders.

My mother was known by the name of Milldred Jackson. She is the mother of seven slaves only, all being sons, of whom I am the eldest. She was also so fortunate or unfortunate, as to have some of what is called the slaveholding blood flowing in her veins. I know not how much; but not enough to prevent her children though fathered by slaveholders, from being bought and sold in the slave markets of the South. It is almost impossible for slaves to give a correct account of their male parentage. All that I know about it is, that my mother informed me that my fathers name was James Bibb. He was doubtless one of the present Bibb family of Kentucky; but I have no personal knowledge of him at all, for he died before my recollection.

The first time I was separated from my mother, I was young and small. I knew nothing of my condition then as a slave. I was living with Mr. White whose wife died and left him a widower with one little girl, who was said to be the legitimate owner of my mother, and all her children. This girl was also my playmate when we were children.

I was taken away from my mother, and hired out to labor for various persons, eight or ten years in succession; and all my wages were expended for the education of Harriet White, my playmate. It was then my sorrows and sufferings commenced. It was then I first commenced seeing and feeling that I was a wretched slave, compelled to work under the lash without wages, and often without clothes enough to hide my nakedness. I have often worked without half enough to eat, both late and early, by day and by night. I have often laid my wearied limbs down at night to rest upon a dirt floor, or a bench, without any covering at all, because I had no where else to rest my wearied body, after having worked hard all the day. I have also been compelled in early life, to go at the bidding of a tyrant, through all kinds of weather, hot or cold, wet or dry, and without shoes frequently, until the month of December, with my bare feet on the cold frosty ground, cracked open and bleeding as I walked. Reader, believe me when I say, that no tongue, nor pen ever has or can express the horrors of American Slavery. Consequently I despair in finding language to express adequately the deep feeling of my soul, as I contemplate the past history of my life. But although I have suffered much from the lash, and for want of food and raiment; I confess that it was no disadvantage to be passed through the hands of so many families, as the only source of information that I had to enlighten my mind, consisted in what I could see and hear from others. Slaves were not allowed books, pen, ink, nor paper, to improve their minds. But it seems to me now, that I was particularly observing, and apt to retain what came under my observation. But more especially, all that I heard about liberty and freedom to the slaves, I never forgot. Among other good trades I learned the art of running away to perfection. I made a regular business of it, and never gave it up, until I had broken the bands of slavery, and landed myself safely in Canada, where I was regarded as a man, and not as a thing.

The first time in my life that I ran away, was for ill treatment, in 1825. I was living with a Mr. Vires, in the village of Newcastle. His wife was a very cross woman. She was every day flogging me, boxing, pulling my ears, and scolding, so that I dreaded to enter the room where she was. This first started me to running away from them. I was often gone several days before I was caught. They would abuse me for going off, but it did no good. The next time they flogged me, I was off again; but after awhile they got sick of their bargain, and returned me back into the hands of my owners. By this time Mr. White had married his second wife. She was what I call a tyrant. I lived with her several months, but she kept me almost half of my time in the woods, running from under the bloody lash. While I was at home she kept me all the time rubbing furniture, washing, scrubbing the floors; and when I was not doing this, she would often seat herself in a large rocking chair, with two pillows about her, and would make me rock her, and keep off the flies. She was too lazy to scratch her own head, and would often make me scratch and comb it for her. She would at other times lie on her bed, in warm weather, and make me fan her while she slept, scratch and rub her feet; but after awhile she got sick of me, and preferred a maiden servant to do such business. I was then hired out again; but by this time I had become much better skilled in running away, and would make calculation to avoid detection, by taking with me a bridle. If any body should see me in the woods, as they have, and asked "what are you doing here sir? you are a runaway?"— I said, "no, sir, I am looking for our old mare;" at other times, "looking for our cows." For such excuses I was let pass. In fact, the only weapon of self defence that I could use successfully, was that of deception. It is useless for a poor helpless slave, to resist a white man in a slaveholding State. Public opinion and the law is against him; and resistance in many cases is death to the slave, while the law declares, that he shall submit or die. The circumstances in which I was then placed, gave me a longing desire to be free. It kindled a fire of liberty within my breast which has never yet been quenched. This seemed to be a part of my nature; it was first revealed to me by the inevitable laws of nature's God. I could see that the All-wise Creator, had made man a free, moral, intelligent and accountable being; capable of knowing good and evil. And I believed then, as I believe now, that every man has a right to wages for his labor; a right to his own wife and children; a right to liberty and the pursuit of happiness; and a right to worship God according to the dictates of his own conscience. But here, in the light of these truths, I was a slave, a prisoner for life; I could possess nothing, nor acquire anything but what must belong to my keeper. No one can imagine my feelings in my reflecting moments, but he who has himself been a slave. Oh! I have often wept over my condition, while sauntering through the forest, to escape cruel punishment.

"No arm to protect me from tyrants aggression;
No parents to cheer me when laden with grief.
Man may picture the bounds of the rocks and the rivers,
The hills and the valleys, the lakes and the ocean,
But the horrors of slavery, he never can trace."

The term slave to this day sounds with terror to my soul,—a word too obnoxious to speak—a system too intolerable to be endured. I know this from long and sad experience. I now feel as if I had just been aroused from sleep, and looking back with quickened perception at the state of torment from whence I fled. I was there held and claimed as a slave; as such I was subjected to the will and power of my keeper, in all respects whatsoever. That the slave is a human being, no one can deny. It is his lot to be exposed in common with other men, to the calamities of sickness, death, and the misfortunes incident to life. But unlike other men, he is denied the consolation of struggling against external difficulties, such as destroy the life, liberty, and happiness of himself and family. A slave may be bought and sold in the market like an ox. He is liable to be sold off to a distant land from his family. He is bound in chains hand and foot; and his sufferings are aggravated a hundred fold, by the terrible thought, that he is not allowed to struggle against misfortune, corporeal punishment, insults and outrages committed upon himself and family; and he is not allowed to help himself, to resist or escape the blow, which he sees impending over him.

This idea of utter helplessness, in perpetual bondage, is the more distressing, as there is no period even with the remotest generation when it shall terminate.

Source: Narrative of the Life and Adventures of Henry Bibb, An American Slave, Written by Himself. With an introduction by Lucius C. Matlack. New York: Henry Bibb, 1849. Library of Congress Rare Book and Special Collections Division, African American Odyssey Collection.

The Life of Josiah Henson, Formerly a Slave, Now an Inhabitant of Canada, as Narrated by Himself

(1849)

Josiah Henson spent 30 years on a plantation in Montgomery County, Maryland, before he escaped slavery and became a Methodist preacher, abolitionist, lecturer, and founder of a cooperative colony of former slaves in Canada. His memoirs were published in 1849 and are said to have been the basis for the novel Uncle Tom's Cabin *by Harriet Beecher Stowe. The following is an excerpt from Henson's autobiography.*

My earliest employments were, to carry buckets of water to the men at work, and to hold a horse-plough, used for weeding between the rows of corn. As I grew older and taller, I was entrusted with the care of master's saddle-horse. Then a hoe was put into my hands, and I was soon required to do the day's work of a man; and it was not long before I could do it, at least as well as my associates in misery.

A description of the everyday life of a slave on a southern plantation illustrates the character and habits of the slave and the slaveholder, created and perpetuated by their relative position. The principal food of those upon my master's plantation consisted of corn-meal and salt herrings; to which was added in summer a little buttermilk, and the few vegetables which each might raise for himself and his family, on the little piece of ground which was assigned to him for the purpose, called a truck-patch.

In ordinary times we had two regular meals in a day: breakfast at twelve o'clock, after laboring from daylight, and supper when the work of the remainder of the day was over. In harvest season we had three. Our dress was of tow-cloth; for the children, nothing but a shirt; for the older ones a pair of pantaloons or a gown in addition, according to the sex. Besides these, in the winter a jacket or overcoat, a wool hat once in two or three years, for the males, and a pair of coarse shoes once a year.

We lodged in log huts, and on the bare ground. Wooden floors were an unknown luxury. In a single room were huddled, like cattle, ten or a dozen persons, men, women, and children. All ideas of refinement and decency were, of course, out of the question. We had neither bedsteads, nor furniture of any description. Our beds were collections of straw and old rags, thrown down in the corners and boxed in with boards; a single blanket the only covering. Our favourite way of sleeping, however, was on a plank, our heads raised on an old jacket and our feet toasting before the smouldering fire. The wind whistled and the rain and snow blew in through the cracks, and the damp earth soaked in the moisture till the floor was miry as a pig-sty. Such were our houses. In these wretched hovels were we penned at night, and fed by day; here were the children born and the sick—neglected.

Source: Uncle Tom's Story of His Life. An Autobiography of the Rev. Josiah Henson (Mrs. Harriet Beecher Stowe's "Uncle Tom"). From 1789 to 1876. With a Preface by Mrs. Harriet Beecher Stowe, and an Introductory Note by George Sturge, and S. Morley, Esq., M.P. London: Christian Age Office, 1876.

Francis Henderson, "Essay on Slavery Conditions"
(1856)

In 1841, 19-year-old Francis Henderson escaped from a slave plantation outside of Washington, DC. In this essay, written 15 years later, he describes the conditions he encountered as a slave on a plantation that was close to the seat of the U.S. government. Freedom had always been a most cherished American ideal—except for millions of black slaves like Henderson.

"MY BEDSTEAD CONSISTED OF A BOARD WIDE ENOUGH TO SLEEP ON"

Our houses were but log huts—the tops partly open—ground floor—rain would come through. My aunt was quite an old woman, and had been sick several years; in rains I have seen her moving from one part of the house to the other, and rolling her bedclothes about to try to keep dry—everything would be dirty and muddy. I lived in the house with my aunt. My bed and bedstead consisted of a board wide enough to sleep on—one end on a stool, the other placed near the fire. My pillow consisted of my jacket—my covering was whatever I could get. My bedtick was the board itself. And this was the way the single men slept—but we were comfortable in this way of sleeping, being used to it. I only remember having but one blanket from my owners up to the age of nineteen, when I ran away.

Our allowance was given weekly—a peck of sifted corn meal, a dozen and a half herrings, two and a half pounds of pork. Some of the boys would eat this up in three days—then they had to steal, or they could not perform their daily tasks. They would visit the hog-pen, sheep-pen, and granaries. I do not remember one slave but who stole some things—they were driven to it as a matter of necessity. I myself did this—many a time have I, with others, run among the stumps in chase of a sheep, that we might have something to eat. . . . In regard to cooking, sometimes many have to cook at one fire, and before all could get to the fire to bake hoe cakes, the overseer's horn would sound: then they must go at any rate. Many a time I have gone along eating a piece of bread and meat, or herring broiled on the coals—I never sat down at a table to eat except at harvest time, all the time I was a slave. In harvest time, the cooking is done at the great house, as the hands they have are wanted in the field. This was more like people, and we liked it, for we sat down then at meals. In the summer we had one pair of linen trousers given us—nothing else; every fall, one pair of woolen pantaloons, one woolen jacket, and two cotton shirts.

My master had four sons in his family. They all left except one, who remained to be a driver. He would often come to the field and accuse the slave of having taken so and so. If we denied it, he would whip the grown-up ones to make them own it. Many a time, when we didn't know he was anywhere around, he would be in the woods watching us—first thing we would know, he would be sitting on the fence looking down upon us, and if any had been idle, the young master would visit him with blows. I have known him to kick my aunt, an old woman who had raised and nursed him, and I have seen him punish my sisters awfully with hickories from the woods.

The slaves are watched by the patrols, who ride about to try to catch them off the quarters, especially at the house of a free person of color. I have known the slaves to stretch clothes lines across the street, high enough to let the horse pass, but not the rider; then the boys would run, and the patrols in full chase would be thrown off by running against the lines. The patrols are poor white men, who live by plundering and stealing, getting rewards for runaways, and setting up little shops on the public roads. They will take whatever the slaves steal, paying in money, whiskey, or whatever the slaves want. They take pigs, sheep, wheat, corn—any thing that's raised they encourage the slaves to steal: these they take to market next day. It's all speculation—all a matter of self-interest, and when the slaves run away, these same traders catch them if they can, to get the reward. If the slave threatens to expose his traffic, he does not care—for the slave's word is good for nothing—it would not be taken.

Source: Drew, Benjamin. *A North-Side View of Slavery.* Boston: J. P. Jewett and Company, 1856.

Dred Scott v. John F. Sanford
(March 6, 1857)

In an appeal of a lower court ruling to the U.S. Supreme Court, former slave Dred Scott and his lawyers claimed that the U.S. Constitution protected his rights to freedom as a citizen. In Scott v. Sanford, *the Court stated that Scott should remain a slave, that as a slave he was not a citizen of the United States and thus not eligible to bring suit in a federal court, and that as a slave he was personal property and thus had never been free. The Dred Scott decision of 1857 was warmly supported in the South, but bitterly denounced by northern opponents of slavery, and as such drove another wedge between the sections on the slavery issue. The following is an excerpt from the Supreme Court's opinion, which was written by Chief Justice Roger B. Taney, speaking for the majority.*

We think they [people of African ancestry] are . . . not included, and were not intended to be included, under the word "citizens" in the Constitution, and can therefore claim none of the rights and privileges which that instrument provides for and secures to citizens of the United States.

Source: Dred Scott v. John F. A. Sandford. 60 U.S. 393 (1857).

Abraham Lincoln, Speech on the Dred Scott Decision and Slavery
(June 26, 1857)

In one of the most telling speeches regarding his position on slavery, Abraham Lincoln, in the 1857 address excerpted here, responds to the U.S. Supreme Court's Dred Scott decision, which had denied Scott's right to sue for his freedom because he was a slave and therefore "property," and not a citizen able to bring suit in federal courts. Lincoln's speech was well received, catapulting him into a famous campaign for the U.S. Senate in Illinois against Stephen A. Douglas in 1858. Although Lincoln would lose that election, his campaigning and speaking skills distinguished him as a possible presidential candidate for the Republican Party in 1860.

And now as to the Dred Scott decision. That decision declares two propositions—first, that a negro cannot sue in the U.S. Courts; and secondly, that Congress cannot prohibit slavery in the Territories. It was made by a divided court—dividing differently on the different points. Judge Douglas does not discuss the merits of the decision; and, in that respect, I shall follow his example, believing I could no more improve on McLean and Curtis, than he could on Taney.

He denounces all who question the correctness of that decision, as offering violent resistance to it. But who resists it? Who has, in spite of the decision, declared Dred Scott free, and resisted the authority of his master over him?

Judicial decisions have two uses—first, to absolutely determine the case decided, and secondly, to indicate to the public how other similar cases will be decided when they arise. For the latter use, they are called "precedents" and "authorities."

We believe, as much as Judge Douglas, (perhaps more) in obedience to, and respect for the judicial department of government. We think its decisions on Constitutional questions, when fully settled, should control, not only the particular cases decided, but the general policy of the country, subject to be disturbed only by amendments of the Constitution as provided in that instrument itself. More than this would be revolution. But we think the Dred Scott decision is erroneous. We know the court that made it, has often over-ruled its own decisions, and we shall do what we can to have it to over-rule this. We offer no resistance to it.

Judicial decisions are of greater or less authority as precedents, according to circumstances. That this should be so, accords both with common sense, and the customary understanding of the legal profession.

If this important decision had been made by the unanimous concurrence of the judges, and without any apparent partisan bias, and in accordance with legal public expectation, and with the steady practice of the departments throughout our history, and had been in no part, based on assumed historical facts which are not really true; or, if wanting in some of these, it had been before the court more than once, and had there been affirmed and re-affirmed through a course of years, it then might be, perhaps would be, factious, nay, even revolutionary, to not acquiesce in it as a precedent.

But when, as it is true we find it wanting in all these claims to the public confidence, it is not resistance, it is not factious, it is not even disrespectful, to treat it as not having yet quite established a settled doctrine for the country—But Judge Douglas considers this view awful. Hear him:

"The courts are the tribunals prescribed by the Constitution and created by the authority of the people to determine, expound and enforce the law. Hence, whoever resists the final decision of the highest judicial tribunal, aims a deadly blow to our whole Republican system of government—a blow, which if successful would place all our rights and liberties at the mercy of passion, anarchy and violence. I repeat, therefore, that if resistance to the decisions of the Supreme Court of the United States, in a matter like the points decided in the Dred Scott case, clearly within their jurisdiction as defined by the Constitution, shall be forced upon the country as a political issue, it will become a distinct and naked issue between the friends and the enemies of the Constitution—the friends and the enemies of the supremacy of the laws."

Why this same Supreme court once decided a national bank to be constitutional; but Gen. Jackson, as President of the United States, disregarded the decision, and vetoed a bill for a re-charter, partly on constitutional ground, declaring that each public functionary must support the Constitution, "as he understands it." But hear the General's own words. Here they are, taken from his veto message:

"It is maintained by the advocates of the bank, that its constitutionality, in all its features, ought to be considered as settled by precedent, and by the decision of the Supreme Court. To this conclusion I cannot assent. Mere precedent is a dangerous source of authority, and should not be regarded as deciding questions of constitutional power, except where the acquiescence of the people and the States can be considered as well settled. So far from this being the case on this subject, an argument against the bank might be based on precedent. One Congress in 1791, decided in favor of a bank; another in 1811, decided against it. One Congress in 1815 decided against a bank; another in 1816 decided in its favor. Prior to the present Congress, therefore the precedents drawn from that source were equal. If we resort to the States, the expressions of legislative, judicial and executive opinions against the bank have been probably to those in its favor as four to one. There is nothing in precedent, therefore, which if its authority were admitted, ought to weigh in favor of the act before me."

I drop the quotations merely to remark that all there ever was, in the way of precedent up to the Dred Scott decision, on the points therein decided, had been against that decision. But hear Gen. Jackson further—

"If the opinion of the Supreme court covered the whole ground of this act, it ought not to control the co-ordinate authorities of this Government. The Congress, the executive and the court, must each for itself be guided by its own opinion of the Constitution. Each public officer, who takes an oath to support the Constitution, swears that he will support it as he understands it, and not as it is understood by others."

Again and again have I heard Judge Douglas denounce that bank decision, and applaud Gen. Jackson for disregarding it. It would be interesting for him to look over his recent speech, and see how exactly his fierce philippics against us for resisting Supreme Court decisions, fall upon his own head. It will call to his mind a long and fierce political war in this country, upon an issue which, in his own language, and, of course, in his own changeless estimation, was "a distinct and naked issue between the friends and the enemies of the Constitution," and in which war he fought in the ranks of the enemies of the Constitution.

I have said, in substance, that the Dred Scott decision was, in part, based on assumed historical facts which were not really true; and I ought not to leave the subject without giving some reasons for saying this; I therefore give an instance or two, which I think fully sustain me. Chief Justice Taney, in delivering the opinion of the majority of the Court, insists at great length that negroes were no part of the people who made, or for whom was made, the Declaration of Independence, or the Constitution of the United States.

On the contrary, Judge Curtis, in his dissenting opinion, shows that in five of the then thirteen states, to wit, New Hampshire, Massachusetts, New York, New Jersey and North Carolina, free negroes were voters, and, in proportion to their numbers, had the same part in making the Constitution that the white people had. He shows this with so much particularity as to leave no doubt of its truth; and, as a sort of conclusion on that point, holds the following language:

"The Constitution was ordained and established by the people of the United States, through the action, in each State, of those persons who were qualified by its laws to act thereon in behalf of themselves and all other citizens of the State. In some of the States, as we have seen, colored persons were among those qualified by law to act on the subject. These colored persons were not only included in the body of 'the people of the United States,' by whom the Constitution was ordained and established; but in at least five of the States they had the power to act, and, doubtless, did act, by their suffrages, upon the question of its adoption."

Again, Chief Justice Taney says: "It is difficult, at this day to realize the state of public opinion in relation to that unfortunate race, which prevailed in the civilized and enlightened portions of the world at the time of the Declaration of Independence, and when the Constitution of the United States was framed and adopted." And again, after quoting from the Declaration, he says: "The general words above quoted would seem to include the whole human family, and if they were used in a similar instrument at this day, would be so understood."

In these the Chief Justice does not directly assert, but plainly assumes, as a fact, that the public estimate of the black man is more favorable now than it was in the days of the Revolution. This assumption is a mistake. In some trifling particulars, the condition of that race has been ameliorated; but, as a whole, in this country, the change between then and now is decidedly the other way; and their ultimate destiny has never appeared so hopeless as in the last three or four years. In two of the five States—New Jersey and North Carolina—that then gave the free negro the right of voting, the right has since been taken away; and in a third—New York—it has been greatly abridged; while it has not been extended, so far as I know, to a single additional State, though the number of the States has more than doubled. In those days, as I understand, masters could, at their own pleasure, emancipate their slaves; but since then, such legal restraints have been made upon emancipation, as to amount almost to prohibition. In those days, Legislatures held the unquestioned power to abolish slavery in their respective States; but now it is

becoming quite fashionable for State Constitutions to withhold that power from the Legislatures. In those days, by common consent, the spread of the black man's bondage to new countries was prohibited; but now, Congress decides that it will not continue the prohibition, and the Supreme Court decides that it could not if it would. In those days, our Declaration of Independence was held sacred by all, and thought to include all; but now, to aid in making the bondage of the negro universal and eternal, it is assailed, and sneered at, and construed, and hawked at, and torn, till, if its framers could rise from their graves, they could not at all recognize it. All the powers of earth seem rapidly combining against him. Mammon is after him; ambition follows, and philosophy follows, and the Theology of the day is fast joining the cry. They have him in his prison house; they have searched his person, and left no prying instrument with him. One after another they have closed the heavy iron doors upon him, and now they have him, as it were, bolted in with a lock of a hundred keys, which can never be unlocked without the concurrence of every key; the keys in the hands of a hundred different men, and they scattered to a hundred different and distant places; and they stand musing as to what invention, in all the dominions of mind and matter, can be produced to make the impossibility of his escape more complete than it is.

It is grossly incorrect to say or assume, that the public estimate of the negro is more favorable now than it was at the origin of the government.

Three years and a half ago, Judge Douglas brought forward his famous Nebraska bill. The country was at once in a blaze. He scorned all opposition, and carried it through Congress. Since then he has seen himself superseded in a Presidential nomination, by one indorsing the general doctrine of his measure, but at the same time standing clear of the odium of its untimely agitation, and its gross breach of national faith; and he has seen that successful rival Constitutionally elected, not by the strength of friends, but by the division of adversaries, being in a popular minority of nearly four hundred thousand votes. He has seen his chief aids in his own State, Shields and Richardson, politically speaking, successively tried, convicted, and executed, for an offense not their own, but his. And now he sees his own case, standing next on the docket for trial.

There is a natural disgust in the minds of nearly all white people, to the idea of an indiscriminate amalgamation of the white and black races; and Judge Douglas evidently is basing his chief hope, upon the chances of being able to appropriate the benefit of this disgust to himself. If he can, by much drumming and repeating, fasten the odium of that idea upon his adversaries, he thinks he can struggle through the storm. He therefore clings to this hope, as a drowning man to the last plank. He makes an occasion for lugging it in from the opposition to the Dred Scott decision. He finds the Republicans insisting that the Declaration of Independence includes ALL men, black as well as white; and forth-with he boldly denies that it includes negroes at all, and proceeds to argue gravely that all who contend it does, do so only because they want to vote, and eat, and sleep, and marry with negroes! He will have it that they cannot be consistent else. Now I protest against that counterfeit logic which concludes that, because I do not want a black woman for a slave I must necessarily want her for a wife. I need not have her for either, I can just leave her alone. In some respects she certainly is not my equal; but in her natural right to eat the bread she earns with her own hands without asking leave of any one else, she is my equal, and the equal of all others.

Chief Justice Taney, in his opinion in the Dred Scott case, admits that the language of the Declaration is broad enough to include the whole human family, but he and Judge Douglas argue that the authors of that instrument did not intend to include negroes, by the fact that they did not at once, actually place them on an equality with the whites. Now this grave argument comes to just nothing at all, by the other fact, that they did not at once, or ever afterwards, actually place all white people on an equality with one or another. And this is the staple argument of both the Chief Justice and

the Senator, for doing this obvious violence to the plain unmistakable language of the Declaration. I think the authors of that notable instrument intended to include all men, but they did not intend to declare all men equal in all respects. They did not mean to say all were equal in color, size, intellect, moral developments, or social capacity. They defined with tolerable distinctness, in what respects they did consider all men created equal—equal in "certain inalienable rights, among which are life, liberty, and the pursuit of happiness." This they said, and this meant. They did not mean to assert the obvious untruth, that all were then actually enjoying that equality, nor yet, that they were about to confer it immediately upon them. In fact they had no power to confer such a boon. They meant simply to declare the right, so that the enforcement of it might follow as fast as circumstances should permit. They meant to set up a standard maxim for free society, which should be familiar to all, and revered by all; constantly looked to, constantly labored for, and even though never perfectly attained, constantly approximated, and thereby constantly spreading and deepening its influence, and augmenting the happiness and value of life to all people of all colors everywhere. The assertion that "all men are created equal" was of no practical use in effecting our separation from Great Britain; and it was placed in the Declaration, nor for that, but for future use. Its authors meant it to be, thank God, it is now proving itself, a stumbling block to those who in after times might seek to turn a free people back into the hateful paths of despotism. They knew the proneness of prosperity to breed tyrants, and they meant when such should re-appear in this fair land and commence their vocation they should find left for them at least one hard nut to crack.

I have now briefly expressed my view of the meaning and objects of that part of the Declaration of Independence which declares that "all men are created equal."

Now let us hear Judge Douglas' view of the same subject, as I find it in the printed report of his late speech. Here it is:

"No man can vindicate the character, motives and conduct of the signers of the Declaration of Independence except upon the hypothesis that they referred to the white race alone, and not to the African, when they declared all men to have been created equal—that they were speaking of British subjects on this continent being equal to British subjects born and residing in Great Britain—that they were entitled to the same inalienable rights, and among them were enumerated life, liberty and the pursuit of happiness. The Declaration was adopted for the purpose of justifying the colonists in the eyes of the civilized world in withdrawing their allegiance from the British crown, and dissolving their connection with the mother country."

My good friends, read that carefully over some leisure hour, and ponder well upon it—see what a mere wreck—mangled ruin—it makes of our once glorious Declaration.

"They were speaking of British subjects on this continent being equal to British subjects born and residing in Great Britain!" Why, according to this, not only negroes but white people outside of Great Britain and America are not spoken of in that instrument. The English, Irish and Scotch, along with white Americans, were included to be sure, but the French, Germans and other white people of the world are all gone to pot along with the Judge's inferior races. I had thought the Declaration promised something better than the condition of British subjects; but no, it only meant that we should be equal to them in their own oppressed and unequal condition. According to that, it gave no promise that having kicked off the King and Lords of Great Britain, we should not at once be saddled with a King and Lords of our own.

I had thought the Declaration contemplated the progressive improvement in the condition of all men everywhere; but no, it merely "was adopted for the purpose of justifying the colonists in the eyes of the civilized world in withdrawing their allegiance from the British crown, and dissolving their connection with the mother country." Why, that object having been effected some eighty years ago, the Declaration is of no practical use now—mere rubbish—old wadding left to rot on the battle-field after the victory is won.

I understand you are preparing to celebrate the "Fourth," tomorrow week. What for? The doings of that day had no reference to the present; and quite half of you are not even descendants of those who were referred to at that day. But I suppose you will celebrate; and will even go so far as to read the Declaration. Suppose after you read it once in the old fashioned way, you read it once more with Judge Douglas' version. It will then run thus: "We hold these truths to be self-evident that all British subjects who were on this continent eighty-one years ago, were created equal to all British subjects born and then residing in Great Britain."

And now I appeal to all—to Democrats as well as others,—are you really willing that the Declaration shall be thus frittered away?—thus left no more at most, than an interesting memorial of the dead past? thus shorn of its vitality, and practical value; and left without the germ or even the suggestion of the individual rights of man in it?

But Judge Douglas is especially horrified at the thought of the mixing blood by the white and black races: agreed for once—a thousand times agreed. There are white men enough to marry all the white women, and black men enough to marry all the black women; and so let them be married. On this point we fully agree with the Judge; and when he shall show that his policy is better adapted to prevent amalgamation than ours we shall drop ours, and adopt his. Let us see. In 1850 there were in the United States, 405,751, mulattoes. Very few of these are the off-spring of whites and free blacks; nearly all have sprung from black slaves and white masters. A separation of the races is the only perfect preventive of amalgamation but as an immediate separation is impossible the next best thing is to keep them apart where they are not already together. If white and black people never get together in Kansas, they will never mix blood in Kansas. That is at least one self-evident truth. A few free colored persons may get into the free States, in any event; but their number is too insignificant to amount to much in the way of mixing blood. In 1850 there were in the free states,

56,649 mulattoes; but for the most part they were not born there—they came from the slave States, ready made up. In the same year the slave States had 348,874 mulattoes all of home production. The proportion of free mulattoes to free blacks—the only colored classes in the free states—is much greater in the slave than in the free states. It is worthy of note too, that among the free states those which make the colored man the nearest to equal the white, have, proportionably the fewest mulattoes the least of amalgamation. In New Hampshire, the State which goes farthest towards equality between the races, there are just 184 Mulattoes while there are in Virginia—how many do you think? 79,775, being 23,126 more than in all the free States together. These statistics show that slavery is the greatest source of amalgamation; and next to it, not the elevation, but the degeneration of the free blacks. Yet Judge Douglas dreads the slightest restraints on the spread of slavery, and the slightest human recognition of the negro, as tending horribly to amalgamation.

This very Dred Scott case affords a strong test as to which party most favors amalgamation, the Republicans or the dear Union-saving Democracy. Dred Scott, his wife and two daughters were all involved in the suit. We desired the court to have held that they were citizens so far at least as to entitle them to a hearing as to whether they were free or not; and then, also, that they were in fact and in law really free. Could we have had our way, the chances of these black girls, ever mixing their blood with that of white people, would have been diminished at least to the extent that it could not have been without their consent. But Judge Douglas is delighted to have them decided to be slaves, and not human enough to have a hearing, even if they were free, and thus left subject to the forced concubinage of their masters, and liable to become the mothers of mulattoes in spite of themselves—the very state of case that produces nine tenths of all the mulattoes—all the mixing of blood in the nation.

Of course, I state this case as an illustration only, not meaning to say or intimate that the master of Dred Scott and his family, or any more than a percentage of masters generally, are inclined to exercise this particular power which they hold over their female slaves.

I have said that the separation of the races is the only perfect preventive of amalgamation. I have no right to say all the members of the Republican party are in favor of this, nor to say that as a party they are in favor of it. There is nothing in their platform directly on the subject. But I can say a very large proportion of its members are for it, and that the chief plank in their platform—opposition to the spread of slavery—is most favorable to that separation.

Such separation, if ever effected at all, must be effected by colonization; and no political party, as such, is now doing anything directly for colonization. Party operations at present only favor or retard colonization incidentally. The enterprise is a difficult one; but "when there is a will there is a way;" and what colonization needs most is a hearty will. Will springs from the two elements of moral sense and self-interest. Let us be brought to believe it is morally right, and, at the same time, favorable to, or, at least, not against, our interest, to transfer the African to his native clime, and we shall find a way to do it, however great the task may be. The children of Israel, to such numbers as to include four hundred thousand fighting men, went out of Egyptian bondage in a body.

How differently the respective courses of the Democratic and Republican parties incidentally bear on the question of forming a will—a public sentiment—for colonization, is easy to see. The Republicans inculcate, with whatever of ability they can, that the negro is a man; that his bondage is cruelly wrong, and that the field of his oppression ought not to be enlarged. The Democrats deny his manhood; deny, or dwarf to insignificance, the wrong of his bondage; so far as possible, crush all sympathy for him, and cultivate and excite hatred and disgust against him; compliment themselves as Union-savers for doing so; and call the indefinite outspreading of his bondage "a sacred right of self-government."

The plainest print cannot be read through a gold eagle; and it will be ever hard to find many men who will send a slave to Liberia, and pay his passage while they can send him to a new country, Kansas for instance, and sell him for fifteen hundred dollars, and the rise.

Source: Lincoln, Abraham. Speech on the Dred Scott Decision at Springfield, Illinois. June 26, 1857. TeachingAmericanHistory.org © 2006 Ashbrook Center for Public Affairs.

Fifth Lincoln-Douglas Debate, Galesburg, Illinois
(October 7, 1858)

In 1858, Stephen A. Douglas and his challenger, Abraham Lincoln, engaged in a series of eight debates across Illinois as they ran against each other for the U.S. Senate seat from Illinois, then held by Douglas. Reproduced here is the Fifth Debate, which was held on October 7, 1858, in Galesburg, a town in Knox County in the northwestern part of the state. The debate was to be held in a park across from Knox College, but inclement weather forced the debaters to move to shelter on the east side of the college's main building. Newspapers put attendance at the debate at about 10,000 people.

During the debate, Douglas minimized the moral issue, arguing that slavery was a local matter and the question of whether or not slavery was to be permitted in a territory could be left to the residents of that territory. Lincoln viewed slavery as an absolute evil that could and should be limited by government action. His most famous line during the Galesburg debate was accusing Douglas of "blowing out the moral lights around us when he maintains that anyone who wants slaves has a right to hold them."

MR. DOUGLAS'S SPEECH

LADIES AND GENTLEMEN: Four years ago I appeared before the people of Knox county for the purpose of defending my political action upon the Compromise measures of 1850 and the passage of the Kansas-Nebraska bill. Those of you before me, who were present then, will remember that I vindicated myself for supporting those two measures by the fact that they rested upon the great fundamental principle that the people of each State and each Territory of this Union have the right, and ought to be permitted to exercise the right, of regulating their own domestic concerns in their own way, subject to no other limitation or restriction than that which the Constitution of the United States imposes upon them. I then called upon the people of Illinois to decide whether that principle of self-government was right or wrong. If it was and is right, then the Compromise measures of 1850 were right, and, consequently, the Kansas and Nebraska bill, based upon the same principle, must necessarily have been right.

The Kansas and Nebraska bill declared, in so many words, that it was the true intent and meaning of the act not to legislate slavery into any State or Territory, nor to exclude it therefrom, but to leave the people thereof perfectly free to form and regulate their domestic institutions in their own way, subject only to the Constitution of the United States. For the last four years I have devoted all my energies, in private and public, to commend that principle to the American people. Whatever else may be said in condemnation or support of my political course, I apprehend that no honest man will doubt the fidelity with which, under all circumstances, I have stood by it.

During the last year a question arose in the Congress of the United States whether or not that principle would be violated by the admission of Kansas into the Union under the Lecompton

Constitution. In my opinion, the attempt to force Kansas in under that Constitution, was a gross violation of the principle enunciated in the Compromise measures of 1850, and Kansas and Nebraska bill of 1854, and therefore I led off in the fight against the Lecompton Constitution, and conducted it until the effort to carry that Constitution through Congress was abandoned. And I can appeal to all men, friends and foes, Democrats and Republicans, Northern men and Southern men, that during the whole of that fight I carried the banner of Popular Sovereignty aloft, and never allowed it to trail in the dust, or lowered my flag until victory perched upon our arms. When the Lecompton Constitution was defeated, the question arose in the minds of those who had advocated it what they should next resort to in order to carry out their views. They devised a measure known as the English bill, and granted a general amnesty and political pardon to all men who had fought against the Lecompton Constitution, provided they would support that bill. I for one did not choose to accept the pardon, or to avail myself of the amnesty granted on that condition. The fact that the supporters of Lecompton were willing to forgive all differences of opinion at that time in the event those who opposed it favored the English bill, was an admission they did not think that opposition to Lecompton impaired a man's standing in the Democratic party. Now the question arises, what was that English bill which certain men are now attempting to make a test of political orthodoxy in this country. It provided, in substance, that the Lecompton Constitution should be sent back to the people of Kansas for their adoption or rejection, at an election which was held in August last, and in case they refused admission under it, that Kansas should be kept out of the Union until she had 93,420 inhabitants. I was in favor of sending the Constitution back in order to enable the people to say whether or not it was their act and deed, and embodied their will; but the other proposition, that if they refused to come into the Union under it, they should be kept out until they had double or treble the population they then had, I never would sanction by my vote. The reason why I could

not sanction it is to be found in the fact that by the English bill, if the people of Kansas had only agreed to become a slaveholding State under the Lecompton Constitution, they could have done so with 35,000 people, but if they insisted on being a free State, as they had a right to do, then they were to be punished by being kept out of the Union until they had nearly three times that population. I then said in my place in the Senate, as I now say to you, that whenever Kansas has population enough for a slave State she has population enough for a free State. I have never yet given a vote, and I never intend to record one, making an odious and unjust distinction between the different States of this Union. I hold it to be a fundamental principle in our republican form of government that all the States of this Union, old and new, free and slave, stand on an exact equality. Equality among the different States is a cardinal principle on which all our institutions rest. Wherever, therefore, you make a discrimination, saying to a slave State that it shall be admitted with 35,000 inhabitants, and to a free State that it shall not be admitted until it has 93,000 or 100,000 inhabitants, you are throwing the whole weight of the Federal Government into the scale in favor of one class of States against the other. Nor would I on the other hand any sooner sanction the doctrine that a free State could be admitted into the Union with 35,000 people, while a slave State was kept out until it had 93,000. I have always declared in the Senate my willingness, and I am willing now to adopt the rule, that no Territory shall ever become a State, until it has the requisite population for a member of Congress, according to the then existing ratio. But while I have always been, and am now willing to adopt that general rule, I was not willing and would not consent to make an exception of Kansas, as a punishment for her obstinacy, in demanding the right to do as she pleased in the formation of her Constitution. It is proper that I should remark here, that my opposition to the Lecompton Constitution did not rest upon the peculiar position taken by Kansas on the subject of slavery. I held then, and hold now, that if the people of Kansas want a slave State, it is their right to make one and be received into the Union under it; if, on the contrary, they want a free State, it is their right to have it, and no man should ever oppose their admission because they ask it under the one or the other. I hold to that great principle of self-government which asserts the right of every people to decide for themselves the nature and character of the domestic institutions and fundamental law under which they are to live.

The effort has been and is now being made in this State by certain postmasters and other Federal office-holders, to make a test of faith on the support of the English bill. These men are now making speeches all over the State against me and in favor of Lincoln, either directly or indirectly, because I would not sanction a discrimination between slave and free States by voting for the English bill. But while that bill is made a test in Illinois for the purpose of breaking up the Democratic organization in this State, how is it in the other States? Go to Indiana, and there you find English himself, the author of the English bill, who is a candidate for re-election to Congress, has been forced by public opinion to abandon his own darling project, and to give a promise that he will vote for the admission of Kansas at once, whenever she forms a Constitution in pursuance of law, and ratifies it by a majority vote of her people. Not only is this the case with English himself, but I am informed that every Democratic candidate for Congress in Indiana takes the same ground. Pass to Ohio, and there you find that Groesbeck, and Pendleton, and Cox, and all the other anti-Lecompton men who stood shoulder to shoulder with me against the Lecompton Constitution, but voted for the English bill, now repudiate it and take the same ground that I do on that question. So it is with the Joneses and others of Pennsylvania, and so it is with every other Lecompton Democrat in the free States. They now abandon even the English bill, and come back to the true platform which I proclaimed at the time in the Senate, and upon which the Democracy of Illinois now stand. And yet, notwithstanding the fact, that every Lecompton and anti-Lecompton Democrat in the free States has abandoned the English bill, you are told that it is to be made a test

upon me, while the power and patronage of the Government are all exerted to elect men to Congress in the other States who occupy the same position with reference to it that I do. It seems that my political offense consists in the fact that I first did not vote for the English bill, and thus pledge myself to keep Kansas out of the Union until she has a population of 93,420, and then return home, violate that pledge, repudiate the bill, and take the opposite ground. If I had done this, perhaps the Administration would now be advocating my re-election, as it is that of the others who have pursued this course. I did not choose to give that pledge, for the reason that I did not intend to carry out that principle. I never will consent, for the sake of conciliating the frowns of power, to pledge myself to do that which I do not intend to perform. I now submit the question to you as my constituency, whether I was not right, first, in resisting the adoption of the Lecompton Constitution; and secondly, in resisting the English bill. I repeat, that I opposed the Lecompton Constitution because it was not the act and deed of the people of Kansas, and did not embody their will. I denied the right of any power on earth, under our system of Government, to force a Constitution on an unwilling people. There was a time when some men could pretend to believe that the Lecompton Constitution embodied the will of the people of Kansas, but that time has passed. The question was referred to the people of Kansas under the English bill last August, and then, at a fair election, they rejected the Lecompton Constitution by a vote of from eight to ten against it to one in its favor. Since it has been voted down by so overwhelming a majority, no man can pretend that it was the act and deed of that people. I submit the question to you whether or not, if it had not been for me, that Constitution would have been crammed down the throats of the people of Kansas against their consent. While at least ninety-nine out of every hundred people here present, agree that I was right in defeating that project, yet my enemies use the fact that I did defeat it by doing right, to break me down and put another man in the United States in my place. The very men who acknowledge that I was right in defeating Lecompton, now form an alliance with Federal office-holders, professed Lecompton men, to defeat me, because I did right. My political opponent, Mr. Lincoln, has no hope on earth, and has never dreamed that he had a chance of success, were it not for the aid that he is receiving from Federal office-holders, who are using their influence and the patronage of the Government against me in revenge for my having defeated the Lecompton Constitution. What do you Republicans think of a political organization that will try to make an unholy and unnatural combination with its professed foes to beat a man merely because he has done right? You know such is the fact with regard to your own party. You know that the ax of decapitation is suspended over every man in office in Illinois, and the terror of proscription is threatened every Democrat by the present Administration, unless he supports the Republican ticket in preference to my Democratic associates and myself. I could find an instance in the postmaster of the city of Galesburgh, and in every other postmaster in this vicinity, all of whom have been stricken down simply because they discharged the duties of their offices honestly, and supported the regular Democratic ticket in this State in the right. The Republican party is availing itself of every unworthy means in the present contest to carry the election, because its leaders know that if they let this chance slip they will never have another, and their hopes of making this a Republican State will be blasted forever.

Now, let me ask you whether the country has any interest in sustaining this organization, known as the Republican party. That party is unlike all other political organizations in this country. All other parties have been national in their character—have avowed their principles alike in the slave and free States, in Kentucky as well as Illinois, in Louisiana as well as in Massachusetts. Such was the case with the old Whig party, and such was and is the case with the Democratic party. Whigs and Democrats could proclaim their principles boldly and fearlessly in the North and in the South, in the East and in the West, wherever the Constitution ruled and the American flag waved over American soil.

But now you have a sectional organization, a party which appeals to the Northern section of the Union against the Southern, a party which appeals to Northern passion, Northern pride, Northern ambition, and Northern prejudices, against Southern people, the Southern States, and Southern institutions. The leaders of that party hope that they will be able to unite the Northern States in one great sectional party, and inasmuch as the North is the strongest section, that they will thus be enabled to out vote, conquer, govern, and control the South. Hence you find that they now make speeches advocating principles and measures which cannot be defended in any slaveholding State of this Union. Is there a Republican residing in Galesburgh who can travel into Kentucky and carry his principles with him across the Ohio? What Republican from Massachusetts can visit the Old Dominion without leaving his principles behind him when he crosses Mason and Dixon's line? Permit me to say to you in perfect good humor, but in all sincerity, that no political creed is sound which cannot be proclaimed fearlessly in every State of this Union where the Federal Constitution is not the supreme law of the land. Not only is this Republican party unable to proclaim its principles alike in the North and in the South, in the free States and in the slave States, but it cannot even proclaim them in the same forms and give them the same strength and meaning in all parts of the same State. My friend Lincoln finds it extremely difficult to manage a debate in the center part of the State, where there is a mixture of men from the North and the South. In the extreme Northern part of Illinois he can proclaim as bold and radical Abolitionism as ever Giddings, Lovejoy, or Garrison enunciated, but when he gets down a little further South he claims that he is an old line Whig, a disciple of Henry Clay, and declares that he still adheres to the old line Whig creed, and has nothing whatever to do with Abolitionism, or negro equality, or Negro citizenship. I once before hinted this of Mr. Lincoln in a public speech, and at Charleston he defied me to show that there was any difference between his speeches in the North and in the South, and that they were not in strict harmony. I will now call your attention to two of them, and you can then say whether you would be apt to believe that the same man ever uttered both. In a speech in reply to me at Chicago in July last, Mr. Lincoln, in speaking of the equality of the negro with the white man, used the following language:

> "I should like to know, if taking this old Declaration of Independence, which declares that all men are equal upon principle, and making exceptions to it, where will it stop? If one man says it does not mean a negro, why may not another man say it does not mean another man? If the Declaration is not the truth, let us get the statute book in which we find it and tear it out. Who is so bold as to do it? If it is not true, let us tear it out."

You find that Mr. Lincoln there proposed that if the doctrine of the Declaration of Independence, declaring all men to be born equal, did not include the negro and put him on an equality with the white man, that we should take the statute book and tear it out. He there took the ground that the negro race is included in the Declaration of Independence as the equal of the white race, and that there could be no such thing as a distinction in the races, making one superior and the other inferior. I read now from the same speech:

> "My friends [he says], I have detained you about as long as I desire to do, and I have only to say let us discard all this quibbling about this man and the other man—this race and that race and the other race being inferior, and therefore they must be placed in an inferior position, discarding our standard that we have left us. Let us discard all these things, and unite as one people throughout this land, until we shall once more stand up declaring that all men are created equal."

["That's right," etc.]

Yes, I have no doubt that you think it is right, but the Lincoln men down in Coles, Tazewell and Sangamon counties do not think it is right. In the conclusion of the same speech, talking to the Chicago Abolitionists, he said: "I leave you, hoping that the lamp of liberty will burn in your bosoms until there shall no longer be a doubt that all men are created free and equal." ["Good, good."] Well, you say good to that, and you are going to vote for Lincoln because he holds that doctrine. I will not blame you for supporting him on that ground, but I will show you in immediate contrast with that doctrine, what Mr. Lincoln said down in Egypt in order to get votes in that locality where they do not hold to such a doctrine. In a joint discussion between Mr. Lincoln and myself, at Charleston, I think, on the 18th of last month, Mr. Lincoln, referring to this subject, used the following language:

> "I will say then, that I am not nor never have been in favor of bringing about in any way the social and political equality of the white and black races; that I am not nor never have been in favor of making voters of the free negroes, or jurors, or qualifying them to hold office, or having them to marry with white people. I will say in addition, that there is a physical difference between the white and black races, which, I suppose, will forever forbid the two races living together upon terms of social and political equality, and inasmuch as they cannot so live, that while they do remain together, there must be the position of superior and inferior, that I as much as any other man am in favor of the superior position being assigned to the white man."

["Good for Lincoln."]

Fellow-citizens, here you find men hurraing for Lincoln and saying that he did right, when in one part of the State he stood up for negro equality, and in another part for political effect, discarded the doctrine and declared that there always must be a superior and inferior race. Abolitionists up north are expected and required to vote for Lincoln because he goes for the equality of the races, holding that by the Declaration of Independence the white man and the negro were created equal, and endowed by the Divine law with that equality, and down south he tells the old Whigs, the Kentuckians, Virginians, and Tennesseeans, that there is a physical difference in the races, making one superior and the other inferior, and that he is in favor of maintaining the superiority of the white race over the negro. Now, how can you reconcile those two positions of Mr. Lincoln? He is to be voted for in the south as a pro-slavery man, and he is to be voted for in the north as an Abolitionist. Up here he thinks it is all nonsense to talk about a difference between the races, and says that we must "discard all quibbling about this race and that race and the other race being inferior, and therefore they must be placed in an inferior position." Down south he makes this "quibble" about this race and that race and the other race being inferior as the creed of his party, and declares that the negro can never be elevated to the position of the white man. You find that his political meetings are called by different names in different counties in the State. Here they are called Republican meetings, but in old Tazewell, where Lincoln made a speech last Tuesday, he did not address a Republican meeting, but "a grand rally of the Lincoln men." There are very few Republicans there, because Tazewell county is filled with old Virginians and Kentuckians, all of whom are Whigs or Democrats, and if Mr. Lincoln had called an Abolition or Republican meeting there, he would not get many votes. Go down into Egypt and you find that he and his party are operating under an alias there, which his friend Trumbull has given them, in order that they may cheat the people. When I was down in Monroe county a few weeks ago addressing the people, I saw handbills posted announcing that Mr. Trumbull was going to speak in behalf of Lincoln, and what do you think the name of his party was there? Why the "Free Democracy." Mr. Trumbull and Mr. Jehu Baker were announced to address the Free Democracy of Monroe county, and the bill was signed "Many Free Democrats." The reason that Lincoln and his party adopted the name of "Free Democracy" down there was because Monroe county has always been an old-fashioned Democratic county, and hence it was necessary to make the people believe that they were Democrats, sympathized with them, and were fighting for Lincoln as Democrats. Come up to Springfield, where Lincoln now lives and always has lived, and you find that the

Convention of his party which assembled to nominate candidates for Legislature, who are expected to vote for him if elected, dare not adopt the name of Republican, but assembled under the title of "all opposed to the Democracy." Thus you find that Mr. Lincoln's creed cannot travel through even one half of the counties of this State, but that it changes its hues and becomes lighter and lighter, as it travels from the extreme north, until it is nearly white, when it reaches the extreme south end of the State. I ask you, my friends, why cannot Republicans avow their principles alike every where? I would despise myself if I thought that I was procuring your votes by concealing my opinions, and by avowing one set of principles in one part of the State, and a different set in another part. If I do not truly and honorably represent your feelings and principles, then I ought not to be your Senator; and I will never conceal my opinions, or modify or change them a hair's breadth in order to get votes. I tell you that this Chicago doctrine of Lincoln's—declaring that the negro and the white man are made equal by the Declaration of Independence and by Divine Providence—is a monstrous heresy. The signers of the Declaration of Independence never dreamed of the negro when they were writing that document. They referred to white men, to men of European birth and European descent, when they declared the equality of all men. I see a gentleman there in the crowd shaking his head. Let me remind him that when Thomas Jefferson wrote that document, he was the owner, and so continued until his death, of a large number of slaves. Did he intend to say in that Declaration, that his negro slaves, which he held and treated as property, were created his equals by Divine law, and that he was violating the law of God every day of his life by holding them as slaves? It must be borne in mind that when that Declaration was put forth, every one of the thirteen Colonies were slaveholding Colonies, and every man who signed that instrument represented a slave-holding constituency. Recollect, also, that no one of them emancipated his slaves, much less put them on an equality with himself, after he signed the Declaration. On the contrary, they all continued to hold their negroes as slaves during the revolutionary war. Now, do you believe—are you willing to have it said—that every man who signed the Declaration of Independence declared the negro his equal, and then was hypocrite enough to continue to hold him as a slave, in violation of what he believed to be the Divine law? And yet when you say that the Declaration of Independence includes the negro, you charge the signers of it with hypocrisy.

I say to you, frankly, that in my opinion, this Government was made by our fathers on the white basis. It was made by white men for the benefit of white men and their posterity forever, and was intended to be administered by white men in all time to come. But while I hold that under our Constitution and political system the negro is not a citizen, cannot be a citizen, and ought not to be a citizen, it does not follow by any means that he should be a slave. On the contrary it does follow that the negro, as an inferior race, ought to possess every right, every privilege, every immunity which he can safely exercise consistent with the safety of the society in which he lives. Humanity requires, and Christianity commands, that you shall extend to every inferior being, and every dependent being, all the privileges, immunities and advantages which can be granted to them consistent with the safety of society. If you ask me the nature and extent of these privileges, I answer that that is a question which the people of each State must decide for themselves. Illinois has decided that question for herself. We have said that in this State the negro shall not be a slave, nor shall he be a citizen. Kentucky holds a different doctrine. New York holds one different from either, and Maine one different from all. Virginia, in her policy on this question, differs in many respects from the others, and so on, until there is hardly two States whose policy is exactly alike in regard to the relation of the white man and the negro. Nor can you reconcile them and make them alike. Each State must do as it pleases. Illinois had as much right to adopt the policy which we have on that subject as Kentucky had to adopt a different policy. The great principle of this Government is, that each State has the right to do as it pleases on all

these questions, and no other State, or power on earth has the right to interfere with us, or complain of us merely because our system differs from theirs. In the Compromise Measures of 1850, Mr. Clay declared that this great principle ought to exist in the Territories as well as in the States, and I reasserted his doctrine in the Kansas and Nebraska bill in 1854.

But Mr. Lincoln cannot be made to understand, and those who are determined to vote for him, no matter whether he is a proslavery man in the south and a negro equality advocate in the north, cannot be made to understand how it is that in a Territory the people can do as they please on the slavery question under the Dred Scott decision. Let us see whether I cannot explain it to the satisfaction of all impartial men. Chief Justice Taney has said in his opinion in the Dred Scott case, that a negro slave being property, stands on an equal footing with other property, and that the owner may carry them into United States territory the same as he does other property. Suppose any two of you, neighbors, should conclude to go to Kansas, one carrying $100,000 worth of negro slaves and the other $100,000 worth of mixed merchandise, including quantities of liquors. You both agree that under that decision you may carry your property to Kansas, but when you get it there, the merchant who is possessed of the liquors is met by the Maine liquor law, which prohibits the sale or use of his property, and the owner of the slaves is met by equally unfriendly legislation, which makes his property worthless after he gets it there. What is the right to carry your property into the Territory worth to either, when unfriendly legislation in the Territory renders it worthless after you get it there? The slaveholder when he gets his slaves there finds that there is no local law to protect him in holding them, no slave code, no police regulation maintaining and supporting him in his right, and he discovers at once that the absence of such friendly legislation excludes his property from the Territory, just as irresistibly as if there was a positive Constitutional prohibition excluding it. Thus you find it is with any kind of property in a Territory, it depends for its protection on the local and municipal law. If the people of a Territory want slavery, they make friendly legislation to introduce it, but if they do not want it, they withhold all protection from it, and then it cannot exist there. Such was the view taken on the subject by different Southern men when the Nebraska bill passed. See the speech of Mr. Orr, of South Carolina, the present Speaker of the House of Representatives of Congress, made at that time, and there you will find this whole doctrine argued out at full length. Read the speeches of other Southern Congressmen, Senators and Representatives, made in 1854, and you will find that they took the same view of the subject as Mr. Orr—that slavery could never be forced on a people who did not want it. I hold that in this country there is no power on the face of the globe that can force any institution on an unwilling people. The great fundamental principle of our Government is that the people of each State and each Territory shall be left perfectly free to decide for themselves what shall be the nature and character of their institutions. When this Government was made, it was based on that principle. At the time of its formation there were twelve slaveholding States and one free State in this Union. Suppose this doctrine of Mr. Lincoln and the Republicans, of uniformity of laws of all the States on the subject of slavery, had prevailed; suppose Mr. Lincoln himself had been a member of the Convention which framed the Constitution, and that he had risen in that august body, and addressing the father of his country, had said as he did at Springfield:

> "A house divided against itself cannot stand. I believe this Government cannot endure permanently half slave and half free. I do not expect the Union to be dissolved—I do not expect the house to fall, but I do expect it will cease to be divided. It will become all one thing or all the other."

What do you think would have been the result? Suppose he had made that Convention believe that doctrine and they had acted upon it, what do you think would have been the result? Do you believe that the one free State would have outvoted the twelve slaveholding States, and thus abolish slavery?

On the contrary, would not the twelve slaveholding States have outvoted the one free State, and under his doctrine have fastened slavery by an irrevocable Constitutional provision upon every inch of the American Republic? Thus you see that the doctrine he now advocates, if proclaimed at the beginning of the Government, would have established slavery everywhere throughout the American continent, and are you willing, now that we have the majority section, to exercise a power which we never would have submitted to when we were in the minority? If the Southern States had attempted to control our institutions, and make the States all slave when they had the power, I ask would you have submitted to it? If you would not, are you willing now, that we have become the strongest under that great principle of self-government that allows each State to do as it pleases, to attempt to control the Southern institutions? Then, my friends, I say to you that there is but one path of peace in this Republic, and that is to administer this Government as our fathers made it, divided into free and slave States, allowing each State to decide for itself whether it wants slavery or not. If Illinois will settle the slavery question for herself, and mind her own business and let her neighbors alone, we will be at peace with Kentucky, and every other Southern State. If every other State in the Union will do the same there will be peace between the North and the South, and in the whole Union.

MR. LINCOLN'S REPLY

MY FELLOW-CITIZENS: A very large portion of the speech which Judge Douglas has addressed to you has previously been delivered and put in print. I do not mean that for a hit upon the Judge at all. If I had not been interrupted, I was going to say that such an answer as I was able to make to a very large portion of it, had already been more than once made and published. There has been an opportunity afforded to the public to see our respective views upon the topics discussed in a large portion of the speech which he has just delivered. I make these remarks for the purpose of excusing myself for not passing over the entire ground that the Judge has traversed. I however desire to take up some of the points that he has attended to, and ask your attention to them, and I shall follow him backwards upon some notes which I have taken, reversing the order by beginning where he concluded.

The Judge has alluded to the Declaration of Independence, and insisted that negroes are not included in that Declaration; and that it is a slander upon the framers of that instrument, to suppose that negroes were meant therein; and he asks you: Is it possible to believe that Mr. Jefferson, who penned the immortal paper, could have supposed himself applying the language of that instrument to the negro race, and yet held a portion of that race in slavery? Would he not at once have freed them? I only have to remark upon this part of the Judge's speech (and that, too, very briefly, for I shall not detain myself, or you, upon that point for any great length of time), that I believe the entire records of the world, from the date of the Declaration of Independence up to within three years ago, may be searched in vain for one single affirmation, from one single man, that the negro was not included in the Declaration of Independence; I think I may defy Judge Douglas to show that he ever said so, that Washington ever said so, that any President ever said so, that any member of Congress ever said so, or that any living man upon the whole earth ever said so, until the necessities of the present policy of the Democratic party, in regard to slavery, had to invent that affirmation. And I will remind Judge Douglas and this audience, that while Mr. Jefferson was the owner of slaves, as undoubtedly he was, in speaking upon this very subject, he used the strong language that "he trembled for his country when he remembered that God was just;" and I will offer the highest premium in my power to Judge Douglas if he will show that he, in all his life, ever uttered a sentiment at all akin to that of Jefferson.

The next thing to which I will ask your attention is the Judge's comments upon the fact, as he assumes it to be, that we cannot call our public meetings as Republican meetings; and he instances

Tazewell county as one of the places where the friends of Lincoln have called a public meeting and have not dared to name it a Republican meeting. He instances Monroe county as another where Judge Trumbull and Jehu Baker addressed the persons whom the Judge assumes to be the friends of Lincoln, calling them the "Free Democracy." I have the honor to inform Judge Douglas that he spoke in that very county of Tazewell last Saturday, and I was there on Tuesday last, and when he spoke there he spoke under a call not venturing to use the word "Democrat." [Turning to Judge Douglas.] What think you of this?

So again, there is another thing to which I would ask the Judge's attention upon this subject. In the contest of 1856 his party delighted to call themselves together as the "National Democracy," but now, if there should be a notice put up any where for a meeting of the "National Democracy," Judge Douglas and his friends would not come. They would not suppose themselves invited. They would understand that it was a call for those hateful postmasters whom he talks about.

Now a few words in regard to these extracts from speeches of mine, which Judge Douglas has read to you, and which he supposes are in very great contrast to each other. Those speeches have been before the public for a considerable time, and if they have any inconsistency in them, if there is any conflict in them, the public have been unable to detect it. When the Judge says, in speaking on this subject, that I make speeches of one sort for the people of the northern end of the State, and of a different sort for the southern people, he assumes that I do not understand that my speeches will be put in print and read north and south. I knew all the while that the speech that I made at Chicago, and the one I made at Jonesboro and the one at Charleston, would all be put in print and all the reading and intelligent men in the community would see them and know all about my opinions. And I have not supposed, and do not now suppose, that there is any conflict whatever between them. But the Judge will have it that if we do not confess that there is a sort of inequality between the white and black races, which justifies us in making them slaves, we must, then, insist that there is a degree of equality that requires us to make them our wives. Now, I have all the while taken a broad distinction in regard to that matter; and that is all there is in these different speeches which he arrays here, and the entire reading of either of the speeches will show that that distinction was made. Perhaps by taking two parts of the same speech, he could have got up as much of a conflict as the one he has found. I have all the while maintained, that in so far as it should be insisted that there was an equality between the white and black races that should produce a perfect social and political equality, it was an impossibility. This you have seen in my printed speeches, and with it I have said, that in their right to "life, liberty and the pursuit of happiness," as proclaimed in that old Declaration, the inferior races are our equals. And these declarations I have constantly made in reference to the abstract moral question, to contemplate and consider when we are legislating about any new country which is not already cursed with the actual presence of the evil—slavery. I have never manifested any impatience with the necessities that spring from the actual presence of black people amongst us, and the actual existence of slavery amongst us where it does already exist; but I have insisted that, in legislating for new countries, where it does not exist, there is no just rule other than that of moral and abstract right! With reference to those new countries, those maxims as to the right of a people to "life, liberty and the pursuit of happiness," were the just rules to be constantly referred to. There is no misunderstanding this, except by men interested to misunderstand it. I take it that I have to address an intelligent and reading community, who will peruse what I say, weigh it, and then judge whether I advance improper or unsound views, or whether I advance hypocritical, and deceptive, and contrary views in different portions of the country. I believe myself to be guilty of no such thing as the latter, though, of course, I cannot claim that I am entirely free from all error in the opinions I advance.

The Judge has also detained us awhile in regard to the distinction between his party and our party. His he assumes to be a national party—ours a sectional one. He does this in asking the question whether this country has any interest in the maintenance of the Republican party? He assumes that our party is altogether sectional—that the party to which he adheres is national; and the argument is, that no party can be a rightful party—can be based upon rightful principles—unless it can announce its principles every where. I presume that Judge Douglas could not go into Russia and announce the doctrine of our national Democracy; he could not denounce the doctrine of kings and emperors and monarchies in Russia; and it may be true of this country, that in some places we may not be able to proclaim a doctrine as clearly true as the truth of Democracy, because there is a section so directly opposed to it that they will not tolerate us in doing so. Is it the true test of the soundness of a doctrine, that in some places people won't let you proclaim it? Is that the way to test the truth of any doctrine? Why, I understood that at one time the people of Chicago would not let Judge Douglas preach a certain favorite doctrine of his. I commend to his consideration the question, whether he takes that as a test of the unsoundness of what he wanted to preach.

There is another thing to which I wish to ask attention for a little while on this occasion. What has always been the evidence brought forward to prove that the Republican party is a sectional party? The main one was that in the Southern portion of the Union the people did not let the Republicans proclaim their doctrines amongst them. That has been the main evidence brought forward—that they had no supporters, or substantially none, in the slave States. The South have not taken hold of our principles as we announce them; nor does Judge Douglas now grapple with those principles. We have a Republican State Platform, laid down in Springfield in June last, stating our position all the way through the questions before the country. We are now far advanced in this canvass. Judge Douglas and I have made perhaps forty speeches apiece, and we have now for the fifth time met face to face in debate, and up to this day I have not found either Judge Douglas or any friend of his taking hold of the Republican platform or laying his finger upon anything in it that is wrong. I ask you all to recollect that. Judge Douglas turns away from the platform of principles to the fact that he can find people somewhere who will not allow us to announce those principles. If he had great confidence that our principles were wrong, he would take hold of them and demonstrate them to be wrong. But he does not do so. The only evidence he has of their being wrong is in the fact that there are people who won't allow us to preach them. I ask again is that the way to test the soundness of a doctrine?

I ask his attention also to the fact that by the rule of nationality he is himself fast becoming sectional. I ask his attention to the fact that his speeches would not go as current now south of the Ohio river as they have formerly gone there. I ask his attention to the fact that he felicitates himself to-day that all the Democrats of the free States are agreeing with him, while he omits to tell us that the Democrats of any slave State agree with him. If he has not thought of this, I commend to his consideration the evidence in his own declaration, on this day, of his becoming sectional too. I see it rapidly approaching. Whatever may be the result of this ephemeral contest between Judge Douglas and myself, I see the day rapidly approaching when his pill of sectionalism, which he has been thrusting down the throats of Republicans for years past, will be crowded down his own throat.

Now in regard to what Judge Douglas said (in the beginning of his speech) about the Compromise of 1850, containing the principle of the Nebraska bill, although I have often presented my views upon that subject, yet as I have not done so in this canvass, I will, if you please, detain you a little with them. I have always maintained, so far as I was able, that there was nothing of the principle of the Nebraska bill in the Compromise of 1850 at all—nothing whatever. Where can you find the principle of the Nebraska bill in that Compromise?

If any where, in the two pieces of the Compromise organizing the Territories of New Mexico and Utah. It was expressly provided in these two acts, that, when they came to be admitted into the Union, they should be admitted with or without slavery, as they should choose, by their own Constitutions. Nothing was said in either of those acts as to what was to be done in relation to slavery during the territorial existence of those Territories, while Henry Clay constantly made the declaration (Judge Douglas recognizing him as a leader) that, in his opinion, the old Mexican laws would control that question during the territorial existence, and that these old Mexican laws excluded slavery. How can that be used as a principle for declaring that during the territorial existence as well as at the time of framing the Constitution, the people, if you please, might have slaves if they wanted them? I am not discussing the question whether it is right or wrong; but how are the New Mexican and Utah laws patterns for the Nebraska bill? I maintain that the organization of Utah and New Mexico did not establish a general principle at all. It had no feature of establishing a general principle. The acts to which I have referred were a part of a general system of Compromises. They did not lay down what was proposed as a regular policy for the Territories; only an agreement in this particular case to do in that way, because other things were done that were to be a compensation for it. They were allowed to come in in that shape, because in another way it was paid for—considering that as a part of that system of measures called the Compromise of 1850, which finally included half a dozen acts. It included the admission of California as a free State, which was kept out of the Union for half a year because it had formed a free Constitution. It included the settlement of the boundary of Texas, which had been undefined before, which was in itself a slavery question; for, if you pushed the line farther west, you made Texas larger, and made more slave Territory; while, if you drew the line toward the east, you narrowed the boundary and diminished the domain of slavery, and by so much increased free Territory. It included the abolition of the slave-trade in the District of Columbia. It included the passage of a new Fugitive Slave law. All these things were put together, and though passed in separate acts, were nevertheless in legislation (as the speeches at the time will show), made to depend upon each other. Each got votes, with the understanding that the other measures were to pass, and by this system of Compromise, in that series of measures, those two bills—the New Mexico and Utah bills—were passed; and I say for that reason they could not be taken as models, framed upon their own intrinsic principle, for all future Territories. And I have the evidence of this in the fact that Judge Douglas, a year afterward, or more than a year afterward, perhaps, when he first introduced bills for the purpose of framing new Territories, did not attempt to follow these bills of New Mexico and Utah; and even when he introduced this Nebraska bill, I think you will discover that he did not exactly follow them. But I do not wish to dwell at great length upon this branch of the discussion. My own opinion is, that a thorough investigation will show most plainly that the New Mexico and Utah bills were part of a system of Compromise, and not designed as patterns for future territorial legislation; and that this Nebraska bill did not follow them as a pattern at all.

The Judge tells, in proceeding, that he is opposed to making any odious distinctions between free and slave States. I am altogether unaware that the Republicans are in favor of making any odious distinctions between the free and slave States. But there still is a difference, I think, between Judge Douglas and the Republicans in this. I suppose that the real difference between Judge Douglas and his friends, and the Republicans on the contrary, is, that the Judge is not in favor of making any difference between slavery and liberty—that he is in favor of eradicating, of pressing out of view, the questions of preference in this country for free or slave institutions; and consequently every sentiment he utters discards the idea that there is any wrong in slavery. Every thing that emanates from him or his coadjutors in their course of policy, carefully excludes the thought that there is any

thing wrong in slavery. All their arguments, if you will consider them, will be seen to exclude the thought that there is any thing whatever wrong in slavery. If you will take the Judge's speeches, and select the short and pointed sentences expressed by him—as his declaration that he "don't care whether slavery is voted up or down" —you will see at once that this is perfectly logical, if you do not admit that slavery is wrong. If you do admit that it is wrong, Judge Douglas cannot logically say he don't care whether a wrong is voted up or voted down. Judge Douglas declares that if any community want slavery they have a right to have it. He can say that logically, if he says that there is no wrong in slavery; but if you admit that there is a wrong in it, he cannot logically say that any body has a right to do wrong. He insists that, upon the score of equality, the owners of slaves and owners of property—of horses and every other sort of property—should be alike and hold them alike in a new Territory. That is perfectly logical, if the two species of property are alike and are equally founded in right. But if you admit that one of them is wrong, you cannot institute any equality between right and wrong. And from this difference of sentiment—the belief on the part of one that the institution is wrong, and a policy springing from that belief which looks to the arrest of the enlargement of that wrong; and this other sentiment, that it is no wrong, and a policy sprung from that sentiment which will tolerate no idea of preventing that wrong from growing larger, and looks to there never being an end of it through all the existence of things, —arises the real difference between Judge Douglas and his friends on the one hand, and the Republicans on the other. Now, I confess myself as belonging to that class in the country who contemplate slavery as a moral, social and political evil, having due regard for its actual existence amongst us and the difficulties of getting rid of it in any satisfactory way, and to all the Constitutional obligations which have been thrown about it; but, nevertheless, desire a policy that looks to the prevention of it as a wrong, and looks hopefully to the time when as a wrong it may come to an end.

Judge Douglas has again, for, I believe, the fifth time, if not the seventh, in my presence, reiterated his charge of a conspiracy or combination between the National Democrats and Republicans. What evidence Judge Douglas has upon his subject I know not, inasmuch as he never favors us with any. I have said upon a former occasion, and I do not choose to suppress it now, that I have no objection to the division in the Judge's party. He got it up himself. It was all his and their work. He had, I think, a great deal more to do with the steps that led to the Lecompton Constitution than Mr. Buchanan had; though at last, when they reached it, they quarreled over it, and their friends divided upon it. I am very free to confess to Judge Douglas that I have no objection to the division; but I defy the Judge to show any evidence that I have in any way promoted that division, unless he insists on being a witness himself in merely saying so. I can give all fair friends of Judge Douglas here to understand exactly the view that Republicans take in regard to that division. Don't you remember how two years ago the opponents of the Democratic party were divided between Fremont and Fillmore? I guess you do. Any Democrat who remembers that division, will remember also that he was at the time very glad of it, and then he will be able to see all there is between the National Democrats and the Republicans. What we now think of the two divisions of Democrats, you then thought of the Fremont and Fillmore divisions. That is all there is of it.

But, if the Judge continues to put forward the declaration that there is an unholy and unnatural alliance between the Republican and the National Democrats, I now want to enter my protest against receiving him as an entirely competent witness upon that subject. I want to call to the Judge's attention an attack he made upon me in the first one of these debates, at Ottawa, on the 21st of August. In order to fix extreme Abolitionism upon me, Judge Douglas read a set of resolutions which he declared had been passed by a Republican State Convention, in October, 1854, at Springfield, Illinois, and he declared I had taken part in that Convention. It turned out that although a few men calling themselves an anti-Nebraska State Convention had sat at Springfield about that time, yet neither did I take any part in it, nor did it pass the resolutions or any such resolutions as Judge Douglas read. So apparent had it become that the resolutions which he read had not been passed at Springfield at all, nor by a State Convention in which I had taken part, that seven days afterward, at Freeport, Judge Douglas declared that he had been misled by Charles H. Lanphier, editor of the *State Register*, and Thomas L. Harris, member of Congress in that District, and he promised in that speech that when he went to Springfield he would investigate the matter. Since then Judge Douglas has been to Springfield, and I presume has made the investigation; but a month has passed since he has been there, and so far as I know, he has made no report of the result of his investigation. I have waited as I think sufficient time for the report of that investigation, and I have some curiosity to see and hear it. A fraud—an absolute forgery was committed, and the perpetration of it was traced to the three—Lanphier, Harris and Douglas. Whether it can be narrowed in any way so as to exonerate any one of them, is what Judge Douglas's report would probably show.

It is true that the set of resolutions read by Judge Douglas were published in the Illinois *State Register* on the 16th of October, 1854, as being the resolutions of an anti-Nebraska Convention, which had sat in that same month of October, at Springfield. But it is also true that the publication in the *Register* was a forgery then, and the question is still behind, which of the three, if not all of them, committed that forgery? The idea that it was done by mistake, is absurd. The article in the Illinois *State Register* contains part of the real proceedings of that Springfield Convention, showing that the writer of the article had the real proceedings before him, and purposely threw out the genuine resolutions passed by the Convention, and fraudulently substituted the others. Lanphier then, as now, was the editor of the *Register*, so that there seems to be but little room for his escape. But then it is to be borne in mind that Lanphier has less interest in the object of that forgery than either of the other two. The main object of that forgery at that time was to beat Yates and elect Harris to Congress, and that object was known to be exceedingly dear to Judge Douglas at that time. Harris and Douglas were both in Springfield when the Convention was in session, and although they both left before the fraud appeared in the *Register*, subsequent events show that they have both had their eyes fixed upon that Convention.

The fraud having been apparently successful upon the occasion, both Harris and Douglas have more than once since then been attempting to put it to new uses. As the fisherman's wife, whose drowned husband was brought home with his body full of eels, said when she was asked, "What was to be done with him?" "Take the eels out and set him again"; so Harris and Douglas have shown a disposition to take the eels out of that stale fraud by which they gained Harris's election, and set the fraud again more than once. On the 9th of July, 1856, Douglas attempted a repetition of it upon Trumbull on the floor of the Senate of the United States, as will appear from the appendix of the *Congressional Globe* of that date.

On the 9th of August, Harris attempted it again upon Norton in the House of Representatives, as will appear by the same documents—the appendix to the *Congressional Globe* of that date. On the 21st of August last, all three—Lanphier, Douglas and Harris—reattempted it upon me at Ottawa. It has been clung to and played out again and again as an exceedingly high trump by this blessed trio. And now that it has been discovered publicly to be a fraud, we find that Judge Douglas manifests no surprise at it at all. He makes no complaint of Lanphier, who must have known it to be a fraud from the beginning. He, Lanphier and Harris, are just as cozy now, and just as active in the concoction of new schemes as they were before the general discovery of this fraud. Now all this is very natural if they are all alike guilty in that fraud, and it is very unnatural if any one of them is innocent. Lanphier perhaps insists that the rule of honor among thieves does not quite require him to take all upon himself, and consequently my friend Judge Douglas finds it difficult to make a satisfactory report upon his investigation. But meanwhile the three are agreed that each is "a most honorable man."

Judge Douglas requires an indorsement of his truth and honor by a re-election to the United States Senate, and he makes and reports against me and against Judge Trumbull, day after day, charges which we know to be utterly untrue, without for a moment seeming to think that this one unexplained fraud, which he promised to investigate, will be the least drawback to his claim to belief. Harris ditto. He asks a re-election to the lower House of Congress without seeming to remember at all that he is involved in this dishonorable fraud! The Illinois *State Register*, edited by Lanphier, then, as now, the central organ of both Harris and Douglas, continues to din the public ear with this assertion without seeming to suspect that these assertions are at all lacking in title to belief.

After all, the question still recurs upon us, how did that fraud originally get into the *State Register*? Lanphier then, as now, was the editor of that paper. Lanphier knows. Lanphier cannot be ignorant of how and by whom it was originally concocted. Can he be induced to tell, or if he has told, can Judge Douglas be induced to tell how it originally was concocted? It may be true that Lanphier insists that the two men for whose benefit it was originally devised, shall at least bear their share of it! How that is, I do not know, and while it remains unexplained, I hope to be pardoned if I insist that the mere fact of Judge Douglas making charges against Trumbull and myself is not quite sufficient evidence to establish them!

While we were at Freeport, in one of these joint discussions, I answered certain interrogatories which Judge Douglas had propounded to me, and there in turn propounded some to him, which he in a sort of way answered. The third one of these interrogatories I have with me and wish now to make some comments upon it. It was in these words: "If the Supreme Court of the United States shall decide that the States cannot exclude slavery from their limits, are you in favor of acquiescing in, adhering to and following such decision, as a rule of political action?"

To this interrogatory Judge Douglas made no answer in any just sense of the word. He contented himself with sneering at the thought that it was possible for the Supreme Court ever to make such a decision. He sneered at me for propounding the interrogatory. I had not propounded it without some reflection, and I wish now to address to this audience some remarks upon it.

In the second clause of the sixth article, I believe it is, of the Constitution of the United States, we find the following language: "This Constitution and the laws of the United States which shall be made in pursuance thereof; and all treaties made, or which shall be made under the authority of the United States, shall be the supreme law of the land; and the judges in every State shall be bound thereby, any thing in the Constitution or laws of any State to the contrary notwithstanding."

The essence of the Dred Scott case is compressed into the sentence which I will now read: "Now, as we have already said in an earlier part of this opinion, upon a different point, the right of property in a slave is distinctly and expressly affirmed in the Constitution." I repeat it, "The right of property in a slave is distinctly and expressly affirmed in the Constitution!" What is it to be "affirmed" in the Constitution? Made firm in the Constitution—so made that it cannot be separated from the Constitution without breaking the Constitution—durable as the Constitution, and part of the Constitution. Now, remembering the provision of the Constitution which I have read, affirming that that instrument is the supreme law of the land; that the Judges of every State shall be bound by it, any law or Constitution of any State to the contrary notwithstanding; that the right of property in a slave is affirmed in that Constitution, is made, formed into, and cannot be separated from it without breaking it; durable as the instrument; part of the instrument; —what follows as a short and even syllogistic argument from it? I think it

follows, and I submit to the consideration of men capable of arguing, whether as I state it, in syllogistic form, the argument has any fault in it?

Nothing in the Constitution or laws of any State can destroy a right distinctly and expressly affirmed in the Constitution of the United States.

The right of property in a slave is distinctly and expressly affirmed in the Constitution of the United States.

Therefore, nothing in the Constitution or laws of any State can destroy the right of property in a slave.

I believe that no fault can be pointed out in that argument; assuming the truth of the premises, the conclusion, so far as I have capacity at all to understand it, follows inevitably. There is a fault in it as I think, but the fault is not in the reasoning; but the falsehood in fact is a fault of the premises. I believe that the right of property in a slave is not distinctly and expressly affirmed in the Constitution, and Judge Douglas thinks it is. I believe that the Supreme Court and the advocates of that decision may search in vain for the place in the Constitution where the right of a slave is distinctly and expressly affirmed. I say, therefore, that I think one of the premises is not true in fact. But it is true with Judge Douglas. It is true with the Supreme Court who pronounced it. They are estopped from denying it, and being estopped from denying it, the conclusion follows that the Constitution of the United States being the supreme law, no constitution or law can interfere with it. It being affirmed in the decision that the right of property in a slave is distinctly and expressly affirmed in the Constitution, the conclusion inevitably follows that no State law or constitution can destroy that right. I then say to Judge Douglas and to all others, that I think it will take a better answer than a sneer to show that those who have said that the right of property in a slave is distinctly and expressly affirmed in the Constitution, are not prepared to show that no constitution or law can destroy that right. I say I believe it will take a far better argument than a mere sneer to show to the minds of intelligent men that whoever has so said, is not prepared, whenever public sentiment is so far advanced as to justify it, to say the other. This is but an opinion, and the opinion of one very humble man; but it is my opinion that the Dred Scott decision, as it is, never would have been made in its present form if the party that made it had not been sustained previously by the elections. My own opinion is, that the new Dred Scott decision, deciding against the right of the people of the States to exclude slavery, will never be made, if that party is not sustained by the elections. I believe, further, that it is just as sure to be made as to-morrow is to come, if that party shall be sustained. I have said, upon a former occasion, and I repeat it now, that the course of argument that Judge Douglas makes use of upon this subject (I charge not his motives in this), is preparing the public mind for that new Dred Scott decision. I have asked him again to point out to me the reasons for his first adherence to the Dred Scott decision as it is. I have turned his attention to the fact that General Jackson differed with him in regard to the political obligation of a Supreme Court decision. I have asked his attention to the fact that Jefferson differed with him in regard to the political obligation of a Supreme Court decision. Jefferson said, that "Judges are as honest as other men, and not more so." And he said, substantially, that "whenever a free people should give up in absolute submission to any department of government, retaining for themselves no appeal from it, their liberties were gone." I have asked his attention to the fact that the Cincinnati platform, upon which he says he stands, disregards a time-honored decision of the Supreme Court, in denying the power of Congress to establish a National Bank. I have asked his attention to the fact that he himself was one of the most active instruments at one time in breaking down the Supreme Court of the State of Illinois, because it had made a decision distasteful to him—a struggle ending in the remarkable circumstance of his sitting down as one of the new Judges who were to overslaugh that decision—getting his title of Judge in that very way.

So far in this controversy I can get no answer at all from Judge Douglas upon these subjects. Not one can I get from him, except that he swells himself up and says, "All of us who stand by the decision of the Supreme Court are the friends of the Constitution; all you fellows that dare question it in any way, are the enemies of the Constitution." Now, in this very devoted adherence to this decision, in opposition to all the great political leaders whom he has recognized as leaders—in opposition to his former self and history, there is something very marked. And the manner in which he adheres to it—not as being right upon the merits, as he conceives (because he did not discuss that at all), but as being absolutely obligatory upon every one simply because of the source from whence it comes—as that which no man can gainsay, whatever it may be—this is another marked feature of his adherence to that decision. It marks it in this respect, that it commits him to the next decision, whenever it comes, as being as obligatory as this one, since he does not investigate it, and won't inquire whether this opinion is right or wrong. So he takes the next one without inquiring whether it is right or wrong. He teaches men this doctrine, and in so doing prepares the public mind to take the next decision when it comes, without any inquiry. In this I think I argue fairly (without questioning motives at all), that Judge Douglas is more ingeniously and powerfully preparing the public mind to take that decision when it comes; and not only so, but he is doing it in various other ways. In these general maxims about liberty—in his assertions that he "don't care whether slavery is voted up or voted down;" that "whoever wants slavery has a right to have it;" that "upon principles of equality it should be allowed to go every where;" that "there is no inconsistency between free and slave institutions." In this he is also preparing (whether purposely or not) the way for making the institution of slavery national! I repeat again, for I wish no misunderstanding, that I do not charge that he means it so; but I call upon your minds to inquire, if you were going to get the best instrument you could, and then set it to work in the most ingenious way, to prepare the public mind for this movement, operating in the free States, where there is now an abhorrence of the institution of slavery, could you find an instrument so capable of doing it as Judge Douglas? or one employed in so apt a way to do it?

I have said once before, and I will repeat it now, that Mr. Clay, when he was once answering an objection to the Colonization Society, that it had a tendency to the ultimate emancipation of the slaves, said that "those who would repress all tendencies to liberty and ultimate emancipation must do more than put down the benevolent efforts of the Colonization Society—they must go back to the era of our liberty and independence, and muzzle the cannon that thunders its annual joyous return—they must blot out the moral lights around us—they must penetrate the human soul, and eradicate the light of reason and the love of liberty!" And I do think—I repeat, though I said it on a former occasion—that Judge Douglas, and whoever like him teaches that the negro has no share, humble though it may be, in the Declaration of Independence, is going back to the era of our liberty and independence, and, so far as in him lies, muzzling the cannon that thunders its annual joyous return; that he is blowing out the moral lights around us, when he contends that whoever wants slaves has a right to hold them; that he is penetrating, so far as lies in his power, the human soul, and eradicating the light of reason and the love of liberty, when he is in every possible way preparing the public mind, by his vast influence, for making the institution of slavery perpetual and national.

There is, my friends, only one other point to which I will call your attention for the remaining time that I have left me, and perhaps I shall not occupy the entire time that I have, as that one point may not take me clear through it.

Among the interrogatories that Judge Douglas propounded to me at Freeport, there was one in about this language: "Are you opposed to the acquisition of any further territory to the United States, unless slavery shall first be prohibited therein?" I answered as I thought, in this way, that I am not generally opposed to the acquisition of additional territory, and that I would support a proposition for the acquisition of additional territory, according as my supporting it was or was not calculated to aggravate this slavery question amongst us. I then proposed to Judge Douglas another interrogatory, which was correlative to that: "Are you in favor of acquiring additional territory in disregard of how it may affect us upon the slavery question?" Judge Douglas answered, that is, in his own way he answered it. I believe that, although he took a good many words to answer it, it was a little more fully answered than any other. The substance of his answer was, that this country would continue to expand—that it would need additional territory—that it was as absurd to suppose that we could continue upon our present territory, enlarging in population as we are, as it would be to hoop a boy twelve years of age, and expect him to grow to man's size without bursting the hoops. I believe it was something like that. Consequently he was in favor of the acquisition of further territory, as fast as we might need it, in disregard of how it might affect the slavery question. I do not say this as giving his exact language, but he said so substantially, and he would leave the question of slavery where the territory was acquired, to be settled by the people of the acquired territory. ["That's the doctrine."] May be it is; let us consider that for a while. This will probably, in the run of things, become one of the concrete manifestations of this slavery question. If Judge Douglas's policy upon this question succeeds and gets fairly settled down, until all opposition is crushed out, the next thing will be a grab for the territory poor Mexico, an invasion of the rich lands of South America, then the adjoining islands will follow, each one of which promises additional slave fields. And this question is to be left to the people of those countries for settlement. When we shall get Mexico, I don't know whether the Judge will be in favor of the Mexican people that we get with it settling that question for themselves and all others; because we know the Judge has a great horror for mongrels, and I understand that the people of Mexico are most decidedly a race of mongrels. I understand that there is not more than one person there out of eight who is pure white, and I suppose from the Judge's previous declaration that when we get Mexico or any considerable portion of it, that he will be in favor of these mongrels settling the question, which would bring him somewhat into collision with his horror of an inferior race.

It is to be remembered, though, that this power of acquiring additional territory is a power confided to the President and Senate of the United States. It is a power not under the control of the representatives of the people any further than they, the President and the Senate, can be considered the representatives of the people. Let me illustrate that by a case we have in our history. When we acquired the territory from Mexico in the Mexican war, the House of Representatives, composed of the immediate representatives of the people, all the time insisted that the territory thus to be acquired should be brought in upon condition that slavery should be forever prohibited therein, upon the terms and in the language that slavery had been prohibited from coming into this country. That was insisted upon constantly, and never failed to call forth an assurance that any territory thus acquired should have that prohibition in it, so far as the House of Representatives was concerned. But at last the President and Senate acquired the territory without asking the House of Representatives any thing about it, and took it without that prohibition. They have the power of acquiring territory without the immediate representatives of the People being called upon to say any thing about it, and thus furnishing a very apt and powerful means of bringing new territory into the Union, and when it is once brought into the country, involving us anew in this slavery agitation. It is, therefore, as I think, a very important question for the consideration of the American people, whether the policy of bringing in additional territory, without considering at all how it will operate upon the safety of the Union in reference to this one great disturbing element in our national politics, shall be adopted as the policy of the country. You will bear in mind that it is to be acquired, according to the Judge's view, as fast as it is needed, and the indefinite part of this proposition is that we have only Judge Douglas and his class of men to decide how fast it is needed. We

have no clear and certain way of determining or demonstrating how fast territory is needed by the necessities of the country. Whoever wants to go out fillibustering, then, thinks that more territory is needed. Whoever wants wider slave fields, feels sure that some additional territory is needed as slave territory. Then it is as easy to show the necessity of additional slave territory as it is to assert any thing that is incapable of absolute demonstration. Whatever motive a man or a set of men may have for making annexation of property or territory, it is very easy to assert, but much less easy to disprove, that it is necessary for the wants of the country.

And now it only remains for me to say that I think it is a very grave question for the people of this Union to consider whether, in view of the fact that this slavery question has been the only one that has ever endangered our Republican institutions—the only one that has ever threatened or menaced a dissolution of the Union—that has ever disturbed us in such a way as to make us fear for the perpetuity of our liberty—in view of these facts, I think it is an exceedingly interesting and important question for this people to consider, whether we shall engage in the policy of acquiring additional territory, discarding altogether from our consideration, while obtaining new territory, the question how it may affect us in regard to this the only endangering element to our liberties and national greatness. The Judge's view has been expressed. I, in my answer to his question, have expressed mine. I think it will become an important and practical question. Our views are before the public. I am willing and anxious that they should consider them fully—that they should turn it about and consider the importance of the question, and arrive at a just conclusion as to whether it is or is not wise in the people of this Union, in the acquisition of new territory, to consider whether it will add to the disturbance that is existing amongst us—whether it will add to the one only danger that has ever threatened the perpetuity of the Union or our own liberties. I think it is extremely important that they shall decide, and rightly decide, that question before entering upon that policy.

And now, my friends, having said the little I wish to say upon this head, whether I have occupied the whole of the remnant of my time or not, I believe I could not enter upon any new topics so as to treat it fully without transcending my time, which I would not for a moment think of doing. I give way to Judge Douglas.

MR. DOUGLAS'S REJOINDER

GENTLEMEN: The highest compliment you can pay me during the brief half hour that I have to conclude is by observing a strict silence. I desire to be heard rather than to be applauded.

The first criticism that Mr. Lincoln makes on my speech was that it was in substance what I have said everywhere else in the State where I have addressed the people. I wish I could say the same of his speech. Why, the reason I complain of him is because he makes one speech north and another south. Because he has one set of sentiments for the Abolition counties and another set for the counties opposed to Abolitionism. My point of complaint against him is that I cannot induce him to hold up the same standard, to carry the same flag in all parts of the State. He does not pretend, and no other man will, that I have one set of principles for Galesburgh and another for Charleston; He does not pretend that I hold to one doctrine in Chicago and an opposite one in Jonesboro. I have proved that he has a different set of principles for each of these localities. All I asked of him was that he should deliver the speech that he has made here to-day in Coles county instead of in old Knox. It would have settled the question between us in that doubtful county. Here I understand him to reaffirm the doctrine of negro equality, and to assert that by the Declaration of Independence the negro is declared equal to the white man. He tells you to-day that the negro was included in the Declaration of Independence when it asserted that all men were created equal. ["We believe it."] Very well.

Mr. Lincoln asserts to-day as he did at Chicago, that the negro was included in that clause of the Declaration of Independence which says that all men were created equal and endowed by the Creator with certain inalienable rights, among which are life, liberty, and the pursuit of happiness. If the negro was made his equal and mine, if that equality was established by Divine law, and was the negro's inalienable right, how came he to say at Charleston to the Kentuckians residing in that section of our State, that the negro was physically inferior to the white man, belonged to an inferior race, and he was for keeping him always in that inferior condition. I wish you to bear these things in mind. At Charleston he said that the negro belonged to an inferior race, and that he was for keeping him in that inferior condition. There he gave the people to understand that there was no moral question involved, because the inferiority being established, it was only a question of degree and not a question of right; here, to-day, instead of making it a question of degree, he makes it a moral question, says that it is a great crime to hold the negro in that inferior condition. ["He's right."] Is he right now or was he right in Charleston? ["Both."] He is right then, sir, in your estimation, not because he is consistent, but because he can trim his principles any way in any section, so as to secure votes. All I desire of him is that he will declare the same principles in the south that he does in the north.

But did you notice how he answered my position that a man should hold the same doctrines throughout the length and breadth of this Republic? He said, "Would Judge Douglas go to Russia and proclaim the same principles he does here?" I would remind him that Russia is not under the American Constitution. If Russia was a part of the American Republic, under our Federal Constitution, and I was sworn to support the Constitution, I would maintain the same doctrine in Russia that I do in Illinois. The slaveholding States are governed by the same Federal Constitution as ourselves, and hence a man's principles, in order to be in harmony with the Constitution, must be the same in the south as they are in the north, the same in the free States as they are in the slave States. Whenever a man advocates one set of principles in one section, and another set in another section, his opinions are in violation of the spirit of the Constitution which he has sworn to support. When Mr. Lincoln went to Congress in 1847, and laying his hand upon the Holy Evangelists, made a solemn vow in the presence of high Heaven that he would be faithful to the Constitution—what did he mean? the Constitution as he expounds it in Galesburg, or the Constitution as he expounds it in Charleston.

Mr. Lincoln has devoted considerable time to the circumstance that at Ottawa I read a series of resolutions as having been adopted at Springfield, in this State, on the 4th or 5th of October, 1854, which happened not to have been adopted there. He has used hard names; has dared to talk about fraud, about forgery, and has insinuated that there was a conspiracy between Mr. Lanphier, Mr. Harris, and myself to perpetrate a forgery. Now, bear in mind that he does not deny that these resolutions were adopted in a majority of all the Republican counties of this State in that year; he does not deny that they were declared to be the platform of this Republican party in the first Congressional District, in the second, in the third, and in many counties of the fourth, and that they thus became the platform of his party in a majority of the counties upon which he now relies for support; he does not deny the truthfulness of the resolutions, but takes exception to the spot on which they were adopted. He takes to himself great merit because he thinks they were not adopted on the right spot for me to use them against him, just as he was very severe in Congress upon the Government of his country when he thought that he had discovered that the Mexican war was not begun in the right spot, and was therefore unjust. He tries very hard to make out that there is something very extraordinary in the place where the thing was done, and not in the thing itself. I never believed before that Abraham Lincoln would be guilty of what he has done this day in regard to those resolutions. In the first place, the moment it was intimated to me that they had been adopted at Aurora and Rockford instead of Springfield, I did not wait for him to call my attention to the fact, but led off and explained in my first meeting after the Ottawa debate, what the mistake was, and how it had been made. I supposed that for

an honest man, conscious of his own rectitude, that explanation would be sufficient. I did not wait for him, after the mistake was made, to call my attention to it, but frankly explained it at once as an honest man would. I also gave the authority on which I had stated that these resolutions were adopted by the Springfield Republican Convention. That I had seen them quoted by Major Harris in a debate in Congress, as having been adopted by the first Republican State Convention in Illinois, and that I had written to him and asked him for the authority as to the time and place of their adoption; that Major Harris being extremely ill, Charles H. Lanphier had written to me for him, that they were adopted at Springfield, on the 5th of October, 1854, and had sent me a copy of the Springfield paper containing them. I read them from the newspaper just as Mr. Lincoln reads the proceedings of meetings held years ago from the newspapers. After giving that explanation, I did not think there was an honest man in the State of Illinois who doubted that I had been led into the error, if it was such, innocently, in the way I detailed; and I will now say that I do not now believe that there is an honest man on the face of the globe who will not regard with abhorrence and disgust Mr. Lincoln's insinuations of my complicity in that forgery, if it was a forgery. Does Mr. Lincoln wish to push these things to the point of personal difficulties here? I commenced this contest by treating him courteously and kindly; I always spoke of him in words of respect, and in return he has sought, and is now seeking, to divert public attention from the enormity of his revolutionary principles by impeaching men's sincerity and integrity, and inviting personal quarrels.

I desired to conduct this contest with him like a gentleman, but I spurn the insinuation of complicity and fraud made upon the simple circumstances of an editor of a newspaper having made a mistake as to the place where a thing was done, but not as to the thing itself. These resolutions were the platform of this Republican party of Mr. Lincoln's of that year. They were adopted in a majority of the Republican counties in the State; and when I asked him at Ottawa whether they formed the platform upon which he stood, he did not answer, and I could not get an answer out of him. He then thought, as I thought, that those resolutions were adopted at the Springfield Convention, but excused himself by saying that he was not there when they were adopted, but had gone to Tazewell court in order to avoid being present at the Convention. He saw them published as having been adopted at Springfield, and so did I, and he knew that if there was a mistake in regard to them, that I had nothing under heaven to do with it. Besides, you find that in all these northern countries where the Republican candidates are running pledged to him, that the Conventions which nominated them adopted that identical platform. One cardinal point in that plat-form which he shrinks from is this—that there shall be no more slave States admitted into the Union, even if the people want them. Lovejoy stands pledged against the admission of any more slave States. ["Right, so do we."] So do you, you say. Farnsworth stands pledged against the admis-sion of any more slave States. Washburne stands pledged the same way. The candidate for the Legislature who is running on Lincoln's ticket in Henderson and Warren, stands committed by his vote in the Legislature to the same thing, and I am informed, but do not know of the fact, that your candidate here is also so pledged. ["Hurra for him, good."] Now, you Republicans all hurra for him, and for the doctrine of "no more slave States," and yet Lincoln tells you that his conscience will not permit him to sanction that doctrine. And com-plains because the resolutions I read at Ottawa made him, as a member of the party, responsible for sanctioning the doctrine of no more slave States. You are one way, you confess, and he is or pretends to be the other, and yet you are both gov-erned by principle in supporting one another. If it be true, as I have shown it is, that the whole Republican party in the northern part of the State stands committed to the doctrine of no more slave States, and that this same doctrine is repudiated by the Republicans in the other part of the State, I wonder whether Mr. Lincoln and his party do not

present the case which he cited from the Scriptures, of a house divided against itself which cannot stand! I desire to know what are Mr. Lincoln's principles and the principles of his party? I hold, and the party with which I am identified hold, that the people of each State, old and new, have the right to decide the slavery question for themselves, and when I used the remark that I did not care whether slavery was voted up or down, I used it in the connection that I was for allowing Kansas to do just as she pleased on the slavery question. I said that I did not care whether they voted slavery up or down, because they had the right to do as they pleased on the question, and therefore my action would not be controlled by any such consideration. Why cannot Abraham Lincoln, and the party with which he acts, speak out their principles so that they may be understood? Why do they claim to be one thing in one part of the State and another in the other part? Whenever I allude to the Abolition doc-trines, which he considers a slander to be charged with being in favor of, you all indorse them, and hurra for them, not knowing that your candidate is ashamed to acknowledge them.

I have a few words to say upon the Dred Scott decision, which has troubled the brain of Mr. Lincoln so much. He insists that that decision would carry slavery into the free States, notwithstanding that the decision says directly the opposite; and goes into a long argument to make you believe that I am in favor of, and would sanction the doctrine that would allow slaves to be brought here and held as slaves contrary to our Constitution and laws. Mr. Lincoln knew better when he asserted this; he knew that one newspaper, and so far as is within my knowledge but one, ever asserted that doctrine, and that I was the first man in either House of Congress that read that article in debate, and denounced it on the floor of the Senate as revolutionary. When the *Washington Union*, on the 17th of last November, published an article to that effect, I branded it at once, and denounced it, and hence the *Union* has been pursuing me ever since. Mr. Toombs, of Georgia, replied to me, and said that there was not a man in any of the slave States south of the Potomac river that held any such doctrine. Mr. Lincoln knows that there is not a member of the Supreme Court who holds that doctrine; he knows that every one of them, as shown by their opinions, holds the reverse. Why this attempt, then, to bring the Supreme Court into disrepute among the people? It looks as if there was an effort being made to destroy public confidence in the highest judicial tribunal on earth. Suppose he succeeds in destroying public confidence in the court, so that the people will not respect its decisions, but will feel at liberty to disregard them, and resist the laws of the land, what will he have gained? He will have changed the Government from one of laws into that of a mob, in which the strong arm of violence will be substituted for the decisions of the courts of justice. He complains because I did not go into an argument reviewing Chief Justice Taney's opinion, and the other opinions of the different judges, to determine whether their reasoning is right or wrong on the questions of law. What use would that be? He wants to take an appeal from the Supreme Court to this meeting to determine whether the questions of law were decided properly. He is going to appeal from the Supreme Court of the United States to every town meeting in the hope that he can excite a prejudice against that court, and on the wave of that prejudice ride into the Senate of the United States, when he could not get there on his own principles, or his own merits. Suppose he should succeed in getting into the Senate of the United States, what then will he have to do with the decision of the Supreme Court in the Dred Scott case? Can he reverse that decision when he gets there? Can he act upon it? Has the Senate any right to reverse it or revise it? He will not pretend that it has. Then why drag the matter into this contest, unless for the purpose of making a false issue, by which he can direct public attention from the real issue.

He has cited General Jackson in justification of the war he is making on the decision of the court. Mr. Lincoln misunderstands the history of the country, if he believes there is any parallel in the two cases. It is true that the Supreme Court once decided that if a Bank of the United States was a necessary fiscal agent of the Government, it was constitutional, and if not, that it was unconstitutional, and also, that whether or not it was necessary for that purpose, was a political question for Congress and not a judicial one for the courts to determine. Hence the court would not determine the bank unconstitutional. Jackson respected the decision, obeyed the law, executed it and carried it into effect during its existence; but after the charter of the bank expired and a proposition was made to create a new bank, General Jackson said, "it is unnecessary and improper, and, therefore, I am against it on Constitutional grounds as well as those of expediency." Is Congress bound to pass every act that is Constitutional? Why, there are a thousand things that are Constitutional, but yet are inexpedient and unnecessary, and you surely would not vote for them merely because you had the right to? And because General Jackson would not do a thing which he had a right to do, but did not deem expedient or proper, Mr. Lincoln is going to justify himself in doing that which he has no right to do. I ask him, whether he is not bound to respect and obey the decisions of the Supreme Court as well as me? The Constitution has created that court to decide all Constitutional questions in the last resort, and when such decisions have been made, they become the law of the land, and you, and he, and myself, and every other good citizen are bound by them. Yet, he argues that I am bound by their decisions and he is not. He says that their decisions are binding on Democrats, but not on Republicans. Are not Republicans bound by the laws of the land as well as Democrats? And when the court has fixed the construction of the Constitution on the validity of a given law, is not their decision binding upon Republicans as well as upon Democrats? Is it possible that you Republicans have the right to raise your mobs and oppose the laws of the land and the constituted authorities, and yet hold us Democrats bound to obey them? My time is within half a minute of expiring, and all I have to say is, that I stand by the laws of the land. I stand by the Constitution as our fathers made it, by the laws as they are enacted, and by the decisions of the court upon all points within their jurisdiction as they are pronounced by the highest tribunal on earth; and any man who resists these must resort to mob law and violence to overturn the government of laws.

Source: The Lincoln Douglas Debates 5th Debate. Galesburg, Illinois, October 7, 1858. TeachingAmerican History.org. © 2006 Ashbrook Center for Public Affairs.

Seventh Lincoln-Douglas Debate, Alton, Illinois (October 15, 1858)

In 1858, Stephen A. Douglas and his challenger, Abraham Lincoln, engaged in a series of eight debates across Illinois as they ran against each other for the U.S. Senate seat from Illinois, then held by Douglas. Reproduced here is the Seventh Debate, which was held on October 15, 1858, in Alton, a town on the Mississippi River in the south-central part of the state. Although the Chicago and Alton Railroad offered half-price fares to the debate from Springfield and elsewhere, the day was cloudy and attendance at the debate was put at only about 5,000 people.

During the debate Douglas again defended the doctrine of popular sovereignty, which stated that the residents of U.S. territories should be allowed to vote on whether or not slavery was to be allowed in their territory, thus removing the federal government from the slavery expansion issue. Douglas also attacked Lincoln's "House Divided" speech, which Lincoln had delivered in Springfield on June 16, 1858, when Republicans chose him as their Senate candidate. The speech was so named because in it Lincoln quoted Jesus, "A house divided against itself cannot stand," as a way of saying that the United States could not stay forever half slave and half free. Even many Republicans considered this statement to be radical.

Lincoln used the Alton debate to attack the Kansas-Nebraska Act of 1854, which was introduced by Douglas and which repealed the Missouri Compromise of 1820, thereby allowing the possibility of slavery north of the old compromise line. To connect with former Whig supporters of the late Henry Clay, Lincoln also mentioned statements by Clay that slavery was an evil.

MR. DOUGLAS' SPEECH.

LADIES AND GENTLEMEN: It is now nearly four months since the canvass between Mr. Lincoln and myself commenced. On the 16th of June the Republican Convention assembled at Springfield and nominated Mr. Lincoln as their candidate for the United States Senate, and he, on that occasion, delivered a speech in which he laid down what he understood to be the Republican creed and the platform on which he proposed to stand during the contest. The principal points in that speech of Mr. Lincoln's were: First, that this Government could not endure permanently divided into free and slave States, as our fathers made it; that they must all become free or all become slave; all become one thing or all become the other, otherwise this Union could not continue to exist. I give you his opinions almost in the identical language he used. His second proposition was a crusade against the Supreme Court of the United States because of the Dred Scott decision; urging as an especial reason for his opposition to that decision that it deprived the negroes of the rights and benefits of that clause in the Constitution of the United States which guaranties to the citizens of each State all the rights, privileges, and immunities of the citizens of the several States. On the 10th of July I returned home, and delivered a speech to the people of Chicago, in which I announced it to be my purpose to appeal to the people of Illinois to sustain the course I had pursued in Congress. In that speech I joined issue with Mr. Lincoln on the points which he had presented. Thus there was an issue clear and distinct made up between us on these two propositions laid down in the speech of Mr. Lincoln at Springfield, and controverted by me in my reply to him at Chicago. On the next day, the 11th of July, Mr. Lincoln replied to me at Chicago, explaining at some length, and reaffirming the positions which he had taken in his Springfield speech. In that Chicago speech he even went further than he had before, and uttered sentiments in regard to the negro being on an equality with the white man. ("That's so.") He adopted in support of this position the argument which Lovejoy and Codding, and other Abolition lecturers had made familiar in the northern and central portions of the State, to wit: that the Declaration of Independence having declared all men free and equal, by Divine law, also that negro equality was an inalienable right, of which they could not be deprived. He insisted, in that speech, that the Declaration of Independence included the negro in the clause, asserting that all men were created equal, and went so far as to say that if one man was allowed to take the position, that it did not include the negro, others might take the position that it did not include other men. He said that all these distinctions between this man and that man, this race and the other race, must be discarded, and we must all stand by the Declaration of Independence, declaring that all men were created equal.

The issue thus being made up between Mr. Lincoln and myself on three points, we went before the people of the State. During the following seven weeks, between the Chicago speeches and our first meeting at Ottawa, he and I addressed large assemblages of the people in many of the central counties. In my speeches I confined myself closely to those three positions which he had taken, controverting his proposition that this Union could not exist as our fathers made it, divided into free and slave States, controverting his proposition of a crusade against the Supreme Court because of the Dred Scott decision, and controverting his proposition that the Declaration of Independence included and meant the negroes as well as the white men, when it declared all men to be created equal. (Cheers for Douglas.) I supposed at that time that these propositions constituted a distinct issue between us, and that the opposite positions we had taken upon them we would be willing to be held to in every part of the State, I never intended to waver one hair's breadth from that issue either in the north or the south, or wherever I should address the people of Illinois. I hold that when the time arrives that I cannot proclaim my political creed in the same terms not only in the northern but the southern part of Illinois, not only in the Northern but the Southern States, and wherever the American flag waves over American soil, that then there must be something wrong in that creed. ("Good, good," and cheers.) So long as we live under a common Constitution, so long as we live in a confederacy of sovereign and equal States, joined together as one for certain purposes, that any political creed is radically wrong which cannot be proclaimed in every State, and every section of that Union, alike. I took up Mr. Lincoln's three propositions in my several speeches, analyzed them, and pointed out what I believed to be the radical errors contained in them. First, in regard to his doctrine that this Government was in violation of the law of God, which says that a house divided against itself cannot stand, I repudiated it as a slander upon the immortal framers of our Constitution. I then said, I have often repeated, and now again assert, that in my opinion our Government can endure forever, (good) divided into free and slave States as our fathers made it,—each State having the right to prohibit, abolish or sustain slavery, just as it pleases. ("Good," "right," and cheers.) This Government was made upon the great basis of the sovereignty of the States, the right of each State to regulate its own domestic institutions to suit itself, and that right was conferred with the understanding and expectation that inasmuch as each locality had separate interests, each locality must have different and distinct local and domestic institutions, corresponding to its wants and interests. Our fathers knew when they made the Government, that the laws and institutions which were well adapted to the green mountains of Vermont, were unsuited to the rice plantations of South Carolina. They knew then, as well as we know now, that the laws and institutions which would be well adapted to the beautiful prairies of Illinois would not be suited to the mining regions of California. They knew that in a Republic as broad as this, having such a variety of soil, climate and interest, there must necessarily be a corresponding variety of local laws— the policy and institutions of each State adapted to its condition and wants. For this reason this Union was established on the right of each State to do as it pleased on the question of slavery, and every other question; and the various States were not allowed to complain of, much less interfere with the policy, of their neighbors. ("That's good doctrine," "that's the doctrine," and cheers.)

Suppose the doctrine advocated by Mr. Lincoln and the abolitionists of this day had prevailed when the Constitution was made, what would have been the result? Imagine for a moment that Mr. Lincoln had been a member of the Convention that framed the Constitution of the United States, and that when its members were about to sign that wonderful document, he had arisen in that Convention as he did at Springfield this summer, and addressing himself to the President, had said, "A house divided against itself cannot stand; (laughter) this Government, divided into free and slave States, cannot endure, they must all be free or all be slave, they must all be one thing or all the other, otherwise, it is a violation of the law of God, and cannot continue to exist;" —suppose Mr. Lincoln had convinced that body of sages that that doctrine was sound, what would have been the result? Remember that the Union was then composed of thirteen States, twelve of which were slaveholding and one free. Do you think that the one free State would have outvoted the twelve slaveholding States, and thus have secured the abolition of slavery? (No, no.) On the other hand, would not the twelve slaveholding States have outvoted the one free State,

and thus have fastened slavery, by a Constitutional provision, on every foot of the American Republic forever? You see that if this Abolition doctrine of Mr. Lincoln had prevailed when the Government was made, it would have established slavery as a permanent institution, in all the States, whether they wanted it or not, and the question for us to determine in Illinois now as one of the free States is, whether or not we are willing, having become the majority section, to enforce a doctrine on the minority, which we would have resisted with our heart's blood had it been attempted on us when we were in a minority. ("We never will," "good, good," and cheers.) How has the South lost her power as the majority section in this Union, and how have the free States gained it, except under the operation of that principle which declares the right of the people of each State and each Territory to form and regulate their domestic institutions in their own way. It was under that principle that slavery was abolished in New Hampshire, Rhode Island, Connecticut, New York, New Jersey, and Pennsylvania; it was under that principle that one half of the slaveholding States became free; it was under that principle that the number of free States increased until from being one out of twelve States, we have grown to be the majority of States of the whole Union, with the power to control the House of Representatives and Senate, and the power, consequently, to elect a President by Northern votes without the aid of a Southern State. Having obtained this power under the operation of that great principle, are you now prepared to abandon the principle and declare that merely because we have the power you will wage a war against the Southern States and their institutions until you force them to abolish slavery every where. (No, never, and great applause.)

After having pressed these arguments home on Mr. Lincoln for seven weeks, publishing a number of my speeches, we met at Ottawa in joint discussion, and he then began to crawfish a little, and let himself down. (Immense applause.) I there propounded certain questions to him. Amongst others, I asked him whether he would vote for the admission of any more slave States in the event the people wanted them. He would not answer. (Applause and laughter.) I then told him that if he did not answer the question there I would renew it at Freeport, and would then trot him down into Egypt and again put it to him. (Cheers.) Well, at Freeport, knowing that the next joint discussion took place in Egypt, and being in dread of it, he did answer my question in regard to no more slave States in a mode which he hoped would be satisfactory to me, and accomplish the object he had in view. I will show you what his answer was. After saying that he was not pledged to the Republican doctrine of "no more slave States," he declared:

"I state to you freely, frankly, that I should be exceedingly sorry to ever be put in the position of having to pass upon that question. I should be exceedingly glad to know that there never would be another slave State admitted into this Union."

Here permit me to remark, that I do not think the people will ever force him into a position against his will. (Great laughter and applause.) He went on to say:

"But I must add in regard to this, that if slavery shall be kept out of the Territory during the territorial existence of any one given Territory, and then the people should, having a fair chance and a clear field when they come to adopt a Constitution, if they should do the extraordinary thing of adopting a slave Constitution, uninfluenced by the actual presence of the institution among them, I see no alternative, if we own the country, but we must admit it into the Union."

That answer Mr. Lincoln supposed would satisfy the old line Whigs, composed of Kentuckians and Virginians, down in the southern part of the State. Now, what does it amount to? I desired to know whether he would vote to allow Kansas to come into the Union with slavery or not, as her people desired. He would not answer; but in a roundabout way said that if slavery should be kept out of a Territory during the whole of its territorial existence, and then the people, when they adopted a State Constitution, asked admission as a slave State, he supposed he would have to let the State

come in. The case I put to him was an entirely different one. I desired to know whether he would vote to admit a State if Congress had not prohibited slavery in it during its territorial existence, as Congress never pretended to do under Clay's Compromise measures of 1850. He would not answer, and I have not yet been able to get an answer from him. (Laughter, "he'll answer this time," "he's afraid to answer," etc.) I have asked him whether he would vote to admit Nebraska if her people asked to come in as a State with a Constitution recognizing slavery, and he refused to answer. ("Put him through," "give it to him," and cheers.) I have put the question to him with reference to New Mexico, and he has not uttered a word in answer. I have enumerated the Territories, one after another, putting the same question to him with reference to each, and he has not said, and will not say, whether, if elected to Congress, he will vote to admit any Territory now in existence with such a Constitution as her people may adopt. He invents a case which does not exist, and cannot exist under this Government, and answers it; but he will not answer the question I put to him in connection with any of the Territories now in existence. ("Hurrah for Douglas," "three cheers for Douglas.") The contract we entered into with Texas when she entered the Union obliges us to allow four States to be formed out of the old State, and admitted with or without slavery as the respective inhabitants of each may determine. I have asked Mr. Lincoln three times in our joint discussions whether he would vote to redeem that pledge, and he has never yet answered. He is as silent as the grave on the subject. (Laughter, "Lincoln must answer," "he will," &c.) He would rather answer as to a state of the case which will never arise than commit himself by telling what he would do in a case which would come up for his action soon after his election to Congress. ("He'll never have to act on any question," and laughter.) Why can he not say whether he is willing to allow the people of each State to have slavery or not as they please, and to come into the Union when they have the requisite population as a slave or a free State as they decide? I have no trouble in answering the question. I have said every where, and now repeat it to you, that if the people of Kansas want a slave State they have a right, under the Constitution of the United States, to form such a State, and I will let them come into the Union with slavery or without, as they determine. ("That's right," "good," "hurrah for Douglas all the time," and cheers.) If the people of any other Territory desire slavery, let them have it. If they do not want it, let them prohibit it. It is their business, not mine. ("That's the doctrine.") It is none of our business in Illinois whether Kansas is a free State or a slave State. It is none of your business in Missouri whether Kansas shall adopt slavery or reject it. It is the business of her people and none of yours. The people of Kansas have as much right to decide that question for themselves as you have in Missouri to decide it for yourselves, or we in Illinois to decide it for ourselves. ("That's what we believe," "We stand by that," and cheers.)

And here I may repeat what I have said in every speech I have made in Illinois, that I fought the Lecompton Constitution to its death, not because of the slavery clause in it, but because it was not the act and deed of the people of Kansas. I said then in Congress, and I say now, that if the people of Kansas want a slave State, they have a right to have it. If they wanted the Lecompton Constitution, they had a right to have it. I was opposed to that Constitution because I did not believe that it was the act and deed of the people, but on the contrary, the act of a small, pitiful minority acting in the name of the majority. When at last it was determined to send that Constitution back to the people, and accordingly, in August last, the question of admission under it was submitted to a popular vote, the citizens rejected it by nearly ten to one, thus showing conclusively, that I was right when I said that the Lecompton Constitution was not the act and deed of the people of Kansas, and did not embody their will. (Cheers.)

I hold that there is no power on earth, under our system of Government, which has the right to force a Constitution upon an unwilling people. (That's

so.) Suppose that there had been a majority of ten to one in favor of slavery in Kansas, and suppose there had been an Abolition President, and an Abolition Administration, and by some means the Abolitionists succeeded in forcing an Abolition Constitution on those slaveholding people, would the people of the South have submitted to that act for one instant? (No, no.) Well, if you of the South would not have submitted to it a day, how can you, as fair, honorable and honest men, insist on putting a slave Constitution on a people who desire a free State? ("That's so," and cheers.) Your safety and ours depend upon both of us acting in good faith, and living up to that great principle which asserts the right of every people to form and regulate their domestic institutions to suit themselves, subject only to the Constitution of the United States. ("That's the doctrine," and immense applause.)

Most of the men who denounced my course on the Lecompton question, objected to it not because I was not right, but because they thought it expedient at that time, for the sake of keeping the party together, to do wrong. (Cheers.) I never knew the Democratic party to violate any one of its principles out of policy or expediency, that it did not pay the debt with sorrow. There is no safety or success for our party unless we always do right, and trust the consequences to God and the people. I chose not to depart from principle for the sake of expediency in the Lecompton question, and I never intend to do it on that or any other question. (Good.)

But I am told that I would have been all right if I had only voted for the English bill after Lecompton was killed. (Laughter and cheers.) You know a general pardon was granted to all political offenders on the Lecompton question, provided they would only vote for the English bill. I did not accept the benefits of that pardon, for the reason that I had been right in the course I had pursued, and hence did not require any forgiveness. Let us see how the result has been worked out. English brought in his bill referring the Lecompton Constitution back to the people, with the provision that if it was rejected Kansas should be kept out of the Union until she had the full ratio of population required for a member of Congress, thus in effect declaring that if the people of Kansas would only consent to come into the Union under the Lecompton Constitution, and have a slave State when they did not want it, they should be admitted with a population of 35,000, but that if they were so obstinate as to insist upon having just such a Constitution as they thought best, and to desire admission as a free State, then they should be kept out until they had 93,420 inhabitants. I then said, and I now repeat to you, that whenever Kansas has people enough for a slave State she has people enough for a free State. I was and am willing to adopt the rule that no State shall ever come into the Union until she has the full ratio of population for a member of Congress, provided that rule is made uniform. I made that proposition in the Senate last winter, but a majority of the Senators would not agree to it; and I then said to them if you will not adopt the general rule I will not consent to make an exception of Kansas.

I hold that it is a violation of the fundamental principles of this Government to throw the weight of federal power into the scale, either in favor of the free or the slave States. Equality among all the States of this Union is a fundamental principle in our political system. We have no more right to throw the weight of the Federal Government into the scale in favor of the slaveholding than the free States, and last of all should our friends in the South consent for a moment that Congress should withhold its powers either way when they know that there is a majority against them in both Houses of Congress.

Fellow-citizens, how have the supporters of the English bill stood up to their pledges not to admit Kansas until she obtained a population of 93,420 in the event she rejected the Lecompton Constitution? How? The newspapers inform us that English himself, whilst conducting his canvass for re-election, and in order to secure it, pledged himself to his constituents that if returned he would disregard his own bill and vote to admit Kansas into the Union with such population as she might have when she made application. We are informed

that every Democratic candidate for Congress in all the States where elections have recently been held, was pledged against the English bill, with perhaps one or two exceptions. Now, if I had only done as these anti-Lecompton men who voted for the English bill in Congress, pledging themselves to refuse to admit Kansas if she refused to become a slave State until she had a population of 93,420, and then returned to their people, forfeited their pledge, and made a new pledge to admit Kansas at any time she applied, without regard to population, I would have had no trouble. You saw the whole power and patronage of the Federal Government wielded in Indiana, Ohio, and Pennsylvania to re-elect anti-Lecompton men to Congress who voted against Lecompton, then voted for the English bill, and then denounced the English bill, and pledged themselves to their people to disregard it. My sin consists in not having given a pledge, and then in not having afterward forfeited it. For that reason, in this State, every postmaster, every route agent, every collector of the ports, and every federal office-holder, forfeits his head the moment he expresses a preference for the Democratic candidates against Lincoln and his Abolition associates. A Democratic Administration which we helped to bring into power, deems it consistent with its fidelity to principle and its regard to duty, to wield its power in this State in behalf of the Republican Abolition candidates in every county and every Congressional District against the Democratic party. All I have to say in reference to the matter is, that if that Administration have not regard enough for principle, if they are not sufficiently attached to the creed of the Democratic party to bury forever their personal hostilities in order to succeed in carrying out our glorious principles, I have. I have no personal difficulty with Mr. Buchanan or his cabinet. He chose to make certain recommendations to Congress, as he had a right to do, on the Lecompton question. I could not vote in favor of them. I had as much right to judge for myself how I should vote as he had how he should recommend. He undertook to say to me, if you do not vote as I tell you, I will take off the heads of your friends. I replied to him, "You did not elect me, I represent Illinois and I am accountable to Illinois, as my constituency, and to God, but not to the President or to any other power on earth."

And now this warfare is made on me because I would not surrender my connections of duty, because I would not abandon my constituency, and receive the orders of the executive authorities how I should vote in the Senate of the United States. I hold that an attempt to control the Senate on the part of the Executive is subversive of the principles of our Constitution. The Executive department is independent of the Senate, and the Senate is independent of the President. In matters of legislation the President has a veto on the action of the Senate, and in appointments and treaties the Senate has a veto on the President. He has no more right to tell me how I shall vote on his appointments than I have to tell him whether he shall veto or approve a bill that the Senate has passed. Whenever you recognize the right of the Executive to say to a Senator, "Do this, or I will take off the heads of your friends," you convert this Government from a republic into a despotism. Whenever you recognize the right of a President to say to a member of Congress, "Vote as I tell you, or I will bring a power to bear against you at home which will crush you," you destroy the independence of the representative, and convert him into a tool of Executive power. I resisted this invasion of the constitutional rights of a Senator, and I intend to resist it as long as I have a voice to speak, or a vote to give. Yet, Mr. Buchanan cannot provoke me to abandon one iota of Democratic principles out of revenge or hostility to his course. I stand by the platform of the Democratic party, and by its organization, and support its nominees. If there are any who choose to bolt, the fact only shows that they are not as good Democrats as I am.

My friends, there never was a time when it was as important for the Democratic party, for all national men, to rally and stand together as it is today. We find all sectional men giving up past differences and continuing the one question of slavery, and when we find sectional men thus uniting, we should unite to resist them and their treasonable designs. Such was the case in 1850, when Clay left the quiet and peace of his home, and again entered upon public life to quell agitation and restore peace to a distracted Union. Then we Democrats, with Cass at our head, welcomed Henry Clay, whom the whole nation regarded as having been preserved by God for the times. He became our leader in that great fight, and we rallied around him the same as the Whigs rallied around old Hickory in 1832, to put down nullification. Thus you see that whilst Whigs and Democrats fought fearlessly in old times about banks, the tariff, distribution, the specie circular, and the subtreasury, all united as a band of brothers when the peace, harmony, or integrity of the Union was imperiled. It was so in 1850, when Abolitionism had even so far divided this country, North and South, as to endanger the peace of the Union; Whigs and Democrats united in establishing the Compromise measures of that year, and restoring tranquillity and good feeling. These measures passed on the joint action of the two parties. They rested on the great principle that the people of each State and each Territory should be left perfectly free to form and regulate their domestic institutions to suit themselves. You Whigs and we Democrats justified them in that principle. In 1854, when it became necessary to organize the Territories of Kansas and Nebraska, I brought forward the bill on the same principle. In the Kansas-Nebraska bill you find it declared to be the true intent and meaning of the act not to legislate slavery into any State or Territory, nor to exclude it therefrom, but to leave the people thereof perfectly free to form and regulate their domestic institutions in their own way. ("That's so," and cheers.) I stand on that same platform in 1858 that I did in 1850, 1854, and 1856. The Washington "Union" pretending to be the organ of the Administration, in the number of the 5th of this month, devotes three columns and a half to establish these propositions: First, that Douglas, in his Freeport speech, held the same doctrine that he did in his Nebraska bill in 1854; second, that in 1854 Douglas justified the Nebraska bill upon the ground that it was based upon the same principle as Clay's Compromise measures of 1850. The "Union" thus proved that Douglas was the same in 1858 that he was in 1856, 1854, and 1850, and consequently argued that he was never a Democrat. Is it not funny that I was never a Democrat? There is no pretense that I have changed a hair's breadth. The "Union" proves by my speeches that I explained the Compromise measures of 1850 just as I do now, and that I explained the Kansas and Nebraska bill in 1854 just as I did in my Freeport speech, and yet says that I am not a Democrat, and cannot be trusted, because I have not changed during the whole of that time. It has occurred to me that in 1854 the author of the Kansas and Nebraska bill was considered a pretty good Democrat. (Cheers) It has occurred to me that in 1856, when I was exerting every nerve and every energy for James Buchanan, standing on the same platform then that I do now, that I was a pretty good Democrat. (Renewed applause.) They now tell me that I am not a Democrat, because I assert that the people of a Territory, as well as those of a State, have the right to decide for themselves whether slavery can or cannot exist in such Territory. Let me read what James Buchanan said on that point when he accepted the Democratic nomination for the Presidency in 1856. In his letter of acceptance, he used the following language:

> "The recent legislation of Congress respecting domestic slavery, derived as it has been from the original and pure fountain of legitimate political power, the will of the majority, promises ere long to allay the dangerous excitement. This legislation is founded upon principles as ancient as free government itself, and in accordance with them has simply declared that the people of a Territory, like those of a State, shall decide for themselves whether slavery shall or shall not exist within their limits."

Dr. Hope will there find my answer to the question he propounded to me before I commenced speaking. (Vociferous shouts of applause.) Of course no man will consider it an answer, who is outside of the Democratic organization, bolts Democratic nominations, and indirectly aids to put Abolitionists into power over Democrats. But whether Dr. Hope considers it an answer or not, every fair-minded man will see that James Buchanan has answered the question, and has asserted that the people of a Territory, like those of a State, shall decide for themselves whether slavery shall or shall not exist within their limits. I answer specifically if you want a further answer, and say that while under the decision of the Supreme Court, as recorded in the opinion of Chief Justice Taney, slaves are property like all other property, and can be carried into any Territory of the United States the same as any other description of property, yet when you get them there they are subject to the local law of the Territory just like all other property. You will find in a recent speech delivered by that able and eloquent statesman, Hon. Jefferson Davis, at Bangor, Maine, that he took the same view of this subject that I did in my Freeport speech. He there said:

> "If the inhabitants of any Territory should refuse to enact such laws and police regulations as would give security to their property or to his, it would be rendered more or less valueless in proportion to the difficulties of holding it without such protection. In the case of property in the labor of man, or what is usually called slave property, the insecurity would be so great that the owner could not ordinarily retain it. Therefore, though the right would remain, the remedy being withheld, it would follow that the owner would be practically debarred, by the circumstances of the case, from taking slave property into a Territory where the sense of the inhabitants was opposed to its introduction. So much for the oft-repeated fallacy of forcing slavery upon any community."

You will also find that the distinguished Speaker of the present House of Representatives, Hon. Jas. L. Orr, construed the Kansas and Nebraska bill in this same way in 1856, and also that great intellect of the South, Alex. H. Stephens, put the same construction upon it in Congress that I did in my Freeport speech. The whole South are rallying to the support of the doctrine that if the people of a

Territory want slavery they have a right to have it, and if they do not want it that no power on earth can force it upon them. I hold that there is no principle on earth more sacred to all the friends of freedom than that which says that no institution, no law, no constitution, should be forced on an unwilling people contrary to their wishes; and I assert that the Kansas and Nebraska bill contains that principle. It is the great principle contained in that bill. It is the principle on which James Buchanan was made President. Without that principle he never would have been made President of the United States. I will never violate or abandon that doctrine if I have to stand alone. (Hurrah for Douglas.) I have resisted the blandishments and threats of power on the one side, and seduction on the other, and have stood immovably for that principle, fighting for it when assailed by Northern mobs, or threatened by Southern hostility. ("That's the truth," and cheers.) I have defended it against the North and the South, and I will defend it against whoever assails it, and I will follow it wherever its logical conclusions lead me. ("So will we all," "hurrah for Douglas.") I say to you that there is but one hope, one safety for this country, and that is to stand immovably by that principle which declares the right of each State and each Territory to decide these questions for themselves. (Hear him, hear him.) This Government was founded on that principle, and must be administered in the same sense in which it was founded.

But the Abolition party really think that under the Declaration of Independence the negro is equal to the white man, and that negro equality is an inalienable right conferred by the Almighty, and hence that all human laws in violation of it are null and void. With such men it is no use for me to argue. I hold that the signers of the Declaration of Independence had no reference to negroes at all when they declared all men to be created equal. They did not mean negro, nor the savage Indians, nor the Fejee Islanders, nor any other barbarous race. They were speaking of white men. ("It's so," "it's so," and cheers.) They alluded to men of European birth and European descent—to white men, and to none others, when they declared that doctrine. ("That's the truth.") I hold that this Government was established on the white basis. It was established by white men for the benefit of white men and their posterity forever, and should be administered by white men, and none others. But it does not follow, by any means, that merely because the negro is not a citizen, and merely because he is not our equal, that, therefore, he should be a slave. On the contrary, it does follow that we ought to extend to the negro race, and to all other dependent races all the rights, all the privileges, and all the immunities which they can exercise consistently with the safety of society. Humanity requires that we should give them all these privileges; Christianity commands that we should extend those privileges to them. The question then arises what are those privileges, and what is the nature and extent of them. My answer is that that is a question which each State must answer for itself. We in Illinois have decided it for ourselves. We tried slavery, kept it up for twelve years, and finding that it was not profitable, we abolished it for that reason, and became a free State. We adopted in its stead the policy that a negro in this State shall not be a slave and shall not be a citizen. We have a right to adopt that policy. For my part I think it is a wise and sound policy for us. You in Missouri must judge for yourselves whether it is a wise policy for you. If you choose to follow our example, very good; if you reject it, still well, it is your business, not ours. So with Kentucky. Let Kentucky adopt a policy to suit herself. If we do not like it we will keep away from it, and if she does not like ours let her stay at home, mind her own business and let us alone. If the people of all the States will act on that great principle, and each State mind its own business, attend to its own affairs, take care of its own negroes and not meddle with its neighbors, then there will be peace between the North and the South, the East and the West, throughout the whole Union. (Cheers.) Why can we not thus have peace? Why should we thus allow a sectional party to agitate this country, to array the North against the South, and convert us into enemies instead of friends, merely that a few ambitious men may ride into power on a sectional hobby? How long is it since these ambitious Northern men wished for a sectional organization? Did any one of them dream of a sectional party as long as the North was the weaker section and the South the stronger? Then all were opposed to sectional parties; but the moment the North obtained the majority in the House and Senate by the admission of California, and could elect a President without the aid of Southern votes, that moment ambitious Northern men formed a scheme to excite the North against the South, and make the people be governed in their votes by geographical lines, thinking that the North, being the stronger section, would outvote the South, and consequently they, the leaders, would ride into office on a sectional hobby. I am told that my hour is out. It was very short.

MR. LINCOLN'S REPLY.

On being introduced to the audience, after the cheering had subsided Mr. Lincoln said:

LADIES AND GENTLEMEN: I have been somewhat, in my own mind, complimented by a large portion of Judge Douglas's speech—I mean that portion which he devotes to the controversy between himself and the present Administration. This is the seventh time Judge Douglas and myself have met in these joint discussions, and he has been gradually improving in regard to his war with the Administration. [Laughter, "That's so."] At Quincy, day before yesterday, he was a little more severe upon the Administration than I had heard him upon any occasion, and I took pains to compliment him for it. I then told him to "Give it to them with all the power he had;" and as some of them were present, I told them I would be very much obliged if they would give it to him in about the same way. [Uproarious laughter and cheers.] I take it he has now vastly improved upon the attack he made then upon the Administration. I flatter myself he has really taken my advice on this subject. All I

can say now is to re-commend to him and to them what I then commended—to prosecute the war against one another in the most vigorous manner. I say to them again—"Go it, husband!—Go it, bear!" [Great laughter.]

There is one other thing I will mention before I leave this branch of the discussion—although I do not consider it much of my business, any way. I refer to that part of the Judge's remarks where he undertakes to involve Mr. Buchanan in an inconsistency. He reads something from Mr. Buchanan, from which he undertakes to involve him in an inconsistency; and he gets something of a cheer for having done so. I would only remind the Judge that while he is very valiantly fighting for the Nebraska bill and the repeal of the Missouri Compromise, it has been but a little while since he was the valiant advocate of the Missouri Compromise. [Cheers.] I want to know if Buchanan has not as much right to be inconsistent as Douglas has? [Loud applause and laughter; "Good, good!" "Hurrah for Lincoln!"] Has Douglas the exclusive right, in this country, of being on all sides of all questions? Is nobody allowed that high privilege but himself? Is he to have an entire monopoly on that subject? [Great laughter.]

So far as Judge Douglas addressed his speech to me, or so far as it was about me, it is my business to pay some attention to it. I have heard the Judge state two or three times what he has stated to-day—that in a speech which I made at Springfield, Illinois, I had in a very especial manner complained that the Supreme Court in the Dred Scott case had decided that a negro could never be a citizen of the United States. I have omitted by some accident heretofore to analyze this statement, and it is required of me to notice it now. In point of fact it is untrue. I never have complained especially of the Dred Scott decision because it held that a negro could not be a citizen, and the Judge is always wrong when he says I ever did so complain of it. I have the speech here, and I will thank him or any of his friends to show where I said that a negro should be a citizen, and complained especially of the Dred Scott decision because it declared he could not be one. I have done no such thing, and

Judge Douglas so persistently insisting that I have done so, has strongly impressed me with the belief of a predetermination on his part to misrepresent me. He could not get his foundation for insisting that I was in favor of this negro equality any where else as well he could by assuming that untrue proposition. Let me tell this audience what is true in regard to that matter; and the means by which they may correct me if I do not tell them truly is by a recurrence to the speech itself. I spoke of the Dred Scott decision in my Springfield speech, and I was then endeavoring to prove that the Dred Scott decision was a portion of a system or scheme to make slavery national in this country. I pointed out what things had been decided by the court. I mentioned as a fact that they had decided that a negro could not be a citizen—that they had done so, as I supposed, to deprive the negro, under all circumstances, of the remotest possibility of ever becoming a citizen and claiming the rights of a citizen of the United States under a certain clause of the Constitution. I stated that, without making any complaint of it at all. I then went on and stated the other points decided in the case, namely: that the bringing of a negro into the State of Illinois and holding him in slavery for two years here was a matter in regard to which they would not decide whether it would make him free or not; that they decided the further point that taking him into a United States Territory where slavery was prohibited by act of Congress, did not make him free, because that act of Congress, as they held, was unconstitutional. I mentioned these three things as making up the points decided in that case. I mentioned them in a lump taken in connection with the introduction of the Nebraska bill, and the amendment of Chase, offered at the time, declaratory of the right of the people of the Territories to exclude slavery, which was voted down by the friends of the bill. I mentioned all these things together, as evidence tending to prove a combination and conspiracy to make the institution of slavery national. In that connection and in that way I mentioned the decision on the point that a negro could not be a citizen, and in no other connection.

Out of this, Judge Douglas builds up his beautiful fabrication—of my purpose to introduce a perfect, social, and political equality between the white and black races. His assertion that I made an "especial objection" (that is his exact language) to the decision on this account, is untrue in point of fact.

Now, while I am upon this subject, and as Henry Clay has been alluded to, I desire to place myself, in connection with Mr. Clay, as nearly right before this people as may be. I am quite aware what the Judge's object is here by all these allusions. He knows that we are before an audience, having strong sympathies southward by relationship, place of birth, and so on. He desires to place me in an extremely Abolition attitude. He read upon a former occasion, and alludes without reading today, to a portion of a speech which I delivered in Chicago. In his quotations from that speech, as he has made them upon former occasions, the extracts were taken in such a way as, I suppose, brings them within the definition of what is called garbling—taking portions of a speech which, when taken by themselves, do not present the entire sense of the speaker as expressed at the time. I propose, therefore, out of that same speech, to show how one portion of it which he skipped over (taking an extract before and an extract after) will give a different idea, and the true idea I intended to convey. It will take me some little time to read it, but I believe I will occupy the time that way.

You have heard him frequently allude to my controversy with him in regard to the Declaration of Independence. I confess that I have had a struggle with Judge Douglas on that matter, and I will try briefly to place myself right in regard to it on this occasion. I said—and it is between the extracts Judge Douglas has taken from this speech, and put in his published speeches:

> "It may be argued that there are certain conditions that make necessities and impose them upon us, and to the extent that a necessity is imposed upon a man he must submit to it. I think that was the condition in which we found ourselves when we established this Government. We had slaves among us, we could not get our Constitution un-

less we permitted them to remain in slavery, we could not secure the good we did secure if we grasped for more; and having by necessity submitted to that much, it does not destroy the principle that is the charter of our liberties. Let the charter remain as our standard."

Now I have upon all occasions declared as strongly as Judge Douglas against the disposition to interfere with the existing institution of slavery. You hear me read it from the same speech from which he takes garbled extracts for the purpose of proving upon me a disposition to interfere with the institution of slavery, and establish a perfect social and political equality between negroes and white people.

Allow me while upon this subject briefly to present one other extract from a speech of mine, more than a year ago, at Springfield, in discussing this very same question, soon after Judge Douglas took his ground that negroes were not included in the Declaration of Independence:

"I think the authors of that notable instrument intended to include all men, but they did not mean to declare all men equal in all respects. They did not mean to say all men were equal in color, size, intellect, moral development or social capacity. They defined with tolerable distinctness in what they did consider all men created equal—equal in certain inalienable rights, among which are life, liberty, and the pursuit of happiness. This they said, and this they meant. They did not mean to assert the obvious untruth, that all were then actually enjoying that equality, or yet, that they were about to confer it immediately upon them. In fact they had no power to confer such a boon. They meant simply to declare the right, so that the enforcement of it might follow as fast as circumstances should permit.

"They meant to set up a standard maxim for free society which should be familiar to all: constantly looked to, constantly labored for, and even, though never perfectly attained, constantly approximated, and thereby constantly spreading and deepening its influence and augmenting the happiness and value of life to all people, of all colors, every where."

There again are the sentiments I have expressed in regard to the Declaration of Independence upon a former occasion—sentiments which have been put in print and read wherever any body cared to know what so humble an individual as myself chose to say in regard to it.

At Galesburgh the other day, I said in answer to Judge Douglas, that three years ago there never had been a man, so far as I knew or believed, in the whole world, who had said that the Declaration of Independence did not include negroes in the term "all men." I reassert it to-day. I assert that Judge Douglas and all his friends may search the whole records of the country, and it will be a matter of great astonishment to me if they shall be able to find that one human being three years ago had ever uttered the astounding sentiment that the term "all men" in the Declaration did not include the negro. Do not let me be misunderstood. I know that more than three years ago there were men who, finding this assertion constantly in the way of their schemes to bring about the ascendancy and perpetuation of slavery, denied the truth of it. I know that Mr. Calhoun and all the politicians of his school denied the truth of the Declaration. I know that it ran along in the mouth of some Southern men for a period of years, ending at last in that shameful though rather forcible declaration of Pettit of Indiana, upon the floor of the United States Senate, that the Declaration of Independence was in that respect "a self-evident lie," rather than a self-evident truth. But I say, with a perfect knowledge of all this hawking at the Declaration without directly attacking it, that three years ago there never had lived a man who had ventured to assail it in the sneaking way of pretending to believe it and then asserting it did not include the negro. I believe the first man who ever said it was Chief Justice Taney in the Dred Scott case, and the next to him was our friend, Stephen A. Douglas. And now it has become the catch-word of the entire party. I would like to call upon his friends every where to consider how they have come in so short a time to view this matter in a way so entirely different from their former belief? to ask whether they are not being borne along by an irresistible current—whither, they know not? [Great applause.]

In answer to my proposition at Galesburgh last week, I see that some man in Chicago has got up a letter addressed to the Chicago "Times," to show, as he professes, that somebody had said so before; and he signs himself "An Old Line Whig," if I remember correctly. In the first place I would say he was not an old line Whig. I am somewhat acquainted with old line Whigs. I was with the old line Whigs from the origin to the end of that party; I became pretty well acquainted with them, and I know they always had some sense, whatever else you could ascribe to them. [Great Laughter.] I know there never was one who had not more sense than to try to show by the evidence he produces that some man had, prior to the time I named, said that negroes were not included in the term "all men" in the Declaration of Independence. What is the evidence he produces? I will bring forward his evidence and let you see what he offers by way of showing that somebody more than three years ago had said negroes were not included in the Declaration. He brings forward part of a speech from Henry Clay—the part of the speech of Henry Clay which I used to bring forward to prove precisely the contrary. [Laughter.] I guess we are surrounded to some extent to-day by the old friends of Mr. Clay, and they will be glad to hear anything from that authority. While he was in Indiana a man presented a petition to liberate his negroes, and he (Mr. Clay) made a speech in answer to it, which I suppose he carefully wrote out himself and caused to be published. I have before me an extract from that speech which constitutes the evidence this pretended "Old Line Whig" at Chicago brought forward to show that Mr. Clay didn't suppose the negro was included in the Declaration of Independence. Hear what Mr. Clay said:

> "And what is the foundation of this appeal to me in Indiana, to liberate the slaves under my care in Kentucky? It is a general declaration in the act announcing to the world the independence of the thirteen American colonies, that all men are created equal. Now, as an abstract principle, there is

no doubt of the truth of that declaration; and it is desirable, in the original construction of society, and in organized societies, to keep it in view as a great fundamental principle. But, then, I apprehend that in no society that ever did exist, or ever shall be formed, was or can the equality asserted among the members of the human race, be practically enforced and carried out. There are portions, large portions, women, minors, insane, culprits, transient sojourners, that will always probably remain subject to the government of another portion of the community.

> "That declaration, whatever may be the extent of its import, was made by the delegations of the thirteen States. In most of them slavery existed, and had long existed, and was established by law. It was introduced and forced upon the colonies by the paramount law of England. Do you believe, that in making that declaration the States that concurred in it intended that it should be tortured into a virtual emancipation of all the slaves within their respective limits? Would Virginia and other Southern States have ever united in a declaration which was to be interpreted into an abolition of slavery among them? Did any one of the thirteen colonies entertain such a design or expectation? To impute such a secret and unavowed purpose, would be to charge a political fraud upon the noblest band of patriots that ever assembled in council—a fraud upon the Confederacy of the Revolution—a fraud upon the union of those States whose Constitution not only recognized the lawfulness of slavery, but permitted the importation of slaves from Africa until the year 1808."

This is the entire quotation brought forward to prove that somebody previous to three years ago had said the negro was not included in the term "all men" in the Declaration. How does it do so? In what way has it a tendency to prove that? Mr. Clay says it is true as an abstract principle that all men are created equal, but that we cannot practically apply it in all cases. He illustrates this by bringing forward the cases of females, minors, and insane persons, with whom it cannot be enforced; but he says it is true as an abstract principle in the organization of society as well as in organized society, and it should be kept in view as a fundamental principle. Let me read a few words more before I add some comments of my own. Mr. Clay says a little further on:

> "I desire no concealment of my opinions in regard to the institution of slavery. I look upon it as a great evil, and deeply lament that we have derived it from the parental Government, and from our ancestors. But here they are, and the question is, how can they be best dealt with? If a state of nature existed, and we were about to lay the foundations of society, no man would be more strongly opposed than I should be, to incorporating the institution of slavery among its elements."

Now, here in this same book—in this same speech—in this same extract brought forward to prove that Mr. Clay held that the negro was not included in the Declaration of Independence—no such statement on his part, but the declaration that it is a great fundamental truth, which should be constantly kept in view in the organization of society and in societies already organized. But if I say a word about it—if I attempt, as Mr. Clay said all good men ought to do, to keep it in view—if, in this "organized society," I ask to have the public eye turned upon it—if I ask, in relation to the organization of new Territories, that the public eye should be turned upon it—forthwith I am vilified as you hear me to-day. What have I done, that I have not the license of Henry Clay's illustrious example here in doing? Have I done aught that I have not his authority for, while maintaining that in organizing new Territories and societies, this fundamental principle should be regarded, and in organized society holding it up to the public view and recognizing what he recognized as the great principle of free government? [Great applause, and cries of "Hurrah for Lincoln."]

And when this new principle—this new proposition that no human being ever thought of three years ago—is brought forward, I combat it as having an evil tendency, if not an evil design. I combat it as having a tendency to dehumanize the negro—to take away from him the right of ever striving to be a man. I combat it as being one of the thousand things constantly done in these days to prepare the public mind to make property, and nothing but property, of the negro in all the States of this Union. [Tremendous applause. "Hurrah for Lincoln." "Hurrah for Trumbull."]

But there is a point that I wish, before leaving this part of the discussion, to ask attention to. I have read and I repeat the words of Henry Clay:

> "I desire no concealment of my opinions in regard to the institution of slavery. I look upon it as a great evil, and deeply lament that we have derived it from the parental Government, and from our ancestors. I wish every slave in the United States was in the country of his ancestors. But here they are; the question is how they can best be dealt with? If a state of nature existed, and we were about to lay the foundations of society, no man would be more strongly opposed than I should be, to incorporate the institution of slavery among its elements."

The principle upon which I have insisted in this canvass, is in relation to laying the foundations of new societies. I have never sought to apply these principles to the old States for the purpose of abolishing slavery in those States. It is nothing but a miserable perversion of what I have said, to assume that I have declared Missouri, or any other slave State, shall emancipate her slaves. I have proposed no such thing. But when Mr. Clay says that in laying the foundations of societies in our Territories where it does not exist, he would be opposed to the introduction of slavery as an element, I insist that we have his warrant—his license for insisting upon the exclusion of that element which he declared in such strong and emphatic language was most hateful to him. [Loud applause.]

Judge Douglas has again referred to a Springfield speech in which I said "a house divided against itself cannot stand." The Judge has so often made the entire quotation from that speech that I can make it from memory. I used this language:

> "We are now far into the fifth year, since a policy was initiated with the avowed object and confident promise of putting an end to the slavery agitation. Under the operation of this policy, that

agitation has not only not ceased, but has constantly augmented. In my opinion it will not cease until a crisis shall have been reached and passed. 'A house divided against itself cannot stand.' I believe this Government cannot endure permanently half slave and half free. I do not expect the house to fall—but I do expect it will cease to be divided. It will become all one thing, or all the other. Either the opponents of slavery will arrest the further spread of it, and place it where the public mind shall rest in the belief that it is in the course of ultimate extinction, or its advocates will push it forward till it shall become alike lawful in all the States—old as well as new, North as well as South."

That extract and the sentiments expressed in it, have been extremely offensive to Judge Douglas. He has warred upon them as Satan wars upon the Bible. [Laughter.] His perversions upon it are endless. Here now are my views upon it in brief.

I said we were now far into the fifth year, since a policy was initiated with the avowed object and confident promise of putting an end to the slavery agitation. Is it not so? When that Nebraska bill was brought forward four years ago last January, was it not for the "avowed object" of putting an end to the slavery agitation? We were to have no more agitation in Congress, it was all to be banished to the Territories. By the way, I will remark here that, as Judge Douglas is very fond of complimenting Mr. Crittenden in these days, Mr. Crittenden has said there was a falsehood in that whole business, for there was no slavery agitation at that time to allay. We were for a little while quiet on the troublesome thing, and that very allaying plaster of Judge Douglas's stirred it up again. [Applause and laughter.] But was it not understood or intimated with the "confident promise" of putting an end to the slavery agitation? Surely it was. In every speech you heard Judge Douglas make, until he got into this "imbroglio," as they call it, with the Administration about the Lecompton Constitution, every speech on that Nebraska bill was full of his felicitations that we were just at the end of the slavery agitation. The last tip of the last joint of the old serpent's tail was just drawing out of view. But has

it proved so? I have asserted that under that policy that agitation "has not only not ceased, but has constantly augmented." When was there ever a greater agitation in Congress than last winter? When was it as great in the country as to-day?

There was a collateral object in the introduction of that Nebraska policy which was to clothe the people of the Territories with a superior degree of self-government, beyond what they had ever had before. The first object and the main one of conferring upon the people a higher degree of "self-government," is a question of fact to be determined by you in answer to a single question. Have you ever heard or known of a people any where on earth who had as little to do, as, in the first instance of its use, the people of Kansas had with this same right of "self-government"? [Loud applause.] In its main policy and in its collateral object, it has been nothing but a living, creeping lie from the time of its introduction till to-day. [Loud cheers.]

I have intimated that I thought the agitation would not cease until a crisis should have been reached and passed. I have stated in what way I thought it would be reached and passed. I have said that it might go one way or the other. We might, by arresting the further spread of it, and placing it where the fathers originally placed it, put it where the public mind should rest in the belief that it was in the course of ultimate extinction. [Great applause.] Thus the agitation may cease. It may be pushed forward until it shall become alike lawful in all the States, old as well as new, North as well as South. I have said, and I repeat, my wish is that the further spread of it may be arrested, and that it may be placed where the public mind shall rest in the belief that it is in the course of ultimate extinction. I have expressed that as my wish. I entertain the opinion upon evidence sufficient to my mind, that the fathers of this Government placed that institution where the public mind did rest in the belief that it was in the course of ultimate extinction. Let me ask why they made provision that the source of slavery—the African slave-trade—should be cut off at the end of twenty years? Why did they make provision that in all the new territory we owned at that time, slavery should be forever inhibited? Why stop its spread in one direction and cut off its source in another, if they did not look to its being placed in the course of ultimate extinction?

Again; the institution of slavery is only mentioned in the Constitution of the United States two or three times, and in neither of these cases does the word "slavery" or "negro race" occur; but covert language is used each time, and for a purpose full of significance. What is the language in regard to the prohibition of the African slave-trade? It runs in about this way: "The migration or importation of such persons as any of the States now existing shall think proper to admit, shall not be prohibited by the Congress prior to the year one thousand eight hundred and eight."

The next allusion in the Constitution to the question of slavery and the black race, is on the subject of the basis of representation, and there the language used is, "Representatives and direct taxes shall be apportioned among the several States which may be included within this Union, according to their respective numbers, which shall be determined by adding to the whole number of free persons, including those bound to service for a term of years, and excluding Indians not taxed—three-fifths of all other persons."

It says "persons," not slaves, not negroes; but this "three-fifths" can be applied to no other class among us than the negroes.

Lastly, in the provision for the reclamation of fugitive slaves, it is said: "No person held to service or labor in one State, under the laws thereof, escaping into another, shall in consequence of any law or regulation therein, be discharged from such service or labor, but shall be delivered up, on claim of the party to whom such service or labor may be due." There again there is no mention of the word "negro" or of slavery. In all three of these places, being the only allusions to slavery in the instrument, covert language is used. Language is used not suggesting that slavery existed or that the black race were among us. And I understand the contemporaneous history of those times to be that covert language was used with a purpose, and that purpose was that in our Constitution, which it was hoped and is still hoped will endure forever—when it should be read by intelligent and patriotic men, after the institution of slavery had passed from among us—there should be nothing on the face of the great charter of liberty suggesting that such a thing as negro slavery had ever existed among us. [Enthusiastic applause.] This is part of the evidence that the fathers of the Government expected and intended the institution of slavery to come to an end. They expected and intended that it should be in the course of ultimate extinction. And when I say that I desire to see the further spread of it arrested, I only say I desire to see that done which the fathers have first done. When I say I desire to see it placed where the public mind will rest in the belief that it is in the course of ultimate extinction, I only say I desire to see it placed where they placed it. It is not true that our fathers, as Judge Douglas assumes, made this Government part slave and part free. Understand the sense in which he puts it. He assumes that slavery is a rightful thing within itself—was introduced by the framers of the Constitution. The exact truth is, that they found the institution existing among us, and they left it as they found it. But in making the Government they left this institution with many clear marks of disapprobation upon it. They found slavery among them, and they left it among them because of the difficulty—the absolute impossibility of its immediate removal. And when Judge Douglas asks me why we cannot let it remain part slave and part free, as the fathers of the Government made it, he asks a question based upon an assumption which is itself a falsehood; and I turn upon him and ask him the question, when the policy that the fathers of the Government had adopted in relation to this element among us was the best policy in the world—the only wise policy—the only policy that we can ever safely continue upon—that will ever give us peace unless this dangerous element masters us all and becomes a national institution—I turn upon him and ask him why he could not let it alone. [Great and prolonged cheering.] I turn and ask him why he was driven to the necessity of introducing a new policy in regard to it? He has himself said he introduced a new policy. He said so in his speech on the 22d of March of the present year, 1858. I ask him why he could not let it remain where our fathers placed it? I ask too of Judge Douglas and his friends why we shall not again place this institution upon the basis on which the fathers left it? I ask you, when he infers that I am in favor of setting the free and slave States at war, when the institution was placed in that attitude by those who made the constitution, did they make any war? ["No;" "no;" and cheers.] If we had no war out of it when thus placed, wherein is the ground of belief that we shall have war out of it if we return to that policy? Have we had any peace upon this matter springing from any other basis? ["No, no."] I maintain that we have not. I have proposed nothing more than a return to the policy of the fathers.

I confess, when I propose a certain measure of policy, it is not enough for me that I do not intend anything evil in the result, but it is incumbent on me to show that it has not a tendency to that result. I have met Judge Douglas in that point of view. I have not only made the declaration that I do not mean to produce a conflict between the States, but I have tried to show by fair reasoning, and I think I have shown to the minds of fair men, that I propose nothing but what has a most peaceful tendency. The quotation that I happened to make in that Springfield speech, that "a house divided against itself cannot stand," and which has proved so offensive to the Judge, was part and parcel of the same thing. He tries to show that variety in the domestic institutions of the different States is necessary and indispensable. I do not dispute it. I have no controversy with Judge Douglas about that. I shall very readily agree with him that it would be foolish for us to insist upon having a cranberry law here, in Illinois, where we have no cranberries, because they have a cranberry law in Indiana, where they have cranberries. [Laughter, "good, good."] I should insist that it would be exceedingly wrong in us to deny to Virginia the right to enact oyster laws where they have oysters, because we want no such laws here. [Renewed laughter.] I understand, I hope, quite as well as Judge Douglas or anybody else, that the variety in the soil and climate and face of the country, and consequent variety in the industrial pursuits and productions of a country, require systems of law conforming to this variety in the natural features of the country. I understand quite as well as Judge Douglas, that if we here raise a barrel of flour more than we want, and the Louisianians raise a barrel of sugar more than they want, it is of mutual advantage to exchange. That produces commerce, brings us together, and makes us better friends. We like one another the more for it. And I understand as well as Judge Douglas, or any body else, that these mutual accommodations are the cements which bind together the different parts of this Union—that instead of being a thing to "divide the house"—figuratively expressing the Union—they tend to sustain it; they are the props of the house tending always to hold it up.

But when I have admitted all this, I ask if there is any parallel between these things and this institution of slavery? I do not see that there is any parallel at all between them. Consider it. When have we had any difficulty or quarrel amongst ourselves about the cranberry laws of Indiana, or the oyster laws of Virginia, or the pine lumber laws of Maine, or the fact that Louisiana produces sugar, and Illinois flour? When have we had any quarrels over these things? When have we had perfect peace in regard to this thing which I say is an element of discord in this Union? We have sometimes had peace, but when was it? It was when the institution of slavery remained quiet where it was. We have had difficulty and turmoil whenever it has made a struggle to spread itself where it was not. I ask, then, if experience does not speak in thunder-tones, telling us that the policy which has given peace to the country heretofore, being returned to, gives the greatest promise of peace again. ["Yes;" "yes;" "yes."] You may say, and Judge Douglas has intimated the same thing, that all this difficulty in regard to the institution of slavery is the mere agitation of office seekers and ambitious Northern politicians. He thinks we want to get "his place," I suppose. [Cheers and laughter.] I agree that there are office seekers amongst us. The Bible says somewhere that we are desperately selfish. I think we would have discovered that fact without the Bible. I do not claim that I am any less so than the average of men, but I do claim that I am not more selfish than Judge Douglas. [Roars of laughter and applause.]

But is it true that all the difficulty and agitation we have in regard to this institution of slavery springs from office seeking—from the mere ambition of politicians? Is that the truth? How many times have we had danger from this question? Go back to the day of the Missouri Compromise. Go back to the Nullification question, at the bottom of which lay this same slavery question. Go back to the time of the Annexation of Texas. Go back to the troubles that led to the Compromise of 1850. You will find that every time, with the single exception of the Nullification question, they sprung from an endeavor to spread this institution. There never was a party in the history of this country, and there probably never will be, of sufficient strength to disturb the general peace of the country. Parties themselves may be divided and quarrel on minor questions, yet it extends not beyond the parties themselves. But does not this question make a disturbance outside of political circles? Does it not enter into the churches and rend them asunder? What divided the great Methodist Church into two parts, North and South? What has raised this constant disturbance in every Presbyterian General Assembly that meets? What disturbed the Unitarian Church in this very city two years ago? What has jarred and shaken the great American Tract Society recently, not yet splitting it, but sure to divide it in the end? Is it not this same mighty, deep-seated power that somehow operates on the minds of men, exciting and stirring them up in every avenue of society—in politics, in religion, in literature, in morals, in all the manifold relations of life? [Applause.] Is this the work of politicians? Is that irresistible power which for fifty years has shaken

the Government and agitated the people to be stilled and subdued by pretending that it is an exceedingly simple thing, and we ought not to talk about it? [Great cheers and laughter.] If you will get every body else to stop talking about it, I assure you I will quit before they have half done so. [Renewed laughter.] But where is the philosophy or statesmanship which assumes that you can quiet that disturbing element in our society which has disturbed us for more than half a century, which has been the only serious danger that has threatened our institutions—I say, where is the philosophy or the statesmanship based on the assumption that we are to quit talking about it, [applause] and that the public mind is all at once to cease being agitated by it? Yet this is the policy here in the north that Douglas is advocating—that we are to care nothing about it! I ask you if it is not a false philosophy? Is it not a false statesmanship that undertakes to build up a system of policy upon the basis of caring nothing about the very thing that every body does care the most about? ["Yes, yes," and applause]—a thing which all experience has shown we care a very great deal about? [Laughter and applause.]

The Judge alludes very often in the course of his remarks to the exclusive right which the States have to decide the whole thing for themselves. I agree with him very readily that the different States have that right. He is but fighting a man of straw when he assumes that I am contending against the right of the States to do as they please about it. Our controversy with him is in regard to the new Territories. We agree that when the States come in as States they have the right and the power to do as they please. We have no power as citizens of the free States or in our federal capacity as members of the Federal Union through the General Government, to disturb slavery in the States where it exists. We profess constantly that we have no more inclination than belief in the power of the Government to disturb it; yet we are driven constantly to defend ourselves from the assumption that we are warring upon the rights of the States. What I insist upon is, that the new Territories shall be kept free from it while in the

Territorial condition. Judge Douglas assumes that we have no interest in them—that we have no right whatever to interfere. I think we have some interest. I think that as white men we have. Do we not wish for an outlet for our surplus population, if I may so express myself? Do we not feel an interest in getting to that outlet with such institutions as we would like to have prevail there? If you go to the Territory opposed to slavery and another man comes upon the same ground with his slave, upon the assumption that the things are equal, it turns out that he has the equal right all his way and you have no part of it your way. If he goes in and makes it a slave Territory, and by consequence a slave State, is it not time that those who desire to have it a free State were on equal ground. Let me suggest it in a different way. How many Democrats are there about here ["A thousand"] who have left slave States and come into the free State of Illinois to get rid of the institution of slavery? [Another voice—"a thousand and one."] I reckon there are a thousand and one. [Laughter.] I will ask you, if the policy you are now advocating had prevailed when this country was in a Territorial condition, where would you have gone to get rid of it? [Applause.] Where would you have found your free State or Territory to go to? And when hereafter, for any cause, the people in this place shall desire to find new homes, if they wish to be rid of the institution, where will they find the place to go to? [Loud cheers.]

Now irrespective of the moral aspect of this question as to whether there is a right or wrong in enslaving a negro, I am still in favor of our new Territories being in such a condition that white men may find a home—may find some spot where they can better their condition—where they can settle upon new soil and better their condition in life. [Great and continued cheering.] I am in favor of this not merely, (I must say it here as I have elsewhere,) for our own people who are born amongst us, but as an outlet for free white people every where, the world over—in which Hans and Baptiste and Patrick, and all other men from all the world, may find new homes and better their conditions in life. [Loud and long continued applause.]

I have stated upon former occasions, and I may as well state again, what I understand to be the real issue in this controversy between Judge Douglas and myself. On the point of my wanting to make war between the free and the slave States, there has been no issue between us. So, too, when he assumes that I am in favor of introducing a perfect social and political equality between the white and black races. These are false issues, upon which Judge Douglas has tried to force the controversy. There is no foundation in truth for the charge that I maintain either of these propositions. The real issue in this controversy—the one pressing upon every mind—is the sentiment on the part of one class that looks upon the institution of slavery as a wrong, and of another class that does not look upon it as a wrong. The sentiment that contemplates the institution of slavery in this country as a wrong is the sentiment of the Republican party. It is the sentiment around which all their actions—all their arguments circle—from which all their propositions radiate. They look upon it as being a moral, social and political wrong; and while they contemplate it as such, they nevertheless have due regard for its actual existence among us, and the difficulties of getting rid of it in any satisfactory way and to all the constitutional obligations thrown about it. Yet having a due regard for these, they desire a policy in regard to it that looks to its not creating any more danger. They insist that it should as far as may be, be treated as a wrong, and one of the methods of treating it as a wrong is to make provision that it shall grow no larger. [Loud applause.] They also desire a policy that looks to a peaceful end of slavery at sometime, as being wrong. These are the views they entertain in regard to it as I understand them; and all their sentiments—all their arguments and propositions are brought within this range. I have said and I repeat it here, that if there be a man amongst us who does not think that the institution of slavery is wrong in any one of the aspects of which I have spoken, he is misplaced and ought not to be with us. And if there be a man amongst us who is so impatient of it as a wrong as to disregard its actual presence among us and the difficulty of getting rid of it suddenly in a satisfactory way, and to disregard the constitutional obligations thrown about it, that man is misplaced if he is on our platform. We disclaim sympathy with him in practical action. He is not placed properly with us.

On this subject of treating it as a wrong, and limiting its spread, let me say a word. Has any thing ever threatened the existence of this Union save and except this very institution of Slavery? What is it that we hold most dear amongst us? Our own liberty and prosperity. What has ever threatened our liberty and prosperity save and except this institution of Slavery? If this is true, how do you propose to improve the condition of things by enlarging Slavery—by spreading it out and making it bigger? You may have a wen or cancer upon your person and not be able to cut it out lest you bleed to death; but surely it is no way to cure it, to engraft it and spread it over your whole body. That is no proper way of treating what you regard a wrong. You see this peaceful way of dealing with it as a wrong—restricting the spread of it, and not allowing it to go into new countries where it has not already existed. That is the peaceful way, the old-fashioned way, the way in which the fathers themselves set us the example.

On the other hand, I have said there is a sentiment which treats it as not being wrong. That is the Democratic sentiment of this day. I do not mean to say that every man who stands within that range positively asserts that it is right. That class will include all who positively assert that it is right, and all who like Judge Douglas treat it as indifferent and do not say it is either right or wrong. These two classes of men fall within the general class of those who do not look upon it as a wrong. And if there be among you any body who supposes that he, as a Democrat can consider himself "as much opposed to slavery as anybody," I would like to reason with him. You never treat it as a wrong. What other thing that you consider as a wrong, do you deal with as you deal with that? Perhaps you say it is wrong, but your leader never does, and you quarrel with any body who says it is wrong. Although you pretend to say so yourself you can

find no fit place to deal with it as a wrong. You must not say any thing about it in the free States, because it is not here. You must not say any thing about it in the slave States, because it is there. You must not say any thing about it in the pulpit, because that is religion and has nothing to do with it. You must not say any thing about it in politics, because that will disturb the security of "my place." There is no place to talk about it as being a wrong, although you say yourself it is a wrong. But finally you will screw yourself up to the belief that if the people of the slave States should adopt a system of gradual emancipation on the slavery question, you would be in favor of it. You would be in favor of it. You say that is getting it in the right place, and you would be glad to see it succeed. But you are deceiving yourself. You all know that Frank Blair and Gratz Brown, down there in St. Louis, undertook to introduce that system in Missouri. They fought as valiantly as they could for the system of gradual emancipation which you pretend you would be glad to see succeed. Now I will bring you to the test. After a hard fight they were beaten, and when the news came over here you threw up your hats and hurraed for Democracy. More than that, take all the argument made in favor of the system you have proposed, and it carefully excludes the idea that there is any thing wrong in the institution of slavery. The arguments to sustain that policy carefully excluded it. Even here to-day you heard Judge Douglas quarrel with me because I uttered a wish that it might sometime come to an end. Although Henry Clay could say he wished every slave in the United States was in the country of his ancestors, I am denounced by those pretending to respect Henry Clay for uttering a wish that it might sometime, in some peaceful way, come to an end. The Democratic policy in regard to that institution will not tolerate the merest breath, the slightest hint, of the least degree of wrong about it. Try it by some of Judge Douglas's arguments. He says he "don't care whether it is voted up or voted down" in the Territories. I do not care myself in dealing with that expression, whether it is intended to be expressive of his individual sentiments on the subject, or only of the national policy he desires to have established. It is alike valuable for my purpose. Any man can say that who does not see any thing wrong in slavery, but no man can logically say it who does see a wrong in it; because no man can logically say he don't care whether a wrong is voted up or voted down. He may say he don't care whether an indifferent thing is voted up or down, but he must logically have a choice between a right thing and a wrong thing. He contends that whatever community wants slaves has a right to have them. So they have if it is not a wrong. But if it is a wrong, he cannot say people have a right to do wrong. He says that upon the score of equality, slaves should be allowed to go in a new Territory, like other property. This is strictly logical if there is no difference between it and other property. If it and other property are equal, his argument is entirely logical. But if you insist that one is wrong and the other right, there is no use to institute a comparison between right and wrong. You may turn over every thing in the Democratic policy from beginning to end, whether in the shape it takes on the statute book, in the shape it takes in the Dred Scott decision, in the shape it takes in conversation, or the shape it takes in short maxim-like arguments—it every where carefully excludes the idea that there is any thing wrong in it.

That is the real issue. That is the issue that will continue in this country when these poor tongues of Judge Douglas and myself shall be silent. It is the eternal struggle between these two principles—right and wrong—throughout the world. They are the two principles that have stood face to face from the beginning of time; and will ever continue to struggle. The one is the common right of humanity and the other the divine right of kings. It is the same principle in whatever shape it develops itself. It is the same spirit that says, "You work and toil and earn bread, and I'll eat it." No matter in what shape it comes, whether from the mouth of a king who seeks to bestride the people of his own nation and live by the fruit of their labor, or from one race of men as an apology for enslaving another race, it is the same tyrannical principle. I was glad to express my gratitude at Quincy, and I re-express it here to Judge Douglas—that he looks to no end of the institution of slavery. That will help the people to see where the struggle really is. It will hereafter place with us all men who really do wish the wrong may have an end. And whenever we can get rid of the fog which obscures the real question—when we can get Judge Douglas and his friends to avow a policy looking to its perpetuation—we can get out from among that class of men and bring them to the side of those who treat it as a wrong. Then there will soon be an end of it, and that end will be its "ultimate extinction." Whenever the issue can be distinctly made, and all extraneous matter thrown out so that men can fairly see the real difference between the parties, this controversy will soon be settled, and it will be done peaceably too. There will be no war, no violence. It will be placed again where the wisest and best men of the world placed it. Brooks of South Carolina once declared that when this Constitution was framed, its framers did not look to the institution existing until this day. When he said this, I think he stated a fact that is fully borne out by the history of the times. But he also said they were better and wiser men than the men of these days; yet the men of these days had experience which they had not, and by the invention of the cotton-gin it became a necessity in this country that slavery should be perpetual. I now say that, willingly or unwillingly, purposely or without purpose, Judge Douglas has been the most prominent instrument in changing the position of the institution of slavery which the fathers of the Government expected to come to an end ere this—and putting it upon Brooks's cotton-gin basis—placing it where he openly confesses he has no desire there shall ever be an end of it.

I understand I have ten minutes yet. I will employ it in saying something about this argument Judge Douglas uses, while he sustains the Dred Scott decision, that the people of the Territories can still somehow exclude slavery. The first thing I ask attention to is the fact that Judge Douglas constantly said, before the decision, that whether they could or not, was a question for the Supreme Court.

But after the court has made the decision he virtually says it is not a question for the Supreme Court, but for the people. And how is it he tells us they can exclude it? He says it needs "police regulations," and that admits of "unfriendly legislation." Although it is a right established by the Constitution of the United States to take a slave into a Territory of the United States and hold him as property, yet unless the Territorial Legislature will give friendly legislation, and, more especially, if they adopt unfriendly legislation, they can practically exclude him. Now, without meeting this proposition as a matter of fact, I pass to consider the real Constitutional obligation. Let me take the gentleman who looks me in the face before me, and let us suppose that he is a member of the Territorial Legislature. The first thing he will do will be to swear that he will support the Constitution of the United States. His neighbor by his side in the Territory has slaves and needs Territorial legislation to enable him to enjoy that Constitutional right. Can he withhold the legislation which his neighbor needs for the enjoyment of a right which is fixed in his favor in the Constitution of the United States which he has sworn to support? Can he withhold it without violating his oath? And more especially, can he pass unfriendly legislation to violate his oath? Why, this is a monstrous sort of talk about the Constitution of the United States! There has never been as outlandish or lawless a doctrine from the mouth of any respectable man on earth. I do not believe it is a Constitutional right to hold slaves in a Territory of the United States. I believe the decision was improperly made and I go for reversing it. Judge Douglas is furious against those who go for reversing a decision. But he is for legislating it out of all force while the law itself stands. I repeat that there has never been so monstrous a doctrine uttered from the mouth of a respectable man.

I suppose most of us (I know it of myself) believe that the people of the Southern States are entitled to a Congressional Fugitive Slave law—that is a right fixed in the Constitution. But it cannot be made available to them without Congressional legislation. In the Judge's language, it is a "barren right" which needs legislation before it can become efficient and valuable to the persons to whom it is guarantied. And as the right is Constitutional I agree that the legislation shall be granted to it—and that not that we like the institution of slavery. We profess to have no taste for running and catching niggers—at least I profess no taste for that job at all. Why then do I yield support to a Fugitive Slave law? Because I do not understand that the Constitution, which guaranties that right, can be supported without it. And if I believed that the right to hold a slave in a Territory was equally fixed in the Constitution with the right to reclaim fugitives, I should be bound to give it the legislation necessary to support it. I say that no man can deny his obligation to give the necessary legislation to support slavery in a Territory, who believes it is a Constitutional right to have it there. No man can, who does not give the Abolitionists an argument to deny the obligation enjoined by the Constitution to enact a Fugitive Slave law. Try it now. It is the strongest Abolition argument ever made. I say if that Dred Scott decision is correct, then the right to hold slaves in a Territory is equally a Constitutional right with the right of a slaveholder to have his runaway returned. No one can show the distinction between them. The one is express, so that we cannot deny it. The other is construed to be in the Constitution, so that he who believes the decision to be correct believes in the right. And the man who argues that by unfriendly legislation, in spite of that Constitutional right, slavery may be driven from the Territories, cannot avoid furnishing an argument by which Abolitionists may deny the obligation to return fugitives, and claim the power to pass laws unfriendly to the right of the slaveholder to reclaim his fugitive. I do not know how such an argument may strike a popular assembly like this, but I defy anybody to go before a body of men whose minds are educated to estimating evidence and reasoning, and show that there is an iota of difference between the Constitutional right to reclaim a fugitive, and the Constitutional right to hold a slave, in a Territory, provided this Dred Scott decision is correct. I defy any man to make an argument that will justify unfriendly legislation to deprive a slaveholder of his right to hold his slave in a Territory, that will not equally, in all its length, breadth and thickness, furnish an argument for nullifying the Fugitive Slave law. Why, there is not such an Abolitionist in the nation as Douglas, after all. [Loud and enthusiastic applause.]

MR. DOUGLAS' REPLY.

Mr. Lincoln has concluded his remarks by saying that there is not such an Abolitionist as I am in all America. (Laughter.) If he could make the Abolitionists of Illinois believe that, he would not have much show for the Senate. (Great laughter and applause.) Let him make the Abolitionists believe the truth of that statement and his political back is broken. (Renewed laughter.)

His first criticism upon me is the expression of his hope that the war of the Administration will be prosecuted against me and the Democratic party of this State with vigor. He wants that war prosecuted with vigor; I have no doubt of it. His hopes of success, and the hopes of his party depend solely upon it. They have no chance of destroying the Democracy of this State except by the aid of federal patronage. ("That's a fact," "good," and cheers.) He has all the federal office-holders here as his allies, ("That's so,") running separate tickets against the Democracy to divide the party, although the leaders all intend to vote directly the Abolition ticket, and only leave the greenhorns to vote this separate ticket who refuse to go into the Abolition camp. (Laughter and cheers.) There is something really refreshing in the thought that Mr. Lincoln is in favor of prosecuting one war vigorously. (Roars of laughter.) It is the first war I ever knew him to be in favor of prosecuting. (Renewed laughter.) It is the first war that I ever knew him to believe to be just or constitutional. (Laughter and cheers.) When the Mexican war [was] being waged, and the American army was surrounded by the enemy in Mexico, he thought that war was unconstitutional, unnecessary, and unjust. ("That's so," "you've got him," "he voted against it," &c.) He thought it was not commenced on the right spot. (Laughter.)

When I made an incidental allusion of that kind in the joint discussion over at Charleston some weeks ago, Lincoln, in replying, said that I, Douglas, had charged him with voting against supplies for the Mexican war, and then he reared up, full length, and swore that he never voted against the supplies—that it was a slander—and caught hold of Ficklin, who sat on the stand, and said, "Here, Ficklin, tell the people that it is a lie." (Laughter and cheers.) Well, Ficklin, who had served in Congress with him, stood up and told them all that he recollected about it. It was that when George Ashmun, of Massachusetts, brought forward a resolution declaring the war unconstitutional, unnecessary, and unjust, that Lincoln had voted for it. "Yes," said Lincoln, "I did." Thus he confessed that he voted that the war was wrong, that our country was in the wrong, and consequently that the Mexicans were in the right; but charged that I had slandered him by saying that he voted against the supplies. I never charged him with voting against the supplies in my life, because I knew that he was not in Congress when they were voted. (Tremendous shouts of laughter.) The war was commenced on the 13th day of May, 1846, and on that day we appropriated in Congress ten millions of dollars and fifty thousand men to prosecute it. During the same session we voted more men and more money, and at the next session we voted more men and more money, so that by the time Mr. Lincoln entered Congress we had enough men and enough money to carry on the war, and had no occasion to vote any more. (Laughter and cheers.) When he got into the House, being opposed to the war, and not being able to stop the supplies, because they had all gone forward, all he could do was to follow the lead of Corwin, and prove that the war was not begun on the right spot, and that it was unconstitutional, unnecessary, and wrong. Remember, too, that this he did after the war had been begun. It is one thing to be opposed to the declaration of a war, another and very different thing to take sides with the enemy against your own country after the war has been commenced. ("Good," and cheers.) Our army was in Mexico at the time, many battles had been fought; our citizens, who were defending the honor of their country's flag, were surrounded by the daggers, the guns and the poison of the enemy. Then it was that Corwin made his speech in which he declared that the American soldiers ought to be welcomed by the Mexicans with bloody hands and hospitable graves; then it was that Ashmun and Lincoln voted in the House of Representatives that the war was unconstitutional and unjust; and Ashmun's resolution, Corwin's speech, and Lincoln's vote, were sent to Mexico and read at the head of the Mexican army, to prove to them that there was a Mexican party in the Congress of the United States who were doing all in their power to aid them. ("That's the truth," "Lincoln's a traitor," etc.) That a man who takes sides with the common enemy against his own country in time of war should rejoice in a war being made on me now, is very natural. (Immense applause.) And in my opinion, no other kind of a man would rejoice in it. ("That's true," "hurrah for Douglas." and cheers.)

Mr. Lincoln has told you a great deal to-day about his being an old line Clay Whig. ("He never was.") Bear in mind that there are a great many old Clay Whigs down in this region. It is more agreeable, therefore, for him to talk about the old Clay Whig party than it is for him to talk Abolitionism. We did not hear much about the old Clay Whig party up in the Abolition districts. How much of an old line Henry Clay Whig was he? Have you read General Singleton's speech at Jacksonville? (Yes, yes, and cheers.) You know that Gen. Singleton was, for twenty-five years, the confidential friend of Henry Clay in Illinois, and he testified that in 1847, when the Constitutional Convention of this State was in session, the Whig members were invited to a Whig caucus at the house of Mr. Lincoln's brother-in-law, where Mr. Lincoln proposed to throw Henry Clay overboard and take up Gen. Taylor in his place, giving, as his reason, that if the Whigs did not take up Gen. Taylor the Democrats would. (Cheers and laughter.) Singleton testifies that Lincoln, in that speech, urged, as another reason for throwing Henry Clay overboard,

that the Whigs had fought long enough for principle and ought to begin to fight for success. Singleton also testifies that Lincoln's speech did have the effect of cutting Clay's throat, and that he (Singleton) and others withdrew from the caucus in indignation. He further states that when they got to Philadelphia to attend the National Convention of the Whig party, that Lincoln was there, the bitter and deadly enemy of Clay, and that he tried to keep him (Singleton) out of the Convention because he insisted on voting for Clay, and Lincoln was determined to have Taylor. (Laughter and applause.) Singleton says that Lincoln rejoiced with very great joy when he found the mangled remains of the murdered Whig statesman lying cold before him. Now, Mr. Lincoln tells you that he is an old line Clay Whig! (Laughter and cheers.) Gen. Singleton testifies to the facts I have narrated, in a public speech which has been printed and circulated broadcast over the State for weeks, yet not a lisp have we heard from Mr. Lincoln on the subject, except that he is an old Clay Whig.

What part of Henry Clay's policy did Lincoln ever advocate? He was in Congress in 1848–9, when the Wilmot proviso warfare disturbed the peace and harmony of the country, until it shook the foundation of the Republic from its center to its circumference. It was that agitation that brought Clay forth from his retirement at Ashland again to occupy his seat in the Senate of the United States, to see if he could not, by his great wisdom and experience, and the renown of his name, do something to restore peace and quiet to a disturbed country. Who got up that sectional strife that Clay had to be called upon to quell? I have heard Lincoln boast that he voted forty-two times for the Wilmot proviso, and that he would have voted as many times more if he could. (Laughter.) Lincoln is the man, in connection with Seward, Chase, Giddings, and other Abolitionists, who got up that strife that I helped Clay to put down. (Tremendous applause.) Henry Clay came back to the Senate in 1849, and saw that he must do something to restore peace to the country. The Union Whigs and the Union Democrats welcomed him the moment he arrived, as the man for the occasion. We believed that he, of all men on earth, had been pre-served by Divine Providence to guide us out of our difficulties, and we Democrats rallied under Clay then, as you Whigs in nullification time rallied under the banner of old Jackson, forgetting party when the country was in danger, in order that we might have a country first, and parties afterwards. ("Three cheers for Douglas.")

And this reminds me that Mr. Lincoln told you that the slavery question was the only thing that ever disturbed the peace and harmony of the Union. Did not nullification once raise its head and disturb the peace of this Union in 1832? Was that the slavery question, Mr. Lincoln? Did not disunion raise its monster head during the last war with Great Britain? Was that the slavery question, Mr. Lincoln? The peace of this country has been disturbed three times, once during the war with Great Britain, once on the tariff question, and once on the slavery question. ("Three cheers for Douglas.") His argument, there-fore, that slavery is the only question that has ever created dissension in the Union falls to the ground. It is true that agitators are enabled now to use this slavery question for the purpose of sectional strife. ("That's so.") He admits that in regard to all things else, the principle that I advocate, making each State and Territory free to decide for itself, ought to pre-vail. He instances the cranberry laws, and the oyster laws, and he might have gone through the whole list with the same effect. I say that all these laws are local and domestic, and that local and domestic con-cerns should be left to each State and each Territory to manage for itself. If agitators would acquiesce in that principle, there never would be any danger to the peace and harmony of the Union. ("That's so," and cheers.)

Mr. Lincoln tries to avoid the main issue by attacking the truth of my proposition, that our fathers made this Government divided into free and slave States, recognizing the right of each to decide all its local questions for itself. Did they not thus make it? It is true that they did not establish slavery in any of the States, or abolish it in any of them; but finding thirteen States, twelve of which were slave and one free, they agreed to form a government uniting them together, as they stood divided into free and slave States, and to guaranty forever to each State the right to do as it pleased on the slavery question. (Cheers.) Having thus made the government, and conferred this right upon each State forever, I assert that this Government can exist as they made it, divided into free and slave States, if any one State chooses to retain slavery. (Cheers.) He says that he looks forward to a time when slavery shall be abolished every where. I look forward to a time when each State shall be allowed to do as it pleases. If it chooses to keep slavery forever, it is not my business, but its own; if it chooses to abolish slavery, it is its own busi-ness—not mine. I care more for the great principle of self-government, the right of the people to rule, than I do for all the negroes in Christendom. (Cheers.) I would not endanger the perpetuity of this Union, I would not blot out the great inaliena-ble rights of the white men for all the negroes that ever existed. (Renewed applause.) Hence, I say, let us maintain this Government on the principles that our fathers made it, recognizing the right of each State to keep slavery as long as its people deter-mine, or to abolish it when they please. (Cheers.) But Mr. Lincoln says that when our fathers made this Government they did not look forward to the state of things now existing, and therefore he thinks the doctrine was wrong; and he quotes Brooks, of South Carolina, to prove that our fathers then thought that probably slavery would be abolished by each State acting for itself before this time. Suppose they did; suppose they did not foresee what has occurred,—does that change the princi-ples of our Government? They did not probably foresee the telegraph that transmits intelligence by lightning, nor did they foresee the railroads that now form the bonds of union between the different States, or the thousand mechanical inventions that have elevated mankind. But do these things change the principles of the Government? Our fathers, I say, made this Government on the principle of the right of each State to do as it pleases in its own domestic affairs, subject to the Constitution, and allowed the people of each to apply to every new change of circumstances such remedy as they may see fit to improve their condition. This right they have for all time to come. (Cheers.)

Mr. Lincoln went on to tell you that he does not at all desire to interfere with slavery in the States where it exists, nor does his party. I expected him to say that down here. (Laughter.) Let me ask him then how he expects to put slavery in the course of ultimate extinction every where, if he does not intend to interfere with it in the States where it exists? He says that he will prohibit it in all Territories, and the inference is, then, that unless they make free States out of them he will keep them out of the Union; for, mark you, he did not say whether or not he would vote to admit Kansas with slavery or not, as her people might apply (he forgot that as usual, etc.); he did not say whether or not he was in favor of bringing the Territories now in existence into the Union on the principle of Clay's Compromise measures on the slavery question. I told you that he would not. His idea is that he will prohibit slavery in all the Territories and thus force them all to become free States, surrounding the slave States with a cordon of free States and hemming them in, keeping the slaves confined to their present limits whilst they go on multiplying until the soil on which they live will no longer feed them, and he will thus be able to put slavery in a course of ultimate extinction by starvation. (Cheers.) He will extinguish slavery in the Southern States as the French general exterminated the Algerines when he smoked them out. He is going to extinguish slavery by surrounding the slave States, hemming in the slaves and starving them out of existence, as you smoke a fox out of his hole. He intends to do that in the name of humanity and Christianity, in order that we may get rid of the terrible crime and sin entailed upon our fathers of holding slaves. (Laughter and cheers.) Mr. Lincoln makes out that line of policy, and appeals to the moral sense of justice and to the Christian feeling of the community to sustain him. He says that any man who holds to the contrary doctrine is in the position of the king who claimed to govern by Divine right. Let us examine for a moment and see what principle it was that overthrew the Divine right of George the

Third to govern us. Did not these colonies rebel because the British parliament had no right to pass laws concerning our property and domestic and private institutions without our consent? We demanded that the British Government should not pass such laws unless they gave us representation in the body passing them,—and this the British government insisting on doing,—we went to war, on the principle that the Home Government should not control and govern distant colonies without giving them a representation. Now, Mr. Lincoln proposes to govern the Territories without giving them a representation, and calls on Congress to pass laws controlling their property and domestic concerns without their consent and against their will. Thus, he asserts for his party the identical principle asserted by George III and the Tories of the Revolution. (Cheers.)

I ask you to look into these things, and then tell me whether the Democracy or the Abolitionists are right. I hold that the people of a Territory, like those of a State (I use the language of Mr. Buchanan in his letter of acceptance,) have the right to decide for themselves whether slavery shall or shall not exist within their limits. ("That's the idea," "Hurrah for Douglas.") The point upon which Chief Justice Taney expresses his opinion is simply this, that slaves being property, stand on an equal footing with other property, and consequently that the owner has the same right to carry that property into a Territory that he has any other, subject to the same conditions. Suppose that one of your merchants was to take fifty or one hundred thousand dollars' worth of liquors to Kansas. He has a right to go there under that decision, but when he gets there he finds the Maine liquor law in force, and what can he do with his property after he gets it there? He cannot sell it, he cannot use it, it is subject to the local law, and that law is against him, and the best thing he can do with it is to bring it back into Missouri or Illinois and sell it. If you take negroes to Kansas, as Col. Jeff. Davis said in his Bangor speech, from which I have quoted to-day, you must take them there subject to the local law. If the people want the institution of slavery they will protect and encourage it; but if they do not want it they will withhold that protection, and the absence of local legislation protecting slavery excludes it as completely as a positive prohibition. ("That's so," and cheers.) You slaveholders of Missouri might as well understand what you know practically, that you cannot carry slavery where the people do not want it. ("That's so.") All you have a right to ask is that the people shall do as they please; if they want slavery let them have it; if they do not want it, allow them to refuse to encourage it.

My friends, if, as I have said before, we will only live up to this great fundamental principle, there will be peace between the North and the South. Mr. Lincoln admits that under the Constitution on all domestic questions, except slavery, we ought not to interfere with the people of each State. What right have we to interfere with slavery any more than we have to interfere with any other question? He says that this slavery question is now the bone of contention. Why? Simply because agitators have combined in all the free States to make war upon it. Suppose the agitators in the States should combine in one-half of the Union to make war upon the railroad system of the other half? They would thus be driven to the same sectional strife. Suppose one section makes war upon any other peculiar institution of the opposite section, and the same strife is produced. The only remedy and safety is that we shall stand by the Constitution as our fathers made it, obey the laws as they are passed, while they stand the proper test and sustain the decisions of the Supreme Court and the constituted authorities.

Source: The Lincoln Douglas Debates, Seventh Debate Part I and Part II. Alton, Illinois, October 15, 1858. TeachingAmericanHistory.org © 2006 Ashbrook Center for Public Affairs.

Letters on American Slavery to the Editor of the *London News*
(1860)

Reproduced here are some of a series of letters written to the editor of the London News *in the 1850s. The letter writers include Victor Hugo, Alexis de Tocqueville, Emile de Girardin, M. Carnot, M. Passy, Joseph Mazzini, Baron Alexander von Humboldt, and O. Lafayette. The letters are in response to the American Tract Society's decision not to publish a tract that touched upon slavery. These letters were later published by the American Anti-Slavery Society in 1860.*

VICTOR HUGO ON JOHN BROWN

To The Editor of *The London News:*

Sir: When our thoughts dwell upon the United States of America, a majestic form rises before the eye of imagination. It is a Washington!

Look, then, to what is taking place in that country of Washington at this present moment.

In the Southern States of the Union there are slaves; and this circumstance is regarded with indignation, as the most monstrous of inconsistencies, by the pure and logical conscience of the Northern States. A white man, a free man, John Brown, sought to deliver these negro slaves from bondage. Assuredly, if insurrection is ever a sacred duty, it must be when it is directed against Slavery. John Brown endeavored to commence the work of emancipation by the liberation of slaves in Virginia. Pious, austere, animated with the old Puritan spirit, inspired by the spirit of the Gospel, he sounded to these men, these oppressed brothers, the rallying cry of Freedom. The slaves, enervated by servitude, made no response to the appeal. Slavery afflicts the soul with weakness. Brown, though deserted, still fought at the head of a handful of heroic men; he was riddled with balls; his two young sons, sacred martyrs, fell dead at his side, and he himself was taken. This is what they call the affair at Harper's Ferry.

John Brown has been tried, with four of his comrades, Stephens, Cowpoke, Green and Copeland.

What has been the character of his trial? Let us sum it up in a few words:—

John Brown, upon a wretched pallet, with six half gaping wounds, a gun-shot wound in his arm, another in his loins, and two in his head, scarcely conscious of surrounding sounds, bathing his mattress in blood, and with the ghastly presence of his two dead sons ever beside him; his four fellow-sufferers wounded, dragging themselves along by his side; Stephens bleeding from four sabre wounds; justice in a hurry, and over-leaping all obstacles; an attorney, Hunter, who wishes to proceed hastily, and a judge, Parker, who suffers, him to have his way; the hearing cut short, almost every application for delay refused, forged and mutilated documents produced, the witnesses for the defense kidnapped, every obstacle thrown in the way of the prisoner's counsel, two cannon loaded with canister stationed in the Court, orders given to the jailers to shoot the prisoners if they sought to escape, forty minutes of deliberation, and three men sentenced to die! I declare on my honor that all this took place, not in Turkey, but in America!

Such things cannot be done with impunity in the face of the civilized world. The universal conscience of humanity is an ever-watchful eye. Let the judges of Charlestown, and Hunter and Parker, and the slaveholding jurors, and the whole population of Virginia, ponder it well: they are watched! They are not alone in the world. At this moment, America attracts the eyes of the whole of Europe.

John Brown, condemned to die, was to have been hanged on the 2d of December—this very day. But news has just reached us. A respite has been granted to him. It is not until the 16th that he is to die. The interval is a brief one. Before it has ended, will a cry of mercy have had time to make itself effectually heard?

No matter! It is our duty to speak out.

Perhaps a second respite may be granted. America is a noble nation. The impulse of humanity springs quickly into life among a free people. We may yet hope that Brown will be saved.

If it were otherwise, if Brown should die on the scaffold on the 16th of December, what a terrible calamity! The executioner of Brown, let us avow it openly (for the day of the kings is past, and the day of the peoples dawns, and to the people we are bound frankly to speak the truth)—the executioner of Brown would be neither the attorney Hunter, nor the judge Parker, nor the Governor Wise, nor the State of Virginia; it would be, though we can scarce think or speak of it without a shudder, the whole American Republic.

The more one loves, the more one admires, the more one venerates that Republic, the more heart-sick one feels at the contemplation of such a catastrophe. A single State ought not to have the power to dishonor all the rest, and in this case there is an obvious justification for a federal intervention. Otherwise, by hesitating to interfere when it might prevent a crime, the Union becomes a participator in its guilt. No matter how intense may be the indignation of the generous Northern States, the Southern States force them to share the opprobrium of this murder. All of us, no matter who we may be, who are bound together as compatriots by the common tie of a democratic creed, feel ourselves in some measure compromised. If the scaffold should be erected on the 16th of December, the incorruptible voice of history would thenceforward testify that the august Confederation of the New World, had added to all its rites of holy brotherhood a brotherhood of blood, and the *fasces* of that splendid Republic would be bound together with the running noose that hung from the gibbet of Brown!

This is a bond that kills.

When we reflect on what Brown, the liberator, the champion of Christ, has striven to effect, and when we remember that he is about to die, slaughtered by the American Republic, the crime assumes an importance co-extensive with that of the nation which commits it—and when we say to ourselves that this nation is one of the glories of the human race; that like France, like England, like Germany, she is one of the great agents of civilization; that she sometimes even leaves Europe in the rear by the sublime audacity of some of her progressive movements; that she is the Queen of an entire world, and that her brow is irradiated with a glorious halo of freedom, we declare our conviction that John Brown will not die; for we recoil horror-struck from the idea of so great a crime committed by so great a people.

Viewed in a political light, the murder of Brown would be an irreparable fault. It would penetrate the Union with a gaping fissure which would lead in the end of its entire disruption. It is possible that the execution of Brown might establish slavery on a firm basis in Virginia, but it is certain that it would shake to its centre the entire fabric of American democracy. You preserve your infamy, but you sacrifice your glory. Viewed in a moral light, it seems to me that a portion of the enlightenment of humanity would be eclipsed, that even the ideas of justice and injustice would be obscured on the day which should witness the assassination of Emancipation by Liberty.

As for myself, though I am but a mere atom, yet being, as I am, in common with all other men, inspired with the conscience of humanity, I fall on my knees, weeping before the great starry banner of the New World; and with clasped hands, and with profound and filial respect, I implore the illustrious American Republic, sister of the French Republic, to see to the safety of the universal moral law, to save John Brown, to demolish the threatening scaffold of the 16th of December, and not to suffer that beneath its eyes, and I add, with a shudder, almost by its fault a crime should be perpetrated surpassing the first fratricide in iniquity.

For—yes, let America know it, and ponder on it well—there is something more terrible than Cain slaying Abel: It is Washington slaying Spartacus!

Victor Hugo.
Hauteville House, Dec. 2d, 1859.

LETTER FROM ALEXIS DE TOCQUEVILLE

I do not think it is for me, a foreigner, to indicate to the United States the time, the measures, or the men by whom Slavery shall be abolished.

Still, as the persevering enemy of despotism everywhere, and under all its forms, I am pained and astonished by the fact that the freest people in the world is, at the present time, almost the only one among civilized and Christian nations which yet maintains personal servitude; and this, while serfdom itself is about disappearing, where it has not already disappeared, from the most degraded nations of Europe.

An old and sincere friend of America, I am uneasy at seeing Slavery retard her progress, tarnish her glory, furnish arms to her detractors, compromise the future career of the Union which is the guaranty of her safety and greatness, and point out beforehand to her, to all her enemies, the spot where they are to strike. As a man too, I am moved at the spectacle of man's degradation by man, and I hope to see the day when the law will grant equal civil liberty to all the inhabitants of the same empire, as God accords the freedom of the will, without distinction, to the dwellers upon earth.

France, 1855.

LETTER FROM EMILE DE GIRARDIN

I seize the occasion now offered me to accuse myself of having too long believed, on the faith of American citizens and French travellers, that the slavery of the blacks neither could nor ought, for their own sakes, to be abolished, without a previous initiation to liberty, by labor, instruction, economy, and redemption—an individual purchase of each one by himself.

But this belief I end by classing among those inveterate errors, which are like the rings of a chain, that even the freest of men drag after them, and even the strongest find it difficult to break.

What I once believed, I believe no longer.

Of all the existing proofs that Liberty is to be conquered or gained, not given, or dealt out by halves, the strongest proof is that, in the United States, the freest of all countries, the maintenance of Slavery is not made a question of time, but of race. Now if the reasons there alleged for the perpetuating and the legalizing of Slavery are true, they will be no less true a thousand years hence than to-day; if they are false, they have no right to impose themselves for a day, for an hour, for a moment. Error has no right against truth; iniquity has no right against equity, for the same reason that the dying have no right against death.

I hold, then, as false—incontestably and absolutely false,—all that blind self-interest and limping common-place are continually repeating, in order to perpetuate and legalize Slavery in the United States; just as I hold as false all that was said and printed before 1789, to perpetuate and legitimate serfdom; and all that is still said in Russia, in favor of the same outrage of men against the nature of man. The slavery of the blacks is the opprobrium of the whites. Thus every wrong brings its own chastisement.

The punishment of the American people is to be the last of the nations, while it is also the first. It is the first, by that Liberty of which it has rolled back the limits, and it is the last by that Slavery whose inconsistency it tolerates; for there are no slaves without tyrants. What matter whether the tyrant be *regal* or *legal*?

Paris, (Office of La Presse), 1855.

LETTER FROM M. CARNOT

The question of Slavery is intimately connected with questions of general policy.

The Pagan republics had Slavery for their basis. They were so organized that they could not subsist without it; and so when Slavery was shaken down, they perished. Liberty for the few, on condition of keeping the many in servitude—such was the principle of the ancient societies.

Christianity bids another morality triumph,—that of human brotherhood. Modern societies recognize the principle that each citizen increases the domain of his own liberty by sharing it with his fellows. Republican France put this principle in practice; at her two great epochs of emancipation, she hastened to send Liberty to her colonial possessions.

North America presents a sad anomaly—a contradiction to the general rule with which we have prefaced these reflections, and thence the enemies of Liberty try to justify their departure from it.

They pretend to believe that the Republic of the United States rests on a basis analogous to that of the Pagan republics; and that the application of the new morality will be dangerous to it. But it is not so. Liberty in the United States is founded on reason, on custom, on patriotism, and on experience already old. She can but gain by diffusion even to prodigality. In the United States, Slavery is more than elsewhere a monstrosity, protected only by private interests. It is a source of corruption and barbarism which delays America in the path of European civilization. It is a fatal example that she presents to Europe, to turn her from the pursuit of American independence.

Paris, 1855.

LETTER FROM M. PASSY

Humanity is governed by laws which continually impel it to extend, without ceasing, the sphere of its knowledge. There is no discovery which does not conduct it to new discoveries; each generation adds its own to the mass which it has received from the past, and thus from age to age are the strength and riches of civilization augmented.

Now it is one of the numerous proofs of the benevolent purposes of the Creator, that every step of mental progress strengthens the ideas of duty and justice, of which humanity makes application in its acts. Human society, as it gains light, does not merely learn thereby the better to profit by its labors. It gains, at the same time, clearer and surer notions of moral order. It discerns evil where it did not at first suspect its existence; and no sooner does it perceive the evil than it seeks the means to suppress it.

This is what, in our day, has awakened so much opposition to Slavery. Thanks to the flood of light already received, society begins to comprehend, not only its iniquity in principle, but all the degradation and suffering it scatters in the lands where it exists. A cry of reprobation arises, and associations are formed to hasten its abolition.

We may, without fear, assert that it will be with Slavery as with all the other remnants of ignorance and original barbarism. The day will come when it must disappear, with the rest of the institutions which have been found inconsistent with the moral feelings to which the development of human reason gives the mastery.

Let those reflect who, at this day, constitute themselves the defenders of Slavery. They have against them the most irresistible of all powers—that of moral truth becoming more and more distinct—that of human conceptions necessarily rising with the growth in knowledge of the divine will. Their defeat is, sooner or later, inevitable.

How much wiser would they be, did they resign themselves to the preparation for a reform, the necessity for which presents itself with such inflexible urgency. It is, doubtless, a work of difficulty. Freemen require other conditions than those to which they were subjected by the lash; but the requisite changes may be effected. Wise precautions and temporary arrangements, united with the injunctions of authority, will not fail of success. Proprietors who dread emancipation! show to your people a little of that benevolence which so promptly subdues those who are unaccustomed to it, and you will find them docile and industrious as freemen. It is Slavery which corrupts and deteriorates the faculties which God has given to all for the amelioration of their destinies and the enjoyment of existence. Liberty, on the contrary, animates and develops them. Human activity rises to extend its conquests, more ingenious and energetic at her reviving breath.

May such assertions as these, conformable as they are to the experience of all ages, no longer meet in America the contradictions which are long extinct in Europe. May those States of the Union where Slavery still counts its partisans, hasten to prepare for its abolition. Storms are gathering over the seat of injustice. Prosperity, gained at the expense of humanity, flows from a source which time will necessarily dry up. There can exist no durable prosperity on earth, but in consistency with the laws of God; and his laws command men to love and serve each other as brethren.

Nice, January 28th, 1855.

LETTER FROM JOSEPH MAZZINI

London, May 1, 1854.

Dear Sir: I have delayed to the present moment my answering your kind invitation, in the hope that I should, perhaps, be enabled to give a better answer than a written one; but I find that neither health nor business will allow me to attend. I must write, and express to you, and through you to your friends, how much I feel grateful for your having asked me to attend the first meeting of the "North of England Anti-Slavery Association;" how earnestly I sympathize with the noble aim you are going to pursue; how deeply I shall commune with your efforts, and help, if I can, their success. No man ought ever to inscribe on his flag the sacred word "Liberty," who is not prepared to shake hands cordially with those, whoever they are, who will attach their names to the constitution of your association. Liberty may be the godlike gift of all races, of all nations, of every being who bears on his brow the stamp of Man, or sink to the level of a narrow and mean self-interest, unworthy of the tears of good and the blood of the brave. I am yours, because I believe in the unity of God; yours, because I believe in the unity of mankind; yours, because I believe in the educatibility of the whole human race, and in a heavenly law of infinite progression for all; yours, because the fulfilment of the law implies the consciousness and the responsibility of the agent, and neither consciousness nor responsibility can exist in slavery; yours, because I have devoted my life to the emancipation of my own country. And I would feel unequal to this task, a mean rebel, not an apostle of truth and justice, had I not felt from my earliest years that the right and duty of revolting against lies and tyranny were grounded on a far higher sphere than that of the welfare of one single nation; that they must start from belief in a principle, which will have sooner or later to be universally applied: "*One God, one humanity, one law, one love from all for all.*" Blessed be your efforts, if they start from this high ground of a common faith; if you do not forget, whilst at work for the emancipation of the black race, the millions of white slaves, suffering, struggling, expiring in Italy, in Poland, in Hungary, throughout all Europe; if you always remember that free men only can achieve the work of freedom, and that Europe's appeal for the abolition of slavery in other lands will not weigh all-powerful before God and men, whilst Europe herself shall be desecrated by arbitrary, tyrannical power, by czars, emperors, and popes.

Every faithfully yours,
Joseph Mazzini

LETTER FROM BARON VON HUMBOLDT

In 1856, Baron von Humboldt caused the following letter to be inserted in the Spenersche Zeitung:—

"Under the title of *Essai Politique sur l'Isle de Cuba*, published in Paris in 1826, I collected together all that the large edition of my *Voyage aux Regions Equinoxiales du Nouveau Continent* contained upon the state of agriculture and slavery in the Antilles. There appeared at the same time an English and a Spanish translation of this work, the latter entitled *Ensayo Politico sobre la Isle de Cuba*, neither of which omitted any of the frank and open remarks which feelings of humanity had inspired. But there appears just now, strangely enough, translated from the Spanish translation, and not from the French original, and published by Derby and Jackson, in New York, an octavo volume of 400 pages, under the title of *The Island of Cuba*, by Alexander Humboldt; with notes and a preliminary essay by J. S. Thrasher. The translator, who has lived a long time on that beautiful island, has enriched my work by more recent *data*

on the subject of the numerical standing of the population, of the cultivation of the soil, and the state of trade, and, generally speaking, exhibited a charitable moderation in his discussion of conflicting opinions. I owe it, however, to a moral feeling, that is now as lively in me as it was in 1826, publicly to complain that in a work which bears my name, the entire seventh chapter of the Spanish translation, with which my *essai politique* ended, has been arbitrarily omitted. To this very portion of my work I attach greater importance than to any astronomical observations, experiments of magnetic intensity, or statistical statements. I have examined with frankness (I here repeat the words I used thirty years ago) whatever concerns the organization of human society in the colonies, the unequal distribution of the rights and enjoyments of life, and the impending dangers which the wisdom of legislators and the moderation of freemen can avert, whatever may be the form of government.

"It is the duty of the traveller who has been an eye-witness of all that torments and degrades human nature to cause the complaints of the unfortunate to reach those whose duty it is to relieve them. I have repeated, in this treatise, the fact that the ancient legislation of Spain on the subject of slavery is less inhuman and atrocious than that of the slave States on the American continent, north or south of the equator.

"A steady advocate as I am for the most unfettered expression of opinion in speech or in writing, I should never have thought of complaining if I had been attacked on account of my statements; but I do think I am entitled to demand that in the free States of the continent of America, people should be allowed to read what has been permitted to circulate from the first year of its appearance in a Spanish translation."

LETTER FROM O. LAFAYETTE

Paris, April 26 1851.

To M. Victor Schaelcher, Representative of the People.

My Dear Colleague,—you have been so obliging as to ask for my views and impressions respecting one of the most important events of our epoch,—the Abolition of Slavery in the French Colonies. I know well that you have an almost paternal interest in this question. You have contributed more than any one to the emancipation of the blacks, in our possessions beyond the seas, and you have enjoyed the double pleasure of seeing the problem completely resolved, and resolved by the Government of the Republic. At the present time, wearied by controversy, the mind loves to repose upon certain and solid progress, which future events can neither alter nor destroy, and which are justly considered as the true conquests of civilization and humanity. In examining the Emancipation of the Slaves in the French Antilles, from the point of view of the material interests of France, it may be variously appreciated; but the immense moral benefit of the act of Emancipation cannot be contested.

In one day, and as by the stroke of a wand, one hundred and fifty thousand of human beings were snatched from the degradation in which they had been held by former legislation, and resumed their rank in the great human family. And we should not omit to state, that this great event was accomplished without our witnessing any of those disorders and struggles which had been threatened, in order to perplex the consciences of the Friends of Abolition.

Will the momentary obstruction of material interests be opposed to these great results? When has it ever been possible in this world to do much good, without seeming at the same time to do a little harm?

I have sometime heard it said that the conditions labor in the Colonies would have been less disturbed, if the preparation and the accomplishment of the Emancipation had been left to the colonists themselves; but you know better than I, my dear Colleague, that these assertions are hardly sincere.

We cannot but recollect with what unanimity and what vehemence the colonial councils opposed, in 1844 and 1845, the Ameliorations that we sought to introduce into the condition of the Slaves.

Is it not evident that this disposition would have rendered impossible the time of a system of transition, which indeed was attempted without success in the English colonies? For myself, I am quite convinced that it would have been impossible to effect the emancipation otherwise than as it was effected, that is to say, in one day, and by a single decree. I would add also, that in my opinion the Abolition of Slavery in our colonies would have remained a long time unaccomplished, if France had not been in Revolution: and if it be easy to understand why all men of the white race do not consent to the Revolution of 1848, I cannot conceive that a single man of color can be found, who does not regard it with benedictions.

Furthermore, my dear colleague, this great question of the Abolition of Negro Slavery, which has my entire sympathy, appears to me to have established its importance throughout the world. At the present time, the States of the Peninsula, if I do not deceive myself, are the only European powers who still continue to possess Slaves; and America, while continuing to uphold Slavery, feel daily more and more how heavily this plague weighs upon her destinies.

In expressing to you, my dear colleague, how much I rejoice in these results, I do not gratify my personal feelings alone. I obey also my family traditions.

You know the interest which my grandfather, General LaFayette, took in the emancipation of the negroes. You know what he had begun to do at the Habitation de la Gabrielle, and what he intended to do there. It was not among the least regrets of his life, that he was stopped in that enterprise.

Pardon, my dear colleague, the details into which I have been led. I know well that I can hardly be indiscreet in speaking on this subject to you. I rely upon those sentiments of friendship which you have always testified for me, and which differences of opinion respecting other political questions cannot weaken.

With fresh assurances of my friendship and consideration,

Your obedient servant and devoted Colleague,

O. LAFAYETTE, Representative of the People, (Seine et Maine.)

Testimony Of Gen. LaFayette. 'When I am indulging in my views of American liberty, it is mortifying to be reminded that a large portion of the people in that very country are SLAVES. It is a dark spot on the face of the nation.' 'I never would have drawn my sword in the cause of American, If I could have conceived that thereby I was helping to found A NATION OF SLAVES.'

Source: Letters on American slavery from Victor Hugo, de Tocqueville, Emile de Girardin, Carnot, Passy, Mazzini, Humboldt, and O. Lafayette. Boston: American Anti-slavery Society, 1860. Library of Congress, Rare Book and Special Collections Division, Daniel A. P. Murray Pamphlets Collection.

Frederick Douglass, "The Constitution of the United States: Is It Pro-Slavery or Anti-Slavery?" (March 26, 1860)

This excerpt is from a speech given by Frederick Douglass in Glasgow, Scotland, on the issue of slavery. Douglass addressed whether or not the Constitution of the United States was pro- or antislavery. He delivered this speech in the winter of 1860, five years before the Civil War ended the debate.

I proceed to the discussion. And first a word about the question. Much will be gained at the outset if we fully and clearly understand the real question. . . . Indeed, nothing is or can be understood. This are often confounded and treated as the same, for no better reason than that they resemble each other, even while they are in their nature and character totally distinct and even directly opposed to each other. This jumbling up of things is a sort of dust-throwing which is often indulged in by small men who argue for victory rather than for truth.

Signed: Frederick Douglass

THE GLASGOW SPEECH

The American Government and the American Constitution are spoken of in a manner which would naturally lead the hearer to believe that one is identical with the other; when the truth is, they are distinct in character as is a ship and a compass. The one may point right and the other steer wrong. A chart is one thing, the course of the vessel is another. The Constitution may be right, the Government is wrong. If the Government has been governed by mean, sordid, and wicked passions, it does not follow that the Constitution is mean, sordid, and wicked.

What, then, is the question? I will state it. It is not whether slavery existed in the United States at the time of the adoption of the Constitution; it is not whether slaveholders took part in the framing of the Constitution; it is not whether those slaveholders, in their hearts, intended to secure certain advantages in that instrument for slavery; it is not whether the American Government has been wielded during seventy-two years in favour of the propagation and permanence of slavery; it is not whether a pro-slavery interpretation has been put upon the Constitution by the American Courts—all these points may be true or they may be false, they may be accepted or they may be rejected, without in any wise affecting the real question in debate.

The real and exact question between myself and the class of persons represented by the speech at the City Hall may be fairly stated thus:

- 1st, Does the United States Constitution guarantee to any class or description of people in that country the right to enslave, or hold as property, any other class or description of people in that country?
- 2nd, Is the dissolution of the union between the slave and free States required by fidelity to the slaves, or by the just demands of conscience? Or, in other words, is the refusal to exercise the elective franchise, and to hold office in America, the surest, wisest, and best way to abolish slavery in America?

To these questions the Garrisonians say Yes. They hold the Constitution to be a slaveholding instrument, and will not cast a vote or hold office, and denounce all who vote or hold office, no matter how faithfully such persons labour to promote the abolition of slavery.

I, on the other hand, deny that the Constitution guarantees the right to hold property in man, and believe that the way to abolish slavery in America is to vote such men into power as well as use their powers for the abolition of slavery. This is the issue plainly stated. . .

[A] very eloquent lecturer at the City Hall doubtless felt some embarrassment from the fact that he had literally to give the Constitution a pro-slavery interpretation; because upon its face it of itself conveys no such meaning, but a very opposite meaning. He thus sums up what he calls the slaveholding provisions of the Constitution. I quote his own words:

"Article 1, section 9, provides for the continuance of the African slave trade for the 20 years, after the adoption of the Constitution.

Art. 4, section 9, provides for the recovery from the other States of fugitive slaves.

Art. 1, section 2, gives the slave States a representation of the three-fifths of all the slave population;

Art. 1, section 8, requires the President to use the military, naval, ordnance, and militia resources of the entire country for the suppression of slave insurrection, in the same manner as he would employ them to repel invasion."

Now any man reading this statement, or hearing it made with such a show of exactness, would unquestionably suppose that the speaker or writer had given the plain written text of the Constitution itself. I can hardly believe that he intended to make any such impression. It would be a scandalous imputation to say he did. Any yet what are we to make of it? How can we regard it? How can he be screened from the charge of having perpetrated a deliberate and point-blank misrepresentation? That individual has seen fit to place himself before the public as my opponent, and yet I would gladly find some excuse for him. I do not wish to think as badly of him as this trick of his would naturally lead me to think. Why did he not read the Constitution? Why did he read that which was not the Constitution? He pretended to be giving chapter and verse, section and clause, paragraph and provision. The words of the Constitution were before him. Why then did he not give you the plain words of the Constitution?

Oh, sir, I fear that the gentleman knows too well why he did not. It so happens that no such words as "African slave trade," no such words as "slave insurrections," are anywhere used in that instrument.

These are the words of that orator, and not the words of the Constitution of the United States. Now you shall see a slight difference between my manner of treating this subject and that which my opponent has seen fit, for reasons satisfactory to himself, to pursue. What he withheld, that I will spread before you: what he suppressed, I will bring to light: and what he passed over in silence, I will proclaim: that you may have the whole case before you, and not be left to depend upon either his, or upon my inferences or testimony. Here then are several provisions of the Constitution to which reference has been made. I read them word for word just as they stand in the paper, called the United States Constitution.

Art. I, sec. 2. "Representatives and direct taxes shall be apportioned among the several States which may be included in this Union, according to their respective numbers, which shall be determined by adding to the whole number of free persons, including those bound to service for a term years, and excluding Indians not taxed, three-fifths of all other persons;

Art. I, sec. 9. The migration or importation of such persons as any of the States now existing shall think fit to admit, shall not be prohibited by the Congress prior to the year one thousand eight hundred and eight, but a tax or duty may be imposed on such importation, not exceeding ten dollars for each person;

Art. 4, sec. 2. No person held to service or labour in one State, under the laws thereof, escaping into another shall, in consequence of any law or regulation therein, be discharged from service or labour; but shall be delivered up on claim of the party to whom such service or labour may be due;

Art. I, sec. 8. To provide for calling for the militia to execute the laws of the Union, suppress insurrections, and repel invasions."

Here then, are those provisions of the Constitution, which the most extravagant defenders of slavery can claim to guarantee a right of property in man. These are the provisions which have been pressed into the service of the human fleshmongers of America.

Let us look at them just as they stand, one by one. Let us grant, for the sake of the argument, that the first of these provisions, referring to the basis of representation and taxation, does refer to slaves. We are not compelled to make that admission, for it might fairly apply to aliens—persons living in the country, but not naturalized. But giving the provisions the very worse construction, what does it amount to? I answer—It is a downright disability laid upon the slaveholding States; one which deprives those States of two-fifths of their natural basis of representation.

A black man in a free State is worth just two-fifths more than a black man in a slave State, as a basis of political power under the Constitution. Therefore, instead of encouraging slavery, the Constitution encourages freedom by giving an increase of "two-fifths" of political power to free over slave States. So much for the three-fifths clause; taking it at its worst, it still leans to freedom, not slavery; for, be it remembered that the Constitution nowhere forbids a coloured man to vote.

. . . Men at that time, both in England and in America, looked upon the (international) slave trade as the life of slavery. The abolition of the slave trade (directly from Africa to the Americas) was supposed to be the certain death of slavery. Cut off the stream, and the pond will dry up, was the common notion at the time.

Wilberforce and Clarkson, clear-sighted as they were, took this view; and the American statesmen, in providing for the abolition of the slave trade, thought they were providing for the abolition of slavery. This view is quite consistent with the history of the times. All regarded slavery as an expiring and doomed system, destined to speedily disappear from the country. But, again, it should be remembered that this very provision, if made to refer to the African slave trade at all, makes the Constitution anti-slavery rather than for slavery; for it says to the slave States, the price you will have to pay for coming into the American Union is, that the slave trade, which you would carry on indefinitely out of the Union, shall be put an end to in twenty years if you come into the Union.

Secondly, if it does apply, it expired by its own limitation more than fifty years ago.

Thirdly, it is anti-slavery, because it looked to the abolition of slavery rather than to its perpetuity.

Fourthly, it showed that the intentions of the framers of the Constitution were good, not bad. I think this is quite enough for this point.

Source: Douglass, Frederick. A Speech Delivered in Glasgow, Scotland. March 26, 1860. Teaching AmericanHistory.org © 2006 Ashbrook Center for Public Affairs.

Frederick Douglass, "Fighting Rebels with Only One Hand," an Editorial in *The North Star*

(September 1861)

In 1861, abolitionist Frederick Douglass wrote "Fighting Rebels with Only One Hand," one of many editorials he wrote in a monthly column, The North Star, *that criticized the United States and its people. In the editorial, Douglass suggested that the government and the American people must somehow "covet the world's ridicule" at the same time the nation was rapidly racing to its own social and political demise. "What are they thinking about, or don't they condescend to think at all?" the abolitionist asked. As always, Douglass was campaigning against the long-standing acceptance and tolerance of slavery.*

Washington, the seat of Government, after ten thousand assurances to the contrary, is now positively in danger of falling before the rebel army. Maryland, a little while ago considered safe for the Union, is now admitted to be studded with the materials for insurrection, and which may flame forth at any moment.—Every resource of the nation, whether of men or money, whether of wisdom or strength, could be well employed to avert the impending ruin. Yet most evidently the demands of the hour are not comprehended by the Cabinet or the crowd. Our Presidents, Governors, Generals and Secretaries are calling, with almost frantic vehemance, for men.—"Men! men! send us men!" they scream, or the cause of the Union is gone, the life of a great nation is ruthlessly sacrificed, and the hopes of a great nation go out in darkness; and yet these very officers, representing the people and Government, steadily and persistently refuse to receive the very class of men which have a deeper interest in the defeat and humiliation of the rebels, than all others.—Men are wanted in Missouri— wanted in Western Virginia, to hold and defend what has been already gained; they are wanted in Texas, and all along the sea coast, and though the Government has at its command a class in the country deeply interested in suppressing the insurrection, it sternly refuses to summon from among the vast multitude a single man, and degrades and insults the whole class by refusing to allow any of their number to defend with their strong arms and brave hearts the national cause. What a spectacle of blind, unreasoning prejudice and pusillanimity is this! The national edifice is on fire. Every man who can carry a bucket of water, or remove a brick, is wanted; but those who have the care of the building, having a profound respect for the feeling of the national burglars who set the building on fire, are determined that the flames shall only be extinguished by Indo-Caucasian hands, and to have the building burnt rather than save it by means of any other. Such is the pride, the stupid prejudice and folly that rules the hour.

Why does the Government reject the Negro? Is he not a man? Can he not wield a sword, fire a gun, march and countermarch, and obey orders like any other? Is there the least reason to believe that a regiment of well-drilled Negroes would deport themselves less soldier-like on the battlefield than the raw troops gathered up generally from the towns and cities of the State of New York? We do believe that such soldiers, if allowed to take up arms in defense of the Government, and made to feel that they are hereafter to be recognized as persons having rights, would set the highest example of order and general good behavior to their fellow soldiers, and in every way add to the national power.

If persons so humble as we can be allowed to speak to the President of the United States, we should ask him if this dark and terrible hour of the nation's extremity is a time for consulting a mere vulgar and unnatural prejudice? We should ask him if national preservation and necessity were not better guides in this emergency than either the tastes of the rebels, or the pride and prejudices of the vulgar? We would tell him that General Jackson in a slave state fought side by side with Negroes at New Orleans, and like a true man, despising meanness, he bore testimony to their bravery at the close of the war. We would tell him that colored men in Rhode Island and Connecticut performed their full share in the war of the Revolution, and that men of the same color, such as the noble Shields Green, Nathaniel Turner and Denmark Vesey stand ready to peril everything at the command of the Government. We would tell him that this is no time

to fight with one hand, when both are needed; that this is no time to fight only with your white hand, and allow your black hand to remain tied.

Whatever may be the folly and absurdity of the North, the South at least is true and wise. The Southern papers no longer indulge in the vulgar expression, "free n——rs." That class of bipeds are now called "colored residents." The Charleston papers say:

"The colored residents of this city can challenge comparison with their class, in any city or town, in loyalty or devotion to the cause of the South. Many of them individually, and without ostentation, have been contributing liberally, and on Wednesday evening, the 7th inst., a very large meeting was held by them, and a committee appointed to provide for more efficient aid. The proceedings of the meeting will appear in results hereinafter to be reported."

It is now pretty well established, that there are at the present moment many colored men in the Confederate army doing duty not only as cooks, servants and laborers, but as real soldiers, having muskets on their shoulders, and bullets in their pockets, ready to shoot down loyal troops, and do all that soldiers may to destroy the Federal Government and build up that of the traitors and rebels. There were such soldiers at Manassas, and they are probably there still. There is a Negro in the army as well as in the fence, and our Government is likely to find it out before the war comes to an end. That the Negroes are numerous in the rebel army, and do for that army its heaviest work, is beyond question. They have been the chief laborers upon those temporary defenses in which the rebels have been able to mow down our men. Negroes helped to build the batteries at Charleston. They relieve their gentlemanly and military masters from the stiffening drudgery of the camp, and devote them to the nimble and dexterous use of arms. Rising above vulgar prejudice, the slaveholding rebel accepts the aid of the black man as readily as that of any other. If a bad cause can do this, why should a good cause be less wisely conducted? We insist upon it, that one black regiment in such a war as this is, without being any more brave and orderly, would be worth to the Government more than two of any other; and that, while the Government continues to refuse the aid of colored men, thus alienating them from the national cause, and giving the rebels the advantage of them, it will not deserve better fortunes than it has thus far experienced.—Men in earnest don't fight with one hand, when they might fight with two, and a man drowning would not refuse to be saved even by a colored hand.

Source: Foner, Philip S. *The Life and Writings of Frederick Douglass.* Vol. III, 152. New York: International Publishers Co. Inc., 1950. Permission of International Publishers/ New York.

Excerpt from *The Gullah Proverbs of 1861*

The Gullah are African Americans whose distinct language and culture were developed in the Low Country regions of North Carolina, South Carolina, Georgia, and parts of Florida. These regions include the coastal plain and the Sea Islands off the coasts of these states. Historically, the Gullah region once extended north to the Cape Fear area on the coast of North Carolina and south to the vicinity of Jacksonville on the coast of Florida. By 2007, however, the Gullah area was confined to the South Carolina (Port Royal and Hilton Head regions) and Georgia Low Country. The Gullah people are also called Geechee, especially in Georgia.

When the U.S. Civil War began, the Union rushed to blockade Confederate shipping. White planters on the Sea Islands, fearing an invasion by U.S. naval forces, abandoned their plantations and fled to the mainland. When Union forces arrived on the Sea Islands in 1861, they found the Gullah people eager for their freedom, and eager as well to defend it. Many Gullahs served with distinction in the Union Army's First South Carolina Volunteers. The Sea Islands were the first place in the South where slaves were freed, including such places as Port Royal and Hilton Head. Before the war ended, Quaker missionaries from Pennsylvania came down to start schools for the newly freed slaves. Penn Center, now a Gullah community organization on Saint Helena Island, South Carolina, began as the very first school for freed slaves.

The Gullah are known for preserving more of their African linguistic and cultural heritage than any other black community in the United States. They speak an English-based Creole language containing many African loanwords and significant influences from African languages in grammar and sentence structure. The Gullah language is related to Jamaican Creole, Bahamian dialect, and the Krio language of Sierra Leone in West Africa. Gullah storytelling, foodways, music, folk beliefs, crafts, and farming and fishing traditions all exhibit strong influences from African cultures. Reproduced here are a series of Gullah proverbs.

GULLAH PROVERBS

Promisin' talk don' cook rice.

Empty sack can't stand upright alone.

Most kill bird don't make stew. (An almost killed bird doesn't make stew.)

Onpossible to get straight wood from crooked timber. (It's impossible to get straight wood from crooked timber.)

Every frog praise its own pond if it dry.

Most hook fish don't help dry hominy. (An almost hooked fish doesn't improve the taste of dry hominy.)

Chip don't fall far from the block.

One clean sheet can' soil another. (A clean sheet cannot soil another.)

It takes a thief to catch a thief.

Det wan ditch you ain' fuh jump. (Death is one ditch you cannot jump.)

There are more ways to kill a dog than to choke him with butter.

Put yuh bess foot fo moss. (Put your best foot foremost.)

Burn child dread fire. (A burned child dreads fire.)

Eby back is fitted to de bu'den. (Every back is fitted to the burden.)

Er good run bettuh dan uh bad stan. (A good run is better than a bad stand.)

Heart don't mean ever thing mouth say. (The heart doesn't mean everything the mouth says.)

Ef you hol' you mad e would kill eby glad. (If you hold your anger, it will kill all your happiness.)

Source: Joyner, Charles. *Down by the Riverside: A South Carolina Slave Community.* Urbana: University of Illinois Press, 1985.

The Negroes at Port Royal, Report of E. L. Pierce, to the Hon. Salmon P. Chase, U.S. Secretary of the Treasury

(1862)

In 1861, the federal government decided to attack the Confederacy in the Deep South with a Union fleet of about 60 ships and 20,000 men. The fleet sailed from Fortress Monroe at Hampton Roads, Virginia, on October 29, 1861, and arrived off the coast of Beaufort, South Carolina, on November 3. The fleet was under the command of Admiral S. F. DuPont, and the Expeditionary Corps troops were under the direction of General W. T. Sherman. The attack on Confederate forts Walker (on Hilton Head) and Beauregard (at Bay Point on St. Phillips Island) began on the morning of November 7. By 3 p.m. the Union fleet had fired nearly 3,000 shots at the two forts and the Confederate forces had retreated, leaving the Beaufort area to Union troops.

This battle marked the first step taken by Sea Island blacks down the long road to freedom. For many slaves in the Port Royal area, the fall of Hilton Head was the single greatest event in their lives. The Civil War changed the lives of planters

and slaves on Hilton Head Island. Gradually, a plan was formulated for the education, welfare, and employment of the blacks, combining government and missionary efforts. The Department of the South, headquartered on Hilton Head Island, became a "Department of Experiments," conducting what a modern historian has called a "dress rehearsal for Reconstruction," and is often called the "Port Royal Experiment."

Reproduced here are excerpts from a report by Edward Lillie Pierce, a U.S. treasury agent, to Secretary of the Treasury Salmon P. Chase regarding conditions among the newly freed Gullah people in February 1862.

THE NEGROES AT PORT ROYAL:

Dear Sir,

My first communication to you was mailed on the third day after my arrival. The same day, I mailed two letters to benevolent persons in Boston, mentioned in my previous communications to you, asking for contributions of clothing, and for a teacher or missionary to be sent, to be supported by the charity of those interested in the movement, to both of which favorable answers have been received. The same day, I commenced a tour of the largest islands, and ever since have been diligently engaged in anxious examinations of the modes of culture—the amount and proportions of the products—the labor required for them—the life and disposition of the laborers upon them—their estimated numbers—the treatment they have received from their former masters, both as to the labor required of them, the provisions and clothing allowed to them, and the discipline imposed their habits, capacities, and desires, with special reference to their being fitted for useful citizenship—and generally whatever concerned the well-being, present and future, of the territory and its people. Visits have also been made to the communities collected at Hilton Head and Beaufort, and conferences held with the authorities, both naval and military, and other benevolent persons interested in the welfare of these people, and the wise and speedy reorganization of society here. No one can be impressed more than myself with the uncertainty of conclusions drawn from experiences and reflections gathered in so brief a period, however industriously and wisely occupied.

Nevertheless, they may be of some service to those who have not been privileged with an equal opportunity. Of the plantations visited, full notes have been taken of seventeen, with reference to number of negroes in all; of field hands; amount of cotton and corn raised, and how much per acre; time and mode of producing and distributing manure; listing, planting, cultivating, picking and ginning cotton; labor required of each hand; allowance of food and clothing; the capacities of the laborers; their wishes and feelings, both as to themselves and their masters. Many of the above points could be determined by other sources, such as persons at the North familiar with the region, and publications. The inquiries were, however, made with the double purpose of acquiring the information and testing the capacity of the persons inquired of. Some of the leading results of the examination will now be submitted. An estimate of the number of plantations open to cultivation, and of the persons upon the territory protected by the forces of the United States, if only approximate to the truth, may prove convenient in providing a proper system of administration. The following islands are thus protected, . . . about two hundred in all. . . . The populous island of North Edisto, lying in the direction of Charleston is still visited by the rebels.

REPORT OF THE GOVERNMENT AGENT

A part near Botany Bay Island is commanded by the guns of one of our war vessels, under which a colony of one thousand negroes sought protection, where they have been temporarily subsisted from its stores. The number has within a few days been stated to have increased to 2,300.

Among these, great destitution is said to prevail. Even to this number, as the negroes acquire confidence in us, large additions are likely every week to be made. The whole island can be safely farmed as soon as troops can be spared for the purpose of occupation. But not counting the plantations of this island, the number on Port Royal, Ladies', St. Helena, Hilton Head, and the smaller islands, may be estimated at 200 plantations. In visiting the plantations, I endeavored to ascertain with substantial accuracy the number of persons upon them, without, however, expecting to determine the precise number.

On that of Thomas Aston Coffin, at Coffin Point, St. Helena, there were 260, the largest found on any one visited. There were 130 on that of Dr. J. W. Jenkins, 120 on that of the Eustis estate, and the others range from 80 to 38, making an average of 81 to a plantation. These, however, may be ranked among the best peopled plantations, and forty to each may be considered a fair average. From these estimates, a population of 8,000 negroes on the islands, now safely protected by our forces, results. Of the 600 at the camp at Hilton Head, about one-half should be counted with the aforesaid plantations whence they have come. Of the 600 at Beaufort, one-third should also be reckoned with the plantations. The other fraction in each case should be added to the 8,000 in computing the population now thrown on our protection. The negroes on Ladies' and St. Helena Islands have quite generally remained on their respective plantations, or if absent, but temporarily, visiting wives or relatives. The dispersion on Port Royal and Hilton Head Islands has been far greater, the people of the former going to Beaufort in considerable numbers, and of the latter to the camp at Hilton Head.

Counting the negroes who have gone to Hilton Head and Beaufort from places now protected by our forces as still attached to the plantations, and to that extent not swelling the 8,000 on plantations, but adding thereto the usual negro population of Beaufort, as also the negroes who have fled to Beaufort and Hilton Head from places not yet occupied by our forces, and adding also the colony at North Edisto, and we must now have thrown upon our hands, for whose present and future we must provide, from 10,000 to 12,000 persons—probably nearer the latter than the former number. This number is rapidly increasing. This week, forty-eight escaped from a single plantation near Grahamville, on the main land, held by the rebels, led by the driver, and after four days of trial and peril, hidden by day and threading the waters with their boats by night, evading the rebel pickets, joyfully entered our camp at Hilton Head. The accessions at Edisto are in larger number, and according to the most reasonable estimates, it would only require small advances by our troops, not involving a general engagement or even loss of life, to double the number which would be brought within our lines. A fact derived from the Census of 1860 may serve to illustrate the responsibility now devolving on the Government. This County of Beaufort had a population of slaves in proportion of 82 8/10 of the whole, a proportion only exceeded by seven other counties in the United States, viz.:

one in South Carolina, that of Georgetown; three in Mississippi, those of Bolivar, Washington and Issequena; and three in Louisiana, those of Madison, Tensas and Concordia.

An impression prevails that the negroes here have been less cared for than in most other rebel districts. If this be so, and a beneficent reform shall be achieved here, the experiment may anywhere else be hopefully attempted. The former white population, so far as can be ascertained, are rebels, with one or two exceptions. In January, 1861, a meeting of the planters on St. Helena Island was held, of which Thomas Aston Coffin was chairman.

A vote was passed, stating its exposed condition, and offering their slaves to the Governor of South Carolina, to aid in building earth mounds, and calling on him for guns to place upon them. A copy of the vote, probably in his own handwriting, and signed by Mr. Coffin, was found in his house. It is worthy of note that the negroes now within our lines are there by the invitation of no one; but they were on the soil when our army began its occupation, and could not have been excluded, except by violent transportation. A small proportion have come in from the main land, evading the pickets of the enemy and our own,—something easily done in an extensive country, with whose woods and creeks they are familiar. The only exportable crop of this region is the long staple Sea Island cotton, raised with more difficulty than the coarser kind, and bringing a higher price. The agents of the Treasury Department expect to gather some 2,500,000 pounds of ginned cotton the present year, nearly all of which had been picked and stored before the arrival of our forces. Considerable quantities have not been picked at all, but the crop for this season was unusually good. Potatoes and corn are raised only for consumption on the plantations,—corn being raised at the rate of only twenty-five bushels per acre. Such features in plantation life as will throw light on the social questions now anxiously weighed deserve notice.

In this region, the master, if a man of wealth, is more likely to have his main residence at Beaufort, sometimes having none on the plantation, but having one for the driver, who is always a negro. He may, however, have one, and an expensive one, too, as in the case of Dr. Jenkins, at St. Helena, and yet pass most of his time at Beaufort, or at the North. The plantation in such cases is left almost wholly under the charge of an overseer. In some cases, there is not even a house for an overseer, the plantation being superintended by the driver, and being visited by the overseer living on another plantation belonging to the same owner.

The houses for the overseers are of an undesirable character. Orchards of orange or fig trees are usually planted near them. The field hands are generally quartered at some distance eighty or one hundred rods from the overseer's or master's house, and are ranged in a row, sometimes in two rows, fronting each other. They are sixteen feet by twelve, each appropriated to a family, and in some cases divided with a partition. They numbered, on the plantations visited, from ten to twenty, and on the Coffin plantation, they are double, numbering twenty-three double houses, intended for forty-six families. The yards seemed to swarm with children, the negroes coupling at an early age.

Except on Sundays, these people do not take their meals at a family table, but each one takes his hominy, bread, or potatoes, sitting on the floor or a bench, and at his own time. They say their masters never allowed them any regular time for meals. Whoever, under our new system, is charged with their superintendence, should see that they attend more to the cleanliness of their persons and houses, and that, as in families of white people, they take their meals together at a table—habits to which they will be more disposed when they are provided with another change of clothing, and when better food is furnished and a proper hour assigned for meals. Upon each plantation visited by me, familiar conversations were had with several laborers, more or less, as time permitted—sometimes inquiries made of them, as they collected in groups, as to what they desired us to do with and for them, with advice as to the course of sobriety and industry which it was for their interest to pursue under

the new and strange circumstances in which they were now placed. Inquiries as to plantation economy, the culture of crops, the implements still remaining, the number of persons in all, and of field hands, and the rations issued, were made of the drivers, as they are called, answering as nearly as the two different systems of labor will permit to foremen on farms in the free States. There is one on each plantation—on the largest one visited, two. They still remained on each visited, and their names were noted. The business of the driver was to superintend the field-hands generally, and see that their tasks were performed fully and properly. He controlled them, subject to the master or overseer. He dealt out the rations.

Another office belonged to him. He was required by the master or overseer, whenever he saw fit, to inflict corporal punishment upon the laborers; nor was he relieved from this office when the subject of discipline was his wife or children. In the absence of the master or overseer, he succeeded to much of their authority. As indicating his position of consequence, he was privileged with four suits of clothing a year, while only two were allowed to the laborers under him. It is evident, from some of the duties assigned to him, that he must have been a person of considerable judgment and knowledge of plantation economy, not differing essentially from that required of the foreman of a farm in the free States. He may be presumed to have known, in many cases, quite as much about the matters with which he was charged as the owner of the plantation, who often passed but a fractional part of his time upon it. The driver, notwithstanding the dispersion of other laborers, quite generally remains on the plantation, as already stated. He still holds the keys of the granary, dealing out the rations of food, and with the same sense of responsibility as before. In one case, I found him in a controversy with a laborer to whom he was refusing his peck of corn, because of absence with his wife on another plantation when the corn was gathered,—it being gathered since the arrival of our army. The laborer protested warmly that he had helped to plant and hoe the corn, and was only absent as charged because of sickness. The driver appealed to me, as the only white man near, and learning from other laborers that the laborer was sick at the time of gathering, I advised the driver to give him his peck of corn, which he did accordingly. The fact is noted as indicating the present relation of the driver to the plantation, where he still retains something of his former authority. This authority is, however, very essentially diminished. The main reason is, as he will assure you, that he has now no white man to back him. Other reasons may, however, concur.

A class of laborers are generally disposed to be jealous of one of their own number promoted to be over them, and accordingly some negroes, evidently moved by this feeling, will tell you that the drivers ought now to work as field hands, and some field hands be drivers in their place. The driver has also been required to report delinquencies to the master or overseer, and upon their order to inflict corporal punishment. The laborers will, in some cases, say that he has been harder than he need to have been, while he will say that he did only what he was forced to do. The complainants who have suffered under the lash may be pardoned for not being sufficiently charitable to him who has unwillingly inflicted it, while, on the other hand, he has been placed in a dangerous position, where a hard nature, or self-interest, or dislike for the victim, might have tempted him to be more cruel than his position required. The truth, in proportions impossible for us in many cases to fix, may lie with both parties. I am, on the whole, inclined to believe that the past position of the driver and his valuable knowledge, both of the plantations and the laborers, when properly advised and controlled, may be made available in securing the productiveness of the plantations and the good of the laborers. It should be added that, in all cases, the drivers were found very ready to answer inquiries and communicate all information, and seemed desirous that the work of the season should be commenced.

There are also on the plantations other laborers, more intelligent than the average, such as the carpenter, the plowman, the religious leader, who may be called a preacher, a watchman or a helper,—the two latter being recognized officers in the churches of these people, and the helpers being aids to the watchman. These persons, having recognized positions among their fellows, either by virtue of superior knowledge or devotion, when properly approached by us, may be expected to have a beneficial influence on the more ignorant, and help to create that public opinion in favor of good conduct which, among the humblest as among the highest, is most useful. I saw many of very low intellectual development, but hardly any too low to be reached by civilizing influences, either coming directly from us or immediately through their brethren. And while I saw some who were sadly degraded, I met also others who were as fine specimens of human nature as one can ever expect to find. Beside attendance on churches on Sundays, there are evening prayer-meetings on the plantations as often as once or twice a week, occupied with praying, singing, and exhortations. In some cases, the leader can read a hymn, having picked up his knowledge clandestinely, either from other negroes or from white children.

Of the adults, about one-half, at least, are members of churches, generally the Baptist, although other denominations have communicants among them. In the Baptist Church on St. Helena Island, which I visited on the 22d January, there were a few pews for the proportionally small number of white attendants, and the much larger space devoted to benches for colored people. On one plantation there is a negro chapel, well adapted for the purpose, built by the proprietor, the late Mrs. Eustis, whose memory is cherished by the negroes and some of whose sons are now loyal citizens of Massachusetts. I have heard among the Negroes scarcely any profane swearing—not more than twice—a striking contrast with my experience among soldiers in the army. It seemed a part of my duty to attend some of their religious meetings, and learn further about these people what could be derived from such a source. Their exhortations to personal piety were fervent, and, though their language was many times confused, at least to my ear, occasionally an important instruction or a felicitous expression could be recognized. In one case, a preacher of their own, commenting on the text, " Blessed are the meek," exhorted his brethren not to be "stout-minded."

On one plantation on Ladies' Island, where some thirty negroes were gathered in the evening, I read passages of Scripture, and pressed on them their practical duties at the present time with reference to the good of themselves, their children, and their people. The passages read were the 1st and 23d Psalms; the 61st chapter of Isaiah, verses 1–4; the Beatitudes in the 5th chapter of Matthew; the 14th chapter of John's Gospel, and the fifth chapter of the Epistle of James. In substance, I told them that their masters had rebelled against the Government, and we had come to put down the rebellion; that we had now met them, and wanted to see what was best to do for them; that Mr. Lincoln, the President or Great Man at Washington, had the whole matter in charge, and was thinking what he could do for them; that the great trouble about doing anything for them was that their masters had always told us, and had made many people believe, that they were lazy, and would not work unless whipped to it; that Mr. Lincoln had sent us down here to see if it was so; that what they did was reported to him, or to men who would tell him; that where I came from all were free, both white and black; that we did not sell children or separate man and wife, but all had to work; that if they were to be free, they would have to work, and would be shut up or deprived of privileges if they did not; that this was a critical hour with them, and if they did not behave well now and respect our agents and appear willing to work, Mr. Lincoln would give up trying to do anything for them, and they must give up all hope for anything better, and their children and grand-children a hundred years hence would be worse off than they had been. I told them they must stick to their plantations and not run about and get scattered, and assured them that what their masters had told them of our intentions to carry them off to Cuba and sell them was a lie, and their masters knew it to be so, and we wanted them to stay on the plantations and raise cotton, and if they behaved well, they should have wages—small,

perhaps, at first; that they should have better food, and not have their wives and children sold off; that their children should be taught to read and write, for which they might be willing to pay something; that by-and-by they would be as well off as the white people, and we would stand by them against their masters ever coming back to take them.

The importance of exerting a good influence on each other, particularly on the younger men, who were rather careless and roving, was urged, as all would suffer in good repute from the bad deeds of a few. At Hilton Head, where I spoke to a meeting of two hundred, and there were facts calling for the counsel, the women were urged to keep away from the bad white men, who would ruin them. Remarks of a like character were made familiarly on the plantations to such groups as gathered about.

At the Hilton Head meeting, a good-looking man, who had escaped from the southern part of Barnwell District, rose and said, with much feeling, that he and many others should do all they could by good conduct to prove what their masters said against them to be false, and to make Mr. Lincoln think better things of them. After the meeting closed, he desired to know if Mr. Lincoln was coming down here to see them, and he wanted me to give Mr. Lincoln his compliments, with his name, assuring the President that he would do all he could for him. The message was a little amusing, but it testified to the earnestness of the simple-hearted man. He had known Dr. Brisbane, who had been compelled some years since to leave the South because of his sympathy for slaves. The name of Mr. Lincoln was used in addressing them, as more likely to impress them than the abstract idea of government. It is important to add that in no case have I attempted to excite them by insurrectionary appeals against their former masters, feeling that such a course might increase the trouble of organizing them into a peaceful and improving system, under a just and healthful temporary discipline; and besides that, it is a dangerous experiment to attempt the improvement of a class of men by appealing to their coarser nature.

The better course toward making them our faithful allies, and therefore the constant enemies of the rebels, seemed to be to place before them the good things to be done for them and their children, and sometimes reading passages of Scripture appropriate to their lot, without, however, note or comment, never heard before by them, or heard only when wrested from their just interpretation; such, for instance, as the last chapter of St. James's Epistle, and the Glad Tidings of Isaiah: "I have come to preach deliverance to the captive." Thus treated and thus educated, they may be hoped to become useful coadjutors, and the unconquerable foes of the fugitive rebels. There are some vices charged upon these people which deserve examination. Notwithstanding their religious professions, in some cases more emotional than practical, the marriage relation, or what answers for it, is not, in many instances, held very sacred by them. The men, it is said, sometimes leave one wife and take another,—something likely to happen in any society where it is permitted or not forbidden by a stern public opinion, and far more likely to happen under laws which do not recognize marriage, and dissolve what answers for it by forced separations, dictated by the mere pecuniary interest of others. The women, it is said, are easily persuaded by white men,—a facility readily accounted for by the power of the master over them, whose solicitation was equivalent to a command, and against which the husband or father was powerless to protect, and increased also by the degraded condition in which they have been placed, where they have been apt to regard what ought to be a disgrace as a compliment, when they were approached by a paramour of superior condition and race. Yet often the dishonor is felt, and the woman, on whose several children her master's features are impressed, and through whose veins his blood flows, has sadly confessed it with an instinctive blush. The grounds of this charge, so far as they may exist, will be removed, as much as in communities of our own race, by a system which shall recognize and enforce the marriage relation among them, protect them against the solicitations of white men as much as law can, still more by putting them in relations were they will be inspired with self-respect

and a consciousness of their rights, and taught by a pure and plainspoken Christianity.

In relation to the veracity of these people, so far as my relations with them have extended, they have appeared, as a class, to intend to tell the truth. Their manner, as much as among white men, bore instinctive evidence of this intention. Their answers to inquiries relative to the management of the plantations have a general concurrence. They make no universal charges of cruelty against their masters. They will say, in some cases, that their own was a very kind one, but another one in that neighborhood was cruel. On St. Helena Island they spoke kindly of "the good William Fripp," as they called him, and of Dr. Clarence Fripp; but they all denounced the cruelty of Alvira Fripp, recounting his inhuman treatment of both men and women.

Another concurrence is worthy of note. On the plantations visited, it appeared from the statements of the laborers themselves, that there were, on an average, about 133 pounds of cotton produced to the acre, and five acres of cotton and corn cultivated to a hand, the culture of potatoes not being noted. An article of the American Agriculturist, published in Turner's Cotton Manual, pp. 132, 133, relative to the culture of Sea Island Cotton, on the plantation of John H. Townsend, states that the land is cultivated in the proportion of 7–12th cotton, 3–12ths corn, and 2–12ths potatoes—in all, less than six acres to a hand—and the average yield of cotton per acre is 135 pounds. I did not take the statistics of the culture of potatoes, but about five acres are planted with them on the smaller plantations, and twenty, or even thirty, on the larger; and the average amount of land to each hand, planted with potatoes, should be added to the five acres of cotton and corn, and thus results not differing substantially are reached in both cases. Thus the standard publications attest the veracity and accuracy of these laborers. Again, there can be no more delicate and responsible position, involving honesty and skill, than that of pilot. For this purpose, these people are every day employed to aid our military and naval operations in navigating these sinuous channels. They were used in the recent reconnoisance in the direction of Savannah; and the success of the affair at Port Royal Ferry depended on the fidelity of a pilot, William, without the aid of whom, or of one like him, it could not have been undertaken. Further information on this point may be obtained of the proper authorities here. These services are not, it is true, in all respects, illustrative of the quality of veracity, but they involve kindred virtues not likely to exist without it. It is proper, however, to state that expressions are sometimes heard from persons who have not considered these people thoughtfully, to the effect that their word is not to be trusted, and these persons, nevertheless, do trust them, and act upon their statements. There may, however, be some color for such expressions.

These laborers, like all ignorant people, have an ill-regulated reason, too much under the control of the imagination. Therefore, where they report the number of soldiers, or relate facts where there is room for conjecture, they are likely to be extravagant, and you must scrutinize their reports. Still, except among the thoroughly dishonest,—no more numerous among them than in other races—there will be found a colorable basis for their statements, enough to show their honest intention to speak truly. It is true also that you will find them too willing to express feelings which will please you. This is most natural. All races, as well as all animals, have their appropriate means of self-defense, and where the power to use physical force to defend one's self is taken away, the weaker animal, or man, or race, resorts to cunning and duplicity. Whatever habits of this kind may appear in these people are directly traceable to the well-known features of their past condition, without involving any essential proneness to deception in the race, further than may be ascribed to human nature.

Upon this point, special inquiries have been made of the Superintendent at Hilton Head, who is brought in direct daily association with them, and whose testimony, truthful as he is, is worth far more than that of those who have had less nice opportunities of observation, and Mr. Lee certifies to the results here presented. Upon the question of

the disposition of these people to work, there are different reports, varied somewhat by the impression an idle or an industrious laborer, brought into immediate relation with the witness, may have made on the mind. In conversations with them, they uniformly answered to assurances that if free they must work, "Yes, massa, we must work to live; that's the law"; and expressing an anxiety that the work of the plantations was not going on. At Hilton Head, they are ready to do for Mr. Lee, the judicious Superintendent, whatever is desired. Hard words and epithets are, however, of no use in managing them, and other parties for whose service they are specially detailed, who do not understand or treat them properly, find some trouble in making their labor available, as might naturally be expected. In collecting cotton, it is sometimes, as I am told, difficult to get them together, when wanted for work. There may be something in this, particularly among the young men. I have observed them a good deal; and though they often do not work to much advantage, a dozen doing sometimes what one or two stout and well-trained Northern laborers would do, and though less must always he expected of persons native to this soil than those bred in Northern latitudes, and under more bracing air, I have not been at all impressed with their general indolence.

As servants, oarsmen, and carpenters, I have seen them working faithfully and with a will. There are some peculiar circumstances in their condition, which no one who assumes to sit in judgment upon them must overlook. They are now, for the first time, freed from the restraint of a master, and like children whose guardian or teacher is absent for the day, they may quite naturally enjoy an interval of idleness. No system of labor for them, outside of the camps, has been begun, and they have had nothing to do except to bale the cotton when bagging was furnished, and we all know that men partially employed are, if anything, less disposed to do the little assigned them than they are to perform the full measure which belongs to them in regular life, the virtue of the latter case being supported by habit. At the camps, they are away from their accustomed places of labor, and have not been so promptly paid as could be desired, and are exposed to the same circumstances which often dispose soldiers to make as little exertion as possible. In the general chaos which prevails, and before the inspirations of labor have been set before them by proper superintendents and teachers who understand their disposition, and show by their conduct an interest in their welfare, no humane or reasonable man would subject them to austere criticism, or make the race responsible for the delinquencies of an idle person, who happened to be brought particularly under his own observation. Not thus would we have ourselves or our own race judged; and the judgment which we would not have meted to us, let us not measure to others. Upon the best examination of these people, and a comparison of the evidence of trustworthy persons, I believe that when properly organized, and with proper motives set before them, they will, as freemen, be as industrious as any race of men are likely to be in this climate. The notions of the sacredness of property as held by these people have sometimes been the subject of discussion here. It is reported they have taken things left in their masters' houses. It was wise to prevent this, and even where it had been done to compel a restoration, at least of expensive articles, lest they should be injured by speedily acquiring, without purchase, articles above their condition. But a moment's reflection will show that it was the most natural thing for them to do. They had been occupants of the estates; had had these things more or less in charge, and when the former owners had left, it was easy for them to regard their title to the abandoned property as better than that of strangers.

Still, it is not true that they have, except as to very simple articles, as soap or dishes, generally availed themselves of such property. It is also stated that in camps where they have been destitute of clothing, they have stolen from each other, but the Superintendents are of opinion that they would not have done this if already well provided. Besides, those familiar with large bodies collected together, like soldiers in camp life, also know how often these charges of mutual pilfering are made among them, often with great injustice. It should be added, to complete the statement, that the agents who have been intrusted with the collection of cotton have reposed confidence in the trustworthiness of the laborers, committing property to their charge—a confidence not found to have been misplaced. To what extent these laborers desire to be free, and to serve us still further in putting down the rebellion, has been a subject of examination The desire to be free has been strongly expressed, particularly among the more intelligent and adventurous. Every day, almost, adds a fresh tale of escapes, both solitary and in numbers, conducted with a courage, a forecast, and a skill, worthy of heroes. But there are other apparent features in their disposition which it would be untruthful to conceal. On the plantations, I often found a disposition to evade the inquiry whether they wished to be free or slaves; and though a preference for freedom was expressed, it was rarely in the passionate phrases which would come from an Italian peasant. The secluded and monotonous life of a plantation, with strict discipline and ignorance enforced by law and custom, is not favorable to the development of the richer sentiments, though even there they find at least a stunted growth, irrepressible as they are. The inquiry was often answered in this way: "The white man do what he pleases with us; we are yours now, massa."

Source: The Negroes at Port Royal. Report of E. L. Pierce, Government Agent, to the Hon. Salmon P. Chase, Secretary of the Treasury. Boston: R. F. Wallcut, 1862.

Emancipation Proclamation
(1863)

President Abraham Lincoln issued the Emancipation Proclamation on January 1, 1863, as the nation approached its third year of bloody civil war. The proclamation declared "that all persons held as slaves" within the rebellious states "are, and henceforward shall be free." Despite this expansive wording, the Emancipation Proclamation was limited in many ways. It applied only to states that had seceded from the Union, leaving slavery untouched in the loyal border states, such as Kentucky and Missouri. It also expressly exempted parts of the Confederacy that had already come under the North's control. Most important, the freedom it promised depended on Union military victory.

Although the Emancipation Proclamation did not immediately free a single slave, it fundamentally transformed the character of the war. After January 1, 1863, every advance of federal troops expanded the domain of freedom. Moreover, the proclamation announced the acceptance of black men into the Union Army and Navy, enabling the liberated to become liberators. By the end of the war, almost 200,000 black soldiers and sailors had fought for the Union and freedom.

Whereas on the 22d day of September in the year of our Lord 1862 a Proclamation was issued by the President of the United States containing among other things the following to wit:

That on the first day of January in the year of our Lord 1863 all persons held as slaves within any State, or designated parts of States, the people whereof shall then be in rebellion against the United States, shall be then thenceforth and forever free, and the Executive Government of the United States, including the military and naval authority thereof, will recognize and maintain the freedom of such persons, and will do no act or acts to repress such persons, or any of them in any effort they may make for their actual freedom.

That the Executive will on the first day of January, aforesaid by proclamation, designate the States and parts of States, if any in which the people therein respectively shall then be in rebellion against the United States, and the fact that any State or the people thereof shall on that day be in good faith represented in Congress of the United States by members, chosen thereto at elections wherein a majority of the qualified voters of such State shall have participated, shall in the absence of strong countervailing testimony be deemed conclusive evidence, that such State and the people thereof are not then in rebellion against the United States.

Now Therefore, I ABRAHAM LINCOLN, President of the United States, by virtue of the power in me invested as commander in chief of the army and navy in time of actual armed rebellion against the authority and government of the *United States*, and as a fit and necessary war measure for suppressing said rebellion, do on this first day of January, in the year of our Lord one thousand eight hundred and sixty three, and in accordance with my purpose so to do publicly proclaimed for the full period of one hundred days from the day of the first above mentioned order, and designate as the States and parts of States, wherein the people thereof respectively are this day in rebellion against the *United States* the following to wit, Arkansas, Texas, Louisiana, except the parishes of St. Bernard, Plaquemines, Jefferson, St. John, St. Charles, St. James, Ascension, Assumption, Terre Bonne, Lafourche, St. Mary, St. Martin and Orleans including the City of New Orleans, Mississippi, Alabama, Florida, Georgia, South Carolina, North Carolina, and Virginia, as West Virginia and also the counties of Berkeley, Accomac, Northampton, Elizabeth City, York,

Princess, Ann and Norfolk, including the cities of Norfolk and Portsmouth, and which excepted parts are for the present left precisely as if this proclamation were not issued. And by virtue of the power, and for the purpose afore said, I do order and declare, that all persons held as slaves, within said designated States and parts of States, are and henceforward shall be free, and that the executive Government of the *United States*, including the military and naval authorities thereof, will recognize and maintain the freedom of said persons. And I hereby enjoin upon the people so declared to be free, to abstain from all violence unless in necessary self-defense, and I recommend to them that in all cases when allowed, they labor faithfully for reasonable wages. And I further declare and make known, that such persons of suitable condition will be received into the armed service of the *United States* to garrison forts, positions, stations, and other places, and to man vessels of all sorts in said service. And upon this sincerely believed to be an act of justice warranted by the *Constitution* upon military necessity. I invoke the considerate judgment of mankind, and the gracious favor of *Almighty God*.

In Witness whereof, I have hereunto set my hand, and caused the Seal of the United States to be affixed. Done at the City of Washington, this first day of January in the year of our Lord, one thousand eight hundred and sixty three, and of the independence of the *United States* of America the eighty-seventh.

By President Abraham Lincoln
William H. Seward, Secretary of State

Source: The Emancipation Proclamation, 1863. U.S. National Archives & Records Administration.

Frederick Douglass, "What the Black Man Wants" (April 1865)

In the spring of 1865, just days before the conclusion of the Civil War, abolitionist Frederick Douglass attended the annual meeting of the Massachusetts Anti-Slavery Society in Boston. In the following excerpts from the speech he delivered at the meeting, Douglass argues for suffrage and equality for blacks, for the opportunity for freed blacks to succeed or fail on their own.

I have felt, since I have lived out West [of Boston, in Rochester, NY], that in going there I parted from a great deal that was valuable; and I feel, every time I come to these meetings, that I have lost a great deal by making my home west of Boston, west of Massachusetts; for, if anywhere in the country there is to be found the highest sense of justice, or the truest demands for my race, I look for it in the East, I look for it here. The ablest discussions of the whole question of our rights occur here, and to be deprived of the privilege of listening to those discussions is a great deprivation.

I do not know, from what has been said, that there is any difference of opinion as to the duty of abolitionists, at the present moment. How can we get up any difference at this point, or any point, where we are so united, so agreed? I went especially, however, with that word of Mr. Phillips, which is the criticism of Gen. Banks and Gen. Banks' policy. Gen. Banks instituted a labor policy in Louisiana that was discriminatory of blacks, claiming that it was to help prepare them to better handle freedom. Wendell Phillips countered by saying, "If there is anything patent in the whole history of our thirty years' struggle, it is that the Negro no more needs to be prepared for liberty than the white man." I hold that that policy is our chief danger at the present moment; that it practically enslaves the Negro, and makes the Proclamation [the Emancipation Proclamation] of 1863 a mockery and delusion. What is freedom? It is the right to choose one's own employment. Certainly it means that, if it means anything; and when any individual or combination of individuals undertakes to decide for any man when he shall work, where he shall work, at what he shall work, and for what he shall work, he or they practically reduce him to slavery. [Applause.] He is a slave. That I understand Gen. Banks to do—to determine for the so-called freedman, when, and where, and at what, and for how much he shall work, when he shall be punished, and by whom punished. It is absolute slavery. It defeats the beneficent intention of the Government, if it has beneficent intentions, in regards to the freedom of our people.

I have had but one idea for the last three years to present to the American people, and the phraseology in which I clothe it is the old abolition phraseology. I am for the "immediate, unconditional, and universal" enfranchisement of the black man, in every State in the Union. [Loud applause.]

Without this, his liberty is a mockery; without this, you might as well almost retain the old name of slavery for his condition; for in fact, if he is not the slave of the individual master, he is the slave of society, and holds his liberty as a privilege, not as a right. He is at the mercy of the mob, and has no means of protecting himself.

It may be objected, however, that this pressing of the Negro's right to suffrage is premature. Let us have slavery abolished, it may be said, let us have labor organized, and then, in the natural course of events, the right of suffrage will be extended to the Negro. I do not agree with this. The constitution of the human mind is such, that if it once disregards the conviction forced upon it by a revelation of truth, it requires the exercise of a higher power to produce the same conviction afterwards. The American people are now in tears. The Shenandoah

has run blood—the best blood of the North. All around Richmond, the blood of New England and of the North has been shed—of your sons, your brothers and your fathers. We all feel, in the existence of this Rebellion, that judgments terrible, wide-spread, far-reaching, overwhelming, are abroad in the land; and we feel, in view of these judgments, just now, a disposition to learn righteousness. This is the hour. Our streets are in mourning, tears are falling at every fireside, and under the chastisement of this Rebellion we have almost come up to the point of conceding this great, this all-important right of suffrage. I fear that if we fail to do it now, if abolitionists fail to press it now, we may not see, for centuries to come, the same disposition that exists at this moment. [Applause.]

Hence, I say, now is the time to press this right.

It may be asked, "Why do you want it? Some men have got along very well without it. Women have not this right." Shall we justify one wrong by another? This is the sufficient answer. Shall we at this moment justify the deprivation of the Negro of the right to vote, because some one else is deprived of that privilege? I hold that women, as well as men, have the right to vote . . . [applause] . . . and my heart and voice go with the movement to extend suffrage to woman; but that question rests upon another basis than which our right rests. We may be asked, I say, why we want it. I will tell you why we want it. We want it because it is our right, first of all. No class of men can, without insulting their own nature, be content with any deprivation of their rights. We want it again, as a means for educating our race. Men are so constituted that they derive their conviction of their own possibilities largely by the estimate formed of them by others. If nothing is expected of a people, that people will find it difficult to contradict that expectation. By depriving us of suffrage, you affirm our incapacity to form an intelligent judgment respecting public men and public measures; you declare before the world that we are unfit to exercise the elective franchise, and by this means lead us to undervalue ourselves, to put a low estimate upon ourselves, and to feel that we have no possibilities like other men. Again, I want the elective franchise, for one, as a colored man, because ours is a peculiar government, based upon a peculiar idea, and that idea is universal suffrage. If I were in a monarchial government, or an autocratic or aristocratic government, where the few bore rule and the many were subject, there would be no special stigma resting upon me, because I did not exercise the elective franchise. It would do me no great violence. Mingling with the mass I should partake of the strength of the mass; I should be supported by the mass, and I should have the same incentives to endeavor with the mass of my fellow-men; it would be no particular burden, no particular deprivation; but here where universal suffrage is the rule, where that is the fundamental idea of the Government, to rule us out is to make us an exception, to brand us with the stigma of inferiority, and to invite to our heads the missiles of those about us; therefore, I want the franchise for the black man.

There are, however, other reasons, not derived from any consideration merely of our rights, but arising out of the conditions of the South, and of the country—considerations which have already been referred to by Mr. Phillips—considerations which must arrest the attention of statesmen. I believe that when the tall heads of this Rebellion shall have been swept down, as they will be swept down, when the Davises and Toombses and Stephenses, and others who are leading this Rebellion shall have been blotted out, there will be this rank undergrowth of treason, to which reference has been made, growing up there, and interfering with, and thwarting the quiet operation of the Federal Government in those states. You will see those traitors, handing down, from sire to son, the same malignant spirit which they have manifested and which they are now exhibiting, with malicious hearts, broad blades, and bloody hands in the field, against our sons and brothers. That spirit will still remain; and whoever sees the Federal Government extended over those Southern States will see that Government in a strange land, and not only in a strange land, but in an enemy's land. A post-master of the United States in the South will find himself surrounded by a hostile spirit; a collector in a Southern port will find himself surrounded by a hostile spirit; a United States marshal or United States judge will be surrounded there by a hostile element. That enmity will not die out in a year, will not die out in an age. The Federal Government will be looked upon in those States precisely as the Governments of Austria and France are looked upon in Italy at the present moment. They will endeavor to circumvent, they will endeavor to destroy, the peaceful operation of this Government. Now, where will you find the strength to counterbalance this spirit, if you do not find it in the Negroes of the South? They are your friends, and have always been your friends. They were your friends even when the Government did not regard them as such. They comprehended the genius of this war before you did. It is a significant fact, it is a marvellous fact, it seems almost to imply a direct interposition of Providence, that this war, which began in the interest of slavery on both sides, bids fair to end in the interest of liberty on both sides. [Applause.]

It was begun, I say, in the interest of slavery on both sides. The South was fighting to take slavery out of the Union, and the North was fighting to keep it in the Union; the South fighting to get it beyond the limits of the United States Constitution, and the North fighting to retain it within those limits; the South fighting for new guarantees, and the North fighting for the old guarantees;—both despising the Negro, both insulting the Negro. Yet, the Negro, apparently endowed with wisdom from on high, saw more clearly the end from the beginning than we did. When Seward said the status of no man in the country would be changed by the war, the Negro did not believe him. [Applause.] When our generals sent their underlings in shoulder-straps to hunt the flying Negro back from our lines into the jaws of slavery, from which he had escaped, the Negroes thought that a mistake had been made, and that the intentions of the Government had not been rightly understood by our officers in shoulder-straps, and they continued to come into our lines, threading their way through bogs and fens, over briers and thorns, fording streams, swimming rivers, bringing us tidings as to the safe path to march, and pointing out the dangers that threatened us. They are our only friends in the South, and we should be true to them in this their trial hour, and see to it that they have the elective franchise.

I know that we are inferior to you in some things—virtually inferior. We walk about you like dwarfs among giants. Our heads are scarcely seen above the great sea of humanity. The Germans are superior to us; the Irish are superior to us; the Yankees are superior to us [Laughter]; they can do what we cannot, that is, what we have not hitherto been allowed to do. But while I make this admission, I utterly deny, that we are originally, or naturally, or practically, or in any way, or in any important sense, inferior to anybody on this globe. [Loud applause.]

This charge of inferiority is an old dodge. It has been made available for oppression on many occasions. It is only about six centuries since the blue-eyed and fair-haired Anglo-Saxons were considered inferior by the haughty Normans, who once trampled upon them. If you read the history of the Norman Conquest, you will find that this proud Anglo-Saxon was once looked upon as of coarser clay than his Norman master, and might be found in the highways and byways of Old England laboring with a brass collar on his neck, and the name of his master marked upon it. You were down then! [Laughter and applause.]

You are up now. I am glad you are up, and I want you to be glad to help us up also. [Applause.]

The story of our inferiority is an old dodge, as I have said; for wherever men oppress their fellows, wherever they enslave them, they will endeavor to find the needed apology for such enslavement and oppression in the character of the people oppressed and enslaved. When we wanted, a few years ago, a slice of Mexico, it was hinted that the Mexicans were an inferior race, that the old Castilian blood had become so weak that it would scarcely run down hill, and that Mexico needed the long, strong

and beneficent arm of the Anglo-Saxon care extended over it. We said that it was necessary to its salvation, and a part of the "manifest destiny" of this Republic, to extend our arm over that dilapidated government. So, too, when Russia wanted to take possession of a part of the Ottoman Empire, the Turks were an "inferior race." So, too, when England wants to set the heel of her power more firmly in the quivering heart of old Ireland, the Celts are an "inferior race." So, too, the Negro, when he is to be robbed of any right which is justly his, is an "inferior man." It is said that we are ignorant; I admit it. But if we know enough to be hung, we know enough to vote. If the Negro knows enough to pay taxes to support the government, he knows enough to vote; taxation and representation should go together. If he knows enough to shoulder a musket and fight for the flag, fight for the government, he knows enough to vote. If he knows as much when he is sober as an Irishman knows when drunk, he knows enough to vote, on good American principles. [Laughter and applause.]

But I was saying that you needed a counterpoise in the persons of the slaves to the enmity that would exist at the South after the Rebellion is put down. I hold that the American people are bound, not only in self-defense, to extend this right to the freedmen of the South, but they are bound by their love of country, and by all their regard for the future safety of those Southern States, to do this—to do it as a measure essential to the preservation of peace there. But I will not dwell upon this. I put it to the American sense of honor. The honor of a nation is an important thing. It is said in the Scriptures, "What doth it profit a man if he gain the whole world, and lose his own soul?" It may be said, also, What doth it profit a nation if it gain the whole world, but lose its honor? I hold that the American government has taken upon itself a solemn obligation of honor, to see that this war—let it be long or short, let it cost much or let it cost little—that this war shall not cease until every freedman at the South has the right to vote. [Applause.] It has bound itself to it. What have you asked the black men of the South, the black men of the whole country to do? Why, you have asked them to incur the enmity of their masters, in order to befriend you and to befriend this Government. You have asked us to call down, not only upon ourselves, but upon our children's children, the deadly hate of the entire Southern people. You have called upon us to turn our backs upon our masters, to abandon their cause and espouse yours; to turn against the South and in favor of the North; to shoot down the Confederacy and uphold the flag—the American flag. You have called upon us to expose ourselves to all the subtle machinations of their malignity for all time. And now, what do you propose to do when you come to make peace? To reward your enemies, and trample in the dust your friends? Do you intend to sacrifice the very men who have come to the rescue of your banner in the South, and incurred the lasting displeasure of their masters thereby? Do you intend to sacrifice them and reward your enemies? Do you mean to give your enemies the right to vote, and take it away from your friends? Is that wise policy? Is that honorable? Could American honor withstand such a blow? I do not believe you will do it. I think you will see to it that we have the right to vote. There is something too mean in looking upon the Negro, when you are in trouble, as a citizen, and when you are free from trouble, as an alien. When this nation was in trouble, in its early struggles, it looked upon the Negro as a citizen. In 1776 he was a citizen. At the time of the formation of the Constitution the Negro had the right to vote in eleven States out of the old thirteen. In your trouble you have made us citizens. In 1812 Gen. Jackson addressed us as citizens—"fellow-citizens." He wanted us to fight. We were citizens then! And now, when you come to frame a conscription bill, the Negro is a citizen again. He has been a citizen just three times in the history of this government, and it has always been in time of trouble. In time of trouble we are citizens. Shall we be citizens in war, and aliens in peace? Would that be just?

I ask my friends who are apologizing for not insisting upon this right, where can the black man look, in this country, for the assertion of his right, if he may not look to the Massachusetts Anti-Slavery Society? Where under the whole heavens can he look for sympathy, in asserting this right, if he may not look to this platform? Have you lifted us up to a certain height to see that we are men, and then are any disposed to leave us there, without seeing that we are put in possession of all our rights? We look naturally to this platform for the assertion of all our rights, and for this one especially. I understand the anti-slavery societies of this country to be based on two principles,—first, the freedom of the blacks of this country; and, second, the elevation of them. Let me not be misunderstood here. I am not asking for sympathy at the hands of abolitionists, sympathy at the hands of any. I think the American people are disposed often to be generous rather than just. I look over this country at the present time, and I see Educational Societies, Sanitary Commissions, Freedmen's Associations, and the like,—all very good: but in regard to the colored people there is always more that is benevolent, I perceive, than just, manifested towards us. What I ask for the Negro is not benevolence, not pity, not sympathy, but simply justice. [Applause.]

The American people have always been anxious to know what they shall do with us. Gen. Banks was distressed with solicitude as to what he should do with the Negro. Everybody has asked the question, and they learned to ask it early of the abolitionists, "What shall we do with the Negro?" I have had but one answer from the beginning. Do nothing with us! Your doing with us has already played the mischief with us. Do nothing with us! If the apples will not remain on the tree of their own strength, if they are wormeaten at the core, if they are early ripe and disposed to fall, let them fall! I am not for tying or fastening them on the tree in any way, except by nature's plan, and if they will not stay there, let them fall. And if the Negro cannot stand on his own legs, let him fall also. All I ask is, give him a chance to stand on his own legs! Let him alone! If you see him on his way to school, let him alone, don't disturb him! If you see him going to the dinner table at a hotel, let him go! If you see him going to the ballot-box, let him alone, don't disturb him! [Applause.]

If you see him going into a work-shop, just let him alone,—your interference is doing him a positive injury. Gen. Banks' "preparation" is of a piece with this attempt to prop up the Negro. Let him fall if he cannot stand alone! If the Negro cannot live by the line of eternal justice, so beautifully pictured to you in the illustration used by Mr. Phillips, the fault will not be yours, it will be his who made the Negro, and established that line for his government. [Applause.]

Let him live or die by that. If you will only untie his hands, and give him a chance, I think he will live. He will work as readily for himself as the white man. A great many delusions have been swept away by this war. One was, that the Negro would not work; he has proved his ability to work. Another was, that the Negro would not fight; that he possessed only the most sheepish attributes of humanity; was a perfect lamb, or an "Uncle Tom;" disposed to take off his coat whenever required, fold his hands, and be whipped by anybody who wanted to whip him. But the war has proved that there is a great deal of human nature in the Negro, and that "he will fight," as Mr. Quincy, our President, said, in earlier days than these, "when there is reasonable probability of his whipping anybody." [Laughter and applause.]

Source: Foner, Philip S. *The Life and Writings of Frederick Douglass.* Vol. IV, 157–165. New York: International Publishers Co. Inc., 1950. Permission of International Publishers/New York.

Paul Jennings, "A Colored Man's Reminiscences of James Madison" (1865)

As a young man, Paul Jennings (1799–1874), a slave born on the Virginia estate of James Madison, served Madison as a body servant during and after his presidency (1809–1817). In 1814, when the British attacked and burned Washington, Jennings helped save some of the treasures of the White House. In 1845, Jennings bought his freedom with the assistance of Massachusetts senator Daniel Webster. In the 1850s, Jennings returned to Virginia to track down members of his family who had been sold to other plantations. Three of his sons fought for the Union during the Civil War. In 1865, Jennings published "A Colored Man's Reminiscences of James Madison," the first White House memoir, excerpts of which are reproduced here.

PREFACE

Among the laborers at the Department of the Interior is an intelligent colored man, Paul Jennings, who was born a slave on President Madison's estate, in Montpelier, Va., in 1799. His reputed father was Benj. Jennings, an English trader there; his mother, a slave of Mr. Madison, and the granddaughter of an Indian. Paul was a "body servant" of Mr. Madison, till his death, and afterwards of Daniel Webster, having purchased his freedom of Mrs. Madison. His character for sobriety, truth, and fidelity, is unquestioned; and as he was a daily witness of interesting events, I have thought some of his recollections were worth writing down in almost his own language.

On the 10th of January, 1865, at a curious sale of books, coins and autographs belonging to Edward M. Thomas, a colored man, for many years Messenger to the House of Representatives, was sold, among other curious lots, an autograph of Daniel Webster, containing these words: "I have paid $120 for the freedom of Paul Jennings; he agrees to work out the same at $8 per month, to be furnished with board, clothes, washing," &c.

REMINISCENCES OF MADISON

When Mr. Madison was chosen President, we came . . . and moved into the White House; the east room was not finished, and Pennsylvania Avenue was not paved, but was always in an awful condition from either mud or dust. The city was a dreary place.

Mr. Robert Smith was then Secretary of State, but as he and Mr. Madison could not agree, he was removed, and Colonel Monroe appointed to his place. Dr. Eustis was Secretary of War—rather a rough, blustering man; Mr. Gallatin, a tip-top man, was Secretary of the Treasury; and Mr. Hamilton, of South Carolina, a pleasant gentleman, who thought Mr. Madison could do nothing wrong, and who always concurred in every thing he said, was Secretary of the Navy.

Before the war of 1812 was declared, there were frequent consultations at the White House as to the expediency of doing it. Colonel Monroe was always fierce for it, so were Messrs. Lowndes, Giles, Poydrass, and Pope—all Southerners; all his Secretaries were likewise in favor of it.

Soon after war was declared, Mr. Madison made his regular summer visit to his farm in Virginia. We had not been there long before an express reached us one evening, informing Mr. M. of Gen. Hull's surrender. He was astounded at the news, and started back to Washington the next morning.

After the war had been going on for a couple of years, the people of Washington began to be alarmed for the safety of the city, as the British held Chesapeake Bay with a powerful fleet and army. Every thing seemed to be left to General Armstrong, then Secretary of war, who ridiculed the idea that there was any danger. But, in August, 1814, the enemy had got so near, there could be no doubt of their intentions. Great alarm existed, and some feeble preparations for defense were made. Com. Barney's flotilla was stripped of men, who were placed in battery, at Bladensburg, where they fought splendidly. A large part of his men were tall, strapping negroes, mixed with white sailors and marines. Mr. Madison reviewed them just before the fight, and asked Com. Barney if his "negroes would not run on the approach of the British?" "No sir," said Barney, "they don't know how to run; they will die by their guns first." They fought till a large part of them were killed or wounded; and Barney himself wounded and taken prisoner. One or two of these negroes are still living here.

Well, on the 24th of August, sure enough, the British reached Bladensburg, and the fight began between 11 and 12. Even that very morning General Armstrong assured Mrs. Madison there was no danger. The President, with General Armstrong, General Winder, Colonel Monroe, Richard Rush, Mr. Graham, Tench Ringgold, and Mr. Duvall, rode out on horseback to Bladensburg to see how things looked. Mrs. Madison ordered dinner to be ready at 3, as usual; I set the table myself, and brought up the ale, cider, and wine, and placed them in the coolers, as all the Cabinet and several military gentlemen and strangers were expected. While waiting, at just about 3, as Sukey, the house-servant was lolling out of a chamber window, James Smith, a free colored man who had accompanied Mr. Madison to Bladensburg, gallopped up to the house, waving his hat, and cried out, "Clear out, clear out! General Armstrong has ordered a retreat!" All then was confusion. Mrs. Madison ordered her carriage, and passing through the dining-room, caught up what silver she could crowd into her old-fashioned reticule, and then jumped into the chariot with her servant girl Sukey, and Daniel Carroll, who took charge of them; Jo. Bolin drove them over to Georgetown Heights; the British were expected in a few minutes. Mr. Cutts, her brother- in-law, sent me to a stable on 14th street, for his carriage. People were running in every direction. John Freeman (the colored butler) drove off in the coachee with his wife, child, and servant; also a feather bed lashed on behind the coachee, which was all the furniture saved, except part of the silver and the portrait of Washington (of which I will tell you by-and-by).

I will here mention that although the British were expected every minute, they did not arrive for some hours; in the mean time, a rabble, taking advantage of the confusion, ran all over the White House, and stole lots of silver and whatever they could lay their hands on.

About sundown I walked over to the Georgetown ferry, and found the President and all hands (the gentlemen named before, who acted as a sort of body-guard for him) waiting for the boat. It soon returned, and we all crossed over, and passed up the road about a mile; they then left us servants to wander about. In a short time several wagons from Bladensburg, drawn by Barney's artillery horses, passed up the road, having crossed the Long Bridge before it was set on fire. As we were cutting up some planks a white wagoner ordered us away, and told his boy Tommy to reach out his gun, and he would shoot us. I told him "he had better have used it at Bladensburg." Just then we came up with Mr. Madison and his friends, who had been wandering about for some hours, consulting what to do. I walked on to a Methodist minister's, and in the evening, while he was at prayer, I heard a tremendous explosion, and, rushing out, saw that the public buildings, navy yard, and ropewalks were on fire.

Mrs. Madison slept that night at Mrs. Love's, two or three miles over the river. After leaving that place she called in at a house, and went up stairs. The lady of the house learning who she was, became furious, and went to the stairs and screamed out, "Miss Madison! if that's you, come down and go out! Your husband has got mine out fighting, and d__ you, you shan't stay in my house; so get out!" Mrs. Madison complied, and went to Mrs. Minor's, a few miles further, where she stayed a day or two, and then returned to Washington, where she found Mr. Madison at her brother-in-law's, Richard Cutts, on F street. All the facts about Mrs. M. I learned from her servant Sukey. We moved into the house of Colonel John B. Taylor [Tayloe], corner of 18th street and New York Avenue, where we lived till the news of peace arrived.

In two or three weeks after we returned, Congress met in extra session, at Blodgett's old shell of a house on 7th street (where the General Post-office now stands). It was three stories high, and had been used for a theatre, a tavern, and an Irish boarding house, but both Houses of Congress managed to get along in it very well, notwithstanding it had to accommodate the Patent-office, City and General Post-office, committee-rooms, and what was left of the Congressional Library, at the same time. Things are very different now.

The next summer, Mr. John Law, a large property-holder about the Capitol, fearing it would not be rebuilt, got up a subscription and built a large brick building (now called the Old Capitol, where the secesh prisoners are confined), and offered it to Congress for their use, till the Capitol could be rebuilt. This coaxed them back, though strong efforts were made to remove the seat of government north; but the southern members kept it here.

It has often been stated in print, that when Mrs. Madison escaped from the White House, she cut out from the frame the large portrait of Washington (now in one of the parlors there), and carried it off. This is totally false. She had no time for doing it. It would have required a ladder to get it down. All she carried off was the silver in her reticule, as the British were thought to be but a few squares off, and were expected every moment. John Suse [Jean-Pierre Sioussat] (a Frenchman, then door-keeper, and still living) and Magraw, the President's gardener, took it down and sent it off on a wagon, with some large silver urns and such other valuables as could be hastily got hold of. When the British did arrive, they ate up the very dinner, and drank the wines, &c., that I had prepared for the President's party.

When the news of peace arrived, we were crazy with joy. Miss Sally Coles, a cousin of Mrs. Madison, and afterwards wife of Andrew Stevenson, since minister to England, came to the head of the stairs, crying out, "Peace! peace!" and told John Freeman (the butler) to serve out wine liberally to the servants and others. I played the President's March on the violin, John Suse and some others were drunk for two days, and such another joyful time was never seen in Washington.

Mr. Madison and all his Cabinet were as pleased as any, but did not show their joy in this manner.

After he retired from the presidency, he amused himself chiefly on his farm. At the election for members of the Virginia Legislature, in 1829 or '30, just after General Jackson's accession, he voted for James Barbour, who had been a strong Adams man. He also presided, I think, over the Convention for amending the Constitution, in 1832.

After the news of peace, and of General Jackson's victory at New Orleans, which reached here about the same time, there were great illuminations. We moved into the Seven Buildings, corner of 19th street and Pennsylvania Avenue, and while there, General Jackson came on with his wife, to whom numerous dinner-parties and levees were given. Mr. Madison also held levees every Wednesday evening, at which wine, punch, coffee, and ice-cream were liberally served, unlike the present custom.

While Mr. Jefferson was President, he and Mr. Madison (then his Secretary of State) were extremely intimate; in fact, two brothers could not have been more so. Mr. Jefferson always stopped over night at Mr. Madison's, in going and returning from Washington.

I have heard Mr. Madison say, that when he went to school, he cut his own wood for exercise. He often did it also when at his farm in Virginia. He was very neat, but never extravagant, in his clothes. He always dressed wholly in black—coat, breeches, and silk stockings, with buckles in his shoes and breeches. He never had but one suit at a time. He had some poor relatives that he had to help, and wished to set them an example of economy in the matter of dress. He was very fond of horses, and an excellent judge of them, and no jockey ever cheated him. He never had less than seven horses in his Washington stables while President.

He often told the story, that one day riding home from court with old Tom Barbour (father of Governor Barbour), they met a colored man, who took off his hat. Mr. M. raised his, to the surprise of old Tom; to whom Mr. M. replied, "I never allow a negro to excel me in politeness." Though a similar story is told of General Washington, I have often heard this, as above, from Mr. Madison's own lips.

Source: "A Colored Man's Reminiscences of James Madison," *White House History* (Collection Set 1), 2004, 51–55. Reprinted from *White House History,* a semiannual journal published by the White House Historical Association,www.whitehousehistory.org.

Black Codes of Mississippi

(1865)

In response to passage of the Reconstruction amendments to the U.S. Constitution, which prohibited slavery and extended citizenship and voting rights to black freedmen, the former slaveholding states of the South enacted laws to restrict the rights of blacks and regulate interaction between the races. Such laws became known as "Black Codes." Reproduced here are several statutes enacted by the legislature of Mississippi in 1865.

AN ACT TO CONFER CIVIL RIGHTS ON FREEDMEN, AND FOR OTHER PURPOSES

Section 1. All freedmen, free negroes and mulattoes may sue and be sued, implead and be impleaded, in all the courts of law and equity of this State, and may acquire personal property, and chooses in action, by descent or purchase, and may dispose of the same in the same manner and to the same extent that white persons may: Provided, That the provisions of this section shall not be so construed as to allow any freedman, free negro or mulatto to rent or lease any lands or tenements except in incorporated cities or towns, in which places the corporate authorities shall control the same.

Section 2. All freedmen, free negroes and mulattoes may intermarry with each other, in the same manner and under the same regulations that are provided by law for white persons: Provided, that the clerk of probate shall keep separate records of the same.

Section 3. All freedmen, free negroes or mulattoes who do now and have here before lived and cohabited together as husband and wife shall be taken and held in law as legally married, and the issue shall be taken and held as legitimate for all purposes; and it shall not be lawful for any freedman, free negro or mulatto to intermarry with any white person; nor for any person to intermarry with any freedman, free negro or mulatto; and any person who shall so intermarry shall be deemed guilty of felony, and on conviction thereof shall be confined in the State penitentiary for life; and those shall be deemed freedmen, free negroes and mulattoes who are of pure negro blood, and those descended from a negro to the third generation, inclusive, though one ancestor in each generation may have been a white person.

Section 4. In addition to cases in which freedmen, free negroes and mulattoes are now by law competent witnesses, freedmen, free negroes or mulattoes shall be competent in civil cases, when a party or parties to the suit, either plaintiff or plaintiffs, defendant or defendants; also in cases where freedmen, free negroes and mulattoes is or are either plaintiff or plaintiffs, defendant or defendants. They shall also be competent witnesses in all criminal prosecutions where the crime charged is alleged to have been committed by a white person upon or against the person or property of a freedman, free negro or mulatto: Provided, that in all cases said witnesses shall be examined in open court, on the stand; except, however, they may be examined before the grand jury, and shall in all cases be subject to the rules and tests of the common law as to competency and credibility.

Section 5. Every freedman, free negro and mulatto shall, on the second Monday of January, one thousand eight hundred and sixty-six, and annually thereafter, have a lawful home or employment, and shall have written evidence thereof as follows, to wit: if living in any incorporated city, town, or village, a license from that mayor thereof; and if living outside of an incorporated city, town, or village, from the member of the board of police of his beat, authorizing him or her to do irregular and job work; or a written contract, as provided in Section 6 in this act; which license may be revoked for cause at any time by the authority granting the same.

Section 6. All contracts for labor made with freedmen, free negroes and mulattoes for a longer period than one month shall be in writing, and a duplicate, attested and read to said freedman, free negro or mulatto by a beat, city or county officer, or two disinterested white persons of the county in which the labor is to be performed, of which each party shall have one: and said contracts shall be taken and held as entire contracts, and if the laborer shall quit the service of the employer before the expiration of his term of service, without good cause, he shall forfeit his wages for that year up to the time of quitting.

Section 7. Every civil officer shall, and every person may, arrest and carry back to his or her legal employer any freedman, free negro, or mulatto who shall have quit the service of his or her employer before the expiration of his or her term of service without good cause; and said officer and person shall be entitled to receive for arresting and carrying back every deserting employee aforesaid the sum of five dollars, and ten cents per mile from the place of arrest to the place of delivery; and the same shall be paid by the employer, and held as a set off for so much against the wages of said deserting employee: Provided, that said arrested party, after being so returned, may appeal to the justice of the peace or member of the board of police of the county, who, on notice to the alleged employer, shall try summarily whether said appellant is legally employed by the alleged employer, and has good cause to quit said employer. Either party shall have the right of appeal to the county court, pending which the alleged deserter shall be remanded to the alleged employer or otherwise disposed of, as shall be right and just; and the decision of the county court shall be final.

Section 8. Upon affidavit made by the employer of any freedman, free negro or mulatto, or other credible person, before any justice of the peace or member of the board of police, that any freedman, free negro or mulatto legally employed by said employer has illegally deserted said employment, such justice of the peace or member of the board of police issue his warrant or warrants, returnable before himself or other such officer, to any sheriff, constable or special deputy, commanding him to arrest said deserter, and return him or her to said employer, and the like proceedings shall be had as provided in the preceding section; and it shall be lawful for any officer to whom such warrant shall be directed to execute said warrant in any county in this State; and that said warrant may be transmitted without endorsement to any like officer of another county, to be executed and returned as aforesaid; and the said employer shall pay the costs of said warrants and arrest and return, which shall be set off for so much against the wages of said deserter.

Section 9. If any person shall persuade or attempt to persuade, entice, or cause any freedman, free negro or mulatto to desert from the legal employment of any person before the expiration of his or her term of service, or shall knowingly employ any such deserting freedman, free negro or mullato, or shall knowingly give or sell to any such deserting freedman, free negro or mulatto, any food, raiment, or other thing, he or she shall be guilty of a misdemeanor, and, upon conviction, shall be fined not less than twenty-five dollars and not more than two hundred dollars and costs; and if the said fine

and costs shall not be immediately paid, the court shall sentence said convict to not exceeding two months imprisonment in the county jail, and he or she shall moreover be liable to the party injured in damages: Provided, if any person shall, or shall attempt to, persuade, entice, or cause any freedman, free negro or mullatto to desert from any legal employment of any person, with the view to employ said freedman, free negro or mullato without the limits of this State, such costs; and if said fine and costs shall not be immediately paid, the court shall sentence said convict to not exceeding six months imprisonment in the county jail.

Section 10. It shall be lawful for any freedman, free negro, or mulatto, to charge any white person, freedman, free negro or mulatto by affidavit, with any criminal offense against his or her person or property, and upon such affidavit the proper process shall be issued and executed as if said affidavit was made by a white person, and it shall be lawful for any freedman, free negro, or mulatto, in any action, suit or controversy pending, or about to be instituted in any court of law equity in this State, to make all needful and lawful affidavits as shall be necessary for the institution, prosecution or defense of such suit or controversy.

Section 11. The penal laws of this state, in all cases not otherwise specially provided for, shall apply and extend to all freedman, free negroes and mulattoes. . . .

AN ACT TO REGULATE THE RELATION OF MASTER AND APPRENTICE, AS RELATES TO FREEDMEN, FREE NEGROES, AND MULATTOES

Section 1. It shall be the duty of all sheriffs, justices of the peace, and other civil officers of the several counties in this State, to report to the probate courts of their respective counties semiannually, at the January and July terms of said courts, all freedmen, free negroes, and mulattoes, under the age of eighteen, in their respective counties, beats, or districts, who are orphans, or whose parent or parents have not the means or who refuse to provide for and support said minors; and thereupon it shall be the duty of said probate court to order the clerk of said court to apprentice said minors to some competent and suitable person on such terms as the court may direct, having a particular care to the interest of said minor: Provided, that the former owner of said minors shall have the preference when, in the opinion of the court, he or she shall be a suitable person for that purpose.

Section 2. The said court shall be fully satisfied that the person or persons to whom said minor shall be apprenticed shall be a suitable person to have the charge and care of said minor, and fully to protect the interest of said minor. The said court shall require the said master or mistress to execute bond and security, payable to the State of Mississippi, conditioned that he or she shall furnish said minor with sufficient food and clothing; to treat said minor humanely; furnish medical attention in case of sickness; teach, or cause to be taught, him or her to read and write, if under fifteen years old, and will conform to any law that may be hereafter passed for the regulation of the duties and relation of master and apprentice: Provided, that said apprentice shall be bound by indenture, in case of males, until they are twenty-one years old, and in case of females until they are eighteen years old.

Section 3. In the management and control of said apprentices, said master or mistress shall have the power to inflict such moderate corporeal chastisement as a father or guardian is allowed to infliction on his or her child or ward at common law: Provided, that in no case shall cruel or inhuman punishment be inflicted.

Section 4. If any apprentice shall leave the employment of his or her master or mistress, without his or her consent, said master or mistress may pursue and recapture said apprentice, and bring him or her before any justice of the peace of the county, whose duty it shall be to remand said apprentice to the service of his or her master or mistress; and

in the event of a refusal on the part of said apprentice so to return, then said justice shall commit said apprentice to the jail of said county, on failure to give bond, to the next term of the county court; and it shall be the duty of said court at the first term thereafter to investigate said case, and if the court shall be of opinion that said apprentice left the employment of his or her master or mistress without good cause, to order him or her to be punished, as provided for the punishment of hired freedmen, as may be from time to time provided for by law for desertion, until he or she shall agree to return to the service of his or her master or mistress: Provided, that the court may grant continuances as in other cases: And provided further, that if the court shall believe that said apprentice had good cause to quit his said master or mistress, the court shall discharge said apprentice from said indenture, and also enter a judgment against the master or mistress for not more than one hundred dollars, from the use and benefit of said apprentice, to be collected on execution as in other cases.

Section 5. If any person entice away any apprentice from his or her master or mistress, or shall knowingly employ an apprentice, or furnish him or her food or clothing without the written consent of his or her master or mistress, or shall sell or give said apprentice spirits without such consent, said person so offending shall be guilty of a misdemeanor, and shall, upon conviction there of before the county court, be punished as provided for the punishment of person enticing from their employer hired freedmen, free negroes or mulattoes.

Section 6. It shall be the duty of all civil officers of their respective counties to report any minors within their respective counties to said probate court who are subject to be apprenticed under the provisions of this act, from time to time as the facts may come to their knowledge, and it shall be the duty of said court from time to time as said minors shall be reported to them, or otherwise come to their knowledge, to apprentice said minors as hereinbefore provided.

Section 9. It shall be lawful for any freedman, free negro, or mulatto, having a minor child or children, as provided for by this act.

Section 10. In all cases where the age of the freedman, free negro, or mulatto cannot be ascertained by record testimony, the judge of the county court shall fix the age. . . .

AN ACT TO AMEND THE VAGRANT LAWS OF THE STATE

Section 1. All rogues and vagabonds, idle and dissipated persons, beggars, jugglers, or persons practicing unlawful games or plays, runaways, common drunkards, common night-walkers, pilferers, lewd, wanton, or lascivious persons, in speech or behavior, common railers and brawlers, persons who neglect their calling or employment, misspend what they earn, or do not provide for the support of themselves or their families, or dependents, and all other idle and disorderly persons, including all who neglect all lawful business, habitually misspend their time by frequenting houses of ill-fame, gaming-houses, or tippling shops, shall be deemed and considered vagrants, under the provisions of this act, and upon conviction thereof shall be fined not exceeding one hundred dollars, with all accruing costs, and be imprisoned, at the discretion of the court, not exceeding ten days.

Section 2. All freedmen, free negroes and mulattoes in this State, over the age of eighteen years, found on the second Monday in January, 1866, or thereafter, with no lawful employment or business, or found unlawful assembling themselves together, either in the day or night time, and all white persons assembling themselves with freedmen, Free negroes or mulattoes, or usually associating with freedmen, free negroes or mulattoes, on terms of equality, or living in adultery or fornication with a freed woman, freed negro or mulatto, shall be deemed vagrants, and on conviction thereof shall be fined in a sum not exceeding, in the case of a

freedman, free negro or mulatto, fifty dollars, and a white man two hundred dollars, and imprisonment at the discretion of the court, the free negro not exceeding ten days, and the white man not exceeding six months.

Section 3. All justices of the peace, mayors, and aldermen of incorporated towns, counties, and cities of the several counties in this State shall have jurisdiction to try all questions of vagrancy in their respective towns, counties, and cities, and it is hereby made their duty, whenever they shall ascertain that any person or persons in their respective towns, and counties and cities are violating any of the provisions of this act, to have said party or parties arrested, and brought before them, and immediately investigate said charge, and, on conviction, punish said party or parties, as provided for herein. And it is hereby made the duty of all sheriffs, constables, town constables, and all such like officers, and city marshals, to report to some officer having jurisdiction all violations of any of the provisions of this act, and in case any officer shall fail or neglect any duty herein it shall be the duty of the county court to fine said officer, upon conviction, not exceeding one hundred dollars, to be paid into the county treasury for county purposes.

Section 4. Keepers of gaming houses, houses of prostitution, prostitutes, public or private, and all persons who derive their chief support in the employment's that militate against good morals, or against law, shall be deemed and held to be vagrants.

Section 5. All fines and forfeitures collected by the provisions of this act shall be paid into the county treasury of general county purposes, and in case of any freedman, free negro or mulatto shall fail for five days after the imposition of any or forfeiture upon him or her for violation of any of the provisions of this act to pay the same, that it shall be, and is hereby, made the duty of the sheriff of the proper county to hire out said freedman, free negro or mulatto, to any person who will, for the shortest period of service, pay said fine and forfeiture and all costs: Provided, a preference shall be given to the employer, if there be one, in which case the employer shall be entitled to deduct and retain the amount so paid from the wages of such freedman, free negro or mulatto, then due or to become due; and in case freedman, free negro or mulatto cannot hire out, he or she may be dealt with as a pauper.

Section 6. The same duties and liabilities existing among white persons of this State shall attach to freedmen, free negroes or mulattoes, to support their indigent families and all colored paupers; and that in order to secure a support for such indigent freedmen, free negroes, or mulattoes, it shall be lawful, and is hereby made the duty of the county police of each county in this State, to levy a poll or capitation tax on each and every freedman, free negro, or mulatto, between the ages of eighteen and sixty years, not to exceed the sum of one dollar annually to each person so taxed, which tax, when collected, shall be paid into the county treasurer's hands, and constitute a fund to be called the Freedman's Pauper Fund, which shall be applied by the commissioners of the poor for the maintenance of the poor of the freedmen, free negroes and mulattoes of this State, under such regulations as may be established by the boards of county police in the respective counties of this State.

Section 7. If any freedman, free negro, or mulatto shall fail or refuse to pay any tax levied according to the provisions of the sixth section of this act, it shall be prima facie evidence of vagrancy, and it shall be the duty of the sheriff to arrest such freedman, free negro, or mulatto, or such person refusing or neglecting to pay such tax, and proceed at once to hire for the shortest time such delinquent taxpayer to any one who will pay the said tax, with accruing costs, giving preference to the employer, if there be one.

Section 8. Any person feeling himself or herself aggrieved by judgment of any justice of the peace, mayor, or alderman in cases arising under this act, may within five days appeal to the next term of the county court of the proper county, upon giving bond and security in a sum not less than twenty-five dollars nor more than one hundred and fifty dollars, conditioned to appear and prosecute said appeal, and abide by the judgment of the county court; and said appeal shall be tried de novo in the county court, and the decision of the said court shall be final.

Laws of the State of Mississippi, Passed at a Regular Session of the Mississippi Legislature, held in Jackson, October, November and December, 1865. Jackson, 1866, 82–93, 165–167.

Andrew Johnson, Civil Rights Bill Veto Message
(1866)

On March 27, 1866, President Andrew Johnson sent the following message to Congress explaining his reasons for vetoing the civil rights bill that Congress had recently passed. The president had vetoed the bill a year earlier because he deemed it race legislation that discriminated in favor of African Americans and against whites. In his 1866 veto, the president raised constitutional arguments against the measure, declaring that it infringed the rights of states. The Republicans in Congress, realizing that they could not work with Johnson to enact their program for granting civil rights to the freedmen, repassed the bill by a two-thirds majority, thus making the Civil Rights Act of 1866 the first major piece of legislation to be enacted over a presidential veto.

Congress responded to Johnson's constitutional arguments against the act by incorporating some of its provisions regarding citizenship into the Fourteenth Amendment, which, upon its ratification in 1868, prohibited the states from depriving citizens of the "equal protection of the laws."

Andrew Johnson
March 27, 1866

To the Senate of the United States:

I regret that the bill which has passed both Houses of Congress, entitled "An Act to protect all persons in the United States in their civil rights, and furnish the means of their vindication," contains provisions which I cannot approve, consistently with my sense of duty to the whole people, and my obligations to the Constitution of the United States. I am, therefore, constrained to return it to the Senate (the House in which it originated) with my objections to its becoming law.

By the first section of the bill, all persons born in the United States, and not subject to any foreign power, excluding Indians not taxed, are declared to be citizens of the United States. This provision comprehends the Chinese of the Pacific States, Indians subject to taxation, the people called Gipsies, as well as the entire race designated as blacks, people of color, negroes, mulattoes, and persons of African blood. Every individual of these races, born in the United States, is by the bill made a citizen of the United States. It does not purport to declare or confer any other right of citizenship than Federal citizenship; it does not propose to give these classes of persons any status as citizens of States, except that which may result from their status as citizens of the United States. The power to confer the right of State citizenship is just as exclusively with the several States, as the power to confer the right of Federal citizenship is with Congress. The right of Federal citizenship, thus to be conferred in the several excepted ratios before mentioned, is now, for the first time, proposed to be given by law. If, as is claimed by many, all persons who are native born, already are, by virtue of the Constitution, citizens of the United States, the passage of the pending bill cannot be necessary to make them such. If, on the other hand, such persons are not citizens, as may be assumed from the proposed legislation to make them such, the grave question presents itself whether, where eleven of the thirty-six States are unrepresented in Congress at the time, it is sound policy to make our entire colored population, and all other excepted classes, citizens of the United States. Four millions of them have just emerged from slavery into freedom. Can it be reasonably supposed that they possess the requisite qualifications to entitle them to all the privileges and immunities of citizenship of the United States? Have the people of the several States expressed such a conviction? It may also be asked, whether it is necessary that they should be declared citizens in order that they may be secured in the enjoyment of the civil rights proposed to be conferred by the bill. Those rights are, by Federals as well as by State laws, secured to all domiciled aliens and foreigners, even before the completion of the process of naturalization; and it may safely be assumed that the same enactments are sufficient to give like protection and benefits to those for whom this bill provides special legislation. Besides the policy of the Government, from its origin to the present time, seems to have been that persons who are strangers to and unfamiliar with our institutions and laws, should pass through a certain probation; at the end of which, before attaining the coveted prize, they must give evidence of their fitness to receive and to exercise the rights of citizens as contemplated by the Constitution of the United States. The bill in effect proposes a discrimination against large numbers of intelligent, worthy and patriotic foreigners, and in favor of the negro, to whom, after long years of bondage, the avenues to freedom and intelligence have just now been suddenly opened. He must of necessity, from his previous unfortunate condition of servitude, be less informed as to the nature and character of our institutions than he who, coming from abroad, has to some extent, at least, familiarized himself with the principles of a Government to which he voluntarily intrusts life, liberty, and the pursuit of happiness. Yet it is now proposed by a single legislative enactment to confer the rights of citizens upon all persons of African descent, born within the excluded limits of the United States, while persons of foreign birth, who make our land their home, must undergo a probation of five years, and can only then become citizens upon proof that they are of good moral character, attached to the principles of the Constitution of the United States, and well disposed to the good order and happiness of the same. The first section of the bill also contains an enumeration of the rights to be enjoyed by those classes so made citizens in every State and Territory of the United States. These rights are, to make and enforce contracts, to sue, be parties and give evidence, to inherit, purchase, lease, sell, hold, or convey real and personal property, and to have full and equal benefit of all laws and proceedings for the security of persons and property as is enjoyed by white citizens. So, too, they are made subject to the same punishments, pains, and penalties common with white citizens, and to none others. Thus a perfect equality of the white and colored races is attempted to be fixed by a Federal law in every State of the Union, over the vast field of State jurisdiction covered by these enumerated rights. In no one of them can any State exercise any power of discrimination between different races. In the exercise of State policy over matters exclusively affecting the people of each State, it has frequently been thought expedient to discriminate between the two races. By the statutes of some of the States, North as well as South, it is enacted, for instance, that no white person shall intermarry with a negro or mulatto. Chancellor Kent says, speaking of the blacks, that marriages between them and the whites are forbidden in some of the States where slavery does not exist, and they are prohibited in all the slaveholding States by law; and when not absolutely contrary to law, they are revolting, and

regarded as an offence against public decorum. I do not say that this bill repeals State laws, on the subject of marriage between the two races, for as the whites are forbidden to intermarry with the blacks, the blacks can only make such contracts as the whites themselves are allowed to make, and therefore cannot, under this bill, enter into the marriage contract with the whites. I take this discrimination, however, as an instance of the State policy as to discrimination, and to inquire whether, if Congress can abrogate all State laws of discrimination between the two races, in the matter of real estate, of suits, and of contracts generally, Congress may not also repeal the State laws as to the contract of marriage between the races? Hitherto, every subject embraced in the enumeration of rights contained in the bill has been considered as exclusively belonging to the States; they all relate to the internal policy and economy of the respective States. They are matters which, in each State, concern the domestic condition of its people, varying in each according to its peculiar circumstances and the safety and well-being of its own citizens. I do not mean to say that upon all these subjects there are not Federal restraints; as, for instance, in the State power of legislation over contracts, there is a Federal limitation that no State shall pass a law impairing the obligations of contracts; and, as to crimes, that no State shall pass an ex-post-facto law; and, as to money, that no State shall make any thing but gold and silver as legal tender. But where can we find a Federal prohibition against the power of any State to discriminate, as do most of them, between aliens and citizens, between artificial persons called corporations, and naturalized persons, in the right to hold real estate? If it be granted that Congress can repeal all State laws discriminating between the two races on the subject of suffrage and office? If Congress shall declare by law who shall hold lands, who shall testify, who shall have capacity to make a contract in a State, that Congress can also declare by law, without regard to race or color, shall have the right to act as a juror or as a judge, to hold any office, and finally to vote, in every State and Territory of the United States. As respects the Territory of the United States, they come within the power of Congress, for as to them the law-making power is the Federal power; but as to the States, no similar provision exists, vesting in Congress the power to make such rules and regulations for them.

The object of the second section of the bill is to afford discriminating protection to colored persons in the full enjoyment of all the rights secured to them by the preceding section. It declares that "any person who, under color of any law, statute, ordinance, regulation, or custom, shall subject or cause to be subjected any inhabitant of any State or Territory to the deprivation of any rights secured or protected by this act, or to different punishment, pains, or penalties on account of such person having at any time been held in a condition of slavery or involuntary servitude, except as a punishment of crime, whereof the party shall have been duly convicted, or by reason of his color or race, than is prescribed for the punishment of white persons, shall be deemed guilty of a misdemeanor, and on conviction shall be punished by fine not exceeding one thousand dollars, or imprisonment not exceeding one year, or both, in the discretion of the court." This section seems to be designed to apply to some existing or future law of a State or Territory, which may conflict with the provisions of the bill now under consideration. It provides for counteracting such forbidden legislation, by imposing fine and imprisonment upon the legislators who may pass such conflicting laws, or upon the officers or agents who shall put or attempt to put them into execution. It means an official offence, not a common crime, committed against law upon the person or property of the black race. Such an act may deprive the black man of his property, but not of his right to hold property. It means a deprivation of the right itself, either by the State Judiciary or the State Legislature. It is, therefore, assumed that, under this section, members of a State Legislature who should vote for laws conflicting with the provisions of the bill, that judges of the State courts who should render judgments in antagonism with its terms, and that marshals and sheriffs who should

as ministerial officers execute processes sanctioned by State laws and issued by State judges in execution of their judgments, could be brought before other tribunals and there subjected to fine and imprisonment, for the performance of the duties which such State laws might impose. The legislation thus proposed invades the judicial power of the State. It says to every State court or judge: If you decide that this act is unconstitutional; if you hold that over such a subject-matter the said law is paramount, under color of a State law refuse the exercise of the right to the negro; your error of judgment, however conscientious, shall subject you to fine and imprisonment. I do not apprehend that the conflicting legislation which the bill seems to contemplate is so likely to occur, as to render it necessary at this time to adopt a measure of such constitutionality. In the next place, this provision of the bill seems to be unnecessary, as adequate judicial remedies could be adopted to secure the desired end without invading the immunities of legislators, always important to be preserved in the interest of public liberty, notwithstanding the independence of the judiciary, always essential to the preservation of individual rights, and without impairing the efficiency of ministerial officers, always necessary for the maintenance of public peace and order. The remedy proposed by this section seems to be in this respect not only anomalous but unconstitutional, for the Constitution guarantees nothing with certainty if it does not insure to the several States the right of making index ruling laws in regard to all matters arising within their jurisdiction, subject only to the restriction, in cases of conflict with the Constitution and constitutional laws of the United States—the latter to be held as the supreme law of the land.

The third section gives the district courts of the United States exclusive cognizance of all crimes and offences committed against the provisions of this act, and concurrent jurisdiction with the circuit courts of the United States, of all civil and criminal cases affecting persons that are denied, or cannot enforce in the courts or judicial tribunals of the State or locality where they may be, any of the rights secured to them by the first section. The construction which I have given to the second section is strengthened by this third section, for it makes clear what kind of denial, or deprivation of rights secured by the first section, was in contemplation. It is a denial or deprivation of such rights in the courts or tribunals of the State. It stands, therefore, clear of doubt that the offence and the penalties provided in the second section are intended for the State judge who, in the clear exercise of his functions as a judge, not acting ministerially but judicially, shall decide contrary to this Federal law. In other words, when a State judge, acting upon a question involving a conflict between a State law and a Federal law, and bound, according to his own judgment and responsibility to give an impartial decision between the two, comes to the conclusion that the State law is valid and the Federal law is invalid, he must not follow the dictates of his own judgment, at the peril of fine and imprisonment. The legislative department of the Government of the United States thus takes from the judicial department of the States the sacred and exclusive duty of judicial decision, and converts the State judge into a mere ministerial officer, bound to decide according to the will of Congress. It is clear that in States which deny to persons, whose rights are secured by the first section of the bill, any one of those rights, all criminal and civil cases affecting them will, by the provisions of the third section, come under the executive cognizance of the Federal tribunals. It follows that if in any State, which denies to a colored person any one of all these rights, that person should commit a crime against the laws of a State—murder, arson, rape, or any other crime—all protection and punishment, through the courts of the State, are taken away, and he can only be tried and punished in the Federal courts. How is the criminal to be tried, if the offence is provided for and punished by Federal law? That law, and not the State law, is to govern. It was only when the offence does not happen to be within the province of Federal law that the Federal courts are to try and punish him under any other law. The resort is to be had to the common law, as modified and changed by State legislation, so far as the same is not inconsistent with the Constitution and laws of the United States. So that over this vast domain of criminal jurisprudence, provided by each State for the protection of its citizens and for the punishment of all persons who violate its criminal laws, Federal law, wherever it can be made to apply, displaces State law. The question naturally arises, from what source Congress derives the power to transfer to Federal tribunals certain classes of cases embraced in this section. The Constitution expressly declares that the judicial power of the United States "shall extend to all cases in law and equity, arising under this Constitution, the laws of the United States, and treaties made, or which shall be made, under their authority; to all cases affecting ambassadors or other public ministers and consuls; to all cases of admiralty and maritime jurisdiction; to controversies to which the United States shall be a party; to controversies between two or more States; between a State and citizens of another State; between citizens of different States; between citizens of the same State claiming land under grants of different States; and between a State, or the citizens thereof, and foreign States, citizens, or subjects."

Here the judicial power of the United States is expressly set forth and defined; and the act of September 24, 1789, establishing the judicial courts of the United States, in conferring upon the Federal courts jurisdiction over cases originating in State tribunals, is careful to confine them to the classes enumerated in the above recited clause of the Constitution. This section of the bill undoubtedly comprehends cases and authorizes the exercise of powers that are not, by the Constitution, within the jurisdiction of the courts of the United States. To transfer them to these courts would be an exercise of authority well calculated to excite distrust and alarm on the part of all the States, for the bill applies alike to all of them, as well as to those who have not been engaged in rebellion. It may be assumed that this authority is incident to the power granted to Congress by the Constitution as recently amended, to enforce, by appropriate legislation, the article declaring that neither slavery nor involuntary servitude, except as a punishment for crime, whereof the party shall have been duly convicted, shall exist within the United States, or any place subject to their jurisdiction. It cannot, however, be justly claimed that, with a view to the enforcement of this article of the Constitution, there is at present any necessity for the exercise of all the powers which this bill confers. Slavery has been abolished, and at present nowhere exists within the jurisdiction of the United States. Nor has there been, nor is it likely there will be any attempts to revive it by the people of the States. If, however, any such attempt shall be made, it will then become the duty of the General Government to exercise any and all incidental powers necessary and proper to maintain inviolate this great law of freedom. The fourth section of the bill provides that officers and agents of the Freedmen's Bureau shall be empowered to make arrests, and also that other officers shall be specially commissioned for that purpose by the President of the United States. It also authorizes the Circuit Courts of the United States and the Superior Courts of the Territories to appoint, without limitation, commissioners, who are to be charged with the performance of quasi judicial duties. The fifth section empowers the commissioners so to be selected by the court, to appoint, in writing, one or more suitable persons from time to time to execute warrants and processes desirable by the bill. These numerous official agents are made to constitute a sort of police in addition to the military, and are authorized to summon a posse commitatus, and even to call to their aid such portion of the land and naval forces of the United States, or of the militia, "as may be necessary to the performance of the duty with which they are charged." This extraordinary power is to be conferred upon agents irresponsible to the Government and to the people, to whose number the discretion of the commissioners is the only limit, and in whose hands such authority might be made a terrible engine of wrong, oppression, and fraud. The general statutes regulating the land and naval forces of the United States, the militia,

and the execution of the laws are believed to be adequate for any emergency which can occur in time of peace. If it should prove otherwise, Congress can at any time amend those laws in such a manner as, while subserving the public welfare, not to jeopard the rights, interests, and liberties of the people.

The seventh section provides that a fee of ten dollars shall be paid to each commissioner in every case brought before him, and a few of five dollars to his deputy or deputies for each person he or they may arrest and take before any such commissioner in general for performing such other duties as may be required in the premises. All these fees are to be paid out of the Treasury of the United States, whether there is a conviction or not; but in case of conviction they are to be recoverable from the defendant. It seems to me that under the influence of such temptations, bad men might convert any law, however beneficent, into an instrument of persecution and fraud. By the eighth section of the bill, the United States Courts, which sit only in one place for white citizens, must migrate with the marshal and district attorney, and necessarily with the clerk (although he is not mentioned), to any part of the district, upon the order of the President, and there hold a court for the purpose of the more speedy arrest and trial of persons charged with the violation of this act; and there the judge and officers of the court must remain, upon the order of the President, for the time therein designated.

The ninth section authorizes the President, or such person as he may empower for that purpose, to employ such part of the land or naval forces of the United States, or of the militia, as shall be necessary to prevent the violation and enforce the due execution of this act. This language seems to imply a permanent military force that is to be always at hand, and whose only business is to be the enforcement of this measure over the vast region where it intended to operate.

I do not propose to consider the policy of this bill. To me the details of the bill are fraught with evil. The white race and black race of the South have hitherto lived together under the relation of master and slave—capital owning labor. Now that relation is changed; and as to ownership, capital and labor are divorced. They stand now, each master of itself. In this new relation, one being necessary to the other, there will be a new adjustment, which both are deeply interested in making harmonious. Each has equal power in settling the terms; and, if left to the laws that regulate capital and labor, it is confidently believed that they will satisfactorily work out the problem. Capital, it is true, has more intelligence; but labor is never ignorant as not to understand its own interests, not to know its own value, and not to see that capital must pay that value. This bill frustrates this adjustment. It intervenes between capital and labor, and attempts to settle questions of political economy through the agency of numerous officials, whose interest it will be to foment discord between the two races; for as the breach widens, their employment will continue; and when it is closed, their occupation will terminate. In all our history, in all our experience as a people living under Federal and State law, no such system as that contemplated by the details of this bill has ever before been proposed or adopted. They establish for the security of the colored race safeguards which go indefinitely beyond any that the General Government has ever provided for the white race. In fact, the distinction of race and color is by the bill made to operate in favor of the colored against the white race. They interfere with the municipal legislation of the States; with relations existing exclusively between a State and its citizens, or between inhabitants of the same State; an absorption and assumption of power by the General Government which, if acquiesced in, must sap and destroy our federative system of limited power, and break down the barriers which preserve the rights of the States. It is another step, or rather stride, towards centralization and the concentration of all legislative powers in the National Government. The tendency of the bill must be to resuscitate the spirit of rebellion, and to arrest the progress of those influences which are more closely drawing around the States the bonds of union and peace.

My lamented predecessor, in his proclamation of the 1st of January, 1863, ordered and declared that all persons held as slaves within certain States and parts of States therein designated, were, and thenceforward should be free; and further, that the Executive Government of the United States, including the military and naval authorities thereof, would recognize and maintain the freedom of such persons. This guaranty has been rendered especially obligatory and sacred by the amendment of the Constitution abolishing slavery throughout the United States. I, therefore, fully recognize the obligation to protect and defend that class of our people whenever and wherever it shall become necessary, and to the full extent, compatible with the Constitution of the United States. Entertaining these sentiments, it only remains for me to say that I will cheerfully co-operate with Congress in any measure that may be necessary for the preservation of civil rights of the freedmen, as well as those of all other classes of persons throughout the United States, by judicial process under equal and impartial laws, or conformably with the provisions of the Federal Constitution.

I now return the bill to the Senate, and regret that in considering the bills and joint resolutions, forty-two in number, which have been thus far submitted for my approval, I am compelled to withhold my assent from a second measure that has received the sanction of both Houses of Congress.

Andrew Johnson
Washington, D.C., March 27, 1866.

Source: Johnson, Andrew. Civil Rights Bill Veto of 1866. In *Andrew Johnson, His Life and Speeches,* edited by Lillian Foster. New York: Richardson & Co., 1866.

Civil Rights Act
(1866)

In 1865, the Republican-controlled Congress passed a civil rights bill that was intended to protect the civil rights of newly freed African Americans. President Andrew Johnson, who was a southern conservative from Tennessee, vetoed the bill, believing that it should not be enacted at a time when 11 states were still unrepresented in Congress and that it ultimately discriminated in favor of blacks and against whites. In 1866, Congress again passed the bill. Although Johnson again vetoed it, Congress this time mustered a two-thirds majority in favor of the measure and thus overrode the veto. The act contained provisions regarding citizenship that were later written into the Fourteenth Amendment to the U.S. Constitution. The Civil Rights Act, which is reproduced here, became effective on April 9, 1866.

AN ACT TO PROTECT ALL PERSONS IN THE UNITED STATES IN THEIR CIVIL RIGHTS, AND FURNISH THE MEANS OF THEIR VINDICATION.

Be it enacted, That all persons born in the United States and not subject to any foreign power, excluding Indians not taxed, are hereby declared to be citizens of the United States; and such citizens, of every race and color, without regard to any previous condition of slavery or involuntary servitude, except as a punishment for crime whereof the party shall have been duly convicted, shall have the same right, in every State and Territory in the United States, to make and enforce contracts, to sue, be parties, and give evidence, to inherit, purchase, lease, sell, hold, and convey real and personal property and to full and equal benefit of all laws and proceedings for the security of person and property, as is enjoyed by white citizens, and shall be subject to like punishment, pains, and penalties, and to none other, any law, statute, ordinance, regulation, or custom, to the contrary notwithstanding.

Section 2. And be it further enacted, That any person who, under color of any law, statute, ordinance, regulation, or custom, shall subject, or cause to be subjected, any inhabitant of any State or Territory to the deprivation of any right secured or protected by this act, or to different punishment, pains, or penalties on account of such person having at any time been held in a condition of slavery or involuntary servitude, except as a punishment for crime whereof the party shall have been duly convicted or by reason of his color, or race, than is prescribed for the punishment of white persons, shall be deemed guilty of a misdemeanor, and, on conviction, shall be punished by fine not exceeding one thousand dollars, or imprisonment not exceeding one year, or both, in the discretion of the court.

Section 3. And be it further enacted, That the district courts of the United States . . . shall have, exclusively of the courts of the several States, cognizance of all crimes and offences committed against the provisions of this act, and also, concurrently with the circuit court of the United States, of all causes, civil and criminal, affecting persons who are denied or cannot enforce in the courts or judicial tribunals of the State or locality where they may be any of the rights secured to them by the first section of this act. . . .

Section 4. And be it further enacted, That the district attorneys, marshals, and deputy marshals of the United States, the commissioners appointed by the Circuit and territorial courts of the United States, with powers of arresting, imprisoning, or bailing offenders against the laws of the United States, the officers and agents of the Freedmen's Bureau, and every other officer who may be specially empowered by the President of the United States, shall be, and they are hereby, specially authorized and required, at the expense of the

United States, to institute proceedings against all and every person who shall violate the provisions of this act, and cause him or them to be arrested and imprisoned, or bailed, as the case may be, for trial before such court of the United States or territorial court as by this act has cognizance of the offence. . . .

Section 8. And be it further enacted, That whenever the President of the United States shall have reason to believe that offences have been or are likely to be committed against the provisions of this act within any judicial district, it shall be lawful for him, in his discretion, to direct the judge, marshal, and district attorney of such district to attend at such place within the district, and for such time as he may designate, for the purpose of the more speedy arrest and trial of persons charged

with a violation of this act; and it shall be the duty of every judge or other officer, when any such requisition shall be received by him, to attend at the place and for the time therein designated.

Section 9. And be it further enacted, That it shall be lawful for the President of the United States, or such person as he may empower for that purpose, to employ such part of the land or naval forces of the United States, or of the militia, as shall be necessary to prevent the violation and enforce the due execution of this act.

Section 10. And be it further enacted, That upon all questions of law arising in any cause under the provisions of this act a final appeal may be taken to the Supreme Court of the United States.

Source: U.S. Statutes at Large, 31 (1866). 27, 39th Cong., 1st sess.

Fourteenth Amendment

(1868)

Proposed on June 13, 1866, and ratified on July 9, 1868, the Fourteenth Amendment to the U.S. Constitution creates a broad definition of citizenship in the United States. It requires the states to provide equal protection under the laws to all persons (not only to citizens) within their boundaries. The significance of the Fourteenth Amendment was exemplified when the U.S. Supreme Court later interpreted it to prohibit racial segregation in public schools and other facilities in the 1954 Brown v. Board of Education *decision.*

Section 1. All persons born or naturalized in the United States, and subject to the jurisdiction thereof, are citizens of the United States and of the State wherein they reside. No State shall make or enforce any law which shall abridge the privileges or immunities of citizens of the United States; nor

shall any State deprive any person of life, liberty, or property, without due process of law; nor deny to any person within its jurisdiction the equal protection of the laws.

Section 2. Representatives shall be apportioned among the several States according to their respective numbers, counting the whole number of persons in each State, excluding Indians not taxed. But when the right to vote at any election for the choice of electors for President and Vice President of the United States, Representatives in Congress, the Executive and Judicial officers of a State, or the members of the Legislature thereof, is denied to any of the male inhabitants of such State, being twenty-one years of age, and citizens of the United States, or in any way abridged, except for participation in rebellion, or other crime, the basis of representation therein shall be reduced in the proportion which the number of such male citizens shall bear to the whole number of male citizens twenty-one years of age in such State.

Section 3. No person shall be a Senator or Representative in Congress, or elector of President and Vice President, or hold any office, civil or military, under the United States, or under any State, who, having previously taken an oath, as a member of Congress, or as an officer of the United States, or as a member of any State legislature, or as an executive or judicial officer of any State, to support the Constitution of the United States, shall have engaged in insurrection or rebellion against the same, or given aid or comfort to the enemies thereof. But Congress may by a vote of two-thirds of each House, remove such disability.

Section 4. The validity of the public debt of the United States, authorized by law, including debts incurred for payment of pensions and bounties for services in suppressing insurrection or rebellion, shall not be questioned. But neither the United States nor any State shall assume or pay any debt or obligation incurred in aid of insurrection or rebellion against the United States, or any claim for the loss or emancipation of any slave; but all such debts, obligations and claims shall be held illegal and void.

Section 5. The Congress shall have power to enforce, by appropriate legislation, the provisions of this article.

Source: Fourteenth Amendment to the Constitution, 1868. Primary Documents in American History, Library of Congress.

Hiram R. Revels, Speech to the U.S. Senate
(February 8, 1871)

Hiram Revels of Mississippi was the first African American to serve as a U.S. senator. On February 8, 1871, Revels delivered a speech, excepted here, advocating the establishment of "mixed" schools containing both black and white students. He also expressed his fear of increasing racism and suggested that desegregation in schools would prevent it.

U.S. Senate Chamber
February 8, 1871

. . . I find that the prejudice in this country to color is very great, and I sometimes fear that it is on the increase. For example, let me remark that it matters not how colored people act, it matters not how they behave themselves, how well they deport themselves, how intelligent they may be, how refined they may be—for there are some colored persons who are persons of refinement; this must be admitted—the prejudice against them is equally as great as it is against the most low and degraded colored man you can find in the streets of this city or in any other place.

This, Mr. President, I do seriously regret. And is this prejudice right? Have the colored people done anything to justify the prejudice against them that does exist in the hearts of so many white persons, and generally of one great political party in this country? Have they done anything to justify it? No, sir. Can any reason be given why this prejudice should be fostered in so many hearts against them simply because they are not white? I make these remarks in all kindness, and from no bitterness of feeling at all.

Mr. President, if this prejudice has no cause to justify it, then we must admit that it is wicked, we must admit that it is wrong; we must admit that it has not the approval of Heaven. Therefore I hold it to be the duty of this nation to discourage it, simply because it is wicked, because it is wrong, because it is not approved of by Heaven. If the nation should take a step for the encouragement of this prejudice against the colored race, can they have any ground upon which to predicate a hope that Heaven will smile upon them and prosper them? It is evident that it is the belief of Christian people in this country and in all other enlightened portions of the world that as a nation we have passed through a severe ordeal, that severe judgments have been poured upon us on account of the manner in which a poor, oppressed race was treated in this country.

Sir, this prejudice should be resisted. Steps should be taken by which to discourage it. . . . Mr. President, I desire to say here that the white race has no better friend than I. The Southern people know this. It is known over the length and breadth of this land. I am true to my own race. I wish to see all done that can be done for their encouragement, to assist them in acquiring property, in becoming intelligent, enlightened, useful, valuable citizens. I wish to see this much done for them, and I believe God makes it the duty of this nation to do this much for them; but at the same time, I would not have anything done which would harm the white race.

Sir, during the canvass in the state of Mississippi I traveled into different parts of that state, and this is the doctrine that I everywhere uttered: That while I was in favor of building up the colored race I was not in favor of tearing down the white race. Sir, the white race need not be harmed in order to build up the colored race. The colored race can be built up and assisted, as I before remarked, in acquiring property, in becoming intelligent, valuable, useful citizens, without one hair upon the head of any white man being harmed.

Let me ask, will establishing such schools as I am now advocating in this District harm our white friends? Let us consider this question for a few minutes. By some it is contended that if we establish mixed schools here a great insult will be given to the white citizens, and that the white schools will be seriously damaged. All that I ask those who assume this position to do is to go with me to Massachusetts, to go with me to some other New England states where they have mixed schools, and there they will find schools in as prosperous and flourishing a condition as any to be found in any part of the world. They will find such schools there; and they will find between the white and colored citizens friendship, peace and harmony. . . .

Then, Mr. President, I hold that establishing mixed schools will not harm the white race. I am their friends. I said in Mississippi, and I say here, and I say everywhere, that I would abandon the Republican party if it went into any measures of legislation really damaging to any portion of the white race; but it is not in the Republican party to do that. . . .

Source: Revels, Hiram. "Speech to U.S. Senate Chamber." February 8, 1871.

Jim Crow

(1877–1920)

D. Augustus Straker, First Annual Address to the Law Graduates of Allen University, Class 1884

(June 12, 1884)

In this address to law graduates at Allen University, a black college in Columbia, South Carolina, Professor Straker, dean of the Law Department, inspired his audience with his precise references to their historical past and culture. He advised these new law graduates to maintain character in their professional lives and to rely on ancient rhetorical devices for effective expression in the courtrooms.

Mr. President, Ladies and Gentlemen, and young gentlemen, graduates:

At the closing moments of your departure from the law department of Allen University, your Alma Mater, in which you have pursued and completed a course of legal study, entitling you to the usual degree of Bachelor of Laws, and by subsequent examination before the Supreme Court of the State, admitting you to practice in all the courts of the State, it is my duty to present you with a few words of parting advice. Before doing so, let us take a retrospect upon mutual labors.

In October, 1882, the Law Department of Allen University was opened, I was chosen by the trustees, Dean and Law Professor in this department. This meant more than I conceived. It did not have its usual meaning, that is a teacher of some legal branch of knowledge, to which I must devote my attention and give instruction, but it meant, by force of circumstances, I should be required to teach all the legal topics prescribed by the curriculum of the university, which are, in a great degree, identical with those prescribed by the 23d rule of the Supreme Court of our State. I was not wanting in diffidence of my ability to perform so herculean a task in which was involved so grave responsibilities. My duty was to educate in the law, colored youth, of a race declared to be inferior in capacity with all others. If I failed I certified to both your and my incapacity. My responsibility then was, the maintenance of an entire race's fitness and capacity. I consoled myself in the belief that I had a heart and will determined enough to commence the work, putting my trust in God, the Father of us all, and believing that he had made of one blood all nations upon the face of the earth. I concluded that he had made them all of like susceptibilities, to glorify him in the comprehension of his handiwork, and the laws of the same. Thus I began my labors. You young gentlemen entered the law school. You did not enter as those of the Caucasian race usually do, with the prestige of a wealthy parentage, a pocket full of gold, and the equal facilities belonging of right, to a common brotherhood in man. At the threshold of the temple, wherein you were to drink deep and full from the fountain of legal knowledge, running from time immemorial in the streamlets of tradition, custom and usage, until, beginning with the Jewish Theocracy to the Justinian age, the confluence was commenced with the fathers of English Common Law, Coke, Littleton, and Sir William Blackstone, and the mighty stream, began to flow down the course of civilization, purified by Christianity.

You were met by the common inquisitor of social life, so frequent at the door of the commencement of the pursuit of knowledge by every young man and woman. He inquired of you, "are you laden with the passport to this world's honors—money? Have you an ancestry of boasted Anglo-Saxon renown, which for more than ten hundred years have made easy the pathway of eminence and fame to that race of people?" To these questions you replied, "none." But, continuing, you were further asked: "Have you a heart full of the desire for knowledge and wisdom—a soul inspired with the truth of the Fatherhood of God and the brotherhood of man, despite a long suffering and oppression of your race? Do you believe in your equal capacity under equal facilities and opportunities with all other men?" To which you eagerly replied: "Aye, and forever aye." Then in clarion voice you were bade enter and be strong, and in the face of poverty and innumerable obstacles you commenced your labors. In the autumn you beheld the sere and yellow leaf falling and decomposing, and testifying, if not to total annihilation, to decay and change, typifying man's mortality. Yet you did not falter, though in some cases, after more than twelve hours of manual as well as mental labor in the engagement of a livelihood you would appear at your recitations and lectures with

faces lined with marks of toil and fatigue; but with a cheerful eye, a determination and a will, gladening the heart of your professor and teaching him and yourself how to learn "to labor and to wait." In the spring time joyous nature clad in floral garb with her hill tops carpeted with green, and her valleys resonant with the music of the rippling brooks, gave new life to your studies which strengthened and made you strong. As the summer, the joyous summer of your life of study advanced and ripened into the fruition of your labors on the 24th day of April, your *alma mater* welcomed her sons to her bounty and conferred upon you your degrees, and on the 27th of May last you entered upon the stage of a lawyer's life, to play your part in the arena of struggle for fame and name and wealth, and I trust, usefulness, by virtue of your diploma and the certificate of your efficiency in examination before the Supreme Court of the State. In this arena of lawyer's life there are several stages. Below is the multitude of pettifoggers struggling for filthy lucre only and degrading the profession of law from the height of its great eminence and glory into the mire of selfishness, lying and trickery. The next stage is where you will find a goodly crowd devoted simply to money-making, and utter strangers to the upbuilding of their fellow man. I bid you tarry not in these paths, but strive for the upper-story in your profession—remembering in the language attributed to Daniel Webster, when asked by a despondent young lawyer how he should rise to greatness in his profession amidst the struggles of the pettifogger below, and the competition just above, replied to him, "young man, there is room enough up stairs."

An experience of not more than ten years as a lawyer myself, gives me but little ability to teach you the ways to great height, but such as I have observed I offer you. First, in order to achieve great eminence in your profession you must fully realize and comprehend the width and the depth and the height of law; you must fully comprehend the extent of the word itself. Not only does law mean a rule of action prescribed by a superior to an inferior which he is bound to obey, as found in constitutions, in statutes and in the ordinances of every civilized government, but it is also co-extensive with every known branch of learning. Ascend the heights of science—it is there; traverse the multifarious avenues of art—it is there too. Go among the poets and philosophers, converse with the healing art—it is there. Investigate the pyramids of Egypt and translate the hieroglyphics of her sons—it is there. Go down into the bowels of the earth and seek for wealth in minerals, or try to prove that every stratum, as shown in geology, is truly the antitype of its prototype, the history of the creation recorded in the first book of Genesis. Enter the halls of legislatures, construe their statutes at the former and there you will find the consummation drawn from history as of necessity. A lawyer has no bounds to the requisite acquirement of knowledge. Beginning with the true source of human law—human necessity—you must continue to erect a superstructure upon the foundation of wisdom, as found revealed in the Bible. You may then adorn the edifice as it should be with the lights of poetry, science, art, established upon the foundation of morality and religion. The lawyer that barely knows the statutes of his State or country is like unto the man who is placed in charge of a locomotive, but has only a superficial knowledge of its several parts, their names and their purposes. He is never safe when danger or emergency arises. He is all right so long as the engine runs smoothly, but should some contesting force appear he soon finds how ignorant he is of that general knowledge of the machinery, its origin and the laws governing its application. In such a condition he wishes he had engaged in some calling of which he was thoroughly the master. You must not only be equipped in general knowledge, but you must be strong of nerve and full of energy. In courts of justice you will encounter some judges who will in some instances endeavor to hold the scales of justice so high as not to be able to see the object weighed in the balance. In such instances you need nerve. You must never cease argument and proof until you have made him bring down his scales before his eyes, or close them shut against any prejudice towards your client. Be never guilty of contempt of court, nor be wanting in courage to show proper contempt for a contemptuous court, nevertheless be not high-minded. Let your humility and good conduct secure the favor of bench and bar.

Be of good character—character is that which we really are. When we labor to gain reputation we are not even taking the first step towards the acquisition of character. In reputation you gain favor by something which pleases your neighbor apart frequently from the virtue of the acts. A wisely trained character never stops to ask what will society think of me if I do this thing or leave it undone. It tests the quality of an action by ascertaining whether it is just when judged by the laws of eternal right. Cultivate the good will of all men—politeness is a branch of good character, and remember that your juries come from the county of which county frequently *you* are. For while I would have you brave and courageous in battle for the right, be not puffed up so as to secure the ill will of men, for it is better to be a "living dog than a dead lion," said the prophet. Have due respect for the patience of juries and remember that they are men having feelings to enjoy pleasure and to suffer pain. Do not let it be ever said of you as it is reported in a late number of the *Central Law Journal* of a young lawyer in his maiden speech. It says "he was florid rhetorical, scattering and windy. For four weary hours he talked at the Court until every body felt like lynching him; when he got through his opponent arose and said "your Honor" I will follow the example of my friend and submit the case without argument." This position frequently arises when the young lawyer disregards plain Saxon in his speech and seeks to illumine his argument with rhetorical flashes, so dazzling as to totally obscure the sight of his point and drive away judgement therefrom. Emulate in your profession, those who as lawyers have handed down to us examples at the forum worthy of emulation. As citizens and sons of South Carolina, you will find among her annals lawyers, judges and jurists who have ennobled the profession by their unparalleled ability. I cite you to O'Neil, McDuffie, Parker, Hunt, and Legare; but it was not only in the field of legal contest that they strove and conquered, but they were in the full sense of the term patriots, an attribute indispensable to the immortal honor and glory of a truly great man. It was more than legal ability which enabled lord Mansfield, in his decision in the celebrated Somerset case brought before him under writ of Habeas Corpus, to try the right of an American master to withdraw his alleged slave from the shores of England to say "that the instant a slave landed in England he became a freeman, as the air of England is too pure for a slave to breathe in." If you would combine that noble virtue, patriotism, with an efficiency in law and thus live for the good you can do, I would point you to a standard the highest achieved in English or American lines aye, the highest the world has ever seen. I point you to an American statesman and lawyer in whose patriotism this continent saw the noblest virtue, the greatest daring for good, the sublimest achievements for love of country and the unparalleled philanthropy of any human age. I point you to Charles Sumner, the American Socrates, Cicero and Demosthenes combined. He whose life as a lawyer was chiefly devoted to the enfranchisement, amelioration and elevation of a race of people oppressed for ages by a cruel bondage.

The basis of all his actions at the forum, in the halls of legislation, on the rostrum, everywhere, was equality, which is true equity, the principles of which you have already listened to this evening from one of your number. He denounced all laws in which the equality of all men was not the primal reason. Never more conspicuously was this virtue seen in Charles Sumner than in his celebrated defense in the United States Senate in 1874 against the unjust annexation of the Black Republic of Havti to the United States. His keen eye and fierce legal acumen quickly saw the political assassin's hand at the throat of the young Republic, and with the eloquence of a Demosthenes, the legal knowledge of a Grotius, Vattel, or Puffendorf he exclaimed. "Foremost among admitted principles of international law is the axiom that all nations are equal without distinction of population, size or power. Nor does international law know any distinction of color. Do unto others as you would have them do unto you, is the plan of law for all nations as for all men."

Thus did he plead for the Black Republic, showing his love and his sympathy, not only for the American negro, but for him and for all men wherever found upon the face of the globe where the strong seek to oppress the weak. He would have done the same for the China-man or the Indian. His law extended to humanity at large, and was found, not in text books, but in the wants of man.

Another good and great lawyer, whose knowledge of law shone forth in principles and not mere abstract theories, was Wendell Phillips. He knew no constitutions, laws, customs, traditions, nor usages which did not recognize the equality of rights for all men. Amidst the persecutions of a cruel slaveocracy which threatened his life, he bore onwards and upwards the banner of freedom for all men, and demanded from the American slave-holder the unconditional surrender of the constitutional and natural right of liberty to the slave. He was but a young lawyer when he commenced battle against slavery and for human rights.

I point you to these men as the noblest and purest embodiment of what the lawyer should be. They have died and are no more with us, but their works and their lives are the brightest example for you. You are the legitimate fruit of the tree planted by them. Then, young gentlemen graduates, "Let all thou aim'st at be thy country, thy God's and truth."

In this struggle you will find conflict, false friends, a want of appreciation of your labors by the prejudiced and narrow-minded, nevertheless continue to battle for the right, and learn "to labor and to wait," a lesson no less a virtue because most willingly taught by those for whom you labor most.

> "Lives of great men remind us
> We can make our lives sublime,
> And departing leave behind us
> Footsteps on the sands of time."
> "Footprints that perchance another

Sailing o'er life's troubled main,
A forlorn and shipwrecked brother
Seeing, shall take heart again."

You will encounter, as I have, and others of my profession and your profession, among our own race, prejudice, hostility and cold cheer, so that you will often feel like abandoning the law and seeking fields of labor more lucrative and congenial. But remember that money perishes with the life that made it, and fortune changes with the changes of time, but good works, built upon the pedestal of truth, will be more enduring than brass or marble. Prejudice once existed, to a great extent, among the white brethren of your profession, owing, as it is said, chiefly to our ignorance. As we grow by education and in knowledge the legal maxim, *cessante ratione cessat lex* applies. This is my experience among my white brethren in this city and elsewhere I have been. I have only asked for and demanded my privilege and my clients' rights. Industry must form a chief feature—seek. "He who seeks shall find, and to him that knocks the door shall be opened." Now that you are about to commence active practice, let me beseech you to be industrious. Action is the soul of life; sympathy is its lever in action. Is there any citizen in this audience who purposes to chill the energy of these young men by refraining to give them their patronage, because they are afraid that they cannot obtain justice through a colored lawyer, thus aiding the very wrong you complain against? If so, let him stand and show his cowardly face, and then be banished as a traitor to his race. I trust there is none.

"His be the praise who, looking down on scorn, consults his own clear heart, and nobly dares to be, not to be thought, an honest man."

It is the boast of the legal profession that it is equally capable of doing work in the elevation of humanity, with any other known calling. It is woven into the fabric of every civilization. Progress must be your watchword; the universe your field. The doctrines taught in Blackstone and Kent will not fully teach you human nature nor human wants. You must read the works of great authors in order to broaden your ideas and enrich your thoughts. Read Dante for depth of conception; Milton for sublimity of idea; Macaulay for force of expression, Charles Dickens and Shakespeare for knowledge of the inner human nature and the Bible for wisdom and understanding."

"Not enjoyment, and not sorrow,
Is our destined end or way—
Put to act that each to-morrow
Finds us farther than to-day."

Agitate! Agitate! Agitate is the surest course for securing right and conquering wrong. But I must warn you, if success attend your labors in any department of intellectual life—be not vain of your learning. Learning or knowledge is only excellent when it is useful to others. Let it be said of you, "His learning savors not the school-like gloss that most consists in echoing words and terms, and soonest wins a man an empty name." Be it said of you, too, as a lawyer in your works of humanity, your love of justice, your conduct in struggling for the honor of your *alma mater*.

Whereof you are a well-deserving pillar, remember that of the profession you have chosen the great ecclesiastic Hooker has said: "Her seat is in the bosom of God, her voice the harmony of the world; all things in heaven and earth do her homage—the very least as feeling her care, the greatest as not exempt from her power, both angels and men and creatures of what condition soever, through each in different sort and manner; yet all with uniform consent, admiring her as the mother of their peace and joy." Noble profession! Is it any wonder that of one of the most learned of its votaries, Sir William Blackstone, it is said that in his public line of life he approved himself an able, upright, impartial judge? That he was ever an active and judicious promoter of whatever he thought useful or advantageous to the public in general, or to any particular society or neighborhood he was connected with? That he was a believer in the great truths of Christianity from a thorough investigation of its evidence? Attached to the Church of England from conviction of its excellence, his principles were those of its genuine members—enlarged and tolerant. His religion was pure and unaffected, and his attendance upon its public duties regular, and those always performed with seriousness and devotion. His earliest wish was that he should die:

> "Untainted by the guilty bribe,
> Uncursed admidst the harpy tribe—
> No orphan's cry to wound my ear—
> My honor and my conscience clear.
> Thus may I calmly meet my end,
> Thus to the grave in peace descend."

And so did Sir William Blackstone live and die, and so likewise, young gentlemen, may your lives be and terminate; for, remember, young gentlemen, the term of life is short. To spend that shortness basely, 'twere too long. Though life did ride upon a dial's point—still ending at the arrival of an hour. And as you go forth into the world in the pursuit of your profession, I bid you farewell and God speed.

Source: First Annual Address to the Law Graduates of Allen University, class 1884, given by D. Augustus Straker, June 12, 1884 at Bethel A.M.E. Church, Columbia, SC. Atlanta, GA: Jas. P. Harrison & Co., printers and publishers, 1885. Library of Congress, Rare Book and Special Collections Division, Daniel A. P. Murray Pamphlets Collection.

"Emigration to Liberia," Report of the Standing Committee on Emigration of the Board of Directors of the American Colonization Society
(January 20, 1885)

Colonization of free blacks in Africa was an issue that divided both whites and blacks. Some blacks supported immigration because they thought black Americans would never receive justice in the United States. Others believed African Americans should remain in the United States to fight against slavery and for full legal rights as American citizens. Some whites saw colonization as a way of ridding the nation of blacks, while others believed black Americans would be happier in Africa or elsewhere, where they could live free of racial discrimination. Still others believed black American colonists could play a central role in Christianizing and civilizing Africa.

The American Colonization Society was formed in 1817 to send free African Americans to Africa as an alternative to emancipation in the United States. In 1822, the society established a colony on the west coast of Africa, which, in 1847, became the independent nation of Liberia. By *1867, the society had sent more than 13,000 immigrants to Liberia. Abolitionists attacked the society, trying to discredit colonization as a slaveholder's scheme. After the Civil War, when many blacks wanted to go to Liberia, financial support for colonization waned. Reproduced here is a report from the Standing Committee on Emigration of the Board of Directors of the American Colonization Society, which was unanimously adopted on January 20, 1885.*

The times are changed! Wondrous events combine to turn the world's thought at this moment to the "Dark Continent." The Congo is drawing to itself the activities of nations as never before since the pyramids were built.

As a spider builds his web, beginning with a single thread here and there, attaching the ends to various objects, so does a power in mankind's history weave the texture of human vicissitude. It is a marvelous chapter in this human story which has been written in America. Slaves torn from home and kindred were forced into this country by cruel European greed. From these slaves, then, the most miserable, have sprung nearly seven millions of the colored race, long held here in bondage, but at the same time brought into contact with Christian civilization, finally emancipated, enfranchised, and beginning to be educated. This is one thread.

About seventy years ago a few philanthropists, with far-seeing vision, organized for the purpose of creating a home on the Western coast of Africa for such of these people as could and would return to the Fatherland. The Republic of Liberia has been the result. There is now a focus of light from which the rays may spread across the whole breadth of that long darkness. This is another thread.

England, the same Power that so long winked at "the middle passage" while the forefathers were dragged across the seas and bound in chains in her colonies here, is to-day hovering on the northwestern borders of the infant nation, having within two years past torn from its grasp a large territory, and, if all signs do not fail, is preparing to repeat the act on the southeast borders. Here is a strip of country ready for occupation, and inviting immigrants to come and possess the virgin soil, with all the richness of its productions. This is another thread.

Social and political equality, however fair in name and theory, is difficult in practice as between races so distinct as African and Caucasian. Twenty years of trial here has been sufficient to convince large numbers of the colored people who at first spurned the idea of going to Africa that their proper home is there, and there the fitting field for working out their destiny. This is another thread. And so the loom of Providence weaves on! Amazing threads they all are, but the pattern is from an Omnipotent hand!

Here stands the old Colonization Society alive to-day, while many thought it dead, and as yet about the only ear to listen at the telephone call and gather up the cry which comes from all parts of the land where these African people dwell; and the cry is louder and more intense and multitudinous

month by month. Consider the appeals which roll in upon the Society almost every day in proof of the singular truth. The last month illustrates what has been going on for some time past, but now apparently there more earnestly than ever:

December 1st, 1884, Landsford, S. C., one of them writes: Tell us how to get to Liberia—to Africa; our people are sick and tired of this country, and want to go home; 500 men and women of whom I am the teacher are ready to go at once.

December 8th, 1884, Denison, Texas, another writes: I wrote you about seven years ago, and received a few papers. The mass of our people are poorer than they were eight years ago. We want now to go to Africa. What is the latest news? Can you tell us all about it? What can you do for sending us? How and when can we get there, and what are the conditions? All early answer will confer a favor "on a great crowd of us."

We do not give the exact language, but the substance.

December 12th, 1884, from the same place, another writes: A great many of us are making preparations to go to Liberia, and we want direct information in regard to the whole affair. He asks these questions:

1st How many families must we collect before we can be sent?

2d Can we go on shipboard at Galveston?

3d Do we send any money, and to whom?

The same day, Darlington, S. C., J. P. Brockenton, pastor of Macedonia Baptist Church, of more than 1,000 members, 48 years old, with wife and children, writes, applying for passage to Liberia. From his own accounts he must be an important man. He is President of the South Carolina State Baptist Convention, Moderator of the District Association, Trustee of the free School Board of Darlington County, and Life Director of the Home Mission Society. He wants to go to Africa, he says—

1st Because I want to continue my good work for the Master.

2d Because I think my Christian influence is more needed there than here.

3d Because the harvest in Africa is great, but the laborers are few.

4th Because my children are trained teachers or mechanics, and as such can assist in building up our Fatherland.

5th Because my condition as a *man* will be better established and my work as a *minister* better appreciated.

Pretty sound and sensible reasons. He says he is poor, and if the Society can aid him he will be thankful.

December 21st, 1884, Waco, Texas, a correspondent, who is a superintendent, writes:

We have organized a Bureau of Home and Foreign Missions in our Baptist State Convention. (The Baptists appear to be plentiful.) They are collecting money to send two messengers to Liberia to obtain information. He is now making up a colony to leave for Liberia in 1886. It will be from 1,500 to 2,000 strong. If they can get sufficient information from the American Colonization Society they will not send the two messengers. He says we may see what they are doing in the South to get to the Fatherland. He wants all kinds of information about the matter. He says they are raising about $500 per month; that it costs the Society $100 per head to take them out and support them for six months. "I mean business. If we come to you 2,000 strong, can't you make it less than that? Help us all you can, and let me know at once how many can go in one ship at a time."

December 24th, 1884, one writes again from Denison, Texas: There are 62 already in our company. What are your lowest terms? We have 35 farmers, 4 school-teachers, 1 cabinet-maker, 6 ministers, 4 hotel and steamboat cooks, 2 brick-makers, 4 blacksmiths, 4 carpenters, 2 well-diggers, and a good many laborers. Please don't get impatient at our asking questions, for we want to be all right when we get to the ship.

December 27th, 1884, Homer, Louisiana, another writes, saying he seeks a home for a poor black man; he wants to know all about Liberia; he wants to get where he can be free; says he is not free here by a long ways. What will it take to put me and my wife over?

December 31st, 1884, from Darlington, S. C., again from our friend Brockenton, who now signs himself Secretary of the Club. He acknowledges receipt of books, papers, &c. Says he can't be ready to go till October; that a colony will go with him. He gives quite a description of the *personnel* of his colony; says they expect to be organized into a church before sailing. He predicts great good from this company. They are in all 43 persons, with more to be added.

The same day, from Lynchburg, S. C., a bright man writes of the progress the colored people are making there and elsewhere in the South for emigration. He says there is the greatest unrest among them ever known. Large numbers are going to the West, but the best portion are preparing to make their way to Liberia. The Clarendon Club wants information, and he writes at their request. He says they will plant large crops of cotton, so as to raise money in the fall. He is Secretary of the Clarendon and Williamsburg Clubs. He is without means to travel as he wishes, to stimulate the people; and in view of this, wants circulars and documents from us to spread ABROAD.

The same day, from Waco, Texas, another writes that the people of his county wish to send him to Liberia to bring back a report of the land. He wants to know if he can go. He says the condition of his people is deplorable; that he learns that a whole county of them are going to Kansas; that hundreds are coming from North Carolina to Arkansas—out of the pan, into the fire. What do horses and cows cost in Liberia? Could you send over my piano? My house is worth $1,000; I was offered $600 for it. He wants to sell and get away; says himself and wife are at our service if we can make any use of them.

January 1st, 1885, Chambersburg, Pa., a colored woman writes: We are now really preparing to leave this country. She has lost a former letter, and wants to hear again; says there are eight of them ready to go in May. "Will they be crowded out?" "We have been a long time getting ready, but the Spirit says, Go! and we must abide God's will." Several other families wish to go, especially one that comes from Alabama, where times are hard for colored people.

January 3d, 1885, Kansas City, Mo., a prudent man writes: Would I be safe to start for Liberia with $100 and five children? A great many people here would be glad to go, but they have no information. I am a kalsominer by trade. Would I be of any use when I get there?

The same day, from Denison, Texas, a sharp man writes, asking for full information about emigration to Liberia. He and several others wish to go there. He says they "are very well equipped, with wealth and literature enough to get there and straighten up and straighten out. Write soon, and let us know."

January 7th, 1885, Forestville, N. C., another writes that he is making preparation to go to Liberia. He sees so many colored people awaking to the project of going, because of their oppressions in this country. "We want to reach Africa, the home of the free. Is there any chance for me?"

Such is the burden of the cry from all quarters of the land. What does it mean? Our Society has absolutely done nothing to awaken this intense longing for Africa among the colored people. No means have been employed by us to stir up so deep and general a feeling, unless our circulars and documents for the spread of information may have contributed to it; otherwise, not a whisper from us has been heard. The cry is spontaneous. One of the correspondents above cited seems to have expressed the secret—"The Spirit says, Go!" What other conclusion can we reach? God's hand is in it, weaving the web of His Providence for Africa.

But we would not just now encourage a wholesale exodus. The vast preparation must no doubt be gradual, as all great things are. In the ancient exodus *from* Africa the people were held for forty years in the wilderness prior to their possession of the Promised Land. The first emigrants to Liberia were sent by this Society in 1820, and we have not

failed to send some each year since. The last company of forty-seven was sent last October—in all nearly 16,000 persons, exclusive of 5,722 recaptured Africans—at the cost of $3,000,000—the munificent gift of American Christian philanthropy. At the present time there are on the soil of Liberia about 25,000 souls, comprising the American immigrants and their children, with the recaptured Africans who have settled there, and one million of the native population, enjoying the advantages of the Republic and amenable to its laws, while remoter tribes are pressing down towards the infant Republic as to a centre of brighter hope. There is a coast-line of 500 miles—extending indefinitely inland. This was recently diminished 40 miles by the arbitrary power of England; and about the same extent is coming into dispute on the southeast. It is believed that Liberia could now absorb and assimilate 10,000 persons, especially immigrants from the mother Republic versed in the customs, manners, and laws of a Republican Christian Government. If this population could be transferred to Liberia in the next two years it would probably settle the boundary question now in dispute, besides being of incalculable advantage in many other ways.

They would hardly be missed among us out of a colored population rapidly multiplying, and which by natural increase has nearly doubled during the last score of years, but immense good might flow through them to Liberia and the whole continent.

That many are waking up to this idea, and are ready to leave this country for the land of their forefathers, is evinced, as we have seen, from the constantly-increasing applications for aid to this end. These come in upon us from all quarters and through all channels—through the correspondence of private individuals, members and officers of churches, clubs, and various organizations, and even through Government Departments and through the Christian agencies of our great commercial cities.

The one fact we would emphasize is this: The only hope of lifting Africa up to continental equality and prominence lies not merely in National diplomacy and the jealousy of States, nor in the greed of misers, nor in the craft of unprincipled traders and sharpers who pour out upon the soil, which their touch pollutes, all the vices and wrongs and refuse of modern civilization, but it is mainly in the Christian colony, which is in some sense a Christian mission among stranger tribes of men. This is the voice of history—certainly of modern history. America was redeemed at last by the Christian pilgrims of Europe, who imbued its growing life with the spirit of Christian civilization, and stamped upon its institutions the impress of morality and of Christian faith. Such a power as this is alone adequate to build another Republic like our own from the Atlantic to the Indian Oceans.

It is a marvelous fact that now, simultaneously with the opening of that Continent, such a general desire among our colored people to go to it should spring up so intensely. What a wonderful thread this is in the stupendous web of Providence! And into our hands the grand mission of opening Africa to the splendid realizations of the future is in a very special sense committed, since we are the only Nation on the face of the earth outside of Africa herself that has the fitting material in our colored population; and all signs point to our duty in this respect. The times are ripe for a powerful onward movement in this direction. The two thrilling reports rendered by the Committee on Emigration—one of a year ago and one of the year preceding—were as a bugle blast, calling mankind to action. No form of words could be more eloquent or piercing than the language of those reports. They state the case to the American people with all the cogency of logic, the fire of poetry, and the pathos almost of inspiration. They have been widely circulated; and this seed, so scattered, may yield—Heaven grant it—a rich and plentiful harvest.

But at the opening of another year in the history of this Society we stand confronted with one great necessity, one specific work, which ought to be immediately taken up and accomplished; this is, to put 10,000 of our choicest colored population into Liberia as soon as it is found to be practicable. It will cost a million dollars!

What are our resources—what our means of doing it? The abundance of our own country, the thousands and millions of money in the hands of prosperous capitalists and churchmen, and the ever-plethoric Treasury of the Government itself. But how shall we open these mighty coffers? What key can unlock our way to the hoarded treasure? We have tried commissioned agents, but the effort has been practically a failure. What, then, is left us?

1. Personal appeals to well-known rich philanthropists.
2. Concise, comprehensive, pointed, specific appeals through the religious and secular press of the country.
3. The same kind of appeal to the Christian clergy, and through them to the entire membership of the churches.
4. An earnest, temperate, emphatic appeal to Congress and the Government.

They have loaned a million dollars to the New Orleans Exposition. Great as that is or ought to be, is it any more; on the welfare of mankind than it would be for the same sum to secure the future of the daughter Republic, and through her the Christian civilization of the entire Continent? This would indeed be a glorious consummation! Everything calls for it—everything incites to it. A million dollars in two years for the redemption of that vast territory with its hundred and fifty or two hundred millions of people—what a splendid golden thread would this be in the mighty loom of Providence; in this Divine pattern of human destiny; this august design of the Infinite Reason; this lofty work of the hands of the Eternal!

B. SUNDERLAND, CHARLES C. NOTT, JAMES SAUL,

Committee. Washington, D. C., *January* 20*th,* 1885.

Source: Sunderland, B., Charles C. Nott, and James Saul. "Emigration to Liberia," *Report of the Standing Committee on Emigration of the Board of Directors of the American Colonization Society.* Library of Congress, Rare Book and Special Collections Division, African American Pamphlet Collection.

Alexander Crummell, "Common Sense in Common Schooling"
(September 13, 1886)

Alexander Crummell, the rector of St. Luke's Episcopal Church in Washington, DC, from 1879 to 1898, delivered the following sermon in 1886. In "Common Sense in Common Schooling," Crummell gives a critique of the trends in African American educational facilities during this time. His belief is that the educators need to educate their students in practical trades and industrial arts. He also criticizes U.S. trade unions for their exclusion of blacks.

> *That the soul should be without knowledge is not good.*—Prov. 9:12

To-morrow morning we shall witness the reopening of the public schools and the beginning of another year's school session. As the training and instruction of our children is a matter of very great interest and importance, I am glad of the opportunity to say a few words upon the whole subject of Common-School education.

I need not pause to explain the special significance of the text. It is so plain and apparent that even the youngest can readily take it in, and you, who are their elders, have years ago become familiar with its point and power.

It has had during the last few years a special and peculiar influence upon us as a people. Rarely in the history of man has any people, "sitting in the region and shadow of death"—a people almost literally enveloped in darkness—rarely, I say, has any such people risen up from their Egyptian darkness with such a craving for light as the black race in this country. It has been almost the repetition of the Homeric incident:—

> Dispel this gloom—the light of heaven restore—
> Give me to see, and Ajax asks no more.

Almost universal ignorance was the mental condition of the race of the previous to emancipation.

Out of millions of people, not more than 30,000 were allowed an acquaintance with letters. To-day, hundreds of schools are in existence, and over a million of our children are receiving the elements of common-school education.

The point of interest in this grand fact is that this intellectual receptivity was no tardy and reluctant faculty. Albeit an ignorant people, yet we did not need either to be goaded or even stimulated to intellectual desire. There was no need of any compulsory laws to force our children into the schools. No; the mental appetite of the Negro was like the resurrection of nature in the spring-time of the far northern regions. To-day, universal congelation and death prevail. To-morrow, the icy bands of winter are broken and there is a sudden upheaval of dead, stolid rivers. The living waters rush from their silent beds and sweep away formidable barriers, and spread abroad over wide and extensive plains.

This craving of the appetite for letters and knowledge knows no abatement. Everywhere throughout the nation there still abides this singular and burning aptitude of the black race for schools and learning.

I am proud of this vast and ardent desire of the race; for the brain of man is the very first instrument of human achievement. Given, a cultivated and elastic brain, and you have the possibility of a man, and, with other qualifications and conditions, the probability of almost a demi-god. Take away the trained and cultivated intellect, and you get the likelihood of an animal, and, possibly, of a reptile.

But while I rejoice in the wide spread of lettered acquaintance among us, I cannot close my eyes to a great evil which has been simultaneous with the increase of our knowledge. This evil is becoming so alarming that I feel it a duty to call the attention of both parents and children to it. The evil itself I call Disproportion! It is that which we mean when we have an excess of somewhat that is pleasing, with a loss of what is convenient and substantial. We are all apt then to say that it is *"too much of a good thing."* The like one-sidedness discovers itself among us in our common-school education. Too many of our parents are ruining their children by this error.

They crave an excess of one kind of education, and at the same time neglect important elements of another and quite as important a kind. This sad fact suggests as a theme for consideration to-day "Common Sense in Common Schooling." The subject presents itself in the two topics, *i.e.*, the *excess* and the *defect* in the training of our youth.

(1.) Education as a system in our day divides itself into two sections, which are called, respectively, the higher and the lower. The former pertains to classical learning, *i.e.*, Latin and Greek, Science, and Art, in which latter are included music, drawing, and painting. It is with regard to the higher education that I feel called upon to express my fears and to give my counsel.

I fear we are overdoing this matter of higher learning. Everywhere I go throughout the country I discover two or three very disagreeable and unhealthy facts. I see, *first* of all, *(a)* the vain ambition of very many mothers to over-educate their daughters, and to give them training and culture unfitted for their position in society and unadapted to their prospects in life. I see, likewise, too many men, forgetful of the occupations they held in society, anxious to shoot their sons suddenly, regardless of fitness, into literary characters and into professional life. This is the first evil. *(b)* Next to this I have observed an ambition among the youth of both sexes for aesthetical culture; an inordinate desire for the ornamental and elegant in educational to the neglect of the solid and practical. And *(c)*, thirdly, to a very large extent school children are educated in letters to a neglect of household industry. Scores of both boys and girls go to school. That is their life business and nothing else; but their parents neglect their training in housework, and so they live in the streets, and during the first twelve or fourteen years of their life are given to

play and pleasure. And *(d)*, lastly, our boys and girls almost universally grow up without trades, looking forward, if they do look forward, many of them, to being servants and waiters; and many more I am afraid, expecting to get a living by chance and hap-hazard.

Doubtless some of you will say that the colored people are not the only people at fault in these respects; that the American people, in general, are running wild about the higher culture—are neglecting trades and mechanism, and are leaving the more practical and laborious duties of life to foreigners. Grant that this is the case; but it only serves to strengthen the allegation I make that we, in common with American people, are running into an excessive ambition for the higher culture to the neglect of industrial arts and duties. I go into families. I ask parents what they are preparing their children for, and the answer I frequently receive is: "Oh, I am going to send my son to college to make him a lawyer, or the daughter is to go to the East or to Europe to be made an accomplished lady." Not long ago I met an old acquaintance, and, while talking about the future of her children, I inquired: "What are you going to do with—I will call him 'Tom'?" Tom is a little fellow about fourteen years old; by no means a genius; more anxious about tops and taffy and cigarettes than about his books; never likely, so far as I can see, to set the Potomac on fire. Her answer was that his father purposed sending him to college to make him a lawyer. On another occasion I was talking to a minister of the Gospel about his daughters, and *he* was anxious to send his two girls to Belgium to be educated for society! Not long ago an acquaintance of mine told me that his sons should never do the work he was doing. He was going to educate one to be a doctor, another to be a lawyer, and the third he hoped to make a minister. I must give him the credit that when I pointed out the danger of ruining his sons by this over-education, and that this sudden rise from a humble condition might turn them into lazy and profligate spendthrifts, he listened to me, and I am glad to say he took my advice. He is now giving them his own trade, and I think they are likely to become quiet and industrious young men.

Let me not be misunderstood. I am not only *not* opposed to the higher culture, but I am exceedingly anxious for it. We *must* have a class of trained and superior men and women. We *must* have cultured, refined society. To live on a dead level of inferiority, or to be satisfied with the plane of uniform mediocrity, would be death to us as a people.

Moreover we need, and in our blood, the great molders and fashioners of thought among us. To delegate the thinking of the race to any other people would be to introduce intellectual stagnation in the race; and when thought declines then a people are sure to fall and fade away.

These, then, are the most sufficient reasons for a large introduction among us of the highest training and culture. But this is no reason or excuse for disproportion or extravagance. Culture *is* a great need; but the greater, wider need of the race is industry and practicality. We need especially multitudinous artizans, and productive toil, and the grand realizations of labor, or otherwise we can never get respect or power in the land.

And this leads me next to the other topic, viz, the employments and occupations of industrial life. Here we encounter one of the most formidable difficulties of our civil life in this country. The state of things in this regard is an outrage upon humanity! And I protest, with all my might, against the mandate of the "Trades' Unions," which declare "You black people must be content with servant life!" I say that this race of ours should demand the right to enter every avenue of enterprise and activity white men enter. They should cry out, too, against our exclusion from any of the trades and businesses of life. But with all this remember that no people can *all*, or even many of them, become lawyers, doctors, ministers, teachers, scholars! No people can get their living and build themselves up by refined style and glittering fashion or indulgence in belle-lettres.

No people can live off of flowers, nor gain strength and robustness by devotion to art.

And it is just this false and artificial tendency which is ruining colored society almost everywhere in the United States. It is especially so in the large cities. The youth want to go to school until they are nineteen or twenty years of age. Meanwhile, the book-idea so predominates that duty and industry are thrown into the shade. Mothers and fathers work hard to sustain their children. After awhile the children look with contempt upon their unlettered, hard-handed parents, and regard them as only born for use and slavish toil. Is this an exaggeration? Have you not seen some of those fine young ladies, whose mothers sweat and toil for them in the wash-tub or cook in the kitchen, boasting that they can't hem a pocket handkerchief or cook a potato? Have not you seen some of these grand gentlemen who forget the humble parents who begot them, forget the humble employments of those parents, turn up their noses at the ordinary occupations of the poor race they belong to, and then begin the fantastic airs of millionaires, while they don't own ground enough to bury themselves in?

You say, perchance, "Such girls and boys are 'sillies,'" and that their brainless folly is no reason why the higher education should not be given in all the schools. It is just here I beg to differ with you. I maintain that parents should exercise discrimination in this matter. They have no right to waste time and expense upon incapable girls and boys. They have no right to raise up a whole regiment of pretentious and lazy fools to plague society and to ruin themselves. They have no right to send out into the world a lot of young men and women with heads crammed with Latin, Greek, and literature; with no heart to labor; with hands of baby softness; interested only in idleness, and given to profligacy and ruinous pleasure. And just this, in numerous cases, is the result of this ambitious system of education in this land. We are turning out annually from the public schools a host of fine scholars, but not a few of them lazy, inflated, senseless, sensual! Whole shoals of girls hating labor, slattern in habits and at the same time bespangled with frippery, devoted to dress, and the easy prey of profligate men! And lots of young men utterly indifferent to the fortunes of their families and the interests of their girls, but scores of them thoroughly unprincipled and profligate!

They live for to-day, but the life they live is for sensual delight, and the culture they have gained is spent in skillful devices to administer to the lusts of the flesh. This I am constrained to say is the result of the higher education in well nigh half of the colored youth who graduate from high schools and colleges, and it is ruinous to our people.

You ask me the remedy for this great evil. MY answer is by avoidance of the excess which I have pointed out and the adoption of the ordinary common-school education. Shun disproportion. Hold on to the higher education, but use it only in fit and exceptional cases. If you have a son or a daughter burning with the desire for learning, give that child every possible opportunity. But you see the condition I present, viz, that it *burns* with intellectual desire. But how often is this the case? The difficulty in the matter is that parents themselves are to blame for the miscarriage of their children's education. Everybody now a days is crazy about education. Fathers and mothers are anxious that their children should shine. However ordinary a boy or girl may be the parents want them to be scholars. The boy may be a numbskull, the girl a noodle. The fond parent thinks the child a prodigy; stimulates its ambition, gives it indulgence, saves it from labor, keeps it at school almost to its majority and then, at last, it finds out that the child has no special talent, dislikes labor, is eager for pleasure, dress, and display, is selfish and cruel to its parents, unable to earn its own living, and expects father and mother to drudge for its support and vanity. I am sure that you all know numerous cases of such failure and ruin.

And it all comes from a neglect of a few plain common-sense rules which belong naturally to the subject of education.

Let me briefly set before you some of these rules:

First of all, secure for your children an acquaintance with reading writing, arithmetic, and geography. When well grounded in these studies, which is ordinarily at 12 or 13, then ascertain whether your children are fitted for the higher branches. If you yourself are educated, form your own judgement; if not, get the advice of a well-qualified friend, or the opinion of your minister, or take counsel of the child's schoolmaster. If convinced that the child gives promise of superiority, keep it at school, give it the best opportunities, and labor hard to make your child a thorough scholar.

(2) On the other hand, if you find your child has but ordinary capacity, take it from school and put it at an early day to work. If you don't you will not only waste time but you are likely to raise up a miserable dolt or a lazy dandy. Such a child, brought up to fruitless inactivity, dawdling for years over unappreciated culture, will, likely as not never want to work for his living, may turn out a gambler or a thief, and in the end may disgrace your name or break your heart. Don't keep your children too long at school; don't think too much about the book and so little about labor. Remember that the end of all true education is to learn to do duty in life and to secure an honorable support and sustenance.

And here (3) let me press upon you the importance of training your children in industrial habits *at home* during the period of their school life. Going to school should never prevent a girl from learning to sew, to cook, to sweep, bed-making, and scrubbing the floor; nor a boy from using a hammer, cleaning the yard, bringing in coal, doing errands, working hard to help his mother, or to assist his father. Home work, moreover, is the natural antidote to the mental strain, and oftentimes the physical decline which, in these days, comes from the excess of study, which is the abnormal feature of the present school system.

From labor health, from health contentment flows.

If you begin your child's school life by the separation of books and learning from manual labor, then you begin his education with poison as the very first portion of his intelligent life! He had better a deal be ignorant and industrious than lettered and slothful, and, perchance, a beggar! Laziness and learning are as incongruous as a "jewel in a swine's snout," and few things are so demoralizing to the young. Witness the large numbers of lettered youth and young men, fresh from schools, academies, and colleges, who fill the jails and prisons of the country, and then think of the large and more skillful numbers outside who ought, in justice, to be companying with those *within*. Nothing is more contemptible than the crowds of these dandaical "clothes-bags," for they deserve no better title, one sees in our large cities, who have, indeed, the varnish of the schools and literature, but who lack common sense, full of vanity and pretense, poisoned with lust and whisky, and, while too proud and too lazy to work, get their living by vice and gambling. This abuse of learning, however, is not confined to men. Alas! that it must be acknowledged, we have all over the land scores of cultured young woman in whose eyes labor is a disgrace and degradation, who live lives of lazy cunning or deception, and plunge determinedly into lust and harlotry. And the poor old fathers and mothers who toiled so painfully for their schooling, and hoped such great things for their daughters, have been cast down to misery and despair, or else have died broken-hearted over their daughters' shame and ruin. And in every such case how sad the reflection: "O, that I had been wise with my child! O, that I had scouted her false notions about style and elegance! O, that I had been more anxious to make her industrious and virtuous! Then all this anguish and distress would never have fallen upon me!" Such cases of folly have their lessons for all of us who are parents. May Almighty God make us both wise in our generation, and prudent and discreet with our children.

The words I have spoken this day have sprung from two or three deep convictions which I am sure are thoroughly scriptural and true, and which, I think, may rightly close this discourse:

1. The first of these is that children are neither toys nor playthings, such as are embroidery and jewels and trinkets. They are moral spiritual beings, endowed with conscience and crowned with the principle of immortality. You may toy and play with your trinkets, but you are accountable to God for the soul, the life, the character, and the conduct of your child. Hence duty and responsibility are the two paramount considerations which are to be allied with the entire training of your children, whether at home or in their school life.

2. Children are trusts for the good and health of society and the commonwealth. The law don't allow you to poison the air with filth and garbage, and for the simple reason that as a householder you are a trustee for your fellow-creatures. But in regards of your children you are, in a far higher sense, a trustee for your fellow-creatures around you. What right have you to send forth from your threshold a senseless fool, full of learning it may be, but with no sense, no idea of responsibility for anybody, impudent to old people, a rowdy in God's Church, a rioter, a gambler, a rake? Ought not the culture you have toiled to give him serve to make him modest, a mild-mannered man, a stay to his humble toilsome parents, a useful man in society, a thrifty and productive citizen in the community? And was it not your duty, all his life long, to strive to realize such a large and high-souled being as the fruit of your family life and training?

Or, if perchance it is a girl, what right have you to send forth into the world a lazy, impertinent creature, bedecked and bejeweled indeed; full perchance, of letters and accomplishments, but with no womanly shame; brazen with boldness; lazy as a sloth, and, yet, proud, pretentious, crazy for ruinous delights; swept away by animal desires; alien from domestic duties, and devoted to pleasure? Go to, now. Is this the fruit of your vineyard? When God and man, too, look that it should bring forth grapes, will you only thrust upon us such wild grapes?

You have no such right! You are a trustee for society, and you should take a pride in rearing up ornaments for society—"Sons," as the psalmist describes them, "who may grow up as the young plants;" "daughters, as the polished corners of the temple." Just such, I am proud to say, as I see in many of your own families is this church, whose children are intelligent, scholarly, and, at the same time, virtuous, modest, obedient, and industrious. God's holy name be praised for such children, such parents, such godly families! May God, for Jesus' sake, multiply them a hundred fold in all our communities!

3. Join to this, thirdly, the most solemn of all considerations, *i.e.*, that your children are the servants of the most high God. All souls are says the Almighty. God made them and sent them into the world. He it is who places living souls in the family, in human society, in the nation, in the church, for His own honor and glory. Not for mere pastime, for trifling, or for pleasure are human beings put amid the relations of life. We are all God's property—our children and ourselves—for God's service and His praise. Beloved, accept this grand prerogative of your human existence; train your children for godly uses in this world; train their minds by proper schooling; their bodies by industry; their immortal souls by teaching, catechising, and family devotion, so that they may glorify God in their bodies and their spirits; and then God will give you family order and success in this world; your children honor and blessing by the Holy Ghost, and everlasting light shall be the inheritance of your seed, and your seeds' seed from generation to generation on earth, and glory, honor, and peace, at the last, in the Kingdom of Heaven above!

Source: Common Sense in Common Schooling: a sermon by Alex. Crummell, Rector of St. Luke's Church, Washington, DC, September 13, 1886. Library of Congress, Rare Book and Special Collections Division, Daniel A. P. Murray Pamphlets Collection.

The Wonderful Eventful Life of Rev. Thomas James, by Himself (1887)

In this excerpt from his autobiography, Rev. Thomas James, a minister in the African Methodist Episcopal Church, writes about his life from slavery to the ministry to the antislavery movement in New York and Massachusetts. The narrative is an account of how James ran a camp for free and refugee African Americans in Kentucky during the Civil War.

The story of my life is a simple one, perhaps hardly worth the telling. I have written it in answer to many and oft repeated requests on the part of my friends for a relation of its incidents, and to them I dedicate this little volume.

The Author
Rochester, [N.Y.] Feb. 15, 1886.

I was born a slave at Canajoharie, this state, in the year 1804. I was the third of four children, and we were all the property of Asa Kimball, who, when I was in the eighth year of my age, sold my mother, brother and elder sister to purchasers from Smithtown, a village not far distant from Amsterdam in the same part of the state. My mother refused to go, and ran into the garret to seek a hiding place. She was pursued, caught, tied hand and foot and delivered to her new owner. I caught my last sight of my mother as they rode off with her. My elder brother and sister were taken away at the same time. I never saw either my mother or sister again. Long years afterwards my brother and I were reunited, and he died in this city a little over a year ago. From him I learned that my mother died about the year 1846, in the place to which she had been taken. My brother also informed me that he and his sister were separated soon after their transfer to a Smithport master, and he never heard of her subsequent fate. Of my father I never had any personal knowledge, and, indeed, never heard anything. My youngest sister, the other member of the family, died when I was yet a youth.

While I was still in the seventeenth year of my age, Master Kimball was killed in a runaway accident; and at the administrator's sale I was sold with the rest of the property, my new master being Cromwell Bartlett, of the same neighborhood. As I remember, my first master was a well-to-do but rough farmer, a skeptic in religious matters, but of better heart than address; for he treated me well. He owned several farms, and my work was that of a farm hand. My new master had owned me but a few months when he sold me, or rather traded me, to George H. Hess, a wealthy farmer of the vicinity of Fort Plain. I was bartered in exchange for a yoke of steers, a colt and some additional property, the nature and amount of which I have now forgotten. I remained with Master Hess from March until June of the same year, when I ran away. My master had worked me hard, and at last undertook to whip me. This led me to seek escape farm slavery. I arose in the night, and taking the newly staked line of the Erie canal for my route, traveled along it westward until, about a week later, I reached the village of Lockport. No one had stopped me in my flight. Men were at work digging the new canal at many points, but they never troubled themselves even to question me. I slept in barns at night and begged food at farmers' houses along my route. At Lockport a colored man showed me the way to the Canadian border. I crossed the Niagara at Youngstown on the ferry-boat, and was free!

Once on free soil, I began to look about for work, and found it at a point called Deep Cut on the Welland Canal, which they were then digging. I found the laborers a rough lot, and soon had a mind to leave them. After three months had passed, I supposed it safe to return to the American side, and acting on the idea I recrossed the river. A farmer named Rich, residing near Youngstown, engaged me as a wood chopper. In the spring I made my way to Rochesterville and found a home with Lawyer Talbert. The chores about his place were left to me, and I performed the same service for Orlando Hastings. I was then nineteen years of age. As a slave I had never been inside of a school or a church, and I knew nothing of letters or religion. The wish to learn awoke in me almost from the moment I set foot in the place, and I soon obtained an excellent chance to carry the wish into effect. After the opening of the Erie canal, I obtained work in the warehouse of the Hudson and Erie line, and found a home with its manager, Mr. Pliny Allen Wheeler. I was taught to read by Mr. Freeman, who had opened a Sunday-school of his own for colored youths, on West Main street, or Buffalo street, as it was then called. But my self-education advanced fastest in the warehouse during the long winter and spring months, when the canal was closed and my only work consisted of chores about the place and at my employer's residence. The clerks helped me whenever I needed help in my studies. Soon I had learning enough to be placed in charge of the freight business of the warehouse, with full direction over the lading of boats. I became a member of the African Methodist Episcopal Society in 1823, when the church was on Ely street, and my studies took the direction of preparation for the ministry. In 1828 I taught a school for colored children on Favor street, and I began holding meetings at the same time. In the following year I first formally commenced preaching, and in 1830 I bought as a site for a religious edifice the lot now occupied by Zion's church. In the meantime the Ely street society had ceased to exist, its death having been hastened by internal quarrels and by dishonesty among its trustees. On the lot already mentioned I built a small church edifice, which was afterwards displaced by a larger one, the latter finally giving way to the present structure on the same site. I was ordained as a minister in May, 1833, by Bishop Rush. I had been called Tom as a Slave, and they called me Jim at the warehouse. I put both together when I reached manhood, and was ordained as Rev. Thomas James.

Two years before the last mentioned event in my life, Judge Sampson, vice-president of the local branch of the African Colonization Society of that day, turned over to me a batch of anti-slavery literature sent him by Arthur Tappan. It was these documents that turned my thoughts into a channel which they never quitted until the colored man became the equal of the white in the eye of the law, if not in the sight of his neighbor of another race. In the early summer of 1833 we held the first of a series of anti-slavery meetings in the court house. The leading promoters of that meeting were William Bloss, Dr. Reid—whose widow, now in the 86th year of her age, still lives in Rochester— and Dr. W. Smith. There was a great crowd in attendance on the first night, but its leading motive was curiosity, and it listened without interfering with the proceedings. The second night we were plied with questions, and on the third they drowned with their noise the voices of the speakers and finally turned out the lights. Not to be baulked of his purpose, Mr. Bloss, who was not a man to be cowed by opposition, engaged the session room of the Third Presbyterian church; but even there we were forced to lock the doors before we could hold our abolition meeting in peace. There we organized our anti-slavery society, and when the journals of the day refused to publish our constitution and by laws, we bought a press for a paper of our own and appointed the three leaders already named to conduct it. It was printed fort-nightly and was called *The Rights of Man*. I was sent out to make a tour of the country in its interest, obtaining subscriptions for the paper and lecturing against slavery. At LeRoy I was mobbed, my meeting was broken up, and I was saved from worse treatment only by the active efforts of Mr. Henry Brewster, who secreted me in his own house. At the village I next visited, Warsaw, I was aided by Seth M. Gates and others, and I was also well received at Perry. At Pike, however, I was arrested and subjected to a mock trial, with the object of scaring me into flight from the place. At Palmyra I found no hall or church in which I could speak. Indeed the place was then a mere hamlet and could boast of but half a dozen dwellings. My tour embraced nearly every village in this and adjourning counties, and the treatment given me varied with the kind of people I happened to find in the budding settlements of the time. In the same fall I attended the first Anti-Slavery State Convention at Utica.

In 1835 I left Rochester to form a colored church at Syracuse. Of course I joined anti-slavery work to the labor which fell upon me as a pastor. In the city last named the opponents of the movement laid a trap for me, by proposing a public discussion of the leading questions at issue. I was a little afraid of my ability to cope with them alone, and therefore, quietly wrote to Gerrett Smith, Beriah Green and Alvin Stewart for help. When the public discussion took place, and these practiced speakers met and answered the arguments of our opponents, the representatives of the latter—the leading editor and the foremost lawyer of the place—left the church in disgust, pleading that they had a good case, but did not expect to face men so well able to handle any question as the friends of mine I had invited. After their retreat from the hall, the two champions of slavery stirred up the salt boilers to mob us, but we adjourned before night, and when the crowd arrived at the edifice they found only prayer meeting of the church people in progress, and slunk away ashamed. I was stationed nearly three years at Syracuse, and was then transferred to Ithaca, where a little colored religious society already existed. I bought a site for a church edifice for them, and saw it built during the two years of my stay in the village. Thence I was sent to Sag Harbor, Long Island, and, finally to New Bedford, Massachusetts.

It was at New Bedford that I first saw Fred. Douglass. He was then, so to speak, right out of slavery, but had already begun to talk in public, though not before white people. He had been given authority to act as an exhorter by the church before my coming, and I some time afterwards licensed him to preach. He was then a member of my church. On one occasion, after I had addressed a white audience on the slavery question, I called upon Fred. Douglass, whom I saw among the auditors, to relate his story. He did so and in a year from that time he was in the lecture field with Parker Pillsbury and other leading abolitionist orators. Not long afterwards a letter was received from him by his fellow church members, in which he said that he had cut loose from the church; he had found that the American Church was the bulwark of American slavery. We did not take the letter to mean that Mr. Douglas had repudiated the Christian religion at the same time that he bade good-by to the churches.

It was soon after this that great excitement arose in New Bedford over the action of Rev. Mr. Jackson, a Baptist minister, who had just returned from a Baltimore clerical convention, which sent a petition to the Maryland Legislature in favor of the passage of a law compelling free Negroes to leave the state, under the plea that the free colored men mingling with the slaves incited the latter to insurrection. Rev. Mr. Jackson was a vice-president of that convention and a party to its action. Printed accounts of the proceedings were sent to me, and at a meeting called to express dissent from the course taken by the minister named and his brethren, I introduced a resolution, of which the following is a copy: "*Resolved*, That the great body of the American clergy, with all their pretensions to sanctity, stand convicted by their deadly hostility to the Anti-Slavery movement, and their support of the slave system, as a brotherhood of thieves, and should branded as such by all honest Christians."

The tone and tenor of this resolution now carry an air of extravagant injustice, but there was at that time only too much truth in the charge it contains. The resolution was tabled, but it was at the same time decided to publish it, and to invite the ministers of the town to appear at an adjourned meeting and defend their course, if they could. Nearly thirty ministers of New Bedford and vicinity appeared at the next meeting, and with one voice denounced the obnoxious resolution and its author. The result was that a strong prejudice was excited against me, a prejudice that was increased by an event which took place soon afterwards—the whole due to the fact that the respectable and wealthy classes, as well as the lower orders, at the time regarded abolitionists with equal aversion and contempt. The conscience of the North had not yet been fairly awakened to the monstrous wrong of human bondage.

On my journey homeward from a visit to New York City, I met Mr. Henry Ludlam, his wife, two children and a slave girl, from Richmond, Va., all bound for New Bedford to spend the summer with Captain Bunbar, father-in-law of the head of this party of visitors. I said that I met them, but the meeting consisted only in this, that they and I were on board the same train, but not in the same car. I was in the "Jim Crow" car, as colored persons were not permitted to enter the others with white people, and the slave girl was sent to the same car by the same rule. I talked with her, and, as I was in duty bound to do, asked her to come to my church during the stay of the family in New Bedford. After some weeks had passed and she did not come, I took with me a colored teacher and another friend to call on her and learn, if we could, why she did not attend the services. Her master or owner met us at the door and gave us this answer: "Lucy is my slave, and slaves don't receive calls." In short, he refused to let us enter the house, whereat we took advice from friends, and applied to Judge Crapo for a writ of *habeas corpus*. The judge sent us about our business with the advice not to annoy Mr. Ludlam, who was entitled to hospitable treatment as a visitor and guest. Instead of taking this advice, we journeyed to Boston, and were given by Judge Wilds the writ his judicial brother in New Bedford had denied us. We had Sheriff Pratt and the writ with us when we made our next call on the slave girl's master. The latter at first refused even the sheriff leave to see the girl, and finally proposed to give bail for her appearance before the judge. The sheriff turned to me inquiringly when this proposal was made, and I answered: "Mr. Sheriff, you were directed to take the person of the girl Lucy, and I call upon you to do your duty." Thus we got possession of the girl, but not before her owner had obtained leave for a few minutes' private conversation with her. In this talk, as we afterwards learned, he frightened Lucy by telling her that our purpose was an evil one, and obtained her promise to display a handkerchief from the room in which she would be confined as a signal for the rescue he promised her. We took the girl to a chamber on the upper floor of the residence of the Rev. Joel Knight, and the evening we prepared to lie down before the door. Lucy displayed the handkerchief as she had promised, and, when we questioned her about it, answered: "Master told me to do it; he is coming to take me home." At this we quietly called together twenty men from the colored district of the place, and they took seats in the church close at hand, ready for any emergency. At one o' clock in the morning Ludlam appeared on the scene, with a backing of a dozen men, carrying a ladder, to effect a rescue. The sheriff hailed them, but they gave no answer, whereat our party of colored men sallied forth, and the rescuers fled in all directions. The entire town was now agog over the affair. So many took sides against us, and such threats were made, that the sheriff was forced to call to his aid the local police, and, thus escorted, the girl was placed aboard the cars for Boston. The other party, to the number of 150 men, chartered a train by another route, with the design of overpowering the sheriff's posse in the streets of Boston; but so large a force of officers was called out by the sheriff that the slaveholder's friends gave up the idea of carrying out their design. Lucy was brought before Judge Wilds, who postponed the hearing until the following Saturday, and meanwhile invited us privately to bring the girl to his home in the course of the day, as he wanted to talk with her. This we did, and the judge told Lucy what her rights were; that by the laws of Massachusetts she was free—her case was not covered by the fugitive slave law—and that if she wanted her freedom she should have it. If, however, she chose to return to her master she could do so; "but," added the judge, "after what has happened, he will probably sell you on your return with the family to a slave state." She asked for her freedom, and received it the next day, when the case was heard in open court. The Sunday night following word was received at the colored church where we were holding services that our enemies were trying to kidnap the girl. That broke up the meeting; the colored people rallied, and the attempt failed. Lucy's master was forced to return to his slave home without his human chattel. The girl afterwards married, had children, and, I believed, live happily among the people of her own color at the North.

One of the earliest cases in which I became interested as a laborer in the anti-slavery cause was that of the Emstead captives. The slaver Emstead was a Spanish vessel which left the African coast in 1836 with a cargo of captive blacks. When four days out the captives rose, and, coming on deck, threw overboard all but two of the officers and crew. The two they saved to navigate the vessel; but instead of taking the vessel back to the coast they had just left, as they were directed by the blacks, the two sailors attempted to make the American main, and the vessel finally drifted ashore near Point Judith, on Long Island Sound. The Spanish Minister demanded the surrender of the blacks to his government. They were taken off the ship and sent to Connecticut for trial. Arthur Tappan and Richard Johnson interested themselves in the captives, and succeeded in postponing their trial for two and a half years. Two young men were meanwhile engaged to instruct the captives, and when their trial at last came they were able to give evidence which set them free. They testified that they had been enticed on board of the slaver in small parties for the ostensible purpose of trade, and had then been thrown into the hold and chained. There were nearly one hundred of the captives, and on their release we tried hard, but vainly, to persuade them to stay in this country. I escorted them on shipboard when they were about to sail from New York for their native land.

After a stay of two years at New Bedford I took charge of a colored church in Boston, and left that to give nearly all my time of lectures and addresses on the anti-slavery issue. It was during this period that I took an active interest in the case of Anthony Burns, a runaway slave, who reached Boston as a stowaway in 1852. His former master learned that Burns had found a home in Boston, and made two futile attempts, with the aid of government officials, to recapture him. They made a third trial of it with such precautions as they thought would surely command success. A posse of twenty five United States Deputy Marshals was collected in Richmond, Washington, Philadelphia and New York, and secretly sent to Boston. They lined the street in the vicinity of the shop in which Burns was employed. Several of them followed him when he emerged from the door, and at the corner of Hanover and Cambridge streets they surrounded, captured and ironed him, telling the crowd which was fast collecting that he was accused of breaking into a jewelry store. The marshals succeeded in getting their prisoner into the court-house before the true state of the case became known to the crowd. A call was at once issued for a meeting of our Anti-Slavery Vigilance Committee, and word was sent to Theodore Parker, Wendell Phillips, and other noted leaders, to attend and give advice as to the wisest course to take under the circumstances. It was at first proposed to buy or ransom Burns, and representatives of the committee accordingly offered $1,300 for him. But the marshals would not take it. They said they would let Boston people see the law—the fugitive slave law—could be executed in spite of their opposition. Two companies of marines from the navy yard were called out to support the marshals. But the people gathered from all quarters; they came in swarms from points as far as Lowell, and it was determined at all hazards to prevent the return of the fugitive to slavery. A beam sixty feet long was procured, and at nine o'clock that night was used as a battering-ram against the court house doors. An incident which happened just before this attempt to force an entrance into the court-house added fuel to the fierce fire of excitement. One of the court attendants who found himself outside the building tried to re-enter it, but received a deadly slash from a sword in the hands of a guard, who mistook the character of the man. The victim of this ghastly mistake ran but a few rods before he fell, bleeding and lifeless. The doors gave way at the first thrust of the beam, and we entered to find ourselves in the midst of the two armed companies already mentioned. We gave the soldiers warning that they would get but one fire before all would be over with them, and at this threat they gave up trying actively to interfere with us. But although it had proved easy to break into the court house, it was not so easy to get at the prisoner. The marshals had him with them in an underground cell. The passage to it was narrow, the doors were strong, and we could for the moment do nothing. We finally hit upon a plan to bring the marshals to reason by threatening to starve them out. When they found that not even a glass of water could be sent in to them they began to talk of terms, offering to take the $1,300 we had in the first instance proposed to give them for their prisoner. We declined the proposition, but now offered them $300 for their trouble. This they consented to take, with the provision that they should be allowed to convey the prisoner unmolested to Richmond, Va., and then return him quietly to Boston, in order that they might be able to say they had succeeded in taking their man out of the state. We made them give a bond in the sum of $10,000 that they would abide by the agreement, and use Burns well while they had him in their hands. It was all done, as people say, according to contract. Benjamin F. Butler said to me at the time—he was then the Democratic collector of the port—"James," these were his characteristic words, "I had rather see the court house, niggers and all, blown up to the seventh heaven than see a slave taken out of the city of Boston." When Burns was taken to the wharf guarded by a large force of marshals and from fifteen to twenty companies of militia, every store along the streets traversed was hung with crape. At one point a black coffin suspended from a wire level with the third story windows was drawn back and forth. Boston was in mourning over the disgrace of even in appearance surrendering as a slave a human being who had once set foot on its soil.

Another case in which I was equally interested was that of the fugitive slaves, William and Ellen Craft. The latter, who had hardly a tinge of African blood in her veins, and who could not in color be distinguished from a white person, was housekeeper for a rich southern planter, and the former, who was quite black, was her husband. In August, 1851, the master and his family departed for a watering place, leaving Ellen in charge of the mansion during their absence, and putting money enough in her hands for the temporary needs of the household. Soon after the departure of the family, Ellen put on men's clothing, and with husband set out on foot at night for the North and freedom! In the morning they stopped at a public house, Ellen representing herself as a planter's son, with a servant—her husband—to attend her. She carried her arm in a sling, and told the clerk she could not use it when he asked her to register their names. In this manner they made their way north, and finally to Boston. Their master at last obtained trace of them, and one day arrived at Boston to recover his human property. He called upon the judge of the proper court for the necessary order, but the judge, pleading pressure of business, directed the applicant to call again later in the day. In the interval the judge notified the abolitionists, and they held a meeting the same evening to decide what to do in the case. They came to the conclusion that as the writ or process issued in conformity with the fugitive slave law was civil, and not criminal, there would be no means of serving it upon the fugitives if the latter kept within the domicile and locked the doors. The Crafts acted upon this advice, and were secretly supplied with food by their abolitionist friends during their confinement within doors. The master was thus prevented from recovering possession of them, but he remained in the city and lingered about the neighborhood in which the fugitives were self-confined until the Boston boys annoyed and pestered him to such a degree that he was forced to ask police protection. He obtained it only on a promise to leave the city, but broke his word and was again persecuted by the boys so persistently that he was forced to leave Boston. The fugitives were not again molested, for they quietly removed to Montreal as soon as their prosecutor was fairly out of the way.

Still another case in which I was concerned was that of a runaway slave girl who was seized in Boston and taken to the court house, where a hearing was obtained for her by the opponents of the fugitive slave law. Our counsel had little hope of gaining anything but time by the proceeding, and arranged a signal by which we who were gathered outside the court room—for the proceedings took place with closed doors—might understand that the case had gone against us. When the decision was given the lawyer started for the door in feigned disgust, and it was partially opened for his exit he gave the signal by raising his hand. Instantly a huge colored man named Clark thrust an iron bar between the door and its frame, so that it could not be closed, and we rushed in, to the terror of the court attendants. We took the girl from their hands, and, placing her in a closed carriage, drove her to Roxbury. Three other carriages were driven from the court house in other directions at the same moment, in order to baffle any attempt at pursuit. The crowd of colored people collected in front of the court house on the occasion included a large number of women, each of them armed with a quarter of a pound of Cayenne pepper to throw into the eyes of the officers should the latter come to blows with their friends. The girl was kept in her hiding place a fortnight, and then as the excitement had abated, safely sent to Canada.

In relating the rescue of the slave girl Lucy, I mentioned the fact that we colored people were in those days obliged to ride in a second class or "Jim Crow" car, even in New England. The same separation was enforced on steamboats and stage-coaches, colored people being compelled to ride on the outside of the latter. It was hard to make headway against the rules of the railroad and steamship companies, because they would only sell us half-fare tickets, and on these we could not demand seats with white people I finally procured two first class or full fare tickets by having a white man buy them for me. A colored friend and myself quietly took seats in the corner of the regular passenger coach. The brakemen did not see us until just before the time for the train to start. Then one of them, approaching us, said: "You have made a mistake." "No," was our answer, as we held up the tickets But the man persisted, "You can't ride in here; you know that." My answer was: "You advertise a fare of nine shillings from New Bedford to Boston, and I have this ticket as a receipt that I have paid the money." He reiterated: "You can't ride here, and I want you to go out." "No," was my answer, "I have bought and paid for this ticket and have the same right here as other people." The ticket agent was called in, and tried to persuade us to leave the car. "Our rules," he said, "forbid your occupation of seats in this car. We want no trouble, and you had better go out peaceably." "We want none," answered I, "and shall make none, but we propose to stay where we are." They sent in trainmen, baggageman, and hackmen; we resisted passively, and three seats to which we clung as they were dragging us along were torn up before they got us out. I obtained a warrant from Judge Crapo, and had them arrested at once. The hearing took place the same day, and on the following morning the judge handed down a long written opinion. He ruled that custom was law, and by custom colored people were not allowed to ride in the company of white people.

Furthermore railway corporations had the right to make their own regulations on such a subject, and consequently we had no cause of action, I paid the costs and gave notice of appeal to the Supreme Court. When the case was heard at Boston the court decided that the word "color," as applied to persons, was unknown to the laws of the commonwealth of Massachusetts, and that the youngest colored child had the same rights as the richest white citizen. No company chartered as a common carrier had a right to enact regulations above the laws of the state. The decision of Judge Crapo was reversed, and I was given $300 damages besides. That broke up the practice of consigning colored railway passengers to "Jim Crow" cars.

I had somewhat similar experience on the steamer plying between New Bedford and Nantucket. They would sell only blue or second-class tickets to colored persons, who were thus prevented from entering the cabin with white people. When I asked for a full fare ticket it was refused me, but they offered to sell me a blue one. This I would not take, and I went on board without a ticket. I visited the cabin and other parts of the boat forbidden to colored passengers, but no trouble occurred until the ticket gatherer made his rounds. I told the man that I had no ticket, but would pay the regular fare, not half fare. The captain began by taking the hat from my head and locking it up in his office. Next, he told me that I

could pay half fare or be put off the boat at her next landing place. He was in such haste to carry out his threat, that he retarded the steamer's headway in sight of a port at which she was not to stop, had a boat lowered over the side and ordered me to enter it. I refused and he swore. "You have men enough to put me ashore if you choose," said I, "but I want the right of redress." At this he ordered the boat raised, and the steamer proceeded to her destination with me still on board. When we came within sight of Nantucket he sent a servant to me with my hat, but I refused to take it. I went ashore with a handkerchief tied about my head. It was well advertised before evening that I would at my lecture—I was already booked to speak there that night—tell the story of my treatment on the boat. When the bells were calling people to the lecture hall, the captain's clerk came to me with the message that that officer wanted to see me; but I sent back word that I would say all I had to say to him at the lecture. After the lecture three ladies presented me a new hat, in accepting which I remarked that Captain Nottfinney was welcome to wear my old one, left in his hands. I went back on the same boat without a ticket, for they still refused to sell me a full fare one; but no one asked for my ticket, and no one said a word to me, although I went where I pleased on the boat.

While stationed at Boston I made the acquaintance of Rev. Mr. Phileo and his wife, the latter being that Prudence Crandall who was sent to a Connecticut jail for teaching a school for colored children at Canterbury Green. As I remember, a special session of the legislature was called by the governor for the express purpose of passing a law to cover such cases, and under the law thus enacted she was sent to jail. She was engaged at the time to the young preacher. He married her in jail, and when she was his wife, claimed and obtained her release. The social persecution to which she had been subjected before her imprisonment was renewed on her release, and she and her husband left the place, never to return to it.

I returned to Rochester in 1856, and took charge of the colored church in this city. In 1862 I received an appointment from the American Missionary Society to labor among the colored people of Tennessee and Louisiana, but I never reached either of these states. I left Rochester with my daughter, and reported at St. Louis, where I received orders to proceed to Louisville, Kentucky. On the train, between St. Louis and Louisville, a party of forty Missouri ruffians entered the car at an intermediate station, and threatened to throw me and my daughter off the train. They robbed me of my watch. The conductor undertook to protect us, but, finding it out of his power, brought a number of Government officers and passengers from the next car to our assistance. At Louisville the government took me out of the hands of the Missionary Society to take charge of freed and refugee blacks, to visit the prisons of that commonwealth, and to set free all colored persons found confined without charge of crime. I served first under the orders of General Burbage, and then under those of his successor, General Palmer. The homeless colored people, for whom I was to care, were gathered in a camp covering ten acres of ground on the outskirts of the city. They were housed in light buildings, and supplied with rations from the commissary stores. Nearly all the persons in the camp were women and children, for the colored men were sworn into the United States service as soldiers as fast as they came in. My first duty, after arranging the affairs of the camp, was to visit the slave pens, of which there were five in the city. The largest, known as Garrison's, was located on Market Street, and to that I made my first visit. When I entered it, and was about to make a thorough inspection of it, Garrison stopped me with the insolent remark, "I guess no nigger will go over me in this pen." I showed him my orders, whereupon he asked time to consult the mayor. He started for the entrance, but was stopped by the guard I had stationed there. I told him he would not leave the pen until I had gone through every part of it. "So," said I, "throw open your doors, or I will put you under arrest." I found hidden away in that pen 260 colored persons, part of them in irons. I took them all to my camp, and they were free. I next called at Otterman's pen on Second Street, from which also I took a large number of slaves. A third large pen was named Clark's, and

there were two smaller ones besides. I liberated the slaves in all of them. One morning it was reported to me that a slave trader had nine colored men locked in a room in the National hotel. A waiter from the hotel brought the information at daybreak. I took a squad of soldiers with me to the place, and demanded the surrender of the blacks. The clerk said there were none in the house. Their owners had gone off with "the boys" at daybreak. I answered that I could take no man's word in such a case, but must see for myself. When I was about to begin the search, a colored man secretly gave me the number of the room the men were in. The room was locked, and the porter refused to give up the keys. A threat to place him under arrest brought him to reason, and I found the colored men inside, as I had anticipated. One of them, an old man, who sat with his face between his hands, said as I entered: "So'thin' tole me last night that so' thin' was a goin' to happen to me." That very day I mustered the nine men into the service of the government, and that made them free men.

So much anger was excited by these proceedings, that the mayor and common council of Louisville visited General Burbage at his headquarters, and warned him that if I was not sent away within forty-eight hours my life would pay the forfeit. The General sternly answered them: "If James is killed, I will hold responsible for the act every man who fills an office under your city government. I will hang them all higher than Haman was hung, and I have 15,000 troops behind me to carry out the order. Your only salvation lies in protecting this colored man's life." During my first year and a half at Louisville, a guard was stationed at the door of my room every night, as a necessary precaution in view of the threats of violence of which I was the object. One night I received a suggestive hint of the treatment the rebel sympathizers had in store for me should I chance to fall into their hands. A party of them approached the house where I was lodged protected by a guard. The soldiers, who were new recruits, ran off in afright. I found escape by the street cut off, and as I ran for the rear alley I discovered that avenue also guarded by a squad of my enemies. As a last resort I jumped a side fence, and stole along until out of sight and hearing of the enemy. Making my way to the house of a colored man named White, I exchanged my uniform for an old suit of his, and then, sallying forth, mingled with the rebel party, to learn, if possible, the nature of their intentions. Not finding me, and not having noticed my escape, they concluded that they must have been misinformed as to my lodging place for that night. Leaving the locality they proceeded to the house of another friend of mine, named Bridle, whose home was on Tenth street. After vainly searching every room in Bridle's house, they dispersed with the threat that if they got me I should hang to the nearest lamp-post. For a long time after I was placed in charge of the camp, I was forced to forbid the display of lights in any of the buildings at night, for fear of drawing the fire of rebel bushwhackers. All the fugitives in the camp made their beds on the floor, to escape danger from rifle balls fired through the thin siding of the frame structures.

I established a Sunday and a day school in my camp and held religious services twice a week as well as on Sundays. I was ordered by General Palmer to marry every colored woman that came into camp to a soldier unless she objected to such a proceeding. The ceremony was a mere form to secure the freedom of the female colored refugees; for Congress had passed a law giving freedom to the wives and children of all colored soldiers and sailors in the service of the government. The Emancipation Proclamation, applying as it did only to states in rebellion, failed to meet the case of slaves in Kentucky, and we were obliged to resort to this ruse to escape the necessity of giving up to their masters many of the runaway slave women and children who flocked to our camp.

I had a contest of this kind with a slave trader known as Bill Hurd. He demanded the surrender of a colored woman in my camp who claimed her freedom on the plea that her husband had enlisted in the federal army. She wished to go to Cincinnati, and General Palmer, giving me a railway pass for her, cautioned me to see her on board the cars for the North before I left her. At the levee I saw Hurd and

a policeman, and suspecting that they intended a rescue, I left the girl with the guard at the river and returned to the general for a detail of one or more men. During my absence Hurd claimed the woman from the guard and the latter brought all the parties to the provost marshal's headquarters, although I had directed him to report to General Palmer with the woman in case of trouble; for I feared that the provost marshal's sympathies were on the slave owner's side. I met Hurd, the policeman and the woman at the corner of Sixth and Green streets and halted them. Hurd said the provost marshal had decided that she was his property. I answered— what I had just learned—that the provost marshal was not at his headquarters and that his subordinate had no authority to decide such a case. I said further that I had orders to take the party before General Palmer and proposed to do it. They saw it was not prudent to resist, as I had a guard to enforce the order. When the parties were heard before the general, Hurd said the girl had obtained her freedom and a pass by false pretenses. She was his property; he had paid $500 for her; she was single when he bought her and she had not married since. Therefore she could claim no rights under the law giving freedom to the wives of colored soldiers. The general answered that the charge of false pretenses was a criminal one and the woman would be held for trial upon it. "But," said Hurd, "she is my property and I want her." "No," answered the general, "we keep our own prisoners." The general said to me privately, after Hurd was gone: "The woman has a husband in our service and I know it; but never mind that. We'll beat these rebels at their own game." Hurd hung about headquarters two or three days until General Palmer said finally: "I have no time to try this case; take it before the provost marshal." The latter, who had been given the hint, delayed action for several days more, and then turned over the case to General Dodge. After another delay, which still further tortured the slave trader, General Dodge said to me one day: "James, bring Mary to my headquarters, supply her with rations, have a guard ready, and call Hurd as a witness." When the slave trader had made his statement to the same effect as before, General

Dodge delivered judgment in the following words: "Hurd, you are an honest man. It is a clear case. All I have to do, Mary, is to sentence you to keep away from this department during the remainder of the present war. James, take her across the river and see her on board the cars." "But, general," whined Hurd, "that won't do. I shall lose her services if you sent her north." "You have nothing to do with it; you are only a witness in this case," answered the general. I carried out the order strictly, to remain with Mary until the cars started; and under the protection of a file of guards, she was soon placed on the train en route for Cincinnati.

Among the slaves I rescued and brought to the refugee camp was a girl named Laura, who had been locked up by her mistress in a cellar and left to remain there two days and as many nights without food or drink. Two refugee slave women were seen by their master making toward my camp, and calling upon a policeman he had then seized and taken them to the house of his brother-in-law on Washington street. When the facts were reported to me, I took a squad of guards to the house and rescued them. As I came out of the house with the slave women, their master asked me: "What are you going to do with them?" I answered that they would probably take care of themselves. He protested that he had always used the runaway women well, and appealing to one of them, asked: "Have I not, Angelina?" I directed the woman to answer the question, saying that she had as good a right to speak as he had, and that I would protect her in that right. She then said: "He tied my dress over my head Sunday and whipped me for refusing to carry victuals to the bushwhackers and guerillas in the woods." I brought the women to camp, and soon afterwards sent them north to find homes. I sent one girl rescued by me under somewhat similar circumstances as far as this city to find a home with Colonel Klinck's family.

Up to that time in my career I had never received serious injury at any man's hands. I was several times reviled and hustled by mobs in my first tour of the district about the city of Rochester, and once when I was lecturing in New Hampshire a reckless, half-drunken fellow in the lobby fired a pistol at me, the ball shattering the plaster a few feet from my head. But, as I said, I had never received serious injury. Now, however, I received a blow, the effects of which I shall carry to my grave. General Palmer sent me to the shop of a blacksmith who was suspected of bushwhacking, with an order requiring the latter to report at headquarters. The rebel, who was a powerful man, raised a short iron bar as I entered and aimed a savage blow at my head. By an instinctive movement I saved my life, but the blow fell on my neck and shoulders, and I was for a long time afterwards disabled by the injury. My right hand remains partially paralyzed and almost wholly useless to this day.

Many a sad scene I witnessed at my camp of colored refugees in Louisville. There was the mother bereaved of her children, who had been sold and sent farther South lest they should escape in the general rush for the federal lines and freedom; children, orphaned in fact if not in name, for separation from parents among the colored people in those days left no hope of reunion this side the grave; wives forever parted from their husbands, and husbands who might never hope to catch again the brightening eye and the welcoming smile of the help-mates whose hearts God and nature had joined to theirs. . . .

I remained at Louisville a little over three years, staying for some months after the war closed in charge of the colored camp, the hospital, dispensary and government stores. In 1865 the colored people of Kentucky were called upon for the first time to celebrate the Fourth of July. I spoke to General Palmer about it, and he, approving the idea, issued a proclamation for the purpose. There was but a single voice raised against it, and that, strange as it may seem, was the voice of a colored Baptist preacher named Adams. But the slave holders had always pursued the policy of buying over to their interest a few unworthy colored ministers who took an active part in the peaceful political revolution which placed the local government of the District of Columbia in loyal hands. In 1878 I was appointed by Bishop Wayman a missionary preacher for the colored churches of Ohio. While engaged in this missionary work I was driven out of Darke county by a terrorizing band of ruffians, who called themselves regulators, and many of whom were from the Kentucky side of the river. A number of leading white citizens were treated in like manner by the same band. In 1880, when the exodus from the South began, I labored under the direction of the Topeka Relief Association in behalf of the homeless throngs of colored people who flocked into Kansas. In the following year this relief was discontinued, and we organized in southern Kansas an agricultural and industrial institute, of which I became general agent. The institute of which Elizabeth L. Comstock was an active advocate, is still in existence, and has done a noble work in the education of people of color. My last charge was the pastorate of the African Methodist Episcopal Church at Lockport. Between three and four years ago both my eyes became affected by cataracts, and I now grope my way in almost complete blindness.

My home is again in the city of Rochester, where I began my life work. In 1829 I married in this city a free colored girl, and by her had four children, two of whom are now married and living at the West. My first wife died in 1841. Sixteen years ago I married again. My wife was a slave, freed by Sherman at the capture of Atlanta and sent north with other colored refugees. I first met her in the State of Pennsylvania. She is the companion of my old age. Two children—my daughter, who is in the fifteenth year of her age, and my son, who is verging on his twelfth year, are the comfort and joy of our household. With them I sing the old "Liberty Minstrel" songs, which carry me back to the days when the conscience of the North was first awakened to the iniquities of slavery. Blessed be God that I have lived to see the liberation and the enfranchisement of the people of my color and blood!

You ask me what change for the better has taken place in the condition of the colored people of this locality in my day. I answer that the Anti-Slavery agitation developed an active and generous sympathy for the free colored man of the North, as well as for his brother in bondage. We felt the good effect of that sympathy and the aid and encouragement which accompanied it. But now that the end of the Anti-Slavery agitation has been fully accomplished, our white friends are inclined to leave us to our own resources, overlooking the fact that social prejudices still close the trades against our youth, and that we are again as isolated as in the days before the wrongs of our race touched the heart of the American people. After breathing for so considerable a period an atmosphere surcharged with sympathy for our race, we feel the more keenly the current of neglect which seems to have chilled against us even the enlightened and religious classes of the communities among which we live, but of which we cannot call ourselves a part.

Source: The Wonderful Eventful Life of Rev. Thomas James, by Himself. 3rd ed. Rochester, NY: Post-Express Printing Company, 1887. Library of Congress, Rare Book and Special Collections Division, Daniel A. P. Murray Pamphlets Collection.

Frances E. W. Harper, "Light beyond the Darkness"
(ca. 1890s)

As a freed African American woman from Baltimore, Frances E. W. Harper expressed her belief in racial cooperation and harmony through her poetry. In the following poem, "Light beyond the Darkness," she refuted the call for black revenge against white society.

From the peaceful heights of a higher life
I heard your maddening cry of strife;
It quivered with anguish, wrath and pain,
Like a demon struggling with his chain.
A chain of evil, heavy and strong,
Rusted with ages of fearful wrong.
Encrusted with blood and burning tears.
The chain I had worn and dragged for years.
It clasped my limbs, but it bound your heart.
And formed of your life a fearful part;
You sowed the wind, but could not control
The tempest wild of a guilty soul.
You saw me stand with my broken chain
Forged in the furnace of fiery pain.
You saw my children around me stand
Lovingly clasping my unbound hand.
But you remembered my blood and tears
'mid the weary wasting flight of years.
You thought of the rice swamps, lone and dank,
When my heart in hopeless anguish sank.
You thought of your fields with harvest white,
Where I toiled in pain from morn till night;
You thought of the days you bought and sold
The children I loved, for paltry gold.
You thought of our shrieks that rent the air—
Our moans of anguish and deep despair;
With chattering teeth and paling face,
You thought of your nation's deep disgrace.
You wove from your fears a fearful fate
To spring from your seeds of scorn and hate;
You imagined the saddest, wildest thing,
That time, with revenges fierce, could bring
The cry you thought from a Voodoo breast
Was the echo of your soul's unrest;
When thoughts too sad for fruitless tears
Loomed like the ghosts of avenging years.
Oh prophet of evil, could not your voice
In our new hopes and freedom rejoice?
'mid the light which streams around our way
Was there naught to see but an evil day?
Nothing but vengeance, wrath and hate,
And the serpent coils of an evil fate—
A fate that shall crush and drag you down;

A doom that shall press like an iron crown?
A fate that shall crisp and curl your hair
And darken your faces now so fair,
And send through your veins like a poisoned flood
The hated stream of the Negro's blood?
A fate to madden the heart and brain
You've peopled with phantoms of dread and pain,
And fancies wild of your daughter's shriek
With Congo kisses upon her cheek?
Beyond the mist of your gloomy fears,
I see the promise of brighter years.
Through the dark I see their golden hem
And my heart gives out its glad amen.
The banner of Christ was your sacred trust,
But you trailed that banner in the dust,
And mockingly told us amid our pain
The hand of your God had forged our chain.
We stumbled and groped through the dreary night
Till our fingers touched God's robe of light;
And we knew He heard, from his lofty throne,
Our saddest cries and faintest moan.
The cross you have covered with sin and shame
We'll bear aloft in Christ's holy name.
Oh, never again may its folds be furled
While sorrow and sin enshroud our world!
God, to whose fingers thrills each heart beat,
Has not sent us to walk with aimless feet,
To cover and crouch, with bated breath
From margins of life to shores of death.
Higher and better than hate for hate,
Like the scorpion fangs that desolate,
Is the hope of a brighter, fairer morn
And a peace and a love that shall yet be born;
When the Negro shall hold an honored place,
The friend and helper of every race;
His mission to build and not destroy.
And gladden the world with love and joy.

Source: Harper, Frances E. W. *Light beyond the Darkness.* Chicago: Donohue and Henneberry, n.d. Library of Congress, Rare Book and Special Collections Division, Daniel A. P. Murray Pamphlets Collection.

George C. Rowe Clinton, "A Noble Life: Memorial Souvenir of Rev. Jos. C. Price, D.D."

(1894)

George C. Rowe Clinton, an African American minister, wrote this speech in the form of a poem for Joseph C. Price, the deceased president of Livingstone College, a black college in Salisbury, North Carolina.

A star arose at close of night:
'tis dark before the dawn;
A brilliant star, a righteous light,
Foretoken of the morn—
The day when the oppressor's hand
Should palsied be throughout the land.
A man of influence and power,
Who laid himself with grace,
Upon the altar of his God,
An offering for his race.
E'er prodigal of strength and thought,
And from his race withholding nought.
He cried: "If I'd a thousand tongues,
And each a thunderbolt;
I'd turn them on in mighty power,
Like an electric volt;
I'd send them forth with lightning pace—
To help and elevate my race!
With purpose firm he lived his creed,
And toiled with might and main,
Each day more clearly saw the need—
Despising worldly gain—
He counted not his life too dear
To spend in raising mortals here.
The manly form now prostrate lies;
The flashing eye is dim;
The hand oft raised for principle,
Touched by the monster grim,
Is laid upon the quiet breast,
The life-work finished—entered rest.
The tongue of fire is silent now;
The loving heart is still;
The mind surcharged with burning thought,
Yet loyal to God's will—
Has ceased to plan for mortals here,
Is active in another sphere.
A sense of loss our hearts shall feel:
Hushed is the sweet voice now;

While we shall miss his thrilling words.
To God we humbly bow;
And thank Him for the sacrifice
So freely made by Joseph Price.
His task on earth was finished soon;
Life's battle nobly won.
He rests from labor ere the noon,
His life race fully run.
He watches still the conflict here,
And perfect love has cast out fear.
He is not dead; but gone to join
The host from care set free!
He is not dead; his spirit lives
Where joys immortal be!
Where noble souls are victors crowned;
Where perfect love at last is found.
Now glorified amid the host,
Whose names in honor stand;
Phillips and Garnet, Garrison,
And all that noble band—
Lincoln and Sumner—heroes brave,
Who sought to free and help the slave.
Yes, there within the pearly gates,
They wait for you and me;
Those men who planned that from the curse
Our people might be free;
Rejoicing in the broadening day
When shadows dark should flee away.
Our hero was a patriot true,
A messenger of truth:
Whose words of faith and hope rang out
Inspiring age and youth.
His life will inspiration give—

Through coming time his influence live!
Rest in peace, beloved brother,
Holy influence will not cease;
Memory of the just is blessed—
Rest in peace, then, rest in peace!
　　　　—G.C.R.

Source: Rowe, George C. *A Noble Life: Memorial Souvenir of Rev. Jos. C. Price, D.D.* Charleston, SC: s.n., 1894. Library of Congress, Rare Book and Special Collections Division, Daniel A. P. Murray Pamphlets Collection.

Sermon Preached by Rev. G. V. Clark, at Second Congregational Church, Memphis, Tenn.
(June 16, 1895)

In the following sermon, Rev. G. V. Clark, pastor of the Second Congregational Church in Memphis, Tennessee, in the late 1890s, delivered a stirring reminder to his congregation that God's plan, not man's, was the most important rule in their lives. By illustrating ambition for the Lord's work, Clark argued, African Americans could overcome the inherent discrimination of post–Civil War America. Clark's notion was very much in line with the position of Booker T. Washington. Clark's church, founded in 1868, was one of the most famous African American churches in the South; its affiliation with LeMoyne-Owen College made Clark quite influential with black students at the turn of the century.

There is a noble ambition in every successful individual or race. Some one has said, "I am charged with ambition. The charge is true and I glory in its truth. Let that ambition be a noble one and who shall blame it."

Rev. G. V. Clark

"I set before you an open door, and no man can shut it."

Rev. iii. 8.

The application of the truth in the text was to the church in Philadelphia, in Asia Minor. Then to all the Christian world. The door opened is emblematic of the opportunities presented to the church. In other words, it was a setting before the church her mission—henceforward the church would not be so handicapped as before. Oppositions, such as had proved an obstacle before, would cease; unbelief would not be so stubborn and unreasonable; the gospel and its messengers would have easier access to the world, Jews and Gentiles. We notice, too, that the opening is by Christ, the great head of the church. Behind the church is his authority. None can, therefore, resist successfully her authority, nor

question with propriety her right to teach truth. The principles to be promulgated are two, namely: Love to God supremely, and to our neighbors as ourselves. The latter command, however, seems to be regarded by men and races after they have reached the zenith of power, as antiquated and abrogated. It is neither antiquated nor abrogated, I boldly declare. The declaration of all the world to the contrary, rich or poor, high or low, of whatever race, country or nationality, do not alter the fact. Putting this truth in a little different form, Christ said, "They that are strong ought to bear the infirmities of the weak." This the Lord means his church shall do, and if she does not do this, for this is a cardinal principle of practical Christianity, then I think he will set aside the church in her present form, purifying her, and bring her forth clad in new, cleaner garments. It is a burning shame that herein her robes are verily stained with guilt. This idea of helpfulness to the weaker is not to be understood as of limited application, but of universal force. A principle binding alike on church and state. It is intended to be placed as a foundation stone for governmental, as well as ecclesiastical righteousness and equity. Moreover, the divine blessing invariably attends the efforts of that people who make it the rule of their lives, and the theme of their discussion, and the object of their every endeavor to do unto others just as they wish to be done by. Christ calls this the fulfillment of the royal law. Creeds, nationality, learning, sciences, philosophy, splendidly equipped armies and navies, with power to successfully resist the invasions of all foes, by wading in their blood, all sink into insignificance when compared with this great and all important principle. All else is worthless in the sight of God when this is wanting. The open door, or opportunities, presented the church of Christ, in the text, carries with it great responsibilities. There is no work necessary to the highest development of the race, or the purity and happiness of mankind that is not here offered through the church, a mission, higher in degree and broader in extent than was ever committed to mortals before. The length, breadth, height and magnitude of this trust hath not yet been fully comprehended, I fear, by even the wisest and best of men. This is due, in part, to inherited prejudices infused into the Christian life, and part, also, from environment. If once the church gets a clear understanding and a just conception of her high calling, much, if not all, that now obstructs her entrance into that "open door" will vanish as mist before the rising sun. To this end I join the poet who said:

"To her my tears shall fall,
To her my prayers ascend,
To her my cares and toils be given,
Till toils and cares shall end."

In this commission the church is to know no race distinction nor condition, but to preach Christ to both Jew and Gentile, bond and free, African and Caucasian, rich and poor, ignorant and learned, all, as equally under necessity to repent and believe in order to receive salvation.

To preach is not sufficient, as practice speaks much louder than words. Sectarianism, the caste spirit and the like are blots on the escutcheon of Christians, by whomsoever practiced. It must be renounced and denounced, else the grand opportunity offered by the "open door" will be closed and barred eternally. It was not until Peter had his housetop vision, and the church held her first council at Jerusalem, did the meanness and exclusiveness of caste and race antagonism appear to these primitive saints. This was an excrescence produced and made to develop on the body of Christ's bride, the church, by the blind hate and racial exclusiveness among the first followers of Christ. As in those days, this evil, with others, hindered the church and caused the rejection of many churches by the Lord, so will it continue to do to races and religions who refuse to practice this spirit as required by Christ, the author of our religion.

Thus I have given you some thoughts on the primary application of this Scripture teaching. I desire now to call attention to a secondary consideration in this connection. There is a warning which comes to us, of this most enlightened age of the world's history, in the rise of four of the greatest nations known to the world, namely: the Greeks, Romans, Hebrews and Anglo-Saxons. Let us consider each in the order mentioned. I assume to begin with that God had a mission of a far-reaching purpose in bringing each of these races into historical notice. That mission I believe was to glorify and serve God. I can conceive no divine purpose in raising up a nation which does not have for its object the purest, most perfect obedience and service of which that people is capable. We know the Greeks were once the foremost race of antiquity, successful alike on the field of battle and in the sphere of arts and letters. Their skill as sculptors stands unsurpassed by any race of past ages. They left to the world monuments of their genius and high achievements, showing their exquisiteness of touch and delicacy of taste. The literary quality of their writings and public addresses show a very advanced stage of scholarship. Their poetry will never cease to be the wonder, and claim the admiration of the literary world. Their philosophers are acknowledged by the great men of this age, who are esteemed as learned, as master minds. To say all this is but to proclaim the Greeks a highly intellectual, artistic people. This is but the verdict of many centuries. It would be but partial praise to say all I have in their behalf and fail to say that they were great educators. When carried as captives from their native land as prisoners of war it was a most common thing for them to be brought as tutors in royal palaces, and among the nobility. This was a result of an eagerness always to learn something new. In war they were aggressive, heroic and skillful. Their language as a vehicle of communication is most admirable in lucidity and laconicalness. In all of this you readily see what the Greeks gave the world showing their mental possibilities. But there is one more thing to mention which shows the spirit of a great race. It is that they were possessed of love of personal liberty. No encroachment upon this sacred ground was ever allowed to the state by them. Their idea of government was that the state existed for the individual and not the individual for good of the state. Having said so much, all of which is true, one may ask why they were not retained and perpetuated. Great warriors, artists, scholars and lovers of individual liberty in a race, are not the chief element to qualify a race or individual for permanence of existence before God. They were lacking in the first and chief essential. God is seeking an ideal people. The Greeks were not that people. Had they religion? The answer is yes. The Apostle Paul declared they were too religious. Gods were more easily found among Athenians than men. Their religion, like all paganism, proved more degrading than elevating. The relation between Jehovah and man was served by the nation rejecting him for carnal things called gods. More still, the relation between man and man was predominated by a debasing, sensual gratification which destroyed all their noble aspirations. Having reached, therefore, the summit of their glory in material and intellectual achievements, and declining more and more rapidly, at the same time, in morality and spiritual discernment, God wrote on the walls of the nation's hall of revelry, "Thou art weighed in the balances and found wanting." Thus their doom came. They achieved greatness in everything but one, and that was *true godliness*. No nation can be truly great without it. The door that was once opened to them finally closed and that forever.

The Romans we next notice before the "open door" of opportunities. Through many vicissitudes this great race passed from a mere clannish state on up into a monarchy, and the world's first great republic. From first to last, however, they were doomed to utter extinction because, mainly, they fell short of the divine ideal of greatness. The Romans possessed, notwithstanding, many noble traits or qualities necessary to produce greatness. They surpassed the Greeks in some respects while they fell behind them in some others. While the former exalted culture, the latter put stress upon unity and order. By diplomacy they succeeded in forming helpful alliances such as afforded them great advantages in times of war. Under her splendidly equipped armies, on sea and land, she became the mistress of the world. The Greeks with all their greatness became subject to Rome. The zenith of her glory was reached about the transition period from a republic to a monarchy. From that time, owing to her vanity and vices, she steadily declined. Before, however, her downfall came she was allowed to contribute something substantial to the world's progress. I mention such as her arts, sculpture, massive architecture, royal highways, a magnificently organized government, matchless orators and statesmen, and a language both exquisite and expressive. By means of these the world is in advance of what it was prior to the rise of the Romans into power and supremacy over the world. For hundreds of years she wielded the scepter. And, mark you, I believe under the controlling hand of God, great blessings to mankind have resulted from the contributions of this race. Their greatness none can dispute. But for one needful indispensable virtue, which Rome lacked, she might to-day still be in the ascendency among nations. This falling short was that they failed to have, as a nation, the religion requiring supreme love to God, and love for "our neighbors as ourselves." On every other achievement without love as the chief element, was written, "weighed and found wanting." This is the central thought in the divine mind and must be with nations. The displacement of this ruling people was an act of God rather than the superior forces of enemies. For the crime of ungodliness Rome, like Greece, was set aside. She failed to enter the "open door." Their love of country, learning and the domestic relation could not save them from ruin.

Let us take another highly favored race for our consideration. These people were more than any other blessed of God. I refer to the Hebrews, the descendants of Abraham. If God could be charged with partiality because he seemed kinder and more considerate of one race than another, it would be because of His great patience and love for Israel. The story of how the race began and developed under Divine providence is fully known to all.

Sacred and secular history have most fully recorded the facts. There was doubtless a far reaching purpose in the mind of God in thus blessing and forbearing with his chosen yet most rebellious children. That purpose I conceive to be to raise up if possible an ideal race. It seemed at times that God would in them accomplish greater results than in any other race. He came nearer exhausting his goodness in helping this nation than with any other. They sprung from faithful Abraham, developed in their government, into families, tribes and ultimately a nation. In it all was the hand of God revealed.

Now as to results. They were a means of direct communication from God to the world. The best code of laws, many of the most beautiful characters of men, women, and finally the world's Redeemer came of that race. To them, as to no other, we are indebted through God for that book, the Bible. It is at once unique, instructive and the only authorized record of God, Christ and the future state, good and bad. The oracles of God were committed to these people to be transmitted to the world. This old world is a better one because they lived and wrought. But like Greece and Rome they were found wanting. Having been elevated to the highest distinction they doomed themselves to a mighty fall. The same old charge of, "I have somewhat against thee," was laid at their door. That old sentence, "thou art weighed in the balances and found wanting" was written on the nation's walls. This, however, was not done until they had many times been warned and entreated to repent. God finished in and with them his work just so far as they were willing. The door swung open before them for 2,500 years. They were free to enter and were plead with to enter. Their final opportunity came. The chances are forever gone now. As a nation, they are without a country, shepherds without sheep. You say their downfall was due to their rejection of Christ, but I say to you the crucifixion of the Messiah was but the culmination of an evil heart of centuries of growth. Yea, it was as much a breaking of the Golden Rule, the sin against their fellowman, as a sin against God. In the fall of Jerusalem the national crash came.

Take still another race, now on trial. I name to you the Anglo-Saxons. In the unfolding of the divine will and providence, as manifested in rearing up of nations, this race comes into history with great promise of permanency. They seem to possess more great qualities than any other hitherto noticed. It is a race of great energy, intelligence, virtue, and courage. The great men and women of the race that adorn the pages of history with a halo of glory exceed all others. From this race have sprung great poets, artists, statesmen, warriors, scholars, reformers, geniuses, philanthropists and devout Christians. Such a race is destined, under God, to a great future. Their foundation is extensive and firm. But one thing, however, can cause their downfall. That one thing, too, seems now to threaten the overthrow, namely, the sin against man, especially the weaker brother. Around this class of human beings God seems to desire to throw protection and encouragement. Diametrically opposed to this (herein is the Golden Rule summed up) is the declaration of the Anglo-Saxons to the effect that all races in the way of their civilization must go to the wall. That means a merciless declaration of war on others. This spirit, let them remember, is irreconcilably at war with the very spirit and genius of Christianity. This spirit and genius are to bring back man to his Creator. That race that is in harmony with this principle grasps in one hand the Almighty, and in the other humanity. Thus there is an uplifting through first and second causes.

The great danger to this race lies in its prosperity and supremacy over the weaker races. When they forget that all they are, or might be, is due to divine favor only, and it seems they are forgetting in the United States, then will come the beginning of the end. If the advantages enjoyed by them but be ascribed to God's blessing, and used to promote his glory and the welfare of his little ones, the Anglo-Saxons will perpetuate their own supremacy and reflect glory upon the name of the God of nations. The failure to deal justly by their brethren will as surely send them into oblivion as that night follows day. The sentence against them in that event will be, "Inasmuch as ye did it not to one of the least of these ye did it not to me." These shall go away to everlasting punishment. The door of opportunity is open before this race. The most honored and blessed of God are such as not only honor him, but who serve their fellowmen best. What a high trust is here committed! The race seems, however, to be committed firmly to their boasted pride and arrogance, regardless of the warning which the fate of the Greeks, Romans and Hebrews experienced will afford.

Has this race of blood and cruelty reached the pinnacle of its glory? Is it in a state of sure, imperceptible decline? Have we reached the beginning of a disgraceful end in the history of this hitherto greatest race known to historians? Should this be the case, then what? I answer, as one of them, it appears to me that the Divine purpose is to place the colored American on trial, as he has the races referred to, and is now doing with the above named race. There are some distinguishing characteristics of this, my race, which if called of God, into the service of mankind, will put a distinctive stamp upon history never before made prominent. These characteristics are: docility, patience under adversity, as shown under American slavery, musical, imaginative, imitative, great endurance in toil, forgiving, lovers of domestic life, religious. The race, moreover, is unequalled in natural oratory. Such a race must have a future.

It is barely possible that the Divine purpose in permitting American slavery was to raise up on this continent a future people, who, catching all that is good of Anglo-Saxon civilization, and by the use of his imitative genius, assimilate it with his own native qualities, and so produce the ideal race which God is seeking. Certain it is that while none can prove this position as the true one, yet none can disapprove it. All I mean is that it is possible. The door is open before us. By the righteous use of the endowments which the race possesses, recognizing them as from God, a civilization distinctively our own will be the country's blessing and salvation. The world, too, will feel a quickening impulse from such a leavening influence. I realize that the American colored man is without a

past, such as is the boast of Anglo-Saxons. There was a time when no race was any better off than we are. They had to begin. So must we make a beginning. All contemporary races have a bloody record to confront them. The colored race is to make its conquests with a sheathed sword. This is an age wherein the peace man, as did the Lord Jesus Christ, is to contend against sin and error with righteousness and the sword of the Spirit, which is the word of God. Therefore that race which approaches most nearly the divine ideal will endure longest and accomplish most for the world's highest welfare. The crown is not to the most intellectual or warlike domineering race, but to the one serving God and man best. Now, I would not have any race serve God less, but I would have my own serve him best. A failure to do this cannot be substituted by one nor all other noble qualities. A holy competition for the Divine favor and honor will greatly accelerate the speed of the race in striving for the goal.

Mark you, hearer, that every other nation yet fully tried has been rejected of God, not for what they were but for what they were not. Each one contributed something to mankind's betterment, but so far as they were concerned it all meant nothing. Greece gave the world culture; Rome, law and order; the Hebrews, revelation and the Savior; the Anglo-Saxon, science, social order and the most advanced civilization. It is left to some race to yet give that best obedience which God requires, namely; give supremacy to God in head and heart and to place our neighbors deep down in the citadel of our heart or affections. I would therefore appeal to the colored American to let the zeal of God and an impartial love for our fellowmen, of all races and conditions, friends and foes, be the all-absorbing passion of daily life. If you really love your race, if you would have it stand on the very summit of the world's elevation, if you would have it without a peer or parallel in the galaxy of the greatest of nations, then let this love for both Divine and human burn on the altar of your heart. With such God is most well pleased. Therefore, seize the opportunity and save the race from degradation and irrevocable ruin. Such is the burden of my heart.

Source: Afro-American encyclopedia, or, the thoughts, doings, and sayings of the race: embracing addresses, lectures, biographical sketches, sermons, poems, names of universities, colleges, seminaries, newspapers, books, and a history of the denominations, giving the numerical strength of each. In fact, it teaches every subject of interest to the colored people, as discussed by more than one hundred of their wisest and best men and women. Compiled and arranged by James T. Haley. Nashville, TN: Haley & Florida, 1895. Documenting the American South, University of North Carolina at Chapel Hill, 2000. http://docsouth.unc.edu/church/haley/haley.html.

Booker T. Washington, "The Atlanta Compromise" Speech (1895)

Booker T. Washington (1856–1915) was an influential political leader, educator, and author whose autobiography, Up From Slavery, *remains widely read. In this address, given to a predominantly white audience at the Cotton States and International Exposition in Atlanta, Georgia, on September 18, 1895, Washington outlines the "Atlanta Compromise," an agreement between African American and southern white leaders, whereby blacks would quietly accept white political dominance in exchange for white funding of basic educational opportunities for blacks.*

Mr. President and Gentlemen of the Board of Directors and Citizens:

One-third of the population of the South is of the Negro race. No enterprise seeking the material, civil, or moral welfare of this section can disregard this element of our population and reach the highest success. I but convey to you, Mr. President and Directors, the sentiment of the masses of my race when I say that in no way have the value and manhood of the American Negro been more fittingly and generously recognized than by the managers of this magnificent Exposition at every stage of its progress. It is a recognition that will do more to cement the friendship of the two races than any occurrence since the dawn of our freedom. Not only this, but the opportunity here afforded will awaken among us a new era of industrial progress. Ignorant and inexperienced, it is not strange that in the first years of our new life we began at the top instead of at the bottom; that a seat in Congress or the state legislature was more sought than real estate or industrial skill; that the political convention or stump speaking had more attractions than starting a dairy farm or truck garden.

A ship lost at sea for many days suddenly sighted a friendly vessel. From the mast of the unfortunate vessel was seen a signal, "Water, water; we die of thirst!" The answer from the friendly vessel at once came back, "Cast down your bucket where you are." A second time the signal, "Water, water; send us water!" ran up from the distressed vessel, and was answered, "Cast down your bucket where you are." And a third and fourth signal for water was answered, "Cast down your bucket where you are." The captain of the distressed vessel, at last heeding the injunction, cast down his bucket, and it came up full of fresh, sparkling water from the mouth of the Amazon River.

To those of my race who depend on bettering their condition in a foreign land or who underestimate the importance of cultivating friendly relations with the Southern white man, who is their next-door neighbor, I would say: "Cast down your bucket where you are"—cast it down in making friends in every manly way of the people of all races by whom we are surrounded.

Cast it down in agriculture, in mechanics, in commerce, in domestic service, and in the professions. And in this connection it is well to bear in mind that whatever other sins the South may be called to bear, when it comes to business, pure and simple, it is in the South that the Negro is given a man's chance in the commercial world, and in nothing is this Exposition more eloquent than in emphasizing this chance. Our greatest danger is that in the great leap from slavery to freedom we may overlook the fact that the masses of us are to live by the productions of our hands, and fail to keep in mind that we shall prosper in proportion as we learn to dignify and glorify common labor, and put brains and skill into the common occupations of life; shall prosper in proportion as we learn to draw the line between the superficial and the substantial, the ornamental gewgaws of life and the useful. No race can prosper till it learns that there is as much dignity in tilling a field as in writing a poem. It is at the bottom of life we must begin, and not at the top. Nor should we permit our grievances to overshadow our opportunities.

To those of the white race who look to the incoming of those of foreign birth and strange tongue and habits for the prosperity of the South, were I permitted I would repeat what I say to my own race, "Cast down your bucket where you are." Cast it down among the eight millions of Negroes whose habits you know, whose fidelity and love you have tested in days when to have proved treacherous meant the ruin of your firesides. Cast down your bucket among these people who have, without strikes and labor wars, tilled your fields, cleared your forests, built your railroads and cities, and brought forth treasures from the bowels of the earth, and helped make possible this magnificent representation of the progress of the South. Casting down your bucket among my people, helping and encouraging them as you are doing on these grounds, and to education of head, hand, and heart, you will find that they will buy your surplus land, make blossom the waste places in your fields, and

run your factories. While doing this, you can be sure in the future, as in the past, that you and your families will be surrounded by the most patient, faithful, law-abiding, and unresentful people that the world has seen. As we have proved our loyalty to you in the past, in nursing your children, watching by the sick-bed of your mothers and fathers, and often following them with tear-dimmed eyes to their graves, so in the future, in our humble way, we shall stand by you with a devotion that no foreigner can approach, ready to lay down our lives, if need be, in defense of yours, interlacing our industrial, commercial, civil, and religious life with yours in a way that shall make the interests of both races one. In all things that are purely social, we can be as separate as the fingers, yet one as the hand in all things essential to mutual progress.

There is no defense or security for any of us except in the highest intelligence and development of all. If anywhere there are efforts tending to curtail the fullest growth of the Negro, let these efforts be turned into stimulating, encouraging, and making him the most useful and intelligent citizen. Effort or means so invested will pay a thousand percent interest. These efforts will be twice blessed—blessing him that gives and him that takes.

There is no escape through law of man or God from the inevitable:

The laws of changeless justice bind Oppressor with oppressed; And close as sin and suffering joined We march to fate abreast.

Nearly sixteen millions of hands will aid you in pulling the load upward, or they will pull against you the load downward. We shall constitute one-third and more of the ignorance and crime of the South, or one-third its intelligence and progress; we shall contribute one-third to the business and industrial prosperity of the South, or we shall prove a veritable body of death, stagnating, depressing, retarding every effort to advance the body politic.

Gentlemen of the Exposition, as we present to you our humble effort at an exhibition of our progress, you must not expect overmuch. Starting thirty years ago with ownership here and there in a few quilts and pumpkins and chickens (gathered from miscellaneous sources), remember the path that has led from these to the inventions and production of agricultural implements, buggies, steam-engines, newspapers, books, statuary, carving, paintings, the management of drug stores and banks, has not been trodden without contact with thorns and thistles.

While we take pride in what we exhibit as a result of our independent efforts, we do not for a moment forget that our part in this exhibition would fall far short of your expectations but for the constant help that has come to our educational life, not only from the southern states, but especially from northern philanthropists, who have made their gifts a constant stream of blessing and encouragement.

The wisest among my race understand that the agitation of questions of social equality is the extremist folly, and that progress in the enjoyment of all the privileges that will come to us must be the result of severe and constant struggle rather than of artificial forcing. No race that has anything to contribute to the markets of the world is long in any degree ostracized. It is important and right that all privileges of the law be ours, but it is vastly more important that we be prepared for the exercise of these privileges. The opportunity to earn a dollar in a factory just now is worth infinitely more than the opportunity to spend a dollar in an opera-house. In conclusion, may I repeat that nothing in thirty years has given us more hope and encouragement, and

drawn us so near to you of the white race, as this opportunity offered by the Exposition; and here bending, as it were, over the altar that represents the results of the struggles of your race and mine, both starting practically empty-handed three decades ago, I pledge that in your effort to work out the great and intricate problem which God has laid at the doors of the South, you shall have at all times the patient, sympathetic help of my race; only let this be constantly in mind, that, while from representations in these buildings of the product of field, of forest, of mine, of factory, letters, and art, much good will come, yet far above and beyond material benefits will be that higher good, that, let us pray God, will come, in a blotting out of sectional differences and racial animosities and suspicions, in a determination to administer absolute justice, in a willing obedience among all classes to the mandates of law. This, coupled with our material prosperity, will bring into our beloved South a new heaven and a new earth.

Source: Afro-American encyclopedia, or, the thoughts, doings, and sayings of the race: embracing addresses, lectures, biographical sketches, sermons, poems, names of universities, colleges, seminaries, newspapers, books, and a history of the denominations, giving the numerical strength of each. In fact, it teaches every subject of interest to the colored people, as discussed by more than one hundred of their wisest and best men and women. Compiled and arranged by James T. Haley. Nashville, TN: Haley & Florida, 1895. Documenting the American South, University of North Carolina at Chapel Hill, 2000. http://docsouth.unc.edu/church/haley/haley.html.

Hugh M. Browne, "The Higher Education of the Colored People of the South"

(1896)

Hugh M. Browne (1851–1923) was an African American educator and civil rights activist who served as principal of the Institute of Colored Youth in Pennsylvania. Browne saw the value of practical education, from the elementary level to

higher education, for African Americans living in Liberia and the southern United States. However, in this speech, delivered in Washington, DC, in 1896, Browne tells a cautionary tale about the miseducation of black men who could easily have found themselves out of touch with the reality of being black when slavery was not yet a distant memory anywhere in the world.

In my invitation to take part in the discussion of the higher education of the colored people of the South, your Vice-President indicated that the fact that I had lived in Liberia would enable me to speak as one having authority. I am not sure that I understand just what Dr. Wayland meant by this hint,—whether he wished me to give an account of Liberia, the republic which began with an imported college, and has not yet established a common school; nor been able, although maintained financially by friends in the United States, to prevent this college from falling into the condition which Mr. Cleveland calls "innocuous desuetude,"—or whether, possessing himself a knowledge of the retrograding effects of higher education upon that republic, he predicates therefrom the position which I shall take in this discussion. If the latter, he is perfectly right. No man whose judgement is worth accepting can live one week in Liberia without becoming a radical advocate of the now celebrated ratio of 16 to 1,—not between gold and silver money, for Liberia has neither, but between higher and industrial education. I mean that, in the matter of the education of my people, one part of industrial is worth, in weight, volume, and potential energy, sixteen parts of the best literary or higher education the world has ever seen. After much thought and prayerful consideration, I have arrived at the conclusion that the Great Creator has permitted the foundation and existence of Liberia in order to give to the world a striking and forcible object-lesson on the folly of attempting to prepare an undeveloped race for the "ceaseless and inevitable struggle and competition of life" by higher education.

In the time allotted, it is impossible to enter into anything like a full presentation of this object-lesson. Happily, this is not necessary for this Association. If, therefore, I can succeed in presenting what a friend of mine once called "a brief epitome of a brief syllabus," it will be hint sufficient to you gentlemen who are wise in matters relating to social evolution.

Zadig, when required to explain his perfect description of the king's horse, which he had never seen, said:—

> Wandering through the paths which traverse the wood, I noticed the marks of horse-shoes. They were all equidistant. "Ah!" said I, "this is a famous galloper." In a narrow alley, only seven feet wide, the dust upon the trunks of the trees was a little disturbed at three feet and a half from the middle of the path. "This horse," said I to myself, "had a tail three feet and a half long, and, lashing it from one side to the other, he has swept away the dust." Branches of the trees meet overhead at the height of five feet, and under them I saw newly-fallen leaves; so I knew the horse had brushed some of the branches, and was, therefore, five feet high. As to his bit, it must have been made of twenty-three carat gold, for he had rubbed it against a stone, which turned out to be a touchstone, with the properties of which I am familiar by experiment. Lastly, by the marks which his shoes left upon the pebbles of another kind, I was led to think that his shoes were of fine silver.

A nineteenth-century Zadig travelling in Liberia—the people having been swept out of existence—could, by a similar retrospective prophecy, describe what manner of man the Americo-Liberian was. His description would be something like this: He was a man who, in every line of life, was a non-producer. All that he possessed came as a gift, either from another race, or from the wild products of nature. A man who had simply used some of the effects of civilization, without ever manipulating the causes which produce these effects. A man who had memorized the higher education of another race, without ever realizing the fact that knowledge is power. He was like the hello-girl in the central office of a telephone system who uses the phone many times in the day, but knows nothing of the induction coil, the variable contact of the carbon and platinum buttons, and the effect of this contact on the strength of the current passing through it. She simply uses a completed instrument which she can neither repair nor reproduce. . . .

In my journey through Liberia I find a few iron implements used by civilized races, but I find no remains of an iron foundry of factory; and the iron ore, though plentiful, rests undisturbed. I find some manufactured cotton wares, but I find no remains of a cotton gin or mill, and the cotton plant is only found in its wild state. I find rubber manufactures, but no remains of the rubber-factory, and the wild rubber-trees have never been tapped. I find ground coffee, but no remains of the pulping-house or pulper; yet the country is overrun with wild-coffee trees of the finest quality. I find cans which contain all kinds of vegetables, but I find no trace whatever of a truck garden or canning factory. I find leather articles, but no remains of a cattle ranch, slaughter-house, or tannery. I find gold coins, but these bear the stamps of other countries; and the rich deposits of gold throughout the country have not been disturbed. I do not find the slightest evidence of the existence of a railroad or a wagon road, nor are there any indications that the streams were ever used as water-ways. I find a few official records, but among these no other evidence of an income to the republic than that derived from import and export duties; and the exports are uncultivated, raw products, furnished by the uncivilized tribes, and exported by white men residing in the country. I do not find one article bearing the stamp of a Liberian manufacture. I find a college in a sad state of decay, but I find no trace whatever of a common school.

I am not slandering Liberia in this "retrospective prophecy." I am but hinting at facts to which I called the attention of her people while in that country, and pleaded with them at the peril of my life for a change from a dependent to an independent existence; from a delusive imitation of civilization to a real living civilization; from a memorized knowledge of higher education to that bread-winning, resource-developing industrial knowledge which is a power unto the salvation of both soul and body and which alone can help an undeveloped people to help themselves. I pleaded and labored in that country for industrial education, as I have never pleaded for God's protection and guidance for myself or labored for my own existence. After studying the country and the condition of the people, I formulated a plan of education for Liberia quite similar to that which has been made famous by Tuskegee. In the letter to the interested white friends in America accompanying this plan occur such passages as the following, which I now quote to show my position on the question we are now discussing thirteen years ago, while in Liberia, and my position to-day while laboring in the cause of education in this country.

There is too much at stake in the trail which Liberia is making for any one connected with her, be that connection ever so remote, to be indifferent to the most indifferent of her concerns; but to neglect or unwisely order the education of her youth is to sound the death knell before she has reached her majority.

There is not royal road to civilization for the negro; nor does he need such. He needs now, in Liberia, an industrial institute, common primary schools, and a crops of well-trained and experienced foreign teachers, and these black or white, only that they believe in the brotherhood of man, and, above all, are such as think it not a sin to work.

It was a serious mistake when the affairs and control of the college were committed to the charge of the trustees in Liberia. A board of trustees, composed principally of unlearned and illiterate men, is no more prepared to conduct the affairs of a college than is a canal boatman to direct safely over the Atlantic one of our great streamers. I don't believe it possible to step out of slavery into such positions,—the distance is too great, and the steps between the two stages too necessary to the securing and maintaining the latter.

Nor do I think it just in those who desire to see a race *rise* undertake to raise it, as so many of our friends have done since the war. Give the negro the opportunity to grow into such positions and he will stand firm, think correctly, act wisely; but make him the holder of such positions and you expect no more fruit from him than one does perfume from the artificial flower. We must *grow*, and those who direct our growth must themselves be *grown*.

This country needs an institution which will put within the reach of the children of the masses, of the Americo-Liberians and of the natives, a common school education coupled with some trade,—mental improvement and muscular development of distinct money value.

They need the knowledge which skillfully grapples with the difficulties attendant on the development of a new country by a poor and untrained people,—an education which not only trains the mind how to observe and think properly, but which prepares one to intelligently understand the various duties and avocations of life, and enables him to earn a competent livelihood. The child crawls before it walks, and the young nation must struggle first in the rougher roads of material development before she essays to tread the higher paths of purely intellectual culture. For the present, provision for higher education should be made only for exceptional cases of talent and merit. Indeed, it would probably be well if this arrangement were permanent; for, after all, only those of exceptional talent and merit succeed in the walks of higher culture.

Liberia needs thousands of intelligent farmers and skilled artisans. Through these must education show its power and attract the people to its ways. The rising generation here must be taught self-reliance and independence. They must be made producers, who shall bring to markets of the world the products, wares, and manufactures of properly conducted farms, workshops, and manufactories. The institution for this country at present is at Hampton. And I have underscored Hampton four times.

These quotations indicate the conviction which my loyalty to race, wide observation, and experience all unite to confirm,—namely, that a people's education should fit them to succeed in the condition and environment in which their lot is cast.

Let us now come nearer home than Liberia. And let us be perfectly frank and outspoken. The trial of the negro before the bar of nations on the question of his title to the brotherhood of man is too near the jury-stage for sentimentality and weak excuses. The time has arrived for plain speaking and acting, for the presentation of substantial evidence of facts.

The same serious mistake made in Liberia, namely, substituting higher for industrial education, was made in the South. There we had the same disregard of the fact that a wilderness exists between Egypt and Canaan in the progress of a race or people. When we reached the opposite shore of our Red Sea, at the close of the late Rebellion, the majority of our saintly white friends of the North, and the colored men who had ear of the nation at that time, believed that we placed our feet upon the land of Canaan. They, therefore, fed us on the milk and honey of that land.

And to us, in our ignorance, this food was sweeter than manna, though the latter was super-charged with the proper nutriment and came directly from heaven. Now that they and we are beginning to realize that the land was not Canaan, but the shores of a wild, rugged, unexplored wilderness, we are both also discovering that the diet of Canaan does not produce the bone and sinew necessary for the journey.

We were given the higher education of the advanced white man, whose race has fought the good fight in the wilderness and is now concerned about the improvement of Canaan; and with this misfit training we have gone to our people in the wilderness, only to discover that we possess the *outfit of leisure* where the *outfit of labor* is needed.

No, my friends, neither man nor race steps from Egypt to Canaan, they journey there through undiscovered roads. The wedding garment of that land is of the crazy-quilt pattern, made of pieces of experience gathered only on this journey. I am, therefore, singing daily, not of "arms and men," but of the sweet uses of this wilderness, where necessity prepares us to win in the struggle for life, and God prepares us to win in the struggle for the life of others. And the burden of my song is that an education and Christian services, which are not adapted to our present condition and environment, are of no more value to us than is a pair of skates to a boy who lives in Madeira.

We have been sent to the Greek and Latin authors, but they do not teach us to bridge the streams we meet nor how to bring bread from the untilled soil. We need schools which put the hoe in one hand and a book on farming in the other; a hammer in one hand and a book on carpentry in the other; a broom in one hand and a book on house-keeping in the other. Christian scientific industrial training is the highway in the wilderness for us. Every circumstance at present makes this way so clear that wayfaring men, though fools shall not err therein, and those colored men who do err are the fools whom the Good Book recommends should be left to perish in their folly.

Labor, though the taste for it is acquired, is the true means of development. That it required, under God's providence, two centuries and a half to introduce us to a mild form of this means, in the South land of this country, is to me a very significant fact. If we will come to a familiar acquaintance and saving knowledge of labor, we must do so by educating our children to cherish labor as the pearl of great price, and to sell all else to purchase it. We must eradicate the idea that labor is degrading, by training our children to labor, and industrial education alone does this.

I favour the industrial, because the higher or purely literary education is not in touch with out present condition and those parts of our environment with which we are in correspondence. Among others, this higher education produces these three effects which are inimical to the progress of any race or people in our present condition:—

First, This purely literary education produces an unmarketable article, thus entailing upon the race three total losses; namely, the cost of its production, the anticipated selling price, and saddest of all, the expense of carrying this article in stock. The avenues of employment which require higher education are to-day over-crowded with white men; among the supply is greater than the demand, and is still increasing. Nor is their higher education a new thing. It is the result of natural growth, and rests upon an *experience* with the *letter* which now celebrates not its birthdays, but its centennials.

Colored men deceive themselves when they fancy color prejudice the obstacle which closes against us the avenues in which higher education

reaps its harvest. That which closes these avenues tightest is our lack, of that factor of proficiency which is acquired only from experience. And this is the factor which our present condition and environment do not furnish. The whites will not let us practised upon. I am thoroughly convinced that the best way to established this factor amongst, us in this country, is to extract the greatest possible life from those parts of our environment with which we are at present in correspondence.

Second, This purely literary education puts the average colored man out of touch with our people. The young white man, squandering the wealth of his parents, because he was reared out of touch with the causes which accumulated that wealth presents to my mind no sadder or more demoralizing picture in the social life of this country than the young colored squandering the knowledge of the university, because his people were reared out of touch with the concrete causes which produced that formulated, abstract knowledge.

This purely literary training does not touch the present social condition of our people in sufficient vital points. Its trend is toward the abstract, while we are wrestling with the coarser forms of concrete. The formulated knowledge of the book is but the experience of those who have succeeded in the struggle with the concrete, and can be of little developing value to one whose study of it is divorced from the concrete. When we step out of these seminaries of higher education, we are quite like the girl who thought she was a cook because she had memorized the better part of a scientific course on cooking. When thus equipped she finally entered the kitchen, it was only to discover that the old cook did not understand her theories and scientific terms, and she herself did not know a rolling-pin from a cullender—hence each was disgusted with the other.

We are just learning to manipulate the causes of the higher civilization; the knowledge of the effects if this civilization, therefore, will not help us, and one equipped therewith is out of touch with us.

We form the working masses engaged in fields of unskilled labor the world over, even in Africa.

The educated men and women who will help us succeed, round by round, to the top of the ladder, must bring us their learning in our own language. Herein lies the difference between the average college-bred man amongst us and our distinguished educator, Booker T. Washington: the former speaks to us *brokenly* in a foreign language, while the latter speaks to us *plainly* in our own language.

Harvard University honored the race which built her, when she honored Booker T. Washington. I have never known the white race to hesitate in their sanction and praise of men, whatever their color or creed, when they find them storing up energy, the motions arising from which produce social efficiency.

Third, This purely literary training puts the average colored man out of touch with himself. I don't believe any man, white or black, can in the first generation of his intellectual life, digest and assimilate the present prescribed course of higher education.

Physically, there is but one way to obtain the full corn in the ear, and that is to give the seed the condition and environment essential to its daily growth. The seed thus provided for gradually and slowly takes in, digests, and assimilates each day its daily bread, and builds up first the blade, then the ear, and after that the full corn in the ear. It is none the less true of the mental development of a people,—they must receive mental food gradually and orderly, first that which pertains to the blade stage, then that which pertains to the ear stage, and after that, that which pertains to the full-corn-in-the-ear stage. To supply all this while in the blade stage produces the worst form of mental indigestion, and a resemblance to an educated man which is ludicrous and yet self-satisfied. In this connection, I do not hesitate to declare that if one should analyze the efforts put forth under this unnatural training, he will find that they aim rather at the impossible task of changing the Ethiopian's skin than at the possible and God ordained one improving the condition of that skin; and in the name God and humanity, what else can the harvest be than impracticability and discontent? Knowledge, like food, is a power to its possessor only when it is

assimilated. There can be very little harmony among the "internal relations" of that man whose head is overloaded with indigested knowledge while his empty stomach is wrestling with the petition, "Give us this day our daily bread."

A man educated out of touch with himself is like poor little David clothed in the mighty armor of Saul. I rejoice, though, that the time has come when we are learning, even though slowly, that there is at the present stage of our progress more virtue in the sling than there is in the mightiest of such armors.

In conclusion, I am not opposing higher education in itself, I am opposing it at a stage in a people's history when it destroys efficiency and power. I am pleading for an education specially adapted to the circumstances and conditions of a specific case. I am beseeching our benevolent white friends to look upon us in the terrific plants, and not as so much clay to be cast into various forms by the potter. I am not asking a change in the system of education which the white man has built up. I am, out of the fullness of my heart, begging that it be kindergartenized when brought among us. I am claiming that the best way to teach the young idea of an undeveloped people how to shoot it to practise it in shooting the seed corn into the furrow and striking the nail upon the head with the hammer.

I see no reason for blaming the white man for the results of my own inactivity. Nor do I look with alarm upon restrictions placed upon my desire to continue in this inactivity. I do know that his former history gives every assurance that when Ethiopia shall unfold her arms and stretch forth her hands in the rivalry of life he will admit her "on a footing of equality of opportunity." The altruistic feeling of his civilization will demand this as truly as it demanded the abolition of slavery the world over. The height to which we shall rise in true civilization depends upon the energy and wisdom with which we shall stretch forth her hands in this rivalry.

Source: Browne, Hugh M. *The higher education of the colored people of the South.* Washington DC, 1896. Library of Congress, Rare Book and Special Collections Division, Daniel A. P. Murray Pamphlets Collection.

Plessy v. Ferguson
(1896)

When and how racial segregation began in the United States remains an open debate. While some southern states erected legal barriers that restricted the movement of African Americans immediately after slavery ended in 1863, other states erected de facto barriers that effectively controlled the movement of blacks for many decades into the 20th century. It is clear that while blacks and whites in the South lived and worked in much the same way after slavery as during it, an extensive system of social and economic segregation enforced by widespread hostility toward blacks reigned in many parts of the nation in the 1880s and 1890s. When northern troops left the South, old patterns of racial divides resurfaced.

Every southern state had enacted black codes immediately after the war to keep the former slaves under tight control. When these laws were voided by the Union, white southerners began exploring other means to maintain their supremacy over blacks. Southern legislatures, for example, enacted criminal statutes that invariably prescribed harsher penalties for blacks than for whites convicted of the same crime, and erected a system of peonage that survived into the early 20th century.

In 1878, the U.S. Supreme Court ruled that the states could not prohibit segregation on railroads, streetcars, or steamboats. Twelve years later, the court approved a Mississippi statute requiring segregation on intrastate carriers. In doing so, the court acquiesced in the South's solution to race relations.

In Plessy v. Ferguson, *163 U.S. 537 (1896), the best known of the early segregation cases before the Supreme Court, Justice Billings Brown asserted that distinctions based on race did not violate the Thirteenth or Fourteenth amendments, two Civil War amendments passed to abolish slavery and*

secure the legal rights of the former slaves. Although the phrase "separate but equal" is not present in the decision, the court's ruling in Plessy *approved legally enforced segregation as long as the law did not make facilities for blacks inferior to those of whites. In his now famous dissent, Justice John Marshall Harlan protested that states could not impose criminal penalties on citizens simply because they wished to use the public highways and common forms of transportation.*

Justice Brown delivered the opinion of the Court.

This case turns upon the constitutionality of an act of the General Assembly of the State of Louisiana, passed in 1890, providing for separate railway carriages for the white and colored races. . . .

The constitutionality of this act is attacked upon the ground that it conflicts both with the Thirteenth Amendment of the Constitution, abolishing slavery, and the Fourteenth Amendment, which prohibits certain restrictive legislation on the part of the States.

1. That it does not conflict with the Thirteenth Amendment, which abolished slavery and involuntary servitude, except as a punishment for crime, is too clear for argument. . . .

The proper construction of the Fourteenth Amendment was first called to the attention of this court in the Slaughter-house cases, . . . which involved, however, not a question of race, but one of exclusive privileges. The case did not call for any expression of opinion as to the exact rights it was intended to secure to the colored race, but it was said generally that its main purpose was to establish the citizenship of the negro; to give definitions of citizenship of the United States and of the States, and to protect from the hostile legislation of the States the privileges and immunities of citizens of the United States, as distinguished from those of citizens of the States.

The object of the amendment was undoubtedly to enforce the absolute equality of the two races before the law, but in the nature of things it could not have been intended to abolish distinctions based upon color, or to enforce social, as distinguished from political equality, or a commingling of the two races upon terms unsatisfactory to either. Laws permitting, and even requiring, their separation in places where they are liable to be brought into contact do not necessarily imply the inferiority of either race to the other, and have been generally, if not universally, recognized as within the competency of the state legislatures in the exercise of their police power. The most common instance of this is connected with the establishment of separate schools for white and colored children, which has been held to be a valid exercise of the legislative power even by courts of States where the political rights of the colored race have been longest and most earnestly enforced. . . .

So far, then, as a conflict with the Fourteenth Amendment is concerned, the case reduces itself to the question whether the statute of Louisiana is a reasonable regulation, and with respect to this there must necessarily be a large discretion on the part of the legislature. In determining the question of reasonableness it is at liberty to act with reference to the established usages, customs and traditions of the people, and with a view to the promotion of their comfort, and the preservation of the public peace and good order. Gauged by this standard, we cannot say that a law which authorizes or even requires the separation of the two races in public conveyances is unreasonable, or more obnoxious to the Fourteenth Amendment than the acts of Congress requiring separate schools for colored children in the District of Columbia, the constitutionality of which does not seem to have been questioned, or the corresponding acts of state legislatures.

We consider the underlying fallacy of the plaintiff's argument to consist in the assumption that the enforced separation of the two races stamps the colored race with a badge of inferiority. If this be so, it is not by reason of any-thing found in the act, but solely because the colored race chooses to put that construction upon it. The argument necessarily assumes that if, as has been more than once the case, and is not unlikely to be so again, the colored race should become the dominant power in the state legislature, and should enact a law in precisely similar terms, it would thereby relegate the white race to an inferior position. We imagine that the white race, at least, would not acquiesce in this assumption. The argument also assumes that social prejudices may be overcome by legislation, and that equal rights cannot be secured to the negro except by an enforced commingling of the two races. We cannot accept this proposition. If the two races are to meet upon terms of social equality, it must be the result of natural affinities, a mutual appreciation of each other's merits and a voluntary consent of individuals . . . Legislation is powerless to eradicate racial instincts or to abolish distinctions based upon physical differences, and the attempt to do so can only result in accentuating the difficulties of the present situation. If the civil and political rights of both races be equal one cannot be inferior to the other civilly or politically. If one race be inferior to the other socially, the Constitution of the United States cannot put them upon the same plane. . . .

Justice Harlan, dissenting.

While there may be in Louisiana persons of different races who are not citizens of the United States, the words in the act, "white and colored races," necessarily include all citizens of the United States of both races residing in that State. So that we have before us a state enactment that compels, under penalties, the separation of the two races in railroad passenger coaches, and makes it a crime for a citizen of either race to enter a coach that has been assigned to citizens of the other race. . . .

In respect of civil rights, common to all citizens, the Constitution of the United States does not, I think, permit any public authority to know the race of those entitled to be protected in the enjoyment of such rights. Every true man has pride of race, and under appropriate circumstances when the rights of others, his equals before the law, are not to be affected, it is his privilege to express such pride and to take such action based upon it as to him seems proper. But I deny that any legislative body or judicial tribunal may have regard to the race of citizens when the civil rights of those citizens are not involved. Indeed, such legislation, as that here in question, is inconsistent not only with that equality of rights which pertains to citizenship, National and State, but with the personal liberty enjoyed by every one within the United States. . . .

The white race deems itself to be the dominant race in this country. And so it is, in prestige, in achievements, in education, in wealth and in power. So, I doubt not, it will continue to be for all time, if it remains true to its great heritage and holds fast to the principles of constitutional liberty. But in view of the Constitution, in the eye of the law, there is in this country no superior, dominant, ruling class of citizens. There is no caste here. Our Constitution is color-blind, and neither knows nor tolerates classes among citizens. In respect of civil rights, all citizens are equal before the law. The humblest is the peer of the most powerful. The law regards man as man, and takes no account of his surroundings or of his color when his civil rights as guaranteed by the supreme law of the land are involved. It is, therefore, to be regretted that this high tribunal, the final expositor of the fundamental law of the land, has reached the conclusion that it is competent for a State to regulate the enjoyment by citizens of their civil rights solely upon the basis of race.

In my opinion, the judgment this day rendered will, in time, prove to be quite as pernicious as the decision made by this tribunal in the Dred Scott case. . . . The present decision, it may well be apprehended, will not only stimulate aggressions, more or less brutal and irritating, upon the admitted rights of colored citizens, but will encourage the belief that it is possible, by means of state enactments, to defeat the beneficent purposes which the people of the United States had in view when they adopted the recent amendments of the Constitution, by one of which the blacks of this country were made citizens of the United States and of the States in which they respectively reside, and whose privileges and immunities, as citizens, the States are forbidden to abridge. Sixty millions of whites are in no danger from the presence here of eight millions of blacks. The destinies of the two races, in this country, are indissolubly linked together, and the interests of both require that the common government of all shall not permit the seeds of race hate to be planted under the sanction of law. What can more certainly arouse race hate, what more certainly create and perpetuate a feeling of distrust between these races, than state enactments, which, in fact, proceed on the ground that colored citizens are so inferior and degraded that they cannot be allowed to sit in public coaches occupied by white citizens? That, as all will admit, is the real meaning of such legislation as was enacted in Louisiana. . . .

If evils will result from the commingling of the two races upon public highways established for the benefit of all, they will be infinitely less than those that will surely come from state legislation regulating the enjoyment of civil rights upon the basis of race. We boast of the freedom enjoyed by our people above all other peoples. But it is difficult to reconcile that boast with a state of the law which, practically, puts the brand of servitude and degradation upon a large class of our fellow-citizens, our equals before the law. . . .

I am of opinion that the statute of Louisiana is inconsistent with the personal liberty of citizens, white and black, in that State, and hostile to both the spirit and letter of the Constitution of the United States. If laws of like character should be enacted in the several States of the Union, the effect would be in the highest degree mischievous. Slavery, as an institution tolerated by law would, it is true, have disappeared from our country, but there would remain a power in the States, by sinister legislation, to interfere with the full enjoyment of the blessings of freedom; to regulate civil rights, common to all citizens upon the basis of race; and to place in a condition of legal inferiority a large body of American citizens, now constituting a part of the political community called the People of the United States, for whom, and by whom through representatives, our government is administered.

Source: Plessy v. Ferguson, 163 U.S. 537 (1896).

A. D. Mayo, "How Shall the Colored Youth of the South Be Educated?"
(1897)

In this essay, A. D. Mayo, an African American minister from Massachusetts, addressed the educational status of African Americans in the rural South in the 1890s. He wrote that the focus of education should center on industrial arts schools, staffed by well-trained African American teachers, for such schools would provide a solid education of political and social advancement for rural southern blacks.

Next to the preservation of the Union the most notable result of the great Civil War was the emancipation of more than six millions of Negroes and their sudden and perilous elevation, in defiance of all historic precedents, from the lowest to the highest position in modern civilizations,—complete legal citizenship of the United States. For more than thirty years the people of the old fifteen slave states have been wrestling with the problem of bringing the actual condition of these new citizens into conformity with their legal civic status as recorded in the Constitution and laws of every American commonwealth. By common consent the only lever that can lift this nation within a nation to its final position in American life is found in that group of agencies which, "working together for good," is known as education. The present essay is an attempt to outline the educational status of the American negro citizen in our Southern states, and to suggest some of the more evident and imperative methods by which the great educational movement of the colored race, begun with its emancipation in 1865, can now be reorganized in the light of past experience and carried forward to a successful issue.

But first let me indicate the point of view from which this observation and estimate are taken.

1. I trace the direct hand of God's providence in the removal of this people from the darkness of pagan barbarism and bondage in the "dark continent," amid the comparative darkness of Christendom three hundred years ago, to a new continent, destined to become the seat of the world's chief republic. No other portion of this race, either in Africa or elsewhere, has at any time been so favored by divine Providence as in this calling out of Egypt, at the beginning of a forty years in the wilderness, in the journey toward the land of promise.

2. I trace the hand of God through the two hundred and fifty years of the life of this people in the English colonies and the southern United States before its final emancipation, a generation ago. I have no apologies for its darker shades, and make no claim for the "peculiar institution" as a missionary enterprise. But this I see: While the masses of the European peoples, without exception, came up to their day of deliverance through a thousand years of war, pestilence and famine, which destroyed as many as now live on that continent, this people was trained for civilization through a prolonged childhood under the direction and by the consent of the superior class in the most progressive nation on earth. This is the only people that has made the passage from barbarism to civilization without passing through a wilderness dominated by the three furies of the prayer-book,—"sword, pestilence and famine." Up to 1860 it never strewed the continent with its bones or watered its fields with its blood in war. Its people never died in thousands, like every European people, by famine. And so well were they guarded against pestilence that no people on earth has so increased and multiplied, until to-day we behold a nation three times as numerous as the American republic under the presidency of George Washington.

3. When at last the republic, like every great people, was called upon to make the grand decision whether it was indeed one nation or a

confederacy of thirty nations which one of the number could sever, this people was providentially so placed that neither the Union nor the confederacy could boast that it had received the greater aid at its hands. Among the three million soldiers and sailors of the Union, at most were found not more than a quarter of a million of colored fighter and workers. But until the close of the great conflict the confederacy received the aid of probably five millions of the colored people, in raising supplies, carrying on the home life, and working in the various ways whereby the effective strength and number of its armies was prodigiously increased. And it was no small gain for the freedmen that, when peace and freedom came, every generous and thoughtful family in the South acknowledged a debt of gratitude to them and laid no charge against them for what had happened. Meanwhile, the North and the nation, which had liberated the slaves as an act of civil war, felt bound by every consideration of justice and humanity to do its uttermost for their protection and elevation.

4. And when the war cloud lifted and the six millions of this people stood up for the first "dress parade" of the grand army of freedmen, the whole civilized world looked on with amazement at what appeared. For during that period of less than three centuries the race had made a greater progress than any other people in the history of mankind. During those memorable years the African negro had learned the three fundamental lessons of civilization: How to work under intelligent supervision; the language and the religion of a civilized, Christian country. And that country was the world's foremost republic, and all the experiences of slave life had been during the years when it was growing from thirteen colonies to the United States of America. It was not remarkable, under those circumstances, that among these five or six millions was found a body of men and women who became the foremost leaders of the race, by the natural selection of superior intelligence, superior character, and superior executive ability. Freedom came to the Negro in a country by climate adapted to his condition; where good land was a drug in every market; so fertile that no family need starve; so sparsely populated that one of its states to-day could support the entire colored population of eight millions and still call aloud for millions more.

5. I do not discuss the wisdom or unwisdom of the last great act of this "strange eventful history"—the conferring on this people at once the world's highest opportunity—the supreme right of full American citizenship world's highest opportunity—the supreme right of full American citizenship, with all that belongs thereto. But I see that, under the same directing providence, even this, the most daring and perilous experiment in government recorded in history, awoke the entire country at once to the necessity and duty of providing that education for the coming generation without which freedom itself would have been only a mockery and a phantasm.

At once the national government stretched forth its hand to the two millions of colored children and youth. The great philanthropist, George Peabody, born and reared in the common schools of Massachusetts, a citizen of the South, a resident in and illustrious benefactor of the metropolis of the British empire, included the Negro children in the greatest personal gift at that time ever made for the education of a whole people. The board of Peabody trustees, the most distinguished body of men that ever served as a "common school board of education," under the presidency of Robert C. Winthrop, the descendant of Governor John Winthrop, the most illustrious of his great family, the model American citizen; through its right and left hand, Dr. Barnas Sears and Dr. J. L. M. Curry, invited the South to make its final effort to establish the common school for "every sort and condition" of its people. And, most wonderful of all the wonders of this era of miracles, the old master class of the South joined hands with the educational public of the North in the glorious enterprise of educating the children of its freedmen for the new American citizenship. All honor to the North and the nation for what it has done in giving to this people the greatest opportunity, to train its superior youth for the leadership of a nation. But we must not forget that for every dollar expended from the marvelous wealth of the richest nation and the wealthiest states of Christendom in behalf of the Negro, the sixteen states of the South, in the day of their poverty, have given four dollars for the education of these children in the new Southern common schools.

6. So here our "nation within a nation" stands to-day. The North and the republic have given the Negro personal emancipation and, as far as constitutions and laws can go, political freedom. But the only highway to the real use and enjoyment of complete American citizenship is the education of the head, the heart and the hand, which leads a people through the paths of peace and by the methods of a Christian civilization, up from every possible depth to every possible height of human achievement. The South has struck hands once and forever with the North and the nation, and in the establishment and support of the American common school, at a cost, during the past twenty-five years, of more than four hundred and eighty-three million dollars for its colored citizens,—has done such a work as no people under similar circumstances ever did before.

The only question now in order is: in view of what God and the Republic have done, what does this people propose to do for itself? What must this "nation within a nation" do to be saved?

I answer, without one word of hesitation: Turn its back upon the past. Return thanks to Almighty God that it now stands on the threshold of the world's highest position, sovereign citizenship in the world's greatest republic. Let it behold in this opportunity for the education of the two millions of its children and youth in the American common school, the final proof of the gracious providence that "thus far has let it on." Now let it gird up its loins, face the sunrise, and along this highway of civilization begin its upward march toward the future that can only be achieved through that education which is but another name for the Christian method of rising out of the lower places of the earth toward the sunlit summits that front the heavens and scan the horizon.

With the best light at my command I therefore hold that the absolute impending duty of the colored citizens of the South is to combine and by every practical method inaugurate a grand revival in behalf of the country and village common school.

The graded school for colored children and youth in the cities and larger towns in these states is now in a fair way to success. But it is in the vast majority of the common schools for the colored children and youth, in the open country and smaller villages, that the great field for educational work in the south is now found.

By the report of the National Bureau of Education for 1892–93 we learn that in sixteen states and the District of Columbia there are now (estimated) 2,630,331 colored children between the ages of five and eighteen. Of these 1,267,828 are enrolled in the common schools. The average daily attendance varies in different states; in Virginia one-half, in South Carolina a larger, in Maryland a smaller proportion; in the District of Columbia, where the colored schools are best, 11,000 of the 14,500 enrolled. It would probably be an approximate estimate to say that one-third the number of colored children in the South between five and eighteen are in average daily attendance on common schools, in session less than five and rarely four months in the year, during a period probably not exceeding four years in the life of the pupil. These children are under the instruction of 25,615 colored teachers.

"In the academies, schools, colleges, etc., for colored youth there are, as far as known, 10,191 male and 11,920 female students. In all these schools reported in 1892–93 there are 25,859 students. In the elementary departments of seventy-five of these institutions are 13,176 pupils; in the secondary 7,365; in the collegiate, 963; and in professional 924. In the collegiate department of these institutions only twenty-five per centage of colored illiteracy of persons above the age of ten in 1890 was found in Alabama; 69.1 per cent. During the twenty years from 1870 to 1890 the per centage of colored illiteracy was reduced from 85 to 60 per cent of the entire population. In Kentucky the colored school enrolment has reached 78 per cent of the colored youth of school age, while in nine states it falls below 60 per cent. Alabama, with the exception of three states, is giving education to the largest number of colored children in secondary schools. In the number of colored students in normal school courses in 1895 Alabama led the entire South, with 785; also in the number of colored students receiving industrial training, 3,427. It is estimated that the Hampton school in Virginia and the Tuskegee in Alabama now receive nearly one-half the entire sum contributed by the North for the education of the Southern Negro; more than three hundred dollars annually. But, with the best effort of the National Bureau of Education, owing to a chronic habit of neglect in forwarding school returns, these statistics of Negro education can be regarded as little better than a tolerable accurate approximation. Other estimates give in the entire South 162 schools of the secondary and higher type, with 37,000 students and 1,550 teachers. But at the highest estimate, of probably 800,000 colored children and youth in daily school attendance, not 50,000 will be found in any grade above the elementary and lower grammar schools.

If these institutions, especially those largely supported by the North for the secondary and higher schooling of the colored youth in all these states are wise in time and correctly gauge the drift of sentiment in the educational and religious public in the nation, they will at once do four things:—

1. With all possible dispatch consistent with existing arrangements they will relieve themselves of their elementary department and concentrate their work on the training of competent youth for leadership in all the positions where superior ability and character are in demand.

2. These institutions are waking up to the importance of giving better instruction and in many cases improving the quality of their teaching force.

3. They will co-operate, to the extent of their ability and with a heart in their co-operation, in the attempt to make sound industrial training for both sexes, not an annex to, but a permanent feature of their course of study and discipline.

4. They will discourage the attempt of some of our Southern educational missionary associations and home churches to force the sectarian parochial system of elementary schools upon the colored people.

With these four reforms these institutions can rely upon the continued favor of the friends of education throughout the country; at present for temporary supplies, and finally for substantial endowment, to establish them as the future collegiate and professional seminaries for this people.

So we are thrown back upon our fundamental position,—the almost absolute dependence of the colored people of the South upon the country district and village common school of the generation of children and youth now on the ground. More than ninety-five per cent of these two million six hundred thousand, from five to eighteen, will there receive the schooling that will largely determine their ability, twenty years hence, to become the American Macedonian phalanx, the chosen ten thousand on which our "nation within a nation" must depend for its direction in all public and private affairs.

Hitherto, this work of education, including a good deal of aid and comfort for the colored churches, has borne very largely upon the white people of both sections of the country. There are no very reliable statistics of the amount of money contributed by the whole country to the schooling of the colored people during the past thirty-five years. It will probably not be very wide of the truth to say that from the outbreak of the Civil War not less than one hundred and ten million dollars has been paid for this purpose. Of this eighty-five million has been expended by the people of the South for the education of the colored children and youth in the common school, and not less than twenty-five million by the national government and churches and people of the states that remained in the Union in 1862.

Probably no hundred million dollars was never expended anywhere with better results. Nothing that has happened south of Mason and Dixon's line since the foundation of the government has been honorable to the leading class of the South as the voluntary contribution of the eighty-five million dollars, under the peculiar condition of the American common school for the children of their former bondmen.

But, as a grim old railroad president once remarked to me, as he very leisurely extracted a five-dollar gold coin from his vest pocket as his contribution to my ministry of education, I don't take much stock in trying to educate two million of Southern children by passing round a hat." Our nation within a nation must realize, as its educated leaders everywhere declare, that the present condition of affairs is temporary and cannot be prolonged without danger of a decided reaction, not only among the benevolent people of the North, but from the roundabout common sense of the American people. The conviction is abroad, even in a more dangerous form in the South than elsewhere, that a people, eight millions strong, virtually the reliable laboring class of a dozen great states, which from a condition of absolute poverty in 1865, in thirty years has gathered together $300,000,000 of taxable property; the church property of one religious denomination amounting to nine million dollars; the majority of its intelligent, moral and industrial people to-day handling more money than the settlers of New England during the first half-century of their occupation; its average church and social gatherings displaying a better style of dress than entire classes of people in all the states; with the sympathy of Christendom behind it; should not so largely as at present rely on the prodigious system of solicitation that makes every Northern city from June to October a lively imitation of a new administration. Ordinary even "sanctified" human nature, cannot forever endure this tremendous pressure.

It is useless to ignore or in any general way to attempt to resist this impression, or to evade the danger of its becoming more influential in certain sections of the country.

The question comes louder every year: "Why cannot the colored people themselves do more to build their own school system, which is practically their one reliance for the training of the generation of their children now on the ground? Why do their people of means so often ignore their own public schools and spend their money on expensive schools and seminaries elsewhere, or even inferior schools at home? And why do so many of these more prosperous families compel their most valuable school men and women, who are needed at their posts of home service, to wear out their lives in tramping from the Atlantic to the Pacific and from the Lakes to the Gulf, beseeching the gift of student aid, which, if applied in their home common schools, would give an additional month of instruction to fifty children instead of supporting one Common school pupil in a "university?"

I repeat,—I see no help in this emergency save by a great revival in behalf of the common school among the colored masses of all these states. That revival must be led by the teachers and the educational public,—that portion of this people which appreciates the situation and feels the tremendous issues impending on the response to the demand. No political party in state or nation, no system of evangelization in any or all of the churches; no new departure of private benevolence can meet the emergency. There is no other way under heaven known among men" whereby this nation within a nation "can be saved"; as far as its salvation concerns its earthly destiny, except by a great awakening among these eight millions aroused by their own trusted and most influential leaders; not a revival that comes as a cyclone and leaves a spiritual wreck in its wake; but an intelligent, far reaching, practical awakening of whole communities, counties, cities, states; "growing while men sleep"; extending from commonwealth to commonwealth; giving the partisan politician notice to be "up and doing" and every enemy of the common school a "fearful looking for of judgment," until it compels the "power that be" to provide for the training of the young American Negro for the momentous duties already thundering at the door.

"The way to resume specie payments is to resume," said Horace Greeley while the statesmen at Washington were pounding their solemn brows over the financial problem of twenty-five years ago. Booker T. Washington, after his own vivid practical manner of speech, has told us the way in which this work was done in one case:

"Ten years ago a young man born in slavery found his way to the Tuskegee school. By small cash payments and work on the farm he finished the course with a good English education and a practical and theoretical knowledge of farming. Returning to his country home, where five-sixth of the citizens were colored, he still found them mortgaging their crops, living on rented land from hand to mouth, and deeply in debt. School had never lasted longer than three months, and was taught in a wreck of a log cabin by an inferior teacher. Finding this condition of things, the young man took the three months public school as a starting point. Soon he organized the older pupils into a club that came together every week. In these meetings the young man instructed as to the value of owning a home, the evils of mortgaging, and the importance of educating their children. He taught them how to save money, how to sacrifice—to live on bread and potatoes until they could get out of debt, beginning buying a home and stop mortgaging. Through the lessons and influence of these meetings the first year of this young man's work, these people built up by their contributions in money and labor a nice farm school-house that replaces the wreck of the cabin. The next year this work continued, and those people, out of their own pockets, added two months to the original three-months school term. Month by month has been added to the school term till it now lasts seven months every year. Already fourteen families within a radius of ten miles have bought and are buying homes, a large proportion have ceased to mortgage their crops and are raising their own food supplies. In the midst of all was the young teacher with a model cottage and a model farm as an example and a center of light for the whole community."

In all save exceptional cases, at first by private contributions, and ultimately by some method of local taxation, it may be possible to extend the common school in the country and village of the South even for two or three months; put the school-house in better repair, insist on a more competent teacher,

and generally to lift up the entire business of country school-keeping to an assured and progressive condition.

Nowhere in this republic is an able, religious, tactful, dead-in-earnest young man or woman so powerful for good as the thousands of teachers in the colored schools of the sixteen states once called the South. Any state association of colored teachers in five years could place their state as far in advance of its present position in the people's common school as it is to-day beyond the old field-school of the grandfathers.

Now, if any reliable or competent man or woman would appear in any metropolitan city of the North or South, properly indorsed and supported, bringing the "good news" that five hundred country and village common schools districts of the colored people of any of these states would, this coming year, by voluntary contribution, raise each the sum of twenty-five dollars that would furnish the salary of one good teacher indorsed by a principal of a state normal school for one additional month's instruction for its thirty to fifty children, I believe an additional twelve thousand five hundred dollars could be raised in a month and all these fifteen to twenty-five thousand pupils receive two additional months of instruction from a teacher who teaches and does not "fumble" with his little consistency.

This proposition is no visionary theory of my own. During my entire ministry of education in the South, since 1880, I have never asked a Southern community to do what many other Southern communities, no better off than itself, had not successfully done. Hundreds of district schools in all these states are thus being improved by the voluntary contributions of their own people, often assisted from without. I am convinced that if this method of local aid were organized and thoroughly tried, with the indorsement of responsible educators in both sections, it would become not only a success, but one of the most popular methods of giving aid and comfort where most needed by the colored people.

There is yet another reason for the inauguration of this people's grand revival in the interest of the children and youth of their nation within a nation.

The American people's common school is a public university of good manhood, good womanhood, good citizenship in a republican government and order of society. It is from beginning to end an arrangement "of the people, for the people, by the people," acting through a flexible majority, for educating the children in the great American art of living together; each pupil acquiring the mastery of his own mental, moral and executive faculty in preparation for a responsible and inspiring career of full American citizenship at the coming of legal manhood or womanhood. Here the people organize, support and, through responsible officials elected by a legislative school board, teach and train their own children. The pupil is neither a slave under a schoolmaster, nor the subject of a government his parents did not create and control. He is a "minor" citizen, in training for his "majority" in a miniature commonwealth, whose "rules and regulations" are the laws enacted or approved by a popular body and administered by a teacher responsible to the people for every act within his jurisdiction.

Here for this time the child steps out from the limited and exclusive life of the family, where he is often the "all in all," into the broad society of a little republic where no superiority in the wealth, ability, culture, social, personal or public positions of his family tells on his standing among his fellows. As in his future life, he stands for himself and rises or falls according to his own personal merit or demerit.

Another superiority of the American common school over all its rivals is that it is no less a seminary for the adult people than for the children. Before the year 1860 several of the states of the South endeavored to put on the ground the public school system for the white race devised by Thomas Jefferson, at the time of its publication in some ways the broadest and most enlightened that had appeared in this or any land. Although the South was not lacking in good scholars, farsighted educational statesmen, and an increasing body of superior people, who realized the peril to the lower class of its population from the illiteracy that like a great pestilential slough, there as in Europe, festered at the bottom of society, there was never satisfactory or permanent result until the close of the war.

All these interesting experiments were finally stranded on the most dangerous reef in the old-time Southern order of society,—the lack of efficient local government. The old-time system of government in the wide, sparsely settled district of a Southern county was at best a government at long range, always in danger of falling into the hands of a court-house "ring" at the country town; in many ways the feeblest possible arrangement.

The most beneficent and powerful influence was the social and moral power exerted by the superior families,—one of the ablest and best of the aristocratic families in Christendom, held together by one central interest, the preservation of the social and political order of which it was the head. This arrangement did good service through the first half-century transition period of the republic and produced a state of affairs that some of its literary admirers even now laud as the golden age of Southern American society. There was little vagrancy, for the colored folk were under the strict police control of the plantation; the poor white man of the district was an easy-going dependent; and the non-slave-holding farmer generally lived in a different portion of the state.

Thomas Jefferson early saw the peril of a such a condition and urged Virginia to adopt the New England system of town local government, which in a modified form, was afterwards extended to the new Northwest.

But that was then possible. The coming of emancipation found the vast rural districts of this section almost destitute of local government, with the drift of the civil war and the criminal and vagrant class of its six millions of freedmen afloat; with no effective labor laws to protect the children from the ignorance or greed of the patent or the tyranny of the corporation; no efficient vagrant law to save the open country from the nuisance and peril of the idle, vicious, depraved, often fiendish tramp who wandered about at his own wicked will until he ran against an indignant man with a shotgun or an infuriated mob, too crazy with drink and revenge to await the slow motion of a trial in a court, where a swarm of furious criminal lawyers were bound to move heaven and earth in defense of the most flagrant offender.

A potent cure of this and other disorders of the present rural Southern society is the building up of a more efficient style of local government; so that in every neighborhood may be found a body of people accustomed to public activity and administration; not merely voting in a fiercely contested election, but making and administering public ordinances for their own protection and the development of all the conditions of a well-ordered state.

This course must be the growth of a generation. But, meanwhile, as by a special political providence, the beginning of this great movement has already come to the Southern people in the establishment and administration of the people's country and village district school.

This school, although a part of the educational system of the state and still to a large extent dependent on the state for support, is in fact a little republic set up in a limited area of territory through the entire vast rural domain of these sixteen states. Here the people may and often do elect their own local board of school trustees, who administer the school law of the state and supervise the school which contains a representative of every style of family in the district. The school house becomes a little state house, the one centre of the local public life. Every family that sends a child is interested in it as in no political party, church or secret society. The goings-on therein are watched as nothing else is watched in the neighborhood. Its teacher is the "observed of all observers." Every good boy is known and encouraged; every bad boy is "spotted"; every superior girl aspiring to the dignity of a school mistress is "booked" for Tuskegee, Hampton, Claflin or one of the one hundred and sixty-two superior institutions where she may be educated into all of which she is capable.

The people, already possessed of additional public influence, will more and more seek to have their way in this great pubic function. Here they are trained to act together for the most important public interest, the education of their own children. The public life that revolves about the little school house is of the most valuable and stimulating sort. It need have none of the vulgarity and ferocity of partisan political contest. It can dispense with the sectarian fury and superstitious fanaticism that too often make a devil's normal school of a quarrelsome church. It steers clear of the bitter rivalries of social ambition; for the child of the humblest mother may become the foremost leader of his race.

What a people's university can this school be made! It is set up in sight of every man's door, always waiting to be improved, able by the self-sacrifice and enlightened cooperation of its families to become anything good they demand. It is the most radical and powerful training school of young and old America for the new republic that we all will face with the rising sun in the twentieth century. It only needs that the people of every school district in all these states rise to the occasion; take the schools into their own hands: if the legislature will not permit them under the law, improve it by calling in the gospel of putting their own shoulder to the wheel, turning their backs to the politicians and doing the work themselves. Nobody will care or dare to resist any sensible, practical, persistent effort of the people in any country or village school district in the South to make its school the best in the country, in the state, in nation.

No Southern Legislature will permanently refuse to come to the relief of a country school system when the people are straining every nerve to make the best of a hard situation and send up a plea to the capitol for aid and encouragement for the children. And, better yet, any people of any state in the Union that goes on educating itself after this fashion, in the self-helping American way of doing business, as it can in the management of the people's common school, will sooner or later become a body politic that no statesman, even the crossroads politician, can safely offend or ignore,—a constituency that will know just what it needs, and just how to get what it wants, in the direct, peaceful, obstinate American way. A people so trained will vote, and be apt to vote right, especially on education, and that vote will be counted. And every aspirant "in a strait" for an office will look that way, and every patriotic and thoughtful man will rejoice that this glorious right of suffrage, given to our "nation within a nation," has finally become a public blessing, the bulwark of the children's right to education in the people's common school.

The colored teachers must become the leaders in the great revival of the country district and village common school. The young colored man or woman graduate from any of the superior seminaries of the race, especially if his instruction has been a reality and not a sham, if he really knows what he has studied and can tell what he knows, and, beyond his function as a pedagogue, has a broad and generous outfit of intelligent, moral and executive manhood or womanhood, at once may become a missionary of the higher Christian civilization to the entire community.

The colored schools of the Southern country and village need a larger number of well qualified women teachers. The colored woman seems endowed by nature with a genius and faculty for the care of children. Amid all the discord and mutual political defamation of the last thirty years, the first Southern man in his sober senses, is yet to be found who has presumed in public to raise his voice against his colored "Mammy." Repeat that venerable name in the Congress of the United States and a freshet of eloquence will burst all the barriers that even Speaker Reed could pile up, and a score of "great statesmen" will again become a mob of juvenile wildcats in praise of a loving black "mammy" who sunk herself so deep down into their hearts that she could never be forgotten. Now send the granddaughter of that woman of the old time to a good school; help her to drink deep from the fountains of the new education, and put her in charge of the children in the country school house; and there will come a revival that will blossom like the flowery April that reigns in glory in the opening Southern spring.

Of course a great need of the Southern Negro youth is a training in the new industrial education.

I say "new industrial education." For after a very practical and effective style the colored citizen of the United States has graduated with respectable standing from a course of two hundred and fifty years in the university of the old-time type of manual labor. The South of to-day is what we see it, largely because the colored men and women at least during the past two hundred and fifty years, have not been lazy "cumberers of the ground," but the grand army of labor that has wrestled with nature and led these sixteen states "out of the woods" thus far on the high road to material prosperity.

But the new industrial education places the emphasis on the last word: Education. it teaches that all effective work done by the hand is first done by the soul. It is the man that works the hand, not the hand that works the man. No ordinary system of labor, however plodding, faithful and persistent, can develop the resources of the least American state, unless it is organized, supervised and directed by intelligence, character and trained executive ability.

The state of Massachusetts, more than two hundred and fifty years ago, "started business" on the bleak north-eastern Atlantic coast with two ideas: 1. That every man and woman should "work for a living." 2. That every boy and girl should be sent to school. The little state "fought it out on that line" for two hundred or more years before there was within its borders what we now call a school of industrial training. But during this time it had raised up a dozen generations of people of more than ordinary intelligence and habit of work as "steady-going" and persistent as the procession of the seasons and days and hours and minutes of the revolving years. To-day the new Bay State is one of the richest in the world. The average wage-earning in the Commonwealth, including every man, woman and child is 73 cents a day,—nearly twice the amount of the average wage of the whole country; and the state earns $250,000,000 per year in excess of the average earning of that number of the American people. And, beside this, there is no especial lack of all that characterized our higher American civilization.

This does not mean that industrial education is useless. Massachusetts was the first state, twenty-five years ago, to move in the introduction of industrial drawing into every common school, and she challenges the republic to-day for the excellence of her school of skilled industry and the various useful ornamental arts. But her example does remind some of our education that a trained mind, a solid character, an intelligent purpose and a determined will behind the hand, are the creators of all the genuine progress in the material development of the republic.

The especial problem of industrial education in the South is: How shall the vast majority of its colored children and youth who cannot live in cities and can attend only the country district or village common school for a few months in the year and a few years in a lifetime be introduced to the wide field of intelligent and skilled labor in its different departments?

It is so evident that we are almost indignant that any man in his sober senses fail to see it, that unless within the coming twenty-five years the young men and women of this race do take up the mechanical and operative occupations, as they have not yet, they will be first invited and finally compelled to "take a back seat" in the ranks of the laboring and producing class.

I have no question that the South has in its colored population the material for one of the most valuable operative classes in the world; a source of boundless prosperity in the development now awaiting it. What is needed just now is a little less newspaper "thundering in the index" about the vast resources of the Southern country to attract a rush of undesirable immigration from abroad, and a good deal more work put in on the practical side of education to bring its own laboring people up to their native capacity as the enlightened and skilled working class which the South now demands.

The colored graduates of the one hundred and sixty schools of the secondary and higher education in the South, if fitly trained, can be sent forth as teachers to the open country and village schools, where the vast majority of the children are found, and in numerous ways can awaken a great interest in all that relates to improved farming, housekeeping, economical living, mechanical training and operative industry. And thus can they explode the most dangerous public fallacy that still holds captive multitudes of well-meaning but ill-informed people—that the education of the masses is only another name for laziness and "big head." They can inaugurate a movement in thousands of rural communities that will crowd the secondary schools with students, well prepared by a good English elementary training for that union of a thorough academical and industrial outfit which will come like a fertilizing flood upon the open country and lift the people above the stagnation and discouragement that now broods over entire regions of the South-land.

The time has come when the colored clergy of the South should be called to the aid of this greatest of needed revivals. The history of every denomination of Christian churches in America proclaims the fact that, in exact proportion to the revival of popular intelligence, good schools, improved industry and moral reform in the affairs of this world, has been the growth of "pure and undefiled religion." The old-time Congregational and Presbyterian clergy of the eastern and middle states of the Union, whose church polity carried along, as upon a strong current, the establishment of schools for the whole people, were the prophets of the prosperity, power and beneficent influence of these churches in the republic. The great revival of interest in popular education in every American church, at present, is one of the most hopeful omens of the future and largely accounts for the fact that the American Christian church as a whole to-day gives to the world the most reasonable, truthful, moral and spiritual interpretation of the Christian religion ever given to any people in any land since the great Teacher lived and taught in Palestine.

And while all this is coming to pass, let every man and woman of the race who seeks the ultimate and highest good of our "nation within a nation" stand fast in his or her own place and watch and pray and work for that "good time coming," which always does come when zeal is married to wisdom and "righteousness and peace have kissed each other" in any great effort for the uplift of mankind. Let not the young men and women waste life in reckless and visionary efforts, or in the attempt to carry by assault the venerable fortress of prejudice and injustice that can only be reduced through a siege of starvation by the grand army of children and youth which is now organizing and drilling for a final campaign of education. Man at the best is slow and obstinate; and the barbarism which is the growth of ages of human ignorance, folly and sin will only yield the gradual but irresistible power of a growing enlightenment, a broader justice and a more profound and comprehensive love. Horace Mann used to say "the difficulty with me is that I am always in a hurry, while God is never in a hurry." Certainly, on the backward look, this people, least of all, has reason to rail against Providence; for never in the world before was a community so numerous, in three brief centuries, so tided over the period of transition from the depths of human abasement to the summit of human opportunity.

It will not be through any crisis of violence and tumult and conflict of races, classes and nationalities that the grand army of the American people, 75,000,000 strong, will attain to its complete organization and be marshalled on the field to confront the united ignorance, superstition, shiftlessness, vulgarity and vice of the world on some perhaps not far distant, eventful day to come. All that can be done at present, in the unity and patience of wisdom and love, to lift the masses of our people to a higher plane of intelligent and skilled industry, better home living, economy, solid prosperity and a wider and loftier view of the life, through the entire range of agencies included in that greatest of all words, Education, will hasten the day of deliverance from every private and public hindrance to the complete success of any class of the American people.

Through a whole week before the battle of Sedan, which closed the dismal era of the despotism of Napoleon III, the different armies of the German powers were silently and steadily marching, each by its own most available road, toward the concentration of the hosts for the decisive conflict. If the leaders and soldiers of any special division had become discouraged and demoralized and gone tramping off on its own account, it would have come to grief and there would have been no united Germany and no republican France to-day. Happily each division of that mighty army, in good faith, marched by others from above which it did not understand, "trusting in God and keeping its power dry." And when on the final morning, the fog lifted from above the doomed city, and the hills all around it were swarming with the combined soldiery of the coming German empire, all men understood that the beginning of a new era for Europe and mankind was at its dawn.

Even so, whenever I "can get into the quiet" of trust in God and hope for man, do I seem to hear the steady tramp of the gathering armies of the republic that is to be; each still a "nation within a nation," but all under orders from the Captain of Salvation up in the heavens; approaching that union of races which shall make the real American people the chosen of God for the leadership of mankind through centuries to come. My prayer to God is that through no "invincible ignorance" concerning the past, no frivolity, no madness of impatience or failure in the common ways of life, this "nation within a nation" may be diverted from its providential line of march and be found wandering through unknown regions to its own confusion and the postponing yet farther the final destiny of the land we love. For this republic is the land that has led this people forth out of the wilderness; and its starry flag is the banner under which we all may one day find ourselves looking upward together, hearing once more the last word of our great commander, "Let us have peace."

Source: Mayo, A. D. "How shall the colored youth of the South be educated?" *New England Magazine*, 1897. Library of Congress, Rare Book and Special Collections Division, Daniel A. P. Murray Pamphlets Collection.

James Weldon Johnson and John R. Johnson, "Lift Every Voice and Sing," or, "The Negro National Anthem"
(ca. 1897–1900)

This song, "Lift Every Voice and Sing," was first written, titled, and deposited with the New England Conservatory of Music sometime between 1897 and 1900 by civil rights leader James Weldon Johnson and composer John Rosamond Johnson. It was sung for decades, well into the 20th century, and throughout the civil rights era of the 1960s, particularly at rallies and demonstrations.

Lift every voice and sing
Till earth and heaven ring,
Ring with the harmonies of Liberty;
Let our rejoicing rise
High as the listening skies,
Let it resound loud as the rolling sea.
Sing a song full of the faith that the dark past has taught us,
Sing a song full of the hope that the present has brought us,
Facing the rising sun of our new day begun
Let us march on till victory is won.

Stony the road we trod,
Bitter the chastening rod,
Felt in the days when hope unborn had died;
Yet with a steady beat,
Have not our weary feet
Come to the place for which our fathers sighed?
We have come over a way that with tears have been watered,
We have come, treading our path through the blood of the slaughtered,
Out from the gloomy past,
Till now we stand at last
Where the white gleam of our bright star is cast.

God of our weary years,
God of our silent tears,
Thou who has brought us thus far on the way;
Thou who has by Thy might
Led us into the light,
Keep us forever in the path, we pray.
Lest our feet stray from the places, Our God, where we met Thee;
Lest, our hearts drunk with the wine of the world, we forget Thee;
Shadowed beneath Thy hand,
May we forever stand.
True to our GOD,
True to our native land.

Source: Johnson, James Weldon. "Lift Every Voice and Sing," or, "The Negro National Anthem." New York: Edward B. Marks Music Corporation, 1949.

Mary Church Terrell, "The Progress of Colored Women"
(1898)

Activist Mary Church Terrell delivered this address to the National American Women's Suffrage Association at the Columbia Theater in Washington, DC, on February 18, 1898, on the occasion of the association's 50th anniversary. In the speech, Terrell recounted her role as the founding president of the National Association of Colored Women's Clubs, a confederation of black women's service clubs dedicated to instilling racial pride. This group's goals included improving social and moral conditions in the African American community and founding settlement houses for migrant women, orphanages, day nurseries, kindergartens, evening schools for adults, clinics, and homes for the aged. People attending the meeting included activists Susan B. Anthony, Isabella Beecher Hooker, Rev. Anna Shaw, Lillie Devereux, Mary Wright Sewell, and Carrie Chapman Catt.

Fifty years ago a meeting such as this, planned, conducted and addressed by women would have been an impossibility. Less than forty years ago, few sane men would have predicted that either a slave or one of his descendants would, in this century at least, address such an audience in the Nation's Capital at the invitation of women representing the highest, broadest, best type of womanhood, that can be found anywhere in the world. Thus to me this semi-centennial of the National American Woman Suffrage Association is a double jubilee, rejoicing as I do, not only in the prospective enfranchisement of my sex but in the emancipation of my race. When Ernestine Rose, Lucretia Mott, Elizabeth Cady Stanton, Lucy Stone and Susan B. Anthony began that agitation by which colleges were opened to women and the numerous reforms inaugurated for the amelioration of their condition along all lines, their sisters who groaned in bondage had little reason to hope that these blessings would ever brighten their crushed and blighted lives, for during those days of oppression and despair, colored women were not only refused admittance to institutions of learning, but the law of the States in which the majority lived made it a crime to teach them to read. Not only could they possess no property, but even their bodies were not their own. Nothing, in short, that could degrade or brutalize the womanhood of the race was lacking in that system from which colored women then had little hope of escape. So gloomy were their prospects, so fatal the laws, so pernicious the customs, only fifty years ago. But, from the day their fetters were broken and their minds released from the darkness of ignorance to which for more than two hundred years they had been doomed, from the day they could stand erect in the dignity of womanhood, no longer bond but free, till tonight, colored women have forged steadily ahead in the acquisition of knowledge and in the cultivation of those virtues which make for good. To use a thought of the illustrious Frederick Douglass, if judged by the depths from which they have come, rather than by the heights to which those blessed with centuries of opportunities have attained, colored women need not hang their heads in shame. Consider if you will, the almost insurmountable obstacles which have confronted colored women in their efforts to educate and cultivate themselves since their emancipation, and I dare assert, not boastfully, but with pardonable pride, I hope, that the progress they have made and the work they have accomplished, will bear a favorable comparison at least with that of their more fortunate sisters, from the opportunity of acquiring knowledge and the means of self-culture have never been entirely withheld. For, not only are colored women with ambition and aspiration handicapped on account of their sex, but they are everywhere baffled and mocked on account of their race. Desperately and continuously they are forced to fight that opposition, born of a cruel, unreasonable prejudice which neither their merit nor their necessity seems able to subdue. Not only because they are women, but because they are colored women, are discouragement and disappointment meeting them at every turn. Avocations opened and opportunities offered to their more favored sisters have been and are tonight closed and barred against them. While those of the dominant race have a variety of trades and pursuits from which they may choose, the woman through whose veins one drop of African blood is known to flow is limited to a pitiful few. So overcrowded are the avocations in which colored women may engage and so poor is the pay in consequence, that only the barest livelihood can be eked out by the rank and file. And yet, in spite of the opposition encountered, the obstacles opposed to their acquisition of knowledge and their accumulation of property, the progress made by colored women along these lines has never been surpassed by that of any people in the history of the world. Though the slaves were liberated less than forty years ago, penniless, and ignorant, with neither shelter nor food, so great was their thirst for knowledge and so herculean were their efforts to secure it, that there are today hundreds of negroes, many of them women, who are graduates, some of them having taken degrees from the best institutions of the land. From Oberlin, that friend of the oppressed, Oberlin, my dear alma mater, whose name will always be loved and whose praise will ever be sung as the first college in the country which was just, broad and benevolent enough to open its doors to negroes and to women on an equal footing with men; from Wellesley and Vassar, from Cornell and Ann Arbor, from the best high schools throughout the North, East and West, Colored girls have been graduated with honors, and have thus forever settled the question of their capacity and worth. But a few years ago in an examination in which a large number of young women and men competed for a scholarship, entitling the successful competitor to an entire course through the Chicago University, the only colored girl among them stood first and captured this great prize. And so, wherever colored girls have studied, their instructors bear testimony to their intelligence, diligence and success.

With this increase of wisdom there has sprung up in the hearts of colored women an ardent desire to do good in the world. No sooner had the favored few availed themselves of such advantages as they could secure than they hastened to dispense these blessings to the less fortunate of their race. With tireless energy and eager zeal, colored women have, since their emancipation, been continuously prosecuting the work of educating and elevating their race, as though upon themselves alone devolved the accomplishment of this great task. Of the teachers engaged in instructing colored youth, it is perhaps no exaggeration to say that fully ninety per cent are women. In the back-woods, remote from the civilization and comforts of the city and town, on the plantations reeking with ignorance and vice, our colored women may be found battling with evils which such conditions always entail. Many a heroine, of whom the world

will never hear, has thus sacrificed her life to her race, amid surroundings and in the face of privations which only martyrs can tolerate and bear. Shirking responsibility has never been a fault with which colored women might be truthfully charged. Indefatigably and conscientiously, in public work of all kinds they engage, that they may benefit and elevate their race. The result of this labor has been prodigious indeed. By banding themselves together in the interest of education and morality, by adopting the most practical and useful means to this end, colored women have in thirty short years become a great power for good. Through the National Association of Colored Women, which was formed by the union of two large organizations in July, 1896, and which is now the only national body among colored women, much good has been done in the past, and more will be accomplished in the future, we hope. Believing that it is only through the home that a people can become really good and truly great, the National Association of Colored Women has entered that sacred domain. Homes, more homes, better homes, purer homes is the text upon which our have been and will be preached. Through mothers' meetings, which are a special feature of the work planned by the Association, much useful information in everything pertaining to the home will be disseminated. We would have heart-to-heart talks with our women, that we may strike at the root of evils, many of which lie, alas, at the fireside. If the women of the dominant race with all the centuries of education, culture and refinement back of them, with all their wealth of opportunity ever present with them—if these women feel the need of a Mothers' Congress that they may be enlightened as to the best methods of rearing children and conducting their homes, how much more do our women, from whom shackles have but yesterday fallen, need information on the same vital subjects? And so throughout the country we are working vigorously and conscientiously to establish Mothers' Congresses in every community in which our women may be found.

Under the direction of the Tuskegee, Alabama, branch of the National Association, the work of bringing the light of knowledge and the gospel of cleanliness to their benighted sisters on the plantations has been conducted with signal success. Their efforts have thus far been confined to four estates, comprising thousand of acres of land, on which live hundreds of colored people, yet in the darkness of ignorance and the grip of sin, miles away from churches and schools. Under the evil influences of plantation owners, and through no fault of their own, the condition of the colored people is, in some sections to-day no better than it was at the close of the war. Feeling the great responsibility resting upon them, therefore, colored women, both in organizations under the National Association, and as individuals are working with might and main to afford their unfortunate sisters opportunities of civilization and education, which without them, they would be unable to secure.

By the Tuskegee club and many others all over the country, object lessons are given in the best way to sweep, dust, cook, wash and iron, together with other information concerning household affairs. Talks on social purity and the proper method of rearing children are made for the benefit of those mothers, who in many instances fall short of their duty, not because they are vicious and depraved, but because they are ignorant and poor. Against the one-room cabin so common in the rural settlements in the South, we have inaugurated a vigorous crusade. When families of eight or ten, consisting of men, women and children, are all huddled together in a single apartment, a condition of things found not only in the South, but among our poor all over the land, there is little hope of inculcating morality or modesty. And yet, in spite of these environments which are so destructive of virtue, and though the safeguards usually thrown around maidenly youth and innocence are in some sections withheld from colored girls, statistics compiled by men, not inclined to falsify in favor of my race, show that immorality among *colored women* is *not* so great as among women in countries like Austria, Italy, Germany, Sweden and France.

In New York City a mission has been established and is entirely supported by colored women under supervision of the New York City Board. It has in operation a kindergarten, classes in cooking and sewing, mothers' meetings, mens' meetings, a reading circle and a manual training school for boys. Much the same kind of work is done by the Colored Woman's League and the Ladies Auxiliary of this city, the Kansas City League of Missouri, the Woman's Era Club of Boston, the Woman's Loyal Union of New York, and other organizations representing almost every State in the Union. The Phyllis Wheatley Club of New Orleans, another daughter of the National Association, has in two short years succeeded in establishing a Sanatorium and a Training School for nurses. The conditions which caused the colored women of New Orleans to choose this special field in which to operate are such as exist in many other sections of our land. From the city hospitals colored doctors are excluded altogether, not even being allowed to practice in the colored wards, and colored patients—no matter how wealthy they are—are not received at all, unless they are willing to go into the charity wards. Thus the establishment of a Sanatorium answers a variety of purposes. It affords colored medical students an opportunity of gaining a practical knowledge of their profession, and it furnishes a well-equipped establishment for colored patients who do not care to go into the charity wards of the public hospitals.

The daily clinics have been a great blessing to the colored poor. In the operating department, supplied with all the modern appliances, two hundred operations have been performed, all of which have resulted successfully under the colored surgeon-in-chief. Of the eight nurses who have registered, one has already passed an examination before the State Medical Board of Louisiana, and is now practicing her profession. During the yellow fever epidemic in New Orleans last summer, there was a constant demand for Phyllis Wheatley nurses. By indefatigable energy and heroic sacrifice of both money and time, these noble women raised nearly one thousand dollars, with which to defray the expenses of the Sanatorium for the first eight months of its existence. They have recently succeeded in securing from the city of New Orleans an annual appropriation of two hundred and forty dollars, which they hope will soon be increased. Dotted all over the country are charitable organizations for the aged, orphaned and poor, which have been established by colored women; just how many, it is difficult to state. Since there is such an imperative need of statistics, bearing on the progress, possessions, and prowess of colored women, the National Association has undertaken to secure this data of such value and importance to the race. Among the charitable institutions, either founded, conducted or supported by colored women, may be mentioned the Hale Infirmary of Montgomery, Alabama; the Carrie Steel Orphanage of Atlanta; the Reed Orphan Home of Covington; the Haines Industrial School of Augusta in the State of Georgia; a Home for the Aged of both races at New Bedford and St. Monica's Home of Boston in Massachusetts; Old Folks' Home of Memphis, Tenn.; colored Orphan's Home, Lexington, Ky., together with others of which time forbids me to speak.

Mt. Meigs Institute is an excellent example of a work originated and carried into successful execution by a colored woman. The school was established for the benefit of colored people on the plantations in the black belt of Alabama, because of the 700,000 negroes living in that State, probably 90 per cent are outside of the cities; and Waugh was selected because in the township of Mt. Meigs, the population is practically all colored. Instruction given in this school is of the kind best suited to the needs of those people for whom it was established. Along with their scholastic training, girls are taught everything pertaining to the management of a home, while boys learn practical farming, carpentering, wheel-wrighting, blacksmithing, and have some military training. Having started with almost nothing, only eight years ago, the trustees of the school now own nine acres of land, and five buildings, in which two thousand pupils have received instruction—all through the courage the industry and sacrifice of one good woman. The Chicago clubs and several others engage in rescue work among fallen women and tempted girls.

Questions affecting or legal status as a race are also constantly agitated by our women. In Louisiana and Tennessee, colored women have several times petitioned the legislatures of their respective States to repeal the obnoxious "Jim Crow Car" laws, nor will any stone be left unturned until this iniquitous and unjust enactment against respectable American citizens be forever wiped from the statutes of the South. Against the barbarous Convict Lease System of Georgia, of which negroes, especially the female prisoners, are the principal victims, colored women are waging a ceaseless war. By two lecturers, each of whom, under the Woman's Christian Temperance Union has been National Superintendent of work among colored people, the cause of temperance has for many years been eloquently espoused.

In business, colored women have had signal success. There is in Alabama a large milling and cotton business belonging to and controlled entirely by a colored woman who has sometimes as many as seventy-five men in her employ. In Halifax, Nova Scotia, the principal ice plant of the city is owned and managed by one of our women. In the professions we have dentists and doctors, whose practice is lucrative and large. Ever since the publication, in 1773, of a book entitled "Poems on Various Subjects, Religious and Moral," by Phyllis Wheatley, negro servant of Mr John Wheatley of Boston, colored women have from time to time given abundant evidence of literary ability. In sculpture we are represented by a woman upon whose chisel Italy has set her seal of approval; in painting, by Bougerean's pupil, whose work was exhibited in the last Paris Salon, and in Music by young women holding diplomas from the first conservatories in the land.

And, finally, as an organization of women nothing lies nearer the heart of the National Association than the children, many of whose lives, so sad and dark, we might brighten and bless. It is the kindergarten we need. Free kindergartens in every city and hamlet of this broad land we must have, if the children are to receive from us what it is our duty to give. Already during the past year kindergartens have been established and successfully maintained by several organizations, from which most encouraging reports have come. May their worthy example be emulated, till in no branch of the Association shall the children of the poor, at least, be deprived of the blessings which flow from the kindergarten alone. The more unfavorable the environments of children, the more necessary is it that steps be taken to counteract baleful influences on innocent victims. How imperative is it then that as colored women, we inculcate correct principles and set good examples for our own youth, whose little feet will have so many thorny paths of prejudice, temptation, and injustice to tread. The colored youth is vicious we are told, and statistics showing the multitudes of our boys and girls who crowd the penetentiaries and fill the jails appall and dishearten us. But side by side with these facts and figures of crime I would have presented and pictured the miserable hovels from which these youth criminals come. Make a tour of the settlements of colored people, who in many cities are relegated to the most noisome sections permitted by the municipal government, and behold the mites of humanity who infest them. Here are our little ones, the future representatives of the race, fairly drinking in the pernicious example of their elders, coming in contact with nothing but ignorance and vice, till at the age of six, evil habits are formed which no amount of civilizing or Christianizing can ever completely break. Listen to the cry of our children. In imitation of the example set by the Great Teacher of men, who could not offer himself as a sacrifice, until he had made an eternal plea for the innocence and helplessness of childhood, colored women are everywhere reaching out after the waifs and strays, who without their aid may be doomed to lives of evil and shame. As an organization, the National Association of Colored Women feels that the establishment of kindergartens is the special mission which we are called to fulfill. So keenly alive are we to the necessity of rescuing our little ones, whose noble qualities are deadened and dwarfed by the very atmosphere which they breathe, that the officers of the Association are now trying to secure means by which to send out a kindergarten organizer, whose duty it shall be both to arouse the conscience of our women, and to establish kindergartens, wherever the means therefore can be secured.

And so, lifting as we climb, onward and upward we go, struggling and striving, and hoping that the buds and blossoms of our desires will burst into glorious fruition ere long. With courage, born of success achieved in the past, with a keen sense of the responsibility which we shall continue to assume, we look forward to a future large with promise and hope. Seeking no favors because of our color, nor patronage because of our needs, we knock at the bar of justice, asking an equal chance.

Source: Terrell, Mary Church. "Commentary on The Progress of Colored Women." In *The Colored American,* edited by Richard T. Greener. Washington, DC: Smith Brothers, Printers, 1898. Library of Congress, Rare Book and Special Collections Division, Daniel A. P. Murray Pamphlets Collection.

Richard T. Greener, Commentary on "The Progress of Colored Women" by Mary Church Terrell

(1898)

Richard T. Greener (1844–1922) became the first African American graduate of Harvard College in 1869, the first African American faculty member of the University of South Carolina in 1873, and the dean of the Howard University School of Law in 1878. Greener was a close friend of Frederick Douglass, who served as his mentor, and he held a position as staff writer at The New National

Era, *which was then edited by Douglass. Excerpted here is Greener's commentary on the address Mary Church Terrell delivered to the National American Women's Suffrage Association at the Columbia Theater in Washington, DC, on February 18, 1898. Greener's article, which appeared in the newspaper* The Colored American, *traced the progress of colored women's rights from the time of Sojourner Truth in the 1840s to the 1890s.*

The distance from Sojourner Truth to Mary Church Terrell is really more than the forty or fifty years of fight for political recognition for women. It is an infinitely greater distance, almost limitless space, between the centuries of debasement and degradation of a sex, and the meteor's flight of education, purity, aplomb, rare scholarly training and literary culture.

The cold type cannot give to those who simply read the following earnest words, full of suggestive thought, of pathos and deepest reflection, that warmth and color which the occasion itself furnished—the brilliant setting, the *entourage* of intellectuality which made this the finest meeting of a most notable assembly.

Nor can the ordinary reader perceive the severity of the test, which set this champion of her sex, in juxtaposition in forensic art, with such war-worn and battle-scarred veterans, as Miss Anthony, Mrs. Blake, Mrs. Shaw, Mrs. Foster, and with the able and eloquent representatives of Norway and Sweden.

Never have I seen a more profound impression nor felt myself more stirred at the romance of the American negro as exemplified in the deeper tragedy of the negro woman, who stands today not merely the forlorn hope of the race; but in her achievements and her attainments, in her sorrows, travailing, and aspirations, the highest type of the race—the portion, psychologically and physiologically, upon which its future mainly depends.

That the opportunity was afforded Mary Church Terrell, to sound the note, and sing so strong, beautifully and pathetically the refrain of her struggling sex, is a source of extreme gratification to those of us, who well know her advantages of training, travel and culture: but even we were surprised most agreeably, and delighted at the able treatment and the signal success of her womanly exposition, judged by its cordial reception and its evident effect upon the audience.

Such occasions rarely occur in a race's history and it is no small privilege to be permitted, as I am here, to call attention to one for the history of the race, whose annals unfortunately are only too brief and at best most imperfectly kept.

Source: Greener, Richard T. *The Colored American*, Washington, DC: February 19, 1898. Library of Congress, Rare Book and Special Collections Division, African American Pamphlet Collection.

Booker T. Washington, Interviewed on the Hardwick Bill in the *Atlanta Constitution*

(1900)

This interview of Booker T. Washington appeared in the Atlanta Constitution *in 1900. The interview illustrates Washington's eloquent demeanor through his response to the defeat of the Hardwick*

Bill, a measure introduced into the Georgia legislature for the purpose of disenfranchising the colored people. Washington respectfully addresses the intellect of all southerners, black and white, in this brief interview. The bill was defeated in the lower house of the legislature by an overwhelming vote—only 3 votes were cast in its favor and 137 votes cast against it.

Professor Booker T. Washington, the head of the famous industrial school for colored youths at Tuskegee, and probably the foremost man of his race today, gave his views on the question of franchise restriction to a representative of the Constitution yesterday. Professor Washington spent the day in the city, having come here on business. When asked for an expression on the Hardwick bill, he said that he did not care to discuss that or any other specific measure, but on the subject of an educational qualification restricting the ballot to the intelligence of the country, he had very decided views.

"I dread the idea of seeming to intrude my views too often upon the public," said Professor Washington, "but I feel that I can speak very frankly upon this subject, because I am speaking to the south and southern people. It has been my experience that when our southern people are convinced that one speaks from the heart and tries to speak that which he feels is for the permanent good of both races, he is always accorded a respectful hearing. No possible influence could tempt me to say that which I thought would tend merely to stir up strife or to induce my own people to return to the old time method of political agitation rather than give their time, as most of them are now doing, to the more fundamental principles of citizenship, education, industry and prosperity.

"The question of the rights and elevation of the negro is not left almost wholly to the south, as it has been long pleaded should be done," added Professor Washington. "The south has over and over said to the north and her representatives have repeated it in congress, that if the north and the federal government would 'hands off,' the south would deal justly and fairly with the negro. The prayer of the south has been almost wholly answered. The world is watching the south as it has never done before.

"Not only have the north and the federal congress practically agreed to leave the matter of the negro's citizenship in the hands of the south, but many conservative and intelligent negroes in recent years have advised the negro to cast his lot more closely with the southern white man and to cease a continued senseless opposition to his interests. This policy has gained ground to such an extent that the white man controls practically every state and every country and township in the south.

"There is a feeling of friendship and mutual confidence growing between the two races that is most encouraging. But in the midst of this condition of things one is surprised and almost astounded at the measures being introduced and passed by the various law-making bodies of the southern states. What is the object of the election laws? Since there is white domination throughout the south, there can be but one object in the passing of these laws— to disfranchise the negro. At the present time the south has a great opportunity as well as responsibility. Will she shirk this opportunity or will she look matters in the face and grapple with it bravely, taking the negro by the hand and seeking to lift him up to the point where he will be prepared for citizenship? None of the laws passed by any southern state, or that are now pending, will do this. These new laws will simply change the form of the present bad election system and widen the breach between the two races, when we might, by doing right, cement the friendship between them.

"To pass an election law with an understanding clause simply means that some individual will be tempted to perjure his soul and degrade his whole life by deciding in too many cases that the negro does not 'understand' the constitution and that a white man, even though he be an ignorant white foreigner with but recently acquired citizenship does 'understand' it. In a recent article President Hadley, of Yale university, covers the whole truth when he says 'We cannot make a law which shall allow the right exercise of a discretionary power and prohibit its wrong use.' The 'understanding' clause may serve to keep negroes from voting, but the time will come when it will also be used to keep white men from voting if any number of them disagree with the election officer who holds the discretionary power.

"While discussing this matter, it would be unfair to the white people of the south and to my race if I were not perfectly frank. What interpretation does the outside world and the negro put upon these 'understanding' clauses? Either that they are meant to leave a loophole so that the ignorant white man can vote or to prevent the educated negro from voting. If this interpretation is correct in either case the law is unjust. It is unjust to the white man because it takes away from him the incentive to prepare himself to become an intelligent voter. It is unjust to the negro because it makes him feel that no matter how well he prepared himself in education for voting he will be refused a vote through the operation of the 'understanding' clause.

"And what is worse this treatment will keep alive in the negro breast the feeling that he is being wrongfully treated by the southern white man and therefore he ought to vote against him, whereas with just treatment the years will not be many before a large portion of the colored people will be willing to vote with the southern white people.

"Then again I believe that such laws put our southern white people in a false position.

"I cannot think that there is any large number of white people in the south who are so ignorant or so poor that they cannot get education and property enough that will enable them to stand the test by the side of the negro in these respects. I do not believe that these white people want it continually advertised to the world that some special law must be passed by which they will seem to be given an unfair advantage over the negro by reason of their ignorance or poverty.

"It is unfair to blame the negro for not preparing himself for citizenship by acquiring intelligence and then when he does get education and property to pass a law that can be so operated as to prevent him from being a citizen even though he may be a large tax payer. The southern white people have reached the point where they can afford to be just and generous; where there will be nothing to hide

and nothing to explain. It is an easy matter, requiring little thought, generosity or statesmanship to push a weak man down when he is struggling to get up. Any one can do that. Greatness, generosity, statesmanship are shown in stimulating, encouraging every individual in the body politic to make of himself the most useful, intelligent and patriotic citizen possible. Take from the negro all incentive to make himself and children useful property-holding citizens and can any one blame him for becoming a beast capable of committing any crime?

"I have the greatest sympathy with the south in its efforts to find a way out of present difficulties, but I do not want to see the south tie its self to a body of death. No form of repression will help matters. Spain tried that for 400 years and was the loser. There is one, and but one way out of our present difficulties and that is the right way. All else but right will fail. We must face the fact that the tendency of the world is forward and not backward. That all civilized countries are growing in the direction of giving liberty to their citizens, not withholding it. Slavery ceased because it was opposed to the progress of both races and so all form of repression, will fail—must fail—in the long run. Whenever a change is thought necessary to be made in the fundamental law of the states, as Governor Candler says in his recent message:

"'The man who is virtuous and intelligent, however poor or humble; or of whatever race or color, may be safely intrusted with the ballot.'

"And as the recent industrial convention at Huntsville, Ala., composed of the best brains of the white south puts it:

"'To move the race problem from the domain of politics, where it has so long and seriously vexed the industrial progress of the south, we recommend to the several states of the south the adoption of an intelligent standard of citizenship that will equally apply to black and white alike.' We must depend upon the mental, industrial and moral elevation of all the people to bring relief. The history of the world proves that there is no other safe cure. We may find a way to stop the negro from selling his vote, but what about the conscience of the man who buys his vote? We must go to the bottom of the evil.

"Our southern states cannot afford to have suspicion of evil intention resting upon them. It not only will hurt them morally, but financially.

"In conclusion let me add that the southern states owe it to themselves not to pass unfair election laws because it is against the constitution of the United States and each state is under a solemn obligation that every citizen, regardless of color, shall be given the full protection of the laws. No state can make a law that can be so interpreted to mean one thing when applied to the black man and another when applied to a white man, without disregarding the constitution of the United States. In the second place, unfair election laws in the long run, I repeat, will injure the white man more than the negro, such laws will not only disfranchise the negro, but the white man as well.

"The history of the country shows that in those states where the election laws are most just, there you will find the most wealth, the most intelligence and the smallest percentage of crime. The best element of white people in the south are not in favor of oppressing the negro, they want to help him up, but they are sometimes mistaken as to the best method of doing this. "While I have spoken very plainly, I do not believe that any one will misinterpret my motives. I am not in politics per se, nor do I intend to be, neither would I encourage my people to become mere politicians, but the question I have been discussing strikes at the very fundamental principles of citizenship."—*Atlanta Constitution*

Source: Interview with Booker T. Washington. *Atlanta Constitution.* Tuskegee, AL: Tuskegee Institute Steam Print., 1900. Library of Congress, Rare Book and Special Collections Division, Daniel A. P. Murray Pamphlets Collection.

W. E. B. Du Bois, "Of the Training of Black Men" (September 1902)

In the fall of 1902, W. E. B. Du Bois published the following article, "Of the Training of Black Men," in The Atlantic. *In the article, Du Bois argued against the then-popular idea of training young black men as tradesmen for economic purposes alone. This approach of teaching black men trades alone seemed to Du Bois a shallow solution to a deeper problem faced by all blacks in the United States—assimilation into mainstream American life. Merely training them to work as carpenters, masons, and other tradesmen belittled them in their own eyes and in the eyes of the world. Du Bois wrote that better race relations required broader education of young black men so that the United States would be populated by two self-respecting, cultured, and educated races, not one elite and the other a resentful minority.*

From the shimmering swirl of waters where many, many thoughts ago the slave-ship first saw the square tower of Jamestown have flowed down to our day three streams of thinking: one from the larger world here and over-seas, saying, the multiplying of human wants in culture lands calls for the world-wide co-operation of men in satisfying them. Hence arises a new human unity, pulling the ends of earth nearer, and all men, black, yellow, and white. The larger humanity strives to feel in this contact of living nations and sleeping hordes a thrill of new life in the world, crying, If the contact of Life and Sleep be Death, shame on such Life. To be sure, behind this thought lurks the afterthought of force and dominion,—the making of brown men to delve when the temptation of beads and red calico cloys.

The second thought streaming from the death-ship and the curving river is the thought of the older South: the sincere and passionate belief that somewhere between men and cattle God created a tertium quid, and called it a Negro,—a clownish, simple creature, at times even lovable within its limitations, but straitly foreordained to walk within the Veil. To be sure, behind the thought lurks the afterthought,—some of them with favoring chance might become men, but in sheer self-defense we dare not let them, and build about them walls so high, and hang between them and the light a veil so thick, that they shall not even think of breaking through.

And last of all there trickles down that third and darker thought, the thought of the things themselves, the confused half-conscious mutter of men who are black and whitened, crying Liberty, Freedom, Opportunity—vouchsafe to us, O boastful World, the chance of living men! To be sure, behind the thought lurks the after-thought: suppose, after all, the World is right and we are less than men? Suppose this mad impulse within is all wrong, some mock mirage from the untrue?

So here we stand among thoughts of human unity, even through conquest and slavery; the inferiority of black men, even if forced by fraud; a shriek in the night for the freedom of men who themselves are not yet sure of their right to demand it. This is the tangle of thought and afterthought wherein we are called to solve the problem of training men for life.

Behind all its curiousness, so attractive alike to sage and dilettante, lie its dim dangers, throwing across us shadows at once grotesque and awful. Plain it is to us that what the world seeks through desert and wild we have within our threshold;—a stalwart laboring force, suited to the semi-tropics; if, deaf to the voice of the Zeitgeist, we refuse to use and develop these men, we risk poverty and loss. If, on the other hand, seized by the brutal afterthought, we debauch the race thus caught in our talons, selfishly sucking their blood and brains in the future as in the past, what shall save us from national decadence? Only that saner selfishness which, Education teaches men, can find the rights of all in the whirl of work.

Source: Du Bois, W. E. B. "Of the Training of Black Men." *The Atlantic Monthly* 90, no. 539 (1902): 289–297.

Oswald Garrison Villard, "The Negro in the Regular Army"
(1903)

Oswald Garrison Villard (1872–1949) was an American journalist and author who championed various causes, including civil rights and anti-imperialism. The author of a well-received biography on abolitionist John Brown, Villard, who graduated from Harvard University in 1893, began to write regularly for the New York Evening Post *and* The Nation *in 1894. In 1903, Villard published the essay "The Negro in the Regular Army," in which he described the achievements of African American soldiers in U.S. military history. In the following excerpt, Villard describes the contributions of black soldiers to the Union war effort during the Civil War.*

When the Fifty-fourth Massachusetts Regiment stormed Fort Wagner on July 18, 1863, it established for all time the fact that the colored soldier would fight and fight well. This had already been demonstrated in Louisiana by colored regiments under the command of General Godfrey Weitzel in the attack upon Port Hudson on May 27 of the same year.

On that occasion regiments composed for the greater part of raw recruits—plantation hands with centuries of servitude under the lash behind them—stormed trenches and dashed upon cold steel in the hands of their former masters and oppressors. After that there was no more talk in the portion of the country of the "natural cowardice" of the negro. But the heroic qualities of regiment Colonel Robert Gould Shaw, his social prominence and that of his officers, and the comparative nearness of their battlefield to the North, attracted greater and more lasting attention to the daring and bravery of their exploit, until it finally became fixed in many minds as the first real baptism of fire of colored American soldiers.

After Wagner the recruiting of colored regiments, originally opposed by both North and South, went on apace, particularly under the Federal government, which organized no less than one hundred and fifty-four, designated as "United States Colored Troops." Colonel Shaw's raising of a colored regiment aroused quite as much comment in the North because of the race prejudice it defied, as because of the novelty of the new organization. General Weitzel tendered his resignation the instant General B. F. Butler assigned black soldiers to his brigade, and was with difficulty induced to serve on. His change of mind was a wise one, and not only because these colored soldiers covered him with glory at Port Hudson. It was his good fortune to be the central figure in one of the dramatic incidents of a war that must ever rank among the most thrilling and tragic the world has seen. The black cavalrymen who rode into Richmond, the first of the Northern troops to enter the Southern capital, went in waving their sabres and crying to the negroes on the sidewalks, "We have come to set you free!" They were from the division of Godfrey Weitzel, and American history has no more stirring moment.

In the South, notwithstanding the raising in 1861 of a colored Confederate regiment by Governor Moore of Louisiana (a magnificent body of educated colored men which afterwards became the First Louisiana National Guards of General Weitzel's brigade and the first colored regiment in the Federal Army), the feeling against negro troops was insurmountable until the last days of the struggle. Then no straw could be overlooked. When, in December, 1863, Major-General Patrick R. Cleburne, who commanded a division of Hardee's Corps of the Confederate Army of the Tennessee, sent in a paper in which the employment of the slaves as soldiers of the South was vigorously advocated, Jefferson Davis indorsed it with the statement, "I deem it inexpedient at this time to give publicity to this paper, and request that it be suppressed." General Cleburne urged that "freedom within a reasonable time" be granted to every slave remaining true to the Confederacy, and was moved to this action by the valor of the Fifty-fourth Massachusetts, saying, "If they [the negroes] can be made to face and fight bravely against their former masters, how much more probable is it that with the allurement of a higher reward, and led by those masters, they would submit to discipline and face dangers?"

With the ending of the civil war the regular army of the United States was reorganized upon a peace footing by an act of Congress dated July 28, 1866. In just recognition of the bravery of the colored volunteers six regiments, the Ninth and Tenth Cavalry and the Thirty-eighth, Thirty-ninth, Fortieth, and Forth-first Infantry, were designated as colored regiments. When the army was again reduced in 1869, the Thirty-eighth and Forty-first became the Twenty-fourth Infantry, and the Thirty-ninth and Fortieth became the Twenty-fifth. This left four colored regiments in the regular army as it was constituted from 1870 until 1901. There has never been a colored artillery organization in the regular service.

Source: Villard, Oswald Garrison. "The Negro in the Regular Army." *The Atlantic Monthly,* June,1903.

The Negro Development and Exposition Company of the U.S.A., "An Address to the American Negro"

(1907)

"An Address to the American Negro" was written by the Negro Development and Exposition Company of the U.S.A. and delivered at an annual exhibition held in Virginia to consolidate and promote Negro thrift, progress, and commerce after emancipation.

To the Ten Million Negroes of the United States, Greeting . . .

Whereas a large number of representative men and women of the race secured, under the laws of Virginia, a charter for the Negro Development and Exposition Company of the United States of America, on the 13th day of August, 1903, which company was organized for the purpose of holding a separate exhibit on the occasion of the 300th anniversary of the landing of the first English speaking people of this country at Jamestown. Va., but before the incorporation of this company, there was organized and chartered the Jamestown Exposition Company, under the laws of Virginia, for the purpose of celebrating the said 300th anniversary, by holding a land and naval exhibition at or near Hampton Roads, Va.

This last company is officered, owned and operated by the white people of this country. The Negro felt that in as much as there was to be a celebration of the said event by the white race, it would be a fit and opportune time for the Negro to come upon the scenes and there present to the nations of the earth, the evidence of his thrift and progress, by putting upon exhibition the articles and things made and invented, created and produced by the race since its emancipation, and that in accordance with the uncertain and unsatisfactory conditions now existing as to the Negro in this country, that a creditable exhibit of his industrial capacities would result in untold good to the entire race, that the Negro question has been and is being discussed all over this country, some taking a favorable view of the situation, others taking different views, leaving him in an unsatisfactory position as to his relation to the government and the country in which he lives. A creditable exhibit would have a tendency to show just what the Negro can do, what he has done, and what he is doing in the solution of the much talked of question, or problem. That in this particular time, such an exhibit would be productive of great results from every point of view. The fact that the nations of the earth have been invited by the President of the United States to participate in the said exposition, is another evidence that such an exhibit would be of untold benefit to the Negro. It would also be stimulating to the Negro to see for himself what he can do, as such an exhibit would bring together the entire race with its exhibits to be thus viewed, which under no other circumstances it could have done.

After the incorporation of the said Negro Development and Exposition Company, its executive officers conferred with the Jamestown Company and secured concessions to hold a separate and distinct exhibit on the occasion of the great national and international exposition to enable the Negro to produce the results above referred to. The concessions were in every way satisfactory and agreeable to both the Negro Development and Exposition Company and the Jamestown Exposition Company. After this concession, the said Negro Development and Exposition Company proceeded to present its claim for a special exhibit on account of the race to the American people regardless of race or color. Its first effort was for the endorsement of the National Negro Business League, of which Dr. Booker T. Washington is president. Its second effort was to secure the endorsement and support of the National Negro Baptist Convention at its session in the city of Chicago on the 27th day of October 1905, which endorsement was unanimously received. It received the endorsement of a number of the State Baptist Conventions, and of the State A. M.

E. Conferences including that of Virginia. It received the endorsement of the State Baptist Conventions of North Carolina, South Carolina and a number of district and other conventions of the race in the various States of the Union. Among them were the Florida State Negro Business League, and the Mississippi State Negro Business League. We carried the cause from State to State. We have had resolutions adopted endorsing our efforts in nearly every State of the Union, where the race population justified the adoption of such resolutions. We have spoken and received the endorsement in mass meetings assembled in the cities in the North and West.

The company's authorized capital stock was fixed at $800,000 at the par value of $10 each. We saw that the money could not be raised in time to have the desired result by the sale of the capital stock among the members of our own race. We, therefore, appealed to the governors of the different States, where the colored people were in large numbers of the colored population justified asking that they recommend to their legislatures the appropriation of an amount of money, justified by the numbers of Negroes, to aid and assist the Negro of their respective States in uniting with their brethren in Virginia in making a creditable exhibit of their achievements from their said States. From them we received favorable response. A large number of the governors recommended such an appropriation, and in a number of States appropriations have been made for the said State's participation in the Jamestown Exposition. We have appealed to the State commissioners, appointed by their respective governors, asking that a proportion of the appropriation thus made, be set apart to assist the Negro of that State in the part he desires to take in connection with the Negro exhibit at the Jamestown Exposition.

We have appeared before the committees of several legislatures. We have presented the cause of the Negroes and asked the legislatures to provide for them. Then, for fear that the States might not act as promptly as we hoped to or as satisfactorily as we hoped they would, we appealed to the president of the United States, and asked for the influence of his good office in securing an appropriation from the national government. The mere calling the President's attention to the situation secured his immediate endorsement and his pledge of support in our effort to get governmental aid in this laudable enterprise. To emphasize his position in the matter on the occasion of his visit in the South in passing through Richmond, Va., on the 18th day of October, 1905, President Roosevelt stopped the procession that was escorting him through the city of Richmond when it reached the head-quarters of the Negro Development and Exposition Company, and there called for Giles B. Jackson, the Director General of the said company, and addressing him, said in part; "Mr. Jackson, I congratulate you and your people on the magnificent showing you have made in your development. I am with you. I assure you and your people that you have my hearty support in the efforts you are making to have a creditable exhibit of the achievements of your race and I commend you in the effort you are making for the betterment of the condition of your race."

Having thus received the public commendation of the President of the United States, we proceeded to Washington with a bill in hand prepared with pains and asking for the appropriation of $250,000 by the Congress of the United States to the Negro Development and Exposition Company, to aid him in his exhibit. This bill was referred to the committee on Industrial Arts and Expositions and after several meetings of the committee once in the city of Norfolk and on other occasions in the city of Washington, it was agreed to recommend the appropriation of $100,000 in the aid of the Negro Development and Exposition Company. This bill was likewise reported by the committee in the senate, and on the 30th day of June, it passed both houses of Congress and was signed by the president and there upon became the law of the land.

It is needless for us to say that we had quite a difficult task in getting this appropriation. We had to fight those whom we had expected would be our friends, and those whom we had expected to meet in compact in opposition to this appropriation, were those who came to our rescue.

We mean there was not a single white man in congress to raise his voice against us. It passed congress with only one vote against us and that was so faint one could not discover the one who said it. He did not mean it. If he had, he would have made himself heard and his identity known, therefore, we regard it that the bill, appropriating this $100,000 to aid the Negro, was passed without a single voice against it. But, strange as it may appear, there were those among our own race, who wrote letters to congress protesting against governmental aid of the Negro Development and Exposition Company, and these were men of learning, as we are told, but their effort was so preposterous that it made friends for us in congress. The white man saw that any Negro who opposed such an appropriation was an enemy to himself and his race, hence, the opposition of the few, simply made friends for us. We have not an unkind word to say against them or anybody else. The fact that the government has put its seal of approval upon the effort of the Negro Development and Exposition Company and its officers by making the appropriation to aid it in its work, is sufficient to commend the said company to the entire Negro race and to the American people. It does commend it, and in no uncertain tone, for when the government of the United States passes an act appropriating $1,000,000, it puts its commendation upon it. When the Congress of the United States passes an act appropriating $1.00 to any cause, it carries with it its commendation to the world. The committee on Industrial Arts and Expositions investigated everything pertaining to the Negro Development and Exposition Company. They had meetings after meetings, and Negro after Negro appeared before them, either in writing or otherwise, and tried to throw cold water upon the efforts of the Negro in Virginia, but every step they made redowned to the benefit of the Negro Development and Exposition Company. The harder the Negro fought it the better faith the white man had in it, because the Negro could not make the argument sufficiently strong against the appropriation to convince an illiterate man, much less a member of congress, that the Negro exhibit was not the thing to be had.

The fact that there was a Negro department at the Atlanta Exposition, which was supported by governmental aid, and the fact that there was a Negro department at the Charleston Exposition, which was supported by governmental aid, and the fact that the Negro exhibit was gathered together by the authorities of the national government and carried to Paris, and there put upon exhibition, all three of which exhibitions were declared a success, have caused our opposers to abandon all opposition, and to unite with the Negro Development and Exposition Company to make the desired success of the exposition. They were the pride of the Negro race. This alone was argument in favor of the Negro exhibit at the Jamestown Exposition, and left no room for the opposers to make a stand.

Now that all of this has happened and the Negro Development and Exposition Company is still marching to the front with the aid of the government, and is planning to have a gigantic exhibit at the Jamestown Exposition, and that the government of the United States, by its act has removed all doubt as to the success of the exhibit and has declared its faith in the management of the Negro Development and Exposition Company, the thing now to do is for the whole race, even those who differ with us, to unite as one and carry forward the great work of creating the gigantic exhibit on behalf of the Negro race of this country at the Jamestown Exposition.

The argument that the Negro exhibit was a Jim Crow affair, has been knocked out by the act of the government and by the act of the Negro Development and Exposition Company.

The fact that the company is owned and officered by the Negro himself and was made and created on his motion, removed any taint of Jim Crowism. If the Negro Development and Exposition Company is a Jim Crow affair, then every institution of learning, owned and officered by Negroes, is likewise a Jim Crow affair; every church, in which Negroes worship and over which our bishops preside, is a Jim Crow affair. If one is a Jim Crow affair, then the others is. We say neither is. The Negro Development and Exposition Company, and the church, and the institution of learning, owned and operated by Negroes, each is a separate institution for the benefit of the Negro exhibit at the Jamestown Exposition.

Argument has been produced against the exhibit because of the Jim Crow car laws, that exist in the Southern States. This we deplore, and our position is known. We were so much opposed to the law, that Giles B. Jackson, the Director General of this company, appeared before the legislative committee on roads and internal navigation of the Virginia legislature, and opposed the enactment of this law. With all his vim, oratory, force, and effect. He made it possible for a committee, that was headed by Dr. Atkins, of Hampton, Va., to appear before the said committee and enter a solemn protest, but after all the bill was enacted. It was only in keeping with all the Southern States. It is now the law, and as law-abiding citizens, we are compelled to bow in humble submission. If the State is insufficient to compel us to obey the law, the United States government, under the constitution, would have to intervene until we were subjected under the laws of the State. Then, too, is it not the proper thing for us to do to make the best terms we can with railroads since they have the power to give equal accommodation to both races, that being the law of different Southern States that the races should be separated that no distinction should be made as to accommodation? It is incumbent on the Negro to stop kicking and quarreling, and go to the law and to the heads of the authorities of the States and ask that the railroads be required to give equal accommodation for the colored passengers, and this will be done. But whether the citizens of the different States do it or not, the Negro Development and Exposition Company, having in charge the Negro exhibit at Jamestown, will see to it that equal and good accommodations will be afforded to the Negro travelers, to and from the exposition. The Negro Development and Exposition Company is making itself busy in looking after this part of the program. It will take up the matter with the heads of the railroad companies. In fact, it has already done so with some of the companies and they have pledged their word and honor that good, clean and satisfactory accommodations will be given to the Negro travelers from the North, South, East and West. That they shall have no reason to complain, other than the fact that they will not be riding with the white folks. They will be riding together in clean, decent and respectable cars with efficient service. Those traveling, who find any fault with the management, will please report the same to Giles B. Jackson, the Director General and the general counsel for the Negro Development and Exposition Company, of U. S. A., and he will take the matter up immediately with the railroad companies and see to it that there shall not be any other occasion for complaint. Col. Jackson is on good terms with the railroad companies, but if they fail to do their duty, the aid of the corporation commission, having charge of the overseeing of all the railroads of Virginia, will adjust matters. This commission was made and created under the constitution of Virginia for the purpose of enforcing the laws, and its aid will be invoked whenever the occasion requires, but it is hoped and believed that the occasion will not require it. The railroad and steamboat companies will make special effort to avoid any complaint from any travelers on all lines and roads.

We issue this address that the members of our race may thoroughly understand the true condition of affairs and that they may not be afraid to come to the exposition. The fact that there will be crowds of people coming from all over the country to the exposition will make it convenient for the reunion of families, that have been separated for ten, twenty, yes, thirty years. The opportunity will be afforded for the meeting of our friends, whom we have not seen since the war. The opportunity will be afforded for the meeting of our kin-folks and relatives, whom we have not seen since our emancipation. Every car coming will bring lots of our race, every boat will be loaded down. On every day there will be those who have not seen each other for years.

Source: Negro Development and Exposition Company of the U.S.A. "An address to the American Negro." Richmond, VA: The Negro Development and Exposition Company of the U.S.A., 1907. Library of Congress, Rare Book and Special Collections Division, Daniel A. P. Murray Pamphlets Collection.

Harlem Renaissance through World War II

(1920–1950)

W. E. B. Du Bois, "The Souls of White Folk"
(1920)

Scholar and activist W. E. B. Du Bois began writing a series of scholarly papers, books, and newspaper and magazine articles early in the 20th century to explore the esoteric varieties of life from the perspective of a black man in the United States. Many of his writings were published in various magazines and journals, including The Atlantic, The Independent, The Crisis, *and* The Journal of Race Development. *Du Bois's works on race were among the first such articles widely circulated to a largely white audience. This essay is from a collection of his essays published in 1920, titled* Darkwater: Voices from Within the Veil.

These are the things of which men think, who live: of their own selves and the dwelling place of their fathers; of their neighbors; of work and service; of rule and reason and women and children; of Beauty and Death and War. To this thinking I have only to add a point of view:

I have been in the world, but not of it. I have seen the human drama from a veiled corner, where all the outer tragedy and comedy have reproduced themselves in microcosm within. From this inner torment of souls the human scene without has interpreted itself to me in unusual and even illuminating ways. For this reason, and this alone, I venture to write again on themes on which great souls have already said greater words, in the hope that I may strike here and there a half-tone, newer even if slighter, up from the heart of my problem and the problems of my people.

Between the sterner flights of logic, I have sought to set some little alightings of what may be poetry. They are tributes to Beauty, unworthy to stand alone; yet perversely, in my mind, now at the end, I know not whether I mean the Thought for the Fancy—or the Fancy for the Thought, or why the book trails off to playing, rather than standing strong on unanswering fact. But this is alway—is it not?—the Riddle of Life.

High in the tower, where I sit above the loud complaining of the human sea, I know many souls that toss and whirl and pass, but none there are that intrigue me more than the Souls of White Folk.

Of them I am singularly clairvoyant. I see in and through them. I view them from unusual points of vantage. Not as a foreigner do I come, for I am native, not foreign, bone of their thought and flesh of their language. Mine is not the knowledge of the traveler or the colonial composite of dear memories, words and wonder. Nor yet is my knowledge that which servants have of masters, or mass of class, or capitalist of artisan. Rather I see these souls undressed and from the back and side. I see the working of their entrails. I know their thoughts and they know that I know. This knowledge makes them now embarrassed, now furious.

They deny my right to live and be and call me misbirth! My word is to them mere bitterness and my soul, pessimism. And yet as they preach and strut and shout and threaten, crouching as they clutch at rags of facts and fancies to hide their nakedness, they go twisting, flying by my tired eyes and I see them ever stripped,—ugly, human.

The discovery of personal whiteness among the world's peoples is a very modern thing,—a nineteenth and twentieth century matter, indeed. The ancient world would have laughed at such a distinction. The Middle Age regarded skin color with mild curiosity; and even up into the eighteenth century we were hammering our national manikins into one, great, Universal Man, with fine frenzy which ignored color and race even more than birth. Today we have changed all that, and the world in a sudden, emotional conversion has discovered that it is white and by that token, wonderful!

This assumption that of all the hues of God whiteness alone is inherently and obviously better than brownness or tan leads to curious acts; even the sweeter souls of the dominant world as they discourse with me on weather, weal, and woe are continually playing above their actual words an obligato of tune and tone, saying:

"My poor, un-white thing! Weep not nor rage. I know, too well, that the curse of God lies heavy on you. Why? That is not for me to say, but be brave! Do your work in your lowly sphere, praying the good Lord that into heaven above, where all is love, you may, one day, be born—white!"

I do not laugh. I am quite straight-faced as I ask soberly:

"But what on earth is whiteness that one should so desire it?" Then always, somehow, some way, silently but clearly, I am given to understand that whiteness is the ownership of the earth forever and ever, Amen!

Now what is the effect on a man or a nation when it comes passionately to believe such an extraordinary dictum as this? That nations are coming to believe it is manifest daily. Wave on wave, each with increasing virulence, is dashing this new religion of whiteness on the shores of our time. Its first effects are funny: the strut of the Southerner, the arrogance of the Englishman amuck, the whoop of the hoodlum who vicariously leads your mob. Next it appears dampening generous enthusiasm in what we once counted glorious; to free the slave is discovered to be tolerable only in so far as it freed his master! Do we sense somnolent writhings in black Africa or angry groans in India or triumphant banzais in Japan? "To your tents, O Israel!" These nations are not white!

After the more comic manifestations and the chilling of generous enthusiasm come subtler, darker deeds. Everything considered, the title to the universe claimed by White Folk is faulty. It ought, at least, to look plausible. How easy, then, by emphasis and omission to make children believe that every great soul the world ever saw was a white man's soul; that every great thought the world ever knew was a white man's thought; that every great deed the world ever did was a white man's deed; that every great dream the world ever sang was a white man's dream. In fine, that if from the world were dropped everything that could not fairly be attributed to White Folk, the world would, if anything, be even greater, truer, better than now. And if all this be a lie, is it not a lie in a great cause?

Here it is that the comedy verges to tragedy. The first minor note is struck, all unconsciously, by those worthy souls in whom consciousness of high descent brings burning desire to spread the gift abroad,—the obligation of nobility to the ignoble.

Such sense of duty assumes two things: a real possession of the heritage and its frank appreciation by the humble-born. So long, then, as humble black folk, voluble with thanks, receive barrels of old clothes from lordly and generous whites, there is much mental peace and moral satisfaction. But when the black man begins to dispute the white man's title to certain alleged bequests of the Fathers in wage and position, authority and training; and when his attitude toward charity is sullen anger rather than humble jollity; when he insists on his human right to swagger and swear and waste,—then the spell is suddenly broken and the philanthropist is ready to believe that Negroes are impudent, that the South is right, and that Japan wants to fight America.

After this the descent to Hell is easy. On the pale, white faces which the great billows whirl upward to my tower I see again and again, often and still more often, a writing of human hatred, a deep and passionate hatred, vast by the very vagueness of its expressions. Down through the green waters, on the bottom of the world, where men move to and fro, I have seen a man—an educated gentleman—grow livid with anger because a little, silent, black woman was sitting by herself in a Pullman car. He was a white man. I have seen a great, grown man curse a little child, who had wandered into the wrong waiting-room, searching for its mother: "Here, you damned black—" He was white. In Central Park I have seen the upper lip of a quiet, peaceful man curl back in a tigerish snarl of rage because black folk rode by in a motor car. He was a white man. We have seen, you and I, city after city drunk and furious with ungovernable lust of blood; mad with murder, destroying, killing, and cursing; torturing human victims because somebody accused of crime happened to be of the same color as the mob's innocent victims and because that color was not white! We have seen,— Merciful God! in these wild days and in the name of Civilization, Justice, and Motherhood,—what have we not seen, right here in America, of orgy, cruelty, barbarism, and murder done to men and women of Negro descent.

Up through the foam of green and weltering waters wells this great mass of hatred, in wilder, fiercer violence, until I look down and know that today to the millions of my people no misfortune could happen,—of death and pestilence, failure and defeat—that would not make the hearts of millions of their fellows beat with fierce, vindictive joy! Do you doubt it? Ask your own soul what it would say if the next census were to report that half of black America was dead and the other half dying.

Unfortunate? Unfortunate. But where is the misfortune? Mine? Am I, in my blackness, the sole sufferer? I suffer. And yet, somehow, above the suffering, above the shackled anger that beats the bars, above the hurt that crazes there surges in me a vast pity,—pity for a people imprisoned and enthralled, hampered and made miserable for such a cause, for such a phantasy!

Conceive this nation, of all human peoples, engaged in a crusade to make the "World Safe for Democracy"! Can you imagine the United States protesting against Turkish atrocities in Armenia, while the Turks are silent about mobs in Chicago and St. Louis; what is Louvain compared with Memphis, Waco, Washington, Dyersburg, and Estill Springs? In short, what is the black man but America's Belgium, and how could America condemn in Germany that which she commits, just as brutally, within her own borders?

A true and worthy ideal frees and uplifts a people; a false ideal imprisons and lowers. Say to men, earnestly and repeatedly: "Honesty is best, knowledge is power; do unto others as you would be done by." Say this and act it and the nation must move toward it, if not to it. But say to a people: "The one virtue is to be white," and the people rush to the inevitable conclusion, "Kill the 'nigger'!"

Is not this the record of present America? Is not this its headlong progress? Are we not coming more and more, day by day, to making the statement "I am white," the one fundamental tenet of our practical morality? Only when this basic, iron rule is involved is our defense of right nation-wide and prompt. Murder may swagger, theft may rule and prostitution may flourish and the nation gives but spasmodic, intermittent and lukewarm attention. But let the murderer be black or the thief brown or the violator of womanhood have a drop of Negro blood, and the righteousness of the indignation sweeps the world. Nor would this fact make the indignation less justifiable did not we all know that it was blackness that was condemned and not crime.

In the awful cataclysm of World War, where from beating, slandering, and murdering us the white world turned temporarily aside to kill each other, we of the Darker Peoples looked on in mild amaze.

Among some of us, I doubt not, this sudden descent of Europe into hell brought unbounded surprise; to others, over wide area, it brought the Schaden Freude of the bitterly hurt; but most of us, I judge, looked on silently and sorrowfully, in sober thought, seeing sadly the prophecy of our own souls.

Here is a civilization that has boasted much. Neither Roman nor Arab, Greek nor Egyptian, Persian nor Mongol ever took himself and his own perfectness with such disconcerting seriousness as the modern white man. We whose shame, humiliation, and deep insult his aggrandizement so often involved were never deceived. We looked at him clearly, with world-old eyes, and saw simply a human thing, weak and pitiable and cruel, even as we are and were.

These super-men and world-mastering demigods listened, however, to no low tongues of ours, even when we pointed silently to their feet of clay. Perhaps we, as folk of simpler soul and more primitive type, have been most struck in the welter of recent years by the utter failure of white religion. We have curled our lips in something like contempt as we have witnessed glib apology and weary explanation. Nothing of the sort deceived us. A nation's religion is its life, and as such white Christianity is a miserable failure.

Nor would we be unfair in this criticism: We know that we, too, have failed, as you have, and have rejected many a Buddha, even as you have

denied Christ; but we acknowledge our human frailty, while you, claiming super-humanity, scoff endlessly at our shortcomings.

The number of white individuals who are practising with even reasonable approximation the democracy and unselfishness of Jesus Christ is so small and unimportant as to be fit subject for jest in Sunday supplements and in *Punch*, *Life*, *Le Rire*, and *Fliegende Blaetter*. In her foreign mission work the extraordinary self-deception of white religion is epitomized: solemnly the white world sends five million dollars worth of missionary propaganda to Africa each year and in the same twelve months adds twenty-five million dollars worth of the vilest gin manufactured. Peace to the augurs of Rome!

We may, however, grant without argument that religious ideals have always far outrun their very human devotees. Let us, then, turn to more mundane matters of honor and fairness. The world today is trade. The world has turned shopkeeper; history is economic history; living is earning a living. Is it necessary to ask how much of high emprise and honorable conduct has been found here? Something, to be sure. The establishment of world credit systems is built on splendid and realizable faith in fellow-men. But it is, after all, so low and elementary a step that sometimes it looks merely like honor among thieves, for the revelations of highway robbery and low cheating in the business world and in all its great modern centers have raised in the hearts of all true men in our day an exceeding great cry for revolution in our basic methods and conceptions of industry and commerce.

We do not, for a moment, forget the robbery of other times and races when trade was a most uncertain gamble; but was there not a certain honesty and frankness in the evil that argued a saner morality? There are more merchants today, surer deliveries, and wider well-being, but are there not, also, bigger thieves, deeper injustice, and more calloused selfishness in well-being? Be that as it may,—certainly the nicer sense of honor that has risen ever and again in groups of forward-thinking men has been curiously and broadly blunted. Consider our chiefest industry,—fighting. Laboriously the Middle Ages built its rules of fairness—equal armament, equal notice, equal conditions. What do we see today? Machine-guns against assegais; conquest sugared with religion; mutilation and rape masquerading as culture,—all this, with vast applause at the superiority of white over black soldiers!

War is horrible! This the dark world knows to its awful cost. But has it just become horrible, in these last days, when under essentially equal conditions, equal armament, and equal waste of wealth white men are fighting white men, with surgeons and nurses hovering near?

Think of the wars through which we have lived in the last decade: in German Africa, in British Nigeria, in French and Spanish Morocco, in China, in Persia, in the Balkans, in Tripoli, in Mexico, and in a dozen lesser places—were not these horrible, too? Mind you, there were for most of these wars no Red Cross funds.

Behold little Belgium and her pitiable plight, but has the world forgotten Congo? What Belgium now suffers is not half, not even a tenth, of what she has done to black Congo since Stanley's great dream of 1880. Down the dark forests of inmost Africa sailed this modern Sir Galahad, in the name of "the noble-minded men of several nations," to introduce commerce and civilization. What came of it? "Rubber and murder, slavery in its worst form," wrote Glave in 1895.

Harris declares that King Leopold's regime meant the death of twelve million natives, "but what we who were behind the scenes felt most keenly was the fact that the real catastrophe in the Congo was desolation and murder in the larger sense. The invasion of family life, the ruthless destruction of every social barrier, the shattering of every tribal law, the introduction of criminal practices which struck the chiefs of the people dumb with horror—in a word, a veritable avalanche of filth and immorality overwhelmed the Congo tribes."

Yet the fields of Belgium laughed, the cities were gay, art and science flourished; the groans that helped to nourish this civilization fell on deaf ears because the world round about was doing the same sort of thing elsewhere on its own account.

As we saw the dead dimly through rifts of battlesmoke and heard faintly the cursings and accusations of blood brothers, we darker men said: This is not Europe gone mad; this is not aberration nor insanity; this is Europe; this seeming Terrible is the real soul of white culture—back of all culture,—stripped and visible today. This is where the world has arrived,—these dark and awful depths and not the shining and ineffable heights of which it boasted. Here is whither the might and energy of modern humanity has really gone.

But may not the world cry back at us and ask: "What better thing have you to show? What have you done or would do better than this if you had today the world rule? Paint with all riot of hateful colors the thin skin of European culture,—is it not better than any culture that arose in Africa or Asia?"

It is. Of this there is no doubt and never has been; but why is it better? Is it better because Europeans are better, nobler, greater, and more gifted than other folk? It is not. Europe has never produced and never will in our day bring forth a single human soul who cannot be matched and over-matched in every line of human endeavor by Asia and Africa. Run the gamut, if you will, and let us have the Europeans who in sober truth over-match Nefertari, Mohammed, Rameses and Askia, Confucius, Buddha, and Jesus Christ. If we could scan the calendar of thousands of lesser men, in like comparison, the result would be the same; but we cannot do this because of the deliberately educated ignorance of white schools by which they remember Napoleon and forget Sonni Ali.

The greatness of Europe has lain in the width of the stage on which she has played her part, the strength of the foundations on which she has builded, and a natural, human ability no whit greater (if as great) than that of other days and races. In other words, the deeper reasons for the triumph of European civilization lie quite outside and beyond Europe,—back in the universal struggles of all mankind.

Why, then, is Europe great? Because of the foundations which the mighty past have furnished her to build upon: the iron trade of ancient, black Africa, the religion and empire-building of yellow Asia, the art and science of the "dago" Mediterranean shore, east, south, and west, as well as north. And where she has builded securely upon this great past and learned from it she has gone forward to greater and more splendid human triumph; but where she has ignored this past and forgotten and sneered at it, she has shown the cloven hoof of poor, crucified humanity,—she has played, like other empires gone, the world fool!

If, then, European triumphs in culture have been greater, so, too, may her failures have been greater. How great a failure and a failure in what does the World War betoken? Was it national jealousy of the sort of the seventeenth century? But Europe has done more to break down national barriers than any preceding culture. Was it fear of the balance of power in Europe? Hardly, save in the half-Asiatic problems of the Balkans. What, then, does Hauptmann mean when he says: "Our jealous enemies forged an iron ring about our breasts and we knew our breasts had to expand,—that we had to split asunder this ring or else we had to cease breathing. But Germany will not cease to breathe and so it came to pass that the iron ring was forced apart."

Whither is this expansion? What is that breath of life, thought to be so indispensable to a great European nation? Manifestly it is expansion overseas; it is colonial aggrandizement which explains, and alone adequately explains, the World War. How many of us today fully realize the current theory of colonial expansion, of the relation of Europe which is white, to the world which is black and brown and yellow? Bluntly put, that theory is this: It is the duty of white Europe to divide up the darker world and administer it for Europe's good.

This Europe has largely done. The European world is using black and brown men for all the uses which men know. Slowly but surely white culture is evolving the theory that "darkies" are born beasts of burden for white folk. It were silly to think otherwise, cries the cultured world, with stronger and shriller accord. The supporting arguments grow and twist themselves in the mouths of merchant, scientist, soldier, traveler, writer, and missionary: Darker peoples are dark in mind as well as in body; of dark, uncertain, and imperfect descent; of frailer, cheaper stuff; they are cowards in the face of mausers and maxims; they have no feelings, aspirations, and loves; they are fools, illogical idiots,—"half-devil and half-child."

Such as they are civilization must, naturally, raise them, but soberly and in limited ways. They are not simply dark white men. They are not "men" in the sense that Europeans are men. To the very limited extent of their shallow capacities lift them to be useful to whites, to raise cotton, gather rubber, fetch ivory, dig diamonds,—and let them be paid what men think they are worth—white men who know them to be well-nigh worthless.

Such degrading of men by men is as old as mankind and the invention of no one race or people. Ever have men striven to conceive of their victims as different from the victors, endlessly different, in soul and blood, strength and cunning, race and lineage. It has been left, however, to Europe and to modern days to discover the eternal world-wide mark of meanness,—color!

Such is the silent revolution that has gripped modern European culture in the later nineteenth and twentieth centuries. Its zenith came in Boxer times: White supremacy was all but world-wide, Africa was dead, India conquered, Japan isolated, and China prostrate, while white America whetted her sword for mongrel Mexico and mulatto South America, lynching her own Negroes the while. Temporary halt in this program was made by little Japan and the white world immediately sensed the peril of such "yellow" presumption! What sort of a world would this be if yellow men must be treated "white"? Immediately the eventual overthrow of Japan became a subject of deep thought and intrigue, from St. Petersburg to San Francisco, from the Key of Heaven to the Little Brother of the Poor.

The using of men for the benefit of masters is no new invention of modern Europe. It is quite as old as the world. But Europe proposed to apply it on a scale and with an elaborateness of detail of which no former world ever dreamed. The imperial width of the thing,—the heaven-defying audacity— makes its modern newness.

The scheme of Europe was no sudden invention, but a way out of long-pressing difficulties. It is plain to modern white civilization that the subjection of the white working classes cannot much longer be maintained. Education, political power, and increased knowledge of the technique and meaning of the industrial process are destined to make a more and more equitable distribution of wealth in the near future. The day of the very rich is drawing to a close, so far as individual white nations are concerned. But there is a loophole. There is a chance for exploitation on an immense scale for inordinate profit, not simply to the very rich, but to the middle class and to the laborers. This chance lies in the exploitation of darker peoples. It is here that the golden hand beckons. Here are no labor unions or votes or questioning onlookers or inconvenient consciences. These men may be used down to the very bone, and shot and maimed in "punitive" expeditions when they revolt. In these dark lands "industrial development" may repeat in exaggerated form every horror of the industrial history of Europe, from slavery and rape to disease and maiming, with only one test of success,—dividends!

This theory of human culture and its aims has worked itself through warp and woof of our daily thought with a thoroughness that few realize. Everything great, good, efficient, fair, and honorable is "white"; everything mean, bad, blundering, cheating, and dishonorable is "yellow"; a bad taste is "brown"; and the devil is "black." The changes of this theme are continually rung in picture and story, in newspaper heading and moving-picture, in sermon and school book, until, of course, the King can do no wrong,—a White Man is always right and a Black Man has no rights which a white man is bound to respect.

There must come the necessary despisings and hatreds of these savage half-men, this unclean canaille of the world—these dogs of men. All through the world this gospel is preaching. It has its literature, it has its secret propaganda and above all—it pays!

There's the rub,—it pays. Rubber, ivory, and palm-oil; tea, coffee, and cocoa; bananas, oranges, and other fruit; cotton, gold, and copper—they, and a hundred other things which dark and sweating bodies hand up to the white world from pits of slime, pay and pay well, but of all that the world gets the black world gets only the pittance that the white world throws it disdainfully.

Small wonder, then, that in the practical world of things-that-be there is jealousy and strife for the possession of the labor of dark millions, for the right to bleed and exploit the colonies of the world where this golden stream may be had, not always for the asking, but surely for the whipping and shooting. It was this competition for the labor of yellow, brown, and black folks that was the cause of the World War. Other causes have been glibly given and other contributing causes there doubtless were, but they were subsidiary and subordinate to this vast quest of the dark world's wealth and toil.

Colonies, we call them, these places where "niggers" are cheap and the earth is rich; they are those outlands where like a swarm of hungry locusts white masters may settle to be served as kings, wield the lash of slave-drivers, rape girls and wives, grow as rich as Croesus and send homeward a golden stream. They belt the earth, these places, but they cluster in the tropics, with its darkened peoples: in Hong Kong and Anam, in Borneo and Rhodesia, in Sierra Leone and Nigeria, in Panama and Havana—these are the El Dorados toward which the world powers stretch itching palms.

Germany, at last one and united and secure on land, looked across the seas and seeing England with sources of wealth insuring a luxury and power which Germany could not hope to rival by the slower processes of exploiting her own peasants and workingmen, especially with these workers half in revolt, immediately built her navy and entered into a desperate competition for possession of colonies of darker peoples. To South America, to China, to Africa, to Asia Minor, she turned like a hound quivering on the leash, impatient, suspicious, irritable, with blood-shot eyes and dripping fangs, ready for the awful word. England and France crouched watchfully over their bones, growling and wary, but gnawing industriously, while the blood of the dark world whetted their greedy appetites. In the background, shut out from the highway to the seven seas, sat Russia and Austria, snarling and snapping at each other and at the last Mediterranean gate to the El Dorado, where the Sick Man enjoyed bad health, and where millions of serfs in the Balkans, Russia, and Asia offered a feast to greed well-nigh as great as Africa.

The fateful day came. It had to come. The cause of war is preparation for war; and of all that Europe has done in a century there is nothing that has equaled in energy, thought, and time her preparation for wholesale murder. The only adequate cause of this preparation was conquest and conquest, not in Europe, but primarily among the darker peoples of Asia and Africa; conquest, not for assimilation and uplift, but for commerce and degradation. For this, and this mainly, did Europe gird herself at frightful cost for war.

The red day dawned when the tinder was lighted in the Balkans and Austro-Hungary seized a bit which brought her a step nearer to the world's highway; she seized one bit and poised herself for another. Then came that curious chorus of challenges, those leaping suspicions, raking all causes for distrust and rivalry and hatred, but saying little of the real and greatest cause.

Each nation felt its deep interests involved. But how? Not, surely, in the death of Ferdinand the Warlike; not, surely, in the old, half-forgotten revanche for Alsace-Lorraine; not even in the neutrality of Belgium. No! But in the possession of land overseas, in the right to colonies, the chance to levy endless tribute on the darker world,—on coolies in China, on starving peasants in India, on black savages in Africa, on dying South Sea Islanders, on Indians of the Amazon—all this and nothing more.

Even the broken reed on which we had rested high hopes of eternal peace,—the guild of the laborers—the front of that very important movement for human justice on which we had builded most, even this flew like a straw before the breath of king and kaiser. Indeed, the flying had been foreshadowed when in Germany and America "international" Socialists had all but read yellow and black men out of the kingdom of industrial justice. Subtly had they been bribed, but effectively: Were they not lordly whites and should they not share in the spoils of rape? High wages in the United States and England might be the skillfully manipulated result of slavery in Africa and of peonage in Asia.

With the dog-in-the-manger theory of trade, with the determination to reap inordinate profits and to exploit the weakest to the utmost there came a new imperialism,—the rage for one's own nation to own the earth or, at least, a large enough portion of it to insure as big profits as the next nation. Where sections could not be owned by one dominant nation there came a policy of "open door," but the "door" was open to "white people only." As to the darkest and weakest of peoples there was but one unanimity in Europe,—that which Hen Demberg of the German Colonial Office called the agreement with England to maintain white "prestige" in Africa,—the doctrine of the divine right of white people to steal.

Thus the world market most wildly and desperately sought today is the market where labor is cheapest and most helpless and profit is most abundant. This labor is kept cheap and helpless because the white world despises "darkies." If one has the temerity to suggest that these workingmen may walk the way of white workingmen and climb by votes and self-assertion and education to the rank of men, he is howled out of court. They cannot do it and if they could, they shall not, for they are the enemies of the white race and the whites shall rule forever and forever and everywhere. Thus the hatred and despising of human beings from whom Europe wishes to extort her luxuries has led to such jealousy and bickering between European nations that they have fallen afoul of each other and have fought like crazed beasts. Such is the fruit of human hatred.

But what of the darker world that watches? Most men belong to this world. With Negro and Negroid, East Indian, Chinese, and Japanese they form two-thirds of the population of the world. A belief in humanity is a belief in colored men. If the uplift of mankind must be done by men, then the destinies of this world will rest ultimately in the hands of darker nations.

What, then, is this dark world thinking? It is thinking that as wild and awful as this shameful war was, it is nothing to compare with that fight for freedom which black and brown and yellow men must and will make unless their oppression and humiliation and insult at the hands of the White World cease. The Dark World is going to submit to its present treatment just as long as it must and not one moment longer.

Let me say this again and emphasize it and leave no room for mistaken meaning: The World War was primarily the jealous and avaricious struggle for the largest share in exploiting darker races. As such it is and must be but the prelude to the armed and indignant protest of these despised and raped peoples. Today Japan is hammering on the door of justice, China is raising her half-manacled hands to knock next, India is writhing for the freedom to knock, Egypt is sullenly muttering, the Negroes of South and West Africa, of the West Indies, and of the United States are just awakening to their shameful slavery. Is, then, this war the end of wars? Can it be the end, so long as sits enthroned, even in the souls of those who cry peace, the despising and robbing of darker peoples? If Europe hugs this delusion, then this is not the end of world war,—it is but the beginning!

We see Europe's greatest sin precisely where we found Africa's and Asia's,—in human hatred, the despising of men; with this difference, however: Europe has the awful lesson of the past before her, has the splendid results of widened areas of tolerance, sympathy, and love among men, and she faces a greater, an infinitely greater, world of men than any preceding civilization ever faced.

It is curious to see America, the United States, looking on herself, first, as a sort of natural peacemaker, then as a moral protagonist in this terrible time. No nation is less fitted for this role. For two or more centuries America has marched proudly in the van of human hatred,—making bonfires of human flesh and laughing at them hideously, and making the insulting of millions more than a matter of dislike,—rather a great religion, a world war-cry: Up white, down black; to your tents, O white folk, and world war with black and parti-colored mongrel beasts!

Instead of standing as a great example of the success of democracy and the possibility of human brotherhood America has taken her place as an awful example of its pitfalls and failures, so far as black and brown and yellow peoples are concerned. And this, too, in spite of the fact that there has been no actual failure; the Indian is not dying out, the Japanese and Chinese have not menaced the land, and the experiment of Negro suffrage has resulted in the uplift of twelve million people at a rate probably unparalleled in history. But what of this? America, Land of Democracy, wanted to believe in the failure of democracy so far as darker peoples were concerned. Absolutely without excuse she established a caste system, rushed into preparation for war, and conquered tropical colonies. She stands today shoulder to shoulder with Europe in Europe's worst sin against civilization. She aspires to sit among the great nations who arbitrate the fate of "lesser breeds without the law" and she is at times heartily ashamed even of the large number of "new" white people whom her democracy has admitted to place and power. Against this surging forward of Irish and German, of Russian Jew, Slav and "dago" her social bars have not availed, but against Negroes she can and does take her unflinching and immovable stand, backed by this new public policy of Europe. She trains her immigrants to this despising of "niggers" from the day of their landing, and they carry and send the news back to the submerged classes in the fatherlands.

Source: Du Bois, W. E. B. "The Souls of White Folk." *Darkwater: Voices from Within the Veil.* New York: Harcourt, Brace & Co., 1920.

Walter White, "The Eruption of Tulsa"
(June 29, 1921)

The Tulsa race riot of 1921, one of the most chilling events in the entire history of race tensions in the United States, reversed generations of economic, social, and political gains made by African Americans in Tulsa, Oklahoma. Beginning on Memorial Day in 1921, a well-armed white mob, some of them deputized by the police department, targeted Tulsa's prosperous black neighborhood, Greenwood— "The black Wall Street"—which had become one of the most vibrant centers of African American life in the country. The riot was sparked by a white girl's claim that she had been assaulted by a black youth. Eventually, the white mob razed 36 square blocks, burned to the ground more than 3,000 homes, and killed as many as 300 people, many of whom were buried in mass graves or simply dumped anonymously into the Arkansas River. By the end of the onslaught, the rioters had destroyed Tulsa's thriving black community, which had numbered 15,000 people and rivaled New York City as a national center of urban black life. This article describing and lamenting the episode was written by Walter White, president of the National Association for the Advancement of Colored People (NAACP), and was published in the NAACP's Crisis *magazine.*

A hysterical white girl related that a nineteen-year-old colored boy attempted to assault her in the public elevator of a public office building of a thriving town of 100,000 in open daylight. Without pausing to find out whether or not the story was true, without bothering with the slight detail of investigating the character of the woman who made the outcry (as a matter of fact, she was of exceedingly doubtful reputation), a mob of 100-percent Americans set forth on a wild rampage that cost the lives of fifty white men; of between 150 and 200 colored men, women and children; the destruction by fire of $1,500,000 worth of property; the looting of many homes; and everlasting damage to the reputation of the city of Tulsa and the State of Oklahoma.

This, in brief, is the story of the eruption of Tulsa on the night of May 31 and the morning of June 1, 1921. One could travel far and find few cities where the likelihood of trouble between the races was as little thought of as in Tulsa. Her reign of terror stands as a grim reminder of the grip mob violence has on the throat of America, and the ever-present possibility of devastating race conflicts where least expected.

Tulsa is a thriving, bustling, enormously wealthy town of between 90,000 and 100,000. In 1910 it was the home of 18,182 souls, a dead and hopeless outlook ahead. Then oil was discovered. The town grew amazingly. On December 29, 1920, it had bank deposits totaling $65,449,985.90; almost $1,000 per capita when compared with the Federal Census figures of 1920, which gave Tulsa 72,075. The town lies in the center of the oil region and many are the stories told of the making of fabulous fortunes by men who were operating on a shoe-string. Some of the stories rival those of the "forty-niners" in California. The town has a number of modern office buildings, many beautiful homes, miles of clean, well-paved streets, and aggressive and progressive businessmen who well exemplify Tulsa's motto of "The City with a Personality."

So much for the setting. What are the causes of the race riot that occurred in such a place?

First, the Negro in Oklahoma has shared in the sudden prosperity that has come to many of his white brothers, and there are some colored men there who are wealthy. This fact has caused a bitter resentment on the part of the lower order of whites, who feel that these colored men, members of an "inferior race," are exceedingly presumptuous in achieving greater economic prosperity than they who are members of a divinely ordered superior race. There are at least three colored persons in Oklahoma who are worth a million dollars each; J.W. Thompson of Clearview is worth $500,000; there are a number of men and women worth $100,000; and many whose possessions are valued at $25,000 and $50,000 each. This was particularly true of Tulsa, where there were two colored men worth $150,000 each; two worth $100,000; three $50,000; and four who were assessed at $25,000. In one case where a colored man owned and operated a printing plant with $25,000 worth of printing machinery in it, the leader of a mob that set fire to and destroyed the plant was a linotype operator employed for years by the colored owner at $48 per week. The white man was killed while attacking the plant. Oklahoma is largely populated by pioneers from other States. Some of the white pioneers are former residents of Mississippi, Georgia, Tennessee, Texas, and other States more typically Southern than Oklahoma. These have brought with them their anti-Negro prejudices. Lethargic and unprogressive by nature, it sorely irks them to see Negroes making greater progress than they themselves are achieving.

One of the charges made against the colored men in Tulsa is that they were "radical." Questioning the whites more closely regarding the nature of this radicalism, I found it means that Negroes were uncompromisingly denouncing "Jim-Crow" cars, lynching, peonage; in short, were asking that the Federal constitutional guaranties of "life, liberty, and the pursuit of happiness" be given regardless of color. The Negroes of Tulsa and other Oklahoma cities are pioneers; men and women who have dared, men and women who have had the initiative and the courage to pull up stakes in other less-favored States and face hardship in a newer one for the sake of eventual progress. That type is ever less ready to submit to insult. Those of the whites who seek to maintain the old white group control

naturally do not relish seeing Negroes emancipating themselves from the old system.

A third cause was the rotten political conditions in Tulsa. A vice ring was in control of the city, allowing open operation of houses of ill fame, of gambling joints, the illegal sale of whiskey, the robbing of banks and stores, with hardly a slight possibility of the arrest of the criminals, and even less of their conviction. For fourteen years Tulsa has been in the absolute control of this element. Most of the better element, and there is a large percentage of Tulsans who can properly be classed as such, are interested in making money and getting away. They have taken little or no interest in the election of city or county officials, leaving it to those whose interest it was to secure officials who would protect them in their vice operations. About two months ago the State legislature assigned two additional judges to Tulsa County to aid the present two in clearing the badly clogged dockets. These judges found more than six thousand cases awaiting trial. Thus in a county of approximately 100,000 population, six out of every hundred citizens were under indictment for some sort of crime, with little likelihood of trial in any of them.

Last July a white man by the name of Roy Belton, accused of murdering a taxicab driver, was taken from the county jail and lynched. According to the statements of many prominent Tulsans, local police officers directed traffic at the scene of the lynching, trying to afford every person present an equal chance to view the event. Insurance companies refuse to give Tulsa merchants insurance on their stocks; the risk is too great. There have been so many automobile thefts that a number of companies have canceled all policies on cars in Tulsa. The net result of these conditions was that practically none of the citizens of the town, white or colored, had very much respect for the law.

Source: White, Walter. "The Eruption of Tulsa." *The Nation*, June 29, 1921, 909–910.

Alain Locke, The Harlem Number of *The Survey Graphic*, Vol. 6, No. 6 (March 1925)

In March 1925, Survey Graphic *magazine commissioned scholar Alain Locke to oversee, as guest editor, a landmark collection of studies, reports, and essays, all dedicated to what seemed like the emergence of a renaissance—a cultural flowering of black life—in the Harlem neighborhood of New York City. The special edition of the magazine edited by Locke was entitled* Harlem, Mecca of the New Negro; *it became the initiating document of the New Negro movement, which associated the Harlem Renaissance with a new attitude on the part of blacks, who refused to any longer quietly submit to racial segregation. In December 1925, Locke republished that edition as an anthology entitled* The New Negro: An Interpretation of Negro Life. *An immediate success, Locke's work became a masterwork of African American literature and the philosophical foundation of the Harlem Renaissance.*

If we were to offer a symbol of what Harlem has come to mean in the short span of twenty years, it would be another statue of liberty on the landward side of New York. It stands for a folk-movement which in human significance can be compared only with the pushing back of the western frontier in the first half of the last century, or the waves of immigration which have swept in from overseas in the last half. Numerically far smaller than either of these movements, the volume of migration is such none the less that Harlem has become the greatest Negro community the world has known—without counterpart in the South or in Africa. But beyond this, Harlem represents the Negro's latest thrust towards Democracy.

The special significance that today stamps it as the sign and center of the renaissance of a people lies, however, layers deep under the Harlem that many know but few have begun to understand. Physically Harlem is little more than a note of sharper color in the kaleidoscope of New York. The metropolis pays little heed to the shifting crystallizations of its own heterogeneous millions. Never having experienced permanence, it has watched, without emotion or even curiosity, Irish, Jew, Italian, Negro, a score of other races drift in and out of the same colorless tenements.

So Harlem has come into being and grasped its destiny with little heed from New York. And to the herded thousands who shoot beneath it twice a day on the subway, or the comparatively few whose daily travel takes them within sight of its fringes or down its main arteries, it is a black belt and nothing more. The pattern of delicatessen store and cigar shop and restaurant and undertaker's shop which repeats itself a thousand times on each of New York's long avenues is unbroken through Harlem. Its apartments, churches and storefronts antedated the Negroes and, for all New York knows, may outlast them there. For most of New York, Harlem is merely a rough rectangle of common-place city blocks, lying between and to east and west of Lenox and Seventh Avenues, stretching nearly a mile north and south—and unaccountably full of Negroes.

Another Harlem is savored by the few—a Harlem of racy music and racier dancing, of cabarets famous or notorious according to their kind, of amusement in which abandon and sophistication are cheek by jowl—a Harlem which draws the connoisseur in diversion as well as the undiscriminating sightseer. This Harlem is the fertile source of the "shuffling" and "rollin'" and "runnin' wild" revues that establish themselves season after season in "downtown" theaters. It is part of the exotic fringe of the metropolis.

Beneath this lies again the Harlem of the newspapers—a Harlem of monster parades and political flummery, a Harlem swept by revolutionary oratory or draped about the mysterious figures of Negro "millionaires," a Harlem pre-occupied with naive adjustments to a white world—a Harlem, in short, grotesque with the distortions of journalism.

Yet in final analysis, Harlem is neither slum, ghetto, resort or colony, though it is in part all of them. It is—or promises at least to be—a race capital. Europe seething in a dozen centers with emergent nationalities, Palestine full of a renascent Judaism—these are no more alive with the spirit of a racial awakening than Harlem; culturally and spiritually it focuses a people. Negro life is not only founding new centers, but finding a new soul. The tide of Negro migration, northward and cityward, is not to be fully explained as a blind flood started by the demands of war industry coupled with the shutting off of foreign migration, or by the pressure of poor crops coupled with increased social terrorism in certain sections of the South and Southwest. Neither labor demand, the boll-weevil nor the Ku Klux Klan is a basic factor, however contributory any or all of them may have been. The wash and rush of this human tide on the beach line of the northern city centers is to be explained primarily in terms of a new vision of opportunity, of social and economic freedom of a spirit to seize, even in the face of an extortionate and heavy toll, a chance for the improvement of conditions. With each successive wave of it, the movement of the Negro migrant becomes more and more like that of the European waves at their crests, a mass movement toward the larger and the more democratic chance—in the Negro's case a deliberate flight not only from countryside to city, but from medieaval America to modern.

The secret lies close to what distinguishes Harlem from the ghettos with which it is sometimes compared. The ghetto picture is that of a slowly dissolving mass, bound by ties of custom and culture and association, in the midst of a freer and more varied society. From the racial standpoint, our Harlems are themselves crucibles. Here in Manhattan is not merely the largest Negro community in the world, but the first concentration in history of so many diverse elements of Negro life. It has attracted the African, the West Indian, the Negro American; has brought together the Negro of the North and the Negro of the South; the man from the city and the man from the town and village; the peasant, the student, the business man, the professional man, artist, poet, musician, adventurer and worker, preacher and criminal, exploiter and social outcast. Each group has come with its own separate motives and for its own special ends, but their greatest experience has been the finding of one another. Proscription and prejudice have thrown these dissimilar elements into a common area of contact and interaction. Within this area, race sympathy and unity have determined a further fusing of sentiment and experience . . . Hitherto, it must be admitted that American Negroes have been a race more in name than in fact, or to be exact, more in sentiment than in experience. The chief bond between them has been that of a common condition rather than a common consciousness; a problem in common rather than a life in common. In Harlem, Negro life is seizing upon its first chances for group expression and self-determination. That is why our comparison is taken with those nascent centers of folk-expression and self-determination which are playing a creative part in the world today. Without pretense to their political significance, Harlem has the same role to play for the New Negro as Dublin has had for the New Ireland or Prague for the New Czechoslovakia.

It is true the formidable centers of our race life, educational, industrial, financial, are not in Harlem, yet here, nevertheless, are the forces that make a group known and felt in the world. The reformers, the fighting advocates, the inner spokesmen, the poets, artists and social prophets are here, and pouring in toward them are the fluid ambitious youth and pressing in upon them the migrant masses. The professional observers, and the enveloping communities as well, are conscious of the physics of this stir and movement, of the cruder and more obvious facts of a ferment and a migration. But they are as yet largely unaware of the psychology of it, of the galvanizing shocks and reactions, which mark the social awakening and internal reorganization which are making a race out of its own disunited elements.

A railroad ticket and a suitcase, like a Baghdad carpet, transport the Negro peasant from the cotton-field and farm to the heart of the most complex urban civilization. Here in the mass, he must and does survive a jump of two generations in social economy and of a century and more in civilization. Meanwhile the Negro poet, student, artist, thinker, by the very move that normally would take him off at a tangent from the masses, finds himself in their midst, in a situation concentrating the racial side of his experience and heightening his race-consciousness. These moving, half-awakened newcomers provide an exceptional seed-bed for the germinating contacts of the enlightened minority. And that is why statistics are out of joint with fact in Harlem, and will be for a generation or so.

Harlem, I grant you, isn't typical—but it is significant, it is prophetic. No sane observer, however sympathetic to the new trend, would contend that the great masses are articulate as yet, but they stir, they move, they are more than physically restless. The challenge of the new intellectuals among them is clear enough—the "race radicals" and realists who have broken with the old epoch of philanthropic guidance, sentimental appeal and protest. But are we after all only reading into the stirrings of a sleeping giant the dreams of an agitator? The answer is in the migrating peasant. It is the "man farthest down" who is most active in getting up. One of the most characteristic symptoms of this is the professional man himself migrating to recapture his constituency after a vain effort to maintain in some Southern corner what for years back seemed an established living and clientele. The clergyman following his errant flock, the physician or lawyer trailing his clients, supply the true clues. In a real sense it is the rank and file who are leading, and the leaders who are following. A transformed and transforming psychology permeates the masses.

When the racial leaders of twenty years ago spoke of developing race-pride and stimulating race-consciousness, and of the desirability of race solidarity, they could not in any accurate degree have anticipated the abrupt feeling that has surged up and now pervades the awakened centers. Some of the recognized Negro leaders and a powerful section of white opinion identified with "race work" of the older order have indeed attempted to discount this feeling as a "passing phase," an attack of "race nerves," so to speak, an "aftermath of the war," and the like. It has not abated, however, if we are to gage by the present tone and temper of the Negro press, or by the shift in popular support from the officially recognized and orthodox spokesmen to those of the independent, popular, and often radical type who are unmistakable symptoms of a new order. It is a social disservice to blunt the fact that the Negro of the Northern centers has reached a stage where tutelage, even of the most interested and well-intentioned sort, must give place to new relationships, where positive self-direction must be reckoned with in ever increasing measure.

As a service to this new understanding, the contributors to this Harlem number have been asked, not merely to describe Harlem as a city of migrants and as a race center, but to voice these new aspirations of a people, to read the clear message of the new conditions, and to discuss some of the new relationships and contacts they involve. First, we shall look at Harlem, with its kindred centers in the Northern and Mid-Western cities, as the way mark of a momentous folk movement; then as the center of a gripping struggle for an industrial and urban foothold. But more significant than either of these, we shall also view it as the stage of the pageant of contemporary Negro life. In the drama of its new and progressive aspects, we may be witnessing the resurgence of a race; with our eyes focused on the Harlem scene we may dramatically glimpse the New Negro. A. L.

Source: Locke, Alain. "Harlem." *The Survey Graphic* VI, no. 6 (March 1925), 629, 630.

Alain Locke, "Enter the New Negro"
(March 1925)

In or around 1915, a new segment of American society—a culture of African Americans—began to gradually make itself evident. This newness was not due to the presence of African Americans, but rather to the flowering of a self-conscious "New Negro." It was an evolution that probably began the minute after the first group of slaves arrived in Jamestown, or when the first slave revolt occurred, or when the first slave escaped bondage anywhere in America and began the trek toward self-discovery.

Regardless of when this liberation movement began, what it flowered was finally recognized in the decade between 1915 and 1925 as "something beyond the watch and guard of statistics . . . in the life of the American Negro." Scholar Alain Locke said these changes went unnoticed by sociologists, philanthropists, and others because this emerging cultural wing of mainstream America seemed to defy any "formulae." As Locke wrote, a "younger generation is vibrant with a new psychology; the new spirit is awake in the masses, and under the very eyes of the professional observers is transforming what has been a perennial problem into the progressive phases of contemporary Negro life." In "Enter the New Negro," one of the essays written by Locke himself for the special Harlem edition of The Survey Graphic *magazine that he guest edited in 1925, Locke explains the unprecedented transformation of black culture in the United States and provides the philosophical underpinnings for the Harlem Renaissance.*

The Old Negro had long become more of a myth than a man. The Old Negro, we must remember, was a creature of moral debate and historical controversy. His has been a stock figure perpetuated as an historical fiction partly in innocent sentimentalism, partly in deliberate reactionism. The Negro himself has contributed his share to this through a sort of protective social mimicry forced upon him by the adverse circumstances of dependence. So for generations in the mind of America, the Negro has been more of a formula than a human being— a something to be argued about, condemned or defended, to be "kept down," or "in his place," or "helped up," to be worried with or worried over, harassed or patronized, a social bogey or a social burden. The thinking Negro even has been induced to share this same general attitude, to focus his attention on controversial issues, to see himself in the distorted perspective of a social problem. His shadow, so to speak, has been more real to him than his personality. Through having had to appeal from the unjust stereotypes of his oppressors and traducers to those of his liberators, friends and benefactors, he has subscribed to the traditional positions from which his case has been viewed. Little true social or self-understanding has or could come from such a situation.

But while the minds of most of us, black and white, have thus burrowed in the trenches of the Civil War and Reconstruction, the actual march of development has simply flanked these positions, necessitating a sudden reorientation of view. We have not been watching in the right direction; set North and South on a sectional axis, we have not noticed the East till the sun has us blinking.

Recall how suddenly the Negro spirituals revealed themselves; suppressed for generations under the stereotypes of Wesleyan hymn harmony, secretive, half-ashamed, until the courage of being natural brought them out—and behold, there was folk-music. Similarly the mind of the Negro seems suddenly to have slipped from under the tyranny of social intimidation and to be shaking off the psychology of imitation and implied inferiority. By shedding the old chrysalis of the Negro problem we are achieving something like a spiritual emancipation. Until recently, lacking self understanding, we have been almost as much of a problem to ourselves as we still are to others. But the decade that found us with a problem has left us with only a task. The multitude perhaps feels as yet only a strange relief and a new vague urge, but the thinking few know that in the reaction the vital inner grip of prejudice has been broken.

With this renewed self-respect and self-dependence, the life of the Negro community is bound to enter a new dynamic phase, the buoyancy from within compensating for whatever pressure there may be of conditions from without. The migrant masses, shifting from countryside to city, hurdle several generations of experience at a leap, but more important, the same thing happens spiritually in the life-attitudes and self-expression of the Young Negro, in his poetry, his art, his education and his new outlook, with the additional advantage, of course, of the poise and greater certainty of knowing what it is all about. From this comes the promise and warrant of a new leadership. As one of them has discerningly put it:

> We have tomorrow
> Bright before us
> Like a flame.
> Yesterday, a night-gone thing
> A sun-down name.
> And dawn today
> Broad arch above the road we came.
> We march!

This is what, even more than any "most creditable record of fifty years of freedom," requires that the Negro of today be seen through other than the dusty spectacles of past controversy. The day of "aunties," "uncles" and "mammies" is equally gone. Uncle Tom and Sambo have passed on, and even the "Colonel" and "George" play barnstorm roles from which they escape with relief when the public spotlight is off. The popular melodrama has about played itself out, and it is time to scrap the fictions, garret the bogeys and settle down to a realistic facing of facts.

First we must observe some of the changes which since the traditional lines of opinion were drawn have rendered these quite obsolete. A main change has been, of course, that shifting of the Negro population which has made the Negro problem no longer exclusively or even predominantly Southern. Why should our minds remain sectionalized, when the problem itself no longer is? Then the trend of migration has not only been toward the North and the Central Midwest, but city-ward and to the great centers of industry—the problems of adjustment are new, practical, local and not peculiarly racial. Rather they are an integral part of the large industrial and social problems of our present-day democracy. And finally, with the Negro rapidly in process of class differentiation, if it ever was warrantable to regard and treat the Negro en masse it is becoming with every day less possible, more unjust and more ridiculous.

The Negro too, for his part, has idols of the tribe to smash. If on the one hand the white man has erred in making the Negro appear to be that which would excuse or extenuate his treatment of him, the Negro, in turn, has too often unnecessarily excused himself because of the way he has been treated. The intelligent Negro of today is resolved not to make discrimination an extenuation for his shortcomings in performance, individual or collective; he is trying to hold himself at par, neither inflated by sentimental allowances nor depreciated by current social discounts. For this he must know himself and be known for precisely what he is, and for that reason he welcomes the new scientific rather than the old sentimental interest. Sentimental interest in the Negro has ebbed. We used to lament this as the falling off of our friends; now we rejoice and pray to be delivered both from self-pity and condescension. The mind of each racial group has had a bitter weaning, apathy or hatred on one side matching disillusionment or resentment on the other; but they face each other today with the possibility at least of entirely new mutual attitudes.

It does not follow that if the Negro were better known, he would be better liked or better treated. But mutual understanding is basic for any subsequent cooperation and adjustment. The effort toward this will at least have the effect of remedying in large part what has been the most unsatisfactory feature of our present stage of race relationships in America, namely the fact that the more intelligent and representative elements of the two race groups have at so many points got quite out of vital touch with one another.

The fiction is that the life of the races is separate and increasingly so. The fact is that they have touched too closely at the unfavorable and too lightly at the favorable levels.

While inter-racial councils have sprung up in the South, drawing on forward elements of both races, in the Northern cities manual laborers may brush elbows in their everyday work, but the community and business leaders have experienced no such interplay or far too little of it. These segments must achieve contact or the race situation in America becomes desperate. Fortunately this is happening. There is a growing realization that in social effort the cooperative basis must supplant long-distance philanthropy, and that the only safeguard for mass relations in the future must be provided in the carefully maintained contacts of the enlightened minorities of both race groups. In the intellectual realm a renewed and keen curiosity is replacing the recent apathy; the Negro is being carefully studied, not just talked about and discussed. In art and letters, instead of being wholly caricatured, he is being seriously portrayed and painted.

To all of this the New Negro is keenly responsive as an augury of a new democracy in American culture. He is contributing his share to the new social understanding. But the desire to be understood would never in itself have been sufficient to have opened so completely the protectively closed portals of the thinking Negro's mind. There is still too much possibility of being snubbed or patronized for that. It was rather the necessity for fuller, truer, self-expression, the realization of the unwisdom of allowing social discrimination to segregate him mentally, and a counter-attitude to cramp and fetter his own living—and so the "spite-wall" that the intellectuals built over the "color-line" has happily been taken down. Much of this reopening of intellectual Contacts has Entered in New York and

has been richly fruitful not merely in the enlarging of personal experience, but in the definite enrichment of American art and letters and in the clarifying of our common vision of the social tasks ahead.

The particular significance in the reestablishment of contact between the more advanced and representative classes is that it promises to offset some of the unfavorable reactions of the past, or at least to re-surface race contacts somewhat for the future. Subtly the conditions that are moulding a New Negro are moulding a new American attitude.

However, this new phase of things is delicate; it will call for less charity but more justice; less help, but infinitely closer understanding. This is indeed a critical stage of race relationships because of the likelihood, if the new temper is not understood, of engendering sharp group antagonism and a second crop of more calculated prejudice. In some quarters, it has already done so. Having weaned the Negro, public opinion cannot continue to paternalize. The Negro today is inevitably moving forward under the control largely of his own objectives. What are these objectives? Those of his outer life are happily already well and finally formulated, for they are none other than the ideals of American institutions and democracy. Those of his inner life are yet in process of formation, for the new psychology at present is more of a consensus of feeling than of opinion, of attitude rather than of program. Still some points seem to have crystallized.

Up to the present one may adequately describe the Negro's "inner objectives" as an attempt to repair a damaged group psychology and reshape a warped social perspective. Their realization has required a new mentality for the American Negro. And as it matures we begin to see its effects; at first, negative, iconoclastic, and then positive and constructive. In this new group psychology we note the lapse of sentimental appeal, then the development of a more positive self-respect and self-reliance; the repudiation of social dependence, and then the gradual recovery from hyper-sensitiveness and "touchy" nerves, the repudiation of the double standard of judgment with its special philanthropic allowances and then the sturdier desire for objective and scientific appraisal; and finally the rise from social disillusionment to race pride, from the sense of social debt to the responsibilities of social contribution, and offsetting the necessary working and commonsense acceptance of restricted conditions, the belief in ultimate esteem and recognition. Therefore the Negro today wishes to be known for what he is, even in his faults and shortcomings, and scorns a craven and precarious survival at the price of seeming to be what he is not. He resents being spoken for as a social ward or minor, even by his own, and to being regarded a chronic patient for the sociological clinic, the sick man of American Democracy. For the same reasons he himself is through with those social nostrums and panaceas, the so-called "solutions" of his "problem," with which he and the country have been so liberally dosed in the past. Religion, freedom, education, money—in turn, he has ardently hoped for and peculiarly trusted these things; he still believes in them, but not in blind trust that they alone will solve his life-problem.

Each generation, however, will have its creed and that of the present is the belief in the efficacy of collective efforts in race cooperation. This deep feeling of race is at present the mainspring of Negro life. It seems to be the outcome of the reaction to proscription and prejudice; an attempt, fairly successful on the whole, to convert a defensive into an offensive position, a handicap into an incentive. It is radical in tone, but not in purpose and only the most stupid forms of opposition, misunderstanding or persecution could make it otherwise. Of course, the thinking Negro has shifted a little toward the left with the world-trend, and there is an increasing group who affiliate with radical and liberal movements. But fundamentally for the present the Negro is radical on race matters, conservative on others, in other words, a "forced radical," a social protestant rather than a genuine radical. Yet under further pressure and injustice iconoclastic thought and motives will inevitably increase. Harlem's quixotic radicalisms call for their ounce of democracy today lest tomorrow they be beyond cure.

The Negro mind reaches out as yet to nothing but American wants, American ideas. But this forced attempt to build his Americanism on race values is a unique social experiment, and its ultimate success is impossible except through the fullest sharing of American culture and institutions. There should be no delusion about this. American nerves in sections unstrung with race hysteria are often fed the opiate that the trend of Negro advance is wholly separatist, and that the effect of its operation will be to encyst the Negro as a benign foreign body in the body politic. This cannot be—even if it were desirable. The racialism of the Negro is no limitation or reservation with respect to American life; it is only a constructive effort to build the obstructions in the stream of his progress into an efficient dam of social energy and power. Democracy itself is obstructed and stagnated to the extent that any of its channels are closed. Indeed they cannot be selectively closed. So the choice is not between one way for the Negro and another way for the rest, but between American institutions frustrated on the one hand and American ideals progressively fulfilled and realized on the other.

There is, of course, a warrantably comfortable feeling in being on the right side of the country's professed ideals. We realize that we cannot be undone without America's undoing. It is within the gamut of this attitude that the thinking Negro faces America, but the variations of mood in connection with it are if anything more significant than the attitude itself. Sometimes we have it taken with the defiant ironic challenge of McKay:

> Mine is the future grinding down today
> Like a great landslip moving to the sea,
> Bearing its freight of debris far away
> Where the green hungry waters restlessly
> Heave mammoth pyramids and break and roar
> Their eerie challenge to the crumbling shore.

Sometimes, perhaps more frequently as yet, in the fervent and almost filial appeal and counsel of Weldon Johnson's:

> O Southland, dear Southland!
> Then why do you still cling

To an idle age and a musty page,
To a dead and useless thing.

But between defiance and appeal, midway almost between cynicism and hope, the prevailing mind stands in the mood of the same author's To America, an attitude of sober query and stoical challenge:

How would you have us, as we are?
Or sinking'neath the load we bear,
Our eyes fixed forward on a star,
Or gazing empty at despair?

Rising or falling? Men or things?
With dragging pace or footsteps fleet?
Strong, willing sinews in your wings,
Or tightening chains about your feet?

More and more, however, an intelligent realization of the great discrepancy between the American social creed and the American social practice forces upon the Negro the taking of the moral advantage that is his. Only the steadying and sobering effect of a truly characteristic gentleness of spirit prevents the rapid rise of a definite cynicism and counter-hate and a defiant superiority feeling. Human as this reaction would be, the majority still deprecate its advent, and would gladly see it forestalled by the speedy amelioration of its causes. We wish our race pride to be a healthier, more positive achievement than a feeling based upon a realization of the shortcomings of others. But all paths toward the attainment of a sound social attitude have been difficult; only a relatively few enlightened minds have been able as the phrase puts it "to rise above" prejudice. The ordinary man has had until recently only a hard choice between the alternatives of supine and humiliating submission and stimulating but hurtful counter-prejudice. Fortunately from some inner, desperate resourcefulness has recently sprung up the simple expedient of fighting prejudice by mental passive resistance, in other words by trying to ignore it. For the few, this manna may perhaps be effective, but the masses cannot thrive on it.

Fortunately there are constructive channels opening out into which the balked social feelings of the American Negro can flow freely.

Without them there would be much more pressure and danger than there is. These compensating interests are racial but in a new and enlarged way. One is the consciousness of acting as the advance-guard of the African peoples in their contact with Twentieth Century civilization; the other, the sense of a mission of rehabilitating the race in world esteem from that loss of prestige for which the fate and conditions of slavery have so largely been responsible. Harlem, as we shall see, is the center of both these movements; she is the home of the Negro's "Zionism." The pulse of the Negro world has begun to beat in Harlem. A Negro newspaper carrying news material in English, French and Spanish, gathered from all quarters of America, the West Indies and Africa has maintained itself in Harlem for over five years. Two important magazines, both edited from New York, maintain their news and circulation consistently on a cosmopolitan scale. Under American auspices and backing, three pan-African congresses have been held abroad for the discussion of common interests, colonial questions and the future cooperative development of Africa. In terms of the race question as a world problem, the Negro mind has leapt, so to speak, upon the parapets of prejudice and extended its cramped horizons. In so doing it has linked up with the growing group consciousness of the dark-peoples and is gradually learning their common interests. As one of our writers has recently put it: "It is imperative that we understand the white world in its relations to the nonwhite world." As with the Jew, persecution is making the Negro international.

As a world phenomenon this wider race consciousness is a different thing from the much asserted rising tide of color. Its inevitable causes are not of our making. The consequences are not necessarily damaging to the best interests of civilization. Whether it actually brings into being new Armadas of conflict or argosies of cultural exchange and enlightenment can only be decided by the attitude of the dominant races in an era of critical change. With the American Negro his new internationalism is primarily an effort to recapture contact with the scattered peoples of African derivation. Garveyism may be a transient, if spectacular, phenomenon, but the possible role of the American Negro in the future development of Africa is one of the most constructive and universally helpful missions that any modern people can lay claim to.

Constructive participation in such causes cannot help giving the Negro valuable group incentives, as well as increased prestige at home and abroad. Our greatest rehabilitation may possibly come through such channels, but for the present, more immediate hope rests in the revaluation by white and black alike of the Negro in terms of his artistic endowments and cultural contributions, past and prospective. It must be increasingly recognized that the Negro has already made very substantial contributions, not only in his folk-art, music especially, which has always found appreciation, but in larger, though humbler and less acknowledged ways. For generations the Negro has been the peasant matrix of that section of America which has most undervalued him, and here he has contributed not only materially in labor and in social patience, but spiritually as well. The South has unconsciously absorbed the gift of his folk-temperament. In less than half a generation it will be easier to recognize this, but the fact remains that a leaven of humor, sentiment, imagination and tropic nonchalance has gone into the making of the South from a humble, unacknowledged source. A second crop of the Negro's gifts promises still more largely. He now becomes a conscious contributor . . . beneficiary and ward for that of a collaborator and participant in American civilization. The great social gain in this is the releasing of our talented group from the arid fields of controversy and debate to the productive fields of creative expression. The especially cultural recognition they win should in turn prove the key to that revaluation of the Negro which must precede or accompany any considerable further betterment of race relationships. But whatever the general effect, the present generation will have added the motives of self-expression and spiritual development to the old and still unfinished task of making material headway and progress. No one who understandingly faces the situation with its substantial accomplishment or views the new scene with its still more abundant promise can be entirely without hope. And certainly, if in our lifetime the Negro should not be able to celebrate his full initiation into American democracy, he can at least, on the warrant of these things, celebrate the attainment of a significant and satisfying new phase of group development, and with it a spiritual Coming of Age.

Source: Locke, Alain. "Enter the New Negro." *The Survey Graphic* VI, no. 6 (March 1925), 631–634.

Dorothy West, Amateur Night in Harlem, "That's Why Darkies Were Born" (1938)

The Apollo Theater in Harlem is legendary. Many African American performers started their musical or acting careers there or performed on this stage at some point. While the names of countless performers graced the stage of this sacred place, the audiences played a bigger role in wowing newcomers with thunderous applause, or booing so loud that stage clowns tugged them offstage, never to be seen or heard from again. Writer Dorothy West, a Harlem Renaissance literary figure best known for her two novels, The Living Is Easy, *and* The Wedding, *captured the atmosphere of this place in the following essay describing one amateur night performance in*

November 1938. In this piece, West delivered a poignant reminder that America outside the doors of this theater was less forgiving than even the most critical audience at the Apollo.

The second balcony is packed. The friendly, familiar usher who scowls all the time without meaning it, flatfoots up and down the stairs trying to find seats for the sweethearts. Through his tireless manipulation, separated couples are reunited, and his pride is pardonable.

The crowd has come early, for it is amateur night. The Apollo Theater is full to overflowing. Amateur night is an institution. Every Wednesday, from eleven until midnight, the hopeful aspirants come to the mike, lift up their voices and sing, and retire to the wings for the roll call, when a fluttering piece of paper dangled above their heads comes to rest determined by the volume of applause to indicate to whom the prizes shall go.

The boxes are filled with sightseeing whites led in tow by swaggering blacks. The floor is chocolate liberally sprinkled with white sauce. But the balconies belong to the hardworking, holidaying Negroes, and the jitterbug whites are intruders, and their surface excitement is silly compared to the earthy enjoyment of the Negroes.

The moving picture ends. The screen shoots out of sight. The orchestra blares out the soul-ticking tune, "I think you're wonderful, I think you're grand." Spontaneously, feet and hands beat out the rhythm, and the show is on.

The regular stage show precedes Amateur Hour. Tonight an all-girls orchestra dominates the stage. A long black girl in flowing pink blows blue notes out of a clarinet. It is hot song, and the audience stomps its approval. A little yellow trumpeter swings out. She holds a high note, and it soars up solid. The fourteen pieces are in the groove.

The comedians are old-timers. Their comedy is pure Harlemese, and their prototypes are scattered throughout the audience. There is a burst of appreciative laughter and a round of applause when the redoubtable Jackie Mabley states that she is doing general housework in the Bronx and adds, with telling emphasis, "When you do housework up there, you really do housework." It is real Negro idiom when one comedian observes to another who is carrying a fine fur coat for his girl, "Anytime I see you with something on your arm, somebody is without something."

The show moves on. The girls of sixteen varying shades dance without precision but with effortless joy. The best of their spontaneous steps will find their way downtown. A long brown boy who looks like Cab Calloway sings, "Papa Tree-Top Tall." The regular stage show comes to an end. The acts file on stage. The chorus girls swing in the background. It is a free-for-all, and to the familiar "I think you're wonderful, I think you're grand", the black-face comic grabs the prettiest chorine and they truck on down. When the curtain descends, both sides of the house are having fun. A Negro show would rather have the plaudits of an Apollo audience than any other applause. For the Apollo is the hard, testing ground of Negro show business, and approval there can make or break an act.

It is eleven now. The house lights go up. The audience is restless and expectant. Somebody has brought a whistle that sounds like a wailing baby. The cry fills the theater and everybody laughs. The orchestra breaks into the theater's theme song again. The curtain goes up. An announcer talks into a mike, explaining to his listeners that the three hundred and first broadcast of Amateur Hour at the Apollo is on the air. He signals to the audience and they obligingly applaud.

The emcee comes out of the wings. The audience knows him. He is Negro to his toes, but even Hitler would classify him as Aryan at first glance. He begins a steady patter of jive. When the audience is ready and mellow, he calls the first amateur out of the wings.

Willie comes out and, on his way to the mike, touches the Tree of Hope. For several years the original Tree of Hope stood in front of the Lafayette Theater on Seventh Avenue until the Commissioner of Parks tore it down. It was to bring good fortune to whatever actor touched it, and some say it was not Mr. Moses who had it cut down, but the steady stream of down-and-out actors since the depression who wore it out.

Willie sings "I surrender Dear" in a pure Georgia accent. "I can' mak' mah way," he moans. The audience hears him out and claps kindly. He bows and starts for the wings. The emcee admonishes, "You got to boogie-woogie off the stage, Willie." He boogie-woogies off, which is as much a part of established ritual as touching the Tree of Hope.

Vanessa appears. She is black and the powder makes her look purple. She is dressed in black, and is altogether unprepossessing. She is the kind of singer who makes faces and regards a mike as an enemy to be wrestled with. The orchestra sobs out her song. "I cried for you, now it's your turn to cry over me." Vanessa is an old-time "coon-shouter." She wails and moans deep blue notes. The audience give her their highest form of approval. They clap their hands in time with the music. She finishes to tumultuous applause, and accepts their approval with proud self-confidence. To their wild delight, she flings her arms around the emcee, and boogie woogies off with him.

Ida comes out in a summer print to sing that beautiful lyric, "I Let a Song Go Out of My Heart," in a nasal, off-key whine. Samuel follows her. He is big and awkward, and his voice is very earnest as he promises, "I Won't Tell a Soul I love you." They are both so inoffensive and sincere that the audience lets them off with light applause.

Coretta steps to the mike. Her first note is so awful that the emcee goes to the Tree of Hope and touches it for her. The audience lets her sing the first bar, then bursts into catcalls and derisive whistling. In a moment the familiar police siren is heard off-stage, and big, dark brown Porto Rico, who is part and parcel of amateur night, comes on stage with nothing covering his nakedness but a brassiere and panties and shoots twice at Coretta's feet. She hurriedly retires to the wings with Porto Rico switching after her, brandishing his gun.

A clarinetist, a lean dark boy, pours out such sweetness in "Body and Soul" that somebody rises and shouts, "Peace, brother!" in heartfelt approval. Margaret follows with a sour note. She has chosen

to sing "Old Folks," and her voice quavers so from stage fright that her song becomes an unfortunate choice, and the audience stomps for Porto Rico who appears in a pink and blue ballet costume to run her off the stage.

David is next on the program. With mounting frenzy he sings the intensely pleading blues song, "Rock it for Me." He clutches his knees, rolls his eyes, sings away from the mike, and works himself up to a pitch of excitement that is only cooled by the appearance of Porto Rico in a red brassiere, an ankle-length red skirt, and an exaggerated picture hat. The audience goes wild. Ida comes out. She is a lumpy girl in a salmon pink blouse. The good-looking emcee leads her to the mike and pats her shoulder encouragingly. She snuggles up to him, and a female onlooker audibly snorts, "She sure wants to be hugged." A male spectator shouts, gleefully, "Give her something!"

Ida sings the plaintive, "My Reverie". Her accent is late West Indian and her voice is so bad that for a minute you wonder if it's an act. Instantly here are whistles, boos, and handclapping. The siren sounds off stage and Porto Rico rushed on in an old-fashioned corset and a marabou-trimmed bed jacket. His shots leave her undisturbed. The audience tries to drown her out with louder applause and whistling. She holds to the mike and sings to the bitter end. It is Porto Rico who trots sheepishly after her when she walks unabashed from the stage.

James come to the mike and is reminded by the audience to touch the Tree of Hope. He hasn't forgotten. He tries to start his song, but the audience will not let him. The emcee explains to him that the Tree of Hope is a sacred emblem. The boy doesn't care, and begins his song again. He has been in New York two days, and the emcee cracks that he's been in New York two days too long. The audience refuses to let the lad sing, and the emcee banishes him to the wings to think it over.

A slight, young girl in a crisp white blouse and neat black shirt comes to the mike to sing "Tisket Tasket." She has lost her yellow basket, and her listeners spontaneously inquire of her, "Was it red?" She shouts back dolefully, "No, no, no, no!"

"Was it blue?" No, it wasn't blue, either."

They go on searching together.

A chastened James reappears and touches the Tree of Hope. A woman states with grim satisfaction, "He teched de tree dat time." He has tried to upset a precedent, and the audience is against him from the start. They boo and whistle immediately. Porto Rico in red flannels and a floppy red hat happily shoots him off the stage.

A high school girl in middy blouse, jumper and socks rocks "Froggy Bottom." She is the youngest thing yet, and it doesn't matter how she sings. The house rocks with her. She winds up triumphantly with a tap dance, and boogie woogies confidently off the stage.

A frightened lad falls upon the mike. It is the only barrier between him and the murderous multitude. The emcee's encouragement falls on frozen ears. His voice starts down in his chest and stays here. The house roars for the kill, and Porto Rico, in a baby's bonnet and a little girl's party frock, finishes him off with dispatch.

A white man comes out of the wings, but nobody minds. They have got accustomed to occasional white performers at the Apollo. There was a dancing act in the regular stage show which received deserved applause. The emcee announces the song, "That's Why——" he omits the next word—"Were Born." He is a Negro emcee. He will not use the word "darky" in announcing a song a white man is to sing.

The white man begins to sing, "Someone had to plough the cotton, Someone had to plant the corn, Someone had to work while the white folks played, That's why darkies were born." The Negroes hiss and boo. Instantly the audience is partisan. The whites applaud vigorously. But the greater volume of hisses and boos drown out the applause. The singer halts. The emcee steps to the house mike and raises his hand for quiet. He does not know what to say, and says ineffectually that the song was written to be sung and urges that the singer be allowed to continue. The man begins again, and on

the instant is booed down. The emcee does not know what to do. They are on a sectional hook-up—the announcer has welcomed Boston and Philadelphia to the program during the station break. The studio officials, the listening audience, largely white, has heard a Negro audience booing a white man. It is obvious that in his confusion the emcee has forgotten what the song connotes.

The Negroes are not booing the white man as such. They are booing him for his categorization of them. The song is not new. A few seasons ago they listened to it in silent resentment. Now they have learned to vocalize their bitterness. They cannot bear that a white man, as poor as themselves, should so separate himself from their common fate and sing paternally for a price of their predestined lot to serve.

For the third time the man begins, and now all the fun that has gone before is forgotten. There is resentment in every heart. The white man will not save the situation by leaving the stage, and the emcee steps again to the house mike with an impassioned plea. The Negroes know this emcee. He is as white as any white man. Now it is ironic that he should be so fair, for the difference between him and the amateur is too undefined. The emcee spreads out his arms and begins, "My people—."

He says without explanation that "his people" should be proud of the song. He begs "his people" to let the song be sung to show that they are ladies and gentlemen. He winds up with a last appeal to "his people" for fair play. He looks for all the world like the plantation owner's yellow boy acting as buffer between the black and the big house.

The whole house breaks into applause, and this time the scattered hisses are drowned out. The amateur begins and ends in triumph. He is the last contestant, and in the lineup immediately following, he is overwhelmingly voted first prize. More of the black man's blood money goes out of Harlem.

The show is over. The orchestra strikes up, "I think you're wonderful, I think you're grand." The audience files out. They are quiet and confused and sad. It is twelve on the dot. Six hours of sleep and then back to the Bronx or up and down an elevator shaft. Yessir, Mr. White Man, I work all day while you-all play. It's only fair. That's why darkies were born.

Source: West, Dorothy. "That's Why Darkies Were Born." Amateur Night in Harlem. New York, 1938. Library of Congress, Manuscript Division, WPA Federal Writers' Project Collection.

Dorothy West, Game Songs and Rhymes, Interview with Mrs. Laura M. (October 1938)

When the United States was plunged into a severe economic depression in the 1930s, many Americans were unemployed. The government launched a variety of programs aimed at putting Americans back to work. One of those programs was the Works Progress Administration, which included the Writers Project. Writers fanned out across the country, interviewing Americans about their lives. This interview, conducted by federal writer and Harlem Renaissance literary figure Dorothy West, is with a woman identified only as Mrs. Laura M. in New York City, who talked about the games she played and the songs she sang as a child.

Mrs. Laura M. (prefers not to have her full name used) 300 West 114th Street, New York, N.Y, originally from South Carolina

I used to hear Mama sing this song and play it on the organ. I don't know where it started but I used to hear it all the time.

The Little Brown Jug

I.
Me and my wife and the little brown jug
Crossed the river on a hickory log.
She fell in and I got wet;
Hung to the little brown jug, you bet.

Chorus:
Ha-ha-ha, you and me,
Little brown jug, don't I love thee?
Ha-ha-ha, you and me,
Little brown jug, don't I love thee?

II.
Me and my wife lived all alone
In a little hut we called our own,
She loved gin and I loved rum;
We two together had a lot of fun.

Chorus:
Ha-ha-ha, you and me,
Little brown jug, don't I love thee?
Ha-ha-ha, you and me,
Little brown jug, I do love thee.

We used to sing this one, too:

O where, o where is my little dog gone?
O where, o where has he gone?
With his tail cut short and his ears cropped off,
O where, o where has he gone?

Chorus:
He's gone, he's gone
O where has he gone?
O where has my little dog gone?

(That was the funny part - 'dog gone'.)

II.
O where, o where is my little dog gone?
O where, o where has he gone?
With his eyes punched out and his nose cut off,
O where, o where has he gone?

Chorus:
He's gone, he's gone,
O where has he gone?
O where has my little dog gone?

We used to sing this a lot when we were kids . . . No, you didn't play any game with it. You just sat around singing it; a bunch could sing it, or just one or two. The number didn't matter since no game was attached to it.

I.
My grandfather had some very fine sheep,
Some very fine sheep had he.
It was a baa, baa here,
A baa, baa there; a baa, baa everywhere.

Chorus:
Come along boys, come along girls,
To the merry green fields away.

II.
My grandfather had some very fine cows,
Some very fine cows had he.
It was a moo, moo here,
A moo, moo there; a moo, moo everywhere.

Chorus:
Come along boys, come along girls,
To the merry green fields away.

III.
My grandfather had some very fine pigs,
Some very fine pigs had he.
It was an oink, oink here,
An oink, oink there; an oink, oink everywhere.

Chorus:
Come along boys, come along girls,
To the merry green fields away.

IV.
My grandfather had some very fine ducks,
Some very fine ducks had he.
It was a quack, quack here,
A quack, quack there; a quack, quack everywhere.

Chorus:
Come along boys, come along girls,
To the merry green fields away.

V.
My grandfather had some very fine chickens,
Some very fine chickens had he.
It was a cluck, cluck here,
A cluck, cluck there; a cluck, cluck everywhere.

Chorus:
Come along boys, come along girls,
To the merry green fields away.

VI.
My grandfather had some very fine horses,
Some very fine horses had he.
It was a neigh, neigh here,
A neigh, neigh there; a neigh, neigh everywhere.

Chorus:
Come along boys, come along girls,
To the merry green fields away.

VII.
My grandfather had some very fine mules,
Some very fine mules had he.
It was a hee-haw here,
A hee-haw there; a hee-haw everywhere.

Chorus:
Come along boys, come along girls,
To the merry green fields away.

VIII.
My grandfather had some very fine dogs,
Some very fine dogs had he.
It was a woof-woof here,
A woof-woof there; a woof-woof everywhere.

Chorus:
Come along boys, come along girls,
To the merry green fields away.

IX.
My grandfather had some very fine cats,
Some very fine cats had he.
It was a meow-meow here,
A meow-meow there; a meow-meow everywhere.

Chorus:
Come along boys, come along girls,
To the merry green fields away.

X.
My grandfather had some very fine pigeons,
Some very fine pigeons had he.
It was a coo-coo here,
A coo-coo there; a coo-coo everywhere.

Chorus:
Come along boys, come along girls,
To the merry green fields away.

XI.
A baa, baa here,
A moo, moo there,
An oink, oink here,
A quack, quack there,
A cluck, cluck here,
A neigh, neigh there,
A hee-haw here,
A woof-woof there,
A meow-meow here,
A coo-coo there.
A baa, baa; a moo, moo; oink, oink; a quack, quack; cluck, cluck; neigh, neigh; hee-haw, hee-haw; woof-woof;
meow, meow; coo-coo everywhere.

Chorus:
Come along boys, come along girls,
To the merry green fields away.

***

Most of the games that I played when I was a child are played today, except for one or two that I remembered . . . No, I don't know whether they're played the same way or not because I haven't stopped to watch 'em play nowadays.

I. We used to play a game, I don't know what it was called, where one kid would hide. It was like hide-and-seek backwards. That kid would hide somewhere and then the whole bunch of us would walk around together singing, "Ain't no bogey-man out tonight".

You never knew where the bogey-man was and sometimes he would sneak up on you and whoever he caught had to be the bogey-man next. You hardly ever went around singing by yourself, but with a whole bunch. There'd be two or three bunches, depending on how many were playing, of five or six. When the bogey-man started chasing you, you'd be scared to death, really thinking it was the bogey-man. If he caught you and you had to be the bogey-man, you'd be almost as scared chasing as you were being chased.

II. Two kids could play this game, or as many as eight. If two played it, one said one line and the other said another, so on 'til you said the last line. It was more fun if eight played it because you were so busy saying the last your line, you didn't have time to figure out who'd say the last line—that was the funny one. If eight played it, it went like this:

1st child: "I went upstairs"
2nd child: "What did you see?"
3rd child: "I saw a monkey"
4th child: "Just like me"
5th child: "I one him"
6th child: "I two him"
7th child: "I three him"
8th child: "I four him"
1st child: "I five him"
2nd child: "I six him"
3rd child: "I seven him"
4th child: "I eight (ate) him"

Then you'd start all over again. The fifth child would say, "I went upstairs", and so on. Nobody wanted to say "Just like me" or "I eight (ate) him". It was a lot of fun. You'd keep on 'til everybody had said "Just like me" and 'til everybody ate him.

III. We played a game called the Prisoner's Game: You formed a circle and held hands with one child in the center. That child was in prison and tried to get out. When he thought you weren't holding hands tight, he'd run and try to break through. After he tried that a couple of times and couldn't get out, he'd come up to you and say:

Prisoner: "Is this door locked?"
Group: "Yes, child, yes."
Prisoner: "Can I get out of here?"
Group: "No, child, no."

Then he'd try to break out again. When he got out, you chased him and whoever caught him got to be the prisoner. Then you'd do it all over again 'til you got tired. . . . Yes, it was a privilege to be the prisoner because you had more to do; you were more active.

IV.

Here we go 'round the rosey-bush,
The rosey-bush, the rosey-bush,
Here we go 'round the rosey-bush
So early in the morning.
The last one stoop shall tell her beau,
Tell her beau, tell her beau,

The last one stoop shall tell her beau
So early in the morning.

The last one to squat when you said, "The last one stoop" had to tell who her beau was. If boys played it too, and a boy was the last one to squat down, he had to name his girl.

V.

Here's another game. Little girls around six or seven played it. It wasn't a game really, wasn't anything to it, but we love it, I guess because our mothers didn't like it. A lot of little girls joined hands and went around in a circle chanting, "Shake, shake, shake, for the batter-cake." Then you'd drop hands and shake your-self all over. When you got through shaking, you'd join hands again and start all over again. Some children said, "Shake, shake, shake, for the good egg bread."

VI.

Then there was the game that everybody knows I guess. One person went around and took something from all the children who were going to play [?] game. Maybe he'd take a handkerchief from you, a button from me—anything that you had to give him as a pawn. One child sat in the center and the one who collected the pawns stood over the one in the center. He held one of the pawns in his closed hand over the one sitting down and said,

Child standing:	"Heavy, heavy hangs over your head."
Child sitting:	"Fine or super-fine?"
Child standing:	"Fine (or super-fine, depending upon what the object was)

"What shall the owner of this pawn do?"

The child who was sitting would name some task or feat and then the child who was standing would open his hand and the owner of the pawn would be identified and would have to do the thing requested. It the owner refused or could not do what was asked, he would have to pay a fine of some kind.

A RIDDLE.

Here's a riddle:

"The black men live in the red men's house,
The red men live in the pink men's house,
The pink men live in the white man's house,
The white men live in the green men's house.
What is it?"

A.: A watermelon; the seeds being the black men, the center being the red men, the outer edge of the meat being the pink men, the white men being the white part of the rind, and the green men being the outer rind.

Source: West, Dorothy. "Game Songs and Rhymes, interview with Mrs. Laura M." New York, October, 1938. Library of Congress, Manuscript Division, WPA Federal Writers' Project Collection.

Frank Byrd, "Afternoon in a Pushcart Peddler's Colony" (December 1938)

Works Progress Administration writer Frank Byrd gathered stories from various places, including New York. This report is about a shanty town along the banks of an uptown river.

It was snowing and, shortly after noontime, the snow changed to sleet and beat a tattoo against the rocks and board shacks that had been carelessly thrown together on the west bank of the Harlem. It was windy too and the cold blasts that came in from the river sent the men shivering for cover behind their shacks where some of them had built huge bonfires to ward off the icy chills that swept down from the hills above.

Some of them, unable to stand it any longer, went below into the crudely furnished cabins that were located in the holds of some old abandoned barges that lay half in, half out of the water. But the men did not seem to mind. Even the rotting barges afforded them some kind of shelter. It was certainly better than nothing, not to mention the fact that it was their home; address, the foot of 133rd Street at Park Avenue on the west bank of the Harlem River; depression residence of a little band of part-time pushcart peddlers whose cooperative colony is one of the most unique in the history of New York City.

These men earn their living by cruising the streets long before daylight, collecting old automobile parts, pasteboard, paper, rags, rubber, magazines, brass, iron, steal [sic], old clothes or anything they can find that is saleable as junk. They wheel their little pushcarts around exploring cellars, garbage cans and refuse heaps. When they have a load, they turn their footsteps in the direction of the American Junk Dealers, Inc., whose site of wholesale and retail operations is located directly opposite the pushcart colony at 134th Street and Park Avenue. Of the fifty odd colonists, many are ex-carpenters, painters, brick-masons, auto-mechanics, upholsterers, plumbers and even an artist or two.

Most of the things the men collect they sell, but once in awhile they run across something useful to themselves, like auto parts, pieces of wire, or any electrical equipment, especially in view of the fact that there are two or three electrical engineers in the group.

Joe Elder, a tall, serious-minded Negro, was the founder of the group that is officially known as the National Negro Civil Association. Under his supervision, electrically inclined members of the group set up a complete power plant that supplied all the barges and shacks with electric light. It was constructed with an old automobile engine and an electrical generator bought from the City of New York.

For a long time it worked perfectly. After awhile, when a city inspector came around, he condemned it and the shacks were temporarily without light. It was just as well, perhaps, since part of the colony was forced to vacate the site in order to make room for a mooring spot for a coal company that rented a section of the waterfront.

A rather modern and up-to-date community hall remains on the site, however. One section of it is known as the gymnasium and many pieces of apparatus are to be found there. There are also original oil paintings in the other sections known as the library and recreation room. Here, one is amazed (to say the least) by the comfortable divans, lounges, bookshelves and, of all things, a drinking fountain. The water is purchased from the City and pumped directly to the hall and barges by a homemade, electrically motored pump. In the recreation room there are also three pianos. On cold nights when the men want companionship and relaxation, they bring the women there and dance to the accompaniment of typical Harlem jazz . . . jazz that is also supplied by fellow colonists. (For what Negro is there who is not able to extract a tune of some sort from every known instrument?)

After being introduced to some of the boys, we went down into Oliver's barge. It was shaky, weather-beaten and sprawling, like the other half-dozen that surrounded it. Inside, he had set up an old iron range and attached a pipe to it that carried the smoke out and above the upper deck. On top of the iron grating that had been laid across the open hole on the back of the stove were some spare-ribs that had been generously seasoned with salt, pepper, sage and hot-sauce. Later I discovered a faint flavor of mace in them. The small and pungency of spices filled the low ceilinged room with an appetizing aroma. The faces of the men were alight and hopeful with anticipation.

There was no real cause for worry, however, since Oliver had more than enough for everybody. Soon he began passing out tin plates for everyone. It makes my mouth water just to think of it. When we had gobbled up everything in sight, all of us sat back in restful contemplation puffing on our freshly lighted cigarettes. Afterwards there was conversation, things the men elected to talk about of their own accord.

"You know one thing," Oliver began, "ain't nothin' like a man being his own boss. Now take today, here we is wit' plenty to eat, ha'f a jug of co'n between us and nairy a woman to fuss aroun' wantin' to wash up dishes or mess aroun' befo' duh grub gits a chance to settle good."

"Dat sho is right," Evans Drake agreed. He was Oliver's helper when there were trucks to be repaired. "A 'oman ain't good fuh nuthin' but one thing."

The conversation drifted along until I was finally able to ease in a query or two.

"Boys," I ventured, "how is it that none of you ever got on Home Relief? You can get a little grub out of it, at least, and that would take a little of the load off you, wouldn't it?"

At this they all rose up in unanimous protest.

"Lis'en," one of them said, "befo' I'd take Home Relief I'd go out in duh street an' hit same bastard oveh de haid an' take myse'f some'n'. I know one uv duh boys who tried to git it an' one of dem uppity little college boys ovah dere talked tuh him lak he was some damn jailbird or some'n'. If it had been me, I'd a bust hell outn' him an' walked outa duh place. What duh hell do we wants wid relief anyhow? We is all able-bodied mens an' can take it. We can make our own livin's."

This, apparently, was the attitude of every man there. They seemed to take fierce pride in the fact that every member of Joe Elder's National Negro Civil Association (it used to be called the National Negro Boat Terminal) was entirely self-supporting. They even had their own unemployment insurance fund that provided an income for any member of the group who was ill and unable to work. Each week the men give a small part of their earnings toward this common fund and automatically agree to allow a certain amount to any temporarily incapacitated member. In addition to that, they divide among themselves their ill brother's work and provide a day and night attendant near his shack if his illness is at all serious.

After chatting awhile longer with them, I finally decided to leave.

"Well boys," I said, getting up, "I guess I'll have to be shoving off. Thanks, a lot, for the ribs. See you again sometime."

Before leaving, however, I gave them a couple of packs of cigarettes I had on me in part payment for my dinner.

"O. K." they said. "Come ovah ag'in some time. Some Sat'd'y. Maybe we'll have a few broads (women) and a little co'n."

"Thanks."

Outside the snow and sleet had turned to rain and the snow that had been feathery and white was running down the river bank in brown rivulets of slush and mud. It was a little warmer but the damp air still had a penetrating sharpness to it. I shuddered, wrapped my muffler a little tighter and turned my coat collar up about my ears.

There was wind in the rain, and behind me lay the jagged outline of the ramshackle dwellings. I hated to think of what it would be like, living in them when there was a scarcity of wood or when the fires went out.

Source: Byrd, Frank. " Afternoon in a Pushcart Peddlers' Colony." December 1938. Library of Congress, Manuscript Division, WPA Federal Writers' Project Collection.

Theodore Poston, "Matt Henson, North Pole Explorer Retires"
(1938–1939)

In 1887, African American explorer Matt Henson met Rear Admiral Robert Perry in Washington, DC, where Henson was then working in a clothing store. Fifty years later, New York reporter Theodore Poston wrote the following article telling Henderson's story about his mad dash for the North Pole on an expedition headed by Admiral Peary.

There was little work that morning in the Chief Clerk's Office of the U.S. Custom House in New York City. The whole staff was gathered, for the last time, around the desk of the genial and unassuming little man who had worked there for 23 years. For Matt Henson, sole survivor of Peary's dash to the North Pole, was retiring from government service that day—on a clerk's pension.

A few reporters had dropped in to record the occasion. Friends from Harlem and other parts of the city had come down also. One by one they assured the bald headed but erect one-time explorer that they would continue the fight for Congressional recognition of his deed. And Matt Henson thanked them and turned to bid the staff farewell.

The reporters asked questions. Reluctantly, Henson answered. He displayed no bitterness against a government which had heaped undying honors on the late Rear Admiral Robert E. Peary and completely ignored the only other American to reach the pole. Of the proposed Congressional pension, repeatedly denied him, he said:

"I could use the money. I think that I deserve it. But I will never ask the government nor anybody else for anything. I have worked sixty of the seventy years of my life, so I guess I can make out on the $87.27 a month pension I've earned here."

Negro leaders had not been so philosophical however. For a quarter of a century they had demanded official recognition and a commensurate pension for Mr. Henson. Through their efforts six bills had been introduced in Congress. All died in committee.

Congressman Arthur W. Mitchell resurrected the fight in 1935. Scores of prominent Negroes appeared before the House committee to support the bill which asked for a gold medal and a $2,500 pension. They pointed out that the late Rear Admiral Peary had been awarded a $6,500 pension and a Congressional medal. They recalled that Henson had twice saved Peary's life. They charged that Henson's race was his only barrier to recognition.

The House passed the bill. The Senate killed it.

At the prompting of the reporters, Matt Henson again described their arrival at the North Pole on April 6, 1909, the culmination of a nineteen-year struggle on their part. Together he and Peary had made eight expeditions into the arctic regions, and five unsuccessful dashes for the pole. Twice a helpless Peary had been brought back to civilization by his Negro companion—once when his feet were frozen and again when he was stricken by pneumonia.

For the last time in the Custom House surroundings, Mr. Henson recalled the climax of the final dash which had started July 8, 1908.

As trail breaker for the party which included the two Americans and four Eskimos, the Negro had been the first to arrive at the pole.

"When the compass started to go crazy," he recalled, "I sat down to wait for Mr. Peary. He arrived about forty-five minutes later, and we prepared to wait for the dawn to check our exact positions. Mr. Peary pulled off his boots and warmed his feet on my stomach. We always did that before going to bed up there."

The next morning when their positions had been verified, Peary said: "Matt, we've reached the North Pole at last."

With his exhausted leader looking on, Henson planted the American flag in the barren area.

"That was the happiest moment of my life," Mr. Henson said.

Henson's early life fitted him admirably for the hardships he was to undergo with Peary. Born in Charles County, Maryland, in 1866, he was orphaned at the age of four. When he was nine, he ran away from his foster parents and signed up as a cabin boy on the old sailing vessel Katie Hines. A few years later, the Katie Hines was ice-bound for several months in the Baltic Sea.

"That was my first experience with bitter cold," he recalled, "and it sure came in handy later."

Peary met Henson in 1887 when the latter was working in a store in Washington. Informed of the youth's love of travel, the explorer offered him a job on a surveying expedition in South America. Henson accepted and for twenty-two years, the two men were never separated.

Criticized for taking a Negro with him on his dash to the pole (his critics held that he was afraid that a white man might steal some of his prestige), Peary once said:

"Matt was a better man than any of my white assistants. He made all our sleds. He was popular with the Eskimos. He could talk their language like a native. He was the greatest man living for handling dogs. I couldn't get along without him."

Despite this tribute, however, and a glowing forward to Henson's book, "Negro Explorer at the North Pole," Peary never publicly joined the forces which fought for Congressional recognition of his Negro assistant, Henson recalled.

"Mr. Peary was a hard man like that," the assistant said, "He didn't want to share his honor and his glory with anybody. He wanted everything for himself and his family. So, according to his lights, I guess he felt justified."

The Chief Clerk came over and shook his hand, his fellow workers gathered around to present him with several small mementos, and Matt Henson bade his friends farewell.

When he walked from the room, he had ended the only recognition the government had given him for his deed. For President Taft had appointed him a clerk in the Customs Service for life.

Source: Poston, Theodore. " Matt Henson, North Pole explorer retires." *New York Post*, 1938–39. Library of Congress, Manuscript Division, WPA Federal Writers' Project Collection.

Alfred O. Phillipp, "Midlothian, Illinois: A Folklore in the Making"
(1939)

In the early years of the 20th century, Midlothian, Illinois, became home to one of the first communities of suburban Negroes. It was a new racial-social phenomenon. The tenement-dwelling city Negro and the plantation Negro were comparatively well known. Residents of Midlothian were true Negro suburbanites in this southwest suburb of Chicago, which was inhabited and run exclusively by Negroes. This article by Works Progress Administration writer Alfred O. Phillipp describes life in Midlothian in 1939.

The village was incorporated in 1917, and was named after Eugene S. Midlothian, a realtor and developer. It was situated directly southwest of the city of Blue Island, and was approximately one mile west of Western Avenue at 139th Street. It has an area of more than four square miles, and the boundary limits are: on the north, 135th Street; on the south, 141 Street; on the east, Sacramento Avenue; and on the west, Central Park Avenue.

The population was about 2,250 in this town of black citizens, one of many that sprang up in the Midwest.

The village officialdom comprises a Mayor and a Board of Trustees, the latter being six in number. All are Negros. There is a Police Dept., a Fire Dept., (volunteer, but possessing a standard fire truck) a post office, and a fine grade school,—all named by Negros. Claire Boulevard (formerly Rexford Road) is the connecting highway between the Midlothian Turnpike and Crawford Ave., and runs directly through the center of the village. Here the dusky village caps, equipped with speedy motorcycles, are ever alert and constantly on duty; and unwary speeders along this highway contribute very largely to the coffers of the village treasury.

The town also has its business aspects; although there are no Lions, Rotarians, or other high-pressure groups of go-getters. There are grocery stores, barber shops, filling stations; beauty parlors, and taverns; about in the same proportions as in the average town of two thousand population. But the total volume of business is low, for the chain stores in Midlothian and Blue Island got most of the grocery trade, while the bargain counters of Chicago are also within easy commuting distance.

In the department of religion Midlothian is outstanding, for the town boasts sixteen churches; although there is little ground for boasting when considering these temples of the Lord from the standpoint of architectural beauty. The principal seats are—Baptist, Methodist, Seven Day Adventist, and Church of God in Christ. There are no Catholic or Episcopal churches, but a small group of Midlothian Negro Catholics attend services at the St. Christopher's Church, in Midlothian. There are eighteen "regular" ministers in Midlothian (sixteen of them are on relief or W. P. A.) and a number of "preachers" and "deacons" of no recognized standing except as purveyors of Bible lore and "bringers of light."

As might be supposed from the preponderance of churches there is practically no lodge activity in Midlothian, the church having supplanted the lodge. This may be explained by the fact that from seventy to eighty per cent of the population is on relief. And lodges cost money, whereas religion (as practised in Midlothian) is almost as free as the air. Despite reports of various "Surveys" there is no "Alpha and Omega Masonic Club" in Midlothian, nor any other official A. F. & A. M. organization. There are a few Masons, mostly elderly men who in better days were employed in well paying occupations. There are no jazz clubs, swing bands, or night clubs; and such limited social activities as prevail are strictly those of a small home-loving community. For, as previously stated, the Midlothian' Negro is a true suburbanite and has little in common with the Harlem swingster or the South Side night club devotee.

The ladies have an organization which staggers along under the cumbreus load of two different names, i. e.— The Community Welfare Club, and The Women's Improvement Club. They meet every Friday, the place of assembly being the parlor of a member's home. The village girls of about high school age have a fast softball team which

functions in natty romper-style uniforms of vivid green. The village grade school, an excellent brick edifice aptly named after the Great Emancipator—"The Abraham Lincoln School"—is located on 139th. St. just west of Claire Boulevard. It is presided over by eight colored teachers, and has an average attendance of about 500 pupils. The town has no newspaper of its own, but there is a local agent for the *Chicago Defender*.

The village has definite topographical advantages, being a level terrain dotted with four park-like lagoons. These are not abandoned quarries, or clay holes, but natural ponds. Thus the town has all the natural facilities for beautiful landscaping, despite the prevalence of shanties and dilapidated houses which mar its potential beauty. One Federal Writer (N. Hoen) tersely describes Midlothian as follows: "The side streets are mudholes. The general appearance of the town is characteristic of a Negro settlement." The implication being, of course, that shabby houses and shanties are Negro characteristics. Let me repudiate this insinuation most emphatically. Shanties and dilapidated houses are *not* racial characteristics, but economic factors. Poor people all over the world (regardless of race or color) live in hovels and inferior dwellings; while rich people live in fine houses. And the Midlothian Negro is striving mightily, under the most adverse economic conditions, to create a home for himself in a community of his own race. And he merits no little credit for his efforts. After this outburst of applause I take the liberty of extending a little criticism to my Midlothian friends:—they might have exerted themselves a little more in the way of weed eradication and tree planting.

Whence came the Midlothian Negro? Well, many of them are naturally from Chicago's teeming south side. They were motivated by the same objectives that prompt the white apartment dweller to throw his accumulated rent receipts into the landlords face as a final gesture of defiance and release. . . . A humble dwelling with a small plot of ground to raise corn, carnations, cabbages, and carrots; a few chickens; a luscious goose or two;

and perhaps a shoat to fatten for next minter's lar-der. This is the perennial dream of the incipient surburbanite. But the Chicago suburban develop-ments were restricted, and Negros more rigidly barred. Then, in 1917, Eugene S. Midlothian sub-divided this area and incorporated it for the express purpose of providing a Chicago suburban village for the colored people. The Negroes of Chicago were not slow to grasp the opportunity. Some of them were workers skilled in the building trades, there was an ex-Pullman porter or two, many com-mon laborers, a few college graduates, and a sprin-kling of share croppers and plantation hands fresh from the south. Some purchased modest dwellings hastily erected by the real estate firm, while many could only muster the down payment for a lot. As there were no building restrictions these latter sub-urban aspirants haphazardly gathered a quantity of second-hand lumbers (perhaps some old car sid-ing) some sheet tin, some cheap roofing paper, and assembled what was merely intended to be a

temporary abode. Later, when they worked and saved a little money, they would build "real" homes. Certainly it was not their fault that these fond hopes were but infrequently consummated.

Thus we find in Midlothian a conglomerate of various Negro elements. And in this melting pot of Suburbia these diverse elements are being welded into a definate type—the suburban Negro. That this classification has already assumed a concrete form is quite evident. A Chicago city Negro meets a friend from Midlothian and the following jovial dialogues ensues:

"Hi yah, plow chauffeur," greets the Chicagoan.
"G'long, yo' flat-footed State Street Susie Q, "answers the suburbanite.
"G'wan, yo' Midlothian hayseed."

Source: Philipp, Alfred O. "Robbins Illinois: A Folklore in the Making." Midlothian, IL: 1939. Library of Congress, Manuscript Division, WPA Federal Writers' Project Collection.

Garnett Laidlaw Eskew, "Coonjine in Manhattan"
(1939)

Although much African American history of the 20th century is recorded in church records, long-defunct community newspapers, and other obscure archives, the bulk of it died with the elders in communities throughout the United States who took what they remembered to their graves. The bulk of African American history is found in an oral tradition that is rapidly disappearing. Works Progress Administration writer and researcher Garnett Laidlaw Eskew reconstituted an obscure piece of that history in this essay entitled "Coonjine in Manhattan"—a scion of river lore about black dock workers who were known as "Coonjine."

On a bright October afternoon I walked along pier-lined West Street that borders the Hudson shore in New York City. Near at hand the city roared past; beyond, rose the Jersey cliffs. Here on West Street there is always a crowding and pushing of ocean vessels—transatlantic and coastwise ships; freighter and "luxury liners"—lying in at their berths, thrusting sharp prows against the very city pavements, or edging away from their wharves in the wake of straining tugboats.

Today there were, as always, crowds of steve-dores, longshoremen, and dock laborers on hand, busy about the loading and unloading of cargoes arriving from, or destined for, the ports of the seven

seas. Solidly these men went about their work—
Hungarians, Italians, Irishmen, Germans, Swedes,
with a fair scattering of the native born product.
They seemed to toil with a grim desperation as
though the work they did was distasteful but
necessary.

Among the crowd of laborers on this particular
day, however, was one—a powerful, gray-haired
old Negro—who alone seemed to be enjoying his
back-breaking duties. For he was singing at his
work. Singing:—chanting, in a rhythmical barbaric sort of regularity, a kind of song that awoke
vague nostalgia longings in my innards. Coonjine!
Was it possible, I asked myself, that here in New
York there was a steamboat roustabout—a
"Coonjine Nigger"—from the Mississippi country? A stray from my native Midlands and South?

Looking at him closely I could not doubt it. He
wore the conventional old battered hat turned up in
front, the gunny sack fastened with nails across his
chest and shoulders.

Anyone reared along the Inland rivers would
know that this was the characteristic dress of the
steamboat roustabout, from Cairo, Ill. to St. Louis;
from Cincinnati to New Orleans.

I listened carefully to his song as he laid down
on the dock a large box from his shoulder and
turned back to the ship again.

> Love her in de sunshine,
> Love her in de rain!
> Treats her like a white gal,
> She give my neck a pain!
> De mo' I does for Sadie Lee
> De less dat woman thinks er me!

I had never heard the words before but his manner of singing them smacked undeniably of the
river Negro. There was a guileless naivete that I
could not mistake. Back in the days when the
queenly white steamboats of the Mississippi,
the Ohio and Illinois Rivers, were busy carrying
the freight and passengers of the American Inland
Empire, an army of freight handlers was necessary
to take care of the loading and unloading. At one
time in the middle of the nineteenth century before

the railroads had fully come, nearly two thousand
steamboats steamed gracefully along the rivers.
One fairly good-sized boat carried fifty roustabouts. Therefore, you can at once apprehend the
great need, for strong arms and backs to do the
loading and unloading at the city landings where
the boats touched.

Along the rivers that border Southern Illinois,
Kentucky and the Southern States, Negroes gravi-
tated instinctively to the river life. Steamboating
appealed to them because of its inherently nomadic
character, its constant change of scene, its hours of
pleasant idleness on deck, between landings, when
a black boy could rest and sleep and roll the spotted ivories with his buddies. The wages were relatively good. Particularly, the food was plentiful
and substantial. And that was an important factor
in any job!

And so from the beginning of steam transportation on the Mississippi (1817) the Negro, as a
freight handler—known locally as a roustabout, or
in the vernacular a "rouster"—became an important figure in the mid-American scene. Especially
after the long arm of emancipation had freed the
slaves and they sought out their own careers.

A roustabout's job while it lasted . . . rolling cotton bales over the stageplanks, carrying tierces of
lard and sides of bacon, swinging a recalcitrant pig
calf over the shoulder, carrying it squealing along,
working in all kinds of weather, and under the constant tongue lashings of a profane and two-fisted
steamboat mate . . . was about as hard a job as could
be found. Yet the Negroes loved it because there was
plenty of time between landings for "restin' up."

And there was another way to lighten the labor.
If a boy put his mind on his work and kept it there,
he could not long stand up under the strain. But if
he sang while he worked, "released his spirit on
the wings of song" while his back bent and the
sweat trickled copiously from his pores, he would
forget his weariness.

There is in every rightly constructed Negro a
profound sense of rhythm, an inherent love for the
beat and timing of music, running back to African
days. He sings as naturally as he eats. It was to

alleviate the weariness of carrying freight on and off the steamboats, that the roustabouts sang. And the songs they sang and the shuffling, loose kneed dance-job-trot to which they timed their movements, became known among themselves as the Coonjine.

It was such a song that I heard this gray haired brawny Negro singing on the West Street docks, a thousand miles away from the Mississippi country, on this October afternoon.

(No one seems to know definitely where the name "coonjine" came from. Harris Dickson, well known author of Vicksburg, Miss., and an authority on Negro lore, says that the word is possibly of African origin and points out the word "Coonjai" was the African term for a tribal dance. But, Judge Dickson explains farther, roustabouts didn't run much to "derivations"—to Greek or Latin roots. Whenever they wanted a word they made it up offhand, and usually the word they coined filled the bill so perfectly that it stuck. It may have been so with Coonjine.)

Coonjine songs were not spirituals—neither the genuine nor the "Broadway" variety. There was nothing spiritual about them that I have been able to discover.

Into these songs the rousters put the problems and the incidents of the day's labor, the characteristics of the people they met. The peculiarities of a mate or captain or fellow rouster; the speed and qualities of a particular boat; the charms or meanness of a woman-friend; domestic matters—all these were subjects which the steamboat roustabouts move into the texture of the Coonjine songs with which they lightened the labor of steamboat work. Composed sometimes on the spur of the moment, or garbled versions of songs previously heard, often the words were ridiculous, sometimes senseless, but nearly always ludicrous with occasionally a touch of pathos:

Old roustabout aint got no home,
Make his living on his shoulder bone!
***

There came a lull in the unloading of the ship. The Negro exhaled gustily, mopped his brow and chancing to glance in my direction, grinned and shook his head.

"Sho' is hot!" he announced, "and man is I tired!"

I beckoned him over to one side.

"What boats you work on?" I asked him. "Ever roust on the Kate Adams?"

At which his smile broadened and he broke out in a loud guffaw.

"Go 'long, Boss! You come frum down on the River? Lawd, Lawd! Yassur, I sho'ly did wuk on de ole Lovin Kate. Dat's whut we useter call de Kate Adams. I wuk on Cap'n Buck Layhe's Golden Eagle, too, an' on de City er Louisville and City er Cincinnati, up on de Ohio River. One time, 'bout fifteen years ago, I rousted fer Ole Cap'n. Cooley up de Ouachita River. Yassuh!" He turned scornfully to the group of laborers still carrying articles of freight, "Dese hyuh dagoes and furriners—dey don't know nuthin' bout roustin'! Dey doan know nothin' bout Coonjine, like us does out on de river."

"Do you remember any more of those Coonjine songs?" I asked him. Whereupon he at once became a trifle reticent and embarrassed.

"Laway, hit wuz so long ago I mos' fergit 'em. I useter know a lot dem songs when I wuz a young buck. But sense I done got ole, I got me a wife and jined de chu'ch and fergit mos' all dem ole Coonjine songs."

"But you were singing just now," I told him.

"Wuz I?" he asked, his eyes wide. "Well, dat—dat wuz jes cause I wuz workin', boss!" Presently he resumed: "I 'members one song we uster sing on de Lizzie Bay, when she was runnin' from Ragtown ter Cairo."

"Ragtown? Where was that?"

"Aw— dat's jes' de name de rousters give her Cincinnati. So many rags wuz sold and shipped out on de boats ter make paper outen.

"Dat song went dish here way:
De ole Lizzie Bay she comin' roun' de ben'
All she's a doin' is killin' up men.
De ole Lizzie Bay she's a mighty fine boat
But hit take nine syphon ter keep her afloat.

An' boss, you member dat song bout

Who been hyuh sints I bin gone?
Big ole rouster wid a derby on,
Layin' right dar in my bed
Wid his heels crack open like cracklin' bread.
I whoop my woman and I black her eye,
But I won't cut her th'oat kaze I skeered she
might die. . . ."

I had heard garbled versions of this epic at various river towns, even as I had heard variations of that well-nigh unprintable song with the recurring refrain of "Rango—Rango" and the often twisted, "Roll, Molly, Roll."

This seemed to please him mightily. Under pressure, and in acknowledgement of some silver change, he recalled others of the songs he had chanted years ago, in the days when the big steamboats ran—recalled them slowly, one by one, each song suggesting another. Standing there with him in the West Street pier shed, I gathered a sizeable collection of Coonjine songs. Many, I have no doubt, bore only a slight resemblance to the original wordings. For roustabouts felt, so long as they preserved the thought and central idea and rhythm of a song, they could change the words at will. Sometimes they abandoned the existing words and made up new words of their own. I have heard different versions of barely recognizable Coonjine songs in various towns from St. Louis to the Delta. Once, an antiquated porter at the old Holliday House, fronting the river at Cairo, Ill., sang this one for me:

"Whar wuz you las' night?
O tell me whar you wuz las' night?
Rattin' on de job
In Saint Chawles Hotel."

Which requires some explanation. "Ratting" in rouster lingo for "loafing." The St. Charles Hotel referred, not to the historical hostelry in New Orleans of that name, but to a warm cleared space beneath the steamboat boilers on the lower deck on any boat where the rousters, whenever they were able to dodge the vigilant eye of the mate, were wont to hide away and sleep.

Many a boat has been loaded, down in the cotton country, to the tune of a two line doggerel:

I chaws my terbacker and I spits my juice,
Gwinter love my gal til hit ain't no use.

Roustabouts were always hungry. Near the steamboat landing in Vicksburg there stood, back in the eighties and nineties, an old brick bakery which specialized in "nigger belly"—that is, long slabs of ginger bread which sold at the rate of two for five cents. The roustabouts called it "boozum bread."

Boozum bread, boozum bread,

I eats dat stuff till I dam near dead!—sang the roustabouts of the Belle of the Bends of the Senator Cordell or the Belle Memphis, or any other of a dozen boats. Which also requires some explanation. In carrying articles of freight up and down the stageplank a roustabout had to use both hands to balance it on his shoulder or head. So he would stuff a strip of ginger bread under his shirt bosom next to his skin, the top extending up almost to his collar. By ducking his chin he could bit out chunks of the stuff (soon softened by sweat) without interference with his work. Hence the name, Boozum (bosom) bread.

Vicksburg roustabouts were also partial to this song, which had reference to a certain one-armed hard-fisted steamboat mate, named Lew Brown.

Taint no use for dodgin' roun'
Dat ole mate jes' behine you.
Better cut dat step and coonjine out
Dat ole jes' behine you!

But the songs eulogising the boats themselves stick longer in my mind than any others. There was something intensely personal about a steamboat. To the men who manned and owned and operated them, steamboats had personality. Hence the qualities of certain boats live today in Coonjine songs. . . .

The boats of the Lee Line, in the Memphis-New Orleans trade until a few years ago, fed the passengers and crews well; but paid notoriously low wages. Still the Negroes liked to work for the Lee Line. The reason is to be found in this song:

Reason I likes de Lee Line trade,
Sleep all night wid de chambermaid.
She gimme some pie and she gimme some cake,
An' I gi' her all de money dat I ever make!

The Anchor Line boats (running from 1869–1911) were each named for a Mississippi River City, and fine St. Louis and New Orleans packets, noted for speed, sumptious cabins and elaborate cuisine. I once met, up on the Ohio River, an old roustabout who called himself Ankline Bob—because, he said, he had worked for the Anchor Line. Bob had the lowdown on the different Anchor Line boats:

Dey wuks you hawd but dey feeds you fine
On dem big boats er de Anchor Line.

There was intense rivalry between the different boats of this line. Notably that between the City of Cairo and the City of Monroe. Both were fine and fast, but the Cairo was once said to have a slight edge for speed on the Monroe. Whereupon the roustabouts on the Monroe would sing:

De City of Cairo's a mighty big gun,
But lemme tell you whut de Monroe done:
She lef' Baton Rouge at haff pass one
An' git ter Vicksburg at de settin' er de sun.

Another Anchor Liner; the City of Providence, was nicknamed by the roustabouts "The Trusty Trus" for the reason that her mate was always willing to trust a rouster with a dollar until pay day. They would sing:

Me and muh woman done had a fus . . .
Gwinter take a little trip on de Trusty Trus!
I owes de lanlady fifty cents,
Gwinter roust on de Providence

A song that was popular in America twenty years ago was "Alabama Bound." An ex-roustabout on the St. Louis levee once explained to me that this song was originally a Coonjine song. The steamboat Saltillo was a doughy little sternwheeler which late in the evening used to pull away periodically from the landing and turn her nose southward down the Mississippi. At Cairo she would turn into the Ohio and up that stream to the mouth of the Tennessee River, following the lovely channel of that river back into the Muscle Shoals section of Alabama which the great government dams are today being built to improve navigation.

With their usual happy facility for conferring euphonious nicknames, the Negroes called the Saltillo the Sal Teller.

Sal Teller leave St. Looey
Wid her lights tu'n down.
And you'll know by dat
She's Alabama bound.
Alabama bound!
She's Alabama bound!
You'll know by dat
She's Alabama bound!
Doan you leave me here!
Doan you leave me here!
Ef you's gwine away and ain comin' back
Leave a dime fer beer!
Leave a dime fer beer
Leave a dime fer beer!
Brother, if yu gwine away
Leave a dime fer beer!
I ask de mate
Ter sell me some gin;
Says, I pay you, mister
When de Stack comes in
When de Stack comes in
When de Stack comes in!
Says, I pay you mister,
When de Stack comes in.

The name Stack, recurring several times in the song, referred to one of the Lee Line boats, the Stacker Lee.

Mates and captain, far from objecting to coonjine, encouraged their roustabouts to sing. There was a sound utilitarian reason for this. Anyone who has worked with Negroes knows that they will work better when they work to music, timing their movements to the beat of the tune. A thousand tons of miscellaneous freight and a few hundred bales of cotton could be loaded, to the beat and time of Coonjine, in half the time that songless labor would demand.

Coming up the Mississippi on Captain Cooley's little sternwheeler Ouachita in company with Roark Bradford, one early spring, I learned this song from that skillful portrayer of the Negro character:

This was a cotton-loading song heard frequently on the docks at New Orleans.

> Catfish swimmin' in de river
> Nigger wid a hook and line
> Says de catfish, Lookyere, Nigger,
> You ain' got me dis time.
> Come on, bale (spoken)—got yuh!

And there was another value to Coonjine. Moving in perfect time meant that the rousters' feet hit the stageplank with uniform precision. A wise thing, too! For if a rouster should step upon the vibrating boards out of time, and thus catch the rebound of the stage-plank, he was very likely to be catapulted with his load over into that muddy bourne from which no roustabout returns—or rarely so.

A general opinion prevails throughout the River Southland that nobody but the Negroes can sing Coonjine. This may be true, for if you have ever tried to capture a Coonjine tune from hearing a Negro sing it, you must have realized how utterly futile it is to put down in cold black and white on paper the color and barbaric beauty of the tones.

However, an attempt is being made—as this is written—by an accomplished musical composer in Paducah, Kentucky, to bring out a book of Coonjine songs with music. Such a collection would be an invaluable addition to our vanishing Americana.

For this phase of American life is fast vanishing. With the coming of the railroads, the steamboats (as we knew them once) have gone. So have the black freight handlers who by their songs and ever-rebounding good nature, added much to the pleasure of steamboat travel. Many of the old roustabouts have died. More have left their native South and come to the north to live with grown-up "chillens." You will find them, not only on the West Street docks in New York, but in Cleveland, Chicago, Cincinnati and other cities.

And to those black "creators of American folk-lore" the writer ascribes this brief tribute.

Source: Eskew, Garnett Laidlaw. "Coonjine in Manhattan." Chicago, 1939. Library of Congress, Manuscript Division, WPA Federal Writers' Project Collection.

Ellis Williams, "Down in the West Indies"
(January 1939)

Although much has been written about the great migration of rural blacks who fled the South for new lives in northern cities in the first part of the 20th century, little has been written in American history books about migrants who were fleeing the widespread poverty among blacks in the Caribbean or merely seeking new lives in the United States as so many before them had done. In this piece written for the Works Progress Administration Federal Writers' Project, a West Indian immigrant named Ellis Williams talks about his experiences.

Down in the West Indies, I am a law clerk and stenographer. I was largely dependent on my parents for existence, and because of that I am discontented with my lot. I am Aquarius, born to travel they say. The nomadic urge engulfs me. I want to leave home and the dependency of my folk. I hear and read a lot of America. People say it is a "bed of roses." A fortune easy to acquire and a profession easier still. I want to go! I want to go!

I am only in my teens and my parents try to discourage me. I listen to their good counsel but cannot be dissuaded. I feel that I have been a parasite on them too long. I am going even if I suffer, and there is one thing certain, if I do, they will never learn it from me.

I saved my pence the lawyer paid me and booked a passage. Dad came to the rescue and furnishing me with a good cabin and placed me in the care of the captain who knows something of the family because of shipments of produce to America by the same line.

The trip is uneventful. America is beautiful, but I am anxious to get adjusted and find employment. I am assured it is only a question of time and perseverance. Encouraged, I go into the tall office buildings on lower Fifth Avenue. I try them all. Not a firm is missed. . . . I walk in and offer my services. . . . I am black, foreign looking. My name is taken and I will be sent for in a short time. "Thank you." "Good day." "Oh don't mention it." I am smiled out. I never hear from them again. . . .

Eventually I am told that this is not the way it is done in America. What typewriter do I use? Oh! . . . Well go to the firm that manufactures them. It maintains an employment bureau for the benefit of users of their machines. There is no discrimination there, go and see them." [Ere I go, I write stating my experience, etc., etc., etc., etc. In reply I get a flattering letter asking me to call. I do so.

The place is crowded. A sea of feminine faces disarms me. But I am no longer sensitive. I have gotten over that . . . long since. I grit my teeth and confidently take my seat with the crowd. At the desks the clerks are busy with the telephones, filling out cards and application blanks. I am sure I am not seen. I am just one of the crowd. One by one the girls, and men too, are sent out after jobs. It has been raining. The air is foul. The girls are sweating in their war paint. They are of the type that paints their lips, pencil their brows, rouge their cheeks. . . .

"Clothes, I am going downtown; if you want to follow . . . hang on." At last they get around to me. It is my turn.

I am in front position. In order to get to me the lady is obliged to do a lot of detouring. At first I thought she was about to go out, to go past me. But I am mistaken. She takes a seat right in front of me, a smile on her wrinkled old-maidish face. I am sure she is head of the department. It is a position that must be handled with tact and diplomacy. She does not send one of her assistants. She comes herself. She is from the Buckeye state. She tries to make me feel at home by smiling broadly in my face.

"Are you Mr. . . . ?" "Yes, I am."

"That's nice. How much experience you say you have had?" She is about to write.

"I have stated that in the letter, I think. I have had . . .

"I worked for . . ."

"Oh yes, I have it right here. Used to be secretary for a lawyer. . . . And you took honors in your class at school. That is interesting, isn't it?"

I murmur unintelligibly.

"Well," continues the lady, "we haven't anything at present. . . ."

"But I thought you said in your letter you had a position for me. I have it here with me. I hope I have not left it at home. . . ."

"That position wouldn't suit you," stammering. "It, t, t, t, t, t, it is a position that requires banking experience. It is one of the largest banks in the country. Secretary to the vice-president. Ah, by the way, come to think of it, you know Mr. . . . of Harlem?

"You do! I think his number is . . . Seventh Avenue. Here is one of his cards. Well if I were you I would go to see him. . . . Good day."

Dusk is on the horizon. I am once more on Fifth Avenue. I am not going to see the gentleman. The man she is sending me to was my father's groom.

January 11, 1939

Source: Williams, Ellis. "Down in the West Indies." New York, January 1939. Library of Congress, Manuscript Division, WPA Federal Writers' Project Collection.

Vivian Morris, "Laundry Workers"
(March 1939)

Works Progress Administration writer Vivian Morris visited a laundry where mostly black women were employed. An uninvited guest, she found a way to get inside the building and a skeptical management failed to notice her as she mingled with the workers inside. What she found offers a glimpse of the working lives of women whose stories were rarely told outside of the neighborhoods where they lived.

It was just about noon, early in March, at the West End Laundry downtown in New York City where black women work in the ironing department. The foreman there eyed me suspiciously and then curtly asked me, "What you want?" I showed him a Laundry Workers Union card (which I borrowed from an unemployed laundry worker, in order to ensure my admittance) and told him that I used to work in this laundry and I thought I would drop in and take a friend of mine who worked there out to lunch.

He squinted at the clock and said, "Forty minutes before lunchtime. Too hot in here and how. Better wait outside."

"But," I remonstrated, "the heat doesn't bother me. I used to work in here."

"Say," he ignored my argument, "no fishy back talk and get outside." He watched me until I was out of sight and then he left the room. I promptly darted back into the ironing room where my friend worked.

The clanging of metal as the pistons banged into the sockets, the hiss of steam, women wearily pushing twelve pound irons, women mechanically tending machines—one, button half of the shirt done; two, top finished; three, sleeves pressed and the shirt is ready for the finishers—that was the scene that greeted me as I stood in the laundry's ironing department.

Shirts, thousands of white shirts that produced such a dazzling glare that the women who work in this department wore dark glasses to protect their eyes. The heat was almost unbearable; there seemed to be gushes of damp heat pushed at you from some invisible force in the mechanism of the machine. The smooth shiny-faced women worked in silence, occasionally dropping a word here and there, slowly wiping away dripping perspiration, then back to the machines, to the heavy irons without any outward show of emotion—no protest. The morning had been long and arduous, this was Wednesday a heavy day, but thank God half the day was nearly over.

The heavy, strong-armed woman paused the iron, arms unflexed, and glanced at the clock. She smiled. Forty-five minutes until eating time. A soft contralto voice gave vent to a hymn, a cry of protest, as only the persecuted can sing, warm, plaintive, yet with a hidden buoyancy of exultation that might escape a person who has not also felt the pathos and hopes of a downtrodden, exploited people.

She sang, a trifle louder, "Could my tears forever flow, could my zeal no languor know. Thou must save, and thou alone, these fo' sin could not atone; In my hand no price I bring. Simply to his cross I cling."

The women tended their machines to the tempo of the hymn. They all joined in on the chorus, their voices blending beautifully, though untrained and unpolished they voiced the same soulful sentiment, "Rock of Ages, cleft for me. Let me hide myself in thee." Stanza after stanza rang from their lips, voicing Oppression centuries old, but the song rang out that the inner struggle for real freedom still lit a fiery spark in the recesses of the souls of these toiling women.

The song ended as it began with soft words and humming. One squat, attractive young woman, who single handedly handled three of the shirt machines, began a spirited hymn in militant tempo, with a gusto that negated the earlier attitude of fatigue the entire crew of the ironing room joined in either humming or singing. They were entering the final hour before lunch but to judge from the speed that the song had spurred them to, you would believe they were just beginning. The perspiration dripped copiously but it was forgotten. The chorus of the hymn zoomed forth.

"Dare to be a Daniel. Dare to stand alone. Dare to have a purpose firm and make it known—and make it known."

The woman who finishes the laces with the twelve pound iron wielded it with feathery swiftness and sang her stanza as the others hummed and put in a word here and there.

"Many a mighty gal is lost darin' not to stand . . ."

The words of the next line were overcome by the rise in the humming, but the last line was clear and resonant . . . "By joinin' Daniel's band." The chorus was filled with many pleasing ad-libs and then another took up a stanza. Finally the song died away.

Then the squat machine handler said to the finisher who guided the big iron, "Come on, baby, sing 'at song you made up by yourself, "The Heavy Iron Blues." Without further coaxing the girl addressed as "baby" cleared her throat and began singing. "I lift my iron, Lawd, heavy as a ton of nails. I lift my iron, Lawd, heavy as a ton of nails, but it pays my rent cause my man's still layin' in jail. Got the blues, blues, got the heavy iron blues; but my feet's in good shoes, so doggone the heavy iron blues." Then she started the second stanza which is equally as light but carried some underlying food for thought. "I lif my iron, Lawd, all the livelong day. I lif my iron, Lawd, all the livelong day, cause dat furniture bill I know I got to pay, Got the blues, blues, got the heavy iron blues, but, I pay my union dues, so doggone the heavy iron blues."

There was a sound of whistles from the direction of the river and the girls dropped whatever they were doing and there were many sighs of relief. Lunchtime.

March 9, 1939

Source: Morris, Vivian. "Laundry Workers." West End Laundry, 41st Street between 10th & 11th Avenues, New York. March, 1939. Library of Congress, Manuscript Division, WPA Federal Writers' Project Collection.

Betty Burke, "Jim Cole, Negro Packinghouse Worker"
(July 1939)

In Chicago, one of the places African American workers who came north from the rural South found steady work, was in the thriving meat packing business. This is the story of these workers, as told by one named Jim Cole to Works Progress Administration writer Betty Burke in Chicago in 1939.

I'm working in the Beef Kill section. Butcher on the chain. Been in the place twenty years, I believe. You got to have a certain amount of skill to do the job I'm doing.

Long ago, I wanted to join the AFL union, the Amalgamated Butchers and Meat Cutters, they called it and wouldn't take me. Wouldn't let me in the union. Never said it to my face, but reason of it was plain. Negro. That's it. Just didn't want a Negro man to have what he should. That's wrong. You know that's wrong.

Long about 1937 the CIO come. Well, I tell you, we Negroes was glad to see it come. Well, you know, sometimes the bosses, or either the company stooges try to keep the white boys from joining the union. They say, "you don't want to belong to a black man's organization. That's all the CIO is." Don't fool nobody, but they got to lie, spread lyin' words around.

There's a many different people, talkin' different speech, can't understand English very well, we have to have us union interpreters for lots of our members, but that don't make no mind, they all friends in the union, even if they can't say nothin' except "Brother," an' shake hands.

Well, my own local, we elected our officers and it's the same all over. We try to get every people represented. President of the local, he's Negro. First V. President, he's Polish. Second V. President, he's Irish. Other officers, Scotchman, Lithuanian, Negro, German.

Well, I mean the people in the yards waited along while for the CIO. When they began organizing in the Steel towns, you know, and out in South Chicago, everybody wanted to know when the CIO was coming out to the yards. Twelve, fourteen men started it, meeting in back of a saloon on Ashland, talking over what to do, first part of 1937. Some of my friends are charter members, well I got in too late. Union asked for 15 extra men on the killing floor, on the chain. Company had enough work for them, just tried to make us carry the load. After we had a stoppage, our union stewards went up to the offices of the company and talked turkey. We got the extra help.

I don't care if the union don't do another lick of work raisin' our pay, or settling grievances about anything, I'll always believe they done the greatest thing in the world gettin' everybody who works in the yards together, breaking up the hate and bad feelings that used to be held against the Negro. We all doing our work now, nothing but good to say about the CIO.

Source: Burke, Betty. "Jim Cole, Negro Packinghouse Worker," May 18, 1939. Library of Congress, Manuscript Division, WPA Federal Writers' Project Collection.

Ina B. Hawkes, "Negro Life on a Farm, Mary Johnson" (October 27, 1939)

This article by Works Progress Administration writer Ina B. Hawkes describes an interview with African American farmworker Mary Johnson in a dilapidated shanty in Athens, Georgia, in October 1939. She is identified as Mary Johnson but was also called Aunt Celia by relatives and locals.

The shack had wobbly banisters, decorated with a couple of torn quilts and a worn out mattress, several chinaberry trees and some widely scattered patches of dry grass in the yard, best describes Aunt Celia's home in Athens, Ga.

As I approached that little alcove faint humming tunes of an old slavery song became quite audible. At the door I hesitated a moment then knocked. The humming stopped; Aunt Celia, with a bedraggled broom in one hand, answered.

"Lawdy me, Miss! You scairt me near to death. Is dere sumpin I can do for you?"

"Well, Aunt Celia, it looks like you are too busy to do what I want," I answered.

"Lawd Miss! I'se done got all dese flo's scoured an' de windows washed an' ev'ything out sunning. We kin sit rat here in de sunshine and you kin tell me what you want. I'se gona rest a little while now till dese flo's dry and den I'se gona fix me some dinner."

After we walked out under the tree and sat on an old bench she continued, "Tell me something ob what you want Miss."

"Well, I said, "Aunty, I would like for you to tell me something of your life."

"All right if I kin remember sumpin to tell you dat will do some good."

I looked at Aunt Celia as she sat down. She was 78 years of age, but active and very pleasant to talk with. She was a short stout woman with a large goiter on the outside of her neck. Her hair was a little streaked with gray. Her hands were wrinkled from the strong soapy water she had been using to clean her windows. She looked at me and continued, "I know you think I looks a sight, Miss, but you know folks kaint stay clean doin' house cleanin' lak dis. I was born de second year after de surrender. We all was big farmers and had to work hard; us chillun would go to de field. At dinner time ma would bring our dinner and a big pail of water fo' us. We crawled up under de wagon to git in de shade. Pa would be tired, too, but he'd finally say, 'Come on out kids, lets go back to de fields now. We'se done rested long enuff.'

"My school days was short *farm worker* cause we was po' folks an' had to work. Co'se Miss, us had plenty to eat and some clo's.

"We lived close to Mr. William Henry Morton. I was getting up pretty good size an' Mr. Morton had a boy workin' fo' him dat he sho did lak. He got to noticin' me. I laked him too. Mr. Morton noticed us an' he knowed I was a smart gal, so he got us married right dere in his own house. He give us a small house to live in an' a mule an' cow an' some farm tools to work with.

"I started right out to havin' babies, but I was stout as a mule an' went to de fields just de same an' went side by side of Peter up dem cotton rows. We picked three hundred pounds of cotton ev'y day. I plowed, too. I would work right up till bedtime. My fust chile was born when I was thirteen; I didn't know what it was all about 'till I had the baby. But Miss, we didn't stop. I had a baby ev'y nine months *farm worker* till I had twenty-five. Now don't look at me lak dat, Miss, 'cause it is de truf.

"We made good as long as Peter lived. We tried to raise all of de chilluns right. Mr. Morton tol' us dat he thought we ought to stop a while.

"Well, some of den chilluns got up big enuff to git married and they started havin' chilluns right

when my las' chile was born. I was just ready to git down an' my daughter was sick with her's. I got dere an' done all I could fo' her an' went home and mine come. I prayed then, Miss, for God to never let me have no mo' babies, an' you know I stopped right then."

"Was Peter good to you during all this time Aunt Celia?"

"Oh, yes," she said, "we loved each other, only one time did he step out on me dat I knows of. A gal lived not far from us dat looked good. Mr. Morton had her there on his place to work. I was stayin' home mo' now an' Peter was in de field with dis gal. When her baby was born de po' gal died and left a baby boy. Nobody could tell who de pa was. Peter was right cute about it when he come and said, 'Ceila I'se dat baby's pa an' I want us to take him an' raise him. I asked him how come he didn't tell me befo' de gal died. He said, 'Celia, I was afraid you would kill dat gal, an' I didn't want you to go to de gallus an' be hund.' I don't think dey had no 'lectrik chairs den. We jus' took de baby an' let de matter drop 'cause we still loved each other.

"Miss, my pa and ma was slaves, but you know dey never would tell us much about it. I cain't remember who wus dere Mistess and Marster, but I remember hearin' dem say one time dat dey sho was good to 'em. Dey allus giv'em good food an' good clo's but dey wouldn't let them have any books. Dey would slip sometimes an' look at de papers an' try to read 'em.

"My grandma an' grandpa was slaves, too, Ma said. They had good white folk's and grandpa an' grandma married 'cause dere white folks owned both of 'em. You know, Miss, I guess dat is who I takes atter, 'cause dey had twenty-eight chilluns. Dat tickled dere white folks to death 'cause dey didn't have to buy no mo' slaves. Long as grandpa and grandma had chilluns dey had a big farm an' dat family of niggers was all dey needed, but I'se kind o' glad I won't born in dem days.

"I'se proud o' all my chilluns an' grandchilluns, too."

Just then a tall black negro girl came up with some sacks.

"Lawdy me, Miss, dis is my baby chile. Bless her heart; she allus thinks o' her ma."

She opened the sack and was surprised to find green peas and some other things. They shelled the peas and talked of some things which didn't interest me so I got up to go. Then Aunt Ceila said, "Wait Miss, I got some of the old folk's pitchers. I think I can git to the old trunk now widout tracking de flo'."

She was gone only a few minutes and then she came back carrying an old album with lots of old pictures taken back when hoop skirts and bustles were in style. Some of them were made in later years. After looking at the book she said, "I don't

live lak I uster 'cause my husband is dead an' gone now an' I'se getting too old to work. I washes sometimes and de chilluns help me out some."

I told her that it was getting late, that I would have to go now and that I enjoyed talking to her.

"Miss," she said, "when you go back to town go to de welfare people for me and tell dem I sho needs a coat an' some dresses 'cause I sho is necked."

I told her I would do my best and left.

Source: Hawkes, Ina B. "Negro Life on a Farm, Mary Johnson." Edited by Mrs. Maggie B. Freeman. Georgia Writers' Project, Athens. October 27, 1939. Library of Congress, Manuscript Division, WPA Federal Writers' Project Collection.

Al Thayer, as Told to Frank Byrd, "Harlem Parties"
(1939–1940)

There were many legends in the Harlem section of Manhattan, and none was more beloved than the one about a socialite named Dixie Lee. This story is about the night she was shot and killed. The story was told by Al Thayer to Works Progress Administration Writer's Project writer Frank Byrd.

Well, almost anybody will tell you that the gayest thing about Harlem in the old days (during the Prohibition Era) was its hectic parties. Everybody had them and they were thrown on the slightest provocation. Anybody's homecoming, dispossess notice, marriage or divorce was a more than reasonable excuse for a party.

Harlemites socialites and their conduct, in short, were much on the order of lower Manhattan's gay "400". Both thought and acted alike: jittery, sophisticated and inevitably bored. I had my fun along with the rest of them. Life was soft for any unattached young male with a passable wardrobe, a smooth line of chatter and a flair for the latest

dances. It was a cinch to get invited from one week-end party to another, where all expenses were footed by a fat, half-amorous hostess. It was also quite easy to put the bite on ones dull host for a ten or a twenty (never to be repaid, of course) whenever these affairs rolled around. I have even wangled myself a berth as a house-guest for as long as three or four months at a time. It was a soft living for all young writers, artists, struggling musicians and pseudo intellectuals. They were the fad in Harlem. Sponsoring them was definitely the smart, fashionable thing, a real diversion for the social upper-crust.

I remember one child whose parties I always loved to attend. They were so screwy and inconsistent that they were a never failing source of amusement—just like the person who gave them—little Dixie Lee, whom I am sure, all the Harlem old-timers remember with a deep, sincere affection.

It was the last party she ever gave, and typical of all the rest. Robert Van Doren came and, to the surprise of every one, brought his wife, Sonia, instead of the chorus boy that was his current weakness; Mamie Jones, Harlem's perrenial two-hundred pound play girl, had called while in the midst of a shower and when she learned that the party was already underway, took just time enough to slip on a bathrobe and mules, grab two bottles of scotch and hop into her roadster; Jay Clayton, the Customs inspector, who like everyone else, had forgotten when he was last sober, came breathless, hatless, and coatless, his bald head shiny with perspiration—somewhere enroute, he had fastened on to Pearl Buck, currently popular for her Pulitzer prize novel that had been dramatized, and presented by the Theatre Guild; Muriel Payne, author and lecturer, resplendent in blood-red transparent velvet and sporting a long ivory cigarette holder, tripped in escorted by her jet-black grinning gigolo; Lady Nancy Aintree, garbed in bright red beret, flat-heeled shoes and a noisy Johnson, the Negro sculptor just back in Harlem after three years in the gay haunts of Montmarte—he had apparently neither shaved nor had a hair cut in all that time.

Martha Lomax, uptown Now York's buxom, good-time night-life czarina, closed shop, bundled her girls into a fleet of taxis and put in her appearance to help celebrate Dixie's triumphant home coming from the country. A dress house customer, his curiosity aroused, bribed her to bring him along; Rusty Freeman, who had just completed a work-out at the gymnasium, came in a high-necked purple sweater and boasted a beautiful eye to match; after the Broadway new Black and Tan musical, Ethel Rainey, the blues singer, came locked in arms with the leading lady's understudy; Paul White, ex-prizefighter and singer, brought the ex-mayor's girl friend; Cherry McAlpin, who headed the uptown list of socially elite matrons sent the party into an uproar when she put in her appearance with her dapper physician husband in tow, thereby shattering a local precedent of ten years standing; young Reverend Milton Mallory, whose pugistically inclined wife kept him constantly indisposed, nursing black-eyes, fractured ribs and other minor injuries, restored things to normal by finally showing up with the person everyone expected him to bring—his chauffer's wife. There was a shortage of men, so Ace Glassman, the party wit, went down into the street and hailed two taxi drivers who willingly came in but soon admitted that the pace was too much for them.

It was a motley crowd, but they did not seem to mind each other. By midnight, the party was officially declared a success. Jeff, Dixie's boyfriend, insisted on making a round of the night clubs, however; so they piled into all the cars that were available, commandeered passing taxicabs for the leftovers, and ten minutes later, all were comfortably seated at and noisily pounding on the tops of ring-side tables at the Cotton Pickers Club. (Several hours later, those who did not go home and all who were able to, did the same thing in another club. What club it was, nobody knew nor apparently seemed to care.)

On the floor at the Cotton Pickers Club, however, a chocolate-brown girl with full breasts, a strong voice and swinging hips was singing. When she reached the high notes, large veins stood out on her throat and her voice became huskier than ever. After a series of slow sensual choruses, the band doubled its tempo and the girl began to tap dance—flinging herself wildly and indiscrimnately in every direction. Her breasts juggled up and down, all out of time with the rythm of her feet.

My mind was in a whirl and I found it increasingly difficult to hold my head up, yet I was vaguely aware of the thumping music, the prancing waiters and Dixie's boisterous friends. Suddenly I wanted to get away from all of this but could not seem to get up. "Damn this crowd, anyhow!" I thought. "Just a lot o damn smirking, highbrows doing back-flips trying to be funny." What the hell did they get out of it? Oh, to hell with them, anyway—they didn't mean anything to me, I thought. I'd probably never see half of them again.

Somebody poured me another drink. Automatically I drank it.

'You look sleepy, Jeff. Are you?' I heard Dixie ask Jeff.

'Well, I could stand a wink or two. Couldn't you?'

'Don't tell me you're ready to leave so soon?'

'Sure, why not?'

'Listen gang.' Jay Allen chirped, 'little Jeffie wants to go home.'

'Dear! Dear!' cooed Van Doren mockingly, 'Does he want his mama to tuck him in'?

'Naw.' Ace said menacingly, 'He's had experience with them kinda mama's.'

No one answered, or seemed to hear this. Then Lady Nancy piped up brightly—'That's it, lets all tuck the dear boy in!'

'Aw be your age, Aintree.' Ace said, turning away.

Lady Nancy was properly shocked but she would not give Ace the satisfaction of knowing it.

There was more entertainment, but it was entirely wasted on Dixie's party. They had a little show all their own that was beginning to provide serious competition for the house entertainers. Finally, they trailed out into the street. It was dawn. Jay, making a little desperate effort for the spotlight, climbed into a waiting milk wagon and drove down Lenox Avenue flourishing one of the women's evening wraps in his best charioteer fashion and announcing his wares to all sundry in a gin-hoarsened tenor. The others, between bursts of laughter and handclaps of approval, climbed into their cars or waiting taxicabs and drove away.

You probably remember "Young" Johnny Morano. He had made quite a name for himself "in the racket" and admitted it. It was a name to be reckoned with too—even in Chicago where he had finally set up headquarters. His few visits to New York marked the occasion for high revelry behind certain closed doors.

Whenever he condescended to make a public appearance, it was the signal in Harlem night life circles, for a welcome of splendor befitting the arrival of a local big shot.

Well, Johnny accepted it all with a silent dignity—a dignity that he thought becoming to the successor of "Tough" Tony Morano, his brother. He felt better than he had felt in many moons and his feelings were reflected in his face this night. He entered the Cotton Pickers Club to a burst of cheers and applause. He went from table to table greeting those of his old friends whom he recognized, but he never drank with them. He always drank alone. That was one of his hard and fast rules. He never was entirely alone, however, no matter how much he appeared to be. If you looked closely enough, you noticed a group of three or four silent but unusually alert young men hovering somewhere in the immediate background.

I'll never forget it even though I was pretty high. Until Johnny saw Dixie and Jeff, his face was a flushed picture of happiness; then it suddenly changed into a colorless mask with a thin white line for lips. He stopped, wheeled about and walked through a door near the orchestra platform. The silent, hardfaced young men followed him. Well, I suppose you know that Dixie Lee was once "Tough" Tony's girl and that during a fight in her apartment with Jeff Davis, Tony had been shot and killed while scuffling for possession of a gun. It was in all the papers.

Johnny spoke a few crisp words to his attentive young men. They did not answer him but two of them lighted cigarettes and sat down. The other two adjusted their hats, buttoned their tight-fitting spring coats and walked out into the street.

When Jeff and Dixie and I got into a cab, the two young men slouched in a long, blue sedan with soft felt hats tilted over their eyes. I saw them but thought nothing of it.

At the entrance to Dixie's apartment house, we stepped out of the cab; Jeff paid the driver and the three of us started in. This same blue sedan, rolling down the wet street, paused momentarily and sped away. During that few seconds hesitation, several shots rang out. At the first shot, Jeff dropped quickly to the ground and the next minute Dixie slumped down into his arms. The doorman who had gone inside the building came running out. A cop came also. Jeff told him what had happened. He called an ambulance.

While they were waiting for the ambulance, they carried Dixie inside and Jeff did what he could to make her comfortable. When the ambulance came, we climbed in with her. Jeff's face was a picture of agony and despair. Dixie smiled up at him and tried to put her arms around his neck but she couldn't. She sank back into the pillows.

'Don't worry about me, darling', she said. 'I'll be all right.'

The ambulance swerved into the courtyard of Harlem Hospital. Two attendants took Dixie in on a stretcher. The doctor told us to wait in the hall and we sat down on a bench. Finally the doctor came out and motioned us into the room where Dixie lay. Jeff looked at her and held her in his arms.

She looked all right but in back of her, the doctor was shaking his head. The next minute we knew what he was trying to say.

Outside Jeff said: 'It just don't seem possible. Only last night she was so alive and happy. I had never seen her so happy.'

Source: Byrd, Frank. "Harlem Parties, August 23, 1928, Al Thayer." Library of Congress, Manuscript Division, WPA Federal Writers' Project Collection.

Mitchell v. United States

(1941)

In April 1937, Congressman Arthur Wergs Mitchell, the first African American elected to Congress as a Democrat, was traveling by train from Chicago to Hot Springs, Arkansas. After the train crossed the Arkansas line, Mitchell, who had purchased a first-class ticket, was ordered to the black section in the second-class coach. The congressman complied to prevent violence, but later filed suit against the railway. Although his claim was dismissed by the Interstate Commerce Commission, Mitchell took his case to the U.S. Supreme Court, which, in Mitchell v. United States *(1941), unanimously declared that the congressman had been denied his "fundamental right of equality of treatment." The* Mitchell *decision, which is reproduced below, led to the immediate integration of first-class railway carriages and also to the eventual end of segregation in second-class coaches.*

Mr. Chief Justice HUGHES delivered the opinion of the Court.

Appellant, Arthur W. Mitchell, filed a complaint with the Interstate Commerce Commission alleging an unjust discrimination in the furnishing of accommodations to colored passengers on the line of the Chicago, Rock Island & Pacific Railway Company from Chicago to Hot Springs, Arkansas, in violation of the Interstate Commerce Act, 49 U.S.C.A. § 1 et seq. The Commission dismissed the complaint (Mitchell v. Chicago, Rock Island & Pac. R. Co., 229 I.C.C. 703), and appellant brought this suit to set aside the Commission's order. Upon a hearing before three judges, the District Court found the facts as stated in the Commission's findings, and held that the latter were supported by substantial evidence and that the Commission's order was supported by its findings. The court then ruled that it was without jurisdiction, and its dismissal of the complaint was stated to be upon that ground. The case comes here on direct appeal.

The following facts were found by the Commission: Appellant, a Negro resident of Chicago, and a member of the House of Representatives of the United States, left Chicago for Hot Springs on the evening of April 20, 1937, over the lines of the Illinois Central Railroad Company to Memphis, Tennessee, and the Rock Island beyond, traveling on a round-trip ticket he had purchased at three cents per mile. He had requested a bedroom on the Chicago-Hot Springs Pullman sleeping car but none being available he was provided with a compartment as far as Memphis in the sleeper destined to New Orleans. Just before the train reached Memphis, on the morning after leaving Chicago, he had a Pullman porter transfer him to the Chicago-Hot Springs sleeper on the same train. Space was there available and the porter assigned him a particular seat in that car for which he was to pay the established fare of ninety cents. Shortly after leaving Memphis and crossing the Mississippi River into Arkansas, the train conductor took up the Memphis-Hot Springs portion of his ticket but refused to accept payment for the Pullman seat from Memphis and, in accordance with custom, compelled him over his protest and finally under threat of arrest to move into the car provided for colored passengers. This was in purported compliance with an Arkansas statute, Pope's Dig. § 1190, requiring segregation of colored from white persons by the use of cars or partitioned sections providing 'equal but separate and sufficient accommodations' for both races. Later the conductor returned the portion of the ticket he had taken up and advised appellant that he could get a refund on the basis of the coach fare of two cents per mile from Memphis. That refund was not claimed from defendants and was not sought before the Commission, but it was found that the carriers stood ready to make it upon application. Appellant has an action at law pending against defendants in Cook County, Illinois, for damages incident to his transfer.

The Commission further found that the Pullman car contained ten sections of berths and two compartment drawing rooms; that the use of one of the drawing room would have amounted to segregation under the state law and ordinarily such combinations are available to colored passengers upon demand, the ninety cent fare being applicable. Occasionally they are used by colored passengers but in this instance both drawing rooms were already occupied by white passengers. The Pullman car was of modern design and had all the usual facilities and conveniences found in standard sleeping cars. It was air-conditioned, had hot and cold running water and separate flushable toilets for men and women. It was in excellent condition throughout. First-class white passengers had, in addition to the Pullman sleeper, the exclusive use of the train's only dining-car and only observation-parlor car, the latter having somewhat the same accommodations for day use as the Pullman car.

The coach for colored passengers, though of standard size and steel construction, was 'an old combination affair', not air-conditioned, divided by partitions into three main parts, one for colored smokers, one for white smokers and one in the center for colored men and women, known as the women's section, in which appellant sat. There was a toilet in each section but only the one in the women's section was equipped for flushing and it was for the exclusive use of colored women. The car was without wash basins, soap, towels or running water, except in the women's section. The Commission stated that, according to appellant, the car was 'filthy and foul smelling', but that the testimony of defendants' witnesses was to the contrary.

The Commission found that in July, 1937, about three months after complainant's journey above mentioned, the old combination coach was replaced by a modern, allsteel, air-conditioned coach, which was divided by a partition into two sections, one for colored and the other for white passengers, and had comfortable seats. In each section there are wash basins, running hot and cold water, and separate flush toilets for men and women. This coach, the Commission said, was 'as fully desirable in all its appointments as the coach used entirely by white passengers traveling at second-class fares'.

The Commission also found that the demand of colored passengers for Pullman accommodations over the route in question was shown to have been negligible for many years; that 'only about 1 negro to 20 white passengers rides this train from and to points on the line between Memphis and Hot Springs', and there is hardly ever a demand from a colored passenger for Pullman accommodations. The conductor estimated that this demand did not amount to one per year. What demand there may have been at ticket offices did not appear.

The Commission's conclusion was thus stated: 'The present coach properly takes care of colored second-class passengers, and the drawing rooms and compartments in the sleeper provide proper Pullman accommodations for colored first-class passengers, but there are no dining-car nor observation-parlor car accommodations for the latter, and they cannot lawfully range through the train'.

The Commission, though treating the enforcement of the state law as a matter for state authorities, thought that in deciding the case on the facts presented it must recognize that the state law required the defendants to segregate colored passengers; that in these circumstances the present colored-passenger coach and the Pullman drawing rooms met the requirements of the Act; and that as there was comparatively little colored traffic and no indication that there was likely to be such demand for dining-car and observation-parlor car accommodations by colored passengers as to warrant the running of any extra cars or the construction of partitions, the discrimination and prejudice was 'plainly not unjust or undue'. The Commission observed that it was only differences in treatment of the latter character that were 'unlawful and within the power of this Commission to condemn, remove, and prevent'.

From the dismissal of the complaint, five Commissioners dissented.

The United States as a party to this suit to set aside the Commissioner's order, and one of the appellees, does not support the judgment of the court below and has filed a memorandum stating its reasons. The Government concludes that the Commission erroneously supposed that the Arkansas Separate Coach Law applied to an interstate passenger and erroneously determined that the small number of colored passengers asking for first-class accommodations justified an occasional discrimination against them because of their race.

The other appellees—the Interstate Commerce Commission and the carriers—appear in support of the judgment.

First.—The Commission challenges the standing of appellant to bring this suit. We find the objection untenable. This question does not touch the merits of the suit, but merely the authority of the District Court to entertain it. The fact that the Commission's order was one of dismissal of appellant's complaint did not foreclose the right of review. Appellant was an aggrieved party and the negative form of the order is not controlling. Rochester Telephone Corporation v. United States.

Nor is it determinative that it does not appear that appellant intends to make a similar railroad journey. He is an American citizen free to travel, and he is entitled to go by this particular route whenever he chooses to take it and in that event to have facilities for his journey without any discrimination against him which the Interstate Commerce Act forbids. He presents the question whether the Act does forbid the conduct of which he complains.

The question of appellant's right to seek review of the Commission's order thus involves the primary question of administrative authority, that is, whether appellant took an appropriate course in seeking a ruling of the Commission. The established function of the Commission gives the answer. The determination whether a discrimination by an interstate carrier is unjust and unlawful necessitates an inquiry into particular facts and the practice of the carrier in a particular relation, and this underlying inquiry is precisely that which the Commission is authorized to make. As to the duty to seek a determination by the Commission in such a case, we do not see that a passenger would be in any better situation than a shipper. Texas & Pacific Railway Co. v. Abilene Cotton Oil Co., 204 U.S. 426, 27 S.Ct. 350, 51 L.Ed. 553, 9 Ann. Cas. 1075; Robinson v. Baltimore & Ohio R.R. Co., 222 U.S. 506, 32 S.Ct. 114, 56 L.Ed. 288; Mitchell Coal Co. v. Pennsylvania R.R. Co., 230 U.S. 247, 33 S.Ct. 916, 57 L.Ed. 1472; Morrisdale Coal Co. v. Pennsylvania R.R. Co., 230 U.S. 304, 33 S.Ct. 938, 57 L.Ed. 1494; General American Tank Car Corp. v. El Dorado Terminal Co., 308 U.S. 422, 60 S.Ct. 325, 84 L.Ed. 361.

The District Court had jurisdiction to review the action of the Commission and the question on that review was whether that action was in accordance with the applicable law.

Second.—The case was submitted to the District Court upon the evidence taken before the Commission. The undisputed facts showed conclusively that, having paid a first-class fare for the entire journey from Chicago to Hot Springs, and having offered to pay the proper charge for a seat which was available in the Pullman car for the trip from Memphis to Hot Springs, he was compelled, in accordance with custom, to leave that car and to ride in a second-class car and was thus denied the standard conveniences and privileges afforded to first-class passengers. This was manifestly a discrimination against him in the course of his interstate journey and admittedly that discrimination was based solely upon the fact that he was a Negro. The question whether this was a discrimination forbidden by the Interstate Commerce Act is not a question of segregation but one of equality of treatment. The denial to appellant of equality of accommodations because of his race would be an invasion of a fundamental individual right which is guaranteed against state action by the Fourteenth Amendment (McCabe v. Atchison, T. & S.F. Rwy. Co., 235 U.S. 151, 160–162, 35 S.Ct. 69, 70, 71, 59 L.Ed. 169; Missouri ex rel. Gaines v. Canada, 305 U.S. 337, 344, 345, 59 S.Ct. 232, 234, 83 L.Ed. 208) and in view of the nature of the right and of our constitutional policy it cannot be maintained that the discrimination as it was alleged was not essentially unjust. In that aspect it could not be deemed to lie outside the purview of the sweeping prohibitions of the Interstate Commerce Act.

We have repeatedly said that it is apparent from the legislative history of the Act that not only was the evil of discrimination the principal thing aimed at, but that there is no basis for the contention that Congress intended to exempt any discriminatory action or practice of interstate carriers affecting interstate commerce which it had authority to reach. The Shreveport Case, 234 U.S. 342, 356, 34 S.Ct. 833, 838, 58 L.Ed. 1341; Louisville & Nashville R. Co. v. United States, 282 U.S. 740, 749, 750, 51 S.Ct. 297, 300, 301, 75 L.Ed. 672;

Merchants' Warehouse Co. v. United States, 283 U.S. 501, 512, 513, 51 S.Ct. 505, 509, 75 L.Ed. 1227. Paragraph 1 of Section 3 of the Act says explicitly that it shall be unlawful for any common carrier subject to the Act 'to subject any particular person to any undue or unreasonable prejudice or disadvantage in any respect whatsoever'. 49 U.S.C. 3, 49 U.S.C.A. § 3. From the inception of its administration the Interstate Commerce Commission has recognized the applicability of this provision to discrimination against colored passengers because of their race and the duty of carriers to provide equality of treatment with respect to transportation facilities; that is, that colored persons who buy first-class tickets must be furnished with accommodations equal in comforts and conveniences to those afforded to first-class white passengers. See Council v. Western & Atlantic R.R. Co., 1 I.C.C. 339; Heard v. Georgia R.R. Co., 1 I.C.C. 428; Heard v. Georgia R.R. Co., 3 I.C.C. 111; Edwards v. Nashville, C. & St. L. Rwy. Co., 12 I.C.C. 247; Cozart v. Southern Rwy. Co., 16 I.C.C. 226; Gaines v. Seaboard Air Line Rwy. Co., 16 I.C.C. 471; Crosby v. St. Louis-San Francisco Rwy. Co., 112 I.C.C. 239.http://www.law.cornell.edu/supremecourt/text/313/80 - fn2

Third.—We find no sound reason for the failure to apply this principle by holding the discrimination from which the appellant suffered to be unlawful and by forbidding it in the future.

That there was but a single incident was not a justification of the treatment of the appellant. Moreover, the Commission thought it plain that 'the incident was mentioned as representative of an alleged practice that was expected to continue'. And the Commission found that the ejection of appellant from the Pullman car and the requirement that he should continue his journey in a second-class car was 'in accordance with custom', that is, as we understand it, according to the custom which obtained in similar circumstances.

Nor does the change in the carrier's practice avail. That did not alter the discrimination to which appellant had been subjected, and as to the future the change was not adequate. It appears that since July, 1937, the carrier had put in service a coach for colored passengers which is of equal quality with that used by second-class white passengers. But, as the Government well observes, the question does not end with travel on second-class tickets. It does not appear that colored passengers who have bought first-class tickets for transportation by the carrier are given accommodations which are substantially equal to those afforded to white passengers. The Government puts the matter succinctly: 'When a drawing room is available, the carrier practice of allowing colored passengers to use one at Pullman seat rates avoids inequality as between the accommodations specifically assigned to the passenger. But when none is available, as on the trip which occasioned this litigation, the discrimination and inequality of accommodation become self-evident. It is no answer to say that the colored passengers, if sufficiently diligent and forehanded, can make their reservations so far in advance as to be assured of first-class accommodations. So long as white passengers can secure first-class reservations on the day of travel and the colored passengers cannot, the latter are subjected to inequality and discrimination because of their race'. And the Commission has recognized that inequality persists with respect to certain other facilities such as dining-car and observation-parlor car accommodations.

We take it that the chief reason for the Commission's action was the 'comparatively little colored traffic'. But the comparative volume of traffic cannot justify the denial of a fundamental right of equality of treatment, a right specifically safeguarded by the provisions of the Interstate Commerce Act. We thought a similar argument with respect to volume of traffic to be untenable in the application of the Fourteenth Amendment. We said that it made the constitutional right depend upon the number of persons who may be discriminated against, whereas the essence of that right is that it is a personal one. McCabe v. Atchison, Topeka & Santa Fe Rwy. Co., supra. While the supply of particular facilities may be conditioned upon there being a reasonable demand therefore, if facilities are provided, substantial equality of treatment of persons traveling under like conditions cannot be refused. It is the individual, we said, who is entitled to the equal protection of the laws,—not merely a group of individuals, or a body of persons according to their numbers. Id. See, also Missouri ex rel. Gaines v. Canada, 305 U.S. pages 350, 351, 59 S.Ct. 236, 237, 83 L.Ed. 208. And the Interstate Commerce Act expressly extends its prohibitions to the subjecting of 'any particular person' to unreasonable discriminations.

On the facts here presented, there is no room, as the Government properly says, for administrative or expert judgment with respect to practical difficulties. It is enough that the discrimination shown was palpably unjust and forbidden by the Act.

The decree of the District Court is reversed and the cause is remanded with directions to set aside the order of the Commission and to remand the case to the Commission for further proceedings in conformity with this opinion.

It is so ordered.

Reversed and remanded with directions.

Source: Mitchell v. United States et al., 313 U.S. 80 (1941).

O'Neill Carrington, "In a Harlem Cabaret"
(1942)

O'Neill Carrington was a student at DeWitt Clinton High School in the Bronx. His poem "In a Harlem Cabaret" was published in 1942 and poignantly captures the legacy of the Harlem Renaissance.

Brown boys, yellah gals bending, swaying
Black boys joking, drinking, swearing
To the strident cry of a brass clarinet
In a Harlem cabaret.
Pegged legged pants and short silk skirts,
Flashy sheiks and buxom flirts
Swaying to the pleas of a shrill clarinet
In a Harlem cabaret.

A flash of steel, a piercing scream
A muffled thud, a shattered dreamy
A brown boy solos on a lone clarinet
In a Harlem cabaret.

Source: Carrington, O'Neill. *The Magpie.* DeWitt Clinton High School literary magazine. Winter 1942, Vol. 26, No. 1, 47. The New Deal Network.

James Baldwin, "Rendezvous with Life: An Interview with Countee Cullen" (1942)

Poet Countee Cullen was a leading figure of the Harlem Renaissance in the 1930s and 1940s. Novelist, essayist, and playwright James Baldwin was a leading African American literary figure of the 1940s, 1950s, and 1960s. Among his best-known works are Notes of a Native Son, The Fire Next Time, *and* Giovanni's Room. *Reproduced here is a poem by Cullen and Baldwin's commentary on Cullen's career, both of which illustrate how even the Great Depression could not prevent the continued emergence of African American cultural and literary achievements.*

I have a rendezvous with Life
And all travailling lovely things
Like groping seeds and beating wings
And cracked lips warring with a fife.
I am betrothed to Beauty, scarred
With suffering though she may be;
In that she bears pain splendidly
Her comeliness may not be marred.

The above lines were written twenty years ago by a Clinton schoolboy who in his senior year became Editor-in-chief of the *Clinton News* and of the Senior Issue of the *Magpie.* He handled both assignments with assurance and ease. Later he was to become one of Clinton's most distinguished alumni. His name is Countee Cullen.

"My first published poem," Mr. Cullen told me in a deserted classroom in the Frederick Douglass Junior High School where he now teaches, "was published without my knowledge in the *Clinton News.* It seems that there was a controversy between a Clinton teacher and an outsider in which the outsider held that high school students were unable to write acceptable verse, and the Clinton teacher held that they were. My poem was published to prove the Clinton teacher's contention— and it did," said Mr. Cullen, modestly.

That was the beginning of a distinguished career as a writer.

Countee Cullen was born May 30, 1903, the son of a Methodist minister and his devout wife. His father is still pastor of a church at One Hundred Twenty-eighth Street and Seventh Avenue. "My parents," Countee said, "had no objection to my being a poet, as writing poetry cannot be considered a means of making a livelihood."

"Why not?" inquired your startled reporter.

"Poetry," explained Mr. Cullen, "is something which few people enjoy and which fewer people understand. A publishing house publishes poetry only to give the establishment tone. It never expects to make much money on the transaction. And it seldom does."

Yours truly, who had been under the impression that one simply published a book, and sat back and watched the shekels roll in, sat aghast. "I never knew that," I said. "I guess a teaching job comes in pretty handy, then."

"Yes," he admitted. "Also, I *like* to teach."

Mr. Cullen then briefly reviewed how he had received his bachelor's degree at New York University, his Master of Arts at Harvard, and how in 1925 his first book of poetry was published. It established him at once as one of the important of the younger Negro poets and brought him in 1926 the post of assistant editor on the Negro magazine, *Opportunity*. In 1928 he received the Guggenheim Fellowship in Paris. The Guggenheim Fellowship, he explained to me, enables an author to live for a year, do nothing but write and still be alive at the end of the year. It sounds like something out of Shangri-la.

When his twelve month paradise had ended, Mr. Cullen came again to grips with earthly practicalities, and the exigencies of making a living. Eventually, he became a teacher of French in the aforementioned junior high school.

To date, Mr. Cullen has published six books of poetry, one of them being an anthology of Negro poetry, called *Caroling Dusk*. His latest, *The Lost Zoo*, written by request, he talked of as follows:

"Some of the children I was teaching had read of my work and wanted to become better acquainted with it. However, most of it was too far over their heads for them to be able to appreciate it. They asked me to write something that they could understand. *The Lost Zoo* is the result."

Needless to say, I rushed home and investigated the book. I found it a very charming fantasy told in verse except for its prologue and epilogue which are in prose. The title page says it was written by Christopher Cat and Countee P. Cullen. The prologue explains that Chris is Mr. Cullen's pet cat who has been with Mr. Cullen so long that they have even learned to talk to each other. Chris tells him the story of the lost zoo and Mr. Cullen passes it on to us. Chris supplies all the footnotes to the text and a wiser or more charming cat you have never met. However, you probably would not be too anxious to see him in a dark alley. There's something eerie about a cat who not only laughs but can, on occasion, be bitingly sarcastic.

The Lost Zoo tells the story of all the animals who were left behind when Noah built the ark. There was a sleep-a-mite more (the name describes him), the Squilililigee (the name gives you a clue as well as anything else might), the Wake-Up-World (who had twelve eyes of different colors) and "the Snake that walked upon his tail" (the female couldn't, just the male). All these animals and a great many more were left behind and drowned, and the story of the mass catastrophe is one of the author's most engaging pieces of work. It was written for children but this blasé grown-up enjoyed it more than the home-work he was supposed to have been doing.

Asking Mr. Cullen, as per custom, for some secret of success, I was told "There is no secret to success except hard work and getting something indefinable which we call the 'breaks.' In order for a writer to succeed, I suggest three things—read and write—and wait."

"Have you found," I asked, "that there is much prejudice against the Negro in the literary world?"

Mr. Cullen shook his head. "No," he said, "in this field one gets pretty much what he deserves. . . . If you're really something, nothing can hold you back. In the artistic field, society recognizes the Negro as an equal and, in some cases, as a superior member. When one considers the social and political plights of the Negro today, that is, indeed, an encouraging sign."

Mr. Cullen expects to have his latest book, "Autobiography of a Cat" published early in 1942. "It will be in prose," he said, "and one of my few attempts to get at the masses."

Source: Baldwin, James. "Rendezvous with Life: An Interview with Countee Cullen." *The Magpie*, DeWitt Clinton High School literary magazine, Winter 1942, Vol. 26, No. 1, 19. The New Deal Network.

President Harry S. Truman, Executive Order 9981
(July 26, 1948)

In July 1948, President Harry S. Truman signed Executive Order 9981, officially ending segregation in the United States military. The decision was prompted by widespread violence, murders, and executions of black military men and their families throughout the United States. Black civil rights leaders, most notably union leader A. Philip Randolph, and activist Grant Reynolds, demanded the president sign the order. Yet the signing of this order was not the end of discrimination against black soldiers in the military. The order made discrimination no longer official in the military, but de facto discrimination of blacks in the U.S. military continued for many decades in the areas of enlistment, promotions, and training opportunities.

EXECUTIVE ORDER 9981

Establishing the President's Committee on Equality of Treatment and Opportunity In the Armed Forces.

WHEREAS it is essential that there be maintained in the armed services of the United States the highest standards of democracy, with equality of treatment and opportunity for all those who serve in our country's defense:

NOW THEREFORE, by virtue of the authority vested in me as President of the United States, by the Constitution and the statutes of the United States, and as Commander in Chief of the armed services, it is hereby ordered as follows:

1. It is hereby declared to be the policy of the President that there shall be equality of treatment and opportunity for all persons in the armed services without regard to race, color, religion or national origin. This policy shall be put into effect as rapidly as possible, having due regard to the time required to effectuate any necessary changes without impairing efficiency or morale.

2. There shall be created in the National Military Establishment an advisory committee to be known as the President's Committee on Equality of Treatment and Opportunity in the Armed Services, which shall be composed of seven members to be designated by the President.

3. The Committee is authorized on behalf of the President to examine into the rules, procedures and practices of the Armed Services in order to determine in what respect such rules, procedures and practices may be altered or improved with a view to carrying out the policy of this order. The Committee shall confer and advise the Secretary of Defense, the Secretary of the Army, the Secretary of the Navy, and the Secretary of the Air Force, and shall make such recommendations to the President and to said Secretaries as in the judgment of the Committee will effectuate the policy hereof.

4. All executive departments and agencies of the Federal Government are authorized and directed to cooperate with the Committee in its work, and to furnish the Committee such information or the services of such persons as the Committee may require in the performance of its duties.

5. When requested by the Committee to do so, persons in the armed services or in any of the executive departments and agencies of the Federal Government shall testify before the Committee and shall make available for use of the Committee such documents and other information as the Committee may require.

6. The Committee shall continue to exist until such time as the President shall terminate its existence by Executive order.

Harry Truman
The White House
July 26, 1948

Source: Truman, Harry S. Executive Order 9981, Issued on July 26, 1948. Harry S. Truman Library, National Archives and Records Administration.

Ralph J. Bunche, Nobel Peace Prize Acceptance Speech (1950)

Reproduced here is the acceptance speech delivered by Ralph J. Bunche before the Nobel Committee. Bunche was the first person of color to win the Nobel Peace Prize. He earned the award because of his tireless efforts to secure peace in the Middle East, particularly in Palestine.

Your Majesty, Your Royal Highnesses, Mr. President of the Nobel Committee, Ladies and Gentlemen:

To be honored by one's fellow men is a rich and pleasant experience. But to receive the uniquely high honor here bestowed today, because of the world view of Alfred Nobel long ago, is an overwhelming experience. To the President and members of the Nobel Committee I may say of their action, which at this hour finds its culmination, only that I am appreciative beyond the puny power of words to convey. I am inspired by your confidence.

I am not unaware, of course, of the special and broad significance of this award—far transcending its importance or significance to me as an individual—in an imperfect and restive World in which inequalities among peoples, racial and religious bigotries, prejudices and taboos are endemic and stubbornly persistent. From this northern land has come a vibrant note of hope and inspiration for vast millions of people whose bitter experience has impressed upon them that color and inequality are inexorably concomitant.

There are many who figuratively stand beside me today and who are also honored here. I am but one of many cogs in the United Nations, the greatest peace organization ever dedicated to the salvation of mankind's future on earth. It is, indeed, itself an honor to be enabled to practise the arts of peace under the aegis of the United Nations.

As I now stand before you, I cannot help but reflect on the never-failing support and encouragement afforded me, during my difficult assignment in the Near East, by Trygve Lie, and by his Executive Assistant, Andrew Cordier. Nor can I forget any of the more than 700 valiant men and women of the United Nations Palestine Mission who loyally served with Count Bernadotte and me, who were devoted servants of the cause of peace, and without whose tireless and fearless assistance our mission must surely have failed. At this moment, too, I recall, all too vividly and sorrowfully, that ten members of that mission gave their lives in the noble cause of peace-making.

But above all, there was my treasured friend and former chief, Count Folke Bernadotte, who made the supreme sacrifice to the end that Arabs and Jews should be returned to the ways of peace. Scandinavia, and the peaceloving world at large, may long revere his memory, as I shall do, as shall all of those who participated in the Palestine peace effort under his inspiring command.

In a dark and perilous hour of human history, when the future of all mankind hangs fatefully in the balance, it is of special symbolic significance that in Norway, this traditionally peace-loving nation, and among such friendly and kindly people of great good-will, this ceremony should be held for the exclusive purpose of paying high tribute to the sacred cause of peace on earth, good-will among men.

May there be freedom, equality and brotherhood among all men. May there be morality in the relations among nations. May there be, in our time, at long last, a world at peace in which we, the people, may for once begin to make full use of the great good that is in us.

Source: Ralph Bunche Biography. From *Les Prix Nobel en 1950*, Editor Arne Holmberg, Nobel Foundation, Stockholm, 1951. Copyright © The Nobel Foundation 1950.

FBI Investigation of Malcolm X
(1953–1964)

Under the leadership of J. Edgar Hoover, director of the U.S. Federal Bureau of Investigation (FBI), the Justice Department launched a series of sweeping, long-term probes of U.S. citizens. Begun in the early 1950s, these domestic intelligence and spying operations were carried out in secret and were part of the Counterintelligence Program (Cointelpro).

According to FBI documents obtained under the Freedom of Information Act, these operations targeted a wide range of citizens, including prominent political figures, such as John F. Kennedy; entertainers, such as actor and singer Paul Robeson; notorious gangsters; and ordinary citizens suspected of affiliations with communist groups; and other people involved in activity deemed to be suspicious by the FBI bureaus or Justice Department officials in Washington.

Some of the primary targets of Cointelpro were black civil rights leaders, such as W. E. B. Du Bois; black union organizers, such as A. Philip Randolph; and "the leadership of so-called Nationalist-Hate Groups," according to FBI documents. Groups and leaders targeted by the program included Stokely Carmichael and H. Rap Brown of the Student Nonviolent Coordinating Committee, Dr. Martin Luther King Jr. of the Southern Christian Leadership Conference, Maxwell Stanford of the Revolutionary Action Movement, and Elijah Muhammad of the Nation of Islam (NOI).

Although political and civil rights activists, community organizers, the U.S. Congress, the courts, and government agencies had begun to take steps to assimilate African Americans into mainstream culture through legislation, court rulings, and political accommodations, the FBI's secret campaign handicapped their efforts to ensure the legal and civil rights of black Americans.

In February 1953, the FBI began an investigation of Malcolm Little, who was then living in Inkster, Michigan, according to official FBI memos. The FBI file said the agency began investigating him to verify communist influence. His FBI file totaled 4,065 pages at the time of his death in 1965. During the 11-year investigation, Malcolm Little became Malcolm X. He also rose to second in command in the ranks of the NOI, a black nationalist organization. By March 1964, however, following a dispute with the NOI leadership in Chicago, he had left the NOI and formed the Muslim Mosque, Inc. and the Organization of Afro-American Unity. He had also became known as the Minister of the NOI.

Malcolm X was assassinated in 1965 while delivering a speech in New York City. Norman Butler, Thomas Johnson, and Talmadge Hayer were convicted of Malcolm X's murder, and all three were sentenced to life in prison. The following is an excerpt from the Malcolm X file compiled by the FBI.

MALCOLM K. LITTLE currently resides at 23–11 97th Street, East Elmhurst, Queens, New York, a one family dwelling....

LITTLE is a key figure of the NYO [New York Nation of Islam Organization] and until December, 1963, he was the Minister of NOI Mosque #7, NYC, and the official national representative of ELIJAH MUHAMMAD the head of the NOI. He was considered to be the number two man in the NOI.

In December, 1963, he was suspended from the NOI for 90 days. Because of an alleged power struggle within the NOI in which members of ELIJAH's family fear that Malcolm will succeed to the leadership of the NOI, the suspension of subject was made indefinite in March, 1964.

On March 8, 1964, LITTLE announced that he was breaking with the NOI, although still a believer, and would speak out on his own forming his own "black nationalist" group. Although LITTLE indicated he would not form a rival organization to the NOI, it cannot yet be definitely determined whether he will or will not form his own defacto organization.

Mar. 19, 1964

NY 105–8999 CONFIDENTIAL

It is felt that a tesur on his telephone would provide invaluable information relative to his proposed activities in his new role, his supporters if any, and whether or not he will in fact establish his own organization.

Because of his split with the NOI, Bureau sources therein are of no value relative to LITTLE. Further, by this split he has deprived himself of working space and it is felt that most of his business will be conducted at his home and over his telephone.

The NYO requests authority to conduct a survey to determine the feasibility of placing a tesur on the telephone of LITTLE.

ROUTE IN ENVELOPE

To: SAC, New York (105–8999)

From: Director, FBI (100–399321)–86

MALCOLM K. LITTLE

INTERNAL SECURITY—NOI CONFIDENTIAL

REWRAIRTEL 3/11/64

Provided full security is assured, you are authorized to conduct a survey looking toward the installation of a technical surveillance on telephone [number] OL1–6320 at the home of Malcolm K. Little, 23–11 97th Street, East Elmhurst, Queens, New York.

Promptly advise results of same together with our recommendation regarding the installation of the technical surveillance.

Note:

Subject is former minister of Muslim Mosque Number 7, New York City, of the National of Islam (NOI) who was indefinitely suspended by Muhammad, national NOI leader, for his remarks concerning the assassination of President Kennedy. Little has now announced he will form a politically oriented organization more militant than the

NOI which will participate in civil rights activities. The New York Office believes technical surveillance on Little's residence would provide valuable information concerning his activities in this connection which would not otherwise be available

CONFIDENTIAL
Mar 23, 1964
UNITED STATES GOVERNMENT
Memorandum
To: Director, FBI DATE 3/30/64
FROM: SAC, NEW YORK (105–8999)
Subject: RECOMMENDATION FOR INSTALLATION OF TECHNICAL OR MICROPHONE SURVEILLANCE
RE; Title Malcolm K. Little aka

1. Name and address of subject: MALCOLM K. LITTLE 23–11 97th Street, East Elmhurst, Queens, NY

2. Location of technical operation: C

3. Other technical surveillance on same subject. NONE

4. Cost and manpower involved: Cost not known until installed.

5. Adequacy or security: Believed to be secured.

6. Type of case involved: Internal security case on Muslim Mosque, Inc., the newly formed black nationalist organization.

7. Connection or status of subject in the case: Leader and founder of the Muslim Mosque, Inc.

8. Specific information being sought: Information concerning contacts and activity of LITTLE and activity and growth of the Muslim Mosque, Inc.

9. Reasons for believing the specific information will be obtained by technical surveillance: LITTLE conducts business from his residence.

10. Importance of case and subject: Organization has philosophy of black nationalism, and has entered racial field where it suggests formation of rifle clubs by negroes to defend themselves.

11. Possibilities of obtaining desired information by other means (Explain in detail): Only other plausible means . . . Since the organization is new (announced 3/12/64).

12. Risks of detection involved: Negligible to none.

13. Probable length of technical surveillance: Unknown.

14. Request made for technical surveillance by any outside agency (name specific officials, title and agency): Not known.

15. Remarks: Recommend approval of installation.

16. Recommendation of Assistant Director.

4/22/64
Airtel
To: SAC, New York (105–8999)
From: Director, FBI (100–399321)
MALCOLM K. LITTE
INTERNAL SECURITY NOI CONFIDENTIAL
Provided full security is assured, authority is granted to install tesur on the residence of Little, 23–11 97th Street, East Elmhurst, Queens, New York telephone number OL 1–6320. Advise time and date of installation and symbol number, Sulet justification 30 days after installation and each three months thereafter.

April 22, 1964
6/4/64
AIRTEL
To: Director, FBI (100–399321)
FROM: SAC, NEW YORK (105–8999)
CONFIDENTIAL
SUBJECT: MALCOLM K. LITTLE aka
(00:New York
ReBuairtel dated 4/22/64.
Tesur on MALCOLM K. LITTLE, 23–11 97TH Street, East Elmhurst, Queens, NY, telephone number OL 1–6320, installed at 4:00 P.M., 6/3/64.

UNITED STATES GOVERNMENT
Memorandum
TO: DIRECTOR, FBI DATE 7/2/64
FROM: SAC, NEW YORK (105–8999)

SUBJECT: JUSTIFICATION FOR CONTINUA-TION OF TECHNICAL OR MICROPHONE SURVEILLANCE RE: Title MALCOLM K. LITTLE, aka

1. Name of person or organization on whom surveillance placed: MALCOLM K. LITTLE.

2. Address where installation made. Also give exact room number or area covered: 23–11 97th Street, East Elmhurst, Queens, New York (single family dwelling)

3. Location of monitoring plant:

4. Dates of initial authorization and installation: Authorized 4/22/64 Installed 4:00 P.M., 6/3/64

5. Previous and other installations on the same subject (with dates and places): None.

6. If installation is a technical surveillance, answer following questions:

7. If a microphone surveillance involved, state number of microphones actually used and location of each: No.

8. Is the installation part of_____? If so, give symbol of other side of the combination: No.

9. Specific examples of valuable information obtained since previous report which indicates specific value of each item and the information received. State what use was made of each item involved: See attached.

10. Could above information have been obtained from other sources and by other means? No.

11. _____
    _____ ?

12. Has security factor changed since installation?

13. Any request for the surveillance by outside agency (give name, title and agency): No.

14. _____
    _____ ?

15. _____
    _____ ?

16. Personnel Costs_____
    _____ ?

17. Remarks (By SAC): It is recommended that this source be continued in view of the prominence of LITTLE as a militant figure in the civil rights field, particularly as the leader of the Muslim Mosque, Inc and the organization of Afro-American Unity. Recommendation by Assistant Director: This technical surveillance is in the single family dwelling occupied by Malcolm K. Little, 23–11 97th Street, East Elmhurst, Queens, New York. It was first installed on 6/3/64. Little is a former national official of the Nation of Islam (NOI) who broke with that organization on 3/8/64 and formed Muslim Mosque, Incorporated (MMI) which he announced would be a broadly based black nationalist movement for Negroes only. Little has urged Negroes to abandon the doctrine of nonviolence and advocated that Negroes should form rifle clubs to protect their lives and property. At MMI rallies, Little has surrounded himself by guards armed with rifles and there have been numerous incidents recently involving gun-wielding MMI members where violence has been averted only by timely police action. At an MMI rally on 6/28/64, Little announced the formation of a new nonwhite civil rights action group called the "Organization of Afro-American Unity" with headquarters at MMI headquarters in New York City the aim of which would be to bring the United States racial problems before the United Nations and which would engage in civil rights demonstrations using the theme "by any means necessary."

In the past 30 days this technical surveillance has furnished valuable information on Little's travel plans, on the new Organization of Afro-American Unity, facts concerning the arrest of MMI members in Boston on a weapons charge following an altercation with Boston NOI members and information on a threat to Little's life by a person unknown. It also furnished information that Little was sending an assistant to Phoenix and Los Angeles to contact two women who had illegitimate children by Elijah Muhammad, NOI leader. Public announcement of these children by Little has caused the virtual state of war now existant (cq) between the NOI and MMI. On 6/30/64 information war between the NOI and MMI. On 6/30/64 information was received that Little sent telegrams to civil rights leaders Dr. Martin Luther King and James Foreman offering to send his followers to teach self-defense to Negroes if the Government did not provide Federal troops for protection.

All of the above information was furnished immediately to the Bureau and was disseminated to the Department and interested agencies. The Domestic Intelligence Division concurs with the recommendation of SAC, New York, that this installation be continued for additional three months.

UNITED STATES GOVERNMENT
Memorandum
DATE: July 28, 1964
TO: Mr. W. C. Sullivan
From: Mr. F. J. Baumgardner
SUBJECT: MUSLIM MOSQUE, INCORPORATED INTERNAL SECURITY—MMI

Reference is made to memorandum C. D. DeLoach to Mr. Mohr, dated 7/25/64, captioned "Racial Riots," and specifically to the last recommendation concerning establishment of additional technical and photographic surveillance coverage Malcolm X Little and the Muslim Mosque, Incorporated (MMI)

In connection with this matter it is noted Malcolm X Little is out of the U.S. on a tour of African nations and is not expected to return until 8/15/64. We presently have technical coverage on the residence of Malcolm X Little which is producing considerable valuable information. The New York Office has conducted surveys to determine whether additional installations are feasible . . .

A survey was also conducted by New York regarding the feasibility of installing microphone surveillances both at Little's residence and at the hotel. New York points out that the headquarters of MMI will be moved as soon as Little returns to the U.S. and such installations at this time would be impractical. New York also points out that microphone surveillances could not be monitored at the hotel or nearby . . . New York points out that the wife and child of Little are constantly at his residence and there are a number of Negroes constantly around the residence. Little has also maintained guards at his residence since receiving threats of bodily harm. Monitoring of microphone surveillances on the residence of Little could not be handled in the immediate neighborhood. Microphone coverage is not feasible at his residence.

CONFIDENTIAL
UNITED STATES GOVERNMENT
Memorandum
To: Director, FBI 10/2/64
FROM: SAC, NEW YORK

It is recommended that this source be continued in view of the prominence of LITTLE as a militant figure in the civil rights field, particularly as the leader of the Muslim Mosque Inc., and the Organization of Afro-American Unity. Plus the fact that source recently advised that MALCOLM, who has been in Egypt since July, 1964, at the expense of the Egyptian Government, and expected to return to New York on 11/15/64, has been appointed to the board of the Supreme Council governing Islamic affairs and is qualified to spread Islam in America among the Afro-Americans . . .

Source has furnished the following valuable information on dates indicated:

7/3/64 Information that MALCOLM notified New York City Police Department that an attempt was made on his life.

7/4/64 Information that MALCOLM and his followers were attempting to make a big issue out of the reported attempt on MALCOLM's life in order to get the Negro people to support Him. (Police believe complaint on an attempt on MALCOLM's life was a publicity stung by MALCOLM) (Teletype to Bureau 7/4/64).

Source: FBI Investigation of Malcolm X, 1953–1964. Freedom of Information request, Federal Bureau of Investigation, Department of Justice. http://foia.fbi.gov/foiaindex/malcolmx.htm.

Brown v. Board of Education
(1954)

One of the most important U.S. Supreme Court cases in American history, Brown v. Board of Education *reversed generations of jurisprudence. Officially overturning the separate but equal doctrine set by the 1896* Plessy v. Ferguson *decision, the Brown decision mandated that states provide for integration of schools. Arguing for the plaintiffs, young African American attorney Thurgood Marshall marked the start of a career that would eventually lead to a seat on the Supreme Court. The firestorm that erupted as a result of the decision provided the impetus for both pro- and anti-civil rights leaders in the 1960s.*

APPEAL FROM THE UNITED STATES DISTRICT COURT FOR THE DISTRICT OF KANSAS

Syllabus

Segregation of white and Negro children in the public schools of a State solely on the basis of race, pursuant to state laws permitting or requiring such segregation, denies to Negro children the equal protection of the laws guaranteed by the Fourteenth Amendment—even though the physical facilities and other "tangible" factors of white and Negro schools may be equal.

A. *The history of the Fourteenth Amendment is inconclusive as to its intended effect on public education.*

B. *The question presented in these cases must be determined not on the basis of conditions existing when the Fourteenth Amendment was adopted, but in the light of the full development of public education and its present place in American life throughout the Nation.*

C. *Where a State has undertaken to provide an opportunity for an education in its public schools, such an opportunity is a right which must be made available to all on equal terms.*

D. *Segregation of children in public schools solely on the basis of race deprives children of the minority group of equal educational opportunities, even though the physical facilities and other "tangible" factors may be equal.*

E. *The "separate but equal" doctrine adopted in* Plessy v. Ferguson, *163 U.S. 537, has no place in the field of public education.*

F. *The cases are restored to the docket for further argument on specified questions relating to the forms of the decrees.*

Opinion

MR. CHIEF JUSTICE EARL WARREN delivered the opinion of the Court.

These cases come to us from the States of Kansas, South Carolina, Virginia, and Delaware. They are premised on different facts and different local conditions, but a common legal question justifies their consideration together in this consolidated opinion.

In each of the cases, minors of the Negro race, through their legal representatives, seek the aid of the courts in obtaining admission to the public schools of their community on a nonsegregated basis. In each instance, they had been denied admission to schools attended by white children under laws requiring or permitting segregation according to race. This segregation was alleged to deprive the plaintiffs of the equal protection of the laws under the Fourteenth Amendment. In each of the cases other than the Delaware case, a three-judge federal district court denied relief to the plaintiffs on the so-called "separate but equal" doctrine announced by this Court in Plessy v. Ferguson, 163 U.S. 537. Under that doctrine, equality of treatment is accorded when the races are provided substantially equal facilities, even though these facilities be separate. In the Delaware case, the Supreme Court of Delaware adhered to that doctrine, but ordered that the plaintiffs be admitted to the white schools because of their superiority to the Negro schools.

The plaintiffs contend that segregated public schools are not "equal" and cannot be made "equal," and that hence they are deprived of the equal protection of the laws. Because of the obvious importance of the question presented, the Court took jurisdiction. Argument was heard in the 1952 Term, and reargument was heard this Term on certain questions propounded by the Court.

Reargument was largely devoted to the circumstances surrounding the adoption of the Fourteenth Amendment in 1868. It covered exhaustively consideration of the Amendment in Congress, ratification by the states, then-existing practices in racial segregation, and the views of proponents and opponents of the Amendment. This discussion and our own investigation convince us that, although these sources cast some light, it is not enough to resolve the problem with which we are faced. At best, they are inconclusive. The most avid proponents of the post-War Amendments undoubtedly intended them to remove all legal distinctions among "all persons born or naturalized in the United States." Their opponents, just as certainly, were antagonistic to both the letter and the spirit of the Amendments and wished them to have the most limited effect. What others in Congress and the state legislatures had in mind cannot be determined with any degree of certainty.

An additional reason for the inconclusive nature of the Amendment's history with respect to segregated schools is the status of public education at that time. In the South, the movement toward free common schools, supported by general taxation, had not yet taken hold. Education of white children was largely in the hands of private groups. Education of Negroes was almost nonexistent, and practically all of the race were illiterate. In fact, any education of Negroes was forbidden by law in some states. Today, in contrast, many Negroes have achieved outstanding success in the arts and sciences, as well as in the business and professional world. It is true that public school education at the time of the Amendment had advanced further in the North, but the effect of the Amendment on Northern States was generally ignored in the congressional debates. Even in the North, the conditions of public education did not approximate those existing today. The curriculum was usually rudimentary; ungraded schools were common in rural areas; the school term was but three months a year in many states, and compulsory school attendance was virtually unknown. As a consequence, it is not surprising that there should be so little in the history of the Fourteenth Amendment relating to its intended effect on public education.

In the first cases in this Court construing the Fourteenth Amendment, decided shortly after its adoption, the Court interpreted it as proscribing all state-imposed discriminations against the Negro race. The doctrine of "separate but equal" did not make its appearance in this Court until 1896 in the case of Plessy v. Ferguson, supra, involving not education but transportation. American courts have since labored with the doctrine for over half a century. In this Court, there have been six cases involving the "separate but equal" doctrine in the field of public education. In Cumming v. County Board of Education, 175 U.S. 528, and Gong Lum v. Rice, 275 U.S. 78, the validity of the doctrine itself was not challenged. In more recent cases, all on the graduate school level, inequality was found in that specific benefits enjoyed by white students were denied to Negro students of the same educational qualifications. Missouri ex rel. Gaines v. Canada, 305 U.S. 337; Sipuel v. Oklahoma, 332 U.S. 631; Sweatt v. Painter, 339 U.S. 629; McLaurin v. Oklahoma State Regents, 339 U.S. 637. In none of these cases was it necessary to reexamine the doctrine to grant relief to the Negro plaintiff. And in Sweatt v. Painter, supra, the Court expressly reserved decision on the question whether Plessy v. Ferguson should be held inapplicable to public education.

In the instant cases, that question is directly presented. Here, unlike Sweatt v. Painter, there are findings below that the Negro and white schools involved have been equalized, or are being equalized, with respect to buildings, curricula, qualifications and salaries of teachers, and other "tangible" factors. Our decision, therefore, cannot turn on merely a comparison of these tangible factors in the Negro and white schools involved in each of the cases. We must look instead to the effect of segregation itself on public education.

In approaching this problem, we cannot turn the clock back to 1868, when the Amendment was adopted, or even to 1896, when Plessy v. Ferguson was written. We must consider public education in the light of its full development and its present place in American life throughout the Nation. Only in this way can it be determined if segregation in public schools deprives these plaintiffs of the equal protection of the laws.

Today, education is perhaps the most important function of state and local governments. Compulsory school attendance laws and the great expenditures for education both demonstrate our recognition of the importance of education to our democratic society. It is required in the performance of our most basic public responsibilities, even service in the armed forces. It is the very foundation of good citizenship. Today it is a principal instrument in awakening the child to cultural values, in preparing him for later professional training, and in helping him to adjust normally to his environment. In these days, it is doubtful that any child may reasonably be expected to succeed in life if he is denied the opportunity of an education. Such an opportunity, where the state has undertaken to provide it, is a right which must be made available to all on equal terms.

We come then to the question presented: Does segregation of children in public schools solely on the basis of race, even though the physical facilities and other "tangible" factors may be equal, deprive the children of the minority group of equal educational opportunities? We believe that it does.

In Sweatt v. Painter, supra, in finding that a segregated law school for Negroes could not provide them equal educational opportunities, this Court relied in large part on "those qualities which are incapable of objective measurement but which make for greatness in a law school." In McLaurin v. Oklahoma State Regents, supra, the Court, in requiring that a Negro admitted to a white graduate school be treated like all other students, again resorted to intangible considerations: " . . . his ability to study, to engage in discussions and exchange views with other students, and, in general, to learn his profession." Such considerations apply with added force to children in grade and high schools. To separate them from others of similar age and qualifications solely because of their race generates a feeling of inferiority as to their status in the community that may affect their hearts and minds in a way unlikely ever to be undone. The effect of this separation on their educational opportunities was well stated by a finding in the Kansas case by a court which nevertheless felt compelled to rule against the Negro plaintiffs:

Segregation of white and colored children in public schools has a detrimental effect upon the colored children. The impact is greater when it has the sanction of the law, for the policy of separating the races is usually interpreted as denoting the inferiority of the negro group. A sense of inferiority affects the motivation of a child to learn. Segregation with the sanction of law, therefore, has a tendency to [retard] the educational and mental development of negro children and to deprive them of some of the benefits they would receive in a racial[ly] integrated school system.

Whatever may have been the extent of psychological knowledge at the time of Plessy v. Ferguson, this finding is amply supported by modern authority. Any language in Plessy v. Ferguson contrary to this finding is rejected.

We conclude that, in the field of public education, the doctrine of "separate but equal" has no place. Separate educational facilities are inherently unequal. Therefore, we hold that the plaintiffs and others similarly situated for whom the actions have been brought are, by reason of the segregation complained of, deprived of the equal protection of the laws guaranteed by the Fourteenth Amendment. This disposition makes unnecessary any discussion whether such segregation also violates the Due Process Clause of the Fourteenth Amendment.

Because these are class actions, because of the wide applicability of this decision, and because of the great variety of local conditions, the formulation of decrees in these cases presents problems of considerable complexity. On reargument, the consideration of appropriate relief was necessarily subordinated to the primary question—the constitutionality of segregation in public education. We have now announced that such segregation is a denial of the equal protection of the laws. In order that we may have the full assistance of the parties in formulating decrees, the cases will be restored to the docket, and the parties are requested to present further argument on Questions 4 and 5 previously propounded by the Court for the reargument this Term. The Attorney General of the United States is again invited to participate. The Attorneys General of the states requiring or permitting segregation in public education will also be permitted to appear as amici curiae upon request to do so by September 15, 1954, and submission of briefs by October 1, 1954.

It is so ordered.

Source: Brown v. Board of Education, 347 U.S. 483 (1954).

Robert C. Weaver, "Negro as an American"
(1963)

Reproduced here is an excerpt from a speech given in Chicago in June 1963 by Robert C. Weaver, the first black cabinet member in the administration of President Lyndon B. Johnson. He served as secretary of Housing and Urban Development from 1966 to 1968.

When the average well-informed and well-intentioned white American discusses the issue of race with his Negro counterpart there are many areas of agreement. There are also certain significant areas of disagreement.

Negro Americans usually feel that whites exaggerate progress; while whites frequently feel that Negroes minimize gains. Then there are differences relative to the responsibility of Negro leadership. It is in these areas of dispute that some of the most subtle and revealing aspects of Negro-white relationships reside. And it is to the subtle and less obvious aspects of this problem that I wish to direct my remarks.

Most middle-class white Americans frequently ask, "Why do Negroes push so? They have made phenomenal progress in 100 years of freedom, so why don't their leaders do something about the crime rate and illegitimacy?" To them I would reply that when Negroes press for full equality now they are behaving as all other Americans would under similar circumstances. Every American has the right to be treated as a human being and striving for human dignity is a national characteristic. Also, there is nothing inconsistent in such action and realistic self-appraisal. Indeed, as I shall develop, self-help programs among non-whites, if they are to be effective, must go hand-in-glove with the opening of new opportunities.

Negroes who are constantly confronted or threatened by discrimination and inequality articulate a sense of outrage. Many react with hostility, sometimes translating their feelings into overt anti-social actions. In parts of the Negro community a separate culture with deviant values develops. To the members of this subculture I would observe that ours is a middle-class society and those who fail to evidence most of its values and behavior are headed toward difficulties. But I am reminded that the rewards for those who do are often minimal, providing insufficient inducement for large numbers to emulate them.

Until the second decade of the twentieth century, it was traditional to compare the then current position of Negroes with that of a decade or several decades ago. The depression revealed the basic marginal economic status of colored Americans and repudiated this concept of progress. By the early 1930s Negroes became concerned about their relative position in the nation.

Of course, there are those who observe that the average income, the incidence of home ownership, the rate of acquisition of automobiles, and the like, among Negroes in the United States are higher than in some so-called advanced nations. Such comparisons mean little. Incomes are significant only in relation to the cost of living, and the other attainments and acquisitions are significant for comparative purposes only when used to reflect the Negro's relative position in the world. The Negro here—as he has so frequently and eloquently demonstrated—is an American. And his status, no less than his aspirations, can be measured meaningfully only in terms of American standards.

Viewed from this point of view what are the facts?

Median family income among non-whites was slightly less than 55 percent of that for whites in 1959; for individuals the figure was 50 percent.

Only a third of the Negro families in 1959 earned sufficient to sustain an acceptable American standard of living. Yet this involved well over a million Negro families, of which 6,000 earned $25,000 or more.

Undergirding these overall figures are many paradoxes. Negroes have made striking gains in historical terms, yet their current rate of unemployment is well over double that among whites. Over two-thirds of our colored workers are still concentrated in five major unskilled and semi-skilled occupations, as contrasted to slightly over a third of the white labor force.

Despite the continuing existence of color discrimination even for many of the well prepared, there is a paucity of qualified Negro scientists, engineers, mathematicians, and highly-trained clerical and stenographic workers. Lack of college-trained persons is especially evident among Negro men. One is prompted to ask why does this exist?

In 1959 non-white males who were high school graduates earned on the average, 32 percent less than whites; for non-white college graduates the figure was 38 percent less. Among women a much different situation exists. Non-white women who were high school graduates earned on the average some 24 percent less than whites. Non-white female college graduates, however, earned but slightly over one percent less average annual salaries than white women college graduates. Significantly, the median annual income of non-white female college graduates was more than double that of non-white women with only high school education.

Is it any wonder that among non-whites, as contrasted to whites, a larger proportion of women than of men attend and finish college? The lack of economic rewards for higher education goes far in accounting for the paucity of college graduates and the high rate of drop-out among non-white males. It also accounts for the fact that in the North, where there are greater opportunities for white-collar Negro males, more Negro men than women are finishing college; whereas in the South, where teaching is the greatest employment outlet for Negro college graduates, Negro women college graduates outnumber men.

There is much in these situations that reflects the continuing matriarchal character of Negro society—in a situation which had its roots in the family composition under slavery where the father, if identified, had no established role. Subsequent and continuing economic advantages of Negro women who found steady employment as domestics during the post–Civil War era and thereafter perpetuated the pattern. This, in conjunction with easy access of white males to Negro females, served to emasculate many Negro men economically and psychologically. It also explains, in part, the high prevalence of broken homes, illegitimacy, and lack of motivation in the Negro community.

The Negro middle-class seems destined to grow and prosper. At the same time, the economic position of the untrained and poorly trained Negro—as of all untrained and poorly trained in our society—will continue to decline. Non-whites are doubly affected. First, they are disproportionately concentrated in occupations particularly susceptible to unemployment at a time when our technology eats up unskilled and semi-skilled jobs at a frightening rate. Secondly, they are conditioned to racial job discrimination. The latter circumstance becomes a justification for not trying, occasioning a lack of incentive for self-betterment.

The tragedy of discrimination is that it provides an excuse for failure while erecting barriers to success.

Most colored Americans still are not only outside the mainstream of our society but see no hope of entering it. The lack of motivation and anti-social behavior which result are capitalized upon by the champions of the status quo. They say that the average Negro must demonstrate to the average white that the latter's fears are groundless. One proponent of this point of view has stated that Negro crime and illegitimacy must decline and Negro neighborhoods must stop deteriorating.

In these observations lie a volume on race relations. In the first place, those who articulate this point of view fail to differentiate between acceptance as earned by individual merit and enjoyment of rights guaranteed to everyone. Implicit, also, is the assumption that Negroes can lift themselves by their bootstraps, and that once they become brown counterparts of white middle-class Americans, they will be accepted on the basis of individual merit. Were this true, our race problem would be no more than a most recent phase in the melting pot tradition of the nation.

As compared to the earlier newcomers to our cities from Europe, the later ones who are colored face much greater impediments in moving from the slums or from the bottom of the economic ladder. At the same time, they have less resources to meet the more difficult problems which confront them.

One of the most obvious manifestations of the Negro's paucity of internal resources is the absence of widespread integrated patterns of voluntary organizations. The latter, as we know, contributed greatly to the adjustment and assimilation of European immigrants. Both the Negro's heritage and the nature of his migration in the United States militated against the development of similar institutions.

Slavery and resulting post–civil war dependence upon whites stifled self-reliance. Movement from the rural south to northern cities was a far cry from immigration from Europe to the new world. This internal migration was not an almost complete break with the past, nor were those who participated in it subjected to feelings of complete foreignness. Thus the Negro tended to preserve his old institutions when he moved from one part of the nation to another; the immigrant created new ones. And most important, the current adjustment of non-whites to an urban environment is occurring at a time when public agencies are rapidly supplanting voluntary organizations.

Although much is written about crime and family disorganization among Negroes, most literate Americans are poorly informed on such matters. The first fallacy which arises is a confusion of what racial crime figures reflect. When people read that more than half the crime in a given community is committed by Negroes they unconsciously translate this into an equally high proportion of Negroes who are criminals. In fact, the latter proportion is extremely small.

In a similar vein, family stability, as indicated by the presence of both husband and wife, which is very low among the poorest non-whites, rises sharply as income increases.

Equally revealing is the fact that, in all parts of the country, the proportion of non-white families with female heads falls as incomes rise. A good, steady paycheck appears to be an important element in family stability. Those Negroes who have been able to improve their economic position have generally taken on many of the attributes of white middle-class Americans.

But poverty still haunts half of the Negroes in the United States, and while higher levels of national productivity are a sine qua non for higher levels of employment in the nation, they alone will not wipe out unemployment, especially for minorities. The labor reserve of today must be trained if it is to find gainful employment. Among non-whites this frequently involves more than exposure to vocational training. Many of them are functionally illiterate and require basic education prior to any specialized job preparation.

The very magnitude of these problems illustrates that society must take the leadership in solving them. But society can only provide greater opportunities. The individual must respond to the new opportunities. And he does so, primarily, in terms of visible evidence that hard work and sacrifice bring real rewards.

Many white Americans are perplexed, confused, and antagonized by Negroes' persistent pressure to break down racial segregation. Few pause to consider what involuntary segregation means to its victims.

To the Negro, as an American, involuntary segregation is degrading, inconvenient and costly. It is degrading because it is a tangible and constant reminder of the theory upon which it is based—biological racial inferiority. It is inconvenient because it means long trips to work, exclusion from certain cultural and recreational facilities, lack of access to restaurants and hotels conveniently located, and, frequently, relegation to grossly inferior accommodations. Sometimes it spells denial of a job and often it prevents upgrading based on ability.

But the principal disadvantage of involuntary segregation is its costliness. Nowhere is this better illustrated than in education and housing. By any

and all criteria, separate schools are generally inferior schools in which the cultural deprivations of the descendants of slaves are perpetuated.

Enforced residential segregation, the most stubborn and universal of the Negro's disadvantages, often leads to exploitation and effects a spatial pattern which facilitates neglect of public services in the well-defined areas where Negroes live. It restricts the opportunities of the more successful as well as the least successful in the group, augmenting artificially the number of non-whites who live in areas of blight and neglect and face impediments to the attainment of values and behavior required for upward social and economic mobility.

The most obvious consequence of involuntary residential segregation is that the housing dollar in a dark hand usually commands less purchasing power than one in a white hand. Clearly, this is a denial of a basic promise of a free economy.

For immigrant groups in the nation, the trend toward improved socioeconomic status has gone hand-in-hand with decreasing residential segregation. The reverse has been true of the Negro. Eli Ginzberg, in his book, *The Negro Potential*, has delineated the consequences.

It must be recognized that the Negro cannot suddenly take his proper place among whites in the adult world if he has never lived, played, and studied with them in childhood and young adulthood. Any type of segregation handicaps a person's preparation for work and life . . . Only when Negro and white families can live together as neighbors . . . Will the Negro grow up properly prepared for his place in the world of work.

Residential segregation based on color cannot be separated from residential segregation based upon income. Both have snob and class appeal in contemporary America. Concentration of higher income families in the suburbs means that many of those whose attitudes and values dominate our society do not see the poor or needy. But more important, cut off by political boundaries, it is to their interest not to see them.

Yet there are over 30,000,000 Americans who experience poverty today. For the most part, we resent them and the outlays required for welfare services. They are a group which is separate from the majority of Americans and for whom the latter accept only the minimum responsibility. Thus we have, for the first time, class unemployment in the United States.

I happen to have been born a Negro and to have devoted a large part of my adult energies to the problem of the role of the Negro in America. But I am also a government administrator, and have devoted just as much energy—if not more—to problems of government administration at the local, the state and the national level.

My responsibilities as a Negro and an American are part of the heritage I received from my parents—a heritage that included a wealth of moral and social values that don't have anything to do with my race. My responsibilities as a government administrator don't have too much to do with my race, either. My greatest difficulty in public life is combating the idea that somehow my responsibilities as a Negro conflict with my responsibilities as a government administrator: and this is a problem which is presented by those Negroes who feel that I represent them exclusively, as well as by those whites who doubt my capacity to represent all elements in the population. The fact is that my responsibilities as a Negro and a government administrator do not conflict; they complement each other.

The challenge frequently thrown to me is why I don't go out into the Negro community and exhort Negro youths to prepare themselves for present and future opportunities. My answer is somewhat ambivalent. I know that emphasis upon values and behavior conducive to success in the dominant culture of America was an important part of my youthful training. But it came largely from my parents in the security and love of a middle-class family. (And believe me, there is nothing more middle-class than a middle-class minority family!)

Many of the youth which I am urged to exhort come from broken homes. They live in communities where the fellow who stays in school and follows the rules is a "square." They reside in a neighborhood where the most successful are often engaged in shady—if not illegal—activities. They know that the very policeman who may arrest them for violation of the law is sometimes the pay-off man for the racketeers. And they recognize that the majority society, which they frequently believe to be the "enemy," condones this situation. Their experience also leads some of them to believe that getting the kind of job the residents in the neighborhood hold is unrewarding—a commitment to hard work and poverty. For almost all of them, the precepts of Ben Franklin are lily-like in their applicability.

Included in the group are the third generation of welfare clients. It is in this area—where they learn all the jargon of the social workers and psychologists—that they demonstrate real creativity. It is in activities which "beat" the system that they are most adept—and where the most visible rewards are concentrated.

All youth is insecure today. Young people in our slums are not only insecure but angry. Their horizons are limited, and, in withdrawing from competing in the larger society, they are creating a peculiar, but effective, feeling of something that approaches, or at least serves as a viable substitute for, security. In the process, new values and aspirations, a new vocabulary, a new standard of dress, and a new attitude toward authority evolve. Each of these serves to demonstrate a separateness from the dominant culture.

As a realist, I know that these youth relate with me primarily in a negative sense. They see me in terms of someone who has been able to penetrate, to a degree, the color line, and to them I have bettered the "enemy." If I should attempt to suggest their surmounting the restrictions of color, they cite instances of persons they know who were qualified—the relatively few boys or girls in their neighborhood who finished high school or even college—only to be ignored while white youths with much less training were selected for good jobs. And such occurrences are not unique or isolated in their experience.

The example which will be an inspiration to the Negro boys and girls whose anti-social behavior distresses most whites and many Negroes is someone they know who has experienced what they have experienced and has won acceptance in the mainstream of America. When the Ralph Bunches, William Hasties, and John Hope Franklins emerge from their environment, the achievements of these successful Negroes will provide models which have meaning for them.

This is reflected in the occupations which provide the greatest incidence of mobility for slum youth. One thinks immediately of prize fighting and jazz music. In these fields there is a well established tradition of Negroes, reared in the ghetto areas of blight and poverty, who have gone to the top. For youth in a similar environment, these are heroes with whom they can and do identify and relate. And in these fields, a significant proportion of the successful are non-whites. For only in those pursuits in which native genius can surmount (if indeed it does not profit from) lack of high level training does the dominant environment of the Negro facilitate large-scale achievement.

For many successful older colored Americans, middle-class status has been difficult. Restricted, in large measure, to racial ghettos, they have expended great effort to protect their children from falling back into the dominant values of that environment. And these values are probably more repugnant to them than to most Americans. This is understandable in terms of their social origins. For the most part, they come from lower-middle-class families, where industry, good conduct, family ties, and a willingness to postpone immediate rewards for future successes are stressed. Their values and standards of conduct are those of success-oriented middle-class Americans.

It is not that responsible Negroes fail to feel shame about muggings, illegitimacy, and boisterousness on the part of other Negroes. Many—particularly the older ones—feel too much shame in this connection. Accordingly, some either repudiate the "culprits" in terms of scathing condemnation or try to escape from the problem lest it endanger their none too secure status.

These attitudes, too, are shifting. The younger middle-class Negroes are more secure and consequently place less stress upon the quest for respectability. But few Negroes are immune from the toll of upward mobility. Frequently their struggle has been difficult, and the maintenance of their status demands a heavy input. As long as this is true, they will have less energy to devote to the problems of the Negro subculture. It is significant, however, that the sit-ins and freedom marches in the south were planned and executed by Negro college students, most of whom come from middle-class families.

Middle-class Negroes have long led the fight for civil rights; today its youthful members do not hesitate to resort to direct action, articulating the impatience which is rife throughout the Negro community. In so doing they are forging a new solidarity in the struggle for human dignity.

There are today, as there always have been, thousands of dedicated colored Americans who don't make the headlines but are successful in raising the horizons of Negroes. These are the less well-known leaders who function at the local level. The teachers, social workers, local political leaders, ministers, doctors, and an assortment of indigenous leaders—many among the latter with little formal education—who are effective have familiarized themselves with the environmental factors which dull and destroy motivation. They become involved with the total Negro community. They demonstrate—rather than verbalize—a concern for Negro youth's problems. They are trying to reach these young people, not by coddling and providing excuses for failure, but through identification of their potentialities and assistance in the development of these. Involved are both genuine affection and sufficient toughness to facilitate and encourage the development of self-reliance.

Those, white and black alike, who reach the newcomers in our urban areas avoid value judgments relative to cultural patterns. When they suggest thrift, good deportment, greater emphasis upon education and training, they do so as a pragmatic approach. For them, it is not a matter of proselytizing, but a matter of delineating those values and patterns of behavior that accelerate upward mobility in contemporary American society. Such a sophisticated approach enables them to identify deviations from dominant values and conduct which are not inconsistent with a productive and healthy life in modern urban communities. The latter are left undisturbed, so that there will be a minimum adjustment of values and concepts and the maximum functional effectiveness on the part of individuals who will not soon become middle-class America.

What are the responsibilities of Negro leadership?

Certainly the first is to keep pressing for first-class citizenship status—an inevitable goal of those who accept the values of this nation.

Another responsibility of Negro leadership is to encourage and assist Negroes to prepare for the opportunities that are now and will be opened to them.

The ultimate responsibilities of Negro leadership, however, are to show results and maintain a following. This means that it cannot be so "responsible" that it forgets the trials and tribulations of others who are less fortunate or less recognized than itself. It cannot stress progress—the emphasis which is so palatable to the majority group—without, at the same time, delineating the unsolved business of democracy. It cannot provide or identify meaningful models unless it effects social changes which facilitate the emergence of these models from the environment which typifies so much of the Negro community.

But Negro leadership must also face up to the deficiencies which plague the Negro community, and it must take effective action to deal with resulting problems. While, of course, crime, poverty, illegitimacy and hopelessness can all be explained, in large measure, in terms of the Negro's history and current status in America, they do exist. We need no longer be self-conscious in admitting these unpleasant facts, for our knowledge of human behavior indicates clearly that anti-social activities are not inherent in any people. What is required is comprehension of these—a part of society's problems—and remedial and rehabilitation measures.

Emphasis upon self-betterment if employed indiscriminately by Negro leaders is seized upon by white supremacists and their apologists to support the assertion that Negroes—and they mean all Negroes—are not ready for full citizenship. This, because of the nature of our society, Negro leadership must continue to stress rights if it is to receive a hearing for programs of self-improvement.

Black Muslims, who identify the white man as the devil, can and do emphasize—with a remarkable degree of success—morality, industry, and good conduct. But, the Negro leader who does not repudiate his or his followers' Americanism can do so effectively only as he, too, clearly repudiates identification with the white supremacists. This he does, of course, when he champions equal rights, just as the black Muslims accomplish it by directing hate toward all white people.

Most Negroes in leadership capacities have articulated the fact that they and those who follow them are a part of America. They have striven for realization of the American dream. Most recognize their responsibilities as citizens and urge others to follow their example. Sophisticated whites realize that the status of Negroes in our society depends not only upon what the Negro does to achieve his goals and prepare himself for opportunities but, even more, upon what all America does to expand these opportunities. And the quality and nature of future Negro leadership depends upon how effective those leaders who relate to the total society can be in satisfying the yearnings for human dignity which reside in the hearts of all Americans.

Source: Weaver, Robert C. Santa Barbara: Center for the Study of Democratic Institutions, 1963. Courtesy of *New Perspectives Quarterly.*

President Lyndon B. Johnson, Address Before a Joint Session of the Congress (November 27, 1963)

Long the brainchild of civil rights pioneer Rev. Martin Luther King Jr., the proposed civil rights bill was finally presented to Congress just days after the assassination of President John F. Kennedy. Just months earlier, Kennedy had pledged to King that he would finally support the bill. True to the fallen president's word, President Lyndon B. Johnson pushed through Congress what would become the Civil Rights Act of 1964. Reproduced here is Johnson's address to Congress in 1963 about the proposed civil rights bill.

President Lyndon B. Johnson's
Address Before a Joint Session of the Congress
November 27, 1963
Mr. Speaker, Mr. President, Members of the House, Members of the Senate, my fellow Americans:

All I have I would have given gladly not to be standing here today.

The greatest leader of our time has been struck down by the foulest deed of our time. Today John Fitzgerald Kennedy lives on in the immortal words and works that he left behind. He lives on in the mind and memories of mankind. He lives on in the hearts of his countrymen.

No words are sad enough to express our sense of loss. No words are strong enough to express our determination to continue the forward thrust of America that he began.

The dream of conquering the vastness of space—the dream of partnership across the Atlantic—and across the Pacific as well—the dream of a Peace Corps in less developed nations—the dream of education for all of our children—the dream of jobs for all who seek them and need them—the dream of care for our elderly—the dream of an all-out attack on mental illness—and above all, the dream of equal rights for all Americans, whatever their race or color—these and other American dreams have been vitalized by his drive and by his dedication.

And now the ideas and the ideals which he so nobly represented must and will be translated into effective action.

Under John Kennedy's leadership, this Nation has demonstrated that it has the courage to seek peace, and it has the fortitude to risk war. We have proved that we are a good and reliable friend to those who seek peace and freedom. We have shown that we can also be a formidable foe to those who reject the path of peace and those who seek to impose upon us or our allies the yoke of tyranny.

This Nation will keep its commitments from South Viet-Nam to West Berlin. We will be unceasing in the search for peace; resourceful in our pursuit of areas of agreement even with those with whom we differ; and generous and loyal to those who join with us in common cause.

In this age when there can be no losers in peace and no victors in war, we must recognize the obligation to match national strength with national restraint. We must be prepared at one and the same time for both the confrontation of power and the limitation of power. We must be ready to defend the national interest and to negotiate the common interest. This is the path that we shall continue to pursue. Those who test our courage will find it strong, and those who seek our friendship will find it honorable. We will demonstrate anew that the strong can be just in the use of strength; and the just can be strong in the defense of justice.

And let all know we will extend no special privilege and impose no persecution. We will carry on the fight against poverty and misery, and disease and ignorance, in other lands and in our own.

We will serve all the Nation, not one section or one sector, or one group, but all Americans. These are the United States—a united people with a united purpose.

Our American unity does not depend upon unanimity. We have differences; but now, as in the past, we can derive from those differences strength, not weakness, wisdom, not despair. Both as a people and a government, we can unite upon a program, a program which is wise and just, enlightened and constructive.

For 32 years Capitol Hill has been my home. I have shared many moments of pride with you, pride in the ability of the Congress of the United States to act, to meet any crisis, to distill from our differences strong programs of national action.

An assassin's bullet has thrust upon me the awesome burden of the Presidency. I am here today to say I need your help; I cannot bear this burden alone. I need the help of all Americans, and all America. This Nation has experienced a profound shock, and in this critical moment, it is our duty, yours and mine, as the Government of the United States, to do away with uncertainty and doubt and delay, and to show that we are capable of decisive action; that from the brutal loss of our leader we will derive not weakness, but strength; that we can and will act and act now.

From this chamber of representative government, let all the world know and none misunderstand that I rededicate this Government to the unswerving support of the United Nations, to the honorable and determined execution of our commitments to our allies, to the maintenance of military strength second to none, to the defense of the strength and the stability of the dollar, to the expansion of our foreign trade, to the reinforcement of our programs of mutual assistance and cooperation in Asia and Africa, and to our Alliance for Progress in this hemisphere.

On the 20th day of January, in 1961, John F. Kennedy told his countrymen that our national work would not be finished "in the first thousand days, nor in the life of this administration, nor even perhaps in our lifetime on this planet. But," he said, "let us begin."

Today, in this moment of new resolve, I would say to all my fellow Americans, let us continue.

This is our challenge—not to hesitate, not to pause, not to turn about and linger over this evil moment, but to continue on our course so that we may fulfill the destiny that history has set for us. Our most immediate tasks are here on this Hill.

First, no memorial oration or eulogy could more eloquently honor President Kennedy's memory than the earliest possible passage of the civil rights bill for which he fought so long. We have talked long enough in this country about equal rights. We have talked for one hundred years or more. It is time now to write the next chapter, and to write it in the books of law.

I urge you again, as I did in 1957 and again in 1960, to enact a civil rights law so that we can move forward to eliminate from this Nation every trace of discrimination and oppression that is based upon race or color. There could be no greater source of strength to this Nation both at home and abroad.

And second, no act of ours could more fittingly continue the work of President Kennedy than the early passage of the tax bill for which he fought all this long year. This is a bill designed to increase our national income and Federal revenues, and to provide insurance against recession. That bill, if passed without delay, means more security for those now working, more jobs for those now without them, and more incentive for our economy.

In short, this is no time for delay. It is a time for action—strong, forward-looking action on the pending education bills to help bring the light of learning to every home and hamlet in America—strong, forward-looking action on youth employment opportunities; strong, forward-looking action on the pending foreign aid bill, making clear that we are not forfeiting our responsibilities to this hemisphere or to the world, nor erasing Executive flexibility in the conduct of our foreign affairs—and strong, prompt, and forward-looking action on the remaining appropriation bills.

In this new spirit of action, the Congress can expect the full cooperation and support of the executive branch. And in particular, I pledge that the expenditures of your Government will be administered with the utmost thrift and frugality. I will insist that the Government get a dollar's value for a dollar spent. The Government will set an example of prudence and economy. This does not mean that we will not meet our unfilled needs or that we will not honor our commitments. We will do both.

As one who has long served in both Houses of the Congress, I firmly believe in the independence and the integrity of the legislative branch. And I promise you that I shall always respect this. It is deep in the marrow of my bones. With equal firmness, I believe in the capacity and I believe in the ability of the Congress, despite the divisions of opinions which characterize our Nation, to act—to act wisely, to act vigorously, to act speedily when the need arises.

The need is here. The need is now. I ask your help.

We meet in grief, but let us also meet in renewed dedication and renewed vigor. Let us meet in action, in tolerance, and in mutual understanding. John Kennedy's death commands what his life conveyed—that America must move forward. The time has come for Americans of all races and creeds and political beliefs to understand and to respect one another. So let us put an end to the teaching and the preaching of hate and evil and violence. Let us turn away from the fanatics of the far left and the far right, from the apostles of bitterness and bigotry, from those defiant of law, and those who pour venom into our Nation's bloodstream.

I profoundly hope that the tragedy and the torment of these terrible days will bind us together in new fellowship, making us one people in our hour of sorrow. So let us here highly resolve that John Fitzgerald Kennedy did not live—or die—in vain. And on this Thanksgiving eve, as we gather together to ask the Lord's blessing, and give Him our thanks, let us unite in those familiar and cherished words:

America, America,
God shed His grace on thee,
And crown thy good With brotherhood,
From sea to shining sea.

Source: Public Papers of the Presidents of the United States: Lyndon B. Johnson, 1963–64. Volume I, entry 11, 8–10. Washington, DC: Government Printing Office, 1965. Retrieved from the Lyndon Baines Johnson Library, National Archives and Records Administration.

Civil Rights Act of 1964

The assassination of President John F. Kennedy in November 1963 left most civil rights leaders grief-stricken. Kennedy had been the first president since Harry Truman to champion equal rights for black Americans, and the civil rights leaders knew little about Kennedy's successor, Lyndon B. Johnson. Although Johnson had helped engineer the Civil Rights Act of 1957, that had been a mild measure, and no one knew if the Texan would continue Kennedy's call for civil rights or move to placate his fellow southerners.

But on November 27, 1963, addressing the Congress and the nation for the first time as president, Johnson called for passage of the civil rights bill as a monument to the fallen Kennedy. "Let us continue," he declared, promising that "the ideas and the ideals which [Kennedy] so nobly represented must and will be translated into effective action." Moreover, where Kennedy had been sound on principle, Lyndon Johnson was the master of parliamentary procedure, and he used his considerable talents and the prestige of the presidency in support of the bill.

On February 10, 1964, the House of Representatives passed the measure by a lopsided 290–130 vote, but everyone knew the real battle would be in the Senate, whose rules had allowed southerners in the past to mount filibusters that had effectively killed nearly all civil rights legislation. But Johnson pulled every string he knew and had the civil rights leaders mount a massive lobbying campaign, including inundating the Capitol with religious leaders of all faiths and colors. The strategy paid off, and in June the Senate voted to close debate; a few weeks later, the Senate passed the most important piece of civil rights legislation in the nation's history, and on July 2, 1964, President Johnson signed the bill into law.

Some members of Congress, however, worried whether the law would pass constitutional muster, since in 1883 the Supreme Court had voided the last civil rights measure, declaring such action beyond the scope of congressional power. They need not have worried this time. The U.S. Supreme Court accepted two cases on an accelerated basis and in both of them unanimously upheld the power of Congress under the Fourteenth Amendment to protect the civil rights of black Americans.

Title II, of which sections are reprinted here, is the heart of the Civil Rights Act of 1964, and deals with public accommodations, providing that African Americans could no longer be excluded from restaurants, hotels, and other public facilities.

Sec. 201. (a) All persons shall be entitled to the full and equal enjoyment of the goods, services, facilities, privileges, advantages, and accommodations of any place of public accommodation, as defined in this section, without discrimination or segregation on the ground of race, color, religion, or national origin.

(b) Each of the following establishments which serves the public is a place of public accommodation within the meaning of this title if its operations affect commerce, or if discrimination or segregation by it is supported by State action:

(1) any inn, hotel, motel, or other establishment which provides lodging to transient guests, other than an establishment located within a building which contains not more than five rooms for rent or hire and which is actually occupied by the proprietor of such establishment as his residence;

(2) any restaurant, cafeteria, lunchroom, lunch counter, soda fountain, or other facility principally engaged in selling food for consumption on the premises, including, but not limited to, any such facility located on the premises of any retail establishment; or any gasoline station;

(3) any motion picture house, theater, concert hall, sports arena, stadium or other place of exhibition or entertainment; and

(4) any establishment (A)(i) which is physically located within the premises of any establishment otherwise covered by this subsection, or (ii) within the premises of which is physically located any such covered establishment, and (b) which holds itself out as serving patrons of such covered establishment.

(c) The operations of an establishment affect commerce within the meaning of this title if (1) it is one of the establishments described in paragraph (1) of subsection (b); (2) in the case of an establishment described in paragraph (2) of subsection (b), it serves or offers to serve interstate travelers or a substantial portion of the food which it serves, or gasoline or other products which it sells, has moved in commerce; (3) in the case of an establishment described in paragraph (3) of subsection (b), it customarily presents films, performances, athletic teams, exhibitions, or other sources of entertainment which move in commerce; and (4) in the case of an establishment described in paragraph (4) of subsection (b), it is physically located within the premises of, or there is physically located within its premises, an establishment the operations of which affect commerce within the meaning of this subsection. For purposes of this section, "commerce" means travel, trade, traffic, commerce, transportation, or communication among the several States, or between the District of Columbia and any State, or between any foreign country or any territory or possession and any State or the District of Columbia, or between points in the same State but through any other State or the District of Columbia or a foreign country.

(d) Discrimination or segregation by an establishment is supported by State action within the meaning of this title if such discrimination or segregation (1) is carried on under color of any law, statute, ordinance, or regulation; or (2) is carried on under color of any custom or usage required or enforced by officials of the State or political subdivision thereof; or (3) is required by action of the State or political subdivision thereof. . .

(e) The provisions of this title shall not apply to a private club or other establishment not in fact open to the public, except to the extent that the facilities of such establishment are made available to the customers or patrons of an establishment within the scope of subsection (b).

Sec 202. All persons shall be entitled to be free, at any establishment or place, from discrimination or segregation of any kind on the ground of race, color, religion, or national origin, if such discrimination or segregation is or purports to be required by any law, statute, ordinance, regulation, rule, or order of a State or any agency or political subdivision thereof.

Sec. 203. No person shall (a) withhold, deny, or attempt to withhold or deny, or deprive or attempt to deprive, any person of any right or privilege secured by section 201 or 202, or (b) intimidate, threaten, or coerce, or attempt to intimidate, threaten, or coerce any person with purpose of interfering with any right or privilege secured by section 201 or 202, or (c) punish or attempt to punish any person for exercising or attempting to exercise any right or privilege secured by section 201 or 202.

Source: The Civil Rights Act of 1964, 78 Stat. 241. General Records of the U.S. Government, National Archives and Records Administration.

President Lyndon B. Johnson, Radio and Television Remarks Upon Signing the Civil Rights Bill
(July 2, 1964)

The 1964 Civil Rights Act is historically significant because it was signed into law after many turbulent years in which blacks, whites, religious leaders, women, and many other groups had waged many serious battles to win equal rights for every American. President John F. Kennedy had promised to sign the act, but his untimely death meant that his successor, President Lyndon B. Johnson, signed it into law instead. The act marked a legal end to decades of violence, segregation, and discrimination that had torn the nation apart. The hope, at the time, was that this law would make a real beginning of equal rights for all Americans. It was a dream many hoped had come true, including President Johnson.

My fellow Americans:

I am about to sign into law the Civil Rights Act of 1964. I want to take this occasion to talk to you about what that law means to every American.

One hundred and eighty-eight years ago this week a small band of valiant men began a long struggle for freedom. They pledged their lives, their fortunes, and their sacred honor not only to found a nation, but to forge an ideal of freedom—not only for political independence, but for personal liberty—not only to eliminate foreign rule, but to establish the rule of justice in the affairs of men.

That struggle was a turning point in our history. Today in far corners of distant continents, the ideals of those American patriots still shape the struggles of men who hunger for freedom.

This is a proud triumph. Yet those who founded our country knew that freedom would be secure only if each generation fought to renew and enlarge its meaning. From the minutemen at Concord to the soldiers in Viet-Nam, each generation has been equal to that trust.

Americans of every race and color have died in battle to protect our freedom. Americans of every race and color have worked to build a nation of widening opportunities. Now our generation of Americans has been called on to continue the unending search for justice within our own borders.

We believe that all men are created equal. Yet many are denied equal treatment.

We believe that all men have certain unalienable rights. Yet many Americans do not enjoy those rights.

We believe that all men are entitled to the blessings of liberty. Yet millions are being deprived of those blessings—not because of their own failures, but because of the color of their skin.

The reasons are deeply imbedded in history and tradition and the nature of man. We can understand—without rancor or hatred—how this all happened.

But it cannot continue. Our Constitution, the foundation of our Republic, forbids it. The principles of our freedom forbid it. Morality forbids it. And the law I will sign tonight forbids it.

That law is the product of months of the most careful debate and discussion. It was proposed more than one year ago by our late and beloved President John F. Kennedy. It received the bipartisan support of more than two-thirds of the Members of both the House and the Senate. An overwhelming majority of Republicans as well as Democrats voted for it.

It has received the thoughtful support of tens of thousands of civic and religious leaders in all parts of this Nation. And it is supported by the great majority of the American people.

The purpose of the law is simple.

It does not restrict the freedom of any American, so long as he respects the rights of others.

It does not give special treatment to any citizen.

It does say the only limit to a man's hope for happiness, and for the future of his children, shall be his own ability.

It does say that there are those who are equal before God shall now also be equal in the polling booths, in the classrooms, in the factories, and in hotels, restaurants, movie theaters, and other places that provide service to the public.

I am taking steps to implement the law under my constitutional obligation to "take care that the laws are faithfully executed."

First, I will send to the Senate my nomination of LeRoy Collins to be Director of the Community Relations Service. Governor Collins will bring the experience of a long career of distinguished public service to the task of helping communities solve problems of human relations through reason and commonsense.

Second, I shall appoint an advisory committee of distinguished Americans to assist Governor Collins in his assignment.

Third, I am sending Congress a request for supplemental appropriations to pay for necessary costs of implementing the law, and asking for immediate action.

Fourth, already today in a meeting of my Cabinet this afternoon I directed the agencies of this Government to fully discharge the new responsibilities imposed upon them by the law and to do it without delay, and to keep me personally informed of their progress.

Fifth, I am asking appropriate officials to meet with representative groups to promote greater understanding of the law and to achieve a spirit of compliance.

We must not approach the observance and enforcement of this law in a vengeful spirit. Its purpose is not to punish. Its purpose is not to divide, but to end divisions—divisions which have all lasted too long. Its purpose is national, not regional.

Its purpose is to promote a more abiding commitment to freedom, a more constant pursuit of justice, and a deeper respect for human dignity.

We will achieve these goals because most Americans are law-abiding citizens who want to do what is right.

This is why the Civil Rights Act relies first on voluntary compliance, then on the efforts of local communities and States to secure the rights of citizens. It provides for the national authority to step in only when others cannot or will not do the job.

This Civil Rights Act is a challenge to all of us to go to work in our communities and our States, in our homes and in our hearts, to eliminate the last vestiges of injustice in our beloved country.

So tonight I urge every public official, every religious leader, every business and professional man, every workingman, every housewife—I urge every American—to join in this effort to bring justice and hope to all our people—and to bring peace to our land.

My fellow citizens, we have come now to a time of testing. We must not fail.

Let us close the springs of racial poison. Let us pray for wise and understanding hearts. Let us lay aside irrelevant differences and make our Nation whole. Let us hasten that day when our unmeasured strength and our unbounded spirit will be free to do the great works ordained for this Nation by the just and wise God who is the Father of us all.

Source: Public Papers of the Presidents of the United States: Lyndon B. Johnson, 1963–64. Volume II, entry 446, 842–844. Washington, DC: Government Printing Office, 1965. Retrieved from the Lyndon Baines Johnson Library, National Archives and Records Administration.

Voting Rights Act of 1965

This is an excerpt from a transcript of the Voting Rights Act of 1965, which outlawed the requirement that would-be voters in the United States take literacy tests to qualify to register to vote. Literacy tests were routinely inflicted on disenfranchised voters in the Deep South to keep them from voting in local and national elections. This act provided for federal registration of voters in areas that had less than 50 percent of eligible minority voters registered.

AN ACT To enforce the fifteenth amendment to the Constitution of the United States, and for other purposes. Be it enacted by the Senate and House of Representatives of the United States of America in Congress assembled, That this Act shall be known as the "Voting Rights Act of 1965."

SEC. 2. No voting qualification or prerequisite to voting, or standard, practice, or procedure shall be imposed or applied by any State or political subdivision to deny or abridge the right of any citizen of the United States to vote on account of race or color.

SEC. 3. (a) Whenever the Attorney General institutes a proceeding under any statute to enforce the guarantees of the fifteenth amendment in any State or political subdivision the court shall authorize the appointment of Federal examiners by the United States Civil Service Commission in accordance with section 6 to serve for such period of time and for such political subdivisions as the court shall determine is appropriate to enforce the guarantees of the fifteenth amendment (1) as part of any interlocutory order if the court determines that the appointment of such examiners is necessary to enforce such guarantees or (2) as part of any final judgment if the court finds that violations of the fifteenth amendment justifying equitable relief have occurred in such State or subdivision: Provided, That the court need not authorize the appointment of examiners if any incidents of denial or abridgement of the right to vote on account of race or color (1) have been few in number and have been promptly and effectively corrected by State or local action, (2) the continuing effect of such incidents has been eliminated, and (3) there is no reasonable probability of their recurrence in the future.

(b) If in a proceeding instituted by the Attorney General under any statute to enforce the guarantees of the fifteenth amendment in any State or political subdivision the court finds that a test or device has been used for the purpose or with the effect of denying or abridging the right of any citizen of the United States to vote on account of race or color, it shall suspend the use of tests and devices in such State or political subdivisions as the court shall determine is appropriate and for such period as it deems necessary.

(c) If in any proceeding instituted by the Attorney General under any statute to enforce the guarantees of the fifteenth amendment in any State or political subdivision the court finds that violations of the fifteenth amendment justifying equitable relief have occurred within the territory of such State or political subdivision, the court, in addition to such relief as it may grant, shall retain jurisdiction for such period as it may deem appropriate and during such period no voting qualification or prerequisite to voting, or standard, practice, or procedure with respect to voting different from that in force or effect at the time the proceeding was commenced shall be enforced unless and until the court finds that such qualification, prerequisite, standard, practice, or procedure does not have the purpose and will not have the effect of denying or abridging the right to vote on account of race or color: Provided, That such qualification, prerequisite, standard, practice, or procedure may be enforced if the qualification, prerequisite, standard, practice, or procedure has been submitted by the chief legal officer or other appropriate official of such State or subdivision to the Attorney General and the Attorney General has not interposed an objection within sixty days after such submission, except that neither the court's finding nor the Attorney General's failure to object shall bar a subsequent action to enjoin enforcement of such qualification, prerequisite, standard, practice, or procedure.

SEC. 4. (a) To assure that the right of citizens of the United States to vote is not denied or abridged on account of race or color, no citizen shall be denied the right to vote in any Federal, State, or local election because of his failure to comply with any test or device in any State with respect to which the determinations have been made under subsection (b) or in any political subdivision with respect to which such determinations have been made as a separate unit, unless the United States District Court for the District of Columbia in an action for a declaratory judgment brought by such State or subdivision against the United States has determined that no such test or device has been used during the five years preceding the filing of the action for the purpose or with the effect of denying or abridging the right to vote on account of race or color: Provided, That no such declaratory judgment shall issue with respect to any plaintiff for a period of five years after the entry of a final judgment of any court of the United States, other than the denial of a declaratory judgment under this section, whether entered prior to or after the enactment of this Act, determining that denials or abridgments of the right to vote on account of race or color through the use of such tests or devices have occurred anywhere in the territory of such plaintiff. An action pursuant to this subsection shall be heard and determined by a court of three judges in accordance with the provisions of section 2284 of title 28 of the United States Code and any appeal shall lie to the Supreme Court. The court shall retain jurisdiction of any action pursuant to this subsection for five years after judgment and shall reopen the action upon motion of the Attorney General alleging that a test or device has been used for the purpose or with the effect of denying or abridging the right to vote on account of race or color. If the Attorney General determines that he has no reason to believe that any such test or device has been used during the five years preceding the filing of the action for the purpose or with the effect of denying or abridging the right to vote on account of race or color, he shall consent to the entry of such judgment.

(b) The provisions of subsection (a) shall apply in any State or in any political subdivision of a state which (1) the Attorney General determines maintained on November 1, 1964, any test or device, and with respect to which (2) the Director of the Census determines that less than 50 percentum of the persons of voting age residing therein were registered on November 1, 1964, or that less than 50 percentum of such persons voted in the presidential election of November 1964.

A determination or certification of the Attorney General or of the Director of the Census under this section or under section 6 or section 13 shall not be reviewable in any court and shall be effective upon publication in the Federal Register.

(c) The phrase "test or device" shall mean any requirement that a person as a prerequisite for voting or registration for voting (1) demonstrate the ability to read, write, understand, or interpret any matter, (2) demonstrate any educational achievement or his knowledge of any particular subject, (3) possess good moral character, or (4) prove his qualifications by the voucher of registered voters or members of any other class.

(d) For purposes of this section no State or political subdivision shall be determined to have engaged in the use of tests or devices for the purpose or with the effect of denying or abridging the right to vote on account of race or color if (1) incidents of such use have been few in number and have been promptly and effectively corrected by State or local action, (2) the continuing effect of such incidents has been eliminated, and (3) there is no reasonable probability of their recurrence in the future.

(e) (1) Congress hereby declares that to secure the rights under the fourteenth amendment of persons educated in American-flag schools in which the predominant classroom language was other than

English, it is necessary to prohibit the States from conditioning the right to vote of such persons on ability to read, write, understand, or interpret any matter in the English language. (2) No person who demonstrates that he has successfully completed the sixth primary grade in a public school in, or a private school accredited by, any State or territory, the District of Columbia, or the Commonwealth of Puerto Rico in which the predominant classroom language was other than English, shall be denied the right to vote in any Federal, State, or local election because of his inability to read, write, understand, or interpret any matter in the English language, except that, in States in which State law provides that a different level of education is presumptive of literacy, he shall demonstrate that he has successfully completed an equivalent level of education in a public school in, or a private school accredited by, any State or territory, the District of Columbia, or the Commonwealth of Puerto Rico in which the predominant classroom language was other than English.

SEC. 5. Whenever a State or political subdivision with respect to which the prohibitions set forth in section 4(a) are in effect shall enact or seek to administer any voting qualification or prerequisite to voting, or standard, practice, or procedure with respect to voting different from that in force or effect on November 1, 1964, such State or subdivision may institute an action in the United States District Court for the District of Columbia for a declaratory judgment that such qualification, prerequisite, standard, practice, or procedure does not have the purpose and will not have the effect of denying or abridging the right to vote on account of race or color, and unless and until the court enters such judgment no person shall be denied the right to vote for failure to comply with such qualification, prerequisite, standard, practice, or procedure: Provided, That such qualification, prerequisite, standard, practice, or procedure may be enforced without such proceeding if the qualification, prerequisite, standard, practice, or procedure has been submitted by the chief legal officer or other appropriate official of such State or subdivision to the Attorney General and the Attorney General has not interposed an objection within sixty days after such submission, except that neither the Attorney General's failure to object nor a declaratory judgment entered under this section shall bar a subsequent action to enjoin enforcement of such qualification, prerequisite, standard, practice, or procedure. Any action under this section shall be heard and determined by a court of three judges in accordance with the provisions of section 2284 of title 28 of the United States Code and any appeal shall lie to the Supreme Court.

SEC. 6. Whenever (a) a court has authorized the appointment of examiners pursuant to the provisions of section 3(a), or (b) unless a declaratory judgment has been rendered under section 4(a), the Attorney General certifies with respect to any political subdivision named in, or included within the scope of, determinations made under section 4(b) that (1) he has received complaints in writing from twenty or more residents of such political subdivision alleging that they have been denied the right to vote under color of law on account of race or color, and that he believes such complaints to be meritorious, or (2) that, in his judgment (considering, among other factors, whether the ratio of nonwhite persons to white persons registered to vote within such subdivision appears to him to be reasonably attributable to violations of the fifteenth amendment or whether substantial evidence exists that bona fide efforts are being made within such subdivision to comply with the fifteenth amendment), the appointment of examiners is otherwise necessary to enforce the guarantees of the fifteenth amendment, the Civil Service Commission shall appoint as many examiners for such subdivision as it may deem appropriate to prepare and maintain lists of persons eligible to vote in Federal, State, and local elections. Such examiners, hearing officers provided for in section 9(a), and other persons deemed necessary by the Commission to carry out the provisions and purposes of this Act shall be appointed, compensated, and separated

without regard to the provisions of any statute administered by the Civil Service Commission, and service under this Act shall not be considered employment for the purposes of any statute administered by the Civil Service Commission, except the provisions of section 9 of the Act of August 2, 1939, as amended (5 U.S.C. 118i), prohibiting partisan political activity: Provided, That the Commission is authorized, after consulting the head of the appropriate department or agency, to designate suitable persons in the official service of the United States, with their consent, to serve in these positions. Examiners and hearing officers shall have the power to administer oaths.

SEC. 7. (a) The examiners for each political subdivision shall, at such places as the Civil Service Commission shall by regulation designate, examine applicants concerning their qualifications for voting. An application to an examiner shall be in such form as the Commission may require and shall contain allegations that the applicant is not otherwise registered to vote.

(b) Any person whom the examiner finds, in accordance with instructions received under section 9(b), to have the qualifications prescribed by State law not inconsistent with the Constitution and laws of the United States shall promptly be placed on a list of eligible voters. A challenge to such listing may be made in accordance with section 9(a) and shall not be the basis for a prosecution under section 12 of this Act. The examiner shall certify and transmit such list, and any supplements as appropriate, at least once a month, to the offices of the appropriate election officials, with copies to the Attorney General and the attorney general of the State, and any such lists and supplements thereto transmitted during the month shall be available for public inspection on the last business day of the month and, in any event, not later than the forty-fifth day prior to any election. The appropriate State or local election official shall place such names on the official voting list. Any person whose name appears on the examiner's list shall be entitled and allowed to vote in the election district of his residence unless and until the appropriate election officials shall have been notified that such person has been removed from such list in accordance with subsection (d): Provided, That no person shall be entitled to vote in any election by virtue of this Act unless his name shall have been certified and transmitted on such a list to the offices of the appropriate election officials at least forty-five days prior to such election.

(c) The examiner shall issue to each person whose name appears on such a list a certificate evidencing his eligibility to vote.

(d) A person whose name appears on such a list shall be removed therefrom by an examiner if (1) such person has been successfully challenged in accordance with the procedure prescribed in section 9, or (2) he has been determined by an examiner to have lost his eligibility to vote under State law not inconsistent with the Constitution and the laws of the United States.

Sec. 8. Whenever an examiner is serving under this Act in any political subdivision, the Civil Service Commission may assign, at the request of the Attorney General, one or more persons, who may be officers of the United States, (1) to enter and attend at any place for holding an election in such subdivision for the purpose of observing whether persons who are entitled to vote are being permitted to vote, and (2) to enter and attend at any place for tabulating the votes cast at any election held in such subdivision for the purpose of observing whether votes cast by persons entitled to vote are being properly tabulated. Such persons so assigned shall report to an examiner appointed for such political subdivision, to the Attorney General, and if the appointment of examiners has been authorized pursuant to section 3(a), to the court.

SEC. 9. (a) Any challenge to a listing on an eligibility list prepared by an examiner shall be heard and determined by a hearing officer appointed by

and responsible to the Civil Service Commission and under such rules as the Commission shall by regulation prescribe. Such challenge shall be entertained only if filed at such office within the State as the Civil Service Commission shall by regulation designate, and within ten days after the listing of the challenged person is made available for public inspection, and if supported by (1) the affidavits of at least two persons having personal knowledge of the facts constituting grounds for the challenge, and (2) a certification that a copy of the challenge and affidavits have been served by mail or in person upon the person challenged at his place of residence set out in the application. Such challenge shall be determined within fifteen days after it has been filed. A petition for review of the decision of the hearing officer may be filed in the United States court of appeals for the circuit in which the person challenged resides within fifteen days after service of such decision by mail on the person petitioning for review but no decision of a hearing officer shall be reversed unless clearly erroneous. Any person listed shall be entitled and allowed to vote pending final determination by the hearing officer and by the court.

(b) The times, places, procedures, and form for application and listing pursuant to this Act and removals from the eligibility lists shall be prescribed by regulations promulgated by the Civil Service Commission and the Commission shall, after consultation with the Attorney General, instruct examiners concerning applicable State law not inconsistent with the Constitution and laws of the United States with respect to (1) the qualifications required for listing, and (2) loss of eligibility to vote.

(c) Upon the request of the applicant or the challenger or on its own motion the Civil Service Commission shall have the power to require by subpoena the attendance and testimony of witnesses and the production of documentary evidence relating to any matter pending before it under the authority of this section. In case of contumacy or refusal to obey a subpoena, any district court of the United States or the United States court of any territory or possession, or the District Court of the United States for the District of Columbia, within the jurisdiction of which said person guilty of contumacy or refusal to obey is found or resides or is domiciled or transacts business, or has appointed an agent for receipt of service of process, upon application by the Attorney General of the United States shall have jurisdiction to issue to such person an order requiring such person to appear before the Commission or a hearing officer, there to produce pertinent, relevant, and nonprivileged documentary evidence if so ordered, or there to give testimony touching the matter under investigation, and any failure to obey such order of the court may be punished by said court as a contempt thereof.

SEC. 10. (a) The Congress finds that the requirement of the payment of a poll tax as a precondition to voting (i) precludes persons of limited means from voting or imposes unreasonable financial hardship upon such persons as a precondition to their exercise of the franchise, (ii) does not bear a reasonable relationship to any legitimate State interest in the conduct of elections, and (iii) in some areas has the purpose or effect of denying persons the right to vote because of race or color. Upon the basis of these findings, Congress declares that the constitutional right of citizens to vote is denied or abridged in some areas by the requirement of the payment of a poll tax as a precondition to voting.

(b) In the exercise of the powers of Congress under section 5 of the fourteenth amendment and section 2 of the fifteenth amendment, the Attorney General is authorized and directed to institute forthwith in the name of the United States such actions, including actions against States or political subdivisions, for declaratory judgment or injunctive relief against the enforcement of any requirement of the payment of a poll tax as a precondition to voting, or substitute therefore enacted after November 1, 1964, as will be necessary to implement the declaration of subsection (a) and the purposes of this section.

(c) The district courts of the United States shall have jurisdiction of such actions which shall be heard and determined by a court of three judges in accordance with the provisions of section 2284 of title 28 of the United States Code and any appeal shall lie to the Supreme Court. It shall be the duty of the judges designated to hear the case to assign the case for hearing at the earliest practicable date, to participate in the hearing and determination thereof, and to cause the case to be in every way expedited.

(d) During the pendency of such actions, and thereafter if the courts, notwithstanding this action by the Congress, should declare the requirement of the payment of a poll tax to be constitutional, no citizen of the United States who is a resident of a State or political subdivision with respect to which determinations have been made under subsection 4(b) and a declaratory judgment has not been entered under subsection 4(a), during the first year he becomes otherwise entitled to vote by reason of registration by State or local officials or listing by an examiner, shall be denied the right to vote for failure to pay a poll tax if he tenders payment of such tax for the current year to an examiner or to the appropriate State or local official at least forty-five days prior to election, whether or not such tender would be timely or adequate under State law. An examiner shall have authority to accept such payment from any person authorized by this Act to make an application for listing, and shall issue a receipt for such payment. The examiner shall transmit promptly any such poll tax payment to the office of the State or local official authorized to receive such payment under State law, together with the name and address of the applicant.

SEC. 11. (a) No person acting under color of law shall fail or refuse to permit any person to vote who is entitled to vote under any provision of this Act or is otherwise qualified to vote, or willfully fail or refuse to tabulate, count, and report such person's vote.

(b) No person, whether acting under color of law or otherwise, shall intimidate, threaten, or coerce, or attempt to intimidate, threaten, or coerce any person for voting or attempting to vote, or intimidate, threaten, or coerce, or attempt to intimidate, threaten, or coerce any person for urging or aiding any person to vote or attempt to vote, or intimidate, threaten, or coerce any person for exercising any powers or duties under section 3(a), 6, 8, 9, 10, or 12(e).

(c) Whoever knowingly or willfully gives false information as to his name, address, or period of residence in the voting district for the purpose of establishing his eligibility to register or vote, or conspires with another individual for the purpose of encouraging his false registration to vote or illegal voting, or pays or offers to pay or accepts payment either for registration to vote or for voting shall be fined not more than $10,000 or imprisoned not more than five years, or both: Provided, however, That this provision shall be applicable only to general, special, or primary elections held solely or in part for the purpose of selecting or electing any candidate for the office of President, Vice President, presidential elector, Member of the United States Senate, Member of the United States House of Representatives, or Delegates or Commissioners from the territories or possessions, or Resident Commissioner of the Commonwealth of Puerto Rico.

(d) Whoever, in any matter within the jurisdiction of an examiner or hearing officer knowingly and willfully falsifies or conceals a material fact, or makes any false, fictitious, or fraudulent statements or representations, or makes or uses any false writing or document knowing the same to contain any false, fictitious, or fraudulent statement or entry, shall be fined not more than $10,000 or imprisoned not more than five years, or both.

SEC. 12. (a) Whoever shall deprive or attempt to deprive any person of any right secured by section 2, 3, 4, 5, 7, or 10 or shall violate section 11(a) or (b), shall be fined not more than $5,000, or imprisoned not more than five years, or both.

(b) Whoever, within a year following an election in a political subdivision in which an examiner has been appointed (1) destroys, defaces, mutilates, or otherwise alters the marking of a paper ballot which has been cast in such election, or (2) alters any official record of voting in such election tabulated from a voting machine or otherwise, shall be fined not more than $5,000, or imprisoned not more than five years, or both

(c) Whoever conspires to violate the provisions of subsection (a) or (b) of this section, or interferes with any right secured by section 2, 3, 4, 5, 7, 10, or 11(a) or (b) shall be fined not more than $5,000, or imprisoned not more than five years, or both.

(d) Whenever any person has engaged or there are reasonable grounds to believe that any person is about to engage in any act or practice prohibited by section 2, 3, 4, 5, 7, 10, 11, or subsection (b) of this section, the Attorney General may institute for the United States, or in the name of the United States, an action for preventive relief, including an application for a temporary or permanent injunction, restraining order, or other order, and including an order directed to the State and State or local election officials to require them (1) to permit persons listed under this Act to vote and (2) to count such votes.

(e) Whenever in any political subdivision in which there are examiners appointed pursuant to this Act any persons allege to such an examiner within forty-eight hours after the closing of the polls that notwithstanding (1) their listing under this Act or registration by an appropriate election official and (2) their eligibility to vote, they have not been permitted to vote in such election, the examiner shall forthwith notify the Attorney General if such allegations in his opinion appear to be well founded. Upon receipt of such notification, the Attorney General may forthwith file with the district court an application for an order providing for the marking, casting, and counting of the ballots of such persons and requiring the inclusion of their votes in the total vote before the results of such election shall be deemed final and any force or effect given thereto. The district court shall hear and determine such matters immediately after the filing of such application. The remedy provided in this subsection shall not preclude any remedy available under State or Federal law.

(f) The district courts of the United States shall have jurisdiction of proceedings instituted pursuant to this section and shall exercise the same without regard to whether a person asserting rights under the provisions of this Act shall have exhausted any administrative or other remedies that may be provided by law

SEC. 13. Listing procedures shall be terminated in any political subdivision of any State (a) with respect to examiners appointed pursuant to clause (b) of section 6 whenever the Attorney General notifies the Civil Service Commission, or whenever the District Court for the District of Columbia determines in an action for declaratory judgment brought by any political subdivision with respect to which the Director of the Census has determined that more than 50 percentum of the nonwhite persons of voting age residing therein are registered to vote, (1) that all persons listed by an examiner for such subdivision have been placed on the appropriate voting registration roll, and (2) that there is no longer reasonable cause to believe that persons will be deprived of or denied the right to vote on account of race or color in such subdivision, and (b), with respect to examiners appointed pursuant to section 3(a), upon order of the authorizing court. A political subdivision may petition the Attorney General for the termination of listing procedures under clause (a) of this section, and may petition the Attorney General to request the Director of the Census to take such survey or census as may be appropriate for the making of the determination provided for in this section. The District Court for the District of Columbia shall have jurisdiction to require such survey or census to be made by the Director of the Census and it shall require him to

do so if it deems the Attorney General's refusal to request such survey or census to be arbitrary or unreasonable.

SEC. 14. (a) All cases of criminal contempt arising under the provisions of this Act shall be governed by section 151 of the Civil Rights Act of 1957 (42 U.S.C. 1995).

(b) No court other than the District Court for the District of Columbia or a court of appeals in any proceeding under section 9 shall have jurisdiction to issue any declaratory judgment pursuant to section 4 or section 5 or any restraining order or temporary or permanent injunction against the execution or enforcement of any provision of this Act or any action of any Federal officer or employee pursuant hereto.

(c) (1) The terms "vote" or "voting" shall include all action necessary to make a vote effective in any primary, special, or general election, including, but not limited to, registration, listing pursuant to this Act, or other action required by law prerequisite to voting, casting a ballot, and having such ballot counted properly and included in the appropriate totals of votes cast with respect to candidates for public or party office and propositions for which votes are received in an election. (2) The term "political subdivision" shall mean any county or parish, except that, where registration for voting is not conducted under the supervision of a county or parish, the term shall include any other subdivision of a State which conducts registration for voting.

(d) In any action for a declaratory judgment brought pursuant to section 4 or section 5 of this Act, subpoenas for witnesses who are required to attend the District Court for the District of Columbia may be served in any judicial district of the United States: Provided, That no writ of subpoena shall issue for witnesses without the District of Columbia at a greater distance than one hundred miles from the place of holding court without the permission of the District Court for the District of Columbia being first had upon proper application and cause shown.

SEC. 15. Section 2004 of the Revised Statutes (42 U.S.C.1971), as amended by section 131 of the Civil Rights Act of 1957 (71 Stat. 637), and amended by section 601 of the Civil Rights Act of 1960 (74 Stat. 90), and as further amended by section 101 of the Civil Rights Act of 1964 (78 Stat. 241), is further amended as follows:

(a) Delete the word "Federal" wherever it appears in subsections (a) and (c);

(b) Repeal subsection (f) and designate the present subsections (g) and (h) as (f) and (g), respectively.

SEC. 16. The Attorney General and the Secretary of Defense, jointly, shall make a full and complete study to determine whether, under the laws or practices of any State or States, there are preconditions to voting, which might tend to result in discrimination against citizens serving in the Armed Forces of the United States seeking to vote. Such officials shall, jointly, make a report to the Congress not later than June 30, 1966, containing the results

of such study, together with a list of any States in which such preconditions exist, and shall include in such report such recommendations for legislation as they deem advisable to prevent discrimination in voting against citizens serving in the Armed Forces of the United States.

SEC. 17. Nothing in this Act shall be construed to deny, impair, or otherwise adversely affect the right to vote of any person registered to vote under the law of any State or political subdivision.

SEC. 18. There are hereby authorized to be appropriated such sums as are necessary to carry out the provisions of this Act

SEC 19. If any provision of this Act or the application thereof to any person or circumstances is held invalid, the remainder of the Act and the application of the provision to other persons not similarly situated or to other circumstances shall not be affected thereby.

Approved August 6, 1965.

Source: The Voting Rights Act of 1965, 42 U.S.C. §§ 1973–1973bb-1.

Equal Employment Opportunity Act

(1965)

The Equal Employment Opportunity Act of 1965 is among the most important pieces of civil rights legislation passed in the United States. The act made it a crime under federal law to discriminate in employment on the basis of race. It was landmark legislation that led to countless groundbreaking class action lawsuits that forced sweeping changes in U.S. employment practices.

Under and by virtue of the authority vested in me as President of the United States by the Constitution and statutes of the United States, it is ordered as follows:

Part I—Nondiscrimination in Government Employment

Part II—Nondiscrimination in Employment by Government Contractors and Subcontractors

Subpart A - Duties of the Secretary of Labor

SEC. 201. The Secretary of Labor shall be responsible for the administration and enforcement of Parts II and III of this Order. The Secretary shall adopt such rules and regulations and issue such orders as are deemed necessary and appropriate to achieve the purposes of Parts II and III of this Order.

[Sec. 201 amended by EO 12086 of Oct. 5, 1978, 43 FR 46501, 3 CFR, 1978 Comp., p. 230]

Subpart B - Contractors' Agreements

SEC. 202. Except in contracts exempted in accordance with Section 204 of this Order, all Government contracting agencies shall include in every Government contract hereafter entered into the following provisions:

During the performance of this contract, the contractor agrees as follows:

(1) The contractor will not discriminate against any employee or applicant for employment because of race, color, religion, sex, or national origin. The contractor will take affirmative action to ensure that applicants are employed, and that employees are treated during employment, without regard to their race, color, religion, sex or national origin. Such action shall include, but not be limited to the following: employment, upgrading, demotion, or transfer; recruitment or recruitment advertising; layoff or termination; rates of pay or other forms of compensation; and selection for training, including apprenticeship. The contractor agrees to post in conspicuous places, available to employees and applicants for employment, notices to be provided by the contracting officer setting forth the provisions of this nondiscrimination clause.

(2) The contractor will, in all solicitations or advancements for employees placed by or on behalf of the contractor, state that all qualified applicants will receive consideration for employment without regard to race, color, religion, sex or national origin.

(3) The contractor will send to each labor union or representative of workers with which he has a collective bargaining agreement or other contract or understanding, a notice, to be provided by the agency contracting officer, advising the labor union or workers' representative of the contractor's commitments under Section 202 of Executive Order No. 11246 of September 24, 1965, and shall post copies of the notice in conspicuous places available to employees and applicants for employment.

(4) The contractor will comply with provisions of Executive Order No. 11246 of Sept. 24, 1965, and of the rules, regulations, and relevant orders of the Secretary of Labor.

(5) The contractor will furnish all information and reports required by Executive Order No. 11246 of September 24, 1965, and by the rules, regulations, and orders of the Secretary of Labor, or pursuant thereto, and will permit access to his books, records, and accounts by the contracting agency and the Secretary of Labor for purposes of investigation to ascertain compliance with such rules, regulations, and orders.

(6) In the event of the contractor's noncompliance with the nondiscrimination clauses of this contract or with any of such rules, regulations, or orders, this contract may be cancelled, terminated, or suspended in whole or in part and the contractor may be declared ineligible for further Government contracts in accordance with procedures authorized in Executive Order No. 11246 of Sept. 24, 1965, and such other sanctions may be imposed and remedies invoked as provided in Executive Order No. 11246 of September 24, 1965, or by rule, regulation, or order of the Secretary of Labor, or as otherwise provided by law.

(7) The contractor will include the provisions of paragraphs (1) through (7) in every subcontract or purchase order unless exempted by rules, regulations, or orders of the Secretary of Labor issued pursuant to Section 204 of Executive Order No.

11246 of September 24, 1965, so that such provisions will be binding upon each subcontractor or vendor. The contractor will take such action with respect to any subcontract or purchase order as may be directed by the Secretary of Labor as a means of enforcing such provisions including sanctions for noncompliance: Provided, however, that in the event the contractor becomes involved in, or is threatened with, litigation with a subcontractor or vendor as a result of such direction, the contractor may request the United States to enter into such litigation to protect the interests of the United States." [Sec. 202 amended by EO 11375 of Oct. 13, 1967, 32 FR 14303, 3 CFR, 1966–1970 Comp., p. 684, EO 12086 of Oct. 5, 1978, 43 FR 46501, 3 CFR, 1978 Comp., p. 230]

SEC. 203(a). Each contractor having a contract containing the provisions prescribed in Section 202 shall file, and shall cause each of his subcontractors to file, Compliance Reports with the contracting agency or the Secretary of Labor as may be directed. Compliance Reports shall be filed within such times and shall contain such information as to the practices, policies, programs, and employment policies, programs, and employment statistics of the contractor and each subcontractor, and shall be in such form, as the Secretary of Labor may prescribe.

(b) Bidders or prospective contractors or subcontractors may be required to state whether they have participated in any previous contract subject to the provisions of this Order, or any preceding similar Executive order, and in that event to submit, on behalf of themselves and their proposed subcontractors, Compliance Reports prior to or as an initial part of their bid or negotiation of a contract.

(c) Whenever the contractor or subcontractor has a collective bargaining agreement or other contract or understanding with a labor union or an agency referring workers or providing or supervising apprenticeship or training for such workers, the Compliance Report shall include such information

as to such labor union's or agency's practices and policies affecting compliance as the Secretary of Labor may prescribe: Provided, That to the extent such information is within the exclusive possession of a labor union or an agency referring workers or providing or supervising apprenticeship or training and such labor union or agency shall refuse to furnish such information to the contractor, the contractor shall so certify to the Secretary of Labor as part of its Compliance Report and shall set forth what efforts he has made to obtain such information.

(d) The Secretary of Labor may direct that any bidder or prospective contractor or subcontractor shall submit, as part of his Compliance Report, a statement in writing, signed by an authorized officer or agent on behalf of any labor union or any agency referring workers or providing or supervising apprenticeship or other training, with which the bidder or prospective contractor deals, with supporting information, to the effect that the signer's practices and policies do not discriminate on the grounds of race, color, religion, sex or national origin, and that the signer either will affirmatively cooperate in the implementation of the policy and provisions of this Order or that it consents and agrees that recruitment, employment, and the terms and conditions of employment under the proposed contract shall be in accordance with the purposes and provisions of the order. In the event that the union, or the agency shall refuse to execute such a statement, the Compliance Report shall so certify and set forth what efforts have been made to secure such a statement and such additional factual material as the Secretary of Labor may require.

[Sec. 203 amended by EO 11375 of Oct. 13, 1967, 32 FR 14303, 3 CFR, 1966–1970 Comp., p. 684; EO 12086 of Oct. 5, 1978, 43 FR 46501, 3 CFR, 1978 Comp., p. 230]

SEC. 204 (a) The Secretary of Labor may, when the Secretary deems that special circumstances in the national interest so require, exempt a contracting agency from the requirement of including any or all of the provisions of Section 202 of this Order in any specific contract, subcontract, or purchase order.

(b) The Secretary of Labor may, by rule or regulation, exempt certain classes of contracts, subcontracts, or purchase orders (1) whenever work is to be or has been performed outside the United States and no recruitment of workers within the limits of the United States is involved; (2) for standard commercial supplies or raw materials; (3) involving less than specified amounts of money or specified numbers of workers; or (4) to the extent that they involve subcontracts below a specified tier.

(c) Section 202 of this Order shall not apply to a Government contractor or subcontractor that is a religious corporation, association, educational institution, or society, with respect to the employment of individuals of a particular religion to perform work connected with the carrying on by such corporation, association, educational institution, or society of its activities. Such contractors and subcontractors are not exempted or excused from complying with the other requirements contained in this Order.

(d) The Secretary of Labor may also provide, by rule, regulation, or order, for the exemption of facilities of a contractor that are in all respects separate and distinct from activities of the contractor related to the performance of the contract: provided, that such an exemption will not interfere with or impede the effectuation of the purposes of this Order: and provided further, that in the absence of such an exemption all facilities shall be covered by the provisions of this Order."

[Sec. 204 amended by EO 13279 of Dec. 16, 2002, 67 FR 77141, 3 CFR, 2002 Comp., p. 77141–77144]

Subpart C - Powers and Duties of the Secretary of Labor and the Contracting Agencies

SEC. 205. The Secretary of Labor shall be responsible for securing compliance by all Government contractors and subcontractors with this Order and any implementing rules or regulations. All contracting agencies shall comply with the terms of this Order and any implementing rules, regulations, or orders of the Secretary of Labor. Contracting agencies shall cooperate with the Secretary of Labor and shall furnish such information and assistance as the Secretary may require.

[Sec. 205 amended by EO 12086 of Oct. 5, 1978, 43 FR 46501, 3 CFR, 1978 Comp., p. 230]

SEC. 206(a). The Secretary of Labor may investigate the employment practices of any Government contractor or subcontractor to determine whether or not the contractual provisions specified in Section 202 of this Order have been violated. Such investigation shall be conducted in accordance with the procedures established by the Secretary of Labor.

(b) The Secretary of Labor may receive and investigate complaints by employees or prospective employees of a Government contractor or subcontractor which allege discrimination contrary to the contractual provisions specified in Section 202 of this Order.

[Sec. 206 amended by EO 12086 of Oct. 5, 1978, 43 FR 46501, 3 CFR, 1978 Comp., p. 230]

SEC. 207. The Secretary of Labor shall use his/her best efforts, directly and through interested Federal, State, and local agencies, contractors, and all other available instrumentalities to cause any labor union engaged in work under Government contracts or any agency referring workers or providing or supervising apprenticeship or training for or in the course of such work to cooperate in the implementation of the purposes of this Order. The Secretary of Labor shall, in appropriate cases, notify the Equal Employment Opportunity Commission, the Department of Justice, or other appropriate Federal agencies whenever it has reason to believe that the practices of any such labor organization or agency violate Title VI or Title VII of the Civil Rights Act of 1964 or other provision of Federal law.

[Sec. 207 amended by EO 12086 of Oct. 5, 1978, 43 FR 46501, 3 CFR, 1978 Comp., p. 230]

SEC. 208(a). The Secretary of Labor, or any agency, officer, or employee in the executive branch of the Government designated by rule, regulation, or order of the Secretary, may hold such hearings, public or private, as the Secretary may deem advisable for compliance, enforcement, or educational purposes.

(b) The Secretary of Labor may hold, or cause to be held, hearings in accordance with Subsection of this Section prior to imposing, ordering, or recommending the imposition of penalties and sanctions under this Order. No order for debarment of any contractor from further Government contracts under Section 209(6) shall be made without affording the contractor an opportunity for a hearing.

Subpart D - Sanctions and Penalties

SEC. 209(a). In accordance with such rules, regulations, or orders as the Secretary of Labor may issue or adopt, the Secretary may:

(1) Publish, or cause to be published, the names of contractors or unions which it has concluded have complied or have failed to comply with the provisions of this Order or of the rules, regulations, and orders of the Secretary of Labor.

(2) Recommend to the Department of Justice that, in cases in which there is substantial or material violation or the threat of substantial or material violation of the contractual provisions set forth in Section 202 of this Order, appropriate proceedings be brought to enforce those provisions, including the enjoining, within the limitations of applicable law, of organizations, individuals, or groups who prevent directly or indirectly, or seek to prevent directly or indirectly, compliance with the provisions of this Order.

(3) Recommend to the Equal Employment Opportunity Commission or the Department of Justice that appropriate proceedings be instituted under Title VII of the Civil Rights Act of 1964.

(4) Recommend to the Department of Justice that criminal proceedings be brought for the furnishing of false information to any contracting agency or to the Secretary of Labor as the case may be.

(5) After consulting with the contracting agency, direct the contracting agency to cancel, terminate, suspend, or cause to be cancelled, terminated, or suspended, any contract, or any portion or portions thereof, for failure of the contractor or subcontractor to comply with equal employment opportunity provisions of the contract. Contracts may be cancelled, terminated, or suspended absolutely or continuance of contracts may be conditioned upon a program for future compliance approved by the Secretary of Labor.

(6) Provide that any contracting agency shall refrain from entering into further contracts, or extensions or other modifications of existing contracts, with any noncomplying contractor, until such contractor has satisfied the Secretary of Labor that such contractor has established and will carry out personnel and employment policies in compliance with the provisions of this Order.

(b) Pursuant to rules and regulations prescribed by the Secretary of Labor, the Secretary shall make reasonable efforts, within a reasonable time limitation, to secure compliance with the contract provisions of this Order by methods of conference, conciliation, mediation, and persuasion before proceedings shall be instituted under subsection (a)(2) of this Section, or before a contract shall be cancelled or terminated in whole or in part under subsection (a)(5) of this Section.

[Sec. 209 amended by EO 12086 of Oct. 5, 1978, 43 FR 46501, 3 CFR, 1978 Comp., p. 230]

SEC. 210. Whenever the Secretary of Labor makes a determination under Section 209, the Secretary shall promptly notify the appropriate agency. The agency shall take the action directed by the Secretary and shall report the results of the action it has taken to the Secretary of Labor within such time as the

Secretary shall specify. If the contracting agency fails to take the action directed within thirty days, the Secretary may take the action directly.

[Sec. 210 amended by EO 12086 of Oct. 5, 1978, 43 FR 46501, 3 CFR, 1978 Comp., p 230]

SEC. 211. If the Secretary shall so direct, contracting agencies shall not enter into contracts with any bidder or prospective contractor unless the bidder or prospective contractor has satisfactorily complied with the provisions of this Order or submits a program for compliance acceptable to the Secretary of Labor.

[Sec. 211 amended by EO 12086 of Oct. 5, 1978, 43 FR 46501, 3 CFR, 1978 Comp., p. 230]

SEC. 212. When a contract has been cancelled or terminated under Section 209(a)(5) or a contractor has been debarred from further Government contracts under Section 209(a)(6) of this Order, because of noncompliance with the contract provisions specified in Section 202 of this Order, the Secretary of Labor shall promptly notify the Comptroller General of the United States.

[Sec. 212 amended by EO 12086 of Oct. 5, 1978, 43 FR 46501, 3 CFR, 1978 Comp., p. 230]

Subpart E – Certificates of Merit

SEC. 213. The Secretary of Labor may provide for issuance of a United States Government Certificate of Merit to employers or labor unions, or other agencies which are or may hereafter be engaged in work under Government contracts, if the Secretary is satisfied that the personnel and employment practices of the employer, or that the personnel, training, apprenticeship, membership, grievance and representation, upgrading, and other practices and policies of the labor union or other agency conform to the purposes and provisions of this Order.

SEC. 214. Any Certificate of Merit may at any time be suspended or revoked by the Secretary of Labor if the holder thereof, in the judgment of the Secretary, has failed to comply with the provisions of this Order.

SEC. 215. The Secretary of Labor may provide for the exemption of any employer, labor union, or other agency from any reporting requirements imposed under or pursuant to this Order if such employer, labor union, or other agency has been awarded a Certificate of Merit which has not been suspended or revoked.

Part III – Nondiscrimination Provisions in Federally Assisted Construction Contracts

SEC. 301. Each executive department and agency, which administers a program involving Federal financial assistance shall require as a condition for the approval of any grant, contract, loan, insurance, or guarantee thereunder, which may involve a construction contract, that the applicant for Federal assistance undertake and agree to incorporate, or cause to be incorporated, into all construction contracts paid for in whole or in part with funds obtained from the Federal Government or borrowed on the credit of the Federal Government pursuant to such grant, contract, loan, insurance, or guarantee, or undertaken pursuant to any Federal program involving such grant, contract, loan, insurance, or guarantee, the provisions prescribed for Government contracts by Section 202 of this Order or such modification thereof, preserving in substance the contractor's obligations thereunder, as may be approved by the Secretary of Labor, together with such additional provisions as the Secretary deems appropriate to establish and protect the interest of the United States in the enforcement of those obligations. Each such applicant shall also undertake and agree (1) to assist and cooperate actively with the Secretary of Labor in obtaining the compliance of contractors and subcontractors with those contract provisions and with the rules, regulations and relevant orders of the Secretary, (2) to obtain and to furnish to the Secretary of Labor such information as the Secretary may require for the supervision of such compliance, (3) to carry out sanctions and penalties for violation of such obligations imposed upon contractors and subcontractors by the Secretary of Labor pursuant to Part II, Subpart D, of this Order, and (4) to refrain from entering into any contract subject to this Order, or extension or other modification of such a contract with a contractor debarred from Government contracts under Part II, Subpart D, of this Order.

[Sec. 301 amended by EO 12086 of Oct. 5, 1978, 43 FR 46501, 3 CFR, 1978 Comp., p. 230]

SEC. 302(a). "Construction contract" as used in this Order means any contract for the construction, rehabilitation, alteration, conversion, extension, or repair of buildings, highways, or other improvements to real property.

(b) The provisions of Part II of this Order shall apply to such construction contracts, and for purposes of such application the administering department or agency shall be considered the contracting agency referred to therein.

(c) The term "applicant" as used in this Order means an applicant for Federal assistance or, as determined by agency regulation, other program participant, with respect to whom an application for any grant, contract, loan, insurance, or guarantee is not finally acted upon prior to the effective date of this Part, and it includes such an applicant after he/she becomes a recipient of such Federal assistance.

SEC. 303(a). The Secretary of Labor shall be responsible for obtaining the compliance of such applicants with their undertakings under this Order. Each administering department and agency is directed to cooperate with the Secretary of Labor and to furnish the Secretary such information and assistance as the Secretary may require in the performance of the Secretary's functions under this Order.

(b) In the event an applicant fails and refuses to comply with the applicant's undertakings pursuant to this Order, the Secretary of Labor may, after consulting with the administering department or agency, take any or all of the following actions: (1) direct any administering department or agency to cancel, terminate, or suspend in whole or in part the agreement, contract or other arrangement with such applicant with respect to which the failure or refusal occurred; (2) direct any administering department or agency to refrain from extending any further assistance to the applicant under the program with respect to which the failure or refusal occurred until satisfactory assurance of future compliance has been received by the Secretary of Labor from such applicant; and (3) refer the case to the Department of Justice or the Equal Employment Opportunity Commission for appropriate law enforcement or other proceedings.

(c) In no case shall action be taken with respect to an applicant pursuant to clause (1) or (2) of subsection (b) without notice and opportunity for hearing.

[Sec. 303 amended by EO 12086 of Oct. 5, 1978, 43 FR 46501, 3 CFR, 1978 Comp., p. 230]

SEC. 304. Any executive department or agency which imposes by rule, regulation, or order requirements of nondiscrimination in employment, other than requirements imposed pursuant to this Order, may delegate to the Secretary of Labor by agreement such responsibilities with respect to compliance standards, reports, and procedures as would tend to bring the administration of such requirements into conformity with the administration of requirements imposed under this Order: Provided,

That actions to effect compliance by recipients of Federal financial assistance with requirements imposed pursuant to Title VI of the Civil Rights Act of 1964 shall be taken into conformity with the procedures and limitations prescribed in Section 602 thereof and the regulations of the administering department or agency issued there under.

Part IV – Miscellaneous

SEC. 401. The Secretary of Labor may delegate to any officer, agency, or employee in the Executive branch of the Government, any function or duty of the Secretary under Parts II and III of this Order.

[Sec. 401 amended by EO 12086 of Oct. 5, 1978, 43 FR 46501, 3 CFR, 1978 Comp., p. 230]

SEC. 402. The Secretary of Labor shall provide administrative support for the execution of the program known as the "Plans for Progress."

SEC. 403(a). Executive Orders Nos. 10590 (January 19, 1955), 10722 (August 5, 1957), 10925 (March 6, 1961), 11114 (June 22, 1963), and 11162 (July 28, 1964), are hereby superseded and the President's Committee on Equal Employment Opportunity established by Executive Order No. 10925 is hereby abolished. All records and property in the custody of the Committee shall be transferred to the Office of Personnel Management and the Secretary of Labor, as appropriate.

(b) Nothing in this Order shall be deemed to relieve any person of any obligation assumed or imposed under or pursuant to any Executive Order superseded by this Order. All rules, regulations, orders, instructions, designations, and other directives issued by the President's Committee on Equal Employment Opportunity and those issued by the heads of various departments or agencies under or pursuant to any of the Executive orders superseded by this Order, shall, to the extent that they are not inconsistent with this Order, remain in full force and effect unless and until revoked or superseded by appropriate authority. References in such directives to provisions of the superseded orders shall be deemed to be references to the comparable provisions of this Order.

[Sec. 403 amended by EO 12107 of Dec. 28, 1978, 44 FR 1055, 3 CFR, 1978 Comp., p, 264]

SEC. 404. The General Services Administration shall take appropriate action to revise the standard Government contract forms to accord with the provisions of this Order and of the rules and regulations of the Secretary of Labor.

SEC. 405. This Order shall become effective thirty days after the date of this Order. employment.

Source: The Equal Employment Opportunity Act. The provisions of Executive Order 11246 of September 24, 1965, appear at 30 FR 12319, 12935, 3 CFR, 1964–1965 Comp., p. 339. U.S. Department of Labor.

Loving v. Virginia
(1967)

In 1959, Virginia residents Mildred and Richard Loving were sentenced to a year in prison for marrying each other. Because Mildred was black and Richard white, their marriage violated a 1924 Virginia antimiscegenation law. Supported by the American Civil Liberties Union the Lovings filed suit in state court arguing that the Virginia law contravened the Fourteenth Amendment. The case eventually reached the Supreme Court, where, in 1967, the justices handed down a unanimous decision invalidating the Virginia law and all race-based legal restrictions on marriage.

U.S. Supreme Court
Loving v. Virginia, 388 U.S. 1 (1967)
No. 395
Argued April 10, 1967
Decided June 12, 1967

388 U.S. 1

APPEAL FROM THE SUPREME COURT OF APPEALS OF VIRGINIA

Syllabus

Virginia's statutory scheme to prevent marriages between persons solely on the basis of racial classifications held to violate the Equal Protection and Due Process Clauses of the Fourteenth Amendment. Pp. 388 U. S. 4-12.

206 Va. 924, 147 S.E.2d 78, reversed.

Page 388 U. S. 2

MR. CHIEF JUSTICE WARREN delivered the opinion of the Court.

This case presents a constitutional question never addressed by this Court: whether a statutory scheme adopted by the State of Virginia to prevent marriages between persons solely on the basis of racial classifications violates the Equal Protection and Due Process Clauses of the Fourteenth Amendment. [Footnote 1] For reasons which seem to us to reflect the central meaning of those constitutional commands, we conclude that these statutes cannot stand consistently with the Fourteenth Amendment.

In June, 1958, two residents of Virginia, Mildred Jeter, a Negro woman, and Richard Loving, a white man, were married in the District of Columbia pursuant to its laws. Shortly after their marriage, the Lovings returned to Virginia and established their marital abode in Caroline County. At the October Term, 1958, of the Circuit Court of Caroline County, a grand jury issued an indictment charging the Lovings with violating Virginia's ban on interracial marriages. The Lovings pled guilty to the charge, and were sentenced to one year in jail; however, the trial judge suspended the sentence for a period of 25 years on the condition that the Lovings leave the State and not return to Virginia together for 25 years. He stated in an opinion that:

> "Almighty God created the races white, black, yellow, malay and red, and he placed them on separate continents. And, but for the interference with his arrangement, there would be no cause for such marriage. The fact that he separated the races shows that he did not intend for the races to mix."

After their convictions, the Lovings took up residence in the District of Columbia. On November 6, 1963, they filed a motion in the state trial court to vacate the judgment and set aside the sentence on the ground that the statutes which they had violated were repugnant to the Fourteenth Amendment. The motion not having been decided by October 28, 1964, the Lovings instituted a class action in the United States District Court for the Eastern District of Virginia requesting that a three-judge court be convened to declare the Virginia anti-miscegenation statutes unconstitutional and to enjoin state officials from enforcing their convictions. On January 22, 1965, the state trial judge denied the motion to vacate the sentences, and the Lovings perfected an appeal to the Supreme Court of Appeals of Virginia. On February 11, 1965, the three-judge District Court continued the case to allow the Lovings to present their constitutional claims to the highest state court.

The Supreme Court of Appeals upheld the constitutionality of the anti-miscegenation statutes and, after modifying the sentence, affirmed the convictions. [Footnote 2] The Lovings appealed this decision, and we noted probable jurisdiction on December 12, 1966, 385 U.S. 986.

The two statutes under which appellants were convicted and sentenced are part of a comprehensive statutory scheme aimed at prohibiting and punishing interracial marriages. The Lovings were convicted of violating § 258 of the Virginia Code:

> "*Leaving State to evade law.* — If any white person and colored person shall go out of this State, for the purpose of being married, and with the intention of returning, and be married out of it, and afterwards return to and reside in it, cohabiting as man and wife, they shall be punished as provided in § 20-59, and the marriage shall be governed by the same law as if it had been solemnized in this State. The fact of their cohabitation here as man and wife shall be evidence of their marriage."

Section 259, which defines the penalty for miscegenation, provides:

"Punishment for marriage. — If any white person intermarry with a colored person, or any colored person intermarry with a white person, he shall be guilty of a felony and shall be punished by confinement in the penitentiary for not less than one nor more than five years."

Other central provisions in the Virginia statutory scheme are § 20-57, which automatically voids all marriages between "a white person and a colored person" without any judicial proceeding, [Footnote 3] and §§ 20-54 and 1-14 which, respectively, define "white persons" and "colored persons and Indians" for purposes of the statutory prohibitions. [Footnote 4] The Lovings have never disputed in the course of this litigation that Mrs. Loving is a "colored person" or that Mr. Loving is a "white person" within the meanings given those terms by the Virginia statutes.

Virginia is now one of 16 States which prohibit and punish marriages on the basis of racial classifications. [Footnote 5] Penalties for miscegenation arose as an incident to slavery, and have been common in Virginia since the colonial period. [Footnote 6] The present statutory scheme dates from the adoption of the Racial Integrity Act of 1924, passed during the period of extreme nativism which followed the end of the First World War. The central features of this Act, and current Virginia law, are the absolute prohibition of a "white person" marrying other than another "white person" [Footnote 7], a prohibition against issuing marriage licenses until the issuing official is satisfied that the applicants' statements as to their race are correct, [Footnote 8] certificates of "racial composition" to be kept by both local and state registrars, [Footnote 9] and the carrying forward of earlier prohibitions against racial intermarriage. [Footnote 10]

I

In upholding the constitutionality of these provisions in the decision below, the Supreme Court of Appeals of Virginia referred to its 1965 decision in *Naim v. Naim,* 197 Va. 80, 87 S.E.2d 749, as stating the reasons supporting the validity of these laws. In *Naim,* the state court concluded that the State's legitimate purposes were "to preserve the racial integrity of its citizens," and to prevent "the corruption of blood," "a mongrel breed of citizens," and "the obliteration of racial pride," obviously an endorsement of the doctrine of White Supremacy. *Id.* at 90, 87 S.E.2d at 756. The court also reasoned that marriage has traditionally been subject to state regulation without federal intervention, and, consequently, the regulation of marriage should be left to exclusive state control by the Tenth Amendment.

While the state court is no doubt correct in asserting that marriage is a social relation subject to the State's police power, *Maynard v. Hill,* 125 U. S. 190 (1888), the State does not contend in its argument before this Court that its powers to regulate marriage are unlimited notwithstanding the commands of the Fourteenth Amendment. Nor could it do so in light of *Meyer v. Nebraska,* 262 U. S. 390 (1923), and *Skinner v. Oklahoma,* 316 U. S. 535 (1942). Instead, the State argues that the meaning of the Equal Protection Clause, as illuminated by the statements of the Framers, is only that state penal laws containing an interracial element as part of the definition of the offense must apply equally to whites and Negroes in the sense that members of each race are punished to the same degree. Thus, the State contends that, because its miscegenation statutes punish equally both the white and the Negro participants in an interracial marriage, these statutes, despite their reliance on racial classifications, do not constitute an invidious discrimination based upon race. The second argument advanced by the State assumes the validity of its equal application theory. The argument is that, if the Equal Protection Clause does not outlaw miscegenation statutes because of their reliance on racial classifications, the question of constitutionality would thus become whether there was any rational basis for a State to treat interracial marriages differently from other marriages. On this question, the State argues, the scientific evidence is substantially in doubt and, consequently, this Court should defer to the wisdom of the state legislature in adopting its policy of discouraging interracial marriages.

Because we reject the notion that the mere "equal application" of a statute containing racial classifications is enough to remove the classifications from the Fourteenth Amendment's proscription of all invidious racial discriminations, we do not accept the State's contention that these statutes should be upheld if there is any possible basis for concluding that they serve a rational purpose. The mere fact of equal application does not mean that our analysis of these statutes should follow the approach we have taken in cases involving no racial discrimination where the Equal Protection Clause has been arrayed against a statute discriminating between the kinds of advertising which may be displayed on trucks in New York City, *Railway Express Agency, Inc. v. New York,* 336 U. S. 106 (1949), or an exemption in Ohio's *ad valorem* tax for merchandise owned by a nonresident in a storage warehouse, *Allied Stores of Ohio, Inc. v. Bowers,* 358 U. S. 522 (1959). In these cases, involving distinctions not drawn according to race, the Court has merely asked whether there is any rational foundation for the discriminations, and has deferred to the wisdom of the state legislatures. In the case at bar, however, we deal with statutes containing racial classifications, and the fact of equal application does not immunize the statute from the very heavy burden of justification which the Fourteenth Amendment has traditionally required of state statutes drawn according to race.

The State argues that statements in the Thirty-ninth Congress about the time of the passage of the Fourteenth Amendment indicate that the Framers did not intend the Amendment to make unconstitutional state miscegenation laws. Many of the statements alluded to by the State concern the debates over the Freedmen's Bureau Bill, which President Johnson vetoed, and the Civil Rights Act of 1866, 14 Stat. 27, enacted over his veto. While these statements have some relevance to the intention of Congress in submitting the Fourteenth Amendment, it must be understood that they pertained to the passage of specific statutes, and not to the broader, organic purpose of a constitutional amendment. As for the various statements directly concerning the Fourteenth Amendment, we have said in connection with a related problem that, although these historical sources "cast some light" they are not sufficient to resolve the problem;

"[a]t best, they are inconclusive. The most avid proponents of the post-War Amendments undoubtedly intended them to remove all legal distinctions among 'all persons born or naturalized in the United States.' Their opponents, just as certainly, were antagonistic to both the letter and the spirit of the Amendments, and wished them to have the most limited effect."

Brown v. Board of Education, 347 U. S. 483, 347 U. S. 489 (1954). *See also Strauder v. West Virginia,* 100 U. S. 303, 100 U. S. 310 (1880). We have rejected the proposition that the debates in the Thirty-ninth Congress or in the state legislatures which ratified the Fourteenth Amendment supported the theory advanced by the State, that the requirement of equal protection of the laws is satisfied by penal laws defining offenses based on racial classifications so long as white and Negro participants in the offense were similarly punished. *McLaughlin v. Florida,* 379 U. S. 184 (1964).

The State finds support for its "equal application" theory in the decision of the Court in *Pace v. Alabama,* 106 U. S. 583 (1883). In that case, the Court upheld a conviction under an Alabama statute forbidding adultery or fornication between a white person and a Negro which imposed a greater penalty than that of a statute proscribing similar conduct by members of the same race. The Court reasoned that the statute could not be said to discriminate against Negroes because the punishment for each participant in the offense was the same. However, as recently as the 1964 Term, in rejecting the reasoning of that case, we stated "*Pace* represents a limited view of the Equal Protection Clause which has not withstood analysis in the subsequent decisions of this Court." *McLaughlin v. Florida, supra,* at 379 U. S. 188. As we there demonstrated, the Equal Protection Clause requires the consideration of whether the classifications drawn by any statute constitute an arbitrary and invidious discrimination. The clear and central purpose of the Fourteenth Amendment was to eliminate all official state sources of invidious racial discrimination in the States. *Slaughter-House Cases,* 16 Wall. 36, 83 U. S. 71 (1873); *Strauder v. West Virginia,* 100 U. S. 303, 100 U. S. 307-308 (1880); *Ex parte Virginia,* 100 U. S. 339, 100 U. S. 334-335 (1880); *Shelley v. Kraemer,* 334 U. S. 1 (1948); *Burton v. Wilmington Parking Authority,* 365 U. S. 715 (1961).

Page 388 U. S. 11

There can be no question but that Virginia's miscegenation statutes rest solely upon distinctions drawn according to race. The statutes proscribe generally accepted conduct if engaged in by members of different races. Over the years, this Court has consistently repudiated "[d]istinctions between citizens solely because of their ancestry" as being "odious to a free people whose institutions are founded upon the doctrine of equality." *Hirabayashi v. United States,* 320 U. S. 81, 320 U. S. 100 (1943). At the very least, the Equal Protection Clause demands that racial classifications, especially suspect in criminal statutes, be subjected to the "most rigid scrutiny," *Korematsu v. United States,* 323 U. S. 214, 323 U. S. 216 (1944), and, if they are ever to be upheld, they must be shown to be necessary to the accomplishment of some permissible state objective, independent of the racial discrimination which it was the object of the Fourteenth Amendment to eliminate. Indeed, two members of this Court have already stated that they "cannot conceive of a valid legislative purpose . . . which makes the color of a person's skin the test of whether his conduct is a criminal offense."

McLaughlin v. Florida, supra, at 379 U. S. 198 (STEWART, J., joined by DOUGLAS, J., concurring).

There is patently no legitimate overriding purpose independent of invidious racial discrimination which justifies this classification. The fact that Virginia prohibits only interracial marriages involving white persons demonstrates that the racial classifications must stand on their own justification, as

measures designed to maintain White Supremacy. [Footnote 11] We have consistently denied the constitutionality of measures which restrict the rights of citizens on account of race. There can be no doubt that restricting the freedom to marry solely because of racial classifications violates the central meaning of the Equal Protection Clause.

II

These statutes also deprive the Lovings of liberty without due process of law in violation of the Due Process Clause of the Fourteenth Amendment. The freedom to marry has long been recognized as one of the vital personal rights essential to the orderly pursuit of happiness by free men.

Marriage is one of the "basic civil rights of man," fundamental to our very existence and survival. *Skinner v. Oklahoma,* 316 U. S. 535, 316 U. S. 541 (1942). *See also Maynard v. Hill,* 125 U. S. 190 (1888). To deny this fundamental freedom on so unsupportable a basis as the racial classifications embodied in these statutes, classifications so directly subversive of the principle of equality at the heart of the Fourteenth Amendment, is surely to deprive all the State's citizens of liberty without due process of law. The Fourteenth Amendment requires that the freedom of choice to marry not be restricted by invidious racial discriminations. Under our Constitution, the freedom to marry, or not marry, a person of another race resides with the individual, and cannot be infringed by the State.

These convictions must be reversed.

It is so ordered.

[Footnote 1]

Section 1 of the Fourteenth Amendment provides:

"All persons born or naturalized in the United States and subject to the jurisdiction thereof, are citizens of the United States and of the State wherein they reside. No State shall make or enforce any law which shall abridge the privileges or immunities of citizens of the United States; nor shall any State deprive any person of life, liberty, or property, without due process of law; nor deny to any person within its jurisdiction the equal protection of the laws."

[Footnote 2]

206 Va. 924, 147 S.E.2d 78 (1966).

[Footnote 3]

Section 257 of the Virginia Code provides:

"*Marriages void without decree.* — All marriages between a white person and a colored person shall be absolutely void without any decree of divorce or other legal process."

Va.Code Ann. § 20-57 (1960 Repl. Vol.).

[Footnote 4]

Section 20-54 of the Virginia Code provides:

"*Intermarriage prohibited; meaning of term 'white persons.'* — It shall hereafter be unlawful for any white person in this State to marry any save a white person, or a person with no other admixture of blood than white and American Indian. For the purpose of this chapter, the term 'white person' shall apply only to such person as has no trace whatever of any blood other than Caucasian; but persons who have one-sixteenth or less of the blood of the American Indian and have no other non-Caucasic blood shall be deemed to be white persons. All laws heretofore passed and now in effect regarding the intermarriage of white and colored persons shall apply to marriages prohibited by this chapter."

Va.Code Ann. § 20-54 (1960 Repl. Vol.).

The exception for persons with less than one-sixteenth "of the blood of the American Indian" is apparently accounted for, in the words of a tract issued by the Registrar of the State Bureau of Vital Statistics, by "the desire of all to recognize as an integral and honored part of the white race the descendants of John Rolfe and Pocahontas. . . ." Plecker, The New Family and Race Improvement, 17 Va.Health Bull., Extra No. 12, at 25-26 (New Family Series No. 5, 1925), cited in Wadlington, The *Loving* Case: Virginia's Anti-Miscegenation Statute in Historical Perspective, 52 Va.L.Rev. 1189, 1202, n. 93 (1966).

Section 1-14 of the Virginia Code provides:

"*Colored persons and Indians defined.* — Every person in whom there is ascertainable any Negro blood shall be deemed and taken to be a colored person, and every person not a colored person having one fourth or more of American Indian blood shall be deemed an American Indian; except that members of Indian tribes existing in this Commonwealth having one fourth or more of Indian blood and less than one sixteenth of Negro blood shall be deemed tribal Indians."

Va.Code Ann. § 1-14 (1960 Repl. Vol.).

[Footnote 5]

After the initiation of this litigation, Maryland repealed its prohibitions against interracial marriage, Md.Laws 1967, c. 6, leaving Virginia and 15 other States with statutes outlawing interracial marriage: Alabama, Ala.Const., Art. 4, § 102, Ala. Code, Tit. 14, § 360 (1958); Arkansas, Ark.Stat. Ann. § 55-104 (1947); Delaware, Del.Code Ann., Tit. 13, § 101 (1953); Florida, Fla.Const., Art. 16, § 24, Fla.Stat. § 741.11 (1965); Georgia, Ga.Code Ann. § 53-106 (1961); Kentucky, Ky.Rev.Stat. Ann. § 402.020 (Supp. 1966); Louisiana, La.Rev. Stat. § 14:79 (1950); Mississippi, Miss.Const., Art. 14, § 263, Miss.Code Ann. § 459 (1956); Missouri, Mo.Rev.Stat. § 451.020 (Supp. 1966); North Carolina, N.C.Const., Art. XIV, § 8, N.C.Gen.Stat. § 14-181 (1953); Oklahoma, Okla.Stat., Tit. 43, § 12 (Supp. 1965); South Carolina, S.C.Const., Art. 3, § 33, S.C.Code Ann. § 20-7 (1962); Tennessee, Tenn. Const., Art. 11, § 14, Tenn.Code Ann. § 36-402 (1955); Texas, Tex.Pen.Code, Art. 492 (1952); West Virginia, W.Va.Code Ann. § 4697 (1961).

Over the past 15 years, 14 States have repealed laws outlawing interracial marriages: Arizona, California, Colorado, Idaho, Indiana, Maryland, Montana, Nebraska, Nevada, North Dakota, Oregon, South Dakota, Utah, and Wyoming.

The first state court to recognize that miscegenation statutes violate the Equal Protection Clause was the Supreme Court of California. *Perez v. Sharp,* 32 Cal.2d 711, 198 P.2d 17 (1948).

[Footnote 6]

For a historical discussion of Virginia's miscegenation statutes, *see* Wadlington, *supra,* n 4.

[Footnote 7]

Va.Code Ann. § 20-54 (1960 Repl. Vol.).

[Footnote 8]

Va.Code Ann. § 20-53 (1960 Repl. Vol.).

[Footnote 9]

Va.Code Ann. § 20-50 (1960 Repl. Vol.).

[Footnote 10]

Va.Code Ann. § 254 (1960 Repl. Vol.).

[Footnote 11]

Appellants point out that the State's concern in these statutes, as expressed in the words of the 1924 Act's title, "An Act to Preserve Racial Integrity," extends only to the integrity of the white race. While Virginia prohibits whites from marrying any nonwhite (subject to the exception for the descendants of Pocahontas), Negroes, Orientals, and any other racial class may intermarry without statutory interference. Appellants contend that this distinction renders Virginia's miscegenation statutes arbitrary and unreasonable even assuming the constitutional validity of an official purpose to preserve "racial integrity." We need not reach this contention, because we find the racial classifications in these statutes repugnant to the Fourteenth Amendment, even assuming an even-handed state purpose to protect the "integrity" of all races.

MR. JUSTICE STEWART, concurring.

I have previously expressed the belief that "it is simply not possible for a state law to be valid under our Constitution which makes the criminality of an act depend upon the race of the actor." *McLaughlin v. Florida,* 379 U. S. 184, 379 U. S. 198 (concurring opinion). Because I adhere to that belief, I concur in the judgment of the Court.

Source: Loving v. Virginia, 388 U.S. 1 (1967).

Post–Civil Rights Era and the New Millennium

(1970–Present)

Combahee River Collective Statement

(1977)

The Combahee River Collective was a black feminist lesbian organization that formed in the Boston area in 1974. Throughout the 1970s, the group met weekly at the Cambridge, Massachusetts, Women's Center, and also held a series of meetings and retreats and various locations through 1980. The collective is best known for its issuance of the Combahee River Collective Statement, which is considered a defining document in the development of black feminism and in the development of concepts of black feminist and lesbian identity.

We are a collective of Black feminists who have been meeting together since 1974. [1] During that time we have been involved in the process of defining and clarifying our politics, while at the same time doing political work within our own group and in coalition with other progressive organizations and movements. The most general statement of our politics at the present time would be that we are actively committed to struggling against racial, sexual, heterosexual, and class oppression, and see

as our particular task the development of integrated analysis and practice based upon the fact that the major systems of oppression are interlocking. The synthesis of these oppressions creates the conditions of our lives. As Black women we see Black feminism as the logical political movement to combat the manifold and simultaneous oppressions that all women of color face.

We will discuss four major topics in the paper that follows: (1) the genesis of contemporary Black feminism; (2) what we believe, i.e., the specific province of our politics; (3) the problems in organizing Black feminists, including a brief herstory of our collective; and (4) Black feminist issues and practice.

1. The Genesis of Contemporary Black Feminism

Before looking at the recent development of Black feminism we would like to affirm that we find our origins in the historical reality of Afro-American women's continuous life-and-death struggle for survival and liberation. Black women's extremely negative relationship to the American political system (a system of white male rule) has always been determined by our membership in two oppressed racial and sexual castes. As Angela Davis points out in "Reflections on the Black Woman's Role in the Community of Slaves," Black women have always embodied, if only in their physical manifestation, an adversary stance to white male rule and have actively resisted its inroads upon them and their communities in both dramatic and subtle ways. There have always been Black women activists—some known, like Sojourner Truth, Harriet Tubman, Frances E. W. Harper, Ida B. Wells Barnett, and Mary Church Terrell, and thousands upon thousands unknown— who have had a shared awareness of how their sexual identity combined with their racial identity to make their whole life situation and the focus of their political struggles unique. Contemporary Black feminism is the outgrowth of countless generations of personal sacrifice, militancy, and work by our mothers and sisters.

A Black feminist presence has evolved most obviously in connection with the second wave of the American women's movement beginning in the late 1960s. Black, other Third World, and working women have been involved in the feminist movement from its start, but both outside reactionary forces and racism and elitism within the movement itself have served to obscure our participation. In 1973, Black feminists, primarily located in New York, felt the necessity of forming a separate Black feminist group. This became the National Black Feminist Organization (NBFO).

Black feminist politics also have an obvious connection to movements for Black liberation, particularly those of the 1960s and 1970s. Many of us were active in those movements (Civil Rights, Black nationalism, the Black Panthers), and all of our lives were greatly affected and changed by their ideologies, their goals, and the tactics used to achieve their goals. It was our experience and disillusionment within these liberation movements, as well as experience on the periphery of the white male left, that led to the need to develop a politics that was anti-racist, unlike those of white women,

and anti-sexist, unlike those of Black and white men.

There is also undeniably a personal genesis for Black Feminism, that is, the political realization that comes from the seemingly personal experiences of individual Black women's lives. Black feminists and many more Black women who do not define themselves as feminists have all experienced sexual oppression as a constant factor in our day-to-day existence. As children we realized that we were different from boys and that we were treated differently. For example, we were told in the same breath to be quiet both for the sake of being "ladylike" and to make us less objectionable in the eyes of white people. As we grew older we became aware of the threat of physical and sexual abuse by men. However, we had no way of conceptualizing what was so apparent to us, what we knew was really happening.

Black feminists often talk about their feelings of craziness before becoming conscious of the concepts of sexual politics, patriarchal rule, and most importantly, feminism, the political analysis and practice that we women use to struggle against our oppression. The fact that racial politics and indeed racism are pervasive factors in our lives did not allow us, and still does not allow most Black women, to look more deeply into our own experiences and, from that sharing and growing consciousness, to build a politics that will change our lives and inevitably end our oppression. Our development must also be tied to the contemporary economic and political position of Black people. The post—World War II generation of Black youth was the first to be able to minimally partake of certain educational and employment options, previously closed completely to Black people. Although our economic position is still at the very bottom of the American capitalistic economy, a handful of us have been able to gain certain tools as a result of tokenism in education and employment which potentially enable us to more effectively fight our oppression.

A combined anti-racist and anti-sexist position drew us together initially, and as we developed politically we addressed ourselves to heterosexism and economic oppression under capitalism.

2. What We Believe

Above all else, Our politics initially sprang from the shared belief that Black women are inherently valuable, that our liberation is a necessity not as an adjunct to somebody else's may because of our need as human persons for autonomy. This may seem so obvious as to sound simplistic, but it is apparent that no other ostensibly progressive movement has ever considered our specific oppression as a priority or worked seriously for the ending of that oppression. Merely naming the pejorative stereotypes attributed to Black women (e.g. mammy, matriarch, Sapphire, whore, bulldagger), let alone cataloguing the cruel, often murderous, treatment we receive, indicates how little value has been placed upon our lives during four centuries of bondage in the Western hemisphere. We realize that the only people who care enough about us to work consistently for our liberation are us. Our politics evolve from a healthy love for ourselves, our sisters and our community which allows us to continue our struggle and work.

This focusing upon our own oppression is embodied in the concept of identity politics. We believe that the most profound and potentially most radical politics come directly out of our own identity, as opposed to working to end somebody else's oppression. In the case of Black women this is a particularly repugnant, dangerous, threatening, and therefore revolutionary concept because it is obvious from looking at all the political movements that have preceded us that anyone is more worthy of liberation than ourselves. We reject pedestals, queenhood, and walking ten paces behind. To be recognized as human, levelly human, is enough.

We believe that sexual politics under patriarchy is as pervasive in Black women's lives as are the politics of class and race. We also often find it difficult to separate race from class from sex oppression because in our lives they are most often experienced simultaneously. We know that there is

such a thing as racial-sexual oppression which is neither solely racial nor solely sexual, e.g., the history of rape of Black women by white men as a weapon of political repression.

Although we are feminists and Lesbians, we feel solidarity with progressive Black men and do not advocate the fractionalization that white women who are separatists demand. Our situation as Black people necessitates that we have solidarity around the fact of race, which white women of course do not need to have with white men, unless it is their negative solidarity as racial oppressors. We struggle together with Black men against racism, while we also struggle with Black men about sexism.

We realize that the liberation of all oppressed peoples necessitates the destruction of the political-economic systems of capitalism and imperialism as well as patriarchy. We are socialists because we believe that work must be organized for the collective benefit of those who do the work and create the products, and not for the profit of the bosses. Material resources must be equally distributed among those who create these resources. We are not convinced, however, that a socialist revolution that is not also a feminist and anti-racist revolution will guarantee our liberation. We have arrived at the necessity for developing an understanding of class relationships that takes into account the specific class position of Black women who are generally marginal in the labor force, while at this particular time some of us are temporarily viewed as doubly desirable tokens at white-collar and professional levels. We need to articulate the real class situation of persons who are not merely raceless, sexless workers, but for whom racial and sexual oppression are significant determinants in their working/economic lives. Although we are in essential agreement with Marx's theory as it applied to the very specific economic relationships he analyzed, we know that his analysis must be extended further in order for us to understand our specific economic situation as Black women.

A political contribution which we feel we have already made is the expansion of the feminist principle that the personal is political. In our consciousness-raising sessions, for example, we have in many ways gone beyond white women's revelations because we are dealing with the implications of race and class as well as sex. Even our Black women's style of talking/testifying in Black language about what we have experienced has a resonance that is both cultural and political. We have spent a great deal of energy delving into the cultural and experiential nature of our oppression out of necessity because none of these matters has ever been looked at before. No one before has ever examined the multilayered texture of Black women's lives. An example of this kind of revelation/conceptualization occurred at a meeting as we discussed the ways in which our early intellectual interests had been attacked by our peers, particularly Black males. We discovered that all of us, because we were "smart" had also been considered "ugly," i.e., "smart-ugly." "Smart-ugly" crystallized the way in which most of us had been forced to develop our intellects at great cost to our "social" lives. The sanctions in the Black and white communities against Black women thinkers is comparatively much higher than for white women, particularly ones from the educated middle and upper classes.

As we have already stated, we reject the stance of Lesbian separatism because it is not a viable political analysis or strategy for us. It leaves out far too much and far too many people, particularly Black men, women, and children. We have a great deal of criticism and loathing for what men have been socialized to be in this society: what they support, how they act, and how they oppress. But we do not have the misguided notion that it is their maleness, per se—i.e., their biological maleness—that makes them what they are. As Black women we find any type of biological determinism a particularly dangerous and reactionary basis upon which to build a politic. We must also question whether Lesbian separatism is an adequate and progressive political analysis and strategy, even for those who practice it, since it so completely denies any but the sexual sources of women's oppression, negating the facts of class and race.

3. Problems in Organizing Black Feminists

During our years together as a Black feminist collective we have experienced success and defeat, joy and pain, victory and failure. We have found that it is very difficult to organize around Black feminist issues, difficult even to announce in certain contexts that we are Black feminists. We have tried to think about the reasons for our difficulties, particularly since the white women's movement continues to be strong and to grow in many directions. In this section we will discuss some of the general reasons for the organizing problems we face and also talk specifically about the stages in organizing our own collective.

The major source of difficulty in our political work is that we are not just trying to fight oppression on one front or even two, but instead to address a whole range of oppressions. We do not have racial, sexual, heterosexual, or class privilege to rely upon, nor do we have even the minimal access to resources and power that groups who possess any one of these types of privilege have.

The psychological toll of being a Black woman and the difficulties this presents in reaching political consciousness and doing political work can never be underestimated. There is a very low value placed upon Black women's psyches in this society, which is both racist and sexist. As an early group member once said, "We are all damaged people merely by virtue of being Black women." We are dispossessed psychologically and on every other level, and yet we feel the necessity to struggle to change the condition of all Black women. In "A Black Feminist's Search for Sisterhood," Michele Wallace arrives at this conclusion:

> We exists as women who are Black who are feminists, each stranded for the moment, working independently because there is not yet an environment in this society remotely congenial to our struggle—because, being on the bottom, we would have to do what no one else has done: we would have to fight the world. [2]

Wallace is pessimistic but realistic in her assessment of Black feminists' position, particularly in her allusion to the nearly classic isolation most of us face. We might use our position at the bottom, however, to make a clear leap into revolutionary action. If Black women were free, it would mean that everyone else would have to be free since our freedom would necessitate the destruction of all the systems of oppression.

Feminism is, nevertheless, very threatening to the majority of Black people because it calls into question some of the most basic assumptions about our existence, i.e., that sex should be a determinant of power relationships. Here is the way male and female roles were defined in a Black nationalist pamphlet from the early 1970s:

> We understand that it is and has been traditional that the man is the head of the house. He is the leader of the house/nation because his knowledge of the world is broader, his awareness is greater, his understanding is fuller and his application of this information is wiser... After all, it is only reasonable that the man be the head of the house because he is able to defend and protect the development of his home... Women cannot do the same things as men—they are made by nature to function differently. Equality of men and women is something that cannot happen even in the abstract world. Men are not equal to other men, i.e. ability, experience or even understanding. The value of men and women can be seen as in the value of gold and silver—they are not equal but both have great value. We must realize that men and women are a complement to each other because there is no house/family without a man and his wife. Both are essential to the development of any life. [3]

The material conditions of most Black women would hardly lead them to upset both economic and sexual arrangements that seem to represent some stability in their lives. Many Black women have a good understanding of both sexism and racism, but because of the everyday constrictions of their lives, cannot risk struggling against them both.

The reaction of Black men to feminism has been notoriously negative. They are, of course, even more threatened than Black women by the possibility that Black feminists might organize around our own needs. They realize that they might not only lose valuable and hardworking allies in their struggles but that they might also be forced to change their habitually sexist ways of interacting with and oppressing Black women. Accusations that Black feminism divides the Black struggle are powerful deterrents to the growth of an autonomous Black women's movement.

Still, hundreds of women have been active at different times during the three-year existence of our group. And every Black woman who came, came out of a strongly felt need for some level of possibility that did not previously exist in her life.

When we first started meeting early in 1974 after the NBFO first eastern regional conference, we did not have a strategy for organizing, or even a focus. We just wanted to see what we had. After a period of months of not meeting, we began to meet again late in the year and started doing an intense variety of consciousness-raising. The overwhelming feeling that we had is that after years and years we had finally found each other. Although we were not doing political work as a group, individuals continued their involvement in Lesbian politics, sterilization abuse and abortion rights work, Third World Women's International Women's Day activities, and support activity for the trials of Dr. Kenneth Edelin, Joan Little, and Inéz García. During our first summer when membership had dropped off considerably, those of us remaining devoted serious discussion to the possibility of opening a refuge for battered women in a Black community. (There was no refuge in Boston at that time.) We also decided around that time to become an independent collective since we had serious disagreements with NBFO's bourgeois-feminist stance and their lack of a clear political focus.

We also were contacted at that time by socialist feminists, with whom we had worked on abortion rights activities, who wanted to encourage us to attend the National Socialist Feminist Conference in Yellow Springs. One of our members did attend and despite the narrowness of the ideology that was promoted at that particular conference, we became more aware of the need for us to understand our own economic situation and to make our own economic analysis.

In the fall, when some members returned, we experienced several months of comparative inactivity and internal disagreements which were first conceptualized as a Lesbian-straight split but which were also the result of class and political differences. During the summer those of us who were still meeting had determined the need to do political work and to move beyond consciousness-raising and serving exclusively as an emotional support group. At the beginning of 1976, when some of the women who had not wanted to do political work and who also had voiced disagreements stopped attending of their own accord, we again looked for a focus. We decided at that time, with the addition of new members, to become a study group. We had always shared our reading with each other, and some of us had written papers on Black feminism for group discussion a few months before this decision was made. We began functioning as a study group and also began discussing the possibility of starting a Black feminist publication. We had a retreat in the late spring which provided a time for both political discussion and working out interpersonal issues. Currently we are planning to gather together a collection of Black feminist writing. We feel that it is absolutely essential to demonstrate the reality of our politics to other Black women and believe that we can do this through writing and distributing our work. The fact that individual Black feminists are living in isolation all over the country, that our own numbers are small, and that we have some skills in writing, printing, and publishing makes us want to carry out these kinds of projects as a means of organizing Black feminists as we continue to do political work in coalition with other groups.

4. Black Feminist Issues and Projects

During our time together we have identified and worked on many issues of particular relevance to Black women. The inclusiveness of our politics makes us concerned with any situation that impinges upon the lives of women, Third World and working people. We are of course particularly committed to working on those struggles in which race, sex, and class are simultaneous factors in oppression. We might, for example, become involved in workplace organizing at a factory that employs Third World women or picket a hospital that is cutting back on already inadequate health care to a Third World community, or set up a rape crisis center in a Black neighborhood. Organizing around welfare and daycare concerns might also be a focus. The work to be done and the countless issues that this work represents merely reflect the pervasiveness of our oppression.

Issues and projects that collective members have actually worked on are sterilization abuse, abortion rights, battered women, rape and health care. We have also done many workshops and educationals on Black feminism on college campuses, at women's conferences, and most recently for high school women.

One issue that is of major concern to us and that we have begun to publicly address is racism in the white women's movement. As Black feminists we are made constantly and painfully aware of how little effort white women have made to understand and combat their racism, which requires among other things that they have a more than superficial comprehension of race, color, and Black history and culture. Eliminating racism in the white women's movement is by definition work for white women to do, but we will continue to speak to and demand accountability on this issue.

In the practice of our politics we do not believe that the end always justifies the means. Many reactionary and destructive acts have been done in the name of achieving "correct" political goals. As feminists we do not want to mess over people in the name of politics. We believe in collective process and a nonhierarchical distribution of power within our own group and in our vision of a revolutionary society. We are committed to a continual examination of our politics as they develop through criticism and self-criticism as an essential aspect of our practice. In her introduction to *Sisterhood is Powerful* Robin Morgan writes:

I haven't the faintest notion what possible revolutionary role white heterosexual men could fulfill, since they are the very embodiment of reactionary-vested-interest-power.

As Black feminists and Lesbians we know that we have a very definite revolutionary task to perform and we are ready for the lifetime of work and struggle before us.

[1] This statement is dated April 1977.

[2] Wallace, Michele. "A Black Feminist's Search for Sisterhood," *The Village Voice*, 28 July 1975, pp. 6–7.

[3] Mumininas of Committee for Unified Newark, Mwanamke Mwananchi (The Nationalist Woman), Newark, N.J., ©1971, pp. 4–5.

Source: The Combahee River Collective. "The Combahee River Collective Statement." copyright © 1978 by Zillah Eisenstein. Used with permission.

Patterson v. McLean Credit Union
(1989)

Patterson v. McLean Credit Union *was a case involving allegations by an African American employee of McLean Credit Union who claimed she was harassed, denied promotion, and then let go from her job because of her race. In its decision, the Supreme Court reiterated that provisions of the Civil Rights Act of 1866 could be used in legal actions against private racial discrimination. However, although the Supreme Court confirmed that the law could be used in private actions, it ruled that the statute had limited application in the employment setting. Therefore,* Patterson *ultimately limited the reach of the Civil Rights Act of 1866.*

JUSTICE KENNEDY delivered the opinion of the Court.

In this case, we consider important issues respecting the meaning and coverage of one of our oldest civil rights statutes, 42 U.S.C. 1981.

I

Petitioner Brenda Patterson, a black woman, was employed by respondent McLean Credit Union as a teller and a file coordinator, commencing in May 1972. In July 1982, she was laid off. After the termination, petitioner commenced this action in the United States District Court for the Middle District of North Carolina. She alleged that respondent, in violation of 14 Stat. 27, 42 U.S.C. 1981, had harassed her, failed to promote her to an intermediate accounting clerk position, and then discharged her, all because of her race. Petitioner also claimed this conduct amounted to an intentional infliction of emotional distress, actionable under North Carolina tort law.

The District Court determined that a claim for racial harassment is not actionable under 1981 and declined to submit that part of the case to the jury. The jury did receive and deliberate upon petitioner's 1981 claims based on alleged discrimination in her discharge and the failure to promote her, and it found for respondent on both claims. As for petitioner's state-law claim, the District Court directed a verdict for respondent on the ground that the employer's conduct did not rise to the level of outrageousness required to state a claim for intentional infliction of emotional distress under applicable standards of North Carolina law.

In the Court of Appeals, petitioner raised two matters which are relevant here. First, she challenged the District Court's refusal to submit to the jury her 1981 claim based on racial harassment. Second, she argued that the District Court erred in instructing the jury that in order to prevail on her 1981 claim of discriminatory failure to promote, she must show that she was better qualified than the white employee who she alleges was promoted in her stead. The Court of Appeals affirmed. On the racial harassment issue, the court held that, while instances of racial harassment "may implicate the terms and conditions of employment under Title VII [of the Civil Rights Act of 1964, 78 Stat. 253, 42 U.S.C. 2000e et seq.] and of course may be probative of the discriminatory intent required to be shown in a 1981 action," racial harassment itself is not cognizable under 1981 because "racial harassment does not abridge the right to 'make' and 'enforce' contracts." On the jury instruction issue, the court held that once respondent had advanced superior qualification as a legitimate nondiscriminatory reason for its promotion decision, petitioner had the burden of persuasion to show that respondent's justification was a pretext and that she was better qualified than the employee who was chosen for the job.

We granted certiorari to decide whether petitioner's claim of racial harassment in her employment is actionable under 1981, and whether the jury instruction given by the District Court on petitioner's 1981 promotion claim was error. After oral argument on these issues, we requested the parties to brief and argue an additional question:

"Whether or not the interpretation of 42 U.S.C. 1981 adopted by this Court in *Runyon v. McCrary* (1976), should be reconsidered." *Patterson v. McLean Credit Union* (1988).

We now decline to overrule our decision in *Runyon v. McCrary* (1976). We hold further that racial harassment relating to the conditions of employment is not actionable under 1981 because that provision does not apply to conduct which occurs after the formation of a contract and which does not interfere with the right to enforce established contract obligations. Finally, we hold that the District Court erred in instructing the jury regarding petitioner's burden in proving her discriminatory promotion claim.

II

In *Runyon,* the Court considered whether 1981 prohibits private schools from excluding children who are qualified for admission, solely on the basis of race. We held that 1981 did prohibit such conduct, noting that it was already well established in prior decisions that 1981 "prohibits racial discrimination in the making and enforcement of private contracts." Id., citing *Johnson v. Railway Express Agency, Inc.* (1975); *Tillman v. Wheaton-Haven Recreation Assn., Inc.* (1973). The arguments about whether *Runyon* was decided correctly in light of the language and history of the statute were examined and discussed with great care in our decision. It was recognized at the time that a strong case could be made for the view that the statute does not reach private conduct, but that view did not prevail. Some Members of this Court believe that *Runyon* was decided incorrectly, and others consider it correct on its own footing, but the question before us is whether it ought now to be overturned. We conclude after reargument that *Runyon* should not be overruled, and we now reaffirm that 1981 prohibits racial discrimination in the making and enforcement of private contracts.

The Court has said often and with great emphasis that "the doctrine of stare decisis is of fundamental importance to the rule of law." *Welch v. Texas Dept. of Highways and Public Transportation* (1987). Although we have cautioned that "stare decisis is a principle of policy and not a mechanical formula of adherence to the latest decision," *Boys Markets, Inc. v. Retail Clerks* (1970), it is indisputable that stare decisis is a basic self-governing principle within the Judicial Branch, which is entrusted with the sensitive and difficult task of fashioning and preserving a jurisprudential system that is not based upon "an arbitrary discretion." *The Federalist,* No. 78. See also *Vasquez v. Hillery* (1986) (stare decisis ensures that "the law will not merely change erratically" and "permits society to presume that bedrock principles are founded in the law rather than in the proclivities of individuals").

Our precedents are not sacrosanct, for we have overruled prior decisions where the necessity and propriety of doing so has been established. See *Patterson v. McLean Credit Union,* supra (citing cases). Nonetheless, we have held that "any departure from the doctrine of stare decisis demands special justification." *Arizona v. Rumsey* (1984). We have said also that the burden borne by the party advocating the abandonment of an established precedent is greater where the Court is asked to overrule a point of statutory construction. Considerations of stare decisis have special force in the area of statutory interpretation, for here, unlike in the context of constitutional interpretation, the legislative power is implicated, and Congress remains free to alter what we have done. See, e. g., *Square D Co. v. Niagara Frontier Tariff Bureau, Inc.* (1986); *Illinois Brick Co. v. Illinois* (1977).

We conclude, upon direct consideration of the issue, that no special justification has been shown for overruling *Runyon*. In cases where statutory precedents have been overruled, the primary reason for the Court's shift in position has been the intervening development of the law, through either the growth of judicial doctrine or further action taken by Congress. Where such changes have removed or weakened the conceptual underpinnings from the prior decision, see, e.g., *Rodriguez de Quijas v. Shearson/American Express, Inc.* (1989); *Andrews v. Louisville & Nashville R. Co.* (1972), or where the later law has rendered the decision irreconcilable with competing legal doctrines or policies, see, e.g., *Braden v. 30th Judicial Circuit Ct. of Ky.* (1973); *Construction Laborers v. Curry* (1963), the Court has not hesitated to overrule an earlier decision. Our decision in *Runyon* has not been undermined by subsequent changes or development in the law.

Another traditional justification for overruling a prior case is that a precedent may be a positive detriment to coherence and consistency in the law, either because of inherent confusion created by an unworkable decision, see, e.g., *Continental T. V., Inc. v. GTE Sylvania, Inc.* (1977); *Swift & Co. v. Wickham* (1965), or because the decision poses a direct obstacle to the realization of important objectives embodied in other laws, see, e.g., *Rodriguez de Quijas,* supra; *Boys Markets, Inc. v. Retail Clerks,* supra. In this regard, we do not find

Runyon to be unworkable or confusing. Respondent and various amici have urged that *Runyon's* interpretation of 1981, as applied to contracts of employment, frustrates the objectives of Title VII. The argument is that a substantial overlap in coverage between the two statutes, given the considerable differences in their remedial schemes, undermines Congress' detailed efforts in Title VII to resolve disputes about racial discrimination in private employment through conciliation rather than litigation as an initial matter. After examining the point with care, however, we believe that a sound construction of the language of 1981 yields an interpretation which does not frustrate the congressional objectives in Title VII to any significant degree.

Finally, it has sometimes been said that a precedent becomes more vulnerable as it becomes outdated and after being "'tested by experience, has been found to be inconsistent with the sense of justice or with the social welfare.'" *Runyon* (STEVENS, J., concurring), quoting B. Cardozo, *The Nature of the Judicial Process* 149 (1921). Whatever the effect of this consideration may be in statutory cases, it offers no support for overruling *Runyon*. In recent decades, state and federal legislation has been enacted to prohibit private racial discrimination in many aspects of our society. Whether *Runyon's* interpretation of 1981 as prohibiting racial discrimination in the making and enforcement of private contracts is right or wrong as an original matter, it is certain that it is not inconsistent with the prevailing sense of justice in this country. To the contrary, *Runyon* is entirely consistent with our society's deep commitment to the eradication of discrimination based on a person's race or the color of his or her skin. See *Bob Jones University v. United States* (1983) ("[E]very pronouncement of this Court and myriad Acts of Congress and Executive Orders attest a firm national policy to prohibit racial segregation and discrimination"); see also *Brown v. Board of Education* (1954); *Plessy v. Ferguson* (1896) (Harlan, J., dissenting) ("The law regards man as man, and takes no account of his . . . color when his civil rights as guaranteed by the supreme law of the land are involved").

We decline to overrule *Runyon* and acknowledge that its holding remains the governing law in this area.

III

Our conclusion that we should adhere to our decision in *Runyon* that 1981 applies to private conduct is not enough to decide this case. We must decide also whether the conduct of which petitioner complains falls within one of the enumerated rights protected by 1981.

A

Section 1981 reads as follows:

"All persons within the jurisdiction of the United States shall have the same right in every State and Territory to make and enforce contracts, to sue, be parties, give evidence, and to the full and equal benefit of all laws and proceedings for the security of persons and property as is enjoyed by white citizens, and shall be subject to like punishment, pains, penalties, taxes, licenses, and exactions of every kind, and to no other."

The most obvious feature of the provision is the restriction of its scope to forbidding discrimination in the "mak[ing] and enforce[ment]" of contracts alone. Where an alleged act of discrimination does not involve the impairment of one of these specific rights, 1981 provides no relief. Section 1981 cannot be construed as a general proscription of racial discrimination in all aspects of contract relations, for it expressly prohibits discrimination only in the making and enforcement of contracts. See also *Jones v. Alfred H. Mayer Co.* (1968) (1982, the companion statute to 1981, was designed "to prohibit all racial discrimination, whether or not under color of law, with respect to the rights enumerated therein"); *Georgia v. Rachel* (1966) ("The legislative history of the 1866 Act clearly indicates that Congress intended to protect a limited category of rights").

By its plain terms, the relevant provision in 1981 protects two rights: "the same right . . . to make . . . contracts" and "the same right . . . to . . . enforce contracts." The first of these protections extends only to the formation of a contract, but not to problems that may arise later from the conditions of continuing employment. The statute prohibits, when based on race, the refusal to enter into a contract with someone, as well as the offer to make a contract only on discriminatory terms. But the right to make contracts does not extend, as a matter of either logic or semantics, to conduct by the employer after the contract relation has been established, including breach of the terms of the contract or imposition of discriminatory working conditions. Such postformation conduct does not involve the right to make a contract, but rather implicates the performance of established contract obligations and the conditions of continuing employment, matters more naturally governed by state contract law and Title VII.

The second of these guarantees, "the same right . . . to . . . enforce contracts . . . as is enjoyed by white citizens," embraces protection of a legal process, and of a right of access to legal process, that will address and resolve contract-law claims without regard to race. In this respect, it prohibits discrimination that infects the legal process in ways that prevent one from enforcing contract rights, by reason of his or her race, and this is so whether this discrimination is attributed to a statute or simply to existing practices. It also covers wholly private efforts to impede access to the courts or obstruct nonjudicial methods of adjudicating disputes about the force of binding obligations, as well as discrimination by private entities, such as labor unions, in enforcing the terms of a contract. Following this principle and consistent with our holding in *Runyon* that 1981 applies to private conduct, we have held that certain private entities such as labor unions, which bear explicit responsibilities to process grievances, press claims, and represent member in disputes over the terms of binding obligations that run from the employer to the employee, are subject to liability under 1981 for racial discrimination in the enforcement of labor contracts. See *Goodman v. Lukens Steel Co.* (1987). The right to enforce contracts does not, however, extend beyond conduct by an employer which impairs an employee's ability to enforce through legal process his or her established contract rights. As JUSTICE WHITE put it with much force in *Runyon,* one cannot seriously "contend that the grant of the other rights enumerated in 1981, [that is, other than the right to "make" contracts,] i.e., the rights 'to sue, be parties, give evidence,' and 'enforce contracts' accomplishes anything other than the removal of legal disabilities to sue, be a party, testify or enforce a contract. Indeed, it is impossible to give such language any other meaning."

B

Applying these principles to the case before us, we agree with the Court of Appeals that petitioner's racial harassment claim is not actionable under 1981. Petitioner has alleged that during her employment with respondent, she was subjected to various forms of racial harassment from her supervisor. As summarized by the Court of Appeals, petitioner testified that "[her supervisor] periodically stared at her for several minutes at a time; that he gave her too many tasks, causing her to complain that she was under too much pressure; that among the tasks given her were sweeping and dusting, jobs not given to white employees. On one occasion, she testified, [her supervisor] told [her] that blacks are known to work slower than whites. According to [petitioner, her supervisor] also criticized her in staff meetings while not similarly criticizing white employees."

Petitioner also alleges that she was passed over for promotion, not offered training for higher level jobs, and denied wage increases, all because of her race.

With the exception perhaps of her claim that respondent refused to promote her to a position as an accountant, none of the conduct which petitioner alleges as part of the racial harassment against her involves either a refusal to make a contract with her or the impairment of her ability to enforce her established contract rights. Rather, the conduct which petitioner labels as actionable racial harassment is postformation conduct by the employer relating to the terms and conditions of continuing employment. This is apparent from petitioner's own proposed jury instruction on her 1981 racial harassment claim:

". . . The plaintiff has also brought an action for harassment in employment against the defendant, under the same statute, 42 USC 1981. An employer is guilty of racial discrimination in employment where it has either created or condoned a substantially discriminatory work environment. An employee has a right to work in an environment free from racial prejudice. If the plaintiff has proven by a preponderance of the evidence that she was subjected to racial harassment by her manager while employed at the defendant, or that she was subjected to a work environment not free from racial prejudice which was either created or condoned by the defendant, then it would be your duty to find for plaintiff on this issue."

Without passing on the contents of this instruction, it is plain to us that what petitioner is attacking are the conditions of her employment.

This type of conduct, reprehensible though it be if true, is not actionable under 1981, which covers only conduct at the initial formation of the contract and conduct which impairs the right to enforce contract obligations through legal process. Rather, such conduct is actionable under the more expansive reach of Title VII of the Civil Rights Act of 1964. The latter statute makes it unlawful for an employer to "discriminate against any individual with respect to his compensation, terms, conditions, or privileges of employment." Racial harassment in the course of employment is actionable under Title VII's prohibition against discrimination in the "terms, conditions, or privileges of employment." "[T]he [Equal Employment Opportunity Commission (EEOC)] has long recognized that harassment on the basis of race . . . is an unlawful employment practice in violation of 703 of Title VII of the Civil Rights Act." While this

Court has not yet had the opportunity to pass directly upon this interpretation of Title VII, the lower federal courts have uniformly upheld this view, and we implicitly have approved it in a recent decision concerning sexual harassment, *Meritor Savings Bank v. Vinson* (1986). As we said in that case, "harassment [which is] sufficiently severe or pervasive 'to alter the conditions of [the victim's] employment and create an abusive working environment,'" is actionable under Title VII because it "affects a 'term, condition, or privilege' of employment."

Interpreting 1981 to cover postformation conduct unrelated to an employee's right to enforce his or her contract, such as incidents relating to the conditions of employment, is not only inconsistent with that statute's limitation to the making and enforcement of contracts, but would also undermine the detailed and well-crafted procedures for conciliation and resolution of Title VII claims. In Title VII, Congress set up an elaborate administrative procedure, implemented through the EEOC, that is designed to assist in the investigation of claims of racial discrimination in the workplace and to work towards the resolution of these claims through conciliation rather than litigation. Only after these procedures have been exhausted, and the plaintiff has obtained a "right to sue" letter from the EEOC, may he or she bring a Title VII action in court. Section 1981, by contrast, provides no administrative review or opportunity for conciliation.

Where conduct is covered by both 1981 and Title VII, the detailed procedures of Title VII are rendered a dead letter, as the plaintiff is free to pursue a claim by bringing suit under 1981 without resort to those statutory prerequisites. We agree that, after *Runyon,* there is some necessary overlap between Title VII and 1981, and that where the statutes do in fact overlap we are not at liberty "to infer any positive preference for one over the other." *Johnson v. Railway Express Agency, Inc.* We should be reluctant, however, to read an earlier statute broadly where the result is to circumvent the detailed remedial scheme constructed in a later

statute. See *United States v. Fausto* (1988). That egregious racial harassment of employees is forbidden by a clearly applicable law (Title VII), moreover, should lessen the temptation for this Court to twist the interpretation of another statute (1981) to cover the same conduct. In the particular case before us, we do not know for certain why petitioner chose to pursue only remedies under 1981, and not under Title VII. But in any event, the availability of the latter statute should deter us from a tortuous construction of the former statute to cover this type of claim.

By reading 1981 not as a general proscription of racial discrimination in all aspects of contract relations, but as limited to the enumerated rights within its express protection, specifically the right to make and enforce contracts, we may preserve the integrity of Title VII's procedures without sacrificing any significant coverage of the civil rights laws. Of course, some overlap will remain between the two statutes: specifically, a refusal to enter into an employment contract on the basis of race. Such a claim would be actionable under Title VII as a "refus[al] to hire" based on race, and under 1981 as an impairment of "the same right . . . to make . . . contracts . . . as . . . white citizens," But this is precisely where it would make sense for Congress to provide for the overlap. At this stage of the employee-employer relation Title VII's mediation and conciliation procedures would be of minimal effect, for there is not yet a relation to salvage.

C

The Solicitor General and JUSTICE BRENNAN offer two alternative interpretations of 1981. The Solicitor General argues that the language of 1981, especially the words "the same right," requires us to look outside 1981 to the terms of particular contracts and to state law for the obligations and covenants to be protected by the federal statute. Under this view, 1981 has no actual substantive content, but instead mirrors only the specific protections that are afforded under the law of contracts of each State. Under this view, racial harassment in the conditions of employment is actionable when, and only when, it amounts to a breach of contract under state law. We disagree. For one thing, to the extent that it assumes that prohibitions contained in 1981 incorporate only those protections afforded by the States, this theory is directly inconsistent with *Runyon,* which we today decline to overrule. A more fundamental failing in the Solicitor's argument is that racial harassment amounting to breach of contract, like racial harassment alone, impairs neither the right to make nor the right to enforce a contract. It is plain that the former right is not implicated directly by an employer's breach in the performance of obligations under a contract already formed. Nor is it correct to say that racial harassment amounting to a breach of contract impairs an employee's right to enforce his contract. To the contrary, conduct amounting to a breach of contract under state law is precisely what the language of 1981 does not cover. That is because, in such a case, provided that plaintiff's access to state court or any other dispute resolution process has not been impaired by either the State or a private actor, see *Goodman v. Lukens Steel Co.* (1987), the plaintiff is free to enforce the terms of the contract in state court, and cannot possibly assert, by reason of the breach alone, that he has been deprived of the same right to enforce contracts as is enjoyed by white citizens.

In addition, interpreting 1981 to cover racial harassment amounting to a breach of contract would federalize all state-law claims for breach of contract where racial animus is alleged, since 1981 covers all types of contracts, not just employment contracts. Although we must do so when Congress plainly directs, as a rule we should be and are "reluctant to federalize" matters traditionally covered by state common law. *Santa Fe Industries, Inc. v. Green* (1977); see also *Sedima, S. P. R. L. v. Imrex Co.* (1985) (MARSHALL, J., dissenting). By confining 1981 to the impairment of the specific rights to make and enforce contracts, Congress cannot be said to have intended such a result with respect to breach of contract claims. It would be no small paradox, moreover, that under the interpretation of 1981 offered by the Solicitor General, the more a State extends its own contract law to protect employees in general and minorities in particular, the greater would be the potential displacement of state law by 1981. We do not think 1981 need be read to produce such a peculiar result.

JUSTICE BRENNAN, for his part, would hold that racial harassment is actionable under 1981 when "the acts constituting harassment [are] sufficiently severe or pervasive as effectively to belie any claim that the contract was entered into in a racially neutral manner." We do not find this standard an accurate or useful articulation of which contract claims are actionable under 1981 and which are not. The fact that racial harassment is "severe or pervasive" does not by magic transform a challenge to the conditions of employment, not actionable under 1981, into a viable challenge to the employer's refusal to make a contract. We agree that racial harassment may be used as evidence that a divergence in the explicit terms of particular contracts is explained by racial animus. Thus, for example, if a potential employee is offered (and accepts) a contract to do a job for less money than others doing like work, evidence of racial harassment in the workplace may show that the employer, at the time of formation, was unwilling to enter into a nondiscriminatory contract. However, and this is the critical point, the question under 1981 remains whether the employer, at the time of the formation of the contract, in fact intentionally refused to enter into a contract with the employee on racially neutral terms. The plaintiff's ability to plead that the racial harassment is "severe or pervasive" should not allow him to boot-strap a challenge to the conditions of employment (actionable, if at all, under Title VII) into a claim under 1981 that the employer refused to offer petitioner the "same right . . . to make" a contract. We think it clear that the conduct challenged by petitioner relates not to her employer's refusal to enter into a contract with her, but rather to the conditions of her employment.

IV

Petitioner's claim that respondent violated 1981 by failing to promote her, because of race, to a position as an intermediate accounting clerk is a different matter. As a preliminary point, we note that the Court of Appeals distinguished between petitioner's claims of racial harassment and discriminatory promotion, stating that although the former did not give rise to a discrete 1981 claim, "[c]laims of racially discriminatory . . . promotion go to the very existence and nature of the employment contract and thus fall easily within 1981's protection." We think that somewhat overstates the case. Consistent with what we have said in Part III, supra, the question whether a promotion claim is actionable under 1981 depends upon whether the nature of the change in position was such that it involved the opportunity to enter into a new contract with the employer. If so, then the employer's refusal to enter the new contract is actionable under 1981. In making this determination, a lower court should give a fair and natural reading to the statutory phrase "the same right . . . to make . . . contracts," and should not strain in an undue manner the language of 1981. Only where the promotion rises to the level of an opportunity for a new and distinct relation between the employee and the employer is such a claim actionable under 1981. Cf. *Hishon v. King & Spaulding* (1984) (refusal of law firm to accept associate into partnership) (Title VII). Because respondent has not argued at any stage that petitioner's promotion claim is not cognizable under 1981, we need not address the issue further here.

This brings us to the question of the District Court's jury instructions on petitioner's promotion claim. We think the District Court erred when it instructed the jury that petitioner had to prove that she was better qualified than the white employee who allegedly received the promotion. In order to prevail under 1981, a plaintiff must prove purposeful discrimination. *General Building Contractors Assn., Inc. v. Pennsylvania* (1982). We have developed, in analogous areas of civil rights law, a carefully designed framework of proof to determine, in the context of disparate treatment, the ultimate issue whether the defendant intentionally discriminated against the plaintiff. See *Texas Dept. of Community Affairs v. Burdine* (1981); *McDonnell*

Douglas Corp. v. Green (1973). We agree with the Court of Appeals that this scheme of proof, structured as a "sensible, orderly way to evaluate the evidence in light of common experience as it bears on the critical question of discrimination," *Furnco Construction Corp. v. Waters* (1978), should apply to claims of racial discrimination under 1981.

Although the Court of Appeals recognized that the *McDonnell Douglas/Burdine* scheme of proof should apply in 1981 cases such as this one, it erred in describing petitioner's burden. Under our well-established framework, the plaintiff has the initial burden of proving, by a preponderance of the evidence, a prima facie case of discrimination. *Burdine.* The burden is not onerous. Here, petitioner need only prove by a preponderance of the evidence that she applied for and was qualified for an available position, that she was rejected, and that after she was rejected respondent either continued to seek applicants for the position, or, as is alleged here, filled the position with a white employee. See id.; *McDonnell Douglas,* supra.

Once the plaintiff establishes a prima facie case, an inference of discrimination arises. See *Burdine.* In order to rebut this inference, the employer must present evidence that the plaintiff was rejected, or the other applicant was chosen, for a legitimate nondiscriminatory reason. Here, respondent presented evidence that it gave the job to the white applicant because she was better qualified for the position, and therefore rebutted any presumption of discrimination that petitioner may have established. At this point, as our prior cases make clear, petitioner retains the final burden of persuading the jury of intentional discrimination.

Although petitioner retains the ultimate burden of persuasion, our cases make clear that she must also have the opportunity to demonstrate that respondent's proffered reasons for its decision were not its true reasons. In doing so, petitioner is not limited to presenting evidence of a certain type. This is where the District Court erred. The evidence which petitioner can present in an attempt to establish that respondent's stated reasons are pretextual may take a variety of forms. See *McDonnell*

Douglas, supra; *Furnco Construction Corp.,* supra; cf. *United States Postal Service Bd. of Governors v. Aikens* (1983). Indeed, she might seek to demonstrate that respondent's claim to have promoted a better qualified applicant was pretextual by showing that she was in fact better qualified than the person chosen for the position. The District Court erred, however, in instructing the jury that in order to succeed petitioner was required to make such a showing. There are certainly other ways in which petitioner could seek to prove that respondent's reasons were pretextual. Thus, for example, petitioner could seek to persuade the jury that respondent had not offered the true reason for its promotion decision by presenting evidence of respondent's past treatment of petitioner, including the instances of the racial harassment which she alleges and respondent's failure to train her for an accounting position. While we do not intend to say this evidence necessarily would be sufficient to carry the day, it cannot be denied that it is one of the various ways in which petitioner might seek to prove intentional discrimination on the part of respondent. She may not be forced to pursue any particular means of demonstrating that respondent's stated reasons are pretextual. It was, therefore, error for the District Court to instruct the jury that petitioner could carry her burden of persuasion only by showing that she was in fact better qualified than the white applicant who got the job.

V

The law now reflects society's consensus that discrimination based on the color of one's skin is a profound wrong of tragic dimension. Neither our words nor our decisions should be interpreted as signaling one inch of retreat from Congress' policy to forbid discrimination in the private, as well as the public, sphere. Nevertheless, in the area of private discrimination, to which the ordinance of the Constitution does not directly extend, our role is limited to interpreting what Congress may do and has done. The statute before us, which is only one part of Congress' extensive civil rights legislation, does not cover the acts of harassment alleged here.

In sum, we affirm the Court of Appeals' dismissal of petitioner's racial harassment claim as not actionable under 1981. The Court of Appeals erred, however, in holding that petitioner could succeed in her discriminatory promotion claim under 1981 only by proving that she was better qualified for the position of intermediate accounting clerk than the white employee who in fact was promoted. The judgment of the Court of Appeals is therefore vacated insofar as it relates to petitioner's discriminatory promotion claim, and the case is remanded for further proceedings consistent with this opinion.

It is so ordered.

Source: Patterson v. McLean Credit Union, 491 U.S. 164 (1989).

Civil Rights Act of 1991

Reproduced here are excerpts from the Civil Rights Act of 1991. Congress passed the act specifically to address a recent series of U.S. Supreme Court decisions that had limited the rights of workers to sue employers on the basis of racial discrimination. Some of the decisions in question, all of which were issued in 1989, included Patterson v. McLean Credit Union,

Wards Cove Packing Co. v. Atonio, Price Waterhouse v. Hoplins, *and* Martin v. Wilks. *The Civil Rights Act of 1991 was the first modification of basic procedural and substantive rights provided by federal law in employment discrimination cases since the passage of the Civil Rights Act of 1964. The 1991 Act provided trial by jury in employment discrimination cases and allowed the possibility of damages for emotional distress. President George H. W. Bush had vetoed an earlier civil rights bill in 1990, fearing the imposition of racial quotas, but he signed the less comprehensive 1991 measure.*

An Act

To amend the Civil Rights Act of 1964 to strengthen and improve Federal civil rights laws, to provide for damages in cases of intentional employment discrimination, to clarify provisions regarding disparate impact actions, and for other purposes.

Be it enacted by the Senate and House of Representatives of the United States of America in Congress assembled,

SECTION 1. SHORT TITLE.

This Act may be cited as the 'Civil Rights Act of 1991'.

SEC. 2. FINDINGS.

The Congress finds that—

(1) additional remedies under Federal law are needed to deter unlawful harassment and intentional discrimination in the workplace;

(2) the decision of the Supreme Court in Wards Cove Packing Co. v. Atonio, 490 U.S. 642 (1989) has weakened the scope and effectiveness of Federal civil rights protections; and

(3) legislation is necessary to provide additional protections against unlawful discrimination in employment.

SEC. 3. PURPOSES.

The purposes of this Act are—

(1) to provide appropriate remedies for intentional discrimination and unlawful harassment in the workplace;

(2) to codify the concepts of 'business necessity' and 'job related' enunciated by the Supreme Court in Griggs v. Duke Power Co., 401 U.S. 424 (1971), and in the other Supreme Court decisions prior to Wards Cove Packing Co. v. Atonio, 490 U.S. 642 (1989);

(3) to confirm statutory authority and provide statutory guidelines for the adjudication of disparate impact suits under title VII of the Civil Rights Act of 1964 (42 U.S.C. 2000e et seq.); and

(4) to respond to recent decisions of the Supreme Court by expanding the scope of relevant civil rights statutes in order to provide adequate protection to victims of discrimination.

TITLE I—FEDERAL CIVIL RIGHTS REMEDIES

SEC. 101. PROHIBITION AGAINST ALL RACIAL DISCRIMINATION IN THE MAKING AND ENFORCEMENT OF CONTRACTS.

Section 1977 of the Revised Statutes (42 U.S.C. 1981) is amended—

(1) by inserting '(a)' before 'All persons within'; and

(2) by adding at the end the following new subsections:

(b) For purposes of this section, the term 'make and enforce contracts' includes the making, performance, modification, and termination of contracts, and the enjoyment of all benefits, privileges, terms, and conditions of the contractual relationship.

(c) The rights protected by this section are protected against impairment by nongovernmental discrimination and impairment under color of State law.'.

SEC. 102. DAMAGES IN CASES OF INTENTIONAL DISCRIMINATION.

The Revised Statutes are amended by inserting after section 1977 (42 U.S.C. 1981) the following new section:

SEC. 1977A. DAMAGES IN CASES OF INTENTIONAL DISCRIMINATION IN EMPLOYMENT.

'(a) RIGHT OF RECOVERY-

'(1) CIVIL RIGHTS- In an action brought by a complaining party under section 706 or 717 of the

Civil Rights Act of 1964 (42 U.S.C. 2000e-5) against a respondent who engaged in unlawful intentional discrimination (not an employment practice that is unlawful because of its disparate impact) prohibited under section 703, 704, or 717 of the Act (42 U.S.C. 2000e-2 or 2000e-3), and provided that the complaining party cannot recover under section 1977 of the Revised Statutes (42 U.S.C. 1981), the complaining party may recover compensatory and punitive damages as allowed in subsection (b), in addition to any relief authorized by section 706(g) of the Civil Rights Act of 1964, from the respondent.

'(2) DISABILITY- In an action brought by a complaining party under the powers, remedies, and procedures set forth in section 706 or 717 of the Civil Rights Act of 1964 (as provided in section 107(a) of the Americans with Disabilities Act of 1990 (42 U.S.C. 12117(a)), and section 505(a)(1) of the Rehabilitation Act of 1973 (29 U.S.C. 794a(a)(1)), respectively) against a respondent who engaged in unlawful intentional discrimination (not an employment practice that is unlawful because of its disparate impact) under section 501 of the Rehabilitation Act of 1973 (29 U.S.C. 791) and the regulations implementing section 501, or who violated the requirements of section 501 of the Act or the regulations implementing section 501 concerning the provision of a reasonable accommodation, or section 102 of the Americans with Disabilities Act of 1990 (42 U.S.C. 12112), or committed a violation of section 102(b)(5) of the Act, against an individual, the complaining party may recover compensatory and punitive damages as allowed in subsection (b), in addition to any relief authorized by section 706(g) of the Civil Rights Act of 1964, from the respondent.

'(3) REASONABLE ACCOMMODATION AND GOOD FAITH EFFORT- In cases where a discriminatory practice involves the provision of a reasonable accommodation pursuant to section 102(b)(5) of the Americans with Disabilities Act of 1990 or regulations implementing section 501 of the Rehabilitation Act of 1973, damages may not be awarded under this section where the covered entity demonstrates good faith efforts, in consultation with the person with the disability who has informed the covered entity that accommodation is needed, to identify and make a reasonable accommodation that would provide such individual with an equally effective opportunity and would not cause an undue hardship on the operation of the business.

'(b) COMPENSATORY AND PUNITIVE DAMAGES-

'(1) DETERMINATION OF PUNITIVE DAMAGES- A complaining party may recover punitive damages under this section against a respondent (other than a government, government agency or political subdivision) if the complaining party demonstrates that the respondent engaged in a discriminatory practice or discriminatory practices with malice or with reckless indifference to the federally protected rights of an aggrieved individual.

'(2) EXCLUSIONS FROM COMPENSATORY DAMAGES- Compensatory damages awarded under this section shall not include backpay, interest on backpay, or any other type of relief authorized under section 706(g) of the Civil Rights Act of 1964.

'(3) LIMITATIONS- The sum of the amount of compensatory damages awarded under this section for future pecuniary losses, emotional pain, suffering, inconvenience, mental anguish, loss of enjoyment of life, and other nonpecuniary losses, and the amount of punitive damages awarded under this section, shall not exceed, for each complaining party—

'(A) in the case of a respondent who has more than 14 and fewer than 101 employees in each of 20 or more calendar weeks in the current or preceding calendar year, $50,000;

'(B) in the case of a respondent who has more than 100 and fewer than 201 employees in each of 20 or more calendar weeks in the current or preceding calendar year, $100,000; and

'(C) in the case of a respondent who has more than 200 and fewer than 501 employees in each of 20 or more calendar weeks in the current or preceding calendar year, $200,000; and

'(D) in the case of a respondent who has more than 500 employees in each of 20 or more calendar weeks in the current or preceding calendar year, $300,000.

'(4) CONSTRUCTION- Nothing in this section shall be construed to limit the scope of, or the relief available under, section 1977 of the Revised Statutes (42 U.S.C. 1981).

'(c) JURY TRIAL- If a complaining party seeks compensatory or punitive damages under this section—

'(1) any party may demand a trial by jury; and

'(2) the court shall not inform the jury of the limitations described in subsection (b)(3).

'(d) DEFINITIONS- As used in this section:

'(1) COMPLAINING PARTY- The term 'complaining party' means—

'(A) in the case of a person seeking to bring an action under subsection (a)(1), the Equal Employment Opportunity Commission, the Attorney General, or a person who may bring an action or proceeding under title VII of the Civil Rights Act of 1964 (42 U.S.C. 2000e et seq.); or

'(B) in the case of a person seeking to bring an action under subsection (a)(2), the Equal Employment Opportunity Commission, the Attorney General, a person who may bring an action or proceeding under section 505(a)(1) of the Rehabilitation Act of 1973 (29 U.S.C. 794a(a)(1)), or a person who may bring an action or proceeding under title I of the Americans with Disabilities Act of 1990 (42 U.S.C. 12101 et seq.).

'(2) DISCRIMINATORY PRACTICE- The term 'discriminatory practice' means the discrimination described in paragraph (1), or the discrimination or the violation described in paragraph (2), of subsection (a).

SEC. 103. ATTORNEY'S FEES.

The last sentence of section 722 of the Revised Statutes (42 U.S.C. 1988) is amended by inserting ', 1977A' after '1977'.

SEC. 104. DEFINITIONS.

Section 701 of the Civil Rights Act of 1964 (42 U.S.C. 2000e) is amended by adding at the end the following new subsections:

'(l) The term 'complaining party' means the Commission, the Attorney General, or a person who may bring an action or proceeding under this title.

'(m) The term 'demonstrates' means meets the burdens of production and persuasion.

'(n) The term 'respondent' means an employer, employment agency, labor organization, joint labor-management committee controlling apprenticeship or other training or retraining program, including an on-the-job training program, or Federal entity subject to section 717.'.

SEC. 105. BURDEN OF PROOF IN DISPARATE IMPACT CASES.

(a) Section 703 of the Civil Rights Act of 1964 (42 U.S.C. 2000e-2) is amended by adding at the end the following new subsection:

'(k)(1)(A) An unlawful employment practice based on disparate impact is established under this title only if—

'(i) a complaining party demonstrates that a respondent uses a particular employment practice that causes a disparate impact on the basis of race, color, religion, sex, or national origin and the respondent fails to demonstrate that the challenged practice is job related for the position in question and consistent with business necessity; or

'(ii) the complaining party makes the demonstration described in subparagraph (C) with respect to an alternative employment practice and the respondent refuses to adopt such alternative employment practice.

'(B)(i) With respect to demonstrating that a particular employment practice causes a disparate impact as described in subparagraph (A)(i), the complaining party shall demonstrate that each particular challenged employment practice causes a disparate impact, except that if the complaining party can demonstrate to the court that the elements of a respondent's decisionmaking process are not capable of separation for analysis, the decisionmaking process may be analyzed as one employment practice.

'(ii) If the respondent demonstrates that a specific employment practice does not cause the disparate impact, the respondent shall not be required to demonstrate that such practice is required by business necessity.

'(C) The demonstration referred to by subparagraph (A)(ii) shall be in accordance with the law as it existed on June 4, 1989, with respect to the concept of 'alternative employment practice'.

'(2) A demonstration that an employment practice is required by business necessity may not be used as a defense against a claim of intentional discrimination under this title.

'(3) Notwithstanding any other provision of this title, a rule barring the employment of an individual who currently and knowingly uses or possesses a controlled substance, as defined in schedules I and II of section 102(6) of the Controlled Substances Act (21 U.S.C. 802(6)), other than the use or possession of a drug taken under the supervision of a licensed health care professional, or any other use or possession authorized by the Controlled Substances Act or any other provision of Federal law, shall be considered an unlawful employment practice under this title only if such rule is adopted or applied with an intent to discriminate because of race, color, religion, sex, or national origin.'.

(b) No statements other than the interpretive memorandum appearing at Vol. 137 Congressional Record S 15276 (daily ed. Oct. 25, 1991) shall be considered legislative history of, or relied upon in any way as legislative history in construing or applying, any provision of this Act that relates to Wards Cove—Business necessity/cumulation/alternative business practice.

SEC. 106. PROHIBITION AGAINST DISCRIMINATORY USE OF TEST SCORES.

Section 703 of the Civil Rights Act of 1964 (42 U.S.C. 2000e-2) (as amended by section 105) is further amended by adding at the end the following new subsection:

'(l) It shall be an unlawful employment practice for a respondent, in connection with the selection or referral of applicants or candidates for employment or promotion, to adjust the scores of, use different cutoff scores for, or otherwise alter the results of, employment related tests on the basis of race, color, religion, sex, or national origin.'.

SEC. 107. CLARIFYING PROHIBITION AGAINST IMPERMISSIBLE CONSIDERATION OF RACE, COLOR, RELIGION, SEX, OR NATIONAL ORIGIN IN EMPLOYMENT PRACTICES.

(a) IN GENERAL- Section 703 of the Civil Rights Act of 1964 (42 U.S.C. 2000e-2) (as amended by sections 105 and 106) is further amended by adding at the end the following new subsection:

'(m) Except as otherwise provided in this title, an unlawful employment practice is established when the complaining party demonstrates that race, color, religion, sex, or national origin was a motivating factor for any employment practice, even though other factors also motivated the practice.'.

(b) ENFORCEMENT PROVISIONS- Section 706(g) of such Act (42 U.S.C. 2000e-5(g)) is amended—

(1) by designating the first through third sentences as paragraph (1);

(2) by designating the fourth sentence as paragraph (2)(A) and indenting accordingly; and

(3) by adding at the end the following new subparagraph:

'(B) On a claim in which an individual proves a violation under section 703(m) and a respondent demonstrates that the respondent would have taken the same action in the absence of the impermissible motivating factor, the court—

'(i) may grant declaratory relief, injunctive relief (except as provided in clause (ii)), and attorney's fees and costs demonstrated to be directly attributable only to the pursuit of a claim under section 703(m); and

'(ii) shall not award damages or issue an order requiring any admission, reinstatement, hiring, promotion, or payment, described in subparagraph (A).'.

SEC. 108. FACILITATING PROMPT AND ORDERLY RESOLUTION OF CHALLENGES TO EMPLOYMENT PRACTICES IMPLEMENTING LITIGATED OR CONSENT JUDGMENTS OR ORDERS.

Section 703 of the Civil Rights Act of 1964 (42 U.S.C. 2000e-2) (as amended by sections 105, 106, and 107 of this title) is further amended by adding at the end the following new subsection:

'(n)(1)(A) Notwithstanding any other provision of law, and except as provided in paragraph (2), an employment practice that implements and is within the scope of a litigated or consent judgment or order that resolves a claim of employment discrimination under the Constitution or Federal civil rights laws may not be challenged under the circumstances described in subparagraph (B).

'(B) A practice described in subparagraph (A) may not be challenged in a claim under the Constitution or Federal civil rights laws—

'(i) by a person who, prior to the entry of the judgment or order described in subparagraph (A), had—

'(I) actual notice of the proposed judgment or order sufficient to apprise such person that such judgment or order might adversely affect the interests and legal rights of such person and that an opportunity was available to present objections to such judgment or order by a future date certain; and

'(II) a reasonable opportunity to present objections to such judgment or order; or

'(ii) by a person whose interests were adequately represented by another person who had previously challenged the judgment or order on the same legal grounds and with a similar factual situation, unless there has been an intervening change in law or fact.

'(2) Nothing in this subsection shall be construed to—

'(A) alter the standards for intervention under rule 24 of the Federal Rules of Civil Procedure or apply to the rights of parties who have successfully intervened pursuant to such rule in the proceeding in which the parties intervened;

'(B) apply to the rights of parties to the action in which a litigated or consent judgment or order was entered, or of members of a class represented or sought to be represented in such action, or of members of a group on whose behalf relief was sought in such action by the Federal Government;

'(C) prevent challenges to a litigated or consent judgment or order on the ground that such judgment or order was obtained through collusion or fraud, or is transparently invalid or was entered by a court lacking subject matter jurisdiction; or

'(D) authorize or permit the denial to any person of the due process of law required by the Constitution.

'(3) Any action not precluded under this subsection that challenges an employment consent judgment or order described in paragraph (1) shall be brought in the court, and if possible before the judge, that entered such judgment or order. Nothing in this subsection shall preclude a transfer of such action pursuant to section 1404 of title 28, United States Code.'. . . .

SEC. 320. COVERAGE OF PRESIDENTIAL APPOINTEES.

(a) IN GENERAL-

(1) APPLICATION- The rights, protections, and remedies provided pursuant to section 302 and 307(h) of this title shall apply with respect to employment of Presidential appointees.

(2) ENFORCEMENT BY ADMINISTRATIVE ACTION- Any Presidential appointee may file a complaint alleging a violation, not later than 180 days after the occurrence of the alleged violation, with the Equal Employment Opportunity Commission, or such other entity as is designated by the President by Executive Order, which, in accordance with the principles and procedures set forth in sections 554 through 557 of title 5, United States Code, shall determine whether a violation has occurred and shall set forth its determination in a final order. If the Equal Employment Opportunity Commission, or such other entity as is designated by the President pursuant to this section, determines that a violation has occurred, the final order shall also provide for appropriate relief.

Source: Civil Rights Act of 1991. Pub. L. 102-166. http://www.eeoc.gov/eeoc/history/35th/thelaw/cra_1991.html.

Anita Hill, Testimony to Senate Judiciary Committee during the Confirmation Hearing of Clarence Thomas to the U.S. Supreme Court (October 11, 1991)

Anita Hill became a national figure in 1991 when she told the Senate Judiciary Committee that Supreme Court nominee Clarence Thomas had made harassing and sexually inappropriate remarks to her when he was her supervisor at the U.S. Department of Education and the Equal Employment Opportunity Commission (EEOC). Thomas denied making the remarks and was confirmed, though Hill's testimony began a national dialogue on sexual harassment in the workplace. Following are excerpts from Hill's testimony. Hill is currently professor of social policy, law, and women's studies at Brandeis University's Heller School for Social Policy and Management.

Mr. Chairman, Senator Thurmond, members of the committee. My name is Anita F. Hill, and I am a professor of law at the University of Oklahoma. I was born on a farm in Okmulgee County, Oklahoma, in 1956. I am the youngest of 13 children.

I had my early education in Okmulgee County. My father, Albert Hill, is a farmer in that area. My mother's name is Irma Hill. She is also a farmer and a housewife.

My childhood was one of a lot of hard work and not much money, but it was one of solid family affection as represented by my parents. I was reared in a religious atmosphere in the Baptist faith, and I have been a member of the Antioch Baptist Church in Tulsa, Oklahoma, since 1983. It is a very warm part of my life at the present time.

For my undergraduate work, I went to Oklahoma State University and graduated from there in 1977. . . . I graduated from the university with academic honors and proceeded to the Yale Law School, where I received my J. D. degree in 1980.

Upon graduation from law school, I became a practicing lawyer with the Washington, D. C., firm of Wald, Hardraker & Ross. In 1981, I was introduced to now-Judge Thomas by a mutual friend.

Judge Thomas told me that he was anticipating a political appointment, and he asked if I would be interested in working with him.

He was in fact appointed as assistant secretary of Education for civil rights. After he was, after he had taken that post, he asked if I would become his assistant, and I accepted that position.

In my early period there, I had two major projects. The first was an article I wrote for Judge Thomas' signature on the education of minority students. The second was the organization of a seminar on high risk students, which was abandoned because Judge Thomas transferred to the EEOC, where he became the chairman of that office.

During this period at the Department of Education my working relationship with Judge Thomas was positive. I had a good deal of responsibility and independence. I thought he respected my work and that he trusted my judgment.

After approximately three months of working there, he asked me to go out socially with him. What happened next, and telling the world about it, are the two most difficult things—experiences of my life.

It is only after a great deal of agonizing consideration and sleepless nights that I am able to talk of these unpleasant matters to anyone but my close friends.

I declined the invitation to go out socially with him and explained to him that I thought it would jeopardize what at the time I considered to be a very good working relationship. I had a normal social life with other men outside the office. I believed then, as now, that having a social relationship with a person who was supervising my work would be ill-advised. I was very uncomfortable with the idea and told him so.

I thought that by saying no and explaining my reasons, my employer would abandon his social suggestions. However, to my regret, in the following few weeks, he continued to ask me out on several occasions. He pressed me to justify my reasons for saying no to him. These incidents took place in his office or mine. They were in the form of private conversations which would not have been overheard by anyone else.

My working relationship became even more strained when Judge Thomas began to use work situations to discuss sex. On these occasions he would call me into his office for reports on education issues and projects, or he might suggest that because of the time pressures of his schedule we go to lunch to a government cafeteria.

After a brief discussions of work, he would turn the conversation to a discussion of sexual matters. His conversations were very vivid. He spoke about acts that he had seen in pornographic films involving such matters as women having sex with animals and films showing group sex or rape scenes.

He talked about pornographic materials depicting individuals with large penises or large breasts involving various sex acts. On several occasions, Thomas told me graphically of his own sexual prowess.

Because I was extremely uncomfortable talking about sex with him at all, and particularly in such a graphic way, I told him that I did not want to talk about this subject. I would also try to change the subject to education matters or to non-sexual personal matters, such as his background or his beliefs.

My efforts to change the subject were rarely successful.

Throughout the period of these conversations, he also from time to time asked me for social engagements. My reaction to these conversations was to avoid them by eliminating opportunities for us to engage in extended conversations.

This was difficult because, at the time, I was his only assistant at the Office of Education—or Office for Civil Rights. During the latter part of my time at the Department of Education, the social pressures, and any conversation of his offensive behavior, ended. I began both to believe and hope that

our working relationship could be a proper, cordial and professional one.

When Judge Thomas was made chair of the EEOC, I needed to face the question of whether to go with him. I was asked to do so, and I did.

The work itself was interesting, and at the time it appeared that the sexual overtures which had so troubled me had ended.

I also faced the realistic fact that I had no alternative job. While I might have gone back to private practice, perhaps in my old firm or at another, I was dedicated to civil rights work, and my first choice was to be in that field. Moreover, at that time, the Department of Education itself was a dubious venture. President Reagan was seeking to abolish the entire department.

For my first months at the EEOC where I continued to be an assistant to Judge Thomas, there were no sexual conversations or overtures. However, during the fall and winter of 1982, these began again. The comments were random and ranged from pressing me about why I didn't go out with him to remarks about my personal appearance. I remember his saying that some day I would have to tell him the real reason that I wouldn't go out with him.

He began to show displeasure in his tone and voice and his demeanor and his continued pressure for an explanation. He commented on what I was wearing in terms of whether it made me more or less sexually attractive. The incidents occurred in his inner office at the EEOC.

One of the oddest episodes I remember was an occasion in which Thomas was drinking a Coke in his office. He got up from the table at which we were working, went over to his desk to get the Coke, looked at the can and asked, "Who has put pubic hair on my Coke?"

On other occasions, he referred to the size of his own penis as being larger than normal, and he also spoke on some occasions of the pleasures he had given to women with oral sex. At this point, late 1982, I began to feel severe stress on the job. I began to be concerned that Clarence Thomas might take out his anger with me by degrading me or not giving me important assignments. I also thought that he might find an excuse for dismissing me. In January of 1983, I began looking for another job. I was handicapped because I feared that if he found out, he might make it difficult for me to find other employment, and I might be dismissed from the job I had. Another factor that made my search more difficult was that there was a period—this was during a period of a hiring freeze in the government.

In February 1983 I was hospitalized for five days on an emergency basis for acute stomach pain, which I attributed to stress on the job. Once out of the hospital I became more committed to find other employment and sought further to minimize my contact with Thomas. This became easier when Allison Duncan became office director, because most of my work was then funneled through her, and I had contact with Clarence Thomas mostly in staff meetings.

In the spring of 1983, and opportunity to teach at Oral Roberts University opened up. I participated in a seminar, taught an afternoon session in a seminar at Oral Roberts University. The dean of the university saw me teaching and inquired as to whether I would be interested in further pursuing a career in teaching beginning at Oral Roberts University. I agreed to take the job, in large part because of my desire to escape the pressures I felt at the EEOC due to Judge Thomas.

When I informed him that I was leaving in July, I recall that his response was that now I would no longer have an excuse for not going out with him. I told him that I still preferred not to do so. At some time after that meeting, he asked if he could take me to dinner at the end of the term. When I declined, he assured me that the dinner was a professional courtesy only and not a social invitation. I reluctantly agreed to accept that invitation but only if it was at the very end of a working day.

On, as I recall, the last day of my employment at the EEOC in the summer of 1983, I did have dinner with Clarence Thomas. We went directly from work to a restaurant near the office. We talked about the work I had done, both at Education and at the EEOC. He told me that he was pleased with

all of it except for an article and speech that I had done for him while we were at the Office for Civil Rights. Finally he made a comment that I will vividly remember. He said that if I ever told anyone of his behavior that it would ruin his career. This was not an apology, nor was it an explanation. That was his last remark about the possibility of our going out or reference to his behavior.

In July of 1983 I left the Washington, D. C. area, and I've had minimal contacts with Judge Clarence Thomas since. I am of course aware from the press that some questions have been raised about conversations I had with Judge Clarence Thomas after I left the EEOC. From 1983 until today, I have seen Judge Thomas only twice. On one occasion I needed to get a reference from him, and on another, he made a public appearance in Tulsa. On one occasion he called me at home, and we had an inconsequential conversation. On one occasion he called me without reaching me, and I returned the call without reaching him, and nothing came of it.

I have, on at least three occasions, been asked to act as a conduit to him for others. I knew his secretary, Diane Holt. We had worked together at both EEOC and Education. There were occasions on which I spoke to her, and on some of the these occasions, undoubtedly, I passed on some casual comment to then-Chairman Thomas.

There were a series of calls in the first three months of 1985 occasioned by a group in Tulsa, which wished to have a civil rights conference. They wanted Judge Thomas to be the speaker and enlisted my assistance for this purpose. I did call in January and February, to no effect, and finally suggested to the person directly involved, Susan Cahall, that she put the matter into her own hands and call directly. She did so in March of 1985.

In connection with that March invitation, Miss Cahall wanted conference materials for the seminar, and some research was needed. I was asked to try to get the information and did attempt to do so. There was another call about the possible conference in July of 1985.

In August of 1987 I was in Washington D.C., and I did call Diane Holt. In the course of his conversation, she asked me how long I was going to be in town, and I told her. It is recorded in the message as August 15. It was in fact August 20. She told me about Judge Thomas' marriage, and I did say congratulate him.

It is only after a great deal of agonizing consideration that I am able to talk of these unpleasant matters to anyone except my closest friends, as I've said before. These last few days have been very trying and very hard for me, and it hasn't just been the last few days this week.

It has actually been over a month now that I have been under the strain of this issue.

Telling the world is the most difficult experience of my life, but it is very close to having to live through the experience that occasioned this meeting. I may have used poor judgment early on in my relationship with this issue. I was aware, however, that telling at any point in my career could adversely affect my future career, and I did not want early on, to burn all the bridges to the EEOC.

As I said, I may have used poor judgment. Perhaps I should have taken angry or even militant steps, both when I was in the agency or after I left it. But I must confess to the world that the course that I took seemed the better, as well as the easier, approach.

I declined any comment to newspapers, but later, when Senate staff asked me about these matters, I felt I had a duty to report. I have no personal vendetta against Clarence Thomas. I seek only to provide the committee with information which it may regard as relevant.

It would have been more comfortable to remain silent. I took no initiative to inform anyone. But when I asked by a representative of this committee to report my experience, I felt that I had to tell the truth. I could not keep silent.

Source: Hill, Anita. "Testimony to Senate Judiciary Committee." Hearings before the Committee on the Judiciary, United States Senate on the nomination of Clarence Thomas to be Associate Justice of the Supreme Court of the United States. Washington, DC, October 11, 1991.

Million Man March: Pledge

(1995)

On October 16, 1995, Nation of Islam leader Louis Farrakhan led close to 1 million African American men in what he declared a "day of atonement and prayer" on the Washington Mall in Washington, DC. More than 80 speakers addressed the large crowd throughout the course of the day, including such notable figures as Jesse Jackson, Betty Shabazz, Rosa Parks, Marion Barry, and Maya Angelou. Farrakhan promoted the march as a way of reinvigorating a black consciousness movement in America. Reproduced here is the text of the pledge Farrakhan asked men to take.

I pledge that from this day forward I will strive to love my brother as I love myself. I, from this day forward, will strive to improve myself spiritually, morally, mentally, socially, politically and economically for the benefit of myself, my family and my people. I pledge that I will strive to build business, build houses, build hospitals, build factories and enter into international trade for the good of myself, my family and my people.

I pledge that from this day forward I will never raise my hand with a knife or a gun to beat, cut, or shoot any member of my family or any human being except in self-defense. I pledge from this day forward I will never abuse my wife by striking her, disrespecting her, for she is the mother of my children and the producer of my future. I pledge that from this day forward I will never engage in the abuse of children, little boys or little girls for sexual gratification. For I will let them grow in peace to be strong men and women for the future of our people.

I will never again use the "B word" to describe any female. But particularly my own black sister. I pledge from this day forward that I will not poison my body with drugs or that which is destructive to my health and my well-being. I pledge from this day forward I will support black newspapers, black radio, black television. I will support black artists who clean up their acts to show respect for themselves and respect for their people and respect for the ears of the human family. I will do all of this so help me God.

Source: Farrakhan, Louis. Pledge presented at the Million Man March, Washington, DC, October 16, 1995.

Clarence Thomas, "I Am a Man, a Black Man, an American" (1998)

In this 1998 speech delivered at the annual meeting of the National Bar Association in Memphis, Tennessee, U.S. Supreme Court Justice Clarence Thomas reflects on his seven years on the court (he joined the court in October 1991). He speaks of the impact that Martin Luther King's death has had on his life and his restored faith in religion and the country. He also addresses racism and celebrates his freedom as a black man.

Mr. Mayor, my fellow colleagues of both bench and bar, it's a pleasure to be here. And one advantage is that similar to being on the bench, I have heard all of the arguments, and will take them under advisement. I have been told recently that Judge Bailey does not take matters under advisement that frequently, so I will stay out of his court. But it is indeed a pleasure to be here.

A friend of mine who passed away some nine years ago was an active member of the NBA. And many of you may remember him, Gil Hardy. Probably one of the most painful tragedies for me of my confirmation was to see the name of one of the nicest, most decent human beings I had ever met, besmirched. And Gil was my best friend at both college and at Yale Law School. He was the best man at my wedding and he is the person to whom I went for solace.

For those of you with whom I do not share the same opinion and perhaps that is many I will take only 30 minutes of your time. And perhaps at least we can part company having known we at least visited for 30 minutes.

Thank you, Judge Keith, for your kind, warm words. As always, I deeply appreciate the manner in which you have made yourself available over the years for counsel and advice. And I appreciate your courteous and dignified example over the past 15 years. And I might add parenthetically here, I met Judge Keith in the early '80s when I was trying to figure out a way to distribute in excess of 10 million dollars to minorities for scholarships, and was being opposed by individuals who should have been supporting us. And it was his advice and counsel that bolstered us in that effort. We who are just commencing our tenures as judges can only hope to emulate your positive spirit and the strength of character that you've always demonstrated.

I'd also like to thank President Jones for his support, Justice Johnson for your strength and your courage and you stick-to-it-tivity, Judge Bailey—who I thought I had gotten into a mess, but having had dinner with him, he got me into a mess—but I have enjoyed your company and the opportunity to learn from you, to get to know you, and perhaps to develop a friendship over the years. And I would like to thank the other members of the Judicial Council for the National Bar Association who have been so courageous and forthright and kind to invite me to join you this afternoon.

As has become the custom, a wearisome one I admit, this invitation has not been without controversy. Though this unfortunate, this controversy has added little value in the calculus of my decision to be here.

Thirty years ago, we all focused intently on this city as the trauma of Dr. King's death first exploded, then sank into our lives. For so many of us who were trying hard to do what we thought was required of us in the process of integrating this society, the rush of hopelessness and isolation was immediate and overwhelming. It seemed that the whole world had gone mad.

I am certain that each of us has his or her memories of that terrible day in 1968. For me it was the final straw in the struggle to retain my vocation to become a Catholic priest. Suddenly, this cataclysmic event ripped me from the moorings of my grandparents, my youth and my faith, and catapulted me headlong into the abyss that Richard Wright seemed to describe years earlier.

It was this event that shattered my faith in my religion and my country. I had spent the mid-'60s as a successful student in a virtually white environment. I had learned Latin, physics and chemistry. I had accepted the loneliness that came with being "the integrator," the first and the only. But this event, this trauma I could not take, especially when one of my fellow seminarians, not knowing that I was standing behind him, declared that he hoped the S.O.B. died. This was a man of God, mortally stricken by an assassin's bullet, and one preparing for the priesthood had wished evil upon him.

The life I had dreamed of so often during those hot summers on the farm in Georgia or during what seemed like endless hours on the oil truck with my grandfather, expired as Dr. King expired. As so many of you do, I still know exactly where I was when I heard the news. It was a low moment in our nation's history and a demarcation between hope and hopelessness for many of us.

But three decades have evaporated in our lives, too quickly and without sufficient residual evidence of their importance. But much has changed since then. The hope that there would be expeditious resolutions to our myriad problems has long since evaporated with those years. Many who debated and hoped then, now do neither. There now seems to be a broad acceptance of the racial divide as a permanent state. While we once celebrated those things that we had in common with our fellow citizens who did not share our race, so many now are triumphal about our differences, finding little, if anything, in common. Indeed, some go so far as to all but define each of us by our race and establish the range of our thinking and our opinions, if not our deeds by our color.

I, for one, see this in much the same way I saw our denial of rights—as nothing short of a denial of our humanity. Not one of us has the "gospel," nor are our opinions based upon some revealed precepts to be taken as faith. As thinking, rational individuals, not one of us can claim infallibility, even from the overwhelming advantage of hindsight and Monday-morning quarterbacking.

This makes it all the more important that our fallible ideas be examined as all ideas are in the realm of reason, not as some doctrinal or racial heresy. None of us—none of us have been appointed by God or appointed God. And if any of us has, then my question is why hasn't he or she solved all these problems.

I make no apologies for this view now, nor do I intend to do so in the future. I have now been on the court for seven terms. For the most part, it has been much like other endeavors in life. It has its challenges and requires much of the individual to master the workings of the institution. We all know that. It is, I must say, quite different from what I might have anticipated if I had the opportunity to do so.

Unlike the unfortunate practice or custom in Washington and in much of the country, the court is a model of civility. It's a wonderful place. Though there have been many contentious issues to come before the court during these initial years of my tenure, I have yet to hear the first unkind words exchanged among my colleagues. And quite frankly, I think that such civility is the sine qua non of conducting the affairs of the court and the business of the country.

As such, I think that it would be in derogation of our respective oaths and our institutional obligations to our country to engage in uncivil behavior. It would also be demeaning to any of us who engages in such conduct. Having worn the robe, we have a lifetime obligation to conduct ourselves as having deserved to wear the robe in the first instance.

One of the interesting surprises is the virtual isolation, even within the court. It is quite rare that the members of the court see each other during those periods when we're not sitting or when we're not in conference. And the most regular contact beyond those two formal events are the lunches we have on conference and court days.

With respect to my following, or, more accurately, being led by other members of the Court, that is silly, but expected since I couldn't possibly think for myself. And what else could possibly be the explanation when I fail to follow the jurisprudential, ideological and intellectual, if not anti-intellectual, prescription assigned to blacks. Since thinking beyond this prescription is presumptively beyond my abilities, obviously someone must be putting these strange ideas into my mind and my opinions.

Though being underestimated has its advantages, the stench of racial inferiority still confounds my olfactory nerves.

As Ralph Ellison wrote more than 35 years ago, "Why is it so often true that when critics confront the American as Negro, they suddenly drop their advanced critical armament and revert with an air of confident superiority to quite primitive modes of analysis?" Those matters accomplished by whites are routinely subjected to sophisticated modes of analysis. But the when the selfsame matters are accomplished by blacks, the opaque racial prism of analysis precludes such sophistication, and all is seen in black and white. And some who would not venture onto the more sophisticated analytical turf are quite content to play in the minor leagues of primitive harping.

The more things change, the more they remain the same.

Of course there is much criticism of the court by this group or that, depending on the court's decisions in various highly publicized cases. Some of the criticism is profoundly uninformed and unhelpful. And all too often, uncivil second-guessing is not encumbered by the constraints of facts, logic or reasoned analysis.

On the other hand, the constructive and often scholarly criticism is almost always helpful in thinking about or rethinking decisions. It is my view that constructive criticism goes with the turf, especially when the stakes are so high and the cases arouse passions and emotions. And, in a free society, [where is found] the precious freedom of speech and the strength of ideas, we at the court could not possibly claim exemption from such criticism. Moreover, we are not infallible, just final.

As I have noted, I find a thoughtful, analytical criticism most helpful. I do not think any judge can address a vast array of cases and issues without testing and re-testing his or her reasoning and opinions in the crucible of debate. However, since we are quite limited in public debate about matters that may come before the court, such debate must, for the most part, occur intramurally, thus placing a premium on outside scholarship.

Unfortunately, from time to time, the criticism of the court goes beyond the bounds of civil debate and discourse. Today it seems quite acceptable to attack the court and other institutions when one disagrees with an opinion or policy. I can still remember traveling along Highway 17 in south

Georgia, the Coastal Highway, during the '50s and '60s, and seeing the "Impeach Earl Warren" signs.

Clearly, heated reactions to the court or to its members are not unusual. Certainly, Justice Blackmun was attacked repeatedly because many disagreed, as I have, with the opinion he offered on behalf of the Court in *Roe v. Wade.* Though I have joined opinions disagreeing with Justice Blackmun, I could not imagine ever being discourteous to him merely because we disagreed.

I've found during my almost 20 years in Washington that the tendency to personalize differences has grown to be an accepted way of doing business. One need not do the hard work of dissecting an argument. One need only attack and thus discredit the person making the argument. Though the matter being debated is not effectively resolved, the debate is reduced to unilateral pronouncements and glib but quotable cliches.

I, for one, have been singled out for particularly bilious and venomous assaults. These criticisms, as near as I can tell, and I admit that it is rare that I take notice of this calumny, have little to do with any particular opinion, though each opinion does provide one more occasion to criticize. Rather, the principal problem seems to be a deeper antecedent offense: I have no right to think the way I do because I'm black.

Though the ideas and opinions themselves are not necessarily illegitimate if held by non-black individuals, they, and the person enunciating them, are illegitimate if that person happens to be black. Thus, there's a subset of criticism that must of necessity be reserved for me, even if every non-black member of the court agrees with the idea or the opinion. You see, they are exempt from this kind of criticism, precisely because they are not black. As noted earlier, they are more often than not subjected to the whites-only sophisticated analysis.

I will not catalogue my opinions to which there have been objections since they are a matter of public record. But I must note in passing that I can't help but wonder if some of my critics can read.

One opinion that is trotted out for propaganda, for the propaganda parade, is my dissent in *Hudson vs. McMillian.* The conclusion reached by the long arms of the critics is that I supported the beating of prisoners in that case. Well, one must either be illiterate or fraught with malice to reach that conclusion.

Though one can disagree with my dissent, and certainly the majority of the court disagreed, no honest reading can reach such a conclusion. Indeed, we took the case to decide the quite narrow issue, whether a prisoner's rights were violated under the "cruel and unusual punishment" clause of the Eighth Amendment as a result of a single incident of force by the prison guards which did not cause a significant injury.

In the first section of my dissent, I stated the following: "In my view, a use of force that causes only insignificant harm to a prisoner may be immoral; it may be tortuous; it may be criminal, and it may even be remediable under other provisions of the Federal Constitution. But it is not cruel and unusual punishment."

Obviously, beating prisoners is bad. But we did not take the case to answer this larger moral question or a larger legal question of remedies under other statutes or provisions of the Constitution. How one can extrapolate these larger conclusions from the narrow question before the court is beyond me, unless, of course, there's a special segregated mode of analysis.

It should be obvious that the criticism of this opinion serves not to present counter-arguments, but to discredit and attack me because I've deviated from the prescribed path. In his intriguing and thoughtful essay on "My Race Problem and Ours," Harvard law professor Randall Kennedy, a self-described social Democrat, correctly observes that "If racial loyalty is deemed essentially and morally virtuous, then a black person's adoption of positions that are deemed racially disloyal will be seen by racial loyalists as a supremely threatening sin, one warranting the harsh punishments that have historically been visited upon alleged traitors." Perhaps this is the defensive solidarity to which

Richard Wright refers. If so, it is a reaction I understand, but resolutely decline to follow.

In the final weeks of my seminary days, shortly after Dr. King's death, I found myself becoming consumed by feelings of animosity and anger. I was disenchanted with my church and my country. I was tired of being in the minority, and I was tired of turning the other cheek. I, along with many blacks, found ways to protest and try to change the treatment we received in this country. Perhaps my passion for Richard Wright novels was affecting me. Perhaps it was listening too intently to Nina Simone. Perhaps, like Bigger Thomas, I was being consumed by the circumstances in which I found myself, circumstances that I saw as responding only to race.

My feelings were reaffirmed during the summer of 1968 as a result of the lingering stench of racism in Savannah and the assassination of Bobby Kennedy. No matter what the reasons were, I closed out the '60s as one angry young man waiting on the revolution that I was certain would soon come. I saw no way out. I, like many others, felt the deep chronic agony of anomie and alienation. All seemed to be defined by race. We became a reaction to the "man," his ominous reflection.

The intensity of my feelings was reinforced by other events of the late '60s: the riots, the marches, the sense that something had to be done, done quickly to resolve the issue of race. In college there was an air of excitement, apprehension and anger. We started the Black Students Union. We protested. We worked in the Free Breakfast Program. We would walk out of school in the winter of 1969 in protest.

But the questioning for me started in the spring of 1970 after an unauthorized demonstration in Cambridge, Massachusetts, to "free the political prisoners." Why was I doing this rather than using my intellect? Perhaps I was empowered by the anger and relieved that I could now strike back at the faceless oppressor. But why was I conceding my intellect and rather fighting much like a brute? This I could not answer, except to say that I was tired of being restrained.

Somehow I knew that unless I contained the anger within me I would suffer the fates of Bigger Thomas and Damon Cross. It was intoxicating to act upon one's rage, to wear it on one's shoulder, to be defined by it. Yet, ultimately, it was destructive, and I knew it.

So in the spring of 1970, in a nihilistic fog, I prayed that I'd be relieved of the anger and the animosity that ate at my soul. I did not want to hate any more, and I had to stop before it totally consumed me. I had to make a fundamental choice. Do I believe in the principles of this country or not? After such angst, I concluded that I did. But the battle between passion and reason would continue, although abated, still intense.

Ironically, many of the people who are critics today were among those we called half-steppers, who had co-opted by "the man" because they were part of the system that oppressed us. When the revolution came, all of the so-called Negroes needed to be dealt with.

It is interesting to remember that someone gave me a copy of Prof. Thomas Sowell's book, "Education, Myths and Tragedies," in which he predicted much of what has happened to blacks and education. I threw it in the trash, unread, declaring that he was not a black man since no black could take the positions that he had taken, whatever they were, since I had only heard his views were not those of a black man.

I was also upset to hear of a black conservative in Virginia named Jay Parker. How could a black man call himself a conservative? In a twist of fate, they both are dear friends today, and the youthful wrath I visited upon them is now being visited upon me, though without the youth.

What goes around does indeed come around.

The summer of 1971 was perhaps one of the most difficult of my life. It was clear to me that the road to destruction was paved with anger, resentment and rage. But where were we to go? I would often spend hours in our small efficiency apartment in New Haven pondering this question and listening to Marvin Gaye's then new album, "What's Going On?" To say the least, it was a depressing summer. What were we to do? What's going on?

As I think back on those years, I find it interesting that many people seemed to have trouble with their identities as black men. Having had to accept my blackness in the caldron of ridicule from some of my black schoolmates under segregation, then immediately thereafter remain secure in that identity during my years at all-white seminary, I had few racial identity problems. I knew who I was and needed no gimmicks to affirm my identity. Nor, might I add, do I need anyone telling me who I am today. This is especially true of the psycho-silliness about forgetting my roots or self-hatred. If anything, this shows that some people have too much time on their hands.

There's a rush today to prescribe who is black, to prescribe what are our differences, or to ignore what our differences are. Of course, those of us who came from the rural South were different from the blacks who came from the large northern cities, such as Philadelphia and New York. We were all black. But that similarity did not mask the richness of our differences. Indeed, one of the advantages of growing up in a black neighborhood was that we were richly blessed with the ability to see the individuality of each black person with all its fullness and complexity. We saw those differences at school, at home, at church, and definitely at the barbershop on Saturday morning.

Intra-racially, we consistently recognized our differences. It is quite counter-factual to suggest that such differences have not existed throughout our history. Indeed, when I was on the other side of the ideological divide, arguing strenuously with my grandfather that the revolution was imminent and that we all had to stick together as black people, he was quick to remind me that he had lived much longer than I had and during far more difficult times, and that, in any case, it took all kinds to make a world.

I agree with Ralph Ellison when he asked, perhaps rhetorically, why is it that so many of those who would tell us the meaning of Negro, of Negro life, never bothered to learn how varied it really is.

That is particularly true of many whites who have elevated condescension to an art form by advancing a monolithic view of blacks in much the same way that the mythic, disgusting image of the lazy, dumb black was advanced by open, rather than disguised, bigots.

Today, of course, it is customary to collapse, if not overwrite, our individual characteristics into new, but now acceptable stereotypes. It no longer matters whether one is from urban New York City or rural Georgia. It doesn't matter whether we came from a highly educated family or a barely literate one. It does not matter if you are a Roman Catholic or a Southern Baptist. All of these differences are canceled by race, and a revised set of acceptable stereotypes have been put in place.

Long gone is the time when we opposed the notion that we all looked alike and talked alike. Somehow we have come to exalt the new black stereotype above all and to demand conformity to that norm. It is this notion—that our race defines us—that Ralph Ellison so eloquently rebuts in his essay, "The World and the Jug." He sees the lives of black people as more than a burden, but also a discipline, just as any human life which has endured so long is a discipline, teaching its own insights into the human condition, its own strategies of survival. There's a fullness and even a richness here. And here despite the realities of politics, perhaps, but nevertheless here and real because it is human life.

Despite some of the nonsense that has been said about me by those who should know better, and so much nonsense, or some of which subtracts from the sum total of human knowledge, despite this all, I am a man, a black man, an American. And my history is not unlike that of many blacks from the deep South. And in many ways it is not that much different from that of many other Americans.

It goes without saying that I understand the comforts and security of racial solidarity, defensive or otherwise. Only those who have not been set upon by hatred and repelled by rejection fail to understand its attraction. As I have suggested, I have been there.

The inverse relationship between the bold promises and the effectiveness of the proposed solutions, the frustrations with the so-called system, the subtle and not-so-subtle bigotry and animus towards members of my race made radicals and nationalists of many of us. Yes, I understand the reasons why this is attractive. But it is precisely this—in its historic form, not its present-day diluted form that I have rejected. My question was whether as an individual I truly believed that I was the equal of individuals who were white. This I had answered with a resounding "yes" in 1964 during my sophomore year in the seminary. And that answer continues to be yes. Accordingly, my words and my deeds are consistent with this answer.

Any effort, policy or program that has as a prerequisite the acceptance of the notion that blacks are inferior is a non-starter with me. I do not believe that kneeling is a position of strength. Nor do I believe that begging is an effective tactic. I am confident that the individual approach, not the group approach, is the better, more acceptable, more supportable and less dangerous one. This approach is also consistent with the underlying principles of this country and the guarantees of freedom through government by consent. I, like Frederick Douglass, believe that whites and blacks can live together and be blended into a common nationality.

Do I believe that my views or opinions are perfect or infallible? No, I do not. But in admitting that I have no claim to perfection or infallibility, I am also asserting that competing or differing views similarly have no such claim. And they should not be accorded a status of infallibility or any status that suggests otherwise.

With differing, but equally fallible views, I think it is best that they be aired and sorted out in an environment of civility, consistent with the institutions in which we are involved. In this case, the judicial system.

It pains me deeply, or more deeply than any of you can imagine, to be perceived by so many members of my race as doing them harm. All the sacrifice, all the long hours of preparation were to help, not to hurt. But what hurts more, much more, is the amount of time and attention spent on manufactured controversies and media sideshows when so many problems cry out for constructive attention.

I have come here today not in anger or to anger, though my mere presence has been sufficient, obviously, to anger some. Nor have I come to defend my views, but rather to assert my right to think for myself, to refuse to have my ideas assigned to me as though I was an intellectual slave because I'm black.

I come to state that I'm a man, free to think for myself and do as I please.

I've come to assert that I am a judge and I will not be consigned the unquestioned opinions of others.

But even more than that, I have come to say that isn't it time to move on? Isn't it time to realize that being angry with me solves no problems?

Isn't it time to acknowledge that the problem of race has defied simple solutions and that not one of us, not a single one of us can lay claim to the solution?

Isn't it time that we respect ourselves and each other as we have demanded respect from others?

Isn't it time to ignore those whose sole occupation is sowing seeds of discord and animus? That is self-hatred.

Isn't it time to continue diligently to search for lasting solutions?

I believe that the time has come today. God bless each of you, and may God keep you.

Source: Thomas, Clarence. "I Am a Man, a Black Man, an American." Speech, annual meeting of the National Bar Association, Memphis, TN, July 29, 1998.

Harold Ford Jr., 2000 Democratic National Convention Keynote Address
(August 15, 2000)

In August 2000, Tennessee congressman Harold Ford spoke before colleagues at the Democratic National Convention. One of the up-and-coming African American leaders of the Democratic Party, Ford captivated the convention delegates with his vision of an America whose next steps of greatness would come on the shoulders of the civil rights pioneers of previous generations. Ford's speech propelled him to national notoriety, including a close, but unsuccessful, campaign for the U.S. Senate in 2006.

I am honored to speak tonight before a convention that will nominate the favorite son of my home state to be the next President of the United States.

I recognize that I stand here tonight because of the brave men and women—many no older than I am today—who were willing to stand up, and in many cases sit down, to create a more perfect union.

But I also stand here representing a new generation—a generation committed to those ideals and inspired by an unshakeable confidence in our future.

In every neighborhood in my hometown of Memphis, and all across America, I see young people tutoring and mentoring, building homes, caring for seniors, and feeding the hungry.

I also see them using their entrepreneurial spirit to build companies, start non-profits, and drive our new economy.

We stand at this magnificent moment with the ability to unleash the American imagination.

I say to all those of this new generation and to all Americans who share in our spirit: if you want a future that belongs to you—if you want a future that is for everyone—then join with us to make Al Gore and Joe Lieberman the next President and Vice President of the United States.

We know there are some people who do understand the future, but too often as they gaze to the distance, they fail to know how, to make sure that it serves all of our people.

And then there are others who fight tirelessly for the people, but who don't see beyond the horizon.

Al Gore is the rare leader, who both has a vision for the future, and understands that we can only realize its full promise when all our people share in it.

I remember meeting Al Gore for the first time.

I sat across from him at my family's kitchen table back home in Memphis.

As often was the case, my brothers Jake, Isaac and I were right where we wanted to be—right beside our daddy as he discussed the issues of the day.

It was a time when, on the heels of Vietnam and Watergate, young Americans were turning away from public service.

But Al Gore didn't turn away.

He jumped feet first into public life and was elected one of Tennessee's youngest congressmen ever.

That's when he became my role model.

As a young Congressman, Al Gore didn't waste any time.

He held some of the first hearings investigating global warming and its effects on our environment, our health, and our economy.

At the height of the Cold War, when those on both sides of the aisle were stuck on how best to bring peace and security to America, Al Gore, at the age of 34, offered a comprehensive strategy to reduce the threat of nuclear war while keeping America safe and strong.

Both superpowers took notice, and Al Gore helped change the debate.

More than 20 years ago, Al Gore called for serious campaign finance reform.

You know, I was only 4 years old when I cut my first political ad.

I got on the radio and told the people of Memphis that they should support my daddy because he supported an improved economy and lower cookie prices.

Even back then it took real money to put that commercial on the air.

While I recognize the importance of political advertising—and I still have a sweet tooth—I feel passionately that we must reform our system if we truly want to engage my generation in American politics.

Some pose for reform in photo-ops, but Al Gore is ready to sign a campaign reform bill his first day in office.

The choice before us—a choice that weighs heavier on my generation than perhaps any other—is what kind of America will we have, not in four years but forty years. Will the amazing advances of tomorrow be fenced off for the few—or will they be tools for all of us to build better lives?

At this critical time, America needs a leader with the intellect to understand the complexities we face.

A leader with experience who can grasp the challenges of our world.

At this critical time, America needs Al Gore.

I remember the fear many of my college classmates in Pennsylvania faced when we graduated eight years ago.

For many of us, finding a good job was tough.

Well, eight years and 22 million jobs later, the future is something to get excited about again.

But some in the other party would have us go back.

Back to a past where prosperity touches only the well-off and well-connected.

Back to a past where children learn from outdated textbooks and parents can't scrape together the money to send their kids to college.

Back to a past where polluters write our environmental laws.

Back to a past where politicians run up enormous deficits, run factories out of business, and run the economy into the ground.

We have a very different vision of the future.

Al Gore and Joe Lieberman believe the future is for everyone.

Imagine a debt-free economy so strong that everyone shares in the American Dream.

Imagine a healthcare system where every American receives the medicine they need, and where no senior is forced to choose between buying food and filling a prescription.

Imagine a society that treats seniors with the respect and dignity they deserve, and where Social Security and Medicare are strengthened, not only for our parents and grandparents, but for our children and grandchildren.

Imagine a nation of clean coastlines, safe drinking water, pristine parks, and air our kids can breathe as they play in those parks.

We all recognize that no issue is more critical to our nation's continued success than how we educate our kids.

If we can find the will and resources to build prison after prison, then we can build new schools, reduce class sizes, connect every classroom up to the Internet.

Surely we can pay teachers what they are worth—surely we must hold schools accountable for results.

Imagine giving all our kids the world-class education they deserve.

Well, it is time to stop imagining.

So, tonight I call on all my reform-minded Republican and Independent friends to join us in our crusade.

To join us in making this bold imagination a reality.

When I first decided to run for Congress in 1996, many political insiders said I didn't stand a chance.

In my first campaign, I wanted to meet with every important group in my district, but as a newcomer I didn't get as many invitations as I'd hoped for.

But one place I was welcomed—a place where I grew as a candidate—was at kindergarten graduations.

I spoke at more kindergarten graduations than anyone in my district knew existed.

Thirty, to be exact.

I continue to attend kindergarten graduations to this day.

As I see the pride in the eyes of those 5-year-olds and their families . . . well, to me, it's just magical.

For those children and their families, we must continue working for a better life and a better world.

Now, as we turn our attention to the choice at hand, let us remember those children, in kindergartens in Memphis and across our nation and remember what this election is really all about: Them.

Yes, there will be talk during the campaign of budget surpluses and tax cuts, but it is really all about them.

And so, with those five year olds in mind, our first step in encouraging their dreams and unleashing their imaginations is electing Al Gore our next President.

For their sake, we can't go back.

For their sake, we must go forward.

For their sake, we must build a future for everyone. Thank you and God bless you.

Source: Ford, Harold, Jr. Democratic National Convention Keynote Address. Delivered August 15, 2000, Los Angeles, CA. Copyright © Democratic National Convention. AmericanRhetoric.com.

President George W. Bush, Directive on Racial Profiling, and Attorney General John Ashcroft, Response to the President's Directive

(2001)

Racial profiling is when law enforcement uses a person's race or ethnicity to determine whether he or she should be questioned, stopped, or arrested. The practice is highly controversial and has led to charges of racism against police departments and other law enforcement agencies, especially in connection with their stopping African American drivers who come under suspicion because of their race. The practice has led to the coining of the term "driving while black" (DWB) to refer to the racial profiling of African Americans.

In response to widespread criticism of racial profiling, President George W. Bush, on February 27, 2001, issued the following directive ordering the attorney general to begin a review of racial profiling practices used by federal law enforcement agencies and to develop specific recommendations for ending such practices. Also

reproduced here is Attorney General John Ashcroft's March 1, 2001, press conference in which he announced two initiatives to comply with the president's directive. These initiatives included working with Congress to pass legislation to prohibit racial profiling and issuing his own directive ordering federal law enforcement agencies to review the practice and devise guidelines for discontinuing it.

President's Directive on Racial Profiling
THE WHITE HOUSE
Office of the Press Secretary
For Immediate Release
February 28, 2001
February 27, 2001
MEMORANDUM FOR THE ATTORNEY GENERAL
SUBJECT: Racial Profiling

I hereby direct you to review the use by Federal law enforcement authorities of race as a factor in conducting stops, searches, and other investigative procedures. In particular, I ask that you work with the Congress to develop methods or mechanisms to collect any relevant data from Federal law enforcement agencies and work in cooperation with State and local law enforcement in order to assess the extent and nature of any such practices.

I further direct that you report back to me with your findings and recommendations for the improvement of the just and equal administration of our Nation's laws.

GEORGE W. BUSH

Source: Bush, George W. Directive on Racial Profiling, 2001. White House. http://www.whitehouse.gov/news/releases/2001/02/20010228-1.html.

Response by Attorney General John Ashcroft

ATTORNEY GENERAL NEWS CONFERENCE

March 1, 2001

ATTY GEN. ASHCROFT: Well, let me thank you for coming. I'm delighted to be with you again. This makes the third time in the last three days, so it's nice to see you, and I'm pleased to be with you.

During 1999, in my work on the Constitution Subcommittee of the United States Committee—Senate Committee on the Judiciary, I had the happy privilege of working with Russ Feingold, senator from Wisconsin, toward legislation which would help us develop an understanding about the impact of racial profiling on American citizens.

In that responsibility, I held a hearing on Senator Feingold's legislation regarding traffic stops and the relationship of those stops to the race of the individuals populating the vehicles. The testimony there galvanized an opinion of mine from the sort of philosophic to the tragic. I had long believed that to treat people based solely on their race was in violation of the 14th Amendment of the United States Constitution.

But when Rosano Gerald (sp) came to the committee and told of what had happened to him and his 12-year-old son in traveling across one of our states, and being stopped twice in the same trip, and the second time his car literally being disassembled and he being left, with his 12-year-old son, on the side of the road, as I said, it changed theory into tragedy and indelibly marked me with an understanding that racial profiling has really human consequences.

From the very first conversations I had with the president of the United States about my opportunity to serve as the attorney general, we had the opportunity to speak of this mutual concern that we shared. And so when the president of the United States, in his first address to the Congress of the United States, elevated this issue into the consciousness of those who were to be carrying forward on legislative agenda during this next year, it was very pleasing to me, and I was eager to respond to the president's remarks not only to the Congress, but to the president's directive to me. . . .

And I think you all have a copy of this directive; I hope you do.

Today I want to announce that I am taking two actions in order to fulfill the directive of the president of the United States, and to work toward this laudable goal that each of us should share of justice that is not dependent upon racial profiling. And the first of those items I want to mention to you that—is a letter sent to the chairman and ranking members of the House and Senate committees. This letter indicates that I want to work with them in the next six months to produce a legislative product which will help us achieve what the president has indicated to us, especially as it relates to the development of data regarding state and local officials, and in regard to measures similar to the measure sponsored by Senator Russ Feingold and Representative Conyers last year, which was a traffic stops measure.

I believe that the Congress can and will respond constructively. And I will work with them to make sure that they do respond constructively. In the event that the Congress of the United States does not produce a legislative output, direction from the Congress—which I think is the superior way for us to handle these issues is to do it in conjunction with the Congress—at the conclusion of a six-month interval, I'll simply launch a study of my own, because I think this is an issue of such importance and magnitude that we should proceed with it to make sure that we do what's necessary to correct any abuse and to inventory the nature of this problem.

Secondly, I will issue today, for release this week, a directive to the acting deputy attorney general regarding the implementation of the president's directive of reviewing the nature and extent of racial profiling of any law enforcement agencies of the federal government. And there will be four major components of this directive that I intend to issue today and should get to you this week, and that is I would hope that we would be able to develop a summary of the types of contacts that exist between federal law enforcement officials and the public, to estimate the extent of such contacts, the numbers of them within specific timeframes.

And number two, I would hope that we would be able to develop an understanding of the current policies of the federal law enforcement agencies as they relate to racial profiling, including what efforts we have to eliminate any indications that a practice would exist; what rules we might have regarding such practices; what kind of guidance, instruction or training programs we have so that law enforcement officials understand that there are ways for us to conduct the law enforcement responsibilities that are absent these problems, and what kind of disciplinary rules exist in relation to any detected inappropriate use of these techniques or practices.

Number three, if there are currently records that relate to any such practices, that we would be able to collect those and summarize them as they might have occurred in other agencies.

And number four, if there are pending inquiries or actions taken that relate to such allegations of racial profiling by federal law enforcement officials, to develop an understanding of what the numbers of those actions would be.

Let me just indicate that I believe that these are a series of first steps to implement the directive of the president of the United States in an effort to assuage what I consider to be—is an important—and a challenge—to meet an important challenge of our culture, and I look forward to it.

Let me—I should mention again what I think is very important, that effective law enforcement has to be one of the primary goals of a culture, and I don't believe anything that seriously undermines the trust between significant components of the culture and the law enforcement authorities can be a part of effective law enforcement.

I believe we'll enhance law enforcement to the extent that we can build and expand upon the trust of individuals, and it's with that in mind that we understand the real value, not only in terms of the equities of our culture, but to the law enforcement community.

And let me indicate one final point on this particular issue. I believe that the law enforcement community in the United States is the best law enforcement community in the world. I believe that it is populated by individuals who are literally making sacrificial devotions of their lives to achieve an objective in which they believe. That's a secure society in which the persons and property of individuals, those persons and property, are guarded. And I believe that's important, and I believe they want to do this in a way which is effective and respectful of the rights of individuals, and I believe this study will be a way of assisting the law enforcement community in a project and a set of endeavors to which they have given and are giving their lives.

It's with that in mind that we are very eager to move forward on this directive of the president of the United States and to participate in its fulfillment.

Yes? Let's start over here this time.

Q Can you tell us why you want to wait for Congress to pass legislation when you could very well begin initiating a study of your own right now?

ATTY. GEN. ASHCROFT: Well, I think the Congress has been working on this and considering this. They have contact with the entire population of the country. They obviously, I think, will respond constructively in a setting where they have a sense of ownership in that which is developed by way of study.

I think the study is, as I indicated, one of the first steps, and if there are steps that are needed to be taken legislatively, I think moving with the Congress, which has indicated a willingness, especially the affected individuals whose legislation that I signaled in my remarks today, I think that's the right way to do this.

While those are benefits, I don't think they are benefits worth waiting for indefinitely, and that's why I've indicated if we have no real output in the next six months or so, I would expect to just—to conduct items on my own.

Yes, sir?

Q On the federalism issue, can you talk a little bit about the voluntary nature of—if you're not looking into any possible requirements that the federal government is placing on state and local agencies at all, how would this work in terms of developing data on state as well as federal agencies?

ATTY GEN. ASHCROFT: Well, there are a growing number of organizations and institutions of law enforcement around the country that are sensitive to this situation that are collecting data. And the ability to share that data, to develop national conclusions, and to benefit from the information, I think is the focus and has been of the Conyers-Feingold measure, which was proposed last year. And it's a good starting place for us to begin in this respect. I respect their awareness of the relationship between the federal agencies and the state agencies. The president has respected that in his order. Read it carefully. Has the idea that we should be respectful of the responsibility of states. I think it's in that context of mutual respect for those rights that we can ask people to be respectful of the rights of individuals and develop the data which will allow us to make real progress here.

Just go right down the list.

Q Having chaired a hearing on this, do you go into this first step with any preconceived notions of how big a problem this is? Do you have any beginning information on the nature of the problem in numbers, any of that going into this first step—

ATTY GEN. ASHCROFT: What the hearing did for me was to make it clear to me that this isn't a problem that can be quantified just in terms of statistics. For Resano Gerald (sp) and his 12-year-old son, this was as big a problem as you could get. And if you're an affected individual here, the statistics about how many it affects or doesn't affect somewhere else in the culture don't mean much to you because for you it's 100 percent. It's like the guy who is unemployed; the unemployment rate for him is 100 percent. For people who have been the victim of racial profiling, the statistic is 100 percent.

So it's — I don't — it's wrong. And we're going to find out. I think the kinds of inquiries that we're proposing and we're working toward, in my judgment, will help us ascertain the nature of it and the extent of it. But the truth of the matter is, if the kind of thing continues to happen that happened to Resano Gerald (sp) and his 12-year-old son, that is a hundred percent offense in that setting, it's too extensive, and it needs to stop.

Yes, sir?

Q General Ashcroft, what would you say is the current state of the relations between minority communities and police since racial profiling sort of colors that?

ATTY GEN. ASHCROFT: Well, I think every American has a right to look to law enforcement officials to protect their rights. And in those instances, regardless of how rare they might be where a law enforcement institution instead of protecting rights violates rights, you have a compound fracture. You disrupt the trust, but you inflict an injury at the same time. And I think that's why you have a lose-lose situation in that circumstance. You lose the potential for the underlying trust that should support the administration of justice as a societal objective, not just as a law enforcement objective, because frankly, law enforcement is too important a role in the culture to leave to professionals alone. We'll only have good law enforcement in the country to the extent that the people participate. As soon as you start to peel off groups of people and say "We're not going to participate with law enforcement, we don't trust it," we erode the fabric of justice that's necessary to sustain a free culture.

So when you get into the lose-lose situation, you lose trust that comes, and you also have injury that comes as a result of it. That's very—that's significantly bad. I can't tell you how extensive it is. That's really the purpose of the president's directive to me to try and develop an understanding of the nature and extent, and then, based on what we learn, to act appropriately to eradicate it.

Yes.

Q Is racial profiling not banned already by federal law enforcement agents? And second, does your directive reach that issue?

ATTY GEN. ASHCROFT: Well, the directive in regard to the—and thank you for this question. There are two parts to what I'm doing.

I'm asking the Congress to make—to act, to design, to help us move forward on a study that would include the data. And secondly, in the federal arena, I want to find out what different agencies are doing, law enforcement agencies. And you know, there are dozens of federal law enforcement agencies, and we need to find out what they're doing, how they're handling allegations; what they do by way of training; if they find items that merit discipline, what kind of discipline is imposed. And there may be other things we learn in this survey.

As I've indicated to you, the four-step memo that I'm developing is a series of first steps. And we hope to be more conversant about this as we develop the data that we're using.

Yes, ma'am?

Q When you use the term "race," are you using it broadly to include—(inaudible)—country of origin? There are some problems in drug cases where—(off mike).

ATTY GEN. ASHCROFT: I think we'd like to have it apply to race. And when race is used as an indicator or marker of individuals so that they are in one way or another apprehended or dealt with by law enforcement based on their race, that's what we want to know about. That's why we're studying this, to learn about those circumstances. And if there are—and by and large I believe that to be inappropriate. So I think we want to—in the information that we are gathering, we want to be very inclusive about that information.

Mr. Sawyer.

Q Do you believe that there are appropriate steps that the federal government could or should do on this issue beyond the collection—(inaudible)—of data?

ATTY GEN. ASHCROFT: I think that's one of the things we would try to determine, and I think there may well be. What the appropriate steps would be, I think, would be one of the things we might learn. And I think what we want to do is we want to aid the law enforcement community in doing its job well. I want to emphasize again that I believe that racial profiling is not doing the job well because it involves us in this compound injury. It injures the trust that communities need to have in order to participate in law enforcement, and it injures as well the individual. That's a lose-lose situation. We want to help law enforcement move to win-win.

Yes, sir?

Q Mr. Ashcroft, you're the highest law enforcement office in the country. Beyond whether it was inappropriate—(off mike)—do you believe racial and ethnic profiling violates existing civil rights law? If so—(off mike)—present law. If not, you'll need some legislation beyond this—(off mike).

ATTY GEN. ASHCROFT: Any violation of the existing civil rights laws that we develop an understanding and learn about, and with evidence of, we will prosecute and we will enforce.

All right.

Q But does racial profiling per se—when someone is stopped solely on the basis of race, singled out solely for prosecution and investigation solely on the basis of race, does that violate existing civil rights law?

ATTY GEN. ASHCROFT: Let me just say this: that if we come to the conclusion that anyone has violated the civil rights law, with credible evidence, we'll take action to correct that violation and to prosecute it.

Yes?

Q Do you intend to use the language in the '94 pattern and practice law as a weapon to take on instances of racial profiling—

ATTY GEN. ASHCROFT: We will continue to enforce the 1994 law. It is my responsibility to enforce that law. And I believe that the law is an opportunity for us to promote the concept of people being free from unwarranted, inappropriate activities by law enforcement officials.

Q You don't have any problem with the idea I believe the president expressed during the campaign—that it was federal meddling in a state or local affair?

ATTY GEN. ASHCROFT: You know, I believe that there are circumstances that warrant the enforcement of that law. And when we find those circumstances, we will enforce the law.

There are ways to help law enforcement agencies do their jobs well. That's another opportunity of the Justice Department. We are law enforcers, but we can also provide assistance to departments in saying, "Here are the ways that you can avoid difficulties in this area that will help you be better servants to your public." And I think that's one of the objectives of this department.

And there are times when various communities invite the department in. Literally, we don't go in on the basis—and I won't talk about individual cases or instances, but the department is currently in settings where it's been invited in to help departments achieve the objectives of even, fair, equitable, compassionate law enforcement that elicits the trust and cooperation of the citizens and results in better outcomes. That's one of the roles and functions.

There are other times when it's simply that it is our role and function to enforce the law as a way of helping to get us to that objective. And both of those things we want the department to be adept at and to devote resources to. And we'll continue —try to work on both of those tracks. We'll work with both carrots and sticks, if that needs to be the characterization. . . .

Q Some people in the minority community, including some in the Black Caucus, see this racial profiling proposal as kind of a window dressing, an attempt to kind of mollify the minorities who have been opposed to you and President Bush in the past. And that while they're hopeful something may come out of it, there's sort of concerned skepticism that there's nothing really behind it or underneath it, there are other things that would—(inaudible)—follow their concerns there.

ATTY GEN. ASHCROFT: Well, it's unfortunate, first of all, to characterize the measure that was sponsored by Congressman Conyers and Senator Feingold as somehow insubstantial—I think underestimates not only the content of their effort and the content of the legislation, but the nature of these individuals. And my own involvement with this over time, and the president's expressed displeasure with racial profiling over a substantial period of time, I think suggests a far different conclusion.

This is a matter of serious concern to me. And I know from both public utterances of the president, and private statements that he's made to me, that this is a matter of very serious concern to the president of the United States.

I skipped over you earlier.

Q Many experts feel that community policing helps break down barriers between law enforcement and the citizens. How will the Justice Department support its expansion if at all?

ATTY GEN. ASHCROFT: Well, I like the concept of community policing. I had the opportunity when I was governor of the state of Missouri several lifetimes ago — I was starting that program in the state of Missouri. I've personally ridden on the bicycle patrols with the policeman and I understand the increased, sort of, intimacy between the police community and the community generally that exists when a person's on a bicycle or walking the beat and you get the exchanges.

And obviously we want to enhance the capacity of law enforcement to have this cooperative participation with our culture because I do believe that law enforcement is too important to leave to police alone. It is something that requires us all.

So, to the extent that our programs can encourage that and assist localities in choosing to do that, they'll do that.

I think the president has made very clear, and it's my position as well, that it's not appropriate for us to try to run local police operations from Washington and to specify how many of your officers have to be in police cars and how many on bicycles and so many on snowshoes or what have you. I mean, that's the kind of thing that can be decided locally.

Yes, ma'am?

Q Okay, after all the data is collected, how long do you think it will take to make recommendations on ending racial profiling?

ATTY. GEN. ASHCROFT: You know, I don't know, and if I could tell you, I would. We will work promptly. My sense of urgency here, I think, is reflected in the fact that if the Congress doesn't move to direct the nature of a study, we will assemble one on our own, after a reasonable interval for the Congress to act; certainly during — within this year. And it's my view that we should

act quickly. We may be able to do things that will be helpful in advance of that, because I have described a two-track approach. One track relates primarily to the federal law enforcement agencies. We may develop information from that track that allows us to take action even before the Congress would act, as it relates to the other things. . . .

Source: Ashcroft, John. Response to the President's Directive on Racial Profiling. U.S. Department of Justice. http://www.usdoj.gov:80/ag/speeches/2001/030101racialp rofconf.htm.

Grutter v. Bollinger

(2003)

This court case was brought by Barbara Grutter, whose application to the University of Michigan Law School was denied; she argued that she was rejected because of the school's discriminatory admissions policies, which used race as a predominant factor. Upholding the law school's admission policy, the U.S. Supreme Court ruled that the school has a "compelling interest in attaining a diverse student body," noting that the law school broadly defined diversity beyond racial considerations. According to the majority opinion, race could be considered a factor, among others, in the overall assessment of candidates since the law school's policies did not include quotas or fixed numbers. This court case, along with Gratz v. Bollinger *(2003), challenged the use of racial preferences in application processes at the University of Michigan. Decided on the same day, the two cases marked the first time the U.S. Supreme Court had ruled on race-based admissions in institutions of higher education since 1978. Reproduced here is the full text of the opinion of the Court in* Grutter v. Bollinger.

JUSTICE O'CONNOR delivered the opinion of the Court.

This case requires us to decide whether the use of race as a factor in student admissions by the University of Michigan Law School (Law School) is unlawful.

I.

A.

The Law School ranks among the Nation's top law schools. It receives more than 3,500 applications each year for a class of around 350 students. Seeking to "admit a group of students who individually and collectively are among the most capable," the Law School looks for individuals with "substantial promise for success in law school" and "a strong likelihood of succeeding in the practice of law and contributing in diverse ways to the well-being of others." App. 110. More broadly, the Law School seeks "a mix of students with varying backgrounds and experiences who will respect and learn from each other." *Ibid.* In 1992, the dean of the Law School charged a faculty committee with crafting a written admissions policy to implement these goals. In particular, the Law School sought to ensure that its efforts to achieve student body diversity complied with this Court's most recent ruling on the use of race in university admissions. See *Regents of Univ. of Cal. v. Bakke*, 438 U. S. 265 (1978). Upon the unanimous adoption of the committee's report by the Law School faculty, it became the Law School's official admissions policy.

The hallmark of that policy is its focus on academic ability coupled with a flexible assessment of applicants' talents, experiences, and potential "to contribute to the learning of those around them." App. 111. The policy requires admissions officials to evaluate each applicant based on all the information available in the file, including a personal statement, letters of recommendation, and an essay describing the ways in which the applicant will contribute to the life and diversity of the Law School. *Id.*, at 83–84, 114–121. In reviewing an applicant's file, admissions officials must consider the applicant's undergraduate grade point average (GPA) and Law School Admission Test (LSAT) score because they are important (if imperfect) predictors of academic success in law school. *Id.*, at 112. The policy stresses that "no applicant should be admitted unless we expect that applicant to do well enough to graduate with no serious academic problems." *Id.*, at 111.

The policy makes clear, however, that even the highest possible score does not guarantee admission to the Law School. *Id.*, at 113. Nor does a low score automatically disqualify an applicant. *Ibid.* Rather, the policy requires admissions officials to look beyond grades and test scores to other criteria that are important to the Law School's educational objectives. *Id.*, at 114. So-called " 'soft' variables" such as "the enthusiasm of recommenders, the quality of the undergraduate institution, the quality of the applicant's essay, and the areas and difficulty of undergraduate course selection" are all brought to bear in assessing an "applicant's likely contributions to the intellectual and social life of the institution." *Ibid.*

The policy aspires to "achieve that diversity which has the potential to enrich everyone's education and thus make a law school class stronger than the sum of its parts." *Id.*, at 118. The policy does not restrict the types of diversity contributions eligible for "substantial weight" in the admissions process, but instead recognizes "many possible bases for diversity admissions." *Id.*, at 118, 120. The policy does, however, reaffirm the Law School's longstanding commitment to "one particular type of diversity," that is, "racial and ethnic diversity with special reference to the inclusion of students from groups which have been historically discriminated against, like African-Americans, Hispanics and Native Americans, who without this commitment might not be represented in our student body in meaningful numbers." *Id.*, at 120. By enrolling a " 'critical mass' of [underrepresented] minority students," the Law School seeks to "ensur[e] their ability to make unique contributions to the character of the Law School." *Id.*, at 120–121.

The policy does not define diversity "solely in terms of racial and ethnic status." *Id.*, at 121. Nor is the policy "insensitive to the competition among all students for admission to the [L]aw [S]chool." *Ibid.* Rather, the policy seeks to guide admissions officers in "producing classes both diverse and academically outstanding, classes made up of students who promise to continue the tradition of outstanding contribution by Michigan Graduates to the legal profession." *Ibid.*

B.

Petitioner Barbara Grutter is a white Michigan resident who applied to the Law School in 1996 with a 3.8 GPA and 161 LSAT score. The Law School initially placed petitioner on a waiting list, but subsequently rejected her application. In December 1997, petitioner filed suit in the United States District Court for the Eastern District of Michigan against the Law School, the Regents of the University of Michigan, Lee Bollinger (Dean of the Law School from 1987 to 1994, and President of the University of Michigan from 1996 to 2002), Jeffrey Lehman (Dean of the Law School), and Dennis Shields (Director of Admissions at the

Law School from 1991 until 1998). Petitioner alleged that respondents discriminated against her on the basis of race in violation of the Fourteenth Amendment; Title VI of the Civil Rights Act of 1964, 78 Stat. 252, 42 U. S. C. § 2000d; and Rev. Stat. § 1977, as amended, 42 U. S. C. § 1981.

Petitioner further alleged that her application was rejected because the Law School uses race as a "predominant" factor, giving applicants who belong to certain minority groups "a significantly greater chance of admission than students with similar credentials from disfavored racial groups." App. 33–34. Petitioner also alleged that respondents "had no compelling interest to justify their use of race in the admissions process." *Id.*, at 34. Petitioner requested compensatory and punitive damages, an order requiring the Law School to offer her admission, and an injunction prohibiting the Law School from continuing to discriminate on the basis of race. *Id.*, at 36. Petitioner clearly has standing to bring this lawsuit. *Northeastern Fla. Chapter, Associated Gen. Contractors of America v. Jacksonville*, 508 U. S. 656, 666 (1993).

The District Court granted petitioner's motion for class certification and for bifurcation of the trial into liability and damages phases. The class was defined as "'all persons who (A) applied for and were not granted admission to the University of Michigan Law School for the academic years since (and including) 1995 until the time that judgment is entered herein; and (B) were members of those racial or ethnic groups, including Caucasian, that Defendants treated less favorably in considering their applications for admission to the Law School.'" App. to Pet. for Cert. 191a–192a.

The District Court heard oral argument on the parties' cross-motions for summary judgment on December 22, 2000. Taking the motions under advisement, the District Court indicated that it would decide as a matter of law whether the Law School's asserted interest in obtaining the educational benefits that flow from a diverse student body was compelling. The District Court also indicated that it would conduct a bench trial on the extent to which race was a factor in the

Law School's admissions decisions, and whether the Law School's consideration of race in admissions decisions constituted a race-based double standard.

During the 15-day bench trial, the parties introduced extensive evidence concerning the Law School's use of race in the admissions process. Dennis Shields, Director of Admissions when petitioner applied to the Law School, testified that he did not direct his staff to admit a particular percentage or number of minority students, but rather to consider an applicant's race along with all other factors. *Id.*, at 206a. Shields testified that at the height of the admissions season, he would frequently consult the so-called "daily reports" that kept track of the racial and ethnic composition of the class (along with other information such as residency status and gender). *Id.*, at 207a. This was done, Shields testified, to ensure that a critical mass of underrepresented minority students would be reached so as to realize the educational benefits of a diverse student body. *Ibid.* Shields stressed, however, that he did not seek to admit any particular number or percentage of underrepresented minority students. *Ibid.*

Erica Munzel, who succeeded Shields as Director of Admissions, testified that "'critical mass'" means "'meaningful numbers'" or "'meaningful representation,'" which she understood to mean a number that encourages underrepresented minority students to participate in the classroom and not feel isolated. *Id.*, at 208a–209a. Munzel stated there is no number, percentage, or range of numbers or percentages that constitute critical mass. *Id.*, at 209a. Munzel also asserted that she must consider the race of applicants because a critical mass of underrepresented minority students could not be enrolled if admissions decisions were based primarily on undergraduate GPAs and LSAT scores. *Ibid.*

The current Dean of the Law School, Jeffrey Lehman, also testified. Like the other Law School witnesses, Lehman did not quantify critical mass in terms of numbers or percentages. *Id.*, at 211a. He indicated that critical mass means numbers such that underrepresented minority students do not feel isolated or like spokespersons for their race. *Ibid*. When asked about the extent to which race is considered in admissions, Lehman testified that it varies from one applicant to another. *Ibid*. In some cases, according to Lehman's testimony, an applicant's race may play no role, while in others it may be a "'determinative'" factor. *Ibid*.

The District Court heard extensive testimony from Professor Richard Lempert, who chaired the faculty committee that drafted the 1992 policy. Lempert emphasized that the Law School seeks students with diverse interests and backgrounds to enhance classroom discussion and the educational experience both inside and outside the classroom. *Id.*, at 213a. When asked about the policy's "'commitment to racial and ethnic diversity with special reference to the inclusion of students from groups which have been historically discriminated against,'" Lempert explained that this language did not purport to remedy past discrimination, but rather to include students who may bring to the Law School a perspective different from that of members of groups which have not been the victims of such discrimination. *Ibid*. Lempert acknowledged that other groups, such as Asians and Jews, have experienced discrimination, but explained they were not mentioned in the policy because individuals who are members of those groups were already being admitted to the Law School in significant numbers. *Ibid*.

Kent Syverud was the final witness to testify about the Law School's use of race in admissions decisions. Syverud was a professor at the Law School when the 1992 admissions policy was adopted and is now Dean of Vanderbilt Law School. In addition to his testimony at trial, Syverud submitted several expert reports on the educational benefits of diversity. Syverud's testimony indicated that when a critical mass of underrepresented minority students is present, racial stereotypes lose their force because nonminority students learn there is no "'minority viewpoint'" but rather a variety of viewpoints among minority students. *Id.*, at 215a.

In an attempt to quantify the extent to which the Law School actually considers race in making admissions decisions, the parties introduced voluminous evidence at trial. Relying on data obtained from the Law School, petitioner's expert, Dr. Kinley Larntz, generated and analyzed "admissions grids" for the years in question (1995–2000). These grids show the number of applicants and the number of admittees for all combinations of GPAs and LSAT scores. Dr. Larntz made "'cell-by-cell'" comparisons between applicants of different races to determine whether a statistically significant relationship existed between race and admission rates. He concluded that membership in certain minority groups " 'is an extremely strong factor in the decision for acceptance,' " and that applicants from these minority groups "'are given an extremely large allowance for admission'" as compared to applicants who are members of nonfavored groups. *Id.*, at 218a–220a. Dr. Larntz conceded, however, that race is not the predominant factor in the Law School's admissions calculus. 12 Tr. 11–13 (Feb. 10, 2001).

Dr. Stephen Raudenbush, the Law School's expert, focused on the predicted effect of eliminating race as a factor in the Law School's admission process. In Dr. Raudenbush's view, a race-blind admissions system would have a "'very dramatic,'" negative effect on underrepresented minority admissions. App. to Pet. for Cert. 223a. He testified that in 2000, 35 percent of underrepresented minority applicants were admitted. *Ibid*. Dr. Raudenbush predicted that if race were not considered, only 10 percent of those applicants would have been admitted. *Ibid*. Under this scenario, underrepresented minority students would have constituted 4 percent of the entering class in 2000 instead of the actual figure of 14.5 percent. *Ibid*.

In the end, the District Court concluded that the Law School's use of race as a factor in admissions decisions was unlawful. Applying strict scrutiny, the District Court determined that the Law School's asserted interest in assembling a diverse student body was not compelling because "the attainment of a racially diverse class . . . was not recognized as such by *Bakke* and it is not a remedy for past discrimination." *Id.*, at 246a. The District Court went on to hold that even if diversity were compelling, the Law School had not narrowly tailored its use of race to further that interest. The District Court granted petitioner's request for declaratory relief and enjoined the Law School from using race as a factor in its admissions decisions. The Court of Appeals entered a stay of the injunction pending appeal.

Sitting en banc, the Court of Appeals reversed the District Court's judgment and vacated the injunction. The Court of Appeals first held that Justice Powell's opinion in *Bakke* was binding precedent establishing diversity as a compelling state interest. According to the Court of Appeals, Justice Powell's opinion with respect to diversity constituted the controlling rationale for the judgment of this Court under the analysis set forth in *Marks v. United States*, 430 U. S. 188 (1977). The Court of Appeals also held that the Law School's use of race was narrowly tailored because race was merely a "potential 'plus' factor" and because the Law School's program was "virtually identical" to the Harvard admissions program described approvingly by Justice Powell and appended to his *Bakke* opinion. 288 F. 3d 732, 746, 749 (CA6 2002).

Four dissenting judges would have held the Law School's use of race unconstitutional. Three of the dissenters, rejecting the majority's Marks analysis, examined the Law School's interest in student body diversity on the merits and concluded it was not compelling. The fourth dissenter, writing separately, found it unnecessary to decide whether diversity was a compelling interest because, like the other dissenters, he believed that the Law School's use of race was not narrowly tailored to further that interest.

We granted certiorari, 537 U. S. 1043 (2002), to resolve the disagreement among the Courts of Appeals on a question of national importance: Whether diversity is a compelling interest that can justify the narrowly tailored use of race in selecting applicants for admission to public universities. Compare *Hopwood v. Texas*, 78 F. 3d 932 (CA5 1996) (*Hopwood I*) (holding that diversity is not a compelling state interest), with *Smith v. University of Wash. Law School*, 233 F. 3d 1188 (CA9 2000) (holding that it is).

II.

A.

We last addressed the use of race in public higher education over 25 years ago. In the landmark *Bakke* case, we reviewed a racial set-aside program that reserved 16 out of 100 seats in a medical school class for members of certain minority groups. 438 U. S. 265 (1978). The decision produced six separate opinions, none of which commanded a majority of the Court. Four Justices would have upheld the program against all attack on the ground that the government can use race to "remedy disadvantages cast on minorities by past racial prejudice." *Id.*, at 325 (joint opinion of Brennan, White, Marshall, and Blackmun, JJ., concurring in judgment in part and dissenting in part). Four other Justices avoided the constitutional question altogether and struck down the program on statutory grounds. *Id.*, at 408 (opinion of Stevens, J., joined by Burger, C. J., and Stewart and Rehnquist, JJ., concurring in judgment in part and dissenting in part). Justice Powell provided a fifth vote not only for invalidating the set-aside program, but also for reversing the state court's injunction against any use of race whatsoever. The only holding for the Court in *Bakke* was that a "State has a substantial interest that legitimately may be served by a properly devised admissions program involving the competitive consideration of race and ethnic origin." *Id.*, at 320. Thus, we reversed that part of the lower court's judgment that enjoined the university "from any consideration of the race of any applicant." *Ibid.*

Since this Court's splintered decision in *Bakke*, Justice Powell's opinion announcing the judgment of the Court has served as the touchstone for constitutional analysis of race conscious admissions policies. Public and private universities across the Nation have modeled their own admissions programs on Justice Powell's views on permissible race conscious policies. See, *e. g.*, Brief for Judith Areen et al. as *Amici Curiae* 12–13 (law school admissions programs employ "methods designed from and based on Justice Powell's opinion in *Bakke*"); Brief for Amherst College et al. as *Amici Curiae* 27 ("After *Bakke*, each of the *amici* (and undoubtedly other selective colleges and universities as well) reviewed their admissions procedures in light of Justice Powell's opinion . . . and set sail accordingly"). We therefore discuss Justice Powell's opinion in some detail.

Justice Powell began by stating that "[t]he guarantee of equal protection cannot mean one thing when applied to one individual and something else when applied to a person of another color. If both are not accorded the same protection, then it is not equal." *Bakke*, 438 U. S., at 289–290. In Justice Powell's view, when governmental decisions "touch upon an individual's race or ethnic background, he is entitled to a judicial determination that the burden he is asked to bear on that basis is precisely tailored to serve a compelling governmental interest." *Id.*, at 299. Under this exacting standard, only one of the interests asserted by the university survived Justice Powell's scrutiny.

First, Justice Powell rejected an interest in "'reducing the historic deficit of traditionally disfavored minorities in medical schools and in the medical profession'" as an unlawful interest in racial balancing. *Id.*, at 306–307. Second, Justice Powell rejected an interest in remedying societal discrimination because such measures would risk placing unnecessary burdens on innocent third parties "who bear no responsibility for whatever harm the beneficiaries of the special admissions program are thought to have suffered." *Id.*, at 310. Third, Justice Powell rejected an interest in "increasing the number of physicians who will practice in communities currently underserved," concluding that even if such an interest could be compelling in some circumstances the program under review was not "geared to promote that goal." *Id.*, at 306, 310. Justice Powell approved the university's use of race to further only one interest: "the attainment of a diverse student body." *Id.*, at 311. With the important proviso that "constitutional limitations protecting individual rights may not be disregarded," Justice Powell grounded his analysis in the academic freedom that "long has been viewed as a special concern of the First Amendment." *Id.*, at 312, 314. Justice Powell emphasized that nothing less than the "'nation's future depends upon leaders trained through wide exposure' to the ideas and mores of students as diverse as this Nation of many peoples." *Id.*, at 313 (quoting *Keyishian v. Board of Regents of Univ. of State of N. Y.*, 385 U. S. 589, 603 (1967)). In seeking the "right to select those students who will contribute the most to the 'robust exchange of ideas,'" a university seeks "to achieve a goal that is of paramount importance in the fulfillment of its mission." 438 U. S., at 313. Both "tradition and experience lend support to the view that the contribution of diversity is substantial." *Ibid.*

Justice Powell was, however, careful to emphasize that in his view race "is only one element in a range of factors a university properly may consider in attaining the goal of a heterogeneous student body." *Id.*, at 314. For Justice Powell, "[i]t is not an interest in simple ethnic diversity, in which a specified percentage of the student body is in effect guaranteed to be members of selected ethnic groups," that can justify the use of race. *Id.*, at 315. Rather, "[t]he diversity that furthers a compelling state interest encompasses a far broader array of qualifications and characteristics of which racial or ethnic origin is but a single though important element." *Ibid.*

In the wake of our fractured decision in *Bakke*, courts have struggled to discern whether Justice Powell's diversity rationale, set forth in part of the opinion joined by no other Justice, is nonetheless binding precedent under *Marks*. In that case, we explained that "[w]hen a fragmented Court decides a case and no single rationale explaining the result enjoys the assent of five Justices, the holding of the Court may be viewed as that position taken by those Members who concurred in the judgments on the narrowest grounds." 430 U. S., at 193 (internal quotation marks and citation omitted). As the divergent opinions of the lower courts demonstrate, however, "[t]his test is more easily stated than applied to the various opinions supporting the result in [*Bakke*]." *Nichols v. United States*, 511 U. S. 738, 745–746 (1994). Compare, *e. g.*, *Johnson v. Board of Regents of Univ. of Ga.*, 263 F. 3d 1234 (CA11 2001) (Justice Powell's diversity rationale was not the holding of the Court); *Hopwood v. Texas*, 236 F. 3d 256, 274–275 (CA5 2000) (*Hopwood II*) (same); *Hopwood I*, 78 F. 3d 932 (CA5 1996) (same), with *Smith v. University of Wash. Law School*, 233 F. 3d, at 1199 (Justice Powell's opinion, including the diversity rationale, is controlling under *Marks*).

We do not find it necessary to decide whether Justice Powell's opinion is binding under *Marks*. It does not seem "useful to pursue the *Marks* inquiry to the utmost logical possibility when it has so obviously baffled and divided the lower courts that have considered it." *Nichols v. United States, supra*, at 745–746. More important, for the reasons set out below, today we endorse Justice Powell's view that student body diversity is a compelling state interest that can justify the use of race in university admissions.

B.

The Equal Protection Clause provides that no State shall "deny to any person within its jurisdiction the equal protection of the laws." U. S. Const., Amdt. 14, § 2. Because the Fourteenth Amendment "protect[s] *persons*, not *groups*," all "governmental action based on race—a *group* classification long recognized as in most circumstances irrelevant and therefore prohibited—should be subjected to detailed judicial inquiry to ensure that the *personal* right to equal protection of the laws has not been infringed." *Adarand Constructors, Inc. v. Peña*, 515 U. S. 200, 227 (1995) (emphasis in original; internal quotation marks and citation omitted). We are a "free people whose institutions are founded upon the doctrine of equality." *Loving v. Virginia*, 388 U. S. 1, 11 (1967) (internal quotation marks and citation omitted). It follows from that

principle that "government may treat people differently because of their race only for the most compelling reasons." *Adarand Constructors, Inc. v. Peña*, 515 U. S., at 227.

We have held that all racial classifications imposed by government "must be analyzed by a reviewing court under strict scrutiny." *Ibid.* This means that such classifications are constitutional only if they are narrowly tailored to further compelling governmental interests. "Absent searching judicial inquiry into the justification for such race-based measures," we have no way to determine what "classifications are 'benign' or 'remedial'" and what classifications are in fact motivated by illegitimate notions of racial inferiority or simple racial politics." *Richmond v. J. A. Croson Co.*, 488 U. S. 469, 493 (1989) (plurality opinion). We apply strict scrutiny to all racial classifications to "'smoke out' illegitimate uses of race by assuring that [government] is pursuing a goal important enough to warrant use of a highly suspect tool." *Ibid.* Strict scrutiny is not "strict in theory, but fatal in fact." *Adarand Constructors, Inc. v. Peña, supra*, at 237 (internal quotation marks and citation omitted). Although all governmental uses of race are subject to strict scrutiny, not all are invalidated by it. As we have explained, "whenever the government treats any person unequally because of his or her race, that person has suffered an injury that falls squarely within the language and spirit of the Constitution's guarantee of equal protection." 515 U. S., at 229–230. But that observation "says nothing about the ultimate validity of any particular law; that determination is the job of the court applying strict scrutiny." *Id.*, at 230. When race-based action is necessary to further a compelling governmental interest, such action does not violate the constitutional guarantee of equal protection so long as the narrow-tailoring requirement is also satisfied.

Context matters when reviewing race-based governmental action under the Equal Protection Clause. See *Gomillion v. Lightfoot*, 364 U. S. 339, 343–344 (1960) (admonishing that, "in dealing with claims under broad provisions of the

Constitution, which derive content by an interpretive process of inclusion and exclusion, it is imperative that generalizations, based on and qualified by the concrete situations that gave rise to them, must not be applied out of context in disregard of variant controlling facts"). In *Adarand Constructors, Inc. v. Peña*, we made clear that strict scrutiny must take " 'relevant differences' into account." 515 U. S., at 228. Indeed, as we explained, that is its "fundamental purpose." *Ibid.* Not every decision influenced by race is equally objectionable, and strict scrutiny is designed to provide a framework for carefully examining the importance and the sincerity of the reasons advanced by the governmental decision-maker for the use of race in that particular context.

III.

A.

With these principles in mind, we turn to the question whether the Law School's use of race is justified by a compelling state interest. Before this Court, as they have throughout this litigation, respondents assert only one justification for their use of race in the admissions process: obtaining "the educational benefits that flow from a diverse student body." Brief for Respondent Bollinger et al. i. In other words, the Law School asks us to recognize, in the context of higher education, a compelling state interest in student body diversity.

We first wish to dispel the notion that the Law School's argument has been foreclosed, either expressly or implicitly, by our affirmative-action cases decided since *Bakke*. It is true that some language in those opinions might be read to suggest that remedying past discrimination is the only permissible justification for race-based governmental action. See, *e. g., Richmond v. J. A. Croson Co., supra,* at 493 (plurality opinion) (stating that unless classifications based on race are "strictly reserved for remedial settings, they may in fact promote notions of racial inferiority and lead to a politics of racial hostility"). But we have never held that the only governmental use of race that can survive strict

scrutiny is remedying past discrimination. Nor, since *Bakke*, have we directly addressed the use of race in the context of public higher education. Today, we hold that the Law School has a compelling interest in attaining a diverse student body.

The Law School's educational judgment that such diversity is essential to its educational mission is one to which we defer. The Law School's assessment that diversity will, in fact, yield educational benefits is substantiated by respondents and their amici. Our scrutiny of the interest asserted by the Law School is no less strict for taking into account complex educational judgments in an area that lies primarily within the expertise of the university. Our holding today is in keeping with our tradition of giving a degree of deference to a university's academic decisions, within constitutionally prescribed limits. See *Regents of Univ. of Mich. v. Ewing*, 474 U. S. 214, 225 (1985); *Board of Curators of Univ. of Mo. v. Horowitz*, 435 U. S. 78, 96, n. 6 (1978); *Bakke*, 438 U. S., at 319, n. 53 (opinion of Powell, J.).

We have long recognized that, given the important purpose of public education and the expansive freedoms of speech and thought associated with the university environment, universities occupy a special niche in our constitutional tradition. See, *e. g., Wieman v. Updegraff*, 344 U. S. 183, 195 (1952) (Frankfurter, J., concurring); *Sweezy v. New Hampshire*, 354 U. S. 234, 250 (1957); *Shelton v. Tucker*, 364 U. S. 479, 487 (1960); *Keyishian v. Board of Regents of Univ. of State of N. Y.*, 385 U. S., at 603. In announcing the principle of student body diversity as a compelling state interest, Justice Powell invoked our cases recognizing a constitutional dimension, grounded in the First Amendment, of educational autonomy: "The freedom of a university to make its own judgments as to education includes the selection of its student body." *Bakke, supra,* at 312. From this premise, Justice Powell reasoned that by claiming "the right to select those students who will contribute the most to the 'robust exchange of ideas,' " a university "seek[s] to achieve a goal that is of paramount importance in the fulfillment of its mission." 438

U. S., at 313 (quoting *Keyishian v. Board of Regents of Univ. of State of N. Y., supra*, at 603). Our conclusion that the Law School has a compelling interest in a diverse student body is informed by our view that attaining a diverse student body is at the heart of the Law School's proper institutional mission, and that "good faith" on the part of a university is "presumed" absent "a showing to the contrary." 438 U. S., at 318–319.

As part of its goal of "assembling a class that is both exceptionally academically qualified and broadly diverse," the Law School seeks to "enroll a 'critical mass' of minority students." Brief for Respondent Bollinger et al. 13. The Law School's interest is not simply "to assure within its student body some specified percentage of a particular group merely because of its race or ethnic origin." *Bakke,* 438 U. S., at 307 (opinion of Powell, J.). That would amount to outright racial balancing, which is patently unconstitutional. *Ibid.*; *Freeman v. Pitts*, 503 U. S. 467, 494 (1992) ("Racial balance is not to be achieved for its own sake"); *Richmond v. J. A. Croson Co.*, 488 U. S., at 507. Rather, the Law School's concept of critical mass is defined by reference to the educational benefits that diversity is designed to produce.

These benefits are substantial. As the District Court emphasized, the Law School's admissions policy promotes "cross-racial understanding," helps to break down racial stereotypes, and "enables [students] to better understand persons of different races." App. to Pet. for Cert. 246a. These benefits are "important and laudable," because "classroom discussion is livelier, more spirited, and simply more enlightening and interesting" when the students have "the greatest possible variety of backgrounds." *Id.*, at 246a, 244a.

The Law School's claim of a compelling interest is further bolstered by its *amici*, who point to the educational benefits that flow from student body diversity. In addition to the expert studies and reports entered into evidence at trial, numerous studies show that student body diversity promotes learning outcomes, and "better prepares students for an increasingly diverse workforce and society, and better prepares them as professionals." Brief for American Educational Research Association et al. as *Amici Curiae* 3; see, *e.g.*, W. Bowen & D. Bok, *The Shape of the River* (1998); *Diversity Challenged: Evidence on the Impact of Affirmative Action* (G. Orfield & M. Kurlaender eds. 2001); *Compelling Interest: Examining the Evidence on Racial Dynamics in Colleges and Universities* (M. Chang, D. Witt, J. Jones, & K. Hakuta eds. 2003).

These benefits are not theoretical but real, as major American businesses have made clear that the skills needed in today's increasingly global marketplace can only be developed through exposure to widely diverse people, cultures, ideas, and viewpoints. Brief for 3M et al. as *Amici Curiae* 5; Brief for General Motors Corp. as *Amicus Curiae* 3–4. What is more, high-ranking retired officers and civilian leaders of the United States military assert that, "[b]ased on [their] decades of experience," a "highly qualified, racially diverse officer corps . . . is essential to the military's ability to fulfill its principle mission to provide national security." Brief for Julius W. Becton, Jr., et al. as *Amici Curiae* 5. The primary sources for the Nation's officer corps are the service academies and the Reserve Officers Training Corps (ROTC), the latter comprising students already admitted to participating colleges and universities. *Ibid.* At present, "the military cannot achieve an officer corps that is *both* highly qualified and racially diverse unless the service academies and the ROTC used limited race-conscious recruiting and admissions policies." *Ibid.* (emphasis in original). To fulfill its mission, the military "must be selective in admissions for training and education for the officer corps, and it must train and educate a highly qualified, racially diverse officer corps in a racially diverse educational setting." *Id.*, at 29 (emphasis in original). We agree that "[i]t requires only a small step from this analysis to conclude that our country's other most selective institutions must remain both diverse and selective." *Ibid.*

We have repeatedly acknowledged the overriding importance of preparing students for work and citizenship, describing education as pivotal to "sustaining our political and cultural heritage" with a fundamental role in maintaining the fabric of society. *Plyler v. Doe*, 457 U. S. 202, 221 (1982). This Court has long recognized that "education . . . is the very foundation of good citizenship." *Brown v. Board of Education*, 347 U. S. 483, 493 (1954). For this reason, the diffusion of knowledge and opportunity through public institutions of higher education must be accessible to all individuals regardless of race or ethnicity. The United States, as *amicus curiae*, affirms that "[e]nsuring that public institutions are open and available to all segments of American society, including people of all races and ethnicities, represents a paramount government objective." Brief for United States as *Amicus Curiae* 13. And, "[n]owhere is the importance of such openness more acute than in the context of higher education." *Ibid.* Effective participation by members of all racial and ethnic groups in the civic life of our Nation is essential if the dream of one Nation, indivisible, is to be realized.

Moreover, universities, and in particular, law schools, represent the training ground for a large number of our Nation's leaders. *Sweatt v. Painter*, 339 U. S. 629, 634 (1950) (describing law school as a "proving ground for legal learning and practice"). Individuals with law degrees occupy roughly half the state governorships, more than half the seats in the United States Senate, and more than a third of the seats in the United States House of Representatives. See Brief for Association of American Law Schools as *Amicus Curiae* 5–6. The pattern is even more striking when it comes to highly selective law schools. A handful of these schools accounts for 25 of the 100 United States Senators, 74 United States Courts of Appeals judges, and nearly 200 of the more than 600 United States District Court judges. *Id.*, at 6.

In order to cultivate a set of leaders with legitimacy in the eyes of the citizenry, it is necessary that the path to leadership be visibly open to talented and qualified individuals of every race and ethnicity. All members of our heterogeneous society must have confidence in the openness and integrity of the educational institutions that provide this training. As we have recognized, law schools "cannot be effective in isolation from the individuals and institutions with which the law interacts." See *Sweatt v. Painter, supra*, at 634. Access to legal education (and thus the legal profession) must be inclusive of talented and qualified individuals of every race and ethnicity, so that all members of our heterogeneous society may participate in the educational institutions that provide the training and education necessary to succeed in America.

The Law School does not premise its need for critical mass on "any belief that minority students always (or even consistently) express some characteristic minority viewpoint on any issue." Brief for Respondent Bollinger et al. 30. To the contrary, diminishing the force of such stereotypes is both a crucial part of the Law School's mission, and one that it cannot accomplish with only token numbers of minority students. Just as growing up in a particular region or having particular professional experiences is likely to affect an individual's views, so too is one's own, unique experience of being a racial minority in a society, like our own, in which race unfortunately still matters. The Law School has determined, based on its experience and expertise, that a "critical mass" of underrepresented minorities is necessary to further its compelling interest in securing the educational benefits of a diverse student body.

B.

Even in the limited circumstance when drawing racial distinctions is permissible to further a compelling state interest, government is still "constrained in how it may pursue that end: [T]he means chosen to accomplish the [government's] asserted purpose must be specifically and narrowly framed to accomplish that purpose." *Shaw v. Hunt*, 517 U. S. 899, 908 (1996) (internal quotation marks and citation omitted). The purpose of the narrow tailoring requirement is to ensure that "the means chosen 'fit' th[e] compelling goal so closely that there is little or no possibility that the motive for the classification was illegitimate racial prejudice or stereotype." *Richmond v. J. A. Croson Co.*, 488 U. S., at 493 (plurality opinion).

Since *Bakke*, we have had no occasion to define the contours of the narrow-tailoring inquiry with respect to race conscious university admissions programs. That inquiry must be calibrated to fit the distinct issues raised by the use of race to achieve student body diversity in public higher education. Contrary to Justice Kennedy's assertions, we do not "abando[n] strict scrutiny," see *post*, at 394 (dissenting opinion). Rather, as we have already explained, *supra*, at 327, we adhere to *Adarand*'s teaching that the very purpose of strict scrutiny is to take such "relevant differences into account." 515 U. S., at 228 (internal quotation marks omitted).

To be narrowly tailored, a race-conscious admissions program cannot use a quota system—it cannot "insulat[e] each category of applicants with certain desired qualifications from competition with all other applicants." *Bakke*, 438 U. S., at 315 (opinion of Powell, J.). Instead, a university may consider race or ethnicity only as a " 'plus' in a particular applicant's file," without "insulat[ing] the individual from comparison with all other candidates for the available seats." *Id.*, at 317. In other words, an admissions program must be "flexible enough to consider all pertinent elements of diversity in light of the particular qualifications of each applicant, and to place them on the same footing for consideration, although not necessarily according them the same weight." *Ibid.*

We find that the Law School's admissions program bears the hallmarks of a narrowly tailored plan. As Justice Powell made clear in *Bakke*, truly individualized consideration demands that race be used in a flexible, nonmechanical way. It follows from this mandate that universities cannot establish quotas for members of certain racial groups or put members of those groups on separate admissions tracks. See *id.*, at 315–316. Nor can universities insulate applicants who belong to certain racial or ethnic groups from the competition for admission. *Ibid.* Universities can, however, consider race or ethnicity more flexibly as a "plus" factor in the context of individualized consideration of each and every applicant. *Ibid.*

We are satisfied that the Law School's admissions program, like the Harvard plan described by Justice Powell, does not operate as a quota. Properly understood, a "quota" is a program in which a certain fixed number or proportion of opportunities are "reserved exclusively for certain minority groups." *Richmond v. J. A. Croson Co.*, *supra*, at 496 (plurality opinion). Quotas " 'impose a fixed number or percentage which must be attained, or which cannot be exceeded,' " *Sheet Metal Workers v. EEOC*, 478 U. S. 421, 495 (1986) (O'Connor, J., concurring in part and dissenting in part), and "insulate the individual from comparison with all other candidates for the available seats," *Bakke*, *supra*, at 317 (opinion of Powell, J.). In contrast, "a permissible goal . . . require[s] only a good-faith effort . . . to come within a range demarcated by the goal itself," *Sheet Metal Workers v. EEOC, supra*, at 495, and permits consideration of race as a "plus" factor in any given case while still ensuring that each candidate "compete[s] with all other qualified applicants," *Johnson v. Transportation Agency, Santa Clara Cty.*, 480 U. S. 616, 638 (1987).

Justice Powell's distinction between the medical school's rigid 16-seat quota and Harvard's flexible use of race as a "plus" factor is instructive. Harvard certainly had minimum goals for minority enrollment, even if it had no specific number firmly in mind. See *Bakke, supra*, at 323 (opinion of Powell, J.) ("10 or 20 black students could not begin to bring to their classmates and to each other the variety of points of view, backgrounds and experiences of blacks in the United States"). What is more, Justice Powell flatly rejected the argument that Harvard's program was "the functional equivalent of a quota" merely because it had some " 'plus' " for race, or gave greater "weight" to race than to some other factors, in order to achieve student body diversity. 438 U. S., at 317–318.

The Law School's goal of attaining a critical mass of underrepresented minority students does not transform its program into a quota. As the Harvard plan described by Justice Powell recognized, there is of course "some relationship between numbers and achieving the benefits to be derived from a diverse student body, and between numbers and providing a reasonable environment for those students admitted." *Id.*, at 323. "[S]ome attention to numbers," without more, does not transform a flexible admissions system into a rigid quota. *Ibid.* Nor, as Justice Kennedy posits, does the Law School's consultation of the "daily reports," which keep track of the racial and ethnic composition of the class (as well as of residency and gender), "sugges[t] there was no further attempt at individual review save for race itself" during the final stages of the admissions process. See *post*, at 392 (dissenting opinion). To the contrary, the Law School's admissions officers testified without contradiction that they never gave race any more or less weight based on the information contained in these reports. Brief for Respondent Bollinger et al. 43, n. 70 (citing App. in Nos. 01–1447 and 01–1516 (CA6), p. 7336). Moreover, as Justice Kennedy concedes, see *post*, at 390, between 1993 and 1998, the number of African-American, Latino, and Native-American students in each class at the Law School varied from 13.5 to 20.1 percent, a range inconsistent with a quota.

The Chief Justice believes that the Law School's policy conceals an attempt to achieve racial balancing, and cites admissions data to contend that the Law School discriminates among different groups within the critical mass. *Post*, at 380–386 (dissenting opinion). But, as The Chief Justice concedes, the number of underrepresented minority students who ultimately enroll in the Law School differs substantially from their representation in the applicant pool and varies considerably for each group from year to year. See post, at 385 (dissenting opinion).

That a race-conscious admissions program does not operate as a quota does not, by itself, satisfy the requirement of individualized consideration. When using race as a "plus" factor in university admissions, a university's admissions program must remain flexible enough to ensure that each applicant is evaluated as an individual and not in a way that makes an applicant's race or ethnicity the defining feature of his or her application. The importance of this individualized consideration in

the context of a race-conscious admissions program is paramount. See *Bakke*, 438 U. S., at 318, n. 52 (opinion of Powell, J.) (identifying the "denial . . . of th[e] right to individualized consideration" as the "principal evil" of the medical school's admissions program).

Here, the Law School engages in a highly individualized, holistic review of each applicant's file, giving serious consideration to all the ways an applicant might contribute to a diverse educational environment. The Law School affords this individualized consideration to applicants of all races. There is no policy, either *de jure* or *de facto*, of automatic acceptance or rejection based on any single "soft" variable. Unlike the program at issue in *Gratz v. Bollinger, ante*, p. 244, the Law School awards no mechanical, predetermined diversity "bonuses" based on race or ethnicity. See *ante*, at 271–272 (distinguishing a race-conscious admissions program that automatically awards 20 points based on race from the Harvard plan, which considered race but "did not contemplate that any single characteristic automatically ensured a specific and identifiable contribution to a university's diversity"). Like the Harvard plan, the Law School's admissions policy "is flexible enough to consider all pertinent elements of diversity in light of the particular qualifications of each applicant, and to place them on the same footing for consideration, although not necessarily according them the same weight." *Bakke, supra*, at 317 (opinion of Powell, J.).

We also find that, like the Harvard plan Justice Powell referenced in *Bakke*, the Law School's race-conscious admissions program adequately ensures that all factors that may contribute to student body diversity are meaningfully considered alongside race in admissions decisions. With respect to the use of race itself, all underrepresented minority students admitted by the Law School have been deemed qualified. By virtue of our Nation's struggle with racial inequality, such students are both likely to have experiences of particular importance to the Law School's mission, and less likely to be admitted in meaningful numbers on criteria that ignore those experiences. See App. 120.

The Law School does not, however, limit in any way the broad range of qualities and experiences that may be considered valuable contributions to student body diversity. To the contrary, the 1992 policy makes clear "[t]here are many possible bases for diversity admissions," and provides examples of admittees who have lived or traveled widely abroad, are fluent in several languages, have overcome personal adversity and family hardship, have exceptional records of extensive community service, and have had successful careers in other fields. *Id.*, at 118–119. The Law School seriously considers each "applicant's promise of making a notable contribution to the class by way of a particular strength, attainment, or characteristic—*e. g.*, an unusual intellectual achievement, employment experience, nonacademic performance, or personal background." *Id.*, at 83–84. All applicants have the opportunity to highlight their own potential diversity contributions through the submission of a personal statement, letters of recommendation, and an essay describing the ways in which the applicant will contribute to the life and diversity of the Law School.

What is more, the Law School actually gives substantial weight to diversity factors besides race. The Law School frequently accepts nonminority applicants with grades and test scores lower than underrepresented minority applicants (and other nonminority applicants) who are rejected. See Brief for Respondent Bollinger et al. 10; App. 121–122. This shows that the Law School seriously weighs many other diversity factors besides race that can make a real and dispositive difference for nonminority applicants as well. By this flexible approach, the Law School sufficiently takes into account, in practice as well as in theory, a wide variety of characteristics besides race and ethnicity that contribute to a diverse student body. Justice Kennedy speculates that "race is likely outcome determinative for many members of minority groups" who do not fall within the upper range of LSAT scores and grades. *Post*, at 389 (dissenting opinion). But the same could be said of the Harvard plan discussed approvingly by Justice Powell in *Bakke*, and indeed of any plan that uses race as one

of many factors. See 438 U. S., at 316 ("'When the Committee on Admissions reviews the large middle group of applicants who are "admissible" and deemed capable of doing good work in their courses, the race of an applicant may tip the balance in his favor'").

Petitioner and the United States argue that the Law School's plan is not narrowly tailored because race-neutral means exist to obtain the educational benefits of student body diversity that the Law School seeks. We disagree. Narrow tailoring does not require exhaustion of every conceivable race-neutral alternative. Nor does it require a university to choose between maintaining a reputation for excellence or fulfilling a commitment to provide educational opportunities to members of all racial groups. See *Wygant v. Jackson Bd. of Ed.*, 476 U. S. 267, 280, n. 6 (1986) (alternatives must serve the interest "'about as well'"); *Richmond v. J. A. Croson Co.*, 488 U. S., at 509–510 (plurality opinion) (city had a "whole array of race-neutral" alternatives because changing requirements "would have [had] little detrimental effect on the city's interests"). Narrow tailoring does, however, require serious, good faith consideration of workable race-neutral alternatives that will achieve the diversity the university seeks. See *id.*, at 507 (set-aside plan not narrowly tailored where "there does not appear to have been any consideration of the use of race-neutral means"); *Wygant v. Jackson Bd. of Ed., supra*, at 280, n. 6 (narrow tailoring "require[s] consideration" of "lawful alternative and less restrictive means").

We agree with the Court of Appeals that the Law School sufficiently considered workable race-neutral alternatives. The District Court took the Law School to task for failing to consider race-neutral alternatives such as "using a lottery system" or "decreasing the emphasis for all applicants on undergraduate GPA and LSAT scores." App. to Pet. for Cert. 251a. But these alternatives would require a dramatic sacrifice of diversity, the academic quality of all admitted students, or both.

The Law School's current admissions program considers race as one factor among many, in an effort to assemble a student body that is diverse in ways broader than race. Because a lottery would make that kind of nuanced judgment impossible, it would effectively sacrifice all other educational values, not to mention every other kind of diversity. So too with the suggestion that the Law School simply lower admissions standards for all students, a drastic remedy that would require the Law School to become a much different institution and sacrifice a vital component of its educational mission. The United States advocates "percentage plans," recently adopted by public undergraduate institutions in Texas, Florida, and California, to guarantee admission to all students above a certain class-rank threshold in every high school in the State. Brief for United States as *Amicus Curiae* 14–18. The United States does not, however, explain how such plans could work for graduate and professional schools. Moreover, even assuming such plans are race neutral, they may preclude the university from conducting the individualized assessments necessary to assemble a student body that is not just racially diverse, but diverse along all the qualities valued by the university. We are satisfied that the Law School adequately considered race-neutral alternatives currently capable of producing a critical mass without forcing the Law School to abandon the academic selectivity that is the cornerstone of its educational mission.

We acknowledge that "there are serious problems of justice connected with the idea of preference itself." *Bakke*, 438 U. S., at 298 (opinion of Powell, J.). Narrow tailoring, therefore, requires that a race-conscious admissions program not unduly harm members of any racial group. Even remedial race-based governmental action generally "remains subject to continuing oversight to assure that it will work the least harm possible to other innocent persons competing for the benefit." *Id.*, at 308. To be narrowly tailored, a race conscious admissions program must not "unduly burden individuals who are not members of the favored racial and ethnic groups." *Metro Broadcasting, Inc. v. FCC*, 497 U. S. 547, 630 (1990) (O'Connor, J., dissenting).

We are satisfied that the Law School's admissions program does not. Because the Law School considers "all pertinent elements of diversity," it can (and does) select nonminority applicants who have greater potential to enhance student body diversity over underrepresented minority applicants. See *Bakke, supra*, at 317 (opinion of Powell, J.). As Justice Powell recognized in *Bakke*, so long as a race-conscious admissions program uses race as a "plus" factor in the context of individualized consideration, a rejected applicant "will not have been foreclosed from all consideration for that seat simply because he was not the right color or had the wrong surname. . . . His qualifications would have been weighed fairly and competitively, and he would have no basis to complain of unequal treatment under the Fourteenth Amendment." 438 U. S., at 318.

We agree that, in the context of its individualized inquiry into the possible diversity contributions of all applicants, the Law School's race-conscious admissions program does not unduly harm nonminority applicants.

We are mindful, however, that "[a] core purpose of the Fourteenth Amendment was to do away with all governmentally imposed discrimination based on race." *Palmore v. Sidoti*, 466 U. S. 429, 432 (1984). Accordingly, race-conscious admissions policies must be limited in time. This requirement reflects that racial classifications, however compelling their goals, are potentially so dangerous that they may be employed no more broadly than the interest demands. Enshrining a permanent justification for racial preferences would offend this fundamental equal protection principle. We see no reason to exempt race-conscious admissions programs from the requirement that all governmental use of race must have a logical end point. The Law School, too, concedes that all "race-conscious programs must have reasonable durational limits." Brief for Respondent Bollinger et al. 32.

In the context of higher education, the durational requirement can be met by sunset provisions in race-conscious admissions policies and periodic reviews to determine whether racial preferences are still necessary to achieve student body diversity. Universities in California, Florida, and Washington State, where racial preferences in admissions are prohibited by state law, are currently engaged in experimenting with a wide variety of alternative approaches. Universities in other States can and should draw on the most promising aspects of these race-neutral alternatives as they develop. Cf. *United States v. Lopez*, 514 U. S. 549, 581 (1995) (Kennedy, J., concurring) ("[T]he States may perform their role as laboratories for experimentation to devise various solutions where the best solution is far from clear").

The requirement that all race-conscious admissions programs have a termination point "assure[s] all citizens that the deviation from the norm of equal treatment of all racial and ethnic groups is a temporary matter, a measure taken in the service of the goal of equality itself." *Richmond v. J. A. Croson Co.*, 488 U. S., at 510 (plurality opinion); see also Nathanson & Bartnik, The Constitutionality of Preferential Treatment for Minority Applicants to Professional Schools, 58 Chicago Bar Rec. 282, 293 (May–June 1977) ("It would be a sad day indeed, were America to become a quota-ridden society, with each identifiable minority assigned proportional representation in every desirable walk of life. But that is not the rationale for programs of preferential treatment; the acid test of their justification will be their efficacy in eliminating the need for any racial or ethnic preferences at all").

We take the Law School at its word that it would "like nothing better than to find a race-neutral admissions formula" and will terminate its race-conscious admissions program as soon as practicable. See Brief for Respondent Bollinger et al. 34; *Bakke, supra*, at 317–318 (opinion of Powell, J.) (presuming good faith of university officials in the absence of a showing to the contrary). It has been 25 years since Justice Powell first approved the use of race to further an interest in student body diversity in the context of public higher education. Since that time, the number of minority applicants with high grades and test scores has indeed increased. See Tr. of Oral Arg. 43. We expect that 25 years from now, the use of racial preferences will no longer be necessary to further the interest approved today.

IV.

In summary, the Equal Protection Clause does not prohibit the Law School's narrowly tailored use of race in admissions decisions to further a compelling interest in obtaining the educational benefits that flow from a diverse student body. Consequently, petitioner's statutory claims based on Title VI and 42 U. S. C. § 1981 also fail. See *Bakke, supra*, at 287 (opinion of Powell, J.) ("Title VI . . . proscribe[s] only those racial classifications that would violate the Equal Protection Clause or the Fifth Amendment"); *General Building Contractors Assn., Inc. v. Pennsylvania*, 458 U. S. 375, 389–391 (1982) (the prohibition against discrimination in § 1981 is coextensive with the Equal Protection Clause). The judgment of the Court of Appeals for the Sixth Circuit, accordingly, is affirmed.

It is so ordered.

Source: Grutter v. Bollinger, 539 U.S. 306 (2003).

Barack Obama, 2004 Democratic National Convention Keynote Address (July 27, 2004)

In 2004, Illinois senator Barack Obama delivered the keynote address before the Democratic National Convention. Essentially serving as a springboard to Obama's successful campaign to be the Democratic nominee for president in 2008, this speech wove together multiple threads of the

American story—immigration, tradition, and opportunity—into very appealing rhetoric. Desiring "to affirm the greatness of our nation," Obama found his speech to be extraordinarily well received inside and outside the convention.

On behalf of the great state of Illinois, crossroads of a nation, Land of Lincoln, let me express my deepest gratitude for the privilege of addressing this convention.

Tonight is a particular honor for me because— let's face it—my presence on this stage is pretty unlikely. My father was a foreign student, born and raised in a small village in Kenya. He grew up herding goats, went to school in a tin-roof shack. His father—my grandfather—was a cook, a domestic servant to the British.

But my grandfather had larger dreams for his son. Through hard work and perseverance my father got a scholarship to study in a magical place, America, that shone as a beacon of freedom and opportunity to so many who had come before.

While studying here, my father met my mother. She was born in a town on the other side of the world, in Kansas. Her father worked on oil rigs and farms through most of the Depression years. The day after Pearl Harbor my grandfather signed up for duty; joined Gen. Patton's army, marched across Europe. Back home, my grandmother raised their baby and went to work on a bomber assembly line. After the war, they studied on the G.I. Bill, bought a house through FHA, and later moved west all the way to Hawaii in search of opportunity.

And they, too, had big dreams for their daughter. A common dream, born of two continents.

My parents shared not only an improbable love, they shared an abiding faith in the possibilities of this nation. They would give me an African name, *Barack*, or *blessed*, believing that in a tolerant America your name is no barrier to success. They imagined me going to the best schools in the land, even though they weren't rich, because in a generous America you don't have to be rich to achieve your potential.

They are both passed away now. And yet, I know that, on this night, they look down on me with great pride.

I stand here today, grateful for the diversity of my heritage, aware that my parents' dreams live on in my two precious daughters. I stand here knowing that my story is part of the larger American story, that I owe a debt to all of those who came before me, and that, in no other country on Earth, is my story even possible.

Tonight, we gather to affirm the greatness of our nation—not because of the height of our skyscrapers, or the power of our military, or the size of our economy. Our pride is based on a very simple premise, summed up in a declaration made over two hundred years ago: "We hold these truths to be self-evident, that all men are created equal. That they are endowed by their Creator with certain inalienable rights. That among these are life, liberty and the pursuit of happiness."

That is the true genius of America—a faith in simple dreams, an insistence on small miracles. That we can tuck in our children at night and know that they are fed and clothed and safe from harm. That we can say what we think, write what we think, without hearing a sudden knock on the door. That we can have an idea and start our own business without paying a bribe. That we can participate in the political process without fear of retribution, and that our votes will be counted—at least, most of the time.

This year, in this election, we are called to reaffirm our values and our commitments, to hold them against a hard reality and see how we are measuring up, to the legacy of our forebears, and the promise of future generations.

And fellow Americans, Democrats, Republicans, Independents—I say to you tonight: we have more work to do. More work to do for the workers I met in Galesburg, Illinois, who are losing their union jobs at the Maytag plant that's moving to Mexico, and now are having to compete with their own children for jobs that pay seven bucks an hour. More to do for the father that I met who was losing his job and choking back the tears, wondering how he would pay $4,500 a month for the drugs his son needs without the health benefits that he counted on. More to do for the young woman in East St. Louis, and thousands more like her, who has the grades, has the drive, has the will, but doesn't have the money to go to college.

Now don't get me wrong. The people I meet—in small towns and big cities, in diners and office parks—they don't expect government to solve all their problems. They know they have to work hard to get ahead—and they want to.

Go into the collar counties around Chicago, and people will tell you they don't want their tax money wasted, by a welfare agency or by the Pentagon.

Go into any inner city neighborhood, and folks will tell you that government alone can't teach our kids to learn—they know that parents have to teach, that children can't achieve unless we raise their expectations and turn off the television sets and eradicate the slander that says a black youth with a book is acting white. They know those things.

People don't expect government to solve all their problems. But they sense, deep in their bones, that with just a slight change in priorities, we can make sure that every child in America has a decent shot at life, and that the doors of opportunity remain open to all.

They know we can do better. And they want that choice.

In this election, we offer that choice. Our party has chosen a man to lead us who embodies the best this country has to offer. And that man is John Kerry. John Kerry understands the ideals of community, faith, and service because they've defined his life. From his heroic service in Vietnam, to his years as a prosecutor and lieutenant governor, through two decades in the United States Senate, he has devoted himself to this country. Again and again, we've seen him make tough choices when easier ones were available.

His values—and his record—affirm what is best in us. John Kerry believes in an America where hard work is rewarded; so instead of offering tax breaks to companies shipping jobs overseas, he offers them to companies creating jobs here at home.

John Kerry believes in an America where all Americans can afford the same health coverage our politicians in Washington have for themselves.

John Kerry believes in energy independence, so we aren't held hostage to the profits of oil companies, or the sabotage of foreign oil fields.

John Kerry believes in the Constitutional freedoms that have made our country the envy of the world, and he will never sacrifice our basic liberties, nor use faith as a wedge to divide us.

And John Kerry believes that in a dangerous world, war must be an option sometimes, but it should never be the first option.

You know, a while back, I met a young man named Seamus in a VFW hall in East Moline, Illinois. He was a good-looking kid—six-two, six-three, clear-eyed, with an easy smile. He told me he'd joined the Marines, and was heading to Iraq the following week. And as I listened to him explain why he'd enlisted, the absolute faith he had in our country and its leaders, his devotion to duty and service, I thought this young man was all that any of us might hope for in a child. But then I asked myself: Are we serving Seamus as well as he is serving us?

I thought of the 900 men and women—sons and daughters, husbands and wives, friends and neighbors, who won't be returning to their own hometowns. I thought of the families I've met who were struggling to get by without a loved one's full income, or whose loved ones had returned with a limb missing or nerves shattered, but who still lacked long-term health benefits because they were reservists.

When we send our young men and women into harm's way, we have a solemn obligation not to fudge the numbers or shade the truth about why they're going, to care for their families while they're gone, to tend to the soldiers upon their return, and to never *ever* go to war without enough troops to win the war, secure the peace, and earn the respect of the world.

Now let me be clear. Let me be clear. We have real enemies in the world. These enemies must be found. They must be pursued—and they must be defeated. John Kerry knows this.

And just as Lieutenant Kerry did not hesitate to risk his life to protect the men who served with him in Vietnam, President Kerry will not hesitate one moment to use our military might to keep America safe and secure.

John Kerry believes in America. And he knows that it's not enough for just some of us to prosper.

For alongside our famous individualism, there's another ingredient in the American saga. A belief that we're all connected as one people.

If there is a child on the south side of Chicago who can't read, that matters to me, even if it's not my child. If there's a senior citizen somewhere who can't pay for their prescription drugs, and has to choose between medicine and the rent, that makes my life poorer, even if it's not my grandparent. If there's an Arab American family being rounded up without benefit of an attorney or due process, that threatens my civil liberties.

It is that fundamental belief, it is that fundamental belief—I am my brother's keeper, I am my sister's keeper—that makes this country work. It's what allows us to pursue our individual dreams and yet still come together as one American family. E pluribus unum. "Out of many, one."

Now even as we speak, there are those who are preparing to divide us, the spin masters, the negative ad peddlers who embrace the politics of anything goes. Well, I say to them tonight, there is not a liberal America and a conservative America—there is the United States of America. There is not a Black America and a White America and Latino America and Asian America—there's the United States of America.

The pundits, the pundits like to slice-and-dice our country into Red States and Blue States; Red States for Republicans, Blue States for Democrats. But I've got news for them, too. We worship an awesome God in the Blue States, and we don't like federal agents poking around in our libraries in the Red States. We coach Little League in the Blue States and yes, we've got some gay friends in the Red States. There are patriots who opposed the war in Iraq and there are patriots who supported the war in Iraq.

We are one people, all of us pledging allegiance to the stars and stripes, all of us defending the United States of America. In the end, that's what this election is about. Do we participate in a politics of cynicism or do we participate in a politics of hope?

John Kerry calls on us to hope. John Edwards calls on us to hope.

I'm not talking about blind optimism here—the almost willful ignorance that thinks unemployment will go away if we just don't think about it, or the health care crisis will solve itself if we just ignore it. That's not what I'm talking about. I'm talking about something more substantial. It's the hope of slaves sitting around a fire singing freedom songs. The hope of immigrants setting out for distant shores. The hope of a young naval lieutenant bravely patrolling the Mekong Delta. The hope of a mill worker's son who dares to defy the odds. The hope of a skinny kid with a funny name who believes that America has a place for him, too.

Hope in the face of difficulty. Hope in the face of uncertainty. The audacity of hope! In the end, that is God's greatest gift to us, the bedrock of this nation. A belief in things not seen. A belief that there are better days ahead.

I believe that we can give our middle class relief and provide working families with a road to opportunity. I believe we can provide jobs to the jobless, homes to the homeless, and reclaim young people in cities across America from violence and despair. I believe that we have a righteous wind at our backs and that as we stand on the crossroads of history, we can make the right choices, and meet the challenges that face us.

America! Tonight, if you feel the same energy that I do, if you feel the same urgency that I do, if you feel the same passion I do, if you feel the same hopefulness that I do—if we do what we must do, then I have no doubts that all across the country, from Florida to Oregon, from Washington to Maine, the people will rise up in November, and John Kerry will be sworn in as president, and John Edwards will be sworn in as vice president, and this country will reclaim its promise, and out of this long political darkness a brighter day will come.

Rev. Al Sharpton, 2004 Democratic National Convention Address
(July 28, 2004)

One of the most controversial African American leaders in modern America, Rev. Al Sharpton, the leader of National Action Network, addressed the 2004 Democratic National Convention in Boston. Invoking the civil rights heroes of generations past—namely, the Freedom Riders and Rev. Martin Luther King Jr.'s group of marchers in Selma, Alabama—Sharpton reminded the convention delegates of the necessity of continuing the party's efforts for civil rights.

Tonight, I want to address my remarks in two parts.

One, I'm honored to address the delegates here.

Last Friday, I had the experience in Detroit of hearing President George Bush make a speech. And in the speech, he [asked] certain questions. I hope he's watching tonight. I would like to answer your questions, Mr. President.

To the/our chairman, our delegates, and all that are assembled, we're honored and glad to be here tonight.

I'm glad to be joined by supporters and friends from around the country. I'm glad to be joined by my family, Kathy, Dominique, who will be 18, and Ashley.

We are here 228 years after right here in Boston we fought to establish the freedoms of America. The first person to die in the Revolutionary War is buried not far from here, a Black man from Barbados, named Crispus Attucks.

Forty years ago, in 1964, Fannie Lou Hamer and the Mississippi Freedom Democratic Party stood at the Democratic convention in Atlantic City fighting to preserve voting rights for all America and all Democrats, regardless of race or gender.

Hamer's stand inspired Dr. King's march in Selma, which brought about the Voting Rights Act of 1965.

Twenty years ago, Reverend Jesse Jackson stood at the Democratic National Convention in San Francisco, again, appealing to the preserve those freedoms.

Tonight, we stand with those freedoms at risk and our security as citizens in question.

I have come here tonight to say the only choice we have to preserve our freedom at this point in history is to elect John Kerry the president of the United States.

I stood with both John Kerry and John Edwards over 30 occasions in debates during the primary season. I not only debated them, I watched them. I observed their deeds. I looked into their eyes. I am convinced that they are men who say what they mean and mean what they say.

I'm also convinced that at a time when a vicious spirit in the body politic of this country that attempts to undermine America's freedoms—our civil rights, our civil liberties—we must leave this city and go forth and organize this nation for victory for our party and John Kerry and John Edwards in November.

But let me quickly say, this is not just about winning an election. It's about preserving the principles on which this very nation was founded.

Look at the current view of our nation worldwide as a result of our unilateral foreign policy. We went from unprecedented international support and solidarity on September 12th, 2001, to hostility and hatred as we stand here tonight. We can't survive in the world by ourselves.

How did we squander this opportunity to unite the world for democracy and to commit to the global fight against hunger and disease? We did it with a go-it-alone foreign policy based on flawed intelligence. We were told that we were going to Iraq because there were weapons of mass destruction. We lost hundreds of soldiers. We spent $200 billion dollars at a time we had record state deficits. And when it became clear that there were no weapons, they changed the premise for the war and said: No, we went because of other reasons.

If I told you tonight to, "Let's leave the FleetCenter; we're in danger," and when you get outside, you ask me, "Reverend Al, What is the danger?" and I say, "It don't matter. We just needed some fresh air," I have misled you—and we were misled.

We—We are also faced with the prospect of in the next four years that two or more Supreme Court Justices' seats will become available. This year we celebrated the anniversary of *Brown versus the Board of Education*.

This court has voted five to four on critical issues of women's rights and civil rights. It is frightening to think that the gains of civil and women rights and those movements in the last century could be reversed if this administration is in the White House in these next four years.

I suggest to you tonight that if George Bush had selected the court in '54, Clarence Thomas would have never got to law school.

This is not about a Party. This is about living up to the promise of America. The promise of America says we will guarantee quality education for all children and not spend more money on metal detectors than computers in our schools.

The promise of America guarantees health care for all of its citizens and doesn't force seniors to travel to Canada to buy prescription drugs they can't afford here at home.

The promise of America provides that those who work in our health care system can afford to be hospitalized in the very beds they clean up every day.

The promise of America is that government does not seek to regulate your behavior in the bedroom, but to guarantee your right to provide food in the kitchen.

The issue of government is not to determine who may sleep together in the bedroom, it's to help those that might not be eatin' in the kitchen.

The promise of America is that we stand for human rights, whether it's fighting against slavery in the Sudan, where right now Joe Madison and others are fasting, around what is going on in Sudan; AIDS in Lesotho; police misconduct in this country.

The promise of America is one immigration policy for all who seek to enter our shores, whether they come from Mexico, Haiti, or Canada, there must be one set of rules for everybody.

We cannot welcome those to come and then try and act as though any culture will not be respected or treated inferior. We cannot look at the Latino community and preach "one language." No one gave them an English test before they sent them to Iraq to fight for America.

The promise of America is that every citizen's vote is counted and protected, and election schemes do not decide the election.

It, to me, is a glaring contradiction that we would fight, and rightfully so, to get the right to vote for the people in the capital of Iraq in Baghdad, but still don't give the federal right to vote for the people in the capital of the United States, in Washington, D.C.

Mr. President, as I close, Mr. President, I heard you say Friday that you had questions for voters, particularly African-American voters. And you [asked] the question: Did the Democratic Party take us for granted? Well, I have raised questions. But let me answer your question.

You said the Republican Party was the party of Lincoln and Frederick Douglass. It is true that Mr. Lincoln signed the Emancipation Proclamation, after which there was a commitment to give 40 acres and a mule.

That's where the argument, to this day, of reparations starts. We never got the 40 acres. We went all the way to Herbert Hoover, and we never got the 40 acres.

We didn't get the mule. So we decided we'd ride this donkey as far as it would take us.

Mr. President, you said would we have more leverage if both parties got our votes, but we didn't come this far playing political games. It was those that earned our vote that got our vote. We got the Civil Rights Act under a Democrat. We got the Voting Rights Act under a Democrat. We got the right to organize under Democrats.

Mr. President, the reason we are fighting so hard, the reason we took Florida so seriously, is our right to vote wasn't gained because of our age. Our vote was soaked in the blood of martyrs, soaked in the blood of Goodman, Chaney and Schwerner, soaked in the blood of four little girls in Birmingham.

This vote is sacred to us.

This vote can't be bargained away.

This vote can't be given away.

Mr. President, in all due respect, Mr. President, read my lips: Our vote is not for sale.

And there's a whole generation of young leaders that have come forward across this country that stand on integrity and stand on their traditions, those that have emerged with John Kerry and John Edwards as partners, like Greg Meeks, like Obama Baracka [Barack Obama], like our voter registration director, Marjorie Harris, like those that are in the trenches.

And we come with strong family values. Family values is not just those with two-car garages and a retirement plan. Retirement plans are good. But family values also are those who had to make nothing stretch into something happening, who had to make ends meet.

I was raised by a single mother who made a way for me. She used to scrub floors as a domestic worker, put a cleaning rag in her pocketbook, and ride the subways in Brooklyn so I'd have food on the table.

But she taught me as I walked her to that subway that life is about not where you start, but where you're going. That's family values.

And I wanted—I wanted somebody in my community—I wanted to show that example. As I ran for President, I hoped that one child that come out of the ghetto like I did, could look at me walk across the stage with governors and senators and know they didn't have to be a drug dealer, they didn't have to be a hoodlum, they didn't have to be a gangster, they could stand up from a broken home, on welfare, and they could run for President of the United States.

As you know, I live in New York. I was there September 11th when that despicable act of terrorism happened.

Few days after, I left home—my family had taken in a young man even who lost his family. And as they gave comfort to him, I had to do a radio show that morning. When I got there, my friend James Entome [sp?] said, "Reverend, we're going to stop at a certain hour and play a song, synchronized with 900 and 90 other stations."

I said, "That's fine."

He said, "We're dedicating it to the victims of 9/11."

I said, "What song are you playing?"

He said, "We're playing 'America the Beautiful.'"

And the particular station I was at, they played that rendition song by Ray Charles.

As you know, we lost Ray a few weeks ago, but I sat there that morning and listened to Ray sing through those speakers, "Oh beautiful for spacious skies, for amber waves of grain, for purple mountains' majesty across the fruited plain."

And it occurred to me as I heard Ray singing, that Ray wasn't singing about what he knew, 'cause Ray had been blind since he was a child. He hadn't seen many purple mountains. He hadn't seen many fruited plains. He was singing about what he believed to be.

Mr. President, we love America, not because of all of us have seen the beauty all the time.

But we believed if we kept on working, if we kept on marching, if we kept on voting, if we kept on believing, we would make America beautiful for everybody.

Starting November, let's make America beautiful again.

Thank you. And God bless you.

Source: Sharpton, Reverend Al. 2004 Democratic National Convention Address. Delivered July 28, 2004, Fleet Center, Boston, MA. Copyright © Democratic National Convention. Retrieved from AmericanRhetoric.com.

Barack Obama, "A More Perfect Union" Speech
(March 18, 2008)

In reaction to inflammatory racial remarks made by his former pastor, Chicago's Rev. Jeremiah Wright Jr., presidential candidate Barack Obama delivered a landmark speech on racism during his 2008 bid for the Democratic nomination for the presidency of the United States. Speaking at the Constitution Center in Philadelphia on March 18, Obama said the aims of his campaign spoke to the need of finding a fundamental path by which all Americans can work to pursue a better future. He said Wright's remarks both in and out of the pulpit were divisive and came at a crossroad in American history.

The speech is significant for many reasons but specifically because it confronted the issue of race head-on in a campaign that had been careful not to portray the candidate as merely being the only viable black candidate to ever run for the presidency. Campaign aides warned Obama against giving the speech because of fears that it would give his critics bait in what had become an increasingly tight race for the Democratic nomination for president against New York senator Hillary Rodham Clinton, the former first lady and wife of former president Bill Clinton.

The significance of Obama's speech on race was noted in a broad range of commentary outlets, including Matthew Yglesias on The Atlantic *magazine's web outlet, TheAtlantic.com. Yglesias said the timing of the speech and the era in which it was given may have signaled an end to media manipulation of the news. In the past, news outlets could alter the interpretation or significance of speeches by printing or broadcasting small segments of statements, known as "sound bites," in radio and television broadcasting. . . . Sound bites are less important today because video recordings or written transcripts of speeches in their entirety are commonly available to anyone online.*

Because the speech was released in advance to the media, The Democratic Strategist, *a journal of public opinion and political strategy, said the speech received widespread praise even before it was given for "its unexpected honesty and candor for saying things such as 'racial anger is real.' Everyone knows this but it is rarely acknowledged."*

Matt Compton, a spokesman for the Democratic Legislative Committee, made this observation the day after the March 18, 2008, speech: "The campaign put the video of the entire speech on YouTube before lunch. Twenty-four hours after Obama walked off the stage in Philadelphia, this 37-minute address has already been viewed more than 1,000,000 times." The New York Times *posted a transcript of the speech in full online shortly after the speech was delivered, and it was among the most popular stories on the Web site. Minutes after Obama walked off stage, radio stations far and wide, and ranging from National Public Radio outlets to hip-hop stations in the Deep South, all interrupted playlists and scheduled programming to broadcast the speech live or in rebroadcasts throughout the country.*

"We the people, in order to form a more perfect union."

Two hundred and twenty one years ago, in a hall that still stands across the street, a group of men gathered and, with these simple words, launched America's improbable experiment in democracy. Farmers and scholars; statesmen and patriots who had traveled across an ocean to escape tyranny and persecution finally made real their declaration of independence at a Philadelphia convention that lasted through the spring of 1787.

The document they produced was eventually signed but ultimately unfinished. It was stained by this nation's original sin of slavery, a question that divided the colonies and brought the convention to a stalemate until the founders chose to allow the slave trade to continue for at least twenty more years, and to leave any final resolution to future generations.

Of course, the answer to the slavery question was already embedded within our Constitution—a Constitution that had at its very core the ideal of equal citizenship under the law; a Constitution that promised its people liberty, and justice, and a union that could be and should be perfected over time.

And yet words on a parchment would not be enough to deliver slaves from bondage, or provide men and women of every color and creed their full rights and obligations as citizens of the United States. What would be needed were Americans in successive generations who were willing to do their part—through protests and struggle, on the streets and in the courts, through a civil war and civil disobedience and always at great risk—to narrow that gap between the promise of our ideals and the reality of their time.

This was one of the tasks we set forth at the beginning of this campaign—to continue the long march of those who came before us, a march for a more just, more equal, more free, more caring and more prosperous America. I chose to run for the presidency at this moment in history because I believe deeply that we cannot solve the challenges of our time unless we solve them together—unless we perfect our union by understanding that we may have different stories, but we hold common hopes; that we may not look the same and we may not have come from the same place, but we all want to move in the same direction—towards a better future for our children and our grandchildren.

This belief comes from my unyielding faith in the decency and generosity of the American people. But it also comes from my own American story.

I am the son of a black man from Kenya and a white woman from Kansas. I was raised with the help of a white grandfather who survived a Depression to serve in Patton's Army during World War II and a white grandmother who worked on a bomber assembly line at Fort Leavenworth while he was overseas. I've gone to some of the best schools in America and lived in one of the world's poorest nations. I am married to a black American who carries within her the blood of slaves and slave owners—an inheritance we pass on to our two precious daughters. I have brothers, sisters, nieces, nephews, uncles and cousins, of every race and every hue, scattered across three continents, and for as long as I live, I will never forget that in no other country on Earth is my story even possible.

It's a story that hasn't made me the most conventional candidate. But it is a story that has seared into my genetic makeup the idea that this nation is more than the sum of its parts—that out of many, we are truly one.

Throughout the first year of this campaign, against all predictions to the contrary, we saw how hungry the American people were for this message of unity. Despite the temptation to view my candidacy through a purely racial lens, we won commanding victories in states with some of the whitest populations in the country. In South Carolina, where the Confederate Flag still flies, we built a powerful coalition of African Americans and white Americans.

This is not to say that race has not been an issue in the campaign. At various stages in the campaign, some commentators have deemed me either "too black" or "not black enough." We saw racial tensions bubble to the surface during the week before the South Carolina primary. The press has scoured every exit poll for the latest evidence of racial polarization, not just in terms of white and black, but black and brown as well.

And yet, it has only been in the last couple of weeks that the discussion of race in this campaign has taken a particularly divisive turn.

On one end of the spectrum, we've heard the implication that my candidacy is somehow an exercise in affirmative action; that it's based solely on the desire of wide-eyed liberals to purchase racial reconciliation on the cheap. On the other end, we've heard my former pastor, Reverend Jeremiah Wright, use incendiary language to express views that have the potential not only to widen the racial divide, but views that denigrate both the greatness and the goodness of our nation; that rightly offend white and black alike.

I have already condemned, in unequivocal terms, the statements of Reverend Wright that have caused such controversy. For some, nagging questions remain. Did I know him to be an occasionally fierce critic of American domestic and foreign policy? Of course. Did I ever hear him make remarks that could be considered controversial while I sat in church? Yes. Did I strongly disagree with many of his political views? Absolutely—just as I'm sure many of you have heard remarks from your pastors, priests, or rabbis with which you strongly disagreed.

But the remarks that have caused this recent firestorm weren't simply controversial. They weren't simply a religious leader's effort to speak out against perceived injustice. Instead, they expressed a profoundly distorted view of this country—a view that sees white racism as endemic, and that elevates what is wrong with America above all that we know is right with America; a view that sees the conflicts in the Middle East as rooted primarily in the actions of stalwart allies like Israel, instead of emanating from the perverse and hateful ideologies of radical Islam.

As such, Reverend Wright's comments were not only wrong but divisive, divisive at a time when we need unity; racially charged at a time when we need to come together to solve a set of monumental problems—two wars, a terrorist threat, a failing economy, a chronic health care crisis and potentially devastating climate change; problems that are neither black or white or Latino or Asian, but rather problems that confront us all.

Given my background, my politics, and my professed values and ideals, there will no doubt be those for whom my statements of condemnation are not enough. Why associate myself with Reverend Wright in the first place, they may ask? Why not join another church? And I confess that if all that I knew of Reverend Wright were the snippets of those sermons that have run in an endless loop on the television and You Tube, or if Trinity United Church of Christ conformed to the caricatures being peddled by some commentators, there is no doubt that I would react in much the same way.

But the truth is, that isn't all that I know of the man. The man I met more than twenty years ago is a man who helped introduce me to my Christian faith, a man who spoke to me about our obligations to love one another; to care for the sick and lift up the poor. He is a man who served his country as a U.S. Marine; who has studied and lectured at some of the finest universities and seminaries in the country, and who for over thirty years led a church that serves the community by doing God's work here on Earth—by housing the homeless, ministering to the needy, providing day care services and scholarships and prison ministries, and reaching out to those suffering from HIV/AIDS.

In my first book, *Dreams from My Father*, I described the experience of my first service at Trinity:

"People began to shout, to rise from their seats and clap and cry out, a forceful wind carrying the reverend's voice up into the rafters.... And in that single note—hope!—I heard something else; at the foot of that cross, inside the thousands of churches across the city, I imagined the stories of ordinary black people merging with the stories of David and Goliath, Moses and Pharaoh, the Christians in the lion's den, Ezekiel's field of dry bones. Those stories—of survival, and freedom, and hope—became our story, my story; the blood that had spilled was our blood, the tears our tears; until this black church, on this bright day, seemed once more a vessel carrying the story of a people into future generations and into a larger world. Our trials and triumphs became at once unique and universal, black and more than black; in chronicling our journey, the stories and songs gave us a means to reclaim memories that we didn't need to feel shame about . . . memories that all people might study and cherish—and with which we could start to rebuild."

That has been my experience at Trinity. Like other predominantly black churches across the country, Trinity embodies the black community in its entirety—the doctor and the welfare mom, the model student and the former gang-banger. Like other black churches, Trinity's services are full of raucous laughter and sometimes bawdy humor. They are full of dancing, clapping, screaming and shouting that may seem jarring to the untrained ear. The church contains in full the kindness and cruelty, the fierce intelligence and the shocking ignorance, the struggles and successes, the love and yes, the bitterness and bias that make up the black experience in America.

And this helps explain, perhaps, my relationship with Reverend Wright. As imperfect as he may be, he has been like family to me. He strengthened my faith, officiated my wedding, and baptized my children. Not once in my conversations with him have I heard him talk about any ethnic group in derogatory terms, or treat whites with whom he interacted with anything but courtesy and respect. He contains within him the contradictions—the good and the bad—of the community that he has served diligently for so many years.

I can no more disown him than I can disown the black community. I can no more disown him than I can my white grandmother—a woman who helped raise me, a woman who sacrificed again and again for me, a woman who loves me as much as she loves anything in this world, but a woman who once confessed her fear of black men who passed by her on the street, and who on more than one occasion has uttered racial or ethnic stereotypes that made me cringe.

These people are a part of me. And they are a part of America, this country that I love.

Some will see this as an attempt to justify or excuse comments that are simply inexcusable. I can assure you it is not. I suppose the politically safe thing would be to move on from this episode and just hope that it fades into the woodwork. We can dismiss Reverend Wright as a crank or a demagogue, just as some have dismissed Geraldine Ferraro, in the aftermath of her recent statements, as harboring some deep-seated racial bias.

But race is an issue that I believe this nation cannot afford to ignore right now. We would be making the same mistake that Reverend Wright made in his offending sermons about America—to simplify and stereotype and amplify the negative to the point that it distorts reality.

The fact is that the comments that have been made and the issues that have surfaced over the last few weeks reflect the complexities of race in this country that we've never really worked through—a part of our union that we have yet to perfect. And if we walk away now, if we simply retreat into our respective corners, we will never be able to come together and solve challenges like health care, or education, or the need to find good jobs for every American.

Understanding this reality requires a reminder of how we arrived at this point. As William Faulkner once wrote, "The past isn't dead and buried. In fact, it isn't even past." We do not need to recite here the history of racial injustice in this country. But we do need to remind ourselves that so many of the disparities that exist in the African-American community today can be directly traced to inequalities passed on from an earlier generation that suffered under the brutal legacy of slavery and Jim Crow.

Segregated schools were, and are, inferior schools; we still haven't fixed them, fifty years after *Brown v. Board of Education*, and the inferior education they provided, then and now, helps explain the pervasive achievement gap between today's black and white students.

Legalized discrimination—where blacks were prevented, often through violence, from owning property, or loans were not granted to African-American business owners, or black homeowners could not access FHA mortgages, or blacks were excluded from unions, or the police force, or fire departments—meant that black families could not amass any meaningful wealth to bequeath to future generations. That history helps explain the wealth and income gap between black and white, and the concentrated pockets of poverty that persists in so many of today's urban and rural communities.

A lack of economic opportunity among black men, and the shame and frustration that came from not being able to provide for one's family, contributed to the erosion of black families—a problem that welfare policies for many years may have worsened. And the lack of basic services in so many urban black neighborhoods—parks for kids to play in, police walking the beat, regular garbage pick-up and building code enforcement—all helped create a cycle of violence, blight and neglect that continue to haunt us.

This is the reality in which Reverend Wright and other African-Americans of his generation grew up. They came of age in the late fifties and early sixties, a time when segregation was still the law of the land and opportunity was systematically constricted. What's remarkable is not how many failed in the face of discrimination, but rather how many men and women overcame the odds; how many were able to make a way out of no way for those like me who would come after them.

But for all those who scratched and clawed their way to get a piece of the American Dream, there were many who didn't make it—those who were ultimately defeated, in one way or another, by discrimination. That legacy of defeat was passed on to future generations—those young men and increasingly young women who we see standing on street corners or languishing in our prisons, without hope or prospects for the future. Even for those blacks who did make it, questions of race, and racism, continue to define their worldview in fundamental ways. For the men and women of Reverend Wright's generation, the memories of humiliation and doubt and fear have not gone away; nor has the anger and the bitterness of those years. That anger may not get expressed in public, in front of white co-workers or white friends. But it does find voice in the barbershop or around the kitchen table. At times, that anger is exploited by politicians, to gin up votes along racial lines, or to make up for a politician's own failings.

And occasionally it finds voice in the church on Sunday morning, in the pulpit and in the pews. The fact that so many people are surprised to hear that anger in some of Reverend Wright's sermons simply reminds us of the old truism that the most segregated hour in American life occurs on Sunday morning. That anger is not always productive; indeed, all too often it distracts attention from solving real problems; it keeps us from squarely facing our own complicity in our condition, and prevents the African-American community from forging the alliances it needs to bring about real change. But the anger is real; it is powerful; and to simply wish it away, to condemn it without understanding its roots, only serves to widen the chasm of misunderstanding that exists between the races.

In fact, a similar anger exists within segments of the white community. Most working- and middle-class white Americans don't feel that they have been particularly privileged by their race. Their experience is the immigrant experience—as far as they're concerned, no one's handed them anything, they've built it from scratch. They've worked hard all their lives, many times only to see their jobs shipped overseas or their pension dumped after a lifetime of labor. They are anxious about their futures, and feel their dreams slipping away; in an era of stagnant wages and global competition, opportunity comes to be seen as a zero sum game, in which your dreams come at my expense. So when they are told to bus their children to a school across town; when they hear that an African American is getting an advantage in landing a good job or a spot in a good college because of an injustice that they themselves never committed; when they're told that their fears about crime in urban neighborhoods are somehow prejudiced, resentment builds over time.

Like the anger within the black community, these resentments aren't always expressed in polite company. But they have helped shape the political landscape for at least a generation. Anger over welfare and affirmative action helped forge the Reagan Coalition. Politicians routinely exploited fears of crime for their own electoral ends. Talk show hosts and conservative commentators built entire careers unmasking bogus claims of racism while dismissing legitimate discussions of racial injustice and inequality as mere political correctness or reverse racism.

Just as black anger often proved counterproductive, so have these white resentments distracted attention from the real culprits of the middle class squeeze—a corporate culture rife with inside dealing, questionable accounting practices, and short-term greed; a Washington dominated by lobbyists and special interests; economic policies that favor the few over the many. And yet, to wish away the resentments of white Americans, to label them as misguided or even racist, without recognizing they are grounded in legitimate concerns—this too widens the racial divide, and blocks the path to understanding.

This is where we are right now. It's a racial stalemate we've been stuck in for years. Contrary to the claims of some of my critics, black and white, I have never been so naïve as to believe that we can get beyond our racial divisions in a single election cycle, or with a single candidacy—particularly a candidacy as imperfect as my own.

But I have asserted a firm conviction—a conviction rooted in my faith in God and my faith in the American people—that working together we can move beyond some of our old racial wounds, and that in fact we have no choice if we are to continue on the path of a more perfect union.

For the African-American community, that path means embracing the burdens of our past without becoming victims of our past. It means continuing to insist on a full measure of justice in every aspect of American life. But it also means binding our particular grievances—for better health care, and better schools, and better jobs—to the larger aspirations of all Americans—the white woman struggling to break the glass ceiling, the white man who's been laid off, the immigrant trying to feed his family. And it means taking full responsibility for own lives—by demanding more from our fathers, and spending more time with our children, and reading to them, and teaching them that while

they may face challenges and discrimination in their own lives, they must never succumb to despair or cynicism; they must always believe that they can write their own destiny.

Ironically, this quintessentially American—and yes, conservative—notion of self-help found frequent expression in Reverend Wright's sermons. But what my former pastor too often failed to understand is that embarking on a program of self-help also requires a belief that society can change.

The profound mistake of Reverend Wright's sermons is not that he spoke about racism in our society. It's that he spoke as if our society was static; as if no progress has been made; as if this country—a country that has made it possible for one of his own members to run for the highest office in the land and build a coalition of white and black, Latino and Asian, rich and poor, young and old—is still irrevocably bound to a tragic past. But what we know—what we have seen—is that America can change. That is the true genius of this nation. What we have already achieved gives us hope—the audacity to hope—for what we can and must achieve tomorrow.

In the white community, the path to a more perfect union means acknowledging that what ails the African-American community does not just exist in the minds of black people; that the legacy of discrimination—and current incidents of discrimination, while less overt than in the past—are real and must be addressed. Not just with words, but with deeds—by investing in our schools and our communities; by enforcing our civil rights laws and ensuring fairness in our criminal justice system; by providing this generation with ladders of opportunity that were unavailable for previous generations. It requires all Americans to realize that your dreams do not have to come at the expense of my dreams; that investing in the health, welfare, and education of black and brown and white children will ultimately help all of America prosper.

In the end, then, what is called for is nothing more, and nothing less, than what all the world's great religions demand—that we do unto others as we would have them do unto us. Let us be our brother's keeper, Scripture tells us. Let us be our sister's keeper. Let us find that common stake we all have in one another, and let our politics reflect that spirit as well.

For we have a choice in this country. We can accept a politics that breeds division, and conflict, and cynicism. We can tackle race only as spectacle—as we did in the OJ trial—or in the wake of tragedy, as we did in the aftermath of Katrina—or as fodder for the nightly news. We can play Reverend Wright's sermons on every channel, every day and talk about them from now until the election, and make the only question in this campaign whether or not the American people think that I somehow believe or sympathize with his most offensive words. We can pounce on some gaffe by a Hillary supporter as evidence that she's playing the race card, or we can speculate on whether white men will all flock to John McCain in the general election regardless of his policies.

We can do that.

But if we do, I can tell you that in the next election, we'll be talking about some other distraction. And then another one. And then another one. And nothing will change.

That is one option. Or, at this moment, in this election, we can come together and say, "Not this time." This time we want to talk about the crumbling schools that are stealing the future of black children and white children and Asian children and Hispanic children and Native American children. This time we want to reject the cynicism that tells us that these kids can't learn; that those kids who don't look like us are somebody else's problem. The children of America are not those kids, they are our kids, and we will not let them fall behind in a 21st century economy. Not this time.

This time we want to talk about how the lines in the Emergency Room are filled with whites and blacks and Hispanics who do not have health care; who don't have the power on their own to overcome the special interests in Washington, but who can take them on if we do it together.

This time we want to talk about the shuttered mills that once provided a decent life for men and women of every race, and the homes for sale that once belonged to Americans from every religion, every region, every walk of life. This time we want to talk about the fact that the real problem is not that someone who doesn't look like you might take your job; it's that the corporation you work for will ship it overseas for nothing more than a profit.

This time we want to talk about the men and women of every color and creed who serve together, and fight together, and bleed together under the same proud flag. We want to talk about how to bring them home from a war that never should've been authorized and never should've been waged, and we want to talk about how we'll show our patriotism by caring for them, and their families, and giving them the benefits they have earned.

I would not be running for President if I didn't believe with all my heart that this is what the vast majority of Americans want for this country. This union may never be perfect, but generation after generation has shown that it can always be perfected. And today, whenever I find myself feeling doubtful or cynical about this possibility, what gives me the most hope is the next generation—the young people whose attitudes and beliefs and openness to change have already made history in this election.

There is one story in particularly that I'd like to leave you with today—a story I told when I had the great honor of speaking on Dr. King's birthday at his home church, Ebenezer Baptist, in Atlanta.

There is a young, twenty-three-year-old white woman named Ashley Baia who organized for our campaign in Florence, South Carolina. She had been working to organize a mostly African-American community since the beginning of this campaign, and one day she was at a roundtable discussion where everyone went around telling their story and why they were there.

And Ashley said that when she was nine years old, her mother got cancer. And because she had to miss days of work, she was let go and lost her health care. They had to file for bankruptcy, and that's when Ashley decided that she had to do something to help her mom.

She knew that food was one of their most expensive costs, and so Ashley convinced her mother that what she really liked and really wanted to eat more than anything else was mustard and relish sandwiches. Because that was the cheapest way to eat.

She did this for a year until her mom got better, and she told everyone at the roundtable that the reason she joined our campaign was so that she could help the millions of other children in the country who want and need to help their parents too.

Now Ashley might have made a different choice. Perhaps somebody told her along the way that the source of her mother's problems were blacks who were on welfare and too lazy to work, or Hispanics who were coming into the country illegally. But she didn't. She sought out allies in her fight against injustice.

Anyway, Ashley finishes her story and then goes around the room and asks everyone else why they're supporting the campaign. They all have different stories and reasons. Many bring up a specific issue. And finally they come to this elderly black man who's been sitting there quietly the entire time. And Ashley asks him why he's there. And he does not bring up a specific issue. He does not say health care or the economy. He does not say education or the war. He does not say that he was there because of Barack Obama. He simply says to everyone in the room, "I am here because of Ashley."

"I'm here because of Ashley." By itself, that single moment of recognition between that young white girl and that old black man is not enough. It is not enough to give health care to the sick, or jobs to the jobless, or education to our children.

But it is where we start. It is where our union grows stronger. And as so many generations have come to realize over the course of the two hundred and twenty-one years since a band of patriots signed that document in Philadelphia, that is where the perfection begins.

Source: Obama, Barack. "A More Perfect Union." Speech. March 18, 2008. United States Senate, Office of Barack Obama, D-Ill., 713 Hart Senate Office Building, Washington, DC 20510.

Barack Obama, Election Day Speech
(November 4, 2008)

On November 5, 2008, Senator Barack Obama (D-IL) was elected the 44th president of the United States. In remarks prepared and provided by his campaign, President-elect Barack Obama called himself the unlikeliest presidential candidate, according to National Public Radio. He thanked his campaign and the many volunteers who joined the campaign but told a crowd in Grant Park in Chicago and a worldwide television audience that an enormous task had just begun for the electorate and the United States.

If there is anyone out there who still doubts that America is a place where all things are possible; who still wonders if the dream of our founders is alive in our time; who still questions the power of our democracy, tonight is your answer.

It's the answer told by lines that stretched around schools and churches in numbers this nation has never seen; by people who waited three hours and four hours, many for the very first time in their lives, because they believed that this time must be different; that their voice could be that difference.

It's the answer spoken by young and old, rich and poor, Democrat and Republican, black, white, Latino, Asian, Native American, gay, straight, disabled and not disabled—Americans who sent a message to the world that we have never been a collection of red states and blue states; we are, and always will be, the United States of America.

It's the answer that led those who have been told for so long by so many to be cynical, and fearful, and doubtful of what we can achieve to put their hands on the arc of history and bend it once more toward the hope of a better day.

It's been a long time coming, but tonight, because of what we did on this day, in this election, at this defining moment, change has come to America.

I just received a very gracious call from Sen. McCain. He fought long and hard in this campaign, and he's fought even longer and harder for the country he loves. He has endured sacrifices for America that most of us cannot begin to imagine, and we are better off for the service rendered by this brave and selfless leader. I congratulate him and Gov. Palin for all they have achieved, and I look forward to working with them to renew this nation's promise in the months ahead.

I want to thank my partner in this journey, a man who campaigned from his heart and spoke for the men and women he grew up with on the streets of Scranton and rode with on that train home to Delaware, the vice-president-elect of the United States, Joe Biden.

I would not be standing here tonight without the unyielding support of my best friend for the last 16 years, the rock of our family and the love of my life, our nation's next first lady, Michelle Obama. Sasha and Malia, I love you both so much, and you have earned the new puppy that's coming with us to the White House. And while she's no longer with us, I know my grandmother is watching, along with the family that made me who I am. I miss them tonight, and know that my debt to them is beyond measure.

To my campaign manager, David Plouffe; my chief strategist, David Axelrod; and the best campaign team ever assembled in the history of politics—you made this happen, and I am forever grateful for what you've sacrificed to get it done.

But above all, I will never forget who this victory truly belongs to—it belongs to you.

I was never the likeliest candidate for this office. We didn't start with much money or many endorsements. Our campaign was not hatched in the halls of Washington—it began in the backyards of Des Moines and the living rooms of Concord and the front porches of Charleston.

It was built by working men and women who dug into what little savings they had to give $5 and $10 and $20 to this cause. It grew strength from the young people who rejected the myth of their generation's apathy; who left their homes and their families for jobs that offered little pay and less sleep; from the not-so-young people who braved the bitter cold and scorching heat to knock on the doors of perfect strangers; from the millions of Americans who volunteered and organized, and proved that more than two centuries later, a government of the people, by the people and for the people has not perished from this earth. This is your victory.

I know you didn't do this just to win an election, and I know you didn't do it for me. You did it because you understand the enormity of the task that lies ahead. For even as we celebrate tonight, we know the challenges that tomorrow will bring are the greatest of our lifetime—two wars, a planet in peril, the worst financial crisis in a century. Even as we stand here tonight, we know there are brave Americans waking up in the deserts of Iraq and the mountains of Afghanistan to risk their lives for us. There are mothers and fathers who will lie awake after their children fall asleep and wonder how they'll make the mortgage, or pay their doctor's bills, or save enough for college. There is new energy to harness and new jobs to be created; new schools to build and threats to meet and alliances to repair.

The road ahead will be long. Our climb will be steep. We may not get there in one year, or even one term, but America—I have never been more hopeful than I am tonight that we will get there. I promise you: We as a people will get there.

There will be setbacks and false starts. There are many who won't agree with every decision or policy I make as president, and we know that government can't solve every problem. But I will always be honest with you about the challenges we face. I will listen to you, especially when we disagree. And, above all, I will ask you join in the work of remaking this nation the only way it's been done in America for 221 years—block by block, brick by brick, callused hand by callused hand.

What began 21 months ago in the depths of winter must not end on this autumn night. This victory alone is not the change we seek—it is only the chance for us to make that change. And that cannot happen if we go back to the way things were. It cannot happen without you.

So let us summon a new spirit of patriotism; of service and responsibility where each of us resolves to pitch in and work harder and look after not only ourselves, but each other. Let us remember that if this financial crisis taught us anything, it's that we cannot have a thriving Wall Street while Main Street suffers. In this country, we rise or fall as one nation—as one people.

Let us resist the temptation to fall back on the same partisanship and pettiness and immaturity that has poisoned our politics for so long. Let us remember that it was a man from this state who first carried the banner of the Republican Party to the White House—a party founded on the values of self-reliance, individual liberty and national unity. Those are values we all share, and while the Democratic Party has won a great victory tonight, we do so with a measure of humility and determination to heal the divides that have held back our progress.

As Lincoln said to a nation far more divided than ours, "We are not enemies, but friends . . . Though passion may have strained, it must not break our bonds of affection." And, to those Americans whose support I have yet to earn, I may not have won your vote, but I hear your voices, I need your help, and I will be your president, too.

And to all those watching tonight from beyond our shores, from parliaments and palaces to those who are huddled around radios in the forgotten corners of our world—our stories are singular, but our destiny is shared, and a new dawn of American leadership is at hand. To those who would tear this world down: We will defeat you. To those who seek peace and security: We support you. And to all those who have wondered if America's beacon still burns as bright: Tonight, we proved once more that the true strength of our nation comes not from the might of our arms or the scale of our wealth, but from the enduring power of our ideals: democracy, liberty, opportunity and unyielding hope.

For that is the true genius of America—that America can change. Our union can be perfected. And what we have already achieved gives us hope for what we can and must achieve tomorrow.

This election had many firsts and many stories that will be told for generations. But one that's on my mind tonight is about a woman who cast her ballot in Atlanta. She's a lot like the millions of others who stood in line to make their voice heard in this election, except for one thing: Ann Nixon Cooper is 106 years old.

She was born just a generation past slavery; a time when there were no cars on the road or planes in the sky; when someone like her couldn't vote for two reasons—because she was a woman and because of the color of her skin.

And tonight, I think about all that she's seen throughout her century in America—the heartache and the hope; the struggle and the progress; the times we were told that we can't and the people who pressed on with that American creed: Yes, we can.

At a time when women's voices were silenced and their hopes dismissed, she lived to see them stand up and speak out and reach for the ballot. Yes, we can.

When there was despair in the Dust Bowl and depression across the land, she saw a nation conquer fear itself with a New Deal, new jobs and a new sense of common purpose. Yes, we can.

When the bombs fell on our harbor and tyranny threatened the world, she was there to witness a generation rise to greatness and a democracy was saved. Yes, we can.

She was there for the buses in Montgomery, the hoses in Birmingham, a bridge in Selma and a preacher from Atlanta who told a people that "We Shall Overcome." Yes, we can.

A man touched down on the moon, a wall came down in Berlin, a world was connected by our own science and imagination. And this year, in this election, she touched her finger to a screen and cast her vote, because after 106 years in America, through the best of times and the darkest of hours, she knows how America can change. Yes, we can.

America, we have come so far. We have seen so much. But there is so much more to do. So tonight, let us ask ourselves: If our children should live to see the next century; if my daughters should be so lucky to live as long as Ann Nixon Cooper,

what change will they see? What progress will we have made?

This is our chance to answer that call. This is our moment. This is our time—to put our people back to work and open doors of opportunity for our kids; to restore prosperity and promote the cause of peace; to reclaim the American Dream and reaffirm that fundamental truth that out of many, we are one; that while we breathe, we hope, and where we are met with cynicism, and doubt, and those who tell us that we can't, we will respond with that timeless creed that sums up the spirit of a people: Yes, we can.

Thank you, God bless you, and may God bless the United States of America.

Source: Obama, Barack. "Address in Chicago Accepting Election as the 44th President of the United States," November 4, 2008.

President Barack Obama, Remarks on the Arrest of Professor Henry Louis Gates

(2009)

On July 16, 2009, Henry Louis Gates, a prominent professor of African American studies at Harvard University, returned to his Cambridge, Massachusetts, home from a research trip to China. Finding the front door jammed, Gates and his driver attempted to force it open. A passerby misinterpreted their actions as an attempt to break into the house and called 911. When a Cambridge police officer, Sergeant James Crowley, responded to the call, he and Gates got into an altercation that led to Gates's arrest for disorderly conduct. Although the charges against Gates were dropped several days later, the incident sparked a national debate about the use of racial profiling by police.

On July 22, President Barack Obama responded to a question about the incident that

was asked at a presidential press conference by saying that the Cambridge police "acted stupidly" in arresting Gates. This comment was highly criticized, and this criticism led the president to invite Gates and Crowley to the White House. The two men talked with Obama and Vice President Joe Biden in the Rose Garden on July 30, 2009, in what became known as the "Beer Summit." Reproduced here is the full question and answer on the Gates incident from the press conference of July 22.

Q Thank you, Mr. President. Recently Professor Henry Louis Gates Jr. was arrested at his home in Cambridge. What does that incident say to you and what does it say about race relations in America?

THE PRESIDENT: Well, I should say at the outset that "Skip" Gates is a friend, so I may be a little biased here. I don't know all the facts. What's been reported, though, is that the guy forgot his keys, jimmied his way to get into the house, there was a report called into the police station that there might be a burglary taking place—so far, so good, right? I mean, if I was trying to jigger into—well, I guess this is my house now so—(laughter)—it probably wouldn't happen. But let's say my old house in Chicago—(laughter)—here I'd get shot. (Laughter.)

But so far, so good. They're reporting—the police are doing what they should. There's a call, they go investigate what happens. My understanding is at that point Professor Gates is already in his house. The police officer comes in, I'm sure there's some exchange of words, but my understanding is, is that Professor Gates then shows his ID to show that this is his house. And at that point, he gets arrested for disorderly conduct—charges which are later dropped.

Now, I don't know, not having been there and not seeing all the facts, what role race played in that, but I think it's fair to say, number one, any of us would be pretty angry; number two, that the Cambridge Police acted stupidly in arresting somebody when there was already proof that they were in their own home; and number three, what I think we know separate and apart from this incident is

that there is a long history in this country of African Americans and Latinos being stopped by law enforcement disproportionately. That's just a fact.

As you know, Lynn, when I was in the state legislature in Illinois, we worked on a racial profiling bill because there was indisputable evidence that blacks and Hispanics were being stopped disproportionately. And that is a sign, an example of how, you know, race remains a factor in this society. That doesn't lessen the incredible progress that has been made. I am standing here as testimony to the progress that's been made.

And yet the fact of the matter is, is that this still haunts us. And even when there are honest misunderstandings, the fact that blacks and Hispanics are picked up more frequently and oftentime for no cause casts suspicion even when there is good cause. And that's why I think the more that we're working with local law enforcement to improve policing techniques so that we're eliminating potential bias, the safer everybody is going to be.

All right, thank you, everybody.

Source: Obama, Barack. "Remarks on the Arrest of Professor Henry Louis Gates." July 16, 2009. White House Website. http://www.whitehouse.gov/video/President-Obamas-Primetime-Press-Conference-on-Health-Reform/# transcript.

Fisher v. University of Texas at Austin
(2013)

In 2008, undergraduate Abigail Fisher brought suit against the University of Texas, claiming that its race-based admissions policy was not consistent with the Supreme Court's 2003 ruling in Grutter v. Bollinger, *which held that race was an appropriate but limited fact in school admissions policies. Lower courts upheld the university's admissions policy, but in* Fisher v. University of Texas, *the Supreme Court remanded the case to the lower courts, declaring that these courts had not applied the principle of strict*

scrutiny called for in Grutter *in making their original decisions. In doing this, the court strictly followed its decisions in* Grutter *and* Bakke *(1978) and made no attempt to end affirmative action.*

Argued October 10, 2012—Decided June 24, No. 11-345. 2013

The University of Texas at Austin considers race as one of various factors in its undergraduate admissions process. The University, which is committed to increasing racial minority enroll-ment, adopted its current program after this Court decided *Grutter* v. *Bollinger*, 539 U.S. 306, uphold-ing the use of race as one of many "plus factors" in an admissions program that considered the overall individual contribution of each candidate, and decided *Gratz* v. *Bollinger*, 539 U.S. 244, holding unconstitutional an admissions program that auto-matically awarded points to applicants from cer-tain racial minorities.

Petitioner, who is Caucasian, was rejected for admission to the University's 2008 entering class. She sued the University and school officials, alleg-ing that the University's consideration of race in admissions violated the Equal Protection Clause. The District Court granted summary judgment to the University. Affirming, the Fifth Circuit held that *Grutter* required courts to give substantial def-erence to the University, both in the definition of the compelling interest in diversity's benefits and in deciding whether its specific plan was narrowly tailored to achieve its stated goal. Applying that standard, the court upheld the University's admis-sions plan.

Held: Because the Fifth Circuit did not hold the University to the demanding burden of strict scru-tiny articulated in *Grutter* and *Regents of Univ. of Cal.* v. *Bakke*, 438 U.S. 265, its decision affirming the District Court's grant of summary judgment to the University was incorrect. Pp.5-13.

(a)*Bakke*, *Gratz*, and *Grutter*, which directly address the question considered here, are taken as given for purposes of deciding this case. In *Bakke*'s principal opinion, Justice Powell recognized that state university "decisions based on race or ethnic origin . . . are reviewable under the Fourteenth Amendment," 438 U.S., at 287, using a strict scru-tiny standard, *id.*, at 299. He identified as a com-pelling interest that could justify the consideration of race the interest in the educational benefits that flow from a diverse student body, but noted that this interest is complex, encompassing a broad array "of qualifications and characteristics of which racial or ethnic origin is but a single though important element." *Id.*, at 315

In *Gratz* and *Grutter*, the Court endorsed these precepts, observing that an admissions process with such an interest is subject to judicial review and must withstand strict scrutiny, *Gratz*, *supra*, at 275, *i.e.*, a university must clearly demonstrate that its "'purpose or interest is both constitutionally permissible and substantial, and that its use of the classification is "necessary . . . to the accomplish-ment" of its purpose,'" *Bakke*, *supra*, at 305. Additional guidance may be found in the Court's broader equal protection jurisprudence. See, *e.g.*, *Rice* v. *Cayetano*, 528 U.S. 495, 517; *Richmond* v. *J. A. Croson Co.*, 488 U.S. 469, 505. Strict scrutiny is a searching examination, and the government bears the burden to prove "'that the reasons for any [racial] classification [are] clearly identified and unquestionably legitimate.'" *Ibid.* Pp.5-8.

(b)Under *Grutter*, strict scrutiny must be applied to any admissions program using racial categories or classifications. A court may give some defer-ence to a university's "judgment that such diversity is essential to its educational mission," 539 U.S., at 328, provided that diversity is not defined as mere racial balancing and there is a reasoned, principled explanation for the academic decision. On this point, the courts below were correct in finding that *Grutter* calls for deference to the University's experience and expertise about its educational mis-sion. However, once the University has established that its goal of diversity is consistent with strict scrutiny, the University must prove that the means it chose to attain that diversity are narrowly tai-lored to its goal. On this point, the University receives no deference. *Id.*, at 333. It is at all times the University's obligation to demonstrate, and the Judiciary's obligation to determine, that admis-sions processes "ensure that each applicant is eval-uated as an individual and not in a way that makes an applicant's race or ethnicity the defining feature of his or her application." *Id.*, at 337. Narrow tai-loring also requires a reviewing court to verify that it is "necessary" for the university to use race to achieve the educational benefits of diversity. *Bakke*, *supra*, at 305. The reviewing court must ultimately be satisfied that no workable race-neutral alternatives would produce the educational benefits of diversity.

Rather than perform this searching examination, the Fifth Circuit held petitioner could challenge only whether the University's decision to use race as an admissions factor "was made in good faith." It presumed that the school had acted in good faith and gave petitioner the burden of rebutting that presumption. It thus undertook the narrow-tailoring requirement with a "degree of deference" to the school. These expressions of the controlling standard are at odds with *Grutter*'s command that "all racial classifications imposed by government 'must be analyzed by a reviewing court under strict scrutiny.'" 539 U.S., at 326. Strict scrutiny does not permit a court to accept a school's assertion that its admissions process uses race in a permissible way without closely examining how the process works in practice, yet that is what the District Court and Fifth Circuit did here. The Court vacates the Fifth Circuit's judgment. But fairness to the litigants and the courts that heard the case requires that it be remanded so that the admissions process can be considered and judged under a correct analysis. In determining whether summary judgment in the University's favor was appropriate, the Fifth Circuit must assess whether the University has offered sufficient evidence to prove that its admissions program is narrowly tailored to obtain the educational benefits of diversity. Pp.8-13.

631 F.3d 213, vacated and remanded.

Kennedy, J., delivered the opinion of the Court, in which *Roberts, C.J.,* and *Scalia, Thomas, Breyer, Alito,* and *Sotomayor, JJ.,* joined. *Scalia, J.,* and *Thomas, J.,* filed concurring opinions. *Ginsburg, J.,* filed a dissenting opinion. *Kagan, J.,* took no part in the consideration or decision of the case.

JUNE 24, 2013 ABIGAIL NOEL FISHER, PETITIONER v. UNIVERSITY OF TEXAS AT AUSTIN et al. 570 U.S. _____ (2013) FISHER S.Ct. 14-8612 Opinion of the Court v. This opinion is subject to formal revision UNIVERSITY OF TEXAS AT AUSTIN NOTICE: before publication in the preliminary print of the United States Readers are requested to notify the Reporter of Decisions, Supreme Reports. Court of the United States, Washington, D.C. 20543, of any typographical or other formal errors, in order that corrections may be made before the preliminary print goes to press. SUPREME COURT OF THE UNITED STATES No. 11-345

ABIGAIL NOEL FISHER, PETITIONER *v.* UNIVERSITY OF TEXAS AT AUSTIN *et al.*

on writ of certiorari to the united states court of appeals for the fifth circuit

[June 24, 2013]

Justice Kennedy delivered the opinion of the Court.

The University of Texas at Austin considers race as one of various factors in its undergraduate admissions process. Race is not itself assigned a numerical value for each applicant, but the University has committed itself to increasing racial minority enrollment on campus. It refers to this goal as a "critical mass." Petitioner, who is Caucasian, sued the University after her application was rejected. She contends that the University's use of race in the admissions process violated the Equal Protection Clause of the Fourteenth Amendment.

The parties asked the Court to review whether the judgment below was consistent with "this Court's decisions interpreting the Equal Protection Clause of the Fourteenth Amendment, including *Grutter* v. *Bollinger*, 539 U.S. 306 (2003)." Pet. for Cert. i. The Court concludes that the Court of Appeals did not hold the University to the demanding burden of strict scrutiny articulated in *Grutter* and *Regents of Univ. of Cal.* v. *Bakke*, 438 U.S. 265, 305 (1978) (opinion of Powell, J.). Because the Court of Appeals did not apply the correct standard of strict scrutiny, its decision affirming the District Court's grant of summary judgment to the University was incorrect. That decision is vacated, and the case is remanded for further proceedings.

I

A

Located in Austin, Texas, on the most renowned campus of the Texas state university system, the University is one of the leading institutions of higher education in the Nation. Admission is prized and competitive. In 2008, when petitioner sought admission to the University's entering class, she was 1 of 29,501 applicants. From this group 12,843 were admitted, and 6,715 accepted and enrolled. Petitioner was denied admission.

In recent years the University has used three different programs to evaluate candidates for admission. The first is the program it used for some years before 1997, when the University considered two factors: a numerical score reflecting an applicant's test scores and academic performance in high school (Academic Index or AI), and the applicant's race. In 1996, this system was held unconstitutional by the United States Court of Appeals for the Fifth Circuit. It ruled the University's consideration of race violated the Equal Protection Clause because it did not further any compelling government interest. *Hopwood* v. *Texas*, 78 F.3d 932, 955 (1996).

The second program was adopted to comply with the *Hopwood* decision. The University stopped considering race in admissions and substituted instead a new holistic metric of a candidate's potential contribution to the University, to be used in conjunction with the Academic Index. This "Personal Achievement Index" (PAI) measures a student's leadership and work experience, awards, extracurricular activities, community service, and other special circumstances that give insight into a student's background. These included growing up in a single-parent home, speaking a language other than English at home, significant family responsibilities assumed by the applicant, and the general socioeconomic condition of the student's family. Seeking to address the decline in minority enrollment after *Hopwood*, the University also expanded its outreach programs.

The Texas State Legislature also responded to the *Hopwood* decision. It enacted a measure known as the Top Ten Percent Law, codified at Tex. Educ. Code Ann. §51.803 (West 2009). Also referred to as H.B. 588, the Top Ten Percent Law grants automatic admission to any public state college, including the University, to all students in the top 10% of their class at high schools in Texas that comply with certain standards.

The University's revised admissions process, coupled with the operation of the Top Ten Percent Law, resulted in a more racially diverse environment at the University. Before the admissions program at issue in this case, in the last year under the post-*Hopwood* AI/PAI system that did not consider race, the entering class was 4.5% African-American and 16.9% Hispanic. This is in contrast with the 1996 pre-*Hopwood* and Top Ten Percent regime, when race was explicitly considered, and the University's entering freshman class was 4.1% African-American and 14.5% Hispanic.

Following this Court's decisions in *Grutter* v. *Bollinger, supra*, and *Gratz* v. *Bollinger*, 539 U.S. 244 (2003), the University adopted a third admissions program, the 2004 program in which the University reverted to explicit consideration of race. This is the program here at issue. In *Grutter*, the Court upheld the use of race as one of many "plus factors" in an admissions program that considered the overall individual contribution of each candidate. In *Gratz*, by contrast, the Court held unconstitutional Michigan's undergraduate admissions program, which automatically awarded points to applicants from certain racial minorities.

The University's plan to resume race-conscious admissions was given formal expression in June 2004 in an internal document entitled Proposal to Consider Race and Ethnicity in Admissions (Proposal). Supp. App. 1a. The Proposal relied in substantial part on a study of a subset of undergraduate classes containing between 5 and 24 students. It showed that few of these classes had significant enrollment by members of racial minorities. In addition the Proposal relied on what it called "anecdotal" reports from students regarding their "interaction in the classroom." The Proposal concluded that the University lacked a "critical mass" of minority students and that to remedy the deficiency it was necessary to give explicit consideration to race in the undergraduate admissions program.

To implement the Proposal the University included a student's race as a component of the PAI score, beginning with applicants in the fall of 2004. The University asks students to classify themselves from among five predefined racial categories on the application. Race is not assigned an explicit numerical value, but it is undisputed that race is a meaningful factor.

Once applications have been scored, they are plotted on a grid with the Academic Index on the x-axis and the Personal Achievement Index on the y-axis. On that grid students are assigned to so-called cells based on their individual scores. All students in the cells falling above a certain line are admitted. All students below the line are not. Each college—such as Liberal Arts or Engineering—admits students separately. So a student is considered initially for her first-choice college, then for her second choice, and finally for general admission as an undeclared major.

Petitioner applied for admission to the University's 2008 entering class and was rejected. She sued the University and various University officials in the United States District Court for the Western District of Texas. She alleged that the University's consideration of race in admissions violated the Equal Protection Clause. The parties cross-moved for summary judgment. The District Court granted summary judgment to the University. The United States Court of Appeals for the Fifth Circuit affirmed. It held that *Grutter* required courts to give substantial deference to the University, both in the definition of the compelling interest in diversity's benefits and in deciding whether its specific plan was narrowly tailored to achieve its stated goal. Applying that standard, the court upheld the University's admissions plan. 631 F.3d 213, 217-218 (2011).

Over the dissent of seven judges, the Court of Appeals denied petitioner's request for rehearing en banc. See 644 F.3d 301, 303 (CA5 2011) (*per curiam*). Petitioner sought a writ of certiorari. The writ was granted. 565 U.S. ___ (2012).

B

Among the Court's cases involving racial classifications in education, there are three decisions that directly address the question of considering racial minority status as a positive or favorable factor in a university's admissions process, with the goal of achieving the educational benefits of a more diverse student body: *Bakke*, 438 U.S. 265; *Gratz*, *supra*; and *Grutter*, 539 U.S. 306. We take those cases as given for purposes of deciding this case.

We begin with the principal opinion authored by Justice Powell in *Bakke*, *supra*. In *Bakke*, the Court considered a system used by the medical school of the University of California at Davis. From an entering class of 100 students the school had set aside 16 seats for minority applicants. In holding this program impermissible under the Equal Protection Clause Justice Powell's opinion stated certain basic premises. First, "decisions based on race or ethnic origin by faculties and administrations of state universities are reviewable under the Fourteenth Amend-ment." *Id.*, at 287 (separate opinion). The principle of equal protection admits no "artificial line of a 'two-class theory'" that "permits the recognition of special wards entitled to a degree of protection greater than that accorded others." *Id.*, at 295. It is therefore irrelevant that a system of racial preferences in admissions may seem benign. Any racial classification must meet strict scrutiny, for when government decisions "touch upon an individual's race or ethnic background, he is entitled to a judicial determination that the burden he is asked to bear on that basis is precisely tailored to serve a compelling governmental interest." *Id.*, at 299.

Next, Justice Powell identified one compelling interest that could justify the consideration of race: the interest in the educational benefits that flow from a diverse student body. Redressing past discrimination could not serve as a compelling interest, because a university's "broad mission [of] education" is incompatible with making the "judicial, legislative, or administrative findings of constitutional or statutory violations" necessary to justify remedial racial classification. *Id.*, at 307-309.

The attainment of a diverse student body, by contrast, serves values beyond race alone, including enhanced class-room dialogue and the lessening of racial isolation and stereotypes. The academic mission of a university is "a special concern of the First Amendment." *Id.*, at 312. Part of "'the business of a university [is] to provide that atmosphere which is most conducive to speculation, experiment, and creation,'" and this in turn leads to the question of "'who may be admitted to study.'" *Sweezy* v. *New Hampshire*, 354 U.S. 234, 263 (1957) (Frankfurter, J., concurring in judgment).

Justice Powell's central point, however, was that this interest in securing diversity's benefits, although a permissible objective, is complex. "It is not an interest in simple ethnic diversity, in which a specified percentage of the student body is in effect guaranteed to be members of selected ethnic groups, with the remaining percentage an undifferentiated aggregation of students. The diversity that furthers a compelling state interest encompasses a far broader array of qualifications and characteristics of which racial or ethnic origin is but a single though important element." *Bakke*, 438 U.S., at 315 (separate opinion).

In *Gratz*, 539 U.S. 244, and *Grutter, supra*, the Court endorsed the precepts stated by Justice Powell. In *Grutter*, the Court reaffirmed his conclusion that obtaining the educational benefits of "student body diversity is a compelling state interest that can justify the use of race in university admissions." *Id.*, at 325.

As *Gratz* and *Grutter* observed, however, this follows only if a clear precondition is met: The particular admissions process used for this objective is subject to judicial review. Race may not be considered unless the admissions process can withstand strict scrutiny. "Nothing in Justice Powell's opinion in *Bakke* signaled that a university may employ whatever means it desires to achieve the stated goal of diversity without regard to the limits imposed by our strict scrutiny analysis." *Gratz, supra*, at 275. "To be narrowly tailored, a race-conscious admissions program cannot use a quota system," *Grutter*, 539 U.S., at 334, but instead must "remain flexible enough to ensure that each applicant is evaluated as an individual and not in a way that makes an applicant's race or ethnicity the defining feature of his or her application," *id.*, at 337. Strict scrutiny requires the university to demonstrate with clarity that its "purpose or interest is both constitutionally permissible and substantial, and that its use of the classification is necessary . . . to the accomplishment of its purpose." *Bakke*, 438 U.S., at 305 (opinion of Powell, J.) (internal quotation marks omitted).

While these are the cases that most specifically address the central issue in this case, additional guidance may be found in the Court's broader equal protection jurisprudence which applies in this context. "Distinctions between citizens solely because of their ancestry are by their very nature odious to a free people," *Rice* v. *Cayetano*, 528 U.S. 495, 517 (2000) (internal quotation marks omitted), and therefore "are contrary to our traditions and hence constitutionally suspect," *Bolling* v. *Sharpe*, 347 U.S. 497, 499 (1954). "'[B]ecause racial characteristics so seldom provide a relevant basis for disparate treatment,'" *Richmond* v. *J. A. Croson Co.*, 488 U.S. 469, 505 (1989) (quoting *Fullilove* v. *Klutznick*, 448 U.S. 448, 533-534 (1980) (Stevens, J., dissenting)), "the Equal Protection Clause demands that racial classifications . . . be subjected to the 'most rigid scrutiny.'" *Loving* v. *Virginia*, 388 U.S. 1, 11 (1967).

To implement these canons, judicial review must begin from the position that "any official action that treats a person differently on account of his race or ethnic origin is inherently suspect." *Fullilove, supra,* at 523 (Stewart, J., dissenting); *McLaughlin* v. *Florida*, 379 U.S. 184, 192 (1964). Strict scrutiny is a searching examination, and it is the government that bears the burden to prove "'that the reasons for any [racial] classification [are] clearly identified and unquestionably legitimate,'" *Croson, supra,* at 505 (quoting *Fullilove,* 448 *supra,* at 533-535 (Stevens, J., dissenting)).

II

Grutter made clear that racial "classifications are constitutional only if they are narrowly tailored to further compelling governmental interests." 539 U.S., at 326. And *Grutter* endorsed Justice Powell's conclusion in *Bakke* that "the attainment of a diverse student body . . . is a constitutionally permissible goal for an institution of higher education." 438 U.S., at 311-312 (separate opinion). Thus, under *Grutter,* strict scrutiny must be applied to any admissions program using racial categories or classifications.

According to *Grutter,* a university's "educational judgment that such diversity is essential to its educational mission is one to which we defer." 539 U.S., at 328. *Grutter* concluded that the decision to pursue "the educational benefits that flow from student body diversity," *id.,* at 330, that the University deems integral to its mission is, in substantial measure, an academic judgment to which some, but not complete, judicial deference is proper under *Grutter.* A court, of course, should ensure that there is a reasoned, principled explanation for the academic decision. On this point, the District Court and Court of Appeals were correct in finding that *Grutter* calls for deference to the University's conclusion, "'based on its experience and expertise,'" 631 F.3d, at 230 (quoting 645 F.Supp. 2d 587, 603 (WD Tex. 2009)), that a diverse student body would serve its educational goals. There is disagreement about whether *Grutter* was consistent with the principles of equal protection in approving this compelling interest in diversity. See *post,* at 1 (*Scalia,* J., concurring); *post,* at 4-5 (*Thomas, J.,* concurring); *post,* at 1-2 (*Ginsburg,* J., dissenting). But the parties here do not ask the Court to revisit that aspect of *Grutter*'s holding.

A university is not permitted to define diversity as "some specified percentage of a particular group merely because of its race or ethnic origin." *Bakke, supra,* at 307 (opinion of Powell, J.). "That would amount to outright racial balancing, which is patently unconstitutional." *Grutter, supra,* at 330. "Racial balancing is not transformed from 'patently unconstitutional' to a compelling state interest simply by relabeling it 'racial diversity.'" *Parents Involved in Community Schools* v. *Seattle School Dist. No. 1*, 551 U.S. 701, 732 (2007).

Once the University has established that its goal of diversity is consistent with strict scrutiny, however, there must still be a further judicial determination that the admissions process meets strict scrutiny in its implementation. The University must prove that the means chosen by the University to attain diversity are narrowly tailored to that goal. On this point, the University receives no deference. *Grutter* made clear that it is for the courts, not for university administrators, to ensure that "[t]he means chosen to accomplish the [government's] asserted purpose must be specifically and narrowly framed to accomplish that purpose." 539 U.S., at 333 (internal quotation marks omitted). True, a court can take account of a university's experience and expertise in adopting or rejecting certain admissions processes. But, as the Court said in *Grutter,* it remains at all times the University's obligation to demonstrate, and the Judiciary's obligation to determine, that admissions processes "ensure that each applicant is evaluated as an individual and not in a way that makes an applicant's race or ethnicity the defining feature of his or her application." *Id.,* at 337.

Narrow tailoring also requires that the reviewing court verify that it is "necessary" for a university to use race to achieve the educational benefits of diversity. *Bakke, supra,* at 305. This involves a careful judicial inquiry into whether a university could achieve sufficient diversity without using racial classifications. Although "[n]arrow tailoring does not require exhaustion of every *conceivable* race-neutral alternative," strict scrutiny does require a court to examine with care, and not defer to, a university's "serious, good faith consideration of workable race-neutral alternatives." See *Grutter,* 539 U.S., at

339-340 (emphasis added). Consideration by the university is of course necessary, but it is not sufficient to satisfy strict scrutiny: The reviewing court must ultimately be satisfied that no workable race-neutral alternatives would produce the educational benefits of diversity. If "'a nonracial approach . . . could promote the substantial interest about as well and at tolerable administrative expense,'" *Wygant* v. *Jackson Bd. of Ed.*, 476 U.S. 267, 280, n.6 (1986) (quoting Greenawalt, Judicial Scrutiny of "Benign" Racial Preference in Law School Admissions, 75 Colum. L.Rev. 559, 578-579 (1975)), then the university may not consider race. A plaintiff, of course, bears the burden of placing the validity of a university's adoption of an affirmative action plan in issue. But strict scrutiny imposes on the university the ultimate burden of demonstrating, before turning to racial classifications, that available, workable race-neutral alternatives do not suffice.

Rather than perform this searching examination, however, the Court of Appeals held petitioner could challenge only "whether [the University's] decision to reintroduce race as a factor in admissions was made in good faith." 631 F.3d, at 236. And in considering such a challenge, the court would "presume the University acted in good faith" and place on petitioner the burden of rebutting that presumption. *Id.*, at 231-232. The Court of Appeals held that to "second-guess the merits" of this aspect of the University's decision was a task it was "ill-equipped to perform" and that it would attempt only to "ensure that [the University's] decision to adopt a race-conscious admissions policy followed from [a process of] good faith consideration." *Id.*, at 231. The Court of Appeals thus concluded that "the narrow-tailoring inquiry—like the compelling-interest inquiry—is undertaken with a degree of deference to the Universit[y]." *Id.*, at 232. Because "the efforts of the University have been studied, serious, and of high purpose," the Court of Appeals held that the use of race in the admissions program fell within "a constitutionally protected zone of discretion." *Id.*, at 231.

These expressions of the controlling standard are at odds with *Grutter*'s command that "all racial classifications imposed by government 'must be analyzed by a reviewing court under strict scrutiny.'" 539 U.S., at 326 (quoting *Adarand Constructors, Inc.* v. *Peña*, 515 U.S. 200, 227 (1995)). In *Grutter*, the Court approved the plan at issue upon concluding that it was not a quota, was sufficiently flexible, was limited in time, and followed "serious, good faith consideration of workable race-neutral alternatives." 539 U.S., at 339. As noted above, see *supra,* at 1, the parties do not challenge, and the Court therefore does not consider, the correctness of that determination.

Grutter did not hold that good faith would forgive an impermissible consideration of race. It must be remembered that "the mere recitation of a 'benign' or legitimate purpose for a racial classification is entitled to little or no weight." *Croson*, 488 U.S., at 500. Strict scrutiny does not permit a court to accept a school's assertion that its admissions process uses race in a permissible way without a court giving close analysis to the evidence of how the process works in practice.

The higher education dynamic does not change the narrow tailoring analysis of strict scrutiny applicable in other contexts. "[T]he analysis and level of scrutiny applied to determine the validity of [a racial] classification do not vary simply because the objective appears acceptable. . . . While the validity and importance of the objective may affect the outcome of the analysis, the analysis itself does not change." *Mississippi Univ. for Women* v. *Hogan*, 458 U.S. 718, 724, n.9 (1982).

The District Court and Court of Appeals confined the strict scrutiny inquiry in too narrow a way by deferring to the University's good faith in its use of racial classifications and affirming the grant of summary judgment on that basis. The Court vacates that judgment, but fairness to the litigants and the courts that heard the case requires that it be remanded so that the admissions process can be considered and judged under a correct analysis. See *Adarand, supra,* at 237. Unlike *Grutter*, which was decided after trial, this case arises from cross-motions for summary judgment. In this case, as in similar cases, in determining whether summary judgment in favor of the University would be appropriate, the Court of Appeals must assess whether the University has offered sufficient evidence that would prove that its admissions program is narrowly tailored to obtain the educational benefits of diversity. Whether this record—and not "simple . . . assurances of good intention," *Croson, supra,* at 500—is sufficient is a question for the Court of Appeals in the first instance.

* * *

Strict scrutiny must not be "'strict in theory, but fatal in fact,'" *Adarand, supra,* at 237; see also *Grutter, supra,* at 326. But the opposite is also true. Strict scrutiny must not be strict in theory but feeble in fact. In order for judicial review to be meaningful, a university must make a showing that its plan is narrowly tailored to achieve the only interest that this Court has approved in this context: the benefits of a student body diversity that "encompasses a . . . broa[d] array of qualifications and characteristics of which racial or ethnic origin is but a single though important element." *Bakke,* 438 U.S., at 315 (opinion of Powell, J.). The judgment of the Court of Appeals is vacated, and the case is remanded for further proceedings consistent with this opinion.

It is so ordered.

Justice Kagan took no part in the consideration or decision of this case.

Source: Fisher v. University of Texas at Austin, 133 S. Ct. 2411 (2013).

President Barack Obama, Remarks on the Trayvon Martin Case
(July 2013)

On February 26, 2012, George Zimmerman, a neighborhood watch volunteer, called police to report a suspicious person in his Sanford, Florida, neighborhood. This person was 17-year-old Trayvon Martin, an African American youth who was visiting Sanford with his father. Martin was on his way back from a local convenience store, where he had purchased candy and juice. Shortly thereafter, an altercation erupted between Martin, who was unarmed, and Zimmerman, which left the former dead with a gunshot wound to the chest.

Zimmerman claimed self-defense, and the Sanford Police Department declined to charge him, citing their inability to do so under Florida's "stand-your-ground" statute, a self-defense law that allows citizens to use deadly force to defend themselves without any requirement to evade or withdraw from a dangerous situation. The case provoked a firestorm of controversy and considerably heightened racial tensions in the country. Zimmerman was eventually charged in Martin's death, but a jury acquitted him of second-degree murder and manslaughter on July 13, 2013.

Reproduced here is President Barack Obama's statement on the case released on July 14, 2013, the day after the verdict was announced, and also the president's address to surprised reporters in the James S. Brady Press Briefing Room at the White House on July 19, 2013, in which he commented on the outcome of the trial and the Florida self-defense law, telling reporters that "Trayvon Martin could have been me 35 years ago."

Statement by the President, July 14, 2013
The death of Trayvon Martin was a tragedy. Not just for his family, or for any one community, but

for America. I know this case has elicited strong passions. And in the wake of the verdict, I know those passions may be running even higher. But we are a nation of laws, and a jury has spoken. I now ask every American to respect the call for calm reflection from two parents who lost their young son. And as we do, we should ask ourselves if we're doing all we can to widen the circle of compassion and understanding in our own communities. We should ask ourselves if we're doing all we can to stem the tide of gun violence that claims too many lives across this country on a daily basis. We should ask ourselves, as individuals and as a society, how we can prevent future tragedies like this. As citizens, that's a job for all of us. That's the way to honor Trayvon Martin.

Source: Obama, Barack. "Remarks on the Trayvon Martin Case." July 14, 2013. White House Website. http://www. whitehouse.gov/the-press-office/2013/07/14/ statement-president.

Remarks by the President on Trayvon Martin, July 19, 2013

THE PRESIDENT: I wanted to come out here, first of all, to tell you that Jay is prepared for all your questions and is very much looking forward to the session. The second thing is I want to let you know that over the next couple of weeks, there's going to obviously be a whole range of issues—immigration, economics, et cetera—we'll try to arrange a fuller press conference to address your questions.

The reason I actually wanted to come out today is not to take questions, but to speak to an issue that obviously has gotten a lot of attention over the course of the last week—the issue of the Trayvon Martin ruling. I gave a preliminary statement right after the ruling on Sunday. But watching the debate over the course of the last week, I thought it might be useful for me to expand on my thoughts a little bit.

First of all, I want to make sure that, once again, I send my thoughts and prayers, as well as Michelle's, to the family of Trayvon Martin, and to remark on the incredible grace and dignity with which they've dealt with the entire situation. I can

only imagine what they're going through, and it's remarkable how they've handled it.

The second thing I want to say is to reiterate what I said on Sunday, which is there's going to be a lot of arguments about the legal issues in the case—I'll let all the legal analysts and talking heads address those issues. The judge conducted the trial in a professional manner. The prosecution and the defense made their arguments. The juries were properly instructed that in a case such as this reasonable doubt was relevant, and they rendered a verdict. And once the jury has spoken, that's how our system works. But I did want to just talk a little bit about context and how people have responded to it and how people are feeling.

You know, when Trayvon Martin was first shot I said that this could have been my son. Another way of saying that is Trayvon Martin could have been me 35 years ago. And when you think about why, in the African American community at least, there's a lot of pain around what happened here, I think it's important to recognize that the African American community is looking at this issue through a set of experiences and a history that doesn't go away.

There are very few African American men in this country who haven't had the experience of being followed when they were shopping in a department store. That includes me. There are very few African American men who haven't had the experience of walking across the street and hearing the locks click on the doors of cars. That happens to me—at least before I was a senator. There are very few African Americans who haven't had the experience of getting on an elevator and a woman clutching her purse nervously and holding her breath until she had a chance to get off. That happens often.

And I don't want to exaggerate this, but those sets of experiences inform how the African American community interprets what happened one night in Florida. And it's inescapable for people to bring those experiences to bear. The African American community is also knowledgeable that there is a history of racial disparities in the application of our criminal laws—everything from the death penalty to enforcement of our drug laws. And that ends up having an impact in terms of how people interpret the case.

Now, this isn't to say that the African American community is naïve about the fact that African American young men are disproportionately involved in the criminal justice system; that they're disproportionately both victims and perpetrators of violence. It's not to make excuses for that fact— although black folks do interpret the reasons for that in a historical context. They understand that some of the violence that takes place in poor black neighborhoods around the country is born out of a very violent past in this country, and that the poverty and dysfunction that we see in those communities can be traced to a very difficult history.

And so the fact that sometimes that's unacknowledged adds to the frustration. And the fact that a lot of African American boys are painted with a broad brush and the excuse is given, well, there are these statistics out there that show that African American boys are more violent—using that as an excuse to then see sons treated differently causes pain.

I think the African American community is also not naïve in understanding that, statistically, somebody like Trayvon Martin was statistically more likely to be shot by a peer than he was by somebody else. So folks understand the challenges that exist for African American boys. But they get frustrated, I think, if they feel that there's no context for it and that context is being denied. And that all contributes I think to a sense that if a white male teen was involved in the same kind of scenario, that, from top to bottom, both the outcome and the aftermath might have been different.

Now, the question for me at least, and I think for a lot of folks, is where do we take this? How do we learn some lessons from this and move in a positive direction? I think it's understandable that there have been demonstrations and vigils and protests, and some of that stuff is just going to have to work its way through, as long as it remains nonviolent. If

I see any violence, then I will remind folks that that dishonors what happened to Trayvon Martin and his family. But beyond protests or vigils, the question is, are there some concrete things that we might be able to do.

I know that Eric Holder is reviewing what happened down there, but I think it's important for people to have some clear expectations here. Traditionally, these are issues of state and local government, the criminal code. And law enforcement is traditionally done at the state and local levels, not at the federal levels.

That doesn't mean, though, that as a nation we can't do some things that I think would be productive. So let me just give a couple of specifics that I'm still bouncing around with my staff, so we're not rolling out some five-point plan, but some areas where I think all of us could potentially focus.

Number one, precisely because law enforcement is often determined at the state and local level, I think it would be productive for the Justice Department, governors, mayors to work with law enforcement about training at the state and local levels in order to reduce the kind of mistrust in the system that sometimes currently exists.

When I was in Illinois, I passed racial profiling legislation, and it actually did just two simple things. One, it collected data on traffic stops and the race of the person who was stopped. But the other thing was it resourced us training police departments across the state on how to think about potential racial bias and ways to further professionalize what they were doing. And initially, the police departments across the state were resistant, but actually they came to recognize that if it was done in a fair, straightforward way that it would allow them to do their jobs better and communities would have more confidence in them and, in turn, be more helpful in applying the law. And obviously, law enforcement has got a very tough job.

So that's one area where I think there are a lot of resources and best practices that could be brought to bear if state and local governments are receptive. And I think a lot of them would be. And let's figure out are there ways for us to push out that kind of training.

Along the same lines, I think it would be useful for us to examine some state and local laws to see if it—if they are designed in such a way that they may encourage the kinds of altercations and confrontations and tragedies that we saw in the Florida case, rather than diffuse potential altercations.

I know that there's been commentary about the fact that the "stand your ground" laws in Florida were not used as a defense in the case. On the other hand, if we're sending a message as a society in our communities that someone who is armed potentially has the right to use those firearms even if there's a way for them to exit from a situation, is that really going to be contributing to the kind of peace and security and order that we'd like to see?

And for those who resist that idea that we should think about something like these "stand your ground" laws, I'd just ask people to consider, if Trayvon Martin was of age and armed, could he have stood his ground on that sidewalk? And do we actually think that he would have been justified in shooting Mr. Zimmerman who had followed him in a car because he felt threatened? And if the answer to that question is at least ambiguous, then it seems to me that we might want to examine those kinds of laws.

Number three—and this is a long-term project—we need to spend some time in thinking about how do we bolster and reinforce our African American boys. And this is something that Michelle and I talk a lot about. There are a lot of kids out there who need help who are getting a lot of negative reinforcement. And is there more that we can do to give them the sense that their country cares about them and values them and is willing to invest in them?

I'm not naïve about the prospects of some grand, new federal program. I'm not sure that that's what we're talking about here. But I do recognize that as President, I've got some convening power, and there are a lot of good programs that are being done across the country on this front. And for us to be able to gather together business leaders and

local elected officials and clergy and celebrities and athletes, and figure out how are we doing a better job helping young African American men feel that they're a full part of this society and that they've got pathways and avenues to succeed—I think that would be a pretty good outcome from what was obviously a tragic situation. And we're going to spend some time working on that and thinking about that.

And then, finally, I think it's going to be important for all of us to do some soul-searching. There has been talk about should we convene a conversation on race. I haven't seen that be particularly productive when politicians try to organize conversations. They end up being stilted and politicized, and folks are locked into the positions they already have. On the other hand, in families and churches and workplaces, there's the possibility that people are a little bit more honest, and at least you ask yourself your own questions about, am I wringing as much bias out of myself as I can? Am I judging people as much as I can, based on not the color of their skin, but the content of their character? That would, I think, be an appropriate exercise in the wake of this tragedy.

And let me just leave you with a final thought that, as difficult and challenging as this whole episode has been for a lot of people, I don't want us to lose sight that things are getting better. Each successive generation seems to be making progress in changing attitudes when it comes to race. It doesn't mean we're in a post-racial society. It doesn't mean that racism is eliminated. But when I talk to Malia and Sasha, and I listen to their friends and I see them interact, they're better than we are—they're better than we were—on these issues. And that's true in every community that I've visited all across the country.

And so we have to be vigilant and we have to work on these issues. And those of us in authority should be doing everything we can to encourage the better angels of our nature, as opposed to using these episodes to heighten divisions. But we should also have confidence that kids these days, I think, have more sense than we did back then, and certainly more than our parents did or our grandparents did; and that along this long, difficult journey, we're becoming a more perfect union—not a perfect union, but a more perfect union.

Thank you, guys.

Source: Obama, Barack. "Remarks on the Trayvon Martin Case." July 19, 2013. White House Website. http://www.whitehouse.gov/the-press-office/2013/07/19/remarks-president-trayvon-martin.

Selected Bibliography

Arts, Music, and Popular Culture

Alexander, George. *Why We Make Movies: Black Filmmakers Talk about the Magic of Cinema*. New York: Harlem Moon, 2003.

Duffy, Damian, John Jennings, and Keith Knight. *Black Comix: African American Independent Comics, Art and Culture*. New York: Mark Batty Publisher, 2010.

Dupri, Jermaine, and Samantha Marshall. *Young, Rich, and Dangerous: The Making of a Music Mogul*. New York: Atria Books, 2007.

Elam, Harry J., Jr., and David Krasner. *African-American Performance and Theater History: A Critical Reader*. New York: Oxford University Press, 2001.

Fern-Banks, Kathleen. *Historical Dictionary of African-American Television*. Lanham, MD: Scarecrow Press, 2006.

Fisher, William, III. *Promises to Keep: Technology, Law, and the Future of Entertainment*. Stanford, CA: Stanford Law and Politics, 2004.

Fleming, Robert. "Beyond Funny: Black Voices in the World of Comics and Graphic Novels." *Black Issues Book Review*, July 1, 2006.

Garofalo, Reebee. "Crossing Over: From Black Rhythm & Blues to White Rock 'n' Roll." In *R & B, Rhythm and Business: The Political Economy of Black Music*, edited by Norman Kelly. New York: Akashic Books, 2005.

George, Nelson. *Where Did Our Love Go? The Rise and Fall of Motown*. London: Omnibus, 2003.

Glass, Barbara S. *African American Dance: An Illustrated History*. Jefferson, NC: McFarland, 2007.

Gottschild, Brenda Dixon. *The Black Dancing Body: A Geography from Coon to Cool*. New York: Palgrave Macmillan, 2003.

Gulla, Bob. *Icons of R & B and Soul: An Encyclopedia of the Artists Who Revolutionized Rhythm*. Westport, CT: Greenwood Press, 2008.

Havers, Richard, and Richard Evans. *Jazz: The Golden Era*. Edison, NJ: Chartwell Books, 2009.

Havranek, Carrie. *Women Icons of Popular Music: The Rebels, Rockers, and Renegades*. Westport, CT: Greenwood Press, 2009.

Hayes, Reginald B. *Evolution of the Club and Juke Joints in America: A Social Renaissance.* Charleston, SC: BookSurge Publishing, 2008.

Hess, Mickey, ed. *Icons of Hip Hop: An Encyclopedia of the Movement, Music, and Culture.* Westport, CT: Greenwood Press, 2007.

Huggins, Nathan, ed. *Harlem Renaissance.* Updated ed. New York: Oxford University Press, 2007.

Jackson, Buzzy. *A Bad Woman Feeling Good: Blues and the Women Who Sing Them.* New York: Norton, 2005.

Keiler, Alan. *Marian Anderson, A Singer's Journey.* New York: Scribner, 2000.

Keyes, Cheryl L. *Rap Music and Street Consciousness.* Urbana: University of Illinois Press, 2002.

Lehman, Christopher P. *The Colored Cartoon: Black Representation in American Animated Short Films, 1907–1954.* Amherst: University of Massachusetts Press, 2007.

Lehman, Christopher P. *A Critical History of Soul on Television.* Jefferson, NC: McFarland, 2008.

Leininger-Miller, Theresa. *New Negro Artists in Paris: African American Painters and Sculptors in the City of Light, 1922–1934.* New Brunswick, NJ: Rutgers University Press, 2001.

Lewis, David Levering. *When Harlem Was Vogue.* New York: Penguin, 1997.

Littleton, Daryl J. *Black Comedians on Black Comedy: How African-Americans Taught Us to Laugh.* New York: Applause Theatre and Cinema Books, 2006.

Manning, Susan. *Modern Dance, Negro Dance: Race in Motion.* Minneapolis: University of Minnesota Press, 2004.

Phinney, Kevin. *Souled American: How Black Music Transformed White Culture.* New York: Billboard Books, 2005.

Pinn, Anthony B., and Benjamín Valentin, eds. *Creating Ourselves: African Americans and Hispanic Americans on Popular Culture and Religious Expression.* Durham, NC: Duke University Press, 2009.

Prahlad, Anand, ed. *The Greenwood Encyclopedia of African American Folklore.* 3 vols. Westport, CT: Greenwood Press, 2006.

Rome, Dennis. *Black Demons: The Media's Depiction of the African American Male Criminal Stereotype.* Westport, CT: Praeger, 2004.

Sampson, Henry T. *Swingin' on the Ether Waves: A Chronological History of African Americans in Radio and Television Broadcasting, 1925–1955.* Lanham, MD: Scarecrow Press, 2005.

Samuels, Allison. *Off the Record: A Reporter Lifts the Velvet Rope on Hollywood, Hip Hop and Sports.* New York: Amistad, 2007.

Walker-Hill, Helen. *From Spirituals to Symphonies: African-American Women Composers and Their Music.* Westport, CT: Greenwood, Press, 2007.

Ward, Andrew. *Dark Midnight When I Rise, the Story of the Fisk Jubilee Singers: How Black Music Changed the World.* New York: Amistad, 2001.

Ward, Geoffrey C., and Ken Burns. *Jazz: A History of America's Music.* New York: Alfred A. Knopf, 2002.

Washburn, Patrick S. *The African American Newspaper: Voice of Freedom.* Evanston, IL: Northwestern University Press, 2006.

Watkins, Mel. *African American Humor: The Best Black Comedy from Slavery to Today.* Chicago: Lawrence Hill Books, 2002.

Werner, Craig. *Higher Ground: Stevie Wonder, Aretha Franklin, Curtis Mayfield, and the Rise and Fall of American Soul.* New York: Crown Publishers, 2004.

Witham, Barry. *The Federal Theatre Project: A Case Study.* New York: Cambridge University Press, 2003.

Zook, Kristal Brent. *I See Black People: The Rise and Fall of African American-Owned Television and Radio.* New York: Nation Books, 2008.

Civil Rights

Arsenault, Raymond. *Freedom Riders: 1961 and the Struggle for Racial Justice.* New York: Oxford University Press, 2006.

Branch, Taylor. *At Canaan's Edge: America in the King Years, 1965–68.* New York: Simon & Schuster, 2006.

Branch, Taylor. *Pillar of Fire: America in the King Years, 1963–65.* New York: Simon & Schuster, 1999.

Carson, Clayborne. *Civil Rights Chronicle: The African American Struggle for Freedom.* Lincolnwood, IL: Legacy Publishing, 2003.

Carson, Clayborne, gen. ed. *The Eyes on the Prize Civil Rights Reader.* New York: Penguin, 1991.

Carson, Clayborne, Tenisha H. Armstrong, Susan A. Carson, Erin K. Cook, and Susan Englander. *The Martin Luther King, Jr. Encyclopedia.* Santa Barbara, CA: Greenwood, 2008.

Chafe, William H. *Civilities and Civil Rights: Greensboro, North Carolina, and the Black Struggle for Freedom.* New York: Oxford University Press, 1981.

Collier-Thomas, Bettye, and V. P. Franklin, eds. *Sisters in the Struggle: African American Women in the Civil Rights–Black Power Movement.* New York: New York University Press, 2001.

Crawford, Vicki L., Jacqueline Anne Rouse, and Barbara Woods. *Women in the Civil Rights Movement: Trailblazers and Torchbearers, 1941–1965.* Bloomington: Indiana University Press, 1993.

Eick, Gretchen Cassel. *Dissent in Wichita: The Civil Rights Movement in the Midwest, 1954–1972.* Urbana: University of Illinois Press, 2007.

Etheridge, Eric. *Breach of Peace: Portraits of the 1961 Mississippi Freedom Riders.* New York: Atlas, 2008.

Field, Ron. *Civil Rights in America, 1865–1980.* New York: Cambridge University Press, 2002.

Finlayson, Reggie. *We Shall Overcome: The History of the Civil Rights Movement.* Minneapolis: Lerner Publications, 2003.

Free, Marvin D., Jr. *Racial Issues in Criminal Justice: The Case of African Americans.* Monsey, NY: Criminal Justice Press, 2004.

Greenberg, Jack. *Crusaders in the Courts: Legal Battles of the Civil Rights Movement.* Anniversary ed. New York: Twelve Tables Press, 2004.

Houck, Davis W., and David E. Dixon. *Women and the Civil Rights Movement, 1954–1965.* Jackson: University of Mississippi Press, 2009.

Iton, Richard. *In Search of the Black Fantastic: Politics & Popular Culture in the Post-Civil Rights Era.* New York: Oxford University Press, 2008.

Knight, Gladys L. *Icons of African American Protest: Trailblazing Activists of the Civil Rights Movement.* 2 vols. Westport, CT: Greenwood Press, 2009.

Levine, Daniel. *Bayard Rustin and the Civil Rights Movement*. Piscataway, NJ: Rutgers University Press, 2000.

Levy, Peter B. *The Civil Rights Movement*. Westport, CT: Greenwood Press, 1988.

Levy, Peter B. *Let Freedom Ring: A Documentary History of the Modern Civil Rights Movement*. Westport, CT: Praeger, 1992.

Lovett, Bobby L. *Civil Rights in Tennessee: A Narrative*. Knoxville: University of Tennessee Press, 2005.

Lowery, Charles D., and John F. Marszalek, eds. *The Greenwood Encyclopedia of African American Civil Rights*. Westport, CT: Greenwood Press, 2003.

McMurry, Linda. *To Keep the Waters Troubled: The Life of Ida B. Wells*. New York: Oxford University Press, 2000.

Peniel, Joseph E. *Black Power Movement: Rethinking the Civil Rights-Black Power Era*. New York: Routledge, 2006.

Peniel, Joseph E. *Waiting 'Til the Midnight Hour: A Narrative History of Black Power in America*. New York: Henry Holt, 2006.

Richardson, Heather Cox. *The Death of Reconstruction: Race, Labor, and Politics in the Post-Civil Rights North, 1865–1901*. Cambridge, MA: Harvard University Press, 2001.

Robnett, Belinda. *How Long? How Long?: African-American Women in the Struggle for Civil Rights*. New York: Oxford University Press, 1997.

Schecter, Patricia. *Ida B. Wells-Barnett and American Reform, 1880–1930*. Chapel Hill: University of North Carolina Press, 2001.

Smith, Jessie Carney, and Linda T. Wynn, eds. *Freedom Facts and Firsts: 400 Years of the African American Civil Rights Experience*. Detroit: Visible Ink Press, 2009.

Wells, Ida B. *Crusade for Justice: The Autobiography of Ida B. Wells*. Chicago: University of Chicago Press, 1970.

Williams, Juan, with the Eyes on the Prize Production Team. *Eyes on the Prize: America's Civil Rights Years, 1954–63*. New York: Viking Penguin, 1987.

Economics, Work, and Education

Abdul-Jabbar, Kareem. *Black Profiles in Courage: A Legacy of African American Achievement*. New York: William Morrow, 1996.

Aldridge, Delores P., and Carlene Young, eds. *Out of the Revolution: The Development of Africana Studies*. Lanham, MD: Lexington Books, 2000.

Anderson, Terry H. *The Pursuit of Fairness: A History of Affirmative Action*. New York: Oxford University Press, 2004.

Asante, Molefi Kete., and Ama Mazama, eds. *Encyclopedia of Black Studies*. Thousand Oaks, CA: Sage Publications, 2005.

Borjas, George, Jeffrey Grogger, and Gordon H. Hanson. "Immigration and African American Employment Opportunities: The Response of Wages, Employment and Incarceration to Labor Supply Shocks." National Bureau of Economic Research Working Paper Series, Washington, DC, September 2006.

Bowser, Benjamin P. *Black Middle Class: Social Mobility and Vulnerability*. Boulder, CO: Lynne Rienner Publishers, 2007.

Dyson, Michael Eric. *Come Hell or High Water: Hurricane Katrina and the Color of Disaster*. New York: Basic Civitas Books, 2006.

Engle, Ron, and Tice L. Miller, eds. *The American Stage: Social and Economic Issues from the Colonial Period to the Present*. New York: Cambridge University Press, 1993.

Gasman, Marybeth. *Envisioning Black Colleges: A History of the United Negro College Fund*. Baltimore: Johns Hopkins University Press, 2007.

Haddad, William F., and Douglas Pugh, eds. *Black Economic Development*. Englewood Cliffs, NJ: Prentice-Hall, 1969.

Hunter, James Davison. *Culture Wars: The Struggle to Control the Family, Art, Education, Law, and Politics in America*. New York: Basic Books, 1991.

Hydra, Derek S. *The New Urban Renewal: The Economic Transformation of Harlem and Bronzeville*. Chicago: University of Chicago Press, 2008.

Irons, Edward D. *On Black Economic Development: Myths and Facts*. Austin: University of Texas at Austin, 1971.

Jackson, Cynthia L., and Eleanor F. Nunn, eds. *Historically Black Colleges and Universities: A Reference Handbook*. Santa Barbara, CA: ABC-CLIO, 2003.

Kruger, Richard. *Simple Justice: The History of* Brown v. Board of Education *and Black America's Struggle for Equality*. New York: Alfred A. Knopf, 1976.

Lomotey, Kofi, ed. *Encyclopedia of African American Education*. 2 vols. Thousand Oaks, CA: Sage Publications, 2009.

Mjagkij, Nina, ed. *Organizing Black America: An Encyclopedia of African American Associations*. New York: Garland Publishing, 2001.

Nadasen, Premil. *Welfare Warriors: The Welfare Rights Movement in the United States*. New York: Routledge, 2005.

Ogbu, John U. *Black American Students in an Affluent Suburb*. Mahwah, NJ: Lawrence Erlbaum Associates, 2003.

Orleck, Annelise. *Storming Caesars Palace: How Black Mothers Fought Their Own War on Poverty*. Boston: Beacon Press, 2005.

Ricard, Ronyelle, and M. Christopher Brown II. *Ebony Towers in Higher Education: The Evolution, Mission, and Presidency of Historically Black Colleges and Universities*. Sterling, VA: Stylus Publishing, 2008.

Smith, Jessie Carney, ed. *Encyclopedia of African American Business*. 2 vols. Westport, CT: Greenwood Press, 2006.

Tillman, Linda, ed. *The SAGE Handbook of African American Education*. Thousand Oaks, CA: Sage Publications, 2009.

Vinovskis, Maris. *The Birth of Head Start: Preschool Education Policies in the Kennedy and Johnson Administrations*. Chicago: University of Chicago Press, 2008.

Walker, Juliet E. K. *The History of Black Business in America: Capitalism, Race, Entrepreneurship*. New York: Macmillan Library Reference USA, 1998.

West, Michael Rudolph. *The Education of Booker T. Washington: American Democracy and the Idea of Race Relations*. New York: Columbia University Press, 2006.

Williams, Juan, with Dwayne Ashley and Shawn Rhea. *I'll Find a Way or Make One: A Tribute to Historically Black Colleges and Universities*. New York: Amistad, 2004.

Williams, Rhonda Y. *The Politics of Public Housing: Black Women's Struggles Against Urban Inequality*. New York: Oxford University Press, 2004.

Witt, Doris. 1999. *Black Hunger*. Oxford: Oxford University Press, 2008.

History

Appiah, Kwame Anthony, and Henry Louis Gates Jr., eds. *Africana: The Encyclopedia of the African and African American Experience.* 5 vols. New York: Oxford University Press, 2005.

Falola, Toyin, and Kevin D. Roberts. *The Atlantic World, 1450–2000.* Bloomington: Indiana University Press, 2008.

Finkelman, Paul, ed. *Encyclopedia of African American History 1896 to the Present.* 2 vols. New York: Oxford University Press, 2009.

Goldman, Robert M. *Reconstruction and Black Suffrage: Losing the Vote in Reese and Cruikshank.* Charlottesville: University of Virginia Press, 2001.

Gregory, James Noble. *The Southern Diaspora: How the Great Migrations of Black and White Southerners Transformed America.* Chapel Hill: University of North Carolina Press, 2005.

Hine, Darlene Clark, ed. *The African-American Odyssey.* Upper Saddle River, NJ: Prentice Hall, 2000.

Hine, Darlene Clark, ed. *Black Women in America.* 2nd ed. 3 vols. New York: Oxford University Press, 2005.

Hine, Darlene Clark, William C. Hine, and Stanley Harrold, eds. *African Americans: A Concise History.* Upper Saddle River, NJ: Pearson Prentice Hall, 2009.

Horman, Lynn M., and Thomas Reilly. *Black Knights: The Story of the Tuskegee Airmen.* Gretna, LA: Pelican Publishing, 2001.

Jaynes, Gerald D., gen. ed. *Encyclopedia of African American Society.* 2 vols. Thousand Oaks, CA: Sage Publications, 2005.

Leckie, William H., with Shirley A. Leckie. *The Buffalo Soldiers: A Narrative of the Black Calvary in the West.* Rev. ed. Norman: University of Oklahoma Press, 2003.

Montgomery, Elvin, Jr. *Collecting African American History: A Celebration of American's Black Heritage through Documents, Artifacts, and Collectibles.* New York: Stewart, Tabor & Chang, 2001.

Painter, Nell Irvin. *Creating Black Americans: African-American History and Its Meanings, 1619 to the Present.* New York: Oxford University Press, 2006.

Palmer, Colin A. *Encyclopedia of African-American Culture and History: The Black Experience in the Americas.* 2nd ed. 6 vols. Detroit: Macmillan Reference USA, 2006.

Schneider, Mark Robert. *African Americans in the Jazz Age: A Decade of Struggle and Promise.* Lanham, MD: Rowman & Littlefield, 2006.

Siebert, Wilbur H. *The Underground Railroad: From Slavery to Freedom.* Mineola, NY: Dover, 2006.

Smith, Jessie Carney. *Black Firsts: 4,000 Ground-Breaking and Pioneering Historical Events.* 2nd ed. Detroit: Visible Ink, 2003.

Stanton, Mary. *Freedom Walk: Mississippi or Burst.* Jackson: University of Mississippi Press, 2003.

Summer, L. S. *The March on Washington.* Mankato, MN: Child's World, 2001.

Winbush, Raymond A. *Belinda's Petition: A Concise History of Reparations for the Transatlantic Slave Trade.* Philadelphia: XLibris, 2009.

Identity, Culture, and Community

Afro-American Life, History and Culture. Developed for USIS Programs by the Collections Development Branch, Library Programs Division, Office of Cultural Centers and Resources,

Bureau of Educational and Cultural Affairs, United States Information Agency. Washington, DC: The Branch, 1985.

Alexander, Amy. *Fifty Black Women Who Changed America*. Secaucus, NJ: Carol Publishing Group, 1999.

Andrews, George Reid. *Afro-Latin America, 1800–2000*. New York: Oxford University Press, 2004.

Asante, Molefi Kete. *Afrocentricity*. Chicago: African American Images, 2003. First published in 1988 by Africa World Press.

Fogg-Davis, Hawley. *The Ethics of Transracial Adoption*. Ithaca, NY: Cornell University Press, 2002.

Foster, William H., III. *Looking for a Face Like Mine*. Waterbury, CT: Fine Tooth Press, 2005.

Fouche, Rayvon. *Black Inventors in the Age of Segregation*. Baltimore: Johns Hopkins University Press, 2003.

Gaines, Fabiola. *The New Soul Food Cookbook for People with Diabetes*. Alexandria, VA: American Diabetes Association, 2006.

Gaunt, Kyra D. *The Games Black Girls Play: Learning the Ropes from Double-Dutch to Hip-Hop*. New York: New York University Press, 2006.

Harris, Cecil, and Larryette Kyle-DeBose. *Charging the Net: A History of Blacks in Tennis from Althea Gibson and Arthur Ashe to the Williams Sisters*. Chicago: Ivan R. Dee, 2007.

Haskins, Jim, and Kathleen Benson. *Black Stars: African American Religious Leaders*. San Francisco: Jossey-Bass, 2007.

Hey, David, ed. *The Oxford Companion to Local and Family History*. New York: Oxford University Press, 2009.

Hitzges, Norm. *The Greatest Team Ever: The Dallas Cowboys Dynasty of the 1990s*. Nashville, TN: Thomas Nelson, 2007.

Kitwana, Bakari. *The Hip Hop Generation: Young Blacks and the Crisis in African-American Culture*. New York: Basic Civitas Books, 2002.

McLoyd, Vonnie, Nancy E. Hill, and Kenneth A. Dodge. *African American Family Life: Ecological and Cultural Diversity*. New York: Guilford Press, 2005.

Opie, Frederick Douglass. *Hog and Hominy: Soul Food from Africa to America*. New York: Columbia University Press, 2008.

Porter, David L., ed. *African-American Sports Greats: A Biographical Dictionary*. Westport, CT: Greenwood Press, 1995.

Taylor, Charles A. *Juneteenth: A Celebration of Freedom*. Greensboro, NC: Open Hand Publishing, 2002.

Thompson, J. Phillip, III. *Double Trouble: Black Mayors, Black Communities, and the Call for Democracy*. New York: Oxford University Press, 2006.

Whitaker, Matthew C., ed. *African American Icons of Sport: Triumph, Courage, and Excellence*. Westport, CT: Greenwood Press, 2008.

Williams-Forson, Psyche. *Building Houses Out of Chicken Legs: Black Women, Food, and Power*. Chapel Hill: University of North Carolina Press, 2006.

Willis, Deborah. *Posing Beauty: African American Images from the 1890s to the Present*. New York: Norton, 2009.

Willis, Deborah. *Reflections in Black: A History of Black Photographers, 1840 to the Present*. New York: Norton, 2000.

Literature, Oral Narratives, and Writing

Alexander, Amy, ed. *The Farrakhan Factor: African-American Writers on Leadership, Nationhood, and Minister Louis Farrakhan.* New York: Grove Press, 1998.

Andrew, William L., Frances Smith Foster, and Trudier Harris, eds. *The Concise Oxford Companion to African American Literature.* New York: Oxford University Press, 2001.

Du Bois, W. E. B. *The Souls of Black Folk.* 1903. New York: Oxford University Press, 1997.

Hill, Lynda Marion. *Social Rituals and the Verbal Art of Zora Neale Hurston.* Washington, DC: Howard University Press, 1996.

Holloway, Karla F. C. *Passed On: African American Stories.* Durham, NC: Duke University Press, 2002.

Hughes, Langston. *Jazz.* New York: Grolier, 1982.

Hull, Gloria T. *Color, Sex, and Poetry.* Bloomington: Indiana University Press, 1987.

Jemison, Mae. *Find Where the Wind Goes: Moments from My Life.* New York: Scholastic Press, 2001.

Johnson, James Weldon. *The Autobiography of an Ex-Colored Man and Other Writings.* New York: Barnes and Noble, 2007.

Kaplan, Carla, ed. *Zora Neale Hurston: A Life in Letters.* New York: Doubleday, 2002.

Morrison, Toni. *Song of Solomon.* New York: Plume, 1977.

Mullen, Edward J. *Critical Essays on Langston Hughes.* Boston: Hall, 1986.

Napier, Winston, ed. *African American Literary Theory: A Reader.* New York: New York University Press, 2000.

Nelson, Emmanuel S., ed. *African American Authors, 1745–1945: A Bio-Bibliographical Critical Sourcebook.* Westport, CT: Greenwood Press, 2000.

Nelson, Emmanuel S., ed. *The Greenwood Encyclopedia of Multiethnic Literature.* Westport, CT: Greenwood Press, 2005.

Oates, Joyce Carol. *On Boxing.* New York: Harper, 2006.

Ostrom, Hans., and J. David Macey, eds. *The Greenwood Encyclopedia of African American Literature.* 5 vols. Westport, CT: Greenwood Press, 2005.

Perata, David D. *Those Pullman Blues: An Oral History of the African American Railroad Attendant.* Lanham, MD: Madison Books, 1999.

Rawick, George P., ed. *The American Slave: A Composite Autobiography.* 17 vols. Westport, CT: Greenwood Publishing Group, 1972–1979.

West, Cornel, and David Ritz. *Brother West: Living and Loving Out Loud, A Memoir.* New York: Smiley Books, 2009.

Wright, Richard. *Black Power: Three Books from Exile: Black Power; The Color Curtain; and White Man Listen!* Introduction by Cornel West. New York: HarperPerennial, 2008.

Yancy, George, ed. *Cornel West: A Critical Reader.* Malden, MA: Blackwell, 2001.

Politics and Activism

Ginsburg, Benjamin, Theodore J. Lowi, Margaret Weir, and Caroline J. Tolbert. *We the People: An Introduction to American Politics.* 7th essentials ed. New York: Norton, 2009.

Hanson, Joyce A. *Mary McLeod Bethune and Black Women's Political Activism*. Columbia: University of Missouri Press, 2003.

Hogan, Wesley C. *Many Minds, One Heart: SNCC's Dream for a New America*. Chapel Hill: University of North Carolina Press, 2007.

Ifill, Gwen. *The Breakthrough: Politics and Race in the Age of Obama*. New York: Doubleday, 2009.

Johnson, Karen Ann. *Uplifting the Women and the Race: The Lives, Educational Philosophies, and Social Activism of Anna Julia Cooper and Nannie Helen Burroughs*. New York: Garland Publishing, 2000.

Lewis, David Levering. *W. E. B. Du Bois: The Fight for Equality and the American Century 1919–1963*. New York: Kensington, 2003.

Obama, Barack. *The Audacity of Hope: Thoughts on Reclaiming the American Dream*. New York: Crown, 2006.

Obama, Barack. *Dreams from My Father: A Story of Race and Inheritance*. New York: Random House, 1995.

Ogbar, Jeffrey O. G. *Black Power: Radical Politics and African American Identity*. Baltimore: Johns Hopkins University Press, 2004.

Ogbar, Jeffrey O. G. *Hip Hop Revolution: The Culture and Politics of Rap*. Lawrence: University Press of Kansas, 2007.

Pattillo, Mary E. *Black on the Block: The Politics of Race and Class in the City*. Chicago: University of Chicago Press, 2007.

Willis, Deborah, and Emily Bernard, eds. *Michelle Obama: The First Lady in Photographs*. New York: Norton, 2010.

Wolffe, Richard. *Renegade: The Making of a President*. New York: Crown Publishers, 2009.

Racial Violence

Abu-Lughod, Janet L. *Race, Space, and Riots in Chicago, New York, and Los Angeles*. New York: Oxford University Press, 2007.

Aretha, David. *The Trial of the Scottsboro Boys*. Greensboro, NC: Morgan Reynolds Publishing, 2008.

Davis, Thomas J. *Race Relations in America: A Reference Guide with Primary Documents*. Westport CT: Greenwood Press, 2006.

Houck, Davis W., and Matt Grindy. *Emmett Till and the Mississippi Press*. Jackson: University Press of Mississippi, 2008.

Jonas, Gilbert. *Freedom's Sword: The NAACP and the Struggle against Racism in America, 1909–1969*. New York: Routledge, Taylor & Francis, 2007.

Joseph, Janice. *Black Youths, Delinquency, and Juvenile Justice*. Westport, CT: Praeger, 1995.

Randall, Vernellia. *Dying While Black*. Dayton, OH: Seven Principles Press, 2006.

Rucker, Walter, and James Nathaniel Upton, eds. *Encyclopedia of American Race Riots*. Westport, CT: Greenwood Press, 2007.

Russell-Brown, Katheryn. *The Color of Crime*. 2nd ed. New York: New York University Press, 2009.

Walker, Samuel, Cassia Spohn, and Miriam DeLone. *The Color of Justice: Race, Ethnicity, and Crime in America*. 4th ed. Belmont, CA: Thomson Wadsworth, 2007.

Slavery

Brundage, W. Fitzhugh. *Booker T. Washington and Black Progress: Up from Slavery 100 Years Later.* Gainesville: University Press of Florida, 2003.

Clarke, John H. *Christopher Columbus and the Afrikan Holocaust: Slavery and the Rise of European Capitalism.* New York: A & B Books, 1999.

Foster, Francis Smith. *Witnessing Slavery: The Development of Ante-bellum Slave Narratives.* 2nd ed. Madison: University of Wisconsin Press, 1994.

Franklin, John Hope., and Evelyn Brooks Higginbotham. *From Slavery to Freedom.* 9th ed. New York: McGraw-Hill, 2011.

Johnson, Charles, and Patricia Smith. *Africans in America: America's Journey through Slavery.* New York: Harcourt Brace, 1998.

Miller, Randall M., and John David Smith, eds. *Dictionary of Afro-American Slavery.* Updated ed. Westport, CT: Greenwood Press, 1997.

Williams, Eric E. *Capitalism & Slavery.* Chapel Hill: University of North Carolina Press, 1998.

Winbush, Raymond A., ed. *Should America Pay? Slavery and the Raging Debate on Reparations.* New York: Amistad, 2003.

Woodson, Carter Godwin, ed. *Free Negro Owners of Slaves in the United States in 1830, Together with Absentee Ownership of Slaves in the United States in 1830.*

Web Resources

African American Odyssey: The Booker T. Washington Era
http://memory.loc.gov/ammem/aaohtml/aopart6.html

African American Odyssey: The Civil Rights Era
http://memory.loc.gov/ammem/aaohtml/exhibit/aopart9.html

African American Oral History Collection
http://digital.library.louisville.edu/cdm/landingpage/collection/afamoh/

African American Women: Online Archival Collections at Duke University
http://library.duke.edu/rubenstein/collections/digitized/african-american-women/

African American World
http://www.pbs.org/wnet/aaworld/

African Americans in the U.S. Army
http://www.history.army.mil/html/topics/afam/index.html

Africans in America, PBS Program
http://www.pbs.org/wgbh/aia/home.html

Black History, American History
http://www.theatlantic.com/past/docs/unbound/flashbks/black/blahisin.htm

Black Soldiers in the Civil War
http://www.archives.gov/education/lessons/blacks-civil-war/

Booker T. Washington Papers
http://www.historycooperative.org/btw/

Famous Trials, "Scottsboro Boys Trial," 1931–1937
http://law2.umkc.edu/faculty/projects/ftrials/scottsboro/scottsb.htm

History of African Americans in the Civil War
http://www.itd.nps.gov/cwss/history/aa_history.htm

Hutchins Center for African and African American Research, Harvard University
http://hutchinscenter.fas.harvard.edu/

Jim Crow Museum of Racist Memorabilia
http://www.ferris.edu/jimcrow/

Library of Congress, African American Sheet Music, 1850–1900
http://memory.loc.gov/ammem/collections/sheetmusic/brown/index.html

Library of Congress, Booker T. Washington: Online Resources
http://www.loc.gov/rr/program/bib/btwashington/

Martin Luther King Jr. Papers Project
http://mlk-kpp01.stanford.edu/index.php/kingpapers/index

National Center for Educational Statistics: Historically Black Colleges and Universities
http://nces.ed.gov/surveys/annualreports/historicallyblack.asp

National Civil Rights Museum
http://www.civilrightsmuseum.org/

National Oceanic and Atmospheric Administration, Hurricane Katrina
http://www.katrina.noaa.gov/

PBS *From Swastika to Jim Crow: Historically Black Colleges and Universities*
http://www.pbs.org/itvs/fromswastikatojimcrow/blackcolleges.html

The Phillips Collection, Washington, DC: Jacob Lawrence, The Migration Series
http://www.phillipscollection.org/migration_series/index.cfm

The Schomburg Center for Research in Black Culture: In Motion: The African-American Migration Experience
http://www.inmotionaame.org/migrations/landing.cfm?migration=8

Scottboro Boys Museum and Cultural Center
http://bama.ua.edu/~jaray4/index.html

Slavery and the Making of America
http://www.pbs.org/wnet/slavery/

Slavery's Legacy in West Africa: Descendants Cope with Complicity in Brutal Trade
http://www.npr.org/programs/re/archivesdate/2004/apr/slavery/

This Day in Black History
http://www.dayinblackhistory.com/

University of Virginia Library: Portraits from the Golden Age of Jazz: Photographs by William P. Gottlieb
http://explore.lib.virginia.edu/exhibits/show/jazz

Virginia Commonwealth University, Virginia Black History Archives: African American
    Richmond: Educational Segregation and Desegregation
http://www.library.vcu.edu/jbc/speccoll/vbha/school/school.html/

White House Initiative on Historically Black Colleges and Universities
http://www.ed.gov/edblogs/whhbcu/

Index

417

About the Editors

Gary Y. Okihiro is a professor of international and public affairs at Columbia University. He is the author of *Pineapple Culture: A History of the Tropical and Temperate Zones,* and *Island World: A History of Hawai'i and the United States*, as well as the *Encyclopedia of Japanese American Internment* (Greenwood, 2013).

Lionel C. Bascom Bascom has written numerous histories, non-fiction books, and literary collections. He is a professor in the department of writing, linguistics and creative process at Western Connecticut State University and a two-time member of the Pulitzer Prize Jury in Journalism at Columbia University. His books include *The Last Leaf of Harlem: A Collection of Dorothy West Stories* and *A Renaissance in Harlem: The Lost Voices of An African American Community.*